DATE DUE

SAN JUAN BAUTISTA

Gateway to Spanish Texas

San Juan Bautista

GATEWAY TO SPANISH TEXAS

By Robert S. Weddle

UNIVERSITY OF TEXAS PRESS, AUSTIN & LONDON

*Dedicado a los ciudadanos amables de
Guerrero con gran aprecio de su
hospitalidad para un extranjero
con mucha curiosidad*

PREFACE

Exactly 250 years ago, in April, 1718, Don Martín de Alarcón and Padre Fray Antonio de San Buenaventura y Olivares set out from San Juan Bautista to establish the mission settlement which would grow into the city of San Antonio. It was the fulfillment of Olivares' favorite dream, and of the prophecy of all who had looked upon the site. The prophets and the dreamers included Don Domingo Terán de los Ríos, Father Isidro Félix de Espinosa, and the agile Frenchman, Louis Juchereau de St. Denis.

Today, in this HemisFair year of 1968, San Antonio is a bustling metropolis, the most noteworthy offspring of San Juan Bautista, the progenitor of many settlements. While the child has prospered, however, the parent has faded into oblivion. What remains of San Juan Bautista is found at the village of Guerrero, Coahuila, thirty-five miles downriver from Piedras Negras.

Guerrero's ancient buildings of native limestone and adobe testify to the skilled observer of historic beginnings. The casual looker may see little to set this hamlet apart from a multitude of small Mexican towns, tucked away out of the mainstream of the twentieth century. But like the storied burro which carried the Holy Mother when she was great with child, Villa de Guerrero is distinguished by a special set of characteristics. Having fulfilled its mission in history, it seems destined to dwell, like the imperturbable little donkey, forever in the afterglow of its great deeds of the past.

Down Guerrero's main street, formerly known as the Calle Real, have marched the processions of history. The steel hooves of the Spanish trooper's steed, the bare feet of the brown-robed missionary, the wooden wheels of the settler's *carreta*—all have helped to wear away the street's surface, now eroded more than two feet deep. In some respects the street may appear ordinary, but the caravans which have traversed its length were not. The imaginative mind's eye may recapture some of these scenes: Captain Don Diego Ramón's return from the other side of the Río Grande in 1707, bringing a procession of half-naked heathen savages to replace those who had died in the smallpox-ravaged missions; St. Denis, as he appeared suddenly out of the wilderness bearing exotic French goods to tease the tastes of the frontier Spaniards and entice them into violation of the laws of the Crown; the doughty old missionary, Olivares; the dedicated and designing Fray Francisco Hidalgo; the young and earnest Padre Espinosa; the venerable Fray Antonio Margil de Jesús, his bare feet blackened and crusted with ugly sores from countless leagues of travel over the apostolic trail, but his face aglow with zeal for spiritual conquest.

Before one's eyes as he beholds this well-worn street seem to pass the procession of Don Domingo Ramón, his soldiers, his settlers, and their women and children, his herds of horses and cattle, outward bound for the pagan land of the Tejas to establish lasting settlements; of Friar Pedro Muñoz and his string of pack mules, setting out to take much-needed succor to his brother missionaries, suffering privation in the Texas wilderness; of the rumbling caravan of Alarcón, going to form the new settlement at San Antonio de Padua; of the legions of the Marqués de Aguayo, bent on driving the French from Spanish territory and on re-establishing the East Texas missions.

One might also glimpse the military figure of Zebulon Pike, homeward bound from Spanish imprisonment; Ben Milam, traveling to the interior in quest of colonization rights; the hastening army of Antonio López de Santa Anna, destined for glory at the Alamo and infamy at San Jacinto; or General John E. Wool, Captain Robert E. Lee, and the American Army of Chihuahua.

Not an ordinary street, the Calle Real. Outside Guerrero the "Royal Street" turned into the Camino Real, the Royal Road to the Spanish frontier, as long as there was a Spanish frontier. This was the first, and the most enduring, gateway to Spanish Texas.

As Father Hidalgo dreamed of going back to minister to the Tejas Indians, and Olivares yearned to plant a mission on the San Antonio River, it has been my desire for several years to set down this story of San Juan Bautista. It seems fitting that attainment of this goal should be timed to coincide with HemisFair. With this gigantic festival San Antonio, spawned by San Juan Bautista two and one-half centuries ago, prepares to observe that important anniversary.

Robert S. Weddle
Austin, Texas

ACKNOWLEDGMENTS

San Juan Bautista del Río Grande is the type of subject about which one might dream of one day writing without ever bringing himself to do it; or the kind of topic which might be investigated for a lifetime before one dared to attempt to produce a narrative. For saving me from these pitfalls I am indebted to many persons who have contributed generously of their interest and encouragement, as well as of material and other forms of valuable assistance.

Outstanding in this regard are Ben E. Pingenot, Charles G. Downing, and John F. Woodhull, all of whom made available to me their fine libraries and intimate knowledge of the border country in the vicinity of the gateway to Spanish Texas. They have served as my personal guides to places of interest in México which bear a relationship to this study. The memory of those safaris across the Río Grande prompts a word of thanks to their wives, who not only have been excellent hostesses in their homes in Eagle Pass, Texas, but who have packed many a fine picnic lunch for *el otro lado*.

I am indebted also to Ben Pingenot and George Stoepler, of Melvin, Texas, for reading the manuscript and giving me the benefit of their suggestions; to E. H. Swaim, of Eden, for permitting me the run of his outstanding library, and for the use of his microfilm reader.

For furnishing material or references, these persons are due acknowledgment: Richard G. Santos, archivist of Bexar County; Mrs. Marie Berry, reference librarian, San Antonio Public Library; Mrs. Linda Schieber, reference librarian, University of California, Berkeley; Mrs. W. G. Westbrook, librarian, Menard Public Library; Robert E. McDonald, of Leander, Texas; the Reverend Father Lino G. Canedo, O. F. M., Academy of American Franciscan History, Washington, D. C.; Rosendo González and Profesora Aurora Botello G. of Guerrero, Coahuila; Sister M. Claude Lane, archivist, Texas Catholic Archives, Austin; and especially Dr. Chester V. Kielman, archivist, The University of Texas Library, Austin.

To the Academy of American Franciscan History I wish to express my thanks for permission to quote material from Isidro Félix de Espinosa, *Crónica de los colegios de propaganda fide de la Nueva España;* to John Howell Books for leave to use material from Paul D. Nathan and Lesley Byrd Simpson, *The San Sabá Papers;* to David S. Hotchkiss for granting the use of the Joseph de Urrutia map of Presidio de San Juan Bautista from his *Spanish Missions of Texas from 1776 Including the Battle of the Alamo—1835;* and to the British Museum, London, holder of the original Urrutia map.

Bob Carter, manager of the Tovar Ranch in Maverick County, has my deep appreciation for permitting me access to the ranch to reconnoiter the Paso de Francia, and the Camino Real at its entry point into Texas.

My wife, Avis, and my daughter, Teresa, have earned acknowledgment in many ways, but especially for those long hours they spent at the typewriter.

Many others have contributed in various ways. All are appreciated, though space forbids their being recognized.

ABBREVIATIONS USED IN NOTES

A.G.I.: Archivo General de Indias

A.G.N.: Archivo General de la Nación, México

A.M.S.F.: Archivo del Marqués de San Francisco

SWHQ: Southwestern Historical Quarterly

CONTENTS

PART III: PRESIDIO OF THE LINE: AFTER 1772

ILLUSTRATIONS

Part I
FRONTIER OUTPOST
1700-1716

1. FINDING THE GATEWAY

FROM THE CAPITAL CITY of México the trail pointed northward. It meandered through the rugged mountains of the Sierra Madre Oriental, out across the tablelands of the Central Plateau. Ever lengthening, its forward extremity advanced like a long snake, the tail remaining stationary. At last the trail reached out onto the arid plains of the North, ringed by mountains from which came wood and water (sometimes in gushing torrents) and *los indios rebeldes*—the dreaded Toboso Indians.[1] Across the desert country the head of the growing snake extended onward till it reached a gateway on the Great River of the North.

Until this time—the late seventeenth century—Spanish trails had approached Texas from the west rather than the south. They had followed Coronado into New Mexico, and thence out onto the Great Plains, as the fearless *adelantados* went in pursuit of phantom treasure and encountered hardship and suffering which were quite real.

From 1629 the Spaniards in New Mexico made periodic journeys to the Jumanos, a group never clearly defined, ethnologically or geographically. But not by these visits from the west did the Europeans leave their

[1] Akin to the Lipan Apaches (Na-Dene group, Atapascan subgroup, and Atapascan family), the Tobosos were a nomadic, warlike, and cannibalistic tribe which ranged in the Serranías del Burro in northwestern Coahuila. The enemy of the Coahuiltecans, they made such daring and frequent attacks on the missions that their name became synonymous with terror. By 1735 the Tobosos had largely disappeared; those who had not been killed by the Spaniards had joined the Apaches (See James Manly Daniel, "The Advance of the Spanish Frontier and the Despoblado," p. 29).

indelible stamp on Texas. The serpentine trail must writhe its way northward from the heart of México to find its gateway on the Río Grande del
Norte.

Not only did this river form a barrier; it also formed a boundary. It
separated the known—or at least the more familiar—from the *tierra incognita*. Beyond was a land filled with mystery. From its hills and brushy
plains came the enemy Indians who made war on their more docile brothers and who did their best to upset the work of the missions. It was said
that even fiercer tribes ranged beyond.

Yet the ferocity of the Indians was not a complete deterrent. For the
humble padres whose sandals stirred the dust of the winding trail through
the Mexican heartland, it presented a challenge. Here were lost souls who
might be brought into "the society of the Holy Mother Church," souls to
be redeemed from the very jaws of hell. The fathers thrilled to the stories
which their half-tame Indian friends brought back from the *gentilidad,*
the pagan land of the North. The day would come when, in the great
service of both Majesties, they would go forth to accomplish the *reducciones,* to settle the savages in missions.

Settlers on New Spain's northern frontier looked curiously toward the
Río Grande del Norte. Their interest in the outer region centered primarily on three factors: trouble with the Indians who lived there; missionary desires for the conversion of these savages; hunger for a new source of
mineral wealth and adventure. Another factor entered the picture when
France intruded upon Spanish territory; the Spaniards had to move to extend the northern boundary.

Much of the difficulty with the natives was of the Spaniards' own making. They conducted senseless raids on the rancherias of some docile tribes
and sold the captives into slavery, some to work in the mines, some in the
haciendas of the wealthy Creoles.

As the line of Spanish settlements moved northward, a new set of circumstances evolved. Instead of sedentary Indian tribes which the Spaniards
had encountered in other parts, they found in northern México a different
breed. Their native spirit was such that they preferred death in the *montes*
to beatings in the haciendas.[2]

Indian warfare broke out anew in 1661 with a general uprising in the
Monterrey-Saltillo area. Major Juan de la Garza pursued the Cacaxtle

---

[2] Vito Alessio Robles, *Coahuila y Texas en la época colonial*, p. 116.

Indians more than seventy leagues to the north of Monterrey. The Spaniards killed 100 natives and took 125 prisoners south to a life of slavery.[3]

Two years later the *alcalde mayor* of Saltillo, Don Fernando de Azcué y Armendárez, led a follow-up campaign against the Cacaxtles. This expedition was the first to cross the lower Río Grande of which there is definite record.[4] Azcué's route cannot be definitely traced. He traveled six days to reach the enemy camp and may well have forded the river at one of the two main crossings which in future years would serve as the primary entry points to Texas.[5] The battle possibly was fought on the Río de las Nueces or the Río Frío in the Texas hill country.

[3] *Ibid.*, p. 196. W. W. Newcomb, Jr. (*The Indians of Texas: From Prehistoric to Modern Times*, p. 36), defines the Cacaxtles as "an important subgroup of the Kesale-Terkdom Coahuiltecans." Paul Horgan (*Great River: The Río Grande in North American History*, p. 257) transforms the Cacaxtles in this instance into the Plains Indians (Apaches and Comanches), but it was almost a century later before the Comanches were seen this far south.

[4] John Francis Bannon (ed.), *Bolton and the Spanish Borderlands*, p. 109.

[5] While many writers acknowledge only one crossing of importance at the gateway to Spanish Texas, actually there were two. Paso de Francia may have been used the most by the important expeditions, but Paso Pacuache, some distance upstream, deserves nearly equal prominence. In later years Paso de Francia, six miles southeast of Guerrero, Coahuila, was referred to as the Lower Crossing, or as Las Islas, or Isletas, Crossing, because of the islands in that part of the river—"where the water course widens out upon a firm bed of limestone and is divided into three wide arms" (Alessio Robles, *Coahuila y Texas*, p. 377). El Paso Pacuache, so-named for the Coahuiltecan Indian nation by that name, six miles northeast of Guerrero, was known also as Paso de Nogal and Paso de Diego Ramón. Some natives of the area maintain that the correct name is Tlacuache, or 'Possum, Crossing. On April 8, 1967, the author visited both these historic fords, on both sides of the Río Grande, and, accompanied by John F. Woodhull of Eagle Pass, waded across the river at Paso de Francia in water never over knee-deep. This was not possible at Pacuache because the International Boundary and Water Commission has constructed a weir across the river a short distance below the crossing in order to measure the river's flow. Instead of finding three channels at Paso de Francia, as Alessio Robles relates, we found five, each separated from the other by an island.

D. E. Egerton, surveyor for the Río Grande Land Company in the early 1830's, observed concerning the river that ". . . smooth ledges of rock cause rapids rather than falls. . . . At about two leagues below the Presidio del Río Grande, one of the ledges traverses the river, in an oblique direction, from one bank to the other, causing a slight fall at low stages of the water, and there having on its edge probably not more than from ten to twelve inches. Immediately below this, the river, for about half a league, is turned into a variety of channels by a vast number of islands from which this place is called 'Las Islitas' " (In William Kennedy, *Texas: The Rise, Progress, and Prospects of the Republic of Texas*, I, 56).

In any event, Spanish military might was felt in Texas. Soon the wilderness north of the Río Grande would know the power of the cross.

The Indian nations which the Spaniards had sought to subdue by armed might and those which they soon would attempt to convert to Christianity were the same ones. They were the Coahuiltecans,[6] divided into a large number of small tribes and bands which dwelt on both sides of the Río Grande.

Like children lost in darkness the Coahuiltecans stood on the northern frontier of New Spain, beckoning to the missionary fathers to come and show them the light. Their apparent thirst for the Christian Gospel may be attributable largely to a child-like curiosity. Yet to the Spanish padres they represented a challenge which could not go unanswered. The first to respond to the opportunity was Friar Juan Larios.

In the year 1670 the thirty-seven–year–old Franciscan friar, returning to his post in the province of Jalisco after visiting his sister in Durango, suddenly found his way blocked by two Indian warriors. The natives presented a frightening appearance, but they assured the solitary priest that they meant him no harm. They asked only that he go with them to the northern region to convert their people to Christianity.

By one of the two Indians Larios dispatched a hastily scribbled note to his superior; with the other he traveled northeastward. In twenty days they came to a rancheria, where the natives accorded the missionary a warm welcome and immediately set about building him a chapel and a dwelling.

Larios began to study the language of the Indians and to give them instruction in the Catholic faith. Natives from neighboring villages came to see and hear him, and before many weeks had passed, the priest was surrounded by more than five hundred Indians. From this first mission in

---

[6] The Coahuiltecans, closely akin to the Karankawas of the coastal country, were poorly equipped, primitive hunters and gatherers. Culturally speaking, they were quite backward. They lived the harshest and most difficult life, inhabiting the region which had the fewest usable natural resources. The many small nomadic bands often were at war with each other, and captives were frequently roasted and eaten. The Coahuiltecans populated the mission settlements of Coahuila, Nuevo León, and some of those in Texas, gradually losing their identity. They quickly fell prey to the white man's diseases, and by 1800 most of the South Texas Coahuiltecans had disappeared, having been destroyed by disease or absorbed into the Mexican populace (Newcomb, *Indians of Texas*, p. 37).

Coahuila, probably about thirty miles north of present Monclova,[7] Larios went out to visit other Coahuiltecan tribes. For three years he reaped an abundant harvest of souls. He fixed the missionary focal point of north-eastern New Spain where it logically belonged: upon the nomadic Coahuiltecans, whose wanderings in quest of wild foods took them back and forth across the Río Grande, between the two regions later to be known as Coahuila and Texas.

It was the wandering of these peripatetic Indians which caused Brother Manuel de la Cruz, and then Father Francisco Peñasco de Lozano, to journey north of the Río Grande in 1674. Brother Manuel spent twenty-one days north of the big river, in the region now comprising the Texas counties of Maverick, Val Verde, and Kinney. He crossed the stream "at two forks and over a wide ford, in the middle of which was an island of sand."[8]

Could this have been the ford later called Paso de Francia? It cannot be known, but Brother Manuel's thrust into the *tierra incognita* was an important step in the finding of the gateway to Spanish Texas.

A short time after Brother Manuel's return, Father Peñasco left the Mission Santa Rosa on a two-month journey which took him four leagues beyond the Río Grande by an unknown route to the camp of the Manos Prietos nation. Like Brother Manuel he returned with many Indians for the Coahuila missions. Among the number, it is said, were some Tejas—"Indians who were to play so prominent a role fifteen years later in the temporary occupation of eastern Texas."[9]

From beyond the Río Grande the Coahuiltecans kept coming, asking the Spaniards to live among them and teach them their religion. In answer to such appeals Father Larios, in 1675, accompanied Captain Fernando del Bosque to the Texas side of the river. Proceeding almost straight north from Monclova, the Larios-Del Bosque expedition reached the Río Grande on May 11. In his report Del Bosque wrote that the river was more than four hundred varas in width. On its banks was desolate wilderness, with only an abandoned rancheria of grass huts to be seen. The

---

[7] Francis Borgia Steck (trans.), *Forerunners of Captain De León's Expedition to Texas, 1670–1675*, p. 6.

[8] *Ibid.*, p. 16.

[9] *Ibid.*, p. 19.

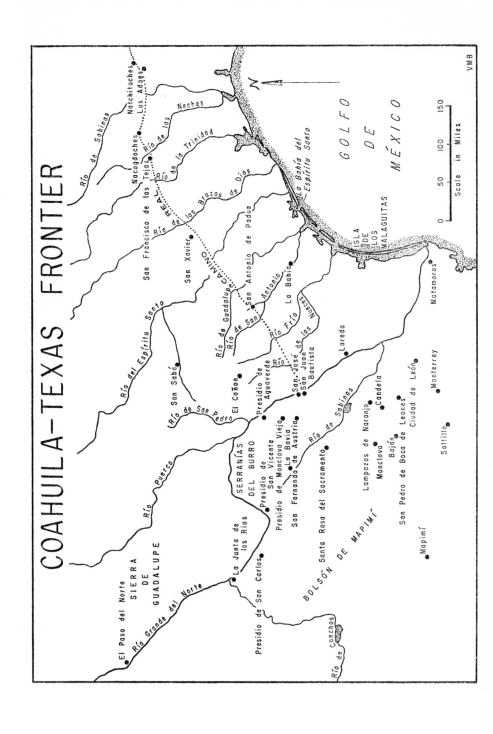

COAHUILA-TEXAS FRONTIER

VMB

GOLFO DE MÉXICO

N

Scale in Miles
0   50   100   150

Río de Sabinas
Natchitoches
Los Adaes
Neches
Nacogdoches
Río de las
Río de la Trinidad
San Francisco de los Tejas
Río de los Brazos de Dios
Río del Espíritu Santo
San Xavier
San Antonio de Padua
Río de Guadalupe
CAMINO REAL
San Antonio
La Bahía del Espíritu Santo
ISLA DE LOS MALAGUITAS
La Bahía
Río de San
Río Frío
Río de los Nueces
San Sabá
Río San Sabá
Río de San Pedro
El Cañon
Presidio de Aguaverde
Río
San José de las
San Juan Bautista
Laredo
Río del Espíritu Santo
Matamoros
Río Puerco
SIERRA DE GUADALUPE
La Junta de los Rios
Presidio de San Vicente
Presidio de Monclova Viejo
La Bavia
San Fernando de Austria
Río de Sabinas
Lampazos de Naranjo
Candela
Monclova
Ciudad de León
Monterrey
SERRANÍAS DEL BURRO
Bajan
San Pedro de Boca de Leones
El Paso del Norte
Presidio de San Carlos
Santa Rosa del Sacramento
BOLSÓN DE MAPIMÍ
Mapimí
Saltillo
Río Grande del Norte
Río de Conchos

Indians in the party advised the leader to proceed upstream from the usual ford and cross at a place where the river had spread itself into three channels. The place where the Spaniards crossed is disputed, but at least one authority holds to Paso de Francia, near the future site of San Juan Bautista, the gateway to Spanish Texas.[10]

The voyageurs visited the same area to which Brother Manuel de la Cruz had come the previous year and recrossed the Río Grande at a point upstream from where they had entered.[11] This expedition induced large numbers of Indians from beyond the river of the North to return to Coahuila and settle themselves in missions.

In such a manner the line of mission establishments on the northern frontier might have continued to advance, had Spanish officialdom been able to resolve its course. But while the Spaniards fussed and floundered, the Coahuiltecans grew restless, and disappointment flared into hostility. Then the difficulty was compounded by the "navigational error" of the Frenchman Robert René Cavelier, Sieur de La Salle. The presence of the French on the Texas coast caused the Spaniards to jump off into an unknown land, far from a supply base. It was a move for which they were not prepared. Yet fear of the foreign invaders caused missionary interest to shift prematurely. The Coahuiltecans were temporarily forgotten, as the religious effort centered upon the Tejas, or Asinais.

The key figures in this venture among the Tejas had come to New Spain in 1683, while La Salle was still in France making preparations for his voyage. Among the twenty-four Franciscan priests who crossed the Atlantic to join in the founding of the Colegio de la Santa Cruz de Querétaro were two who would be most intimately associated with the enterprise: Fathers Damián Massanet and Francisco Hidalgo. Of the two,

[10] Alessio Robles, *Coahuila y Texas*, p. 253 n. The description fits that of Paso de Francia given in *ibid.*, and looking upon that ford, one can easily visualize the crossing at this point as described by Del Bosque. But the river has many other islands dividing its channel, and the description might fit any one of several places on the stream. Steck *(Forerunners*, p. 26) says the crossing probably was made a little below Eagle Pass—the description applied by some historians to the location of San Juan Bautista, thirty-five miles downstream.

[11] Steck *(Forerunners*, p. 30) says the expedition probably touched on the lower reaches of the Pecos River. Ben Cuellar Ximenes *(Gallant Outcasts: Texas Turmoil, 1519–1734*, pp. 46–51), on the other hand, seems hard put to point the *entrada* toward San Antonio, and to make it a preliminary to that settlement, which it was not.

one would be defeated by the experience. The other would marshal the spiritual forces for another attack on paganism.

The founders of México's first missionary college, after a three-month voyage with the silver fleet, reached Veracruz at the darkest hour of that port city's history. More than two thousand pirates had completed the rape and pillage of the city just in time to sail from the harbor before the cargo fleet arrived. The maimed and dying lay unattended while the living moaned in anguish at the loss of their young women, borne away on the pirate ships, their bodies to be used until they were broken.[12] Gone, too, was the gold and silver bullion, which had been piled on the docks to await the fleet's arrival for shipment to Spain. But so great was the toll of human life and dignity that the loss of the treasure hardly seemed worth mentioning.

The work of the Franciscan religious lay before them. The twenty-four-year-old Father Hidalgo was foremost among the priests as they consoled and confessed the living, administered final rites, and gave proper burial to the dead. They labored incessantly until the commissary of the Franciscans, Father Antonio Llinás de Jesús María, thought best to remove them because of the shortage of provisions in the stricken city. With crucifix and breviary, they marched in twos for Querétaro, stopping at villages along the way to hold preaching missions. Father Hidalgo, while waiting for the time for the missionaries to gather at Querétaro, preached at San Juan del Río.

Little is known of the background of this dedicated priest. It appears likely that he was an orphan; the name of his parents and the place of his birth are nowhere found. At the age of fifteen he completed the pre-requisite courses of study and took the religious habit. "He was a completely artless religious, and very zealous for the conversion of the Indians among whom he passed most of his life . . . incapable of all duplicity, cunning, and malice."[13] His guileless nature and religious mortification would help him to bear with patience the labors and hardships which he would meet in New Spain.

---

[12] Juan Domingo Arricivita, *Crónica seráfica y apostólica del Colegio de propaganda fide de la Santa Cruz de Querétaro en la Nueva España, segunda parte,* p. 206. For a dramatic account of this episode see Hodding Carter, *Doomed Road of Empire: The Spanish Trail of Conquest,* pp. 34–38.

[13] Arricivita, *Crónica seráfica,* p. 206. For a biographical sketch of Hidalgo see *ibid.,* Chapters X–XII, pp. 206–226.

Hidalgo applied himself with diligence to the tasks of the missionary college. From his zeal in preaching against vice his reputation grew, and he was called to join with other priests on missions to various villages surrounding Querétaro. He preached in the monasteries, in the plazas, and in the streets. A mission in the Bishopry of Puebla in 1684 was especially fruitful: "Indecent costumes were abandoned, thefts and usuries were restored, ancient enmities reconciled, illicit and dishonest trade stopped; and above all, general confessions and public penitences were seen on every hand."[14]

After the Puebla mission, Hidalgo traveled during the year 1686 with Friar Pedro Medina, hearing confessions and preaching to huge crowds in the Villa de San Miguel el Grande. Without rest for twenty days, Friar Francisco fell gravely ill and was forced to return to the college for recuperation. When he was able to travel the evangelist's trail again, he joined with Friar Antonio de Escaray. His abounding love, his zeal, and his personal magnetism won many souls, as he illumined the understanding and imparted memorable moral lessons, "contrasting the light of the faith with the darkness of vice."[15]

Hidalgo made a practice of illustrating each sermon with an example. With apostolic invective he moved his hearers to make the act of contrition with such fervent spirit that the church often would be flooded with tears.

As the missionary group passed from the Villa de Lagos to Our Lady of San Juan, the people followed them in the roads. All the pueblos along their way were evangelized. At Hacienda de Mata so many came to confess that the plantation was populated like a major town. At Aguascalientes, Friar Francisco Estévez joined Escaray and Hidalgo. The three went together into the city of Zacatecas, whose people were so moved that they proposed the establishment of a new missionary college there.[16]

---

[14] *Ibid.*, p. 208.   [15] *Ibid.*, p. 209.

[16] *Ibid.*, p. 210. Although the people of Zacatecas asked them to establish an apostolic college, offering the church of Nuestra Señora de Guadalupe and the means to build a friary, the friars declined, saying the College of Querétaro lacked sufficient personnel to staff such a college. The College of Nuestra Señora de Guadalupe de Zacatecas was not established until 1702. See Carlos E. Castañeda, *Our Catholic Heritage in Texas,* II, 21–22, and Isidro Félix de Espinosa, *Crónica de los colegios de propaganda fide de la Nueva España,* new edition with notes and introduction by Lino G. Canedo, pp. 805–810.

The three missionaries departed from Zacatecas followed by more than three thousand persons. They continued their mission in the mining camps of La Veta and Pánuco, preaching and hearing confessions at all hours of day and night.

In 1688 the same three priests again departed from the College of the Holy Cross, this time with a different goal: conversion of the Indians. With the blessing of the bishop of Guadalajara, they took the northward trail. Traveling on foot "with the chamber of holy poverty," they slept where darkness found them; they ate what was offered. In all the villages along the winding road which measured the distance to Saltillo they held preaching missions.

In Saltillo the multitudes gathered to hear the Gospel preached and to make their confessions. The priests labored incessantly in pulpit and confessionary to fill the need. The task was too great for Father Escaray; from seventy leagues of travel and unstinting work along the way, his health broke. While he returned to the college, the other two priests pressed on to the Villa de la Monclova, which lay at the edge of the *gentilidad,* the pagan land, where they longed to go and convert the savage.

But when they presented their credentials to their superiors in Monclova, they received no encouragement. All but rebuffed by the local officials and churchmen, they resolved to go ahead, without the support they had hoped for, to the banks of the Río Grande, there to give the Holy Gospel to the nations who lived along its banks. Then their zeal was frustrated further: the officials at Monclova declared the road beyond to be closed.

It was a severe blow, but fervent prayers soon were answered. Three Tlaxcalteco Indians who had joined them in Saltillo sought out the priests in the monastery to offer a plan. The Indians would take them to Boca de Leones. The three would go out and bring in other natives for the missionaries to convert.[17]

At first the padres were disappointed in Boca de Leones, for they failed to find the thirsting souls they had hoped for. The Tlaxcaltecos went out to the Indian villages, however, and soon were bringing in prospects for the mission. A church was built and instruction was given the natives.

Not all the wealth to be gained at Boca de Leones was spiritual. The

[17] Arricivita, *Crónica seráfica,* p. 211. Boca de Leones was at the present site of Villadama, Nuevo León.

Alasapa Indians brought word of some heavy stones found on a mountain overlooking the pleasant valley. After assays revealed that the stones contained great quantities of silver, Boca de Leones grew into a prosperous mining camp, and the King's treasury was enriched. But the missionary priests sought a different kind of wealth. From their mission they went out to mountain and desert, seeking conversions. They drew many natives from the wilds, gathered them at the mission, and instructed them in the Christian Gospel.

As the settlement prospered from the mines, the mission also thrived. So successful was the endeavor that the superior prelate, after two years, decided that it should be turned over to the ecclesiastical judge and the missionaries withdrawn. The Alasapas and other Indians of the mission soon reverted to their former haunts. The padres were grieved; but the year now was 1690, and other important tasks lay ahead.

While Hidalgo and Estévez were laboring in the mission at Boca de Leones, Friar Damián Massanet also had moved out onto the northern frontier. Between Monclova and Boca de Leones he had founded the Mission San Bernardino de la Caldera. He had been called away from the mission the previous year to accompany Governor Alonso de León on his reconnaissance of Espíritu Santo Bay in search of the Frenchman La Salle's Fort St. Louis.

For four years, 1685–1689, the Spaniards had sought La Salle's colony. Five maritime expeditions combed the Gulf Coast, from México to Florida. They found remains of French vessels but somehow managed to misinterpret the evidence, thwarting their own success.

In June, 1686, Alonso de León was chosen to lead the search by land. He twice crossed the lower Río Grande, in 1686 and 1687, from Cadereyta and Cerralvo in Nuevo León, to explore the Texas coast. Then, on July 13, 1687, he was appointed governor of Coahuila. His first few months in office consisted of almost continuous warfare with the Tobosos, assisted by an officer whose name soon would rise to prominence: Diego Ramón.

In May, 1688, De León went in search of an Indian village said to be ruled by a white chief, taking eleven soldiers from Nuevo León under Martín Mendiondo and six from Presidio de San Francisco de Coahuila under Ramón. Crossing the Río Grande, probably at Paso de Francia, the Spaniards went fourteen leagues beyond the river in a northeasterly direc-

tion to find the rancheria of the Frenchman, who said his name was Jean
Géry. Though the man evidently was demented, and there was doubt that
he had knowledge of La Salle's colony, he was sent for interrogation to
México. There it was determined that a new *entrada* should be led by
De León with the Frenchman as a guide. Accompanied by two priests—
one of them Father Damián Massanet—the expedition passed on April 1
near the future site of San Juan Bautista and crossed the Río Grande at the
ford which some say from this date forth was called "Paso de Francia," or
France Way.[18]

On April 22, after three weeks of difficult travel beyond the Río
Grande, they found the gruesome ruins of La Salle's colony, its threat to
New Spain horribly and completely removed by the sanguinary Karan-
kawa Indians.

The Spaniards met a Tejas chief who had a phenomenal knowledge of
the Catholic religion, carrying with him a portable altar adorned with the
figures of the saints. His ancestors, he explained, had seen the Lady in
Blue;[19] he wished that the Spaniards would send missionaries to live
among his people.

Thus the course of future colonization efforts was fixed upon the land
of the Tejas, four hundred miles from the nearest Spanish settlement. It
would be many a day before official wheels would turn faster in New
Spain. The expedition back in México, General De León received on July
27 the decision of the junta to establish a Tejas mission and to place
Father Massanet in charge of conversions. Among those whom Massanet
chose to accompany him was Father Francisco Hidalgo. Hidalgo, however,
stopped off at the Mission de la Caldera in Coahuila and did not accompany the founding expedition.

Departing from Santiago de la Monclova on March 27, the new *entrada*

18 Castañeda (*Our Catholic Heritage*, I, 334–335) goes to some length to dis-
prove the theory that De León's crossing was near the future site of San Juan
Bautista but fails because he has this location misplaced by some thirty miles. He
locates San Juan Bautista "five or six miles below Eagle Pass" and places De
León's crossing at "perhaps a little below present Guerrero," which actually coin-
cides with the location of Paso de Francia.

19 Mother María de Jesús de Ágreda, known as the Lady in Blue, claimed that
her spirit had left a Spanish convent on innumerable occasions to traverse the
thousands of miles into the Texas wilderness, carrying the holy message to the
heathen Indians. The Indians on several occasions reported having seen a beautiful
woman in a blue habit who exhorted them to enter missions.

crossed again at Paso de Francia and proceeded eastward to the ruins of the French fort on Matagorda Bay. On the banks of the Neches the Mission San Francisco de los Tejas was founded, with a second mission, Santísimo Nombre de María, to be established later. After the initial founding the main body of soldiers began the return to Coahuila with Father Massanet and General De León.

De León, on reaching Coahuila, found himself in official disfavor. Early in 1691 Domingo Terán de los Ríos, who had never been to Texas, was named governor of the province. De León, who had led five *entradas*, was denied. A short two months later death ended his career of service to Spain.

The influence of such a forceful leader, however, was not done with. Named governor *ad interim* was one of his captains: Diego Ramón, who evidently had remained behind to defend the settlements of Coahuila during the last two *entradas*, after having made the previous one.

The first man to hold the title of governor of Texas, General Terán de los Ríos moved his fifty troops out of Presidio de San Francisco de Coahuila on May 16, 1691, bound for the Kingdom of the Tejas. The same day Father Damián Massanet and his religious—this time including Friar Francisco Hidalgo—departed from the Mission of San Salvador del Valle de Santiago. The two groups met on the Sabinas River on Sunday, May 20.

Reaching the Río Grande on May 28, the Terán expedition marched six leagues along its banks to arrive at the crossing called Paso de Francia. That night the horses stampeded, and the camp remained four days on the right bank, while an effort was made to round them up. Less than one-third of the sixty-nine missing animals could be found. "We crossed to the other side [says Terán] with a loss of forty-nine saddle horses. While transferring the whole train composing my expedition, three head of stock were drowned. The current is exceedingly rapid where it is narrowest. . . . Here the river's width must be about a gunshot."[20]

The expedition was forced to hurry the crossing, as the river began to rise rapidly. Since the water was too deep for the small stock to wade, and there was no wood for a raft, the soldiers and friars swam their horses back and forth across the swollen stream, carrying armloads of sheep and

[20] Mattie Austin Hatcher (trans.), *The Expedition of Don Domingo Terán de los Ríos into Texas*, p. 12.

goats—seventeen hundred in all. The chore lasted from noon until five o'clock. That night a three-hour storm wrought havoc with the Spaniards' camp. Lightning bolts split the dark sky, and high winds blew down all the tents, leaving the people and their possessions exposed to a heavy downpour of rain. The waters of an arroyo swept over the tent and trunks of General Terán. The storm raged from one o'clock to four in the morning. It was a memorable entry into Texas.[21]

On June 13, the day of St. Anthony of Padua, the expedition camped on the banks of a beautiful stream. Terán named it San Antonio de Padua and recorded his vision that one day *reducciones* would be formed, with mission settlements planted first on the Río Grande and then at this place, which he termed the most beautiful in New Spain.

On reaching the land of the Tejas, the travelers found the Indians insolent, more interested in stealing the Spaniards' horses than in hearing the Christian Gospel. Governor Terán was too preoccupied with the task that lay before him to take much notice of the worsened situation at the missions. His force set out on November 28 for the land of the Cadodacho Indians, on the Red River, a journey marked by the loss of almost all his horses in severe winter weather. Back on the Neches, Terán commandeered the mission's horses for the return to Coahuila, on which he was accompanied by six of Father Massanet's disheartened friars.

In January, 1693, Diego Ramón, acting governor of Coahuila since the death of Alonso de León, reported to the Viceroy the dire circumstances facing the missionaries in East Texas. The crops had failed and their cattle had died. Ramón's successor as governor, Gregorio de Salinas Varona, set out from Monclova the following May 3 to take them the needed supplies. The expedition reached San Francisco de los Tejas on June 8 to find missionaries and soldiers, on meager rations, ready to withdraw. Illness raged among the Indians, and one of the missionaries had died. The Indians, blaming the fathers for the deaths among them, steadfastly refused to be congregated in the mission; they were convinced that the waters of baptism were fatal.

[21] Terán de los Ríos, as he advanced into Texas, established a trail which with some variations would be the main route in years to come. Like many another traveler, he spent his first night after crossing the Río Grande at Charco de Cuervo (or Real de Cuervo), so named because of the thousands of crows which roosted nearby. Thence the trail dissected Arroyo de Ramos, Arroyo de Caramanchel, El Río de las Nueces, and so on to San Antonio.

When Salinas Varona started back for Coahuila, two more missionaries went with him.

Conditions at the mission worsened still. A soldier stood beside a cannon ready to light the fuse as the Indians threatened a massacre. In October the priests finally decided, in the face of repeated threats, to withdraw. They packed the religious ornaments, buried the cannon and the bells, and set fire to the log mission. Stalked by the savages, they trudged back through the wilderness which they had entered with such high hopes. Four of the soldiers deserted to remain with the Indians. Among them was Joseph de Urrutia,[22] who later would return to Spanish service as an interpreter of the Tejas language.

Father Massanet and his companions came again to the crossing on the Río Grande and passed on to Monclova, which they reached on February 17, 1694. The Viceroy asked Massanet to suggest new mission sites in northern Coahuila, but the padre was sick at heart. He was ready to return to Querétaro, to leave the founding of missions to other hands.

Among the missionaries returning from the Tejas, however, was one who would have chosen to remain. He withdrew with resolution in his heart that he would go back to the unfinished work among the East Texas Indians. This priest was Francisco Hidalgo.

The Sieur de La Salle had caused the Spaniards to make an inordinate expenditure of resources to penetrate Texas at a time and under circumstances which were not of their own choosing. It would be so again, though not without the connivance of Father Hidalgo.

The years immediately following the withdrawal of the missionaries from East Texas were dead ones, so far as establishment of new missions on the northern frontier is concerned. The priests returned to their college, and at this point Father Massanet disappears from history.[23] To most of

[22] Urrutia, who entered with Terán, is said to have suffered an accident on the Colorado which forced him to remain with the Indians. He lived with the Kanohatino, Too, and Xarame nations seven years and was made chief of all the nations hostile to the Apaches, against whom he led several campaigns. He returned to San Juan Bautista about the time of its founding and was serving as protector of Indians of Nuevo León at the time of the 1716 *entrada* to re-establish the Tejas missions. He was made captain of the Presidio de San Antonio de Béjar in 1733, and in 1739 led an expedition against the Apaches on the San Sabá River. He died in 1740, to be succeeded as commandant at Béjar by his son, Toribio.

[23] Herbert Eugene Bolton (ed.), *Spanish Exploration in the Southwest, 1542–1706*, p. 350.

the missionaries who had accompanied him, the name "Tejas" was so
odious that they cared not even to pronounce it.[24] Hidalgo was the one
exception to the rule. Having left the Tejas mission against his will, he
longed to return. The road back was long, and well he knew it. But it
seems that each step he took in the intervening years moved him in that
direction. He came at last to the gateway on the Río Grande, where he
worked for years among the various Coahuiltecan nations. Despite the
wealth of opportunity at his fingertips, however, he looked beyond the
Coahuiltecans to fix his gaze upon the Tejas.

Alonso de León had opened the road; he had indelibly marked the
gateway to Spanish Texas. The settlement soon to be placed there would
be, for a time, the most advanced point on the northeast frontier of New
Spain. But such a circumstance could not long endure. Over the two strategic river crossings near San Juan Bautista—Paso Pacuache and Paso de
Francia—would flow the lifeblood of Texas. For a century and a half the
fords would serve as beachheads for invasions, while the nearby mission
settlement functioned as supply depot, station for reinforcements, ecclesiastical headquarters, haven for wayfarers, and starting point for explorations.

The way station at the gateway would receive travelers from both directions: bearers of sword and cross from the south; from the north the
"pagan" souls who were curious about, if not actually thirsting for, the
Christian religion.

2. THE MISSION BUILDERS

FOR SEVERAL YEARS after his return to México from Texas, Father
Hidalgo held preaching missions in the villages surrounding the col-
lege, much as he had done during the first few years of his ministry in the
New World. In 1697 one of the founders of the College of the Holy

---

[24] Arricivita, *Crónica seráfica*, p. 221.

Cross, Friar Antonio Margil de Jesús, returned to the institution to serve as its guardian. During Margil's thirteen-year absence the Colegio de la Santa Cruz had widened its field of apostolic endeavor to include Yucatán and New Galicia, Chiapas and Coahuila, Michoacán and New Mexico. The founders had been reinforced in 1692 by twenty-three priests and four lay brothers from Spain, as well as by native Franciscans from México. They propagated the faith, founded towns, and opened roads into unknown territories.[1]

When Father Margil became guardian, a sprinkling of missions already existed in Coahuila, though it had been several years since a mission had been founded in that northern province. During the term of Governor Gregorio de Salinas Varona (1692–1697), there is record of only one mission having been planted. The fault, however, lay not so much with the Governor as with the hostility of the natives.

While the Indians of the central region had yielded meekly to the Spaniards' requirement that they work their land, those of the North did not acquiese so readily. Still, the Spaniards, few as they were, sought to use the hands of the savages to cultivate their great expanses of land, acquired at little or no cost by means of royal grant. Such methods created for the mission builders a handicap which was difficult to overcome.

During Margil's term as guardian, however, the ceiling lifted. In 1698, "having news of the copious harvest of pagan souls in the north who were without the light of the Gospel," he sent Fathers Diego de Salazar and Francisco Hidalgo to establish missions on the borders of Coahuila and Nuevo Reino de León.[2] For Father Hidalgo it was the first big step on the road back to the Tejas.

The new governor of Coahuila, Don Francisco Cuerbo y Valdés, commissioned Captain Juan Méndez Tobar to go with the padres and give possession of the necessary lands and waters. They arrived at the place called El Ojo de Agua de Lampazos, Lampazos Spring, on November 7, 1698. Here they found a rancheria of Indians, containing both Christians and *gentiles*.[3]

---

[1] Eduardo Enrique Ríos, *Life of Fray Antonio Margil, O. F. M.,* p. 61.

[2] Isidro Félix de Espinosa, *Crónica de los colegios de propaganda fide de la Nueva España,* p. 751.

[3] This word would be translated *heathens* or *pagans,* which the Indians were from the Spanish point of view. Inasmuch as a heathen or a pagan may be con-

Before the padres' arrival, the heavens had given what the good fathers took as a special sign. On a dark night fifty spheres of light, "which seemed as stars loosed from their moorings," fell around the spring. The excited populace looked with awe upon the "charged tongues of descending fire." The priests received news of the incident as a clear indication of the spot where they should build the mission church.[4]

A chapel of straw was begun November 12, the holy day of San Diego de Alcalá. The participants, all barefooted, marched in solemn procession to the new hermitage, holding high a wooden cross "as a royal banner of our redemption."[5] They sang a hymn and celebrated the mass of the saint, giving thanks to the Lord for the new harvest of souls.

"The judge of commission, demonstrating the great extent of his Christianity, kissed the feet of the priests and required that all the other Indians do likewise, paying obedience to the Supreme Pontiff, visible head of the church. All gave vassalage to the King our Lord, in whose royal name they were given possession of this place." The name of Santa María de los Dolores de la Punta was given the mission. "And how could the aid of the Lady of Sorrows fail for those who, as sons of the Cross, were so much the sons of its sorrows?"[6]

Father Salazar departed for the capital to inform the viceroy, Conde de Moctezuma, of his new mission. The Viceroy ordered governors of both Coahuila and Nuevo León to nurture and protect the new settlement. The governors responded by providing sixteen families of Tlaxcaltecos from Saltillo to aid in the mission's work. Salazar wrote of the new undertaking to Father Francisco Estévez, Father Hidalgo's old missionary teammate, now in the court in Madrid. As a result a mission of twelve religious was granted at government expense. The Viceroy, the bishop of Guadalajara, and governors of the two provinces received instructions from the King to lend all protection and encouragement possible to this new mission and to others yet to be founded.

From jubilation over his success in the capital, Father Salazar returned

---

sidered by some to be godless, or at least unreligious, I have chosen not to apply those words except in quoting, directly or indirectly, from Spanish sources.

[4] Espinosa, *Crónica*, p. 752. This location is the present site of Lampazos de Naranjo, Nuevo León.

[5] *Ibid.*, p. 752.   [6] *Ibid.*

to grim reality at St. Mary of Sorrows Mission. He found Father Hidalgo, though happy in his work, suffering many hardships. The hardy friar's daily diet consisted of rabbits, snails, and field rats.

Together the two friars prosecuted the work of the mission. With the few yokes of oxen given them in charity, they cultivated the land. As their work progressed, other natives came to ask a mission on the Río de Sabinas, ten leagues north of the Mission Dolores. Father Hidalgo was about to take his second big step on the road back to the Tejas: founding of the first Mission of San Juan Bautista, at the place significantly known as "Camino de la Nueva Francia y de los Tejas."[7]

On June 15, 1699, in the village of Monclova, the governor of Coahuila, General Don Francisco Cuerbo y Valdés, received a petition from Father Diego de Salazar. The viceroy, Count of Moctezuma, the priest related, had encouraged him in the newly founded Mission of Dolores, as well as in plans for founding still another mission. "I have many nations of heathen Indians of the Sabinas River,[8] of this jurisdiction, who have desire and enthusiasm for gathering themselves to our Holy Faith and placing themselves in a village and being reduced to a political body."[9]

The place on the Sabinas was quite suitable, Salazar observed, with all necessities for founding a pueblo in conformity with other establishments for the natives of Coahuila. The Viceroy had ordered that possession be given him for the establishment of a new mission.

The Governor, in his endorsement, spoke favorably of the proposal; the missions founded previously had served well to extend the faith, and this new one, in a location offering both fertile lands and abundant water, would bring further enhancement of the Royal Crown. The Governor himself dared not leave his own village, which was "pregnant with the live war against the Royal Crown, with which the rebel Toboso Indians

[7] Charles Wilson Hackett and Charmion Clair Shelby (trans.), *Pichardo's Treatise on the Limits of Louisiana and Texas,* II, 93.

[8] The Río de Sabinas rises in the Sierra del Carmen and flows southeastward to reach the Río Grande below Laredo. Known as Arroyo de la Bavia in its upper reaches, it becomes Río de Álamos, then Río de Sabinas, and finally, on entering Nuevo León, it is known as the Río Salado. See James Manly Daniel, "The Advance of the Spanish Frontier and the Despoblado," p. 6.

[9] San Juan Bautista, "Testimonio de la Fundación de la Misión de San Juan Bautista, 1699–1701," A.G.N., Historia, Vol. 29, p. 6.

are harassing us daily on these frontiers of the north." He therefore dele-
gated the tasks of reconnoitering the site, giving possession, and establishing pueblo and mission, to Juan Martín Treviño.[10]

On June 19, 1699, Treviño moved to carry out his orders. He left
Monclova with Friar Francisco Hidalgo and with Pedro Viscarra and
Diego de Minchaca, soldiers of the presidio. That night they reached the
Mission of San Felipe de Valladares, twenty leagues east, where they re-
mained the following day. On June 21 they traveled eight leagues to Santa
María de los Dolores. There Father Salazar waited with two Indian na-
tions, the Chaguanes and the Pachales, the ones who were asking for the
mission on the Río de Sabinas. Treviño instructed the Indians to go to the
Sabinas and wait there for the arrival of the Spaniards the following day.

The company, joined by Salazar, proceeded on June 22 to the Sabinas,
where they found not only the Chaguanes and the Pachales but the Mescales and Xarames nations as well. All four were asking for a village, and
large numbers were coming to be settled "in the society of our Holy
Mother Church and to obedience of His Majesty." Treviño proceeded
with the founding of the Mission San Juan Bautista.

On June 23 preparations were made for building a hut in which to celebrate
Mass, and for founding the village, by virtue of the commission which I hold
for this purpose. . . . Said hut was built, large and capacious.

On June 24 of said year, day of the glorious precursor, Saint John Baptist,
the Reverend Fathers Friar Diego de Salazar y San Buenaventura and Friar
Francisco Hidalgo rang a bell at the door of the hut. At the sound of the bell
more than 150 Indians gathered. There were men, women, and children, of the
Chaguanes, Pachales, Mescales, and Sarames nations. Father Friar Diego, filled
with enthusiasm, visited the site, and, appropriately, a cross was erected in the
earth. The Father took off his shoes and worshiped it and sang the *Imno ves-
tilla Regispro de uinte*. With the prayer of the raising of the cross, he raised it
high. In the name of His Majesty he delivered it to me. I kept us in procession

[10] *Ibid.*, p. 7. Such an assignment was not new to Treviño. He had officiated the
previous December (1698) in the founding of the Mission of Dulce Nombre de
Jesús de Peyotes, fifty leagues from Monclova, between the Río de Sabinas and
the Río Grande. En route to Peyotes he had marched in company with Diego
Ramón, on his way to establish, one day later, the Mission San Francisco Xavier,
forty leagues northwest of Monclova. The Mission San Juan Bautista in the Valle
de Santo Domingo on the Sabinas was the fourth to be planted under the jurisdiction of the Coahuila governor in less than eight months (Vito Alessio Robles,
Coahuila y Texas en la época colonial, p. 373).

until the cross was placed on the altar which was made in the hut for celebration of the holy sacrifice of the Mass. He finished vesting himself and the Mass was sung, for which the said Father Friar Francisco Hidalgo was minister. After the Mass was finished, he bade them pray the prayers of the Christian doctrine and the declaration of the faith, and the Alabado.[11]

Treviño named Andrés de Gámez interpreter, after he had taken the prescribed oath. Through the interpreter he gave the Indians to understand "the great care and solicitude which the Catholic Majesty of our Lord and King, Don Carlos II, has for serving God" and for attracting all the natives to the Catholic faith. The King, he told them, had sent apostolic ministers to teach them the Christian Doctrine in order that they might be saved; the faith and doctrine had been embraced in all the provinces and settlements which were under his royal obedience, and they enjoyed great benefits: peace and justice, personal safety, lands and waters for their pueblos and fields. They were even taught to be polite, and to wear clothes and shoes. With all these advantages went the knowledge of the Holy Catholic Faith and obedience to His Majesty.

To be deserving of these blessings, the interpreter told them, they must preserve and fulfill the precepts of the church and abide by what the fathers taught them. They must give obedience to His Majesty and keep his royal laws. The Indians responded by begging Treviño to give them possession of the lands and water from the river in order that they might continue in the foundation of the village.

Captain Treviño was encouraged by the "great desire and fervor" which the Indians displayed. He was impressed also by the territory: the site was fertile, with abundant pastures, firewood, evergreen hardwoods; there were no swamps; crops of corn, wheat, and beans could be grown. He granted their request for possession of the land and rights to water from the Río de Sabinas.

Proudly the Indians walked about their new fields, symbolizing their possession by cutting branches from the trees and taking water from the stream and sprinkling it over the land. "These," they said pridefully, "are the lands and the water he has given us, and has marked for founding our village."

From placing this foundation at this site, said Treviño, many benefits would be realized for God: the mission would bring peace and quietude

[11] San Juan Bautista, "Testimonio," pp. 8–11.

to Coahuila and Nuevo Reino de León and the camp of Boca de Leones by being the key post for the heathens from the northern region. When communication was established with these Indians, many souls would settle themselves in the society of the Church.

"Therefore, adjusting myself in every circumstance to the Royal ordinances of my commission, for the greater reverence of God and his most Holy Mother, the Virgin Mary, our Lady and Advocate, I found on this site this pueblo and Mission and place upon them the name of San Juan Bautista and Valley of Santo Domingo."[12]

Treviño marked off sufficient area for a church and a cemetery, convent and hospital. For royal houses, jail, and other necessities he staked off the block adjacent to the church, with the main plaza located just to the north of the church. For each block, 120 varas were allowed, and the streets were laid out in such a manner as to provide for future growth. The houses had to be neatly arranged according to established plan; they were made with flat roofs *(casas de terrado)*, with "roosts for the Castillian hens placed high, and nesting places on the ground."[13]

When it came time to name officials of the settlement, Francisco of the Chaguane Nation was chosen as governor. Others of the Chaguane and Pachale nations were appointed alcalde, aldermen, and constable. Badges were awarded each one "to stimulate competition for office." The new officials were charged with their responsibilities through the interpreter: they must uphold justice and see after the good of the village in building its church, completing the houses, and making the aqueduct. And each must obey the governor and alcaldes, for his turn might soon come, and in such a case he would receive obedience in the same manner in which he had given it. They must heed all orders in the service of both Majesties, and for the good of pueblo and mission, observing the Christian Doctrine which the missionaries would teach them.

[12] *Ibid.,* p. 11.

[13] *Ibid.,* p. 12. The Ordinances of Segovia gave detailed specifications for laying out a town. The main plaza was to be in the center, at least one and a half times as long as it was wide, a shape more suitable for festivities involving horsemen. The four main streets were to lead off from the mid-points of the sides of the plaza, while the corners of the plaza were to face the cardinal points, so that the streets would not be exposed to the four winds. Church, *cabildo,* and other buildings were to be located on the square and placed so as to form a defense complex (Daniel, "Advance of the Spanish Frontier," p. 54).

"All were obligated in this manner to do what they could to maintain their residence in the Pueblo and Mission of San Juan Bautista y Valle de Santo Domingo." Father Salazar, as apostolic commissary of the missions of Querétaro, named Father Hidalgo as missionary of the Mission of San Juan Bautista. Father Hidalgo accepted the appointment and remained "with great pleasure and rejoicing" in the mission.[14]

On completion of his report, Juan Martín Treviño presented it to all the Spaniards present for their examination, signed it along with the two priests and the interpreter, and forwarded it on to Governor Cuerbo y Valdés. The Governor approved and confirmed the new mission as well founded and as an enhancement of the Royal Crown, and extended to it the royal protection. He warned that anyone who disturbed or molested the Indians of the mission would be subject to a fine of two hundred pesos, "and he will be prosecuted with all the vigor at our command."[15]

The founding of the Mission San Juan Bautista on the Río de Sabinas was a glorious occasion, marked by optimism. The participants visualized a thriving settlement along the margins of the fertile flood plain, which would produce crops in abundance. But such fond hopes were not to be realized. Within a few short months the huts of the mission stood abandoned, the fields still barren, and the livestock scattered over the countryside.

Records of those few months apparently have been lost, and details of the circumstances which resulted in abandonment of the first site and removal of the Mission San Juan Bautista to a new location are not known. Vito Alessio Robles says:

Shortly after the 150 Indian neophytes were gathered in the mission, they fled from it, stealing the livestock. The missionary Hidalgo, following them to the Río Grande, gathered some of the fugitives and, with them and other Indians which he managed to congregate, placed anew the mission of San Juan Bautista in the vicinity of the Río Bravo.[16]

Soon after the mission was established on the Río de Sabinas, on the Camino de la Nueva Francia y de los Tejas, Father Salazar returned to Querétaro to ask the guardian of the apostolic college for missionaries to

---

[14] San Juan Bautista, "Testimonio," p. 13.
[15] *Ibid.*, p. 15.
[16] Alessio Robles, *Coahuila y Texas,* p. 474.

work in northern Coahuila. Father Margil, desirous of extending the missionary activity among the Coahuiltecans, sent two of the best he had. One was Antonio de San Buenaventura y Olivares, aging and crotchety from his years of service in the mission field in the province of Zacatecas, but with his most important work still ahead. The other was Marcos de Guereña, who suffered pain from the wounds of the Crucified Savior as though they were inflicted upon his own flesh.

"They were known for the strictest observance of the Gospel Rule."[17]

Fathers Olivares and Guereña went immediately to the Río de Sabinas, where they joined Father Hidalgo at San Juan Bautista. Together the three priests suffered the "inevitable labors" of the new mission. But the labors were short-lived, for the troubles which caused the mission to be abandoned soon began.

The mission Indians became unruly, ostensibly under the influence of other savages from the unsettled region to the north. A Christian Tejas Indian whom the missionaries had engaged to serve as interpreter, when they should again be able to enter Texas, was killed by the Indians from *la tierra adentro*. The ministers feared a major uprising, should word of the death reach the Indian's kinsmen.

Late summer drouth seized the land, and the fields were barren. The prospect of winter at this advanced outpost, without provisions or military protection, and with the Indians increasingly hostile, caused the missionaries to abandon the project. They retreated to the Mission of Dolores de la Punta. Yet they could not give up gracefully; their thoughts were ever upon the "pagan souls which lived in darkness"; their burning desire was to disperse this darkness with the light of the Gospel. "The spirit of these operators could not be appeased without looking for new harvests in which they could employ their talents."[18] Father Olivares soon departed for Santiago de la Monclova to negotiate with Governor Cuerbo y Valdés for the protection which would enable the apostolic missionaries to continue their work among the heathens.

The meeting with the Governor bore favorable results. As the year 1699 drew to a close, orders went out from Cuerbo y Valdés to the frontier veteran, Major (Sargento Mayor) Diego Ramón, the Governor's gen-

---

[17] Espinosa, *Crónica*, p. 753.
[18] *Ibid.*

eral lieutenant. On December 16 the Governor reported that he had sent twenty men to Ramón's hacienda of El Carrizalejo. Ramón was standing by, ready to leave for the unsettled land beyond. He would accompany the reverend father missionaries of the College of the Holy Cross of Querétaro to the north and northeast "where countless heathens live without knowledge of the light of the Gospel. He will ascertain whether there are some nations which wish to be settled in the society of our Holy Mother Church and to obedience to His Majesty."[19]

Should Ramón find it necessary to form these Indians into pueblo, he should proceed to do so, the Governor wrote. Cuerbo y Valdés gave the officer commission for such action as proved necessary for finding natives who wished to be settled in missions. Furthermore, he observed, Ramón was qualified by rank and experience to make such decisions, carrying out the proper ceremonies of settling the natives in pueblos in accord with the law, and naming governor and *cabildo* to see after them.

In such terms did Governor Cuerbo y Valdés square himself with the Viceroy for the action he was about to take. He purposely failed to spell out the true situation, or state specifically what his intentions were. He chose not to reveal that the new Mission San Juan Bautista y Valle de Santo Domingo on the Río de Sabinas already was a failure, and his instructions actually were designed to give Ramón authority to help the priests in establishing it at a new location. After all, the Governor wrote, the missionary priests who would administer the holy sacraments to the Indians, and who would teach them the Christian doctrine, should locate themselves in the places which the Indians chose to inhabit.

The Governor signed the instrument in the presence of two witnesses, Don Joseph Antonio de Ecay Múzquiz and Blas de Yruegas, and Ramón marched off at the head of his twenty men in the direction of the Great River of the North. Ramón set his course for the point on the river at which he had crossed with Alonso de León in 1688. With him went Fathers Olivares, Hidalgo, and Guereña.

Because Cuerbo y Valdés and the missionaries were exceeding their authority, or perhaps because some of the key documents have been misplaced, the account of the new foundation on the Río Grande is not found. We have only the version of Padre Espinosa, who himself served at the

[19] Francisco Cuerbo y Valdés, Report, December 16, 1699, in A.G.N., Provincias Internas, Vol. 28, p. 23.

Mission San Juan Bautista del Río Grande. "They arrived at some marshes some two leagues from the Río del Norte on January 1, 1700, Day of the Circumcision of the Lord. They named this site the Valley of the Circumcision, and with more than five hundred Indians of the same nations which they had gathered on the Sabinas River, the first mission, San Juan Bautista, was planted, restoring the name which had been used previously."[20]

The settlement established on this New Year's Day would serve thereafter as the gateway to Spanish Texas. For Father Hidalgo and his secret plan it was a giant step indeed.

[20] Espinosa, *Crónica*, p. 753. In 1790 the interim governor of Coahuila and *ayudante inspector* of missions noted confusion in the records of San Juan Bautista's move and explained it by quoting a 1752 report of Friar Alonso Giraldo de Terreros: A fire in the mission had burned the papers of its archives (Juan Gutiérrez de la Cueva, "Informe de las Misiones de la Provincia de Coahuila hecho por Don Juan Gutiérrez de la Cueva, February 15, 1790," A.G.N., Californias, Vol. 29, folio 224).

3. NEW SPIRITUAL CONQUESTS

MAJOR Diego Ramón, who led the expedition which resulted in the placing of the Mission San Juan Bautista near the Río Grande, was an extraordinary person. Indications are that he was a native of the parish of Santiago de Querétaro, for in the baptism record, 1670–1692, appears the name of Juana, daughter of Diego Ramón and María de los Ríos. "This origin of the family," says Canedo, "may explain the close relations which it maintained with the missionaries of the College of the Cross."[1]

Ramón's name is first found in connection with the history of the mission movement on the northern México frontier in 1674. He was then a young soldier with Francisco de Elizondo when the latter led an expedi-

[1] Lino G. Canedo in Isidro Félix de Espinosa, *Crónica de los colegios de propaganda fide de la Nueva España*, p. 727 n.

tion to the mission of Father Juan Larios at San Ildefonso de la Paz, four-teen leagues north of the Río de Sabinas. In 1687 he was in charge of Governor Alonso de León's post at Santiago de la Monclova, while the Governor made a trip to Mission de la Caldera. He later was with De León on his trip to Texas when the Frenchman Jean Géry was found. After De León's death in 1691 Ramón served as interim governor of Coahuila and, in 1699, he led the expedition which founded Mission San Francisco Xavier, forty miles northwest of Monclova. His association with San Juan Bautista del Río Grande would endure until his natural death in 1724, fifty years after he first appeared on the northern frontier.[2] It was fitting, therefore, that he should lead the founding expedition, giving possession of land and waters in the name of the King.

San Juan Bautista was the first of three missions to be established in the Valle de la Circuncisión. The first buildings were made of straw, including the church and dwelling houses. For several months all three priests lived in one tiny grass hut, which Father Olivares viewed as grossly inadequate, for it failed to turn the weather. After a rainy spring, he expressed his gratitude for a Tlaxcalteco Indian named Marcos who came from Mission de la Caldera to finish the house which the priests would occupy and to make a door for the structure.[3]

Soon after arriving at Valle de la Circuncisión, the new settlers were joined by a man from the land of the Tejas. He was the soldier José de Urrutia, who had elected to remain—some had called it desertion—among the Indians of East Texas in 1693, when the beleaguered Fathers Massanet and Hidalgo had retreated to México. Urrutia had become adept at the Tejas language, had been elevated to a chief's status, and undoubtedly had taken an Indian wife. What now prompted his return to the fringe of civilization is not recorded. If indeed he had deserted and defaulted in his duty, he now was forgiven; the priests on the northern frontier were looking again toward work among the Tejas, and Urrutia's knowledge of the language was invaluable.

Urrutia evidently had just returned from Texas when Father Olivares, eager to increase the number of Indians at the new settlement on the Río

[2] Charles Wilson Hackett and Charmion Clair Shelby (trans.), *Pichardo's Treatise on the Limits of Louisiana and Texas*, I, 224.

[3] Fray Antonio de San Buenaventura y Olivares to Governor Francisco Cuerbo y Valdés, May 6, 1700, in A.G.N., Provincias Internas, Vol. 28, p. 33.

Grande, and to know more of the country which the savages inhabited, prevailed upon the ex-soldier to accompany him on an expedition.

Leaving Fathers Hidalgo and Guereña in charge of the mission, they took a few soldiers and crossed the Río Grande del Norte. They penetrated some thirty leagues beyond the river, to the Río Frío, where they found a multitude of friendly Indians of various Coahuiltecan nations. In the days which followed, the Indians gathered to pray with the priests and demonstrated affection for baptism. They promised to come to a mission if one were established close at hand.[4]

The missionary rejoiced at such an abundant and ready harvest of souls, and yet his feelings were mixed. He must leave these willing ones in the wild country without ministers to teach them. For a moment he considered the possibility of remaining with them, but other considerations dissuaded him. He must go back to assist his companions at San Juan Bautista, for the mission was not yet well established. Too, the site on the Río Grande, so far removed from other settlements, already was at the outer limits. To attempt to establish and maintain others still farther out would be unwise. Regretfully he turned about, but with the vow that one day he would congregate all these nations in missions.

On his return to San Juan, Olivares eagerly told his companions of the many souls awaiting conversion beyond the Río Grande. Together the friars discussed the possibilities, congratulating themselves on having the Mission San Juan Bautista to serve as a base from which to carry the Gospel to the waiting hordes.

The year 1700 was filled with activity at the new settlement in the Valle de la Circuncisión, five miles from the Río Grande. The missionaries were as wood cutters who had gone into the forest without an axe; they had the material with which to work, but they were without tools. Indians were present, and they began to teach them. Yet the mission village could not be established nor lands worked without many necessities which the priests did not have. Furthermore, they could not ask for assistance for the Mis-

---

[4] Espinosa, *Crónica*, p. 754. Robert Carleton Clark ("Louis Juchereau de Saint-Denis and the Re-establishment of the Tejas Missions," *SWHQ*, 6, No. 1 [July, 1902], 4) says Olivares accomplished nothing but stimulation of his own zeal. Clark adds that Fray Hidalgo set out alone from San Juan Bautista for the country of the Asinais, where he lived and labored several years. I have failed to find anything to substantiate this statement.

sion San Juan Bautista; they had not yet reported its removal from the Río de Sabinas.

Early in 1700 a decision was reached which may have been aimed at circumventing this dilemma. A second mission would be founded, under the authority of the commission which Governor Cuerbo y Valdés had given to the *sargento mayor*, Diego Ramón. Ramón reported the founding of the new mission, San Francisco Solano, under that authority on March 1, 1700. Had the ardent Spanish soldier had any inkling of the role this mission would play in history, his pen would have faltered as he wrote the words:

In the Valle de la Circuncisión on the first day of the month of March, 1700, I, Major Diego Ramón . . . placed for execution the founding of a new mission, some two leagues, more or less, from the banks of the same river or copious water spring. [It is] on a pleasant and fertile site, with abundant land and much facility, on the source of water for irrigation. I brought with me, with the assistance of the Father Predicator Friar Antonio de San Buenaventura y Olivares and of the Father Friar Francisco Hidalgo, the heathen Indians gathered from *la tierra adentro* by means of the most sufficient diligence of myself as well as by Father Olivares.[5]

These Indians from the interior land—which probably meant from the region beyond the Río Grande in Texas—were "Sarames, Papanac, Paiaguan, Ysiaguan" nations, all components of the loosely bound Coahuiltecans. On arrival at the new mission they spoke in their own language through the interpreter, Félix Sánchez, from whom Ramón had extracted the customary oath of office. Sánchez agreed thereby to relay the full message and to "tell the truth in everything about which I might ask him."

Both Indians and Spaniards were pleased at the prospects for the mission settlement, for it was located in the Indians' own land, where they were accustomed to living in certain seasons.

Thus I told the interpreter that he might give them to understand first that His Majesty (God keep him) would favor, protect, and succor them only with the motive of converting them to the Catholic faith and to obedience to him, and for the usefulness which will follow the salvation of their souls so that, at the end of their days on earth, they may enjoy the benefits of eternal life.[6]

[5] Diego Ramón in *autos* of the founding of San Francisco Solano, A.G.N., Provincias Internas, Vol. 28, p. 24.

[6] *Ibid.*, p. 25.

Father Olivares reiterated the message in the Mexican language, which some of the Indians were able to understand.

In such a manner the heathen savages were offered "more earthly conveniences than they were able to appreciate."[7] Not only would they have land and irrigation water, and peaceful intercourse with the Spaniards, but they would be taught to wear clothing—a blessing which few of them cared for. Their women and children would be protected and would live with decency.

The Indians, not understanding the full import of what was being told them, responded with enthusiasm. How could they understand that two alien cultures were meeting, and that their own could but be the loser? In accepting the conditions imposed by the Spaniards, they gave none of their own. Thenceforth they would be expected to do as these strange and interesting intruders bade them. There would be no alternative but revolt, no course but to flee to the *montes*. And back to the wilds they would often be driven by the tactics of these foreign people who sometimes seemed to understand as little of the Indians' way as the Indians comprehended of theirs.

The interpreter marked for them the site of their pueblo, and the *sargento mayor* provided for instruction to be given the Indians. Ramón gave them possession of their village and lands with the proper ceremonies set forth in the King's royal decrees: "For the great honor of God and of His Most Holy Mother I found this site and place this pueblo and mission and give it the name San Francisco Solano. In the name of His Majesty I give it the civil and criminal jurisdiction which is accorded the other pueblos and missions of this province."[8]

Thus was the mission born which one day would go down in history as the Alamo. Ramón himself designated the necessary areas for church, cemetery, convent, and hospital, setting aside another block for government buildings and jail, and one for the main plaza, in keeping with custom. He chose from the various tribes those who would serve in various offices of the civil government of the village: governor, alcalde, aldermen, and constable. Through the interpreter they accepted, with the goodwill of their respective nations, and the *sargento mayor*, in His Majesty's name, gave to each the proper insignia of his office. In accepting the tokens of

[7] *Ibid.,* p. 25.
[8] *Ibid.,* p. 25.

authority they obligated themselves to maintain their residence at San Francisco Solano and agreed to hear the Christian doctrine.[9] Friar Olivares began at once to teach them.

The priest first rang a hand bell, and the group recited the four principal prayers with the protestation of the faith and sang hymns of praise. Then the padre said Mass. The various nations, under the urging of their alcaldes, joined in. "Everyone gave obedience . . . to the Reverend Father Missionary, who would order them in the service of God and King and the increase of their pueblo by virtue of which I make this edict of foundation . . ."[10]

Signing the edict of founding in place of the interpreter Sánchez and at his request was José de Urrutia. Ramón, Joseph Valdés, and Father Olivares signed, with Diego Minchaca and Antonio Maldonado as witnesses.

The *autos* of the founding went on to Don Francisco Cuerbo y Valdés, who forwarded them to the viceroy, Conde de Moctezuma y de la Tula, to the bishop of Guadalajara, Felipe de Galindo, and to Father Antonio Margil de Jesús, guardian of the College of Querétaro. The Governor approved the new mission and pueblo as being well founded and issued a reminder of the penalty to be imposed against any citizen or inhabitant who molested or disturbed the mission Indians. He neglected to mention that this actually was the second mission to be placed at the site, and not the first.[11]

The new mission founded, Major Diego Ramón took his twenty soldiers and returned to Santiago de la Monclova, leaving the three missionaries to their own devices. With the help of their Indian neophytes the padres were able to get a corn crop planted before the rains set in. It was a cold, wet spring, and the priests shivered inside their grass hut, which hardly turned the weather at all. The corn grew, but when it was near the roasting ear stage, heavy rains and high wind came, and the stalks fell to the ground. The natives could not understand the concern which this circumstance caused the padres. It was not the way of the Indian to grow crops to be harvested and saved for another day. "They want to consume what they have the same day they receive it,"[12] Olivares wrote. The savages

---

[9] *Ibid.,* p. 26.   [10] *Ibid.,* p. 26.
[11] *Ibid.,* pp. 27–28.
[12] Olivares to Cuerbo y Valdés, May 6, 1700, *ibid.,* p. 33.

did not share this priest's capacity for concern for the future. Their faith, though unenlightened, was in some ways greater than his.

Furthermore, the missionary complained, the Indians were ungrateful for the benefits they received: "They are to Jesus our pastor and the most Holy Virgin Lady as was Judas, who betrayed him."[13]

The Indians came under the easy influence of their kinsmen from the wilds. The devil was at work to "change the spirits of these creatures in order to occasion discord with apocryphal pretexts and sinister imagination and to see that the good of those souls is not advanced, the honor of God less visible . . ."[14] Three or four crafty savages from the Mission de la Caldera came and helped themselves to the provisions and the livestock of the Río Grande missions, killing ten goats. The Indians were apprehended as they returned to kill more animals, but there was little the priests could do to stop them. Father Olivares attempted to reason with the leader but was rebuffed, and the quarrelsome savage tried to persuade some of the mission Indians to kill the priest. José de Urrutia and the Tlaxcalteco, Marcos, of Caldera, who had come to help with the building, said Olivares, were witnesses to the fact.

> I pray to Your Lordship and ask for God our Lord and Father St. Francis to look after these creatures, that they may not be completely lost, and that we might not be obliged to leave them. It would be a pity for the work to be wasted . . . The goal is not attained by beginning works but by finishing them.
> With what has been done the fire of Hell is kindled.[15]

The missionary called upon the Governor to send the soldiers he had promised in order that the troublesome savages might be returned to their own mission. "Without them we cannot live in such retirement, for the word 'soldiers' alone is not much of a bridle to these miserable ones."[16] The Indians of the Río Grande missions did not understand why the priests let Indians from other pueblos take their food and livestock without trying to stop them. They could not comprehend, as Father Olivares put it, that "our institution is not of war but of preaching and planting the faith."[17]

---

[13] *Ibid.*, p. 31.   [14] *Ibid.*, pp. 31–32.
[15] *Ibid.*, p. 32.   [16] *Ibid.*, p. 32.
[17] *Ibid.*, p. 33.

With weather threatening to destroy the corn crop and the Indians from La Caldera having taken their goats, Father Olivares reminded the Governor that he still was waiting for the yoke of oxen he was to receive, and that planting time was rapidly going past. But the greatest need was for the soldiers, and it therefore was decided that the Father Predicator Friar Francisco Hidalgo would go to bear the petition to Cuerbo y Valdés, and to learn whether the soldiers were coming to help the missionaries in planting the faith. Otherwise the ministers would be forced to retire to the Mission de los Dolores de la Punta until help should come from the city of México.

The priest dated this letter "San Juan Bautista and Valle de la Circuncisión de la Ciénaga, May 6, 1700."[18] In his endorsement, May 13, witnessed by Blas de Yruegas and José Antonio de Ecay Múzquiz, Cuerbo y Valdés ordered that the document be placed with the *autos* of the founding of the new Mission San Francisco Solano and sent on to the Viceroy.

Five days later the Coahuila governor wrote to the Viceroy, requesting the soldiers to protect the missions of his province. By dispatch of January 2 that same year, he wrote, His Excellency had approved and confirmed the new foundation of the Pueblo and Mission of San Juan Bautista in the new valley and Río de las Sabinas. The high official had ordered the Governor to report to him what was necessary for the subsistence, conservation, and permanence of this mission and others which would be established in the same valley and in the surrounding territory. The Governor now had determined that those needs consisted principally of just one thing: a garrison of fifty men to "serve as guard, custodians, and halter for the barbarous nations which molest the dominions of His Majesty."[19]

Such a garrison would not only serve this mission but would also accrue to "the total correction and defense of this entire province" and its new conversions, including the newly established San Francisco Solano, reports of which were being sent by that same mail. It would serve to protect the province of Nuevo Reino de León and the mining camp of Boca de Leones; the Villa del Saltillo, and the Pueblo and Valley of Parras, the mining camp of Mazapíl, Niebes, and Charcas—making it easy to settle many *gentiles* to villages and missions which would become permanent.

---

[18] *Ibid.,* p. 34.
[19] Cuerbo y Valdés to the Viceroy, Count of Moctezuma y Tula, May 18, 1700, in *ibid.,* p. 36.

Furthermore, such a presidio would prevent Frenchmen from entering the province. Indians from *la tierra adentro,* Cuerbo said, informed him with certainty and personal knowledge that Frenchmen lived on the banks of a river beyond the pueblos of the Cadodacho, yonder in the province of the Tejas.

The increased protection would also serve to thwart the enemy Toboso Indians from the west and keep them from joining the multitude of heathen Indians of Coahuila in revolt against the Spaniards. In the same manner the Indians from the coast would be prevented from uniting with those of the interior in a similar cause.

Aside from the protection a presidio would offer, he wrote, each new mission founded in the province had need of one hundred fanegas of corn to tide it over the first year until it should be able to sustain itself. Each one needed to be furnished with six large axes for felling trees and clearing lands for farms, six hoes for digging and cleaning the irrigation ditches, three heavy plowshares for breaking land, cultivating, and planting, one adz, one chisel, and three yokes of gentle oxen for plowing and cultivating the lands.

It seemed appropriate also, for the service of both Majesties, that the principal Indian chiefs, particularly those holding the offices of *cabildo,* be provided with some clothing to encourage them to behave decently, and to cause others of the new pueblos and missions to imitate them.

Attracting the natives from the interior would be made easier if a quantity of tobacco, some strawberries, and some turnips were supplied, the Governor continued. Some *cascabeles,* the small bells of the kind which the Indians seemed to like the best, would aid in winning many to the Catholic faith, since most of the Indians in the settlements were asking the water of baptism.

The bishop of Guadalajara, Felipe Galindo, was greatly pleased with the new missions and had promised to foster the spiritual side of the endeavor to whatever extent necessary, the Governor related. Friar Antonio Margil, guardian of the College of the Holy Cross at Querétaro, also was giving thanks to God for the achievement; he had offered all assistance possible.[20]

On June 5 the *fiscal* in the capital, Doctor Don Joseph Antonio de

[20] *Ibid.,* p. 38.

Espinosa Ocampo y Cornejo, received the letter and the *autos* of founding. More than three weeks later he got around to reviewing the contents for the Viceroy. As for the help asked by Cuerbo y Valdés for the new mission in Valle de la Circuncisión—as well as that of San Juan Bautista in the valley of the Sabinas River—it was no more than had been provided for all new conversions "for the attraction of Indians in order that they may become industrious in the labor and cultivation of the lands."[21] That which had been done for the others should be done for these also, since it did not exceed what the Governor proposed.

The appraisal of the *fiscal,* together with the *autos,* did not reach the Viceroy until September 15. By that time action already had been taken which precluded reasonable dispensation of the requests Cuerbo y Valdés made four months earlier.

[21] Joseph Antonio de Espinosa to the Viceroy, June 28, 1700, in *ibid.,* p. 40. Note that this report clearly indicates that no official notice had been given of the moving of San Juan Bautista from the Sabinas River to the Río Grande.

4. THE FLYING COMPANY

WHILE Fathers Olivares and Hidalgo, joined by Father Marcos de Guereña, had gone to establish missions on the Río Grande del Norte, Father Salazar, the president of the missions, remained at Mission Santa María de los Dolores. In the summer of 1700—before the *autos* from Cuerbo y Valdés had yet reached the Viceroy—Salazar undertook the long journey to the city of México to confer with the Count of Moctezuma on the needs of the three missions of his jurisdiction.[1]

These missions, with proper care, he informed the high official, should be able to attain many more conversions than had yet been possible.

[1] Representation of Fray Diego de San Buenaventura y Salazar to the Viceroy, July 16, 1700, in A.G.N., Provincias Internas, Vol. 28, p. 6.

Many were the "pagans" who inhabited the region, he reported; the area was fertile, with an abundance of buffalo meat—"which is like beef"—as well as deer, wild turkey, fish, salt, and other necessities, including wild grapevines. With care and cultivation, the wild grapes could be used to make wine, he noted.[2]

The Indians presently in the Río Grande missions, Salazar claimed, were well instructed in the doctrine, since three religious priests and one layman were on hand for that purpose. San Juan Bautista, San Francisco Solano, and Santa María de los Dolores had in their charge more than nine hundred persons. "In order that these which are already gathered may continue [to receive instruction], and so that more of those who are asking for the Holy Baptism may be gathered, it has seemed appropriate [for me] to come and give report to Your Excellency."[3]

Specifically, the new missions needed sixteen families of Tlaxcalteco Indians from the Pueblo of San Estevan del Saltillo, eighty leagues away. These Indians, allies of the Spaniards since the conquest, were of similar temperament to the Coahuiltecans, the padre observed. They would be most useful in attracting prospects and teaching the neophytes, whom they could instruct in civil matters, in farming, and in the Catholic faith. To encourage the Tlaxcaltecans to such holy employment, Salazar suggested that the government pay fifty pesos to each family to help with the cost of moving. They should be provided with oxen and should receive lands and water rights sufficient for planting and raising livestock, separate from the Indians of the missions. With such incentive, he believed, others would be encouraged to populate the mission outpost. Then missions could be located farther out on the Camino Real. This road which led to the land of the Tejas and to Espíritu Santo Bay had in years past been populated with Frenchmen. "Today we have definite news that they [the French] now are in the Mexican interior which borders with these lands."[4]

Father Salazar's traveling companions on the road to the capital city were two Indians of the Tejas nation. They came, the priest told the Viceroy, to give information concerning the Frenchmen who had entered their land. The white visitors had been well received and treated kindly by

2 *Ibid.*, p. 6.
3 *Ibid.*, p. 6.
4 *Ibid.*, p. 7.

the Indian governor, who had sent these two tribesmen to carry the news to México and to ask the Spaniards to come and defend them.

The Viceroy ordered that the two Tejas Indians be examined by a Spanish interpreter, whom Father Salazar had had the foresight to bring with him. The interpreter was none other than José de Urrutia, who had lived ten years among the Tejas before returning to the fringe of civilization in northern Coahuila.

Salazar, while seeking help in bringing the Tlaxcaltecans, also asked the Viceroy for farm equipment for the new foundations. Each mission needed four yokes of gentle oxen, with plowshares and other tools for clearing and working the lands of the mission Indians: six axes, six hoes, six saws, six chisels, and six adzes. Also needed were two hundred varas of blue cloth to clothe the natives and other goods to serve as an inducement for the various tribes to come. Instead of glass beads, which it was the custom to give but which served no useful purpose, he suggested that two loads of tobacco should be sent. Two bells were needed—for the missions of San Francisco Solano and San Juan Bautista.

Forty leagues separated these two missions on the Río Grande from the Presidio of Coahuila, by Father Salazar's calculations; to that of Nuevo León the distance was sixty leagues. Such remoteness, in his view, made necessary the establishment of a presidio to assist the missionaries in subduing the many Indian nations. "Considering the cost it will be to the Royal Hacienda, I do not propose it to Your Excellency now."[5]

Instead he suggested that a Spanish captain protector be named to "direct, govern, and protect" the Indians, and that he be paid a salary in line with that of others in this type of employment. The religious, noted the padre, were no expense to the Royal Hacienda, because they did not receive stipends. All he was asking was thirteen hundred pesos, a one-time expense.

On July 19, a general junta was convened to consider the padre's rep-representation. Meeting with the junta was Don Gregorio de Salinas Varona, who had made more trips to Texas than perhaps any other man, prior to having served as governor of Coahuila.

The junta considered the news brought by the Tejas Indians. The *fiscal* was ordered to have the natives examined by the secretary of war, through

[5] *Ibid.*, p. 8.

the interpreter, with particular emphasis on the matter of Frenchmen occupying the land of the Tejas.[6]

Interpreter Urrutia "swore by God our Lord and the sign of the Holy Cross to interpret truthfully all which the Indians said, and to keep it a secret to all his loyal knowledge and understanding."[7]

Through him the Indian spokesman gave his testimony: Thirty Frenchmen, whom he had seen previously on Espíritu Santo Bay, had come among the Tejas at the place called Los Nazones, in the midst of the Cadodachos and Tejas. The Frenchmen had presented the Indians with two long muskets, in return for which they received two horses. The Frenchmen had come on foot, dressed in long coats of different colors, wearing white hats with feathers. Others wore shawl-like peasant caps which covered the face.

The Indian witness said he had heard that fifty or sixty leagues beyond, the Frenchmen had received aid from the Cadodachos and had built many earthen houses on the banks of the river. With the Frenchmen had come religious who wore habits like those of St. Francis, with cowls. The foreigners came in large numbers, building earthen houses as if to settle permanently. The Indian related that his uncle, the governor of the Tejas, concerned over such an influx, had sent him on this mission, in the month when the corn was tall. His purpose was to ask for missionaries to come to "the Three Crosses," one hundred leagues beyond their land, which lay on the San Marcos River. His people wished to be settled on the Trinity, the Indian said, because of the good lands.

Concluded Father Salazar, "So much for the news which they have reported as the truth regarding all that has happened. It is not received under oath because he is a heathen and not baptized. It is not signed because he says he does not know how to write."[8] The *fiscal*, Doctor Don Joseph Antonio de Espinosa Ocampo y Cornejo, reviewed the memorial of Father Salazar. The official pointed out that what the padre asked for would facilitate the conversion of the Indian land and the increase of the missions. These attainments were the primary concern of His Majesty, who had re-

---

[6] José Sarmiento Valladares (Conde de Moctezuma y Tula), Viceroy, to *fiscal*, July 19, 1700, in A.G.N., Provincias Internas, Vol. 28, p. 2.

[7] "Declaraciones de los Indios de los Tejas," July 20, 1700, in *ibid.,* p. 10.

[8] *Ibid.,* p. 11.

peatedly given such a charge in the Code of the Indies and the Royal Decrees.

Doctor Espinosa agreed also that the new missions should have a protector, as other missions of Coahuila had, if their controversies were to be settled and they were to be maintained in peace. The Indians, he noted, were accustomed to taking up arms to defend themselves against grievances that were all but imaginary; it would be well that they have someone whom they respected to control them, for "only with difficulty can they be contained."[9]

As for the Frenchmen said to be inhabiting the land of the Tejas and the Cadodachos, the viceregal adviser held that further inquiry should be made.

The junta, which met two days later, ruled that the Tlaxcalteco Indians should be sent to the new missions, with government help in transporting them from Saltillo; the necessary implements should be provided, with annual allocations of corn and livestock to maintain the new conversions; a protector—someone of utmost satisfaction to Father Salazar—should be named, and he should be paid the same salary as a soldier in the presidios of Coahuila.

As for the Frenchmen in Texas, the governors of Coahuila and Nuevo Reino de León were called upon to make inquiry to ascertain the true state of affairs.[10]

No sooner had his requests been approved than Father Salazar asked that José de Urrutia be named protector of the missions, "since he is a suitable subject and has served His Majesty in the land of the Tejas. . . . He knows and understands the languages of the Indians of those regions. The Indians for whom we have attained the progress of the two missions of the Río Grande both love and fear him." He would protect the Indians, encouraging their labors and helping them with their oxen and implements "in order to give constant aid to the furtherance of said missions."[11] The missionary's request was promptly approved by the Viceroy.

In a separate letter Father Salazar asked that the Tlaxcalteco Indian families of the Pueblo of San Estevan del Saltillo be sent under orders to

[9] Fiscal Espinosa to the Viceroy, July 21, 1700, in *ibid.*, p. 3.
[10] Report of Junta, *ibid.*, pp. 14–18.
[11] Diego de San Buenaventura y Salazar to the Viceroy, *ibid.*, p. 19.

the protector, governor, and *cabildo* of the pueblo for division among the three missions, and that the promised help with the cost of moving them be paid. This request was approved July 24.

However quickly the government was able to provide the equipment, supplies, and personnel which the Río Grande missions were to receive, it was not soon enough. Less than six months later the two infant missions in Valle de la Circuncisión were in dire circumstances. Father Antonio de San Buenaventura y Olivares, still with Fathers Francisco Hidalgo and Marcos de Guereña at the missions of San Juan Bautista and San Francisco Solano, wrote on December 12 to Governor Cuerbo y Valdés: "The Lords of heaven and earth shall guide my pen that it may not falter in speaking of the afflictions with which my heart is found at present."[12]

Friar Hidalgo, he wrote, would carry the letter to the Governor, along with one to the bishop of Guadalajara, the Reverend Father Friar Don Felipe Galindo, who was en route to the province to make his official visit to the missions. He wrote to the Bishop:

> We are found alone at this place of San Juan Bautista and San Francisco Solano, the Indians having taken flight because there is nothing for them to eat and the force to protect them is lacking. . . . At present the grief is great because of the Indians of Don Tomás having killed the soldiers in Coahuila [Monclova].[13]

After the attack on the soldiers—details are missing—the rebel Yerbipiame Indians had come in the guise of friendship to the Río Grande Missions. They ate and drank with the Spaniards while they familiarized themselves with the place.

About the same time sixteen hostile Indians came to the Mission of Peyotes and attempted to persuade the Xijames to join with them in a plot to kill the missionaries and depopulate the missions. The enemy Indians were most persuasive in extolling the advantages of rebellion. But in truth, Olivares asserted, they harbored secret intentions of murdering any mission Indians who showed reluctance, and of kidnaping their women and children. This type of vengeance had been visited before on Indians who had manifested a desire to become Christians and to place themselves

[12] Fray Antonio de San Buenaventura y Olivares to Francisco Cuerbo y Valdés, December 12, 1700, *ibid.*, p. 42.

[13] Padre Olivares to Fray Felipe Galindo, December 13, 1700, *ibid.*, p. 48.

in mission and village. The hostiles, luring the Payayes away from their mission under guise of friendship, had viciously fallen upon them and killed fourteen. They carried off the women and children as prisoners. "This ended their inclination to place themselves in missions; we need not waste talk regarding their settlement."[14]

The incident at the Peyotes Mission was coupled with others at San Juan Bautista. One of the Yerbipiames stole from San Juan an Indian woman, whom he took to his rancheria. This wily one had tried to persuade the mission Indians that, without risk to themselves, they could kill the missionaries and end the mission settlement once and for all. Such reports caused growing apprehension in the missions.

Other Indians made raids upon the cattle, goats, and supplies which the priests had gathered for use in the missions. "That [theft] was very easy, our being alone and with no defense whatever."[15]

Again the enemy Indians swept down upon the stockade, killing nine of the ten mission neophytes who attempted to stand them off. The lone survivor was wounded by an arrow. Repeatedly the natives who had manifested their intention of becoming Christians were harassed by the hostiles, who robbed them of their women and children.

But then a band of *indios rebeldes* came with the intention of persuading some of the mission Indians to forsake the pueblo and join in the murder and plunder. The savages confronted four Moso Indians and the Indian Ignacio, *vecino* of La Caldera, who had come to help the priests at San Juan Bautista, as they were butchering meat. The "heathens" disclosed the plan of Don Tomás and his Yerbipiames. It was a grievous error.

Ignacio and the four Mosos acted quickly. By prearranged signal they summoned the Indians of the vicinity, who formed themselves around the enemy, gave a mighty shout, and pounced upon the troublemakers. With their butcher knives they killed most of the hostiles, allowing only a few to escape to carry the news back to their comrades in the *montes*.

In this [wrote Father Olivares to the Bishop] Your Lordship will see how much God loves us, how much he desires the souls and ardor which our lukewarm spirits have collected for the goal of the redemption of these poor souls. But finding ourselves alone, without any protection and without the necessary

14 *Ibid.,* p. 49.
15 *Ibid.,* p. 48.

means for sustaining them for the peace and permanence of the missions, our souls are chilled and our spirits cooled.[16]

He asked His Grace to "see if he can alleviate such pains and give succor to such necessities."[17] Badly needed was corn to feed the Indians and armed men to protect the missions. A garrison of twenty men was needed, to subdue and defend them, said Father Olivares; he hoped the Bishop would send word to the Viceroy, and that His Excellency would provide.

All the natives now had fled from the missions, with no intention of returning unless the Spaniards should send a force to protect and discipline them. Without Indians to teach and apparently forsaken by the government, Father Olivares felt he had ample justification for deserting the missions on the Río Grande and retreating to La Punta. If food and defense were not provided, he would have no choice; there would be little chance that the missions could be maintained, and no chance at all that the faith could be extended to the region beyond.

Our forces are not sufficient to achieve the conquest of souls because in these regions the goal of settlement is not attained with nakedness and virtue but with arms and Christian deeds . . . The establishment of Christianity is not very certain because of the circumstances which have befallen . . . All the Indians of our side have asked me to write to Your Lordship for assistance of one company in order that they may avenge themselves on their enemies and to see if they can get back their women and children who are prisoners. They say they cannot plow the land and can do nothing without having security, because the enemies distract them with disturbances. All the Indians are retired . . .[18]

If the help could not be sent, Olivares concluded emphatically, he hoped the Governor would provide an escort to take the missionaries to La Punta, and some mules to carry the mission ornaments and furniture. Father Hidalgo, now on his way to Querétaro to relieve Father Margil as guardian of the missionary college, would go to present himself at His Lordship's feet. "With his usual religion and humility he will tell of the necessity and the affliction in which we find ourselves."[19]

[16] *Ibid.*, p. 50.
[17] *Ibid.*, p. 50.
[18] Olivares to Cuerbo y Valdés, December 12, 1700, *ibid.*, pp. 43–44.
[19] *Ibid.*, p. 45.

Going with Father Hidalgo would be the Indian Ignacio and the wounded survivor of the attack on the stockade. The versatile Ignacio had served as interpreter when two Indians had come from the region beyond Espíritu Santo Bay in Texas, giving news that ten Frenchmen had come to their rancherías. He would give the Governor more information by word of mouth on the French, who came bringing missionary priests clad in white habits, believed to be Dominicans.

The Bishop of Guadalajara arrived one week later—December 20, 1700—at the Mission Santa María de los Dolores de la Punta, and on the day of St. Thomas the Apostle he celebrated Mass and confirmed twenty-five persons, both young and old. Included were Indians who had been baptized in the Mission and some Spaniards who had settled in the vicinity. The Bishop proceeded to San Juan Bautista, where he consecrated the bells of the two missions and assisted at the sung vespers and in the procession of the Holy Rosary.[20]

On the first day of Passover the Bishop ordered that a committee be formed to report the needs for stability and growth of the missions. Fathers Diego de Salazar, Olivares, Jerónimo Prieto, and Francisco Moreno were members, along with Governor Cuerbo y Valdés, the *sargento mayor*, Diego Ramón, and Captain Bernardo de Benavides. Father Hidalgo had already departed for Querétaro. The resulting report to the Viceroy, Conde de Moctezuma, asked for formation of a garrison which would help gather the Indians and would defend the missionaries of San Juan Bautista.[21]

Father Olivares was chosen to make the long trip to the city of México to plead the case of the northern missions before the general junta. He filled the assignment well. With the horrors of the Indian killings still fresh in his mind, with visions of screaming women carried by force away from their husbands and children, he spoke in a strong voice, filled with warmth and conviction. Olivares also presented exhibits in writing. These consisted of a written report by Bishop Galindo, copies of the letters which Olivares himself had written to Galindo and to the governor, Cuerbo y Valdés, and the replies to those letters.

The *fiscal*, Espinosa, reviewed the *autos* for the Viceroy, offering his

[20] Isidro Félix de Espinosa, *Crónica de los colegios de propaganda fide de la Nueva España,* p. 755.
[21] *Ibid.,* p. 756.

own conclusions. Despite the efforts of the missionaries, he noted, some of the Indians had reacted badly to being settled in missions; their "depraved malevolence" was worse than before. Hence the murders which the Indians had committed in the settlements. Having shot and killed several soldiers, they cut off their heads and carried them as signs of honor and triumph.[22]

The *fiscal* was impressed with Olivares' plea. The official noted that the padre had requested, in the event military protection could not be granted, that mules be sent to move the mission ornaments and furniture back to La Punta. "He [Olivares] would absent himself from the settled Catholics with great regret; and if with dying he might increase faith in God among these barbarians, he would gladly stay. But such a sacrifice would not achieve the desired result, without the help needed to carry out the enterprise."[23] His Majesty, noted Doctor Espinosa, had ordered the placing of an escort of soldiers at such missionary establishments to resist attacks. Yet for want of such protection the Río Grande missions were failing in their purpose and stood in danger of having to be abandoned. Furthermore, Father Olivares had reported other distressing news passed on by his co-worker, Friar Marcos Guereña. Two Indians from beyond the Río Grande had told Friar Marcos that the French were settling above the Bay of Espíritu Santo, where a village was being built.

The *fiscal*, reviewing other documents contained in the *autos* brought by Olivares, noted that 800 pesos had been given by the royal house of Zacatecas to help transport sixteen families of Tlaxcaltecos from Saltillo to the Río Grande. The amount already was in the hand of one Juan Antonio Montalvo in Zacatecas. The rest of the 1,302 pesos collected had been used for purchase of implements, oxen, plows, cloth, tobacco, and other items to aid the Indians of the Río Grande missions.

Bishop Galindo, in his report to the junta, pointed out that only military protection now was needed to assure the increase of the northern missions: the populous nation of the Tecocodames was waiting, the chiefs having

---

[22] San Juan Bautista, "Testimonio del Decreto de Fundación del Presidio de San Juan Bautista," A.G.N., Historia, Vol. 29, p. 70 (José Antonio de Espinosa to Viceroy Moctezuma). It appears the *fiscal* is referring to the murders at San Francisco de Coahuila, mentioned earlier by Olivares.

[23] *Ibid.*, p. 71.

promised to congregate at a new mission near San Juan Bautista. He also entered a plea that the missionaries should be paid a stipend.[24]

The junta agreed that military protection should be provided, and the Viceroy so ordered on March 28, 1701:

I order that there be created and formed a flying company without station or form of a presidio. The Reverend Father Missionaries and the officer to be named will designate the place where it is formed, not to stay permanently but for going from it for the places where it is needed. It shall consist of thirty men and an officer, who shall be the Captain Diego Ramón, in whom the needed attributes are found, according to the information from the Most Illustrious Señor Bishop of Guadalajara. The appointment is sent this date for assisting the Mission of San Juan Bautista del Río Grande del Norte, in Coahuila, for use in going over the lands in order to free the Missionaries and inhabitants from the invasions of the barbarians. The soldiers of the Presidio of Coahuila also will help them in these operations . . . for which is designated the annual salary of three hundred pesos in common gold to each one, and five hundred for the captain and leader . . . From this company three squads of ten men each shall be formed. Two, with the company of said Presidio of Coahuila, must travel continually over all the land, according to what the missions are doing, for protection of the religious, the increase and conversion of Christianity, discovering of the settlements and designs of the French, of which the letters of the Religious tell, communicating to me and the soldiers the news which they may acquire, in order that proper action may be taken. The other squad shall be maintained always in company and assistance of the missionaries, without losing them from sight, in order that it may defend them against the barbarous nations.

I request and charge the said Religious Missionaries to see that the settled Indians and those who will be settled are dedicated to the work and labor of the lands . . . in order that they may harvest the crops needed for them to maintain themselves and not live idly. This should be attained by the end of two years because I order to be given them provisions of corn and cattle that they might have what is necessary for their maintenance [during that time].

As for the eight hundred pesos in the custody of said Juan Antonio Montalvo, I order that it be used to purchase the things which will be most needed in the conversion and encouragement of all the new missions of the Province of Coahuila and its environs.[25]

[24] *Ibid.,* p. 72.
[25] *Ibid.,* pp. 72–75.

Captain Diego Ramón, at the Presidio of San Francisco de Coahuila, received orders for forming the Flying Company of the Río Grande del Norte on May 4, 1701. Toward the end of July he left with his company for the Río Grande, to establish headquarters for his *compañía volante,* the flying company, at San Juan Bautista.

The settlement, with two missions and a company of soldiers, now was established. The flying company, in a short time, would give way to a formal presidio, still with Don Diego in charge. Another mission would be added to the two already established. And without a doubt, when new *entradas* were launched to the country beyond the Great River, this would be the gateway to Spanish Texas.

Captain Diego Ramón, like Father Hidalgo, would play a key role in future entries. When the years overtook him, and he could no longer go himself, he would send sons and daughters in his stead.

Now fifty years old, this one-time lieutenant of Alonso de León is a historical enigma. He appears to have been dedicated to the cause of Christianizing the Indians; he dealt with them wisely. At the same time, however, he evolved a lucrative business for himself and his sons which was contrary to the Laws of the Indies. The business was contraband trade with the French. For the Spanish colonization effort in Texas it opened a Pandora's box, difficult indeed to close again.

Yet in many respects he was peculiarly suited to command the military arm of the mission settlement which lay at the most advanced point on the northeastern frontier of New Spain. In Father Espinosa's words he was "subject of the best accomplishments for subduing the Indians known in this land, since great valor would aid him to conquer fear. His special star would be to be loved by the Infidels."[26]

[26] Espinosa, *Crónica,* p. 756.

5. HARVESTERS IN THE VINEYARD

FATHER OLIVARES, jubilant over the success of his journey to the capital, hastened to Querétaro for a visit with his old friend and co-worker, Father Francisco Hidalgo, who had been called from his post at San Juan Bautista on November 11, 1700, to serve as guardian of the Colegio de la Santa Cruz. Occupied with the problems of the new mission, however, he was unable to leave immediately, and did not reach Querétaro until January 1, 1701.

Happy as the two priests were to see each other, each of them recognized that the visit was more than a social call. Father Hidalgo heard with enthusiasm the news of the flying company to be established on the Río Grande. He had a strong personal interest in the northerly missions, which he had helped to found; yet he could not use his office as guardian to advance his own desires. What was it that Friar Antonio had in mind?

The two of them talked over the needs of the missions, and when they finally came to Olivares' request, the guardian found it within his power to grant. To aid the new conversions he assigned two additional missionaries, who would return with Olivares to the Río Grande. They were Friars Jorge de Puga and Alonso González. The three priests traveled together to San Juan Bautista to join the lonely and penitent Friar Marcos de Guereña.

Father Olivares, his enthusiasm bolstered by the establishment of the presidio adjacent to the two missions, set happily about his task of instructing the Indians of San Francisco Solano. Some three hundred natives of the Xarames, Siabanes, and Payuguanes, not counting the small children, had presented themselves, "all of them so docile that in a short time they gave indications of being very affected with the Catholic doctrine and requested with eagerness the holy baptism."[1]

---

[1] Isidro Félix de Espinosa, *Crónica de los colegios de propaganda fide de la Nueva España,* p. 756.

After proper instruction in the catechism, more than 150 persons were baptized, says Father Espinosa, and many were married in ecclesiastical ceremonies.[2] This mission was the delight of the missionaries. Father Olivares, now its minister, had brought from the city of México many ornaments for the church. Each day the Indians decorated the sanctuary with wild flowers and branches. They gave themselves to instruction each morning and evening. In the fields the neophytes worked industriously, planting and tending the corn.

While Friar Olivares applied himself to the labors of San Francisco Solano Mission, Friar Guereña was at work in that of San Juan Bautista, where he strove to learn the language of the natives. He lived in extreme penitence and austerity.

Native of the Spanish province of Cantabria, Father Guereña, like Father Hidalgo, had entered the religious life at the age of fifteen, taking the habit of the priesthood when he reached maturity. "In his flowering years," says Espinosa, "he came to Campeche and maintained himself ten years in the province of Yucatán, always keeping the holy rule as a true son of Our Father St. Francis."[3]

His great longing was to work in the apostolic institute at Querétaro. He petitioned Father Antonio Margil, the guardian (April, 1697, to November, 1700), and was admitted to the company of missionaries of the College of the Holy Cross. Once in the college he took the guardian as his spiritual father. Margil, recognizing the attributes of his new disciple, relaxed the rein in order that Guereña might practice extraordinary mortification and penitence. The obsession of Friar Marcos was to pattern his deeds after the flagellant Margil. The pupil kept pace with the teacher in penitent exercises, taking no rest from the self-torment except when illness required him to cease the punishment of his body.

Among other practices, he wore a horsehair jacket, the stiff bristles irritating his tender skin. In his belt were steel barbs which constantly

---

[2] According to Edward W. Heusinger *(Early Explorations and Mission Establishments in Texas,* p. 55 n.) there were 24 baptisms and 6 burials at San Francisco Solano in 1703. In 1704—apparently after the mission was moved to San Ildefonso—there were 143 baptisms, mostly of the Xarame, Payuguan, and Siaban tribes.

[3] Espinosa, *Crónica,* p. 844.

pricked him. His countenance, however, reflected the meekness of a lamb. He preached almost continuously and applied himself to the confession-ary, where remorseful sinners were never lacking. Often the penitent in-cluded gamblers who had heard him earnestly preaching in the streets against their particular form of vice; Friar Marcos was a most vigorous prosecutor of the games. Unsurpassed in continued prayer and pursuit of the Way of the Cross, he was instrumental in renewing the fervent spirit with which the College of the Holy Cross had been founded.[4]

Still Friar Marcos was unfulfilled, for he saw that the most needful souls were those of the heathen Indians, who lived in darkness in the *gentilidad* of the North. "At the foot of the crucified Christ he renounced all the comforts of the College and entered the Mission of San Juan Bautista, where in the beginning each minister could portray the Precursor in the wilderness."[5]

Provisions were short. Corn—the wheat of the Indians—was scarce. Guereña may not have developed a fondness for this strange kind of bread, but when tortillas were to be had, he would eat but one, saving the others for some ailing Indian or other person whose need was greater than his own.

Soon after coming to San Juan Bautista he began to apply himself to the study of the language of the Indians. With the words he learned he exhorted the natives to become Christians and to abandon their barbarous customs. That which could not be said with words was expressed with the hands.

When the soldiers of Captain Diego Ramón's flying company came, Father Guereña preached to them also, urging them to live as Christians and to set a good example for the mission Indians. "For this reason he preached to them almost every day, seeking them in their houses."[6]

The customary diversion of these poorly disciplined soldiers was gam-bling with cards. They frequently lost what little they earned, thus de-priving themselves and their families. For this the ardent minister re-proached them.

---

[4] *Ibid.*, p. 845.

[5] The mission having been named for the precursor, St. John the Baptist, *Ibid.*, p. 845.

[6] *Ibid.*, p. 846.

Those who persisted in the vice soon learned better than to practice it in public. On one feast day, following Mass, the gambling crowd gathered in a nearby wood, where, in the cool shade of the dense trees, they thought themselves safe from the prying eyes of the padre. One by one they went by diverse routes to the rendezvous. As they were congratulating themselves on this clever bit of deception, the padre suddenly appeared. So touched were they by the reprimand he delivered that all the soldiers are said to have resolved never to gamble again.

Father Guereña was known to spend long hours in prayer, lying face down upon the ground, prostrate before his God.

Every day he walked the Sacred Way, carrying a heavy cross, wearing a rope around his neck and a crown of sharp-pointed thorns upon his head, his feet bare. He sought to imitate in every possible way the Beloved of his soul. Almost all year long he fasted. Looking for new ways to scourge his body, the penitent Padre went at night to the bank of a *ciénaga* near the mission, removed his habit, and allowed the mosquitoes from the marsh to cover his body and suck his blood, covering him with whelps. [This extraordinary mortification, says Espinosa, would have remained unknown if by chance a soldier had not passed the place at night and seen it.] This same one told it to me many times, with many tears.[7]

The attrition of such penitence and the continued work of the mission broke Friar Marcos' health, and he became so gravely ill that his fellow missionaries, not finding remedy in that mission, determined to carry him to the Mission of Santa María de los Dolores, forty leagues distant. At St. Mary of Sorrows it was hoped his persistent illness might be cured. A litter was fashioned from two sticks, to be borne by two horses. Before Friar Marcos was placed on the litter he was confessed as for death and received the sacred viaticum for this journey and for the passage to heaven. Friar Jorge de Puga and some soldiers set out with him for the Mission of Dolores de la Punta. His condition worsened on the road, and Father Puga administered extreme unction. While they were yet ten leagues from La Punta, with night approaching, a light rain began to fall. With great difficulty they pressed on along the tortuous road. After a time the horses suddenly stopped, and, not being able to see what lay ahead, Father Puga

---

[7] I.e., to Father Espinosa. *Ibid.,* p. 846.

struck a light. As the flickering rays fell upon the form of Father Guereña, it was evident that he was breathing his last.

At the hour of his death the church bell at Mission Dolores is said to have pealed forth mysteriously. When a lay religious went to see who was ringing it, he found no one. Only when the travelers arrived with the body of the deceased priest, and gave testimony of his religious virtues, was the ringing of the church bell, to his satisfaction, explained.[8]

Father Guereña's spirit passed to his Creator sometime before midnight October 16, 1702. The following day his body was buried at the Mission of Santa María de los Dolores, with many tears. Twenty years later his remains were removed to the College of the Holy Cross at Querétaro.

The two missions, San Francisco Solano and San Juan Bautista, were situated close together, and the headquarters for the new flying company had just been placed beside them. Yet, early in 1702, still a third mission was placed but "two musket shots" from the Mission San Juan. Founded in devotion to the Duchess of Sessa (or César), second wife of the viceroy, Conde de Moctezuma, was the Mission San Bernardo. The Duchess provided the new mission, established at her own request, with the necessities for divine worship. Friar Alonso González, who had come from Querétaro with Father Olivares, assumed the ministry, gathering in three rancherias of Indians of the Ocanes, Pacuacian, and Pachales nations. By May 20 some four hundred Indians had gathered.[9]

In 1703 General Francisco Cuerbo y Valdés was replaced as governor of Coahuila by Matías de Aguirre. During the two years of his administration Aguirre paid particular attention to the armament and discipline of the few scattered settlements of the province, in order to aid San Juan Bautista and Santiago de la Monclova in the unending battle with the Indians.[10]

During the year 1703 Captain Diego Ramón was absent from his command. In his place was Buenaventura de Aguirre, probably a kinsman of the Governor sent by him to see after the material improvement of San

---

[8] *Ibid.,* p. 847.

[9] *Ibid.,* p. 756. Aurora Botello G., *Datos Históricos sobre la fundación de la Misión de San Bernardo y la Villa de Guerrero Coah. Antes Real Presidio de Río Grande del Norte,* p. 3.

[10] Vito Alessio Robles, *Coahuila y Texas en la época colonial,* p. 414.

Juan Bautista. At this point the flying company headquarters took the form of a presidio, acquiring for the first time an adequate *plaza de armas,* on which were built ten new flat-roofed houses. Surrounding the presidio were placed three churches with double walls and terraced roofs, one for each of the three missions. These accomplishments were attested to September 23, 1703, by the missionary friars.[11]

But no sooner had the settlement made these strides than the mistake was realized. Sound principles had been ignored in the planning. The presidio formed the hub of the settlement, the three missions clustered around it. Each had demands for pastures and fields close at hand which could not be met because of the notable lack of foresight. Water was scarce also. Before the year was out, the Indians of San Francisco Solano, which a short time before had shown such promise, fled the mission because of the water shortage.

Friar Olivares went out in search of the Indians, at the same time looking for a more suitable place to settle them. Soon joined by Friar Hidalgo, who had completed his term as guardian of the College of Querétaro in October, 1703, he established a new mission site sixteen leagues to the west. Near the present town of Zaragoza the two friars congregated a small band of Xarames. Most of the natives from the previous site refused to come because of the multitude of hostiles who lurked nearby. Nevertheless, some four hundred Terocodames, Ticmamares, Tripas Blancas, Piedras Chiquitas, and some from many other Coahuiltecan subtribes (Julimes, Dedepos, and Gavilanes) gathered. Wood, land, and water were abundant, and the mission kept the Indians pacified at this site until 1708. During this time the mission carried the name of San Ildefonso.

In that fateful year the rebel Toboso Indians who inhabited the country surrounding the missions made incursions which provoked the natives congregated at San Ildefonso to flee to the *montes.* In the brush they could better defend themselves against the troublesome enemy, who had slain eight Christian Indians but two leagues from the mission and carried off two children as prisoners. The flight of the mission Indians occasioned "no little grief for all the missionaries, who charitably and delicately loved them." The priests returned the sacred ornaments of San Ildefonso to San Juan Bautista, "praying to God for the return of the fugitives."[12]

11 Botello, *Datos Históricos,* p. 4.
12 Espinosa, *Crónica,* p. 757.

Prayer was applied in conjunction with persistent effort, and the "stray sheep" were at last gathered back to their folds. The mission was maintained about one year longer by a "dedicated brother," whose name apparently has been lost to posterity.

In order that he might have the comfort of the holy sacrifice of Mass on feast days, and that he might assist the other priests, Father Espinosa has recorded, this solitary friar frequently made the round trip from San Ildefonso to San Juan Bautista—a distance of thirty-two leagues—in one twenty-four–hour period. When the College became aware of this great effort, it was determined to remove the mission to the banks of the Río Grande, three leagues north of the other missions. At the new site, called San José,[13] a capacious church was built, with all the necessities for a pueblo. At this place, which was better defended from attack by the *indios rebeldes,* the remaining fugitives were gathered. The Mission San Francisco Solano, predecessor of the Alamo, remained at San José until 1718, when Friar Olivares moved it to the San Antonio River in Texas.[14]

[13] See Herbert Eugene Bolton, "Spanish Mission Records at San Antonio," *SWHQ,* 10, No. 4 (April, 1907), 303. The record entries for San Francisco Solano covering the years 1710–1713, says Bolton *(ibid.),* made before the mission was moved to San Antonio, throw valuable light on the mission's change of names. First known as San Francisco Solano, it became San Ildefonso at the second site. Records of 1712, at the third site, refer to "Mission del Señor S. Joseph, Yglesia de San Francisco Solano." See also Edmond J. P. Schmitt, "The Name Alamo," *SWHQ,* 3, No. 1 (July, 1899), 68, concerning the various name changes.

[14] Espinosa, *Crónica,* p. 757. San José today is an obscure village of less than one hundred persons, most of whom raise goats on open range. Surrounding the village are numerous rock ruins, perhaps of buildings of the old Mission San Francisco, or of later buildings constructed with mission stone. (See Chapter 38 of this study.)

6. FROM THORNS OF PAGANISM

WHEN Friar Francisco Hidalgo returned to the Río Grande after completing his tenure as guardian of the College of Querétaro, his traveling companion likely was a young priest named Isidro Félix de Espinosa. The future author of the *Crónica de los Colegios de Propaganda Fide de la Nueva España* was then approaching his twenty-fourth birthday. He was born November 16, 1679, at Querétaro, where his parents were longtime residents. He studied under the Jesuit priests in the modest Colegio de la Compañía de Jesús, taking courses in grammar and rhetoric, as well as philosophy.

"This early contact with the Jesuits," says Father Canedo, "explains the particular affection which he always had for them, and which he never passed an opportunity to express in his writings. Nevertheless, his vocation took him to the Franciscans."[1]

On March 18, 1696, Espinosa entered the Colegio de la Santa Cruz as a novitiate. A year later he made his religious profession under Padre Francisco Estévez, then guardian, pending arrival of Friar Antonio Margil to take charge a little over a month later. Having made the profession, Espinosa launched upon the study of theology. He was ordained a subdeacon at the Convento de San Francisco de Valladolid (Morelia), December 17, 1700, at the same time his older brother, Juan Antonio, was ordained as priest. In 1702 he was ordained a deacon, and on February 26, 1703, he became a full-fledged priest.

On October 20 of that year he served as secretary of the Guardian's Assembly which elected Father José Díez as superior of the College of Santa Cruz. Father Hidalgo then returned to the Río Grande, and, as

---

[1] Lino G. Canedo in Isidro Félix de Espinosa, *Crónica de los colegios de propaganda fide de la Nueva España,* Introduction, p. xxiv.

Father Canedo points out, "Espinosa must have accompanied him or followed shortly afterward."[2]

Young Espinosa was assigned as minister of the Mission San Juan Bautista. He was to remain at the Río Grande missions a number of years, during which time the stage was being set for renewal of the missionary effort in Texas and permanent colonization of that region. Then he was to take part in the re-entry and the founding of missions among the Tejas. In December, 1726, he would be named *cronista* of the missionary colleges, and the *Crónica* would be the result. On this work the years at San Juan Bautista had a strong influence. Much of what appears as generalized description actually applies to the missions of the Río Grande, because it was here that Espinosa first served, and these missions which impressed him first and to the greatest degree.

Not only was Espinosa a writer of history; he was a maker of history. He was one of four persons who appear to have had a vital influence on the Río Grande missions in their early stages. The others were Fathers Olivares and Hidalgo and Captain Diego Ramón, all participants in the founding. Father Espinosa traveled with them, hand in hand. He accompanied three important expeditions into Texas, writing well-known diaries of two of them.[3] In his *Crónica* he recorded many of his own observations from his day-to-day life on the frontier, imaginatively, though sometimes with a proclivity for exaggeration. As far as the gateway to Spanish Texas is concerned, these observations began with his trip northward from Querétaro, probably in company with Father Hidalgo, the latter part of 1703.

To reach the missions of the Río Grande, fifty leagues beyond the village of Santiago de Monclova, he says, one would go north from Querétaro by "the ordinary pasture road."[4]

The road would take him to the village of Saltillo and Nuevo Reino de León (Monterrey), and thence to the mining camp of San Pedro de Boca de Leones (Villadama). He would find some settled ranches along the

---

[2] *Ibid.*, pp. xxv–xxxvii.

[3] See Gabriel Tous (trans.), *The Espinosa-Olivares-Aguirre Expedition of 1709,* and *Ramón Expedition: Espinosa's Diary of 1716.*

[4] Espinosa, *Crónica,* p. 761. Canedo (in *ibid.,* p. 765 n.) says this road was that "by which one went to the large pastures which were found principally in the provinces of Nuevo León and Coahuila. Residents of Querétaro, and even of farther south, had their *haciendas* yonder."

route before coming to the first mission, Santa María de los Dolores de la
Punta (Lampazos), in Nuevo León. From this point it was forty leagues
to the inland missions. Ten leagues beyond La Punta was the river called
Sabinas—because of the many evergreens along its banks. "It would be
possible to place a mission on the banks of said river, there being such an
abundance of water, or on the Río del Álamo, which flows west to east
and joins the above mentioned Sabinas River."[5]

Between the Mission Dolores and the Río Grande were arid plains
broken by high, rocky hills adorned only with *lechuguilla,* runty mesquite,
and other thorny bushes called *ramones* (hackberries). The trail crossed
the San Diego River and the salty Santa Mónica to approach the missions
of the Río Grande.

Although the "inland missions" lay upon a plain, they were situated in
a depression, relates Father Espinosa, and the heat was oppressive. The
character of the land was—and is—hot and dry: "very much like that of
our Spain, of which it is said that there are four months of winter and
eight of hell."[6]

In the warm season, the padre noted, a hot, dry wind blew strong. In
the winter the wind was nearly always from the north, so cold that it froze
water underground and brought snow that lasted several days. Many domestic animals died of the cold, which had been known, said the padre, to
freeze baby chicks beneath the mother hen.[7]

Although the country ordinarily was arid, the rains sometimes began in
February. By June they would increase to such an extent that the fields
would be flooded. Generally the rains lasted only a month or two, then
gave way to the rigor of summer heat. Because of the high temperatures
neither Indians nor Spaniards did much work, their bodies being weakened by continuous perspiration. Yet the air was pure and healthful, and
such ailments as chills, rheumatism, and convulsions were virtually unknown, though heat rash was common. In order to remain healthful, it

[5] *Ibid.,* p. 761. Espinosa makes no mention of the fact that this river was the
first site of San Juan Bautista. The Sabinas River referred to is known as the
Salado today. The Río de Sabinas in Coahuila, and the Río Salado de los Nadadores join in Don Martín Lake, and below the lake the river is known as the Río
Salado. Maps of colonial times show it as the Río de Sabinas.

[6] *Ibid.,* p. 761.

[7] *Ibid.,* p. 761. A notable example of Espinosa's bent for exaggeration.

was well to eat little, bathe often, keep out of the sun, and avoid eating certain fruits which produced chills and fever.

The Río Grande del Norte was a fluent river, Espinosa observed. With a few heavy showers its waters would rise to such an extent that it would be impossible to ford the stream, or even to swim it. When the rise was small, the Indians used rafts made of buffalo skins to cross the river. Four persons would cross at a time, each holding to the edge of the raft with one hand and swimming with the other. Along the river were found many swamps, caused by small springs which formed large estuaries. The water of the *ciénagas* was somewhat brackish and impure; sediment from it would form itself into stone. But in the missions this water was not used, for there were other springs whose waters were sweet and clear.

Beyond the Río Grande, on the route to the Tejas, lay smaller rivers— the Nueces, the Frío, the Medina, the Guadalupe, the San Antonio, the San Marcos, the Espíritu Santo or Colorado, and the Trinity—each with sweet, clear waters. Looking eastward from the mission across the Great River of the North, one saw an open land with neither hills nor woods. To the north, distant by two days' travel, began the vast range of hills where the rivers had their source. The hills extended to the edge of the plains, whence the Apaches came.

To the west of the missions, twenty-five leagues distant, were the hills and mountains inhabited by *los indios rebeldes* called Tobosos, who infested all of Parral, Saltillo, and the province of Coahuila.

The land was black and spongy, and because it was loose and crumbly it was most fertile. Proof of the fertility was to be had in the abundance of fruits of the land. Harvests of corn, beans, and wheat, of vegetables and Castillian fruits, including grapes for wine, were bountiful. Green grama grass covered the lowlands between the spreading hills. Patches of mesquite and oak dotted the otherwise treeless expanse. Growing upon the watered slopes were ash, poplar, elm, beech, and willows. Wild fruits and nuts were abundant, including walnuts, grapes, persimmons, and blackberries, as well as some which the Indians feasted upon that were unknown to the Spaniards.

"In flower, the land which today belongs to the pagan seems a pleasant garden, an uncultivated paradise."[8]

[8] *Ibid.,* p. 763. Part of this description—particularly that of black, spongy soil—

The natives gathered enough wild nuts to last them most of the year, storing them in holes in the ground. The particular variety of nut to which Espinosa referred—of varying shapes, sizes, and taste—undoubtedly was the pecan. All of them, he noted, had better taste and flavor than the nuts of Castile.

Grapevines entwined the tallest elms to the very top, and the fruit was delicious, though seedy. There was a species of wild cherry, called *capulines*. Mulberries, better than the tame varieties, abounded along the banks of the streams. The Indians used the mesquite bean to great benefit: They dried it in the sun, and then ground it into dough called *mezquitamal,* which they put up in a year's supply. From the fresh bean a pulp drink called *bebida moliéndole* was made. Another delightful refreshment was made from the prickly pear, which also was used to make tarts. A sweet fruit came from a species of beech tree, and wild roots, similar to the sweet potato, which were hot, were cooked with barbecue. Date palms and wild onions were also found. "They have other roots and fruits unknown to us, which the magnanimous hand of the sovereign Creator of nature provides them."[9]

The mountainous area abounded with wild creatures of beauty, including lions, bears, and wild boars. There were many deer, which furnished food and leather for clothing. The smaller animals included hares, rabbits, skunks, and rats. The rats, "like a rabbit in size," were eaten by the Indians, and there are instances on record when the missionaries had to eat them also. Wolves, coyotes, and foxes ranged the *montes,* but the animal which held a special place of importance in the life of the Indian was the bison, or buffalo. Describing this animal vividly, Espinosa adds, "If the painters seek to portray a demon accurately, they may achieve it with a portrayal of the bison."[10]

The meat was likened to that of the cows of Castile. It provided the most common sustenance of the nations which lived in the vicinity of the Tejas, as well as the tribes which dwelt in the hills. But the *ganado de cíbola* was scarce in the vicinity of the missions, because the Spaniards

---

appears to apply more to the San Antonio area than to that of San Juan Bautista. See Jack M. Inglis, *A History of Vegetation on the Rio Grande Plain,* for a discussion of the area involved here.

[9] *Ibid.,* p. 764.
[10] *Ibid.,* p. 764.

"abuse this sustenance which the all-powerful Lord has given them, killing hundreds of these beasts each day, only to get the tongues, the tallow, and the skin, leaving the meat to feed the birds without serving themselves from it. In order to get buffalo meat now it is necessary to cover many leagues."[11]

But in the remote land of Texas where the Spaniards did not ordinarily go, thousands of bison were found in one herd. Espinosa had seen them that very year, he says, when two religious and fifteen soldiers had penetrated beyond the Colorado River in the month of April to look for the Texas Indians, and had obtained an abundance of meat.[12]

Indeed the land which belonged to the heathen did seem like a paradise in many ways. To the pagan soul who came to suffer the regimentation and discipline of the missions, it seemed most attractive at times.

What was it which prompted the Indians to give up their traditional nomadic way of life and their ancient religion to live in pueblos, under tutelage of the padres? Fear of Spanish military chastisement was one factor. A wish to have the Spaniards as allies in intertribal wars was another. Curiosity regarding this strange intruder in their land perhaps played a bigger part than is generally realized. In any event, it seems that the Indians' desire for self-improvement—either physical or spiritual—played no significant part.

The Coahuiltecans who came to the settlement of San Juan Bautista took their mission vows far more lightly than the padres had intended. When the restraining halter became uncomfortable, they felt free to cast it off and return to the *montes,* to their former way of life in the wilds. Although many of them came to love the missionary fathers, there were a number of facts which their primitive minds were not able to understand.

These were the *indios altaneros,* the arrogant ones, "the most uncultivated people who inhabit these regions of the north."[13] At the beginning

---

[11] *Ibid.,* p. 764. Here is an indication that San Juan Bautista had its hide hunters like Fort Griffin and other United States outposts in "buffalo country" during the century which followed.

[12] *Ibid.,* p. 764. Canedo says Espinosa refers to the expedition ordered by Captain Pedro de Aguirre, and accompanied by Fathers Espinosa and Olivares. Espinosa wrote the diary of the *entrada,* which left from the Mission San Juan Bautista on April 5, 1709 (See Tous, *The Espinosa-Olivares-Aguirre Expedition*).

[13] *Ibid.,* p. 771. Espinosa is not specific on this point, but the entire discussion appears to refer to the Coahuiltecans.

of the conquest, the Spaniards were doubtful as to whether these wild creatures were men or beasts. It had been necessary to ask a ruling of the Pontiffs as to whether they were rational and should be treated as men: whether the missionary priests should attempt to convert their souls to Christianity, or the military should wage upon them a war of extermination, hunting them down like wild animals.[14] But at last it was determined that their souls were to be saved, and the missionaries carried the light of the Gospel into the pagan land, which knew neither *ley* nor *rey,* neither law nor king, for their language included the initial letter of neither word.

The *indios altaneros* were a people who enjoyed natural abundance at the cost of little effort. The skins of wild animals were their clothing, wild meat their sustenance, branches of the trees their shelter. Their arms consisted only of the bow and arrow. They had no stable domicile and remained at one place only until its sustenance was finished. Because they moved with the seasons, they were content to live in huts covered with skins to turn the rain and the rays of the sun, though they afforded no protection from the sun's heat. Espinosa found the huts so sultry that it was possible to stay in them only when a favorable wind was blowing.

The Indians went about naked, with only a deer skin girding their waist. The women generally were covered with two goat skins; Espinosa considered these inadequate, because they were short, scarcely reaching the knees. The male children went naked almost all year long; the females, although at breast, were always covered, a matter which the Christians found somewhat confusing.

The many Coahuiltecan tribes were divided into groups which maintained amity with each other in order to defend themselves against the Apaches who, during the early part of the eighteenth century, molested them continually. The Apache nation, Espinosa noted, "is so numerous and widespread that its rancherias extend for more than three hundred leagues, reaching from northern New Mexico to the vicinity of the Tejas."[15] Fear of the Apaches and the unfulfilled needs in the *montes* compelled many of the *altaneros* to ask the ministers for shelter in the

[14] See Lewis Hanke, *The Spanish Struggle for Justice in the Conquest of America,* pp. 42–53, for a discussion of this point.
[15] Espinosa, *Crónica,* p. 772.

missions. Once they came, however, they were not always constant. They longed to return to the wilds—and frequently did so—to enjoy their "pretended liberty." Many who did stay in the missions shunned the work. Often those who went back to the brush found their former way of life not as appealing as they had remembered it; penitently, they returned to the missions, where they were content to remain.

The padres found it necessary to tolerate many transgressions on the part of the Indians, and to forgive them numerous times before they became industrious in their work. The friars recognized that mission life was a radical change from that in the wilds, where the natives lived in such a manner as to make vagabonds of themselves. Slow and tedious was the missionaries' work. The padres, while attempting to acquaint the Indians with the Christian faith, and to teach them to apply themselves industriously to work in the fields or the shops, had to overcome the language barrier. Patiently the friars employed sign language. "With their uneven and difficult accents," the Indians worked at learning Spanish, going over and over certain words, while the friars pointed with the finger or interpreted by signs "that which it is not possible to reach with words."[16] As many as six different languages were found among the Coahuiltecans who came to the Río Grande missions. "The total difficulty which is encountered at every turn in such a diversity of idioms" occasionally caused the padres to despair of the task and "to raise the eyes to the heavens, asking light to understand."[17]

Making the missions self-sustaining and providing nourishment for all the Indians who might come hungering in soul or body was a mammoth task. Sowing was done in community, a soldier who served as overseer assisting the Indians. The crops were gathered in a common granary, to which the missionary kept the key. He issued provisions weekly to those who had become a part of the political life. Those who had not yet learned to provide for the future were provisioned day by day. All which remained at the end of the year was sold to the captain of the presidio or to other Spanish inhabitants of the community. The priest stood by while the trade was being made to make sure the Indians were not cheated. He also endeavored to see that they converted the price into clothing, or other

[16] *Ibid.*, p. 771.
[17] *Ibid.*, p. 771.

needs for the maintenance of their pueblo, without indulging frivolous tastes.

"With this industry the Indians generally are found dressed."[18] As the work of the missionaries took hold, the Indians learned to weave their blankets of wool and cotton. They became a part of community life, exercising the responsibilities of citizenship and of the various political offices to which they were appointed.

In all the missions of the Río Grande, it was the custom for the entire pueblo to go to the church each morning and evening to hear the Christian doctrine. The padre led a procession into the church, and the prayers were recited in Spanish, taught to the Indians as children. The natives who had been baptized assisted with the instruction of those newly gathered. The ringing of a bell signaled the time for instruction of the neophytes: The *fiscal* of the church and his assistant would go to the houses, gathering the people for instruction. Only those who were sick abed were allowed to miss the service. If one should fail willingly for any other reason, he would be taken after the instruction to the cross at the cemetery gate. Kneeling in front of the cross, with the entire village present, he would be given four or five lashes across the shoulders by the assistant to the *fiscal*.

At such a time the culprit often felt himself irresistibly beckoned by the wilds from which he had come.

When new Indians were gathered to the mission, the missionary took each one individually and explained to him through an interpreter that which he was expected to learn: "all the truths of our holy Catholic faith." After much instruction, when the priest recognized the pupil to be ready for baptism, it was "conferred with all the solemnity to which the Roman ritual is disposed."[19] Those already confirmed usually joined in, and it was a grand and joyous day.

In the beginning days at the missions of San Juan Bautista and San Bernardo, when as many as forty children of both sexes were presented for baptism at one time, it was a high occasion indeed. The priest notified the soldiers of the presidio, and they came with their wives to the church. From the row of tidy youngsters the godparents from the presidio would choose one, and the child would be given a name, selected from a list of

[18] *Ibid.*, p. 772.
[19] *Ibid.*, p. 773.

the saints, at the time of baptizing, which was done according to the Manual. The godparents then caressed their godchild and clothed it to the best of their ability.

When one of the baptized children died, the missionaries rejoiced that the soul of the innocent one had been saved, that "from among the thorns of paganism, God chooses it to be a beautiful flower of the celestial paradise." Such a death was treated as a cause for celebration. As the Spaniards carried the body of the child toward the cemetery, others marched among the procession discharging their muskets. Chimes sounded, and amid other festive demonstrations, "it is a day of glory which passes in this desert land."[20]

The padres derived much satisfaction from seeing gathered in their missions "those drawn from among the briars and savage beasts which they have converted to docile sheep."[21] But many were prone to crave their native haunts, "the pastures where they are fed in paganism." Many times it was news of kinsmen still in the wilds, free to hunt and fish as they chose, which stirred dissatisfaction in the breasts of the mission neophytes, more than any discipline or abuse they suffered in the missions. With visions of the freedom in the *montes,* where they would not be required to work the fields, they would steal away in the night, putting many leagues behind them before sunrise. After the Indians were missed at morning prayers, the padre would take a few soldiers and go in search. Rarely would he return until he found the fugitives, whom he would bring back to the mission. The Indians at the gateway missions often would wait until the waters of the Río Grande were rising. Then, possibly with the aid of a buffalo-skin raft, they would cross the stream. Before they were missed the water would be so high that it could not be crossed on horseback, and the fugitives would make good their escape. Once, when the river was too turbulent to permit the fleeing Indians to cross before dawn, a priest and a detail of soldiers disrobed at the bank of the river "despite the great cold of October" and pursued on horseback. Moved by the tears of the priest, the *alférez* overtook the Indians and "with only his sword" made them return to their mission.

False rumors set afoot by "the common enemy" also were known to work havoc for the missionaries and to disrupt the mission settlement. In

---

[20] *Ibid.,* p. 773.
[21] *Ibid.,* p. 775.

1707 enemy Indians instigated a report that the captain and some soldiers were coming to San Bernardo to punish some of the mission Indians for butchering some livestock. Those who were guilty were advised to flee, which they did in the middle of the night. The Indians, with a head start of several hours, took diverse paths. Next day the minister and a number of soldiers from the presidio took up their pursuit, but only after five days were they able to round up the fugitives and return them to the missions. None of the neophytes was punished, but all were admonished against repeating the flight, which had been caused by the enemy Indians in the first place. They were advised that should some enemy give them bad counsel in the future, they should report to their minister, who would prescribe the appropriate remedy.

7. STRANGER FROM THE WILDERNESS

ACTIVITIES OF THE FRENCH in Texas were a matter of grave concern for officials of New Spain during the early years of the Río Grande settlement. The government had decreed abandonment of the region beyond the River of the North in 1693, when the first East Texas missions had become untenable; yet Spain did not wish to forfeit her right of possession.

In 1700, it will be recalled, two Tejas Indians had come to the northern missions bringing word that Frenchmen had settled among their people and the Cadodachos.[1] The Viceroy ordered the governors of Coahuila and Nuevo Reino de León to investigate the matter further. Some three years later a different governor of Coahuila, Matías de Aguirre, finally acted upon these instructions.

In 1703 Buenaventura de Aguirre, serving as commander of Presidio de San Juan Bautista del Río Grande during one of the several unex-

[1] See Chapter 3 of this study.

plained absences of Captain Diego Ramón, was commissioned by the new governor to investigate the reports of white men living among the Tejas and Cadodacho Indians in eastern Texas. From San Juan Bautista a band of Indian explorers crossed the river to search for the Frenchmen. On their return they reported that they had failed to find the settlements referred to in the Viceroy's order.[2]

Absence of detailed information regarding the expedition of the Indian explorers seems to indicate its lack of importance. No Spaniard accompanied it, apparently, and hence no written report was made. But when out of the wilds to the north a lone lost Spaniard appeared at San Juan Bautista, telling a weird tale of a trip across the continent from Florida, he caused no end of excitement.

His name was Felipe de Mendoza. He claimed to have been sent by Major Francisco Martínez, from the Presidio of Santa María de Galve (Pensacola), to reconnoiter the Bay of San Bernardo (Espíritu Santo, present Lavaca Bay). His purpose was to investigate reports, communicated to Martínez by the commandant of the French fort at Mobile, that the strategic area of the Texas coast was populated by Europeans. In this endeavor he had failed, having lost one of his two Spanish companions to illness, the other to murder.[3]

Who was this Felipe Mendoza? Was he telling the truth? Or was he, like the Frenchman Jean Géry, a demented victim of the wilderness who knew neither where he had been nor where he was going? To find the answers to these questions Mendoza's testimony was subjected to the careful scrutiny of the Spanish officer who had penetrated the land of the Tejas and the Cadodacho more than any other. This officer was the *capitán de caballos,* Don Gregorio de Salinas Varona, former governor of Coahuila (1692–1697), who had crossed Texas with both Alonso de León and Domingo Terán de los Ríos.

Mendoza claimed to have left the fort of Santa María de Galve by land with two other Spaniards, proceeding to Mobile Bay and thence by canoe, or pirogue, to the French fort at the mouth of the Río de la Palisada (Mississippi). Here one of the three Spaniards became ill and was left behind. The officer in charge of the French fort provided Mendoza with

---

[2] Vito Alessio Robles, *Coahuila y Texas en la época colonial,* p. 415.

[3] Declaration of Felipe Mendoza, October 4, 1703, A.G.N., Provincias Internas, Vol. 28, pp. 75–78.

three men to assist him in the reconnaissance of the Bay of San Bernardo. To reach the bay on the Texas gulf coast they took a circuitous route.

For thirty days the small party traveled by canoe up the Río de la Palisada. They came at last to a village of Indians at a place called Umandón de Dejo, on the Río de la Empalisada (the Missouri). Turning west at this point, the five men proceeded to a small village of Tesenacula, and from there turned southward, over plains, then mountains covered with pine and walnut trees (the Ozarks). They followed this route until they encountered a nomadic tribe of Indians who lived along the coast. At this time, as near as can be determined, Mendoza's Spanish companion tried to steal away from the party and make a reconnaissance of the coast without the knowledge of the three Frenchmen; the Frenchmen caught him in the act of forsaking the camp and killed him.

Mendoza was forced not only to abandon the idea of the reconnaissance for which he had been sent but also to flee for his life. He followed the sun westward, over a marshy land, onto plains dotted with live oak groves, and across rivers whose banks were lined with willows and cottonwoods. Coming to a large river, he followed it upstream until he came to the plain at the edge of the range of hills which the Apaches inhabited.[4] He crossed this plain to reach the Río Colorado, which, it was noted, had previously been named the Espíritu Santo River.

Continuing up the Colorado, Mendoza fell ill and was taken in by a tribe of natives whose name he did not know. He was with the savages fifteen days. After leaving them he traveled westward four days more to encounter a Coahuiltecan nation called Pallalles (Payayes). Among them was one wise man who spoke both the Spanish and the Mexican languages.[5] Mendoza stayed among the Payayes eight days. He asked the crafty Indian if he knew anything about distant settlements of Spaniards,

[4] Salinas Varona (in *ibid.*, p. 76) says this was the stream which was named Santa Sicilia in 1691. Mattie Austin Hatcher (*The Expedition of Don Domingo Terán de los Ríos into Texas*, p. 31) shows the place named Santa Cecilia by Terán to have been in the vicinity of the Sulphur River in present Miller County, Arkansas. Mendoza obviously was much nearer the coast, and the Sulphur River would not take him to "the plain at the edge of the range of hills which the Apaches inhabited." It seems likely that the stream which Mendoza followed was the Brazos.

[5] Salinas (A.G.N., Provincias Internas, Vol. 28, p. 77) interpolated that he knew this tribe, and that their habitation was known to be between the Medina and the Hondo Rivers, on the slopes of "the mountain range of Parral."

and the Indian told him of Captain Diego Ramón, who had penetrated this region, and whose fort was not far distant. Mendoza offered to pay the Indian to guide him to Ramón's presidio, but he refused, saying he wanted the white sojourner to remain, that he would make him chief of the Payayes if he would stay.

Mendoza, however, was eager to return to civilization and be among his own people. In sign language he took his leave from the friendly savages and began his lonely journey anew, searching for the Río Grande del Norte. For eleven days he wandered about lost. At last he came to a giant live oak and climbed it to get a view of the surrounding country. From the tree top he could see the Great River winding its way from the direction of the setting sun, and beyond it a vast plain. He lost little time in locating the ford on the river, and from there he made his way to the settlement of San Juan Bautista, the wilderness outpost.

Felipe de Mendoza, after a rest at San Juan Bautista, was sent on to the capital city, where his story was of interest to the Viceroy. Don Gregorio de Salinas Varona, whose service in Texas qualified him, was asked to appraise the testimony of this illiterate wanderer, given October 24, 1703, and his conclusion was that Mendoza definitely had knowledge of the land he claimed to have crossed. He knew the wild *indios bravos* of the coastal region—the same who had destroyed La Salle's colony—though Mendoza mentioned some Indians beyond the province of the Cadocachos of whom Salinas had no knowledge. The wanderer had described the terrain over which Salinas himself had traveled years before with Alonso de León, then with Domingo Terán de los Ríos.

Mendoza appeared to have established a route between the Spanish settlements in Florida and that on the Río Grande, though in Salinas' opinion it would be necessary to send an expedition over the same route, led by a person of wider knowledge and experience, to examine the route. Mendoza had failed to explore the Bay of San Bernardo, which was the logical place for any landing which the French might make in Texas. Such a reconnaissance could be made easily, he suggested, from the province of Coahuila and the missions of the Río del Norte, with twenty-five men from the presidios of El Reino and Coahuila. The bay was no farther than sixty leagues from San Juan Bautista.[6]

Mendoza's story was of two-fold significance to the officials of New

[6] Gregorio de Salinas Varona, "Informe," October 12, 1703, in *ibid.*, p. 74.

Spain. First, he had proved it was possible to travel by land from Florida
to México, a route which had long been sought. Secondly, he had covered
this vast distance without having found any sign of French settlement in
the Spanish-claimed territory of Texas. The Spaniards could breathe easily
a while longer. There would be no hurry about sending out an expedition
such as that suggested by Salinas, especially since the *capitán de caballos*
himself held that it was most unlikely such a French settlement existed.

In his reconnaisance of 1689 and 1691, said Salinas, he had seen no
suitable place for settlement among either the Tejas or the Cadodachos.
All the land was low and subject to overflow, especially when the snows
melted. The Indians, who planted crops of corn, beans, calabashes, watermelons, and tobacco in the creek and river bottoms, were forced in such
times to seek higher ground. Their crops would be left in elevated storage
bins to keep the moisture from spoiling them. It was doubtful, said Salinas, that any Europeans had gone to settle in such places, with the possible
exception of some French missionaries occupied in conversion of the
Indians. Between the mouth of the Río de la Palisada and the Bay of San
Bernardo, he said, there was no one.[7]

Always ready to seize upon an excuse for inaction, the viceregal government of New Spain saw such in the report of Captain Don Gregorio de
Salinas Varona. As for Mendoza, his route from Florida might be of some
advantage later on, if ever the need should arise; but right now such a
need seemed hardly to exist; the matter would keep. East Texas, it seemed,
was hardly a prize, and the French would think twice before trying to
penetrate its wilderness. All the expense of mounting a new expedition to
the land of the Tejas and the Cadodacho could be saved.

At the farflung outpost of San Juan Bautista, meanwhile, life went on
as usual. The priests worked with the savages who came to the missions
expressing interest in the Gospel, teaching them the ways of civilized life
and allegiance to God and king. At the same time the roving Coahuiltecans
were their link with the uninhabited region beyond the Great River, their
pipeline of information. From the Indians who came in from north of the
river, the padres gleaned a knowledge of what was going on among the
Tejas, and among the Apaches. They were ever alert to the circumstance
which would take them back across the river to work among the Indians

[7] *Ibid.,* pp. 73–74.

who had been abandoned in 1693. Their interest was kept alive by constant reports that *más allá,* farther on, was a tribe of natives who wished the Spaniards to come and live among them and bring them news of the Crucified Savior.

At the Presidio de San Juan Bautista del Río Grande the military leaders, too, were alert to the word from *el otro lado,* and the wealth that was to be found there on the other side of the river. They felt the pulse of the natives and reacted accordingly. "Early in the Eighteenth Century," says Bolton, "Captain Diego Ramón pursued Indians above San Juan Bautista. Having crossed the hills called 'Yacasol,' he reached wide plains, beyond them the Pecos River."[8]

Sometime prior to the year of Mendoza's phenomenal trek, Diego Ramón is said also to have explored the Cerro de la Plata, the Mountain of Silver, in Texas, on order of the Viceroy.[9] The probing was constant; the thirst for information from the other side of the river was insatiable.

On June 15, 1705, Martín de Alarcón became governor of the province of Coahuila. The ex-soldier of fortune and major of the militia of Guadalajara visited the missions of the Río Grande the following year and made a report to the Viceroy on their condition and progress, under date of January 27, 1707. The recommendations contained in the report are most interesting.

Some populous Indian nations from the other side of the Río del Norte, he said, had asked him for missionaries. These tribes lived on the Río Frío, which Alarcón stated he had personally reconnoitered and found to be quite suitable for missions, since it was situated in the center of the country inhabited by the friendly heathens.

In order to establish a mission on the Frío River without increased costs to the Royal Hacienda, Alarcón suggested that Mission San Bernardo be moved from the Río Grande. "Only an arroyo separates the mission of

[8] Herbert Eugene Bolton (*Spanish Exploration in the Southwest: 1542–1706,* p. 297 n.) concludes that Yacasol was between San Juan Bautista and the Pecos, possibly the same Sierra de Dacate, visited in 1675 by the Larios-Del Bosque expedition, and identifies it with Anacacho Mountain in southwestern Kinney County, fifteen miles southeast of Brackettville. See also Walter Prescott Webb and H. Bailey Carroll (eds.), *The Handbook of Texas,* I, 42.

[9] Herbert Eugene Bolton, "Preliminaries to 'The Spanish Occupation of Texas, 1519–1690'," in John Francis Bannon, *Bolton and the Spanish Borderlands,* p. 97 n., citing Fray Francisco Hidalgo, "Relacion de la Quivira," MS.

San Juan Bautista and that of San Bernardo," he noted, adding that maintaining two missions in such close proximity was hardly necessary. Mission
San Juan Bautista was so abundant in all the necessities—fourteen yokes
of oxen with implements, and forty-eight head of cattle besides—that it
could well provide for the people and land of San Bernardo also. With
the implements and livestock of San Bernardo—consisting of twelve yokes
of farming oxen and thirty-seven head of cattle and all other necessities—
"I would move and found this mission in the place referred to as Río Frío,
which will result in the great service to both Majesties without increased
costs to the Royal Hacienda."[10]

Many were the Indians, he said, who would come to the new mission,
and it would be closer to the Tejas. Commerce would be facilitated which
previously had been impossible. Governor Alarcón even had a plan for
communicating readily between the proposed mission and the settlement
of San Juan Bautista, farfetched as it may seem in the light of later geographical knowledge. While no hardwoods grew on the banks of the Río
del Norte near San Juan Bautista, he had determined that walnut trees
grew some thirty or forty leagues upstream. He had had two large trees
cut to be cured and brought to Mission San Juan to be used in making
two large canoes. With these vessels he thought it would be possible to
communicate between the mission of the Río Frío and the missions on the
Río Grande.[11]

All was in readiness for the new venture, wrote the Governor from the
Villa de Santiago de la Monclova; he awaited only the Viceroy's superior
wishes.

The following February 18, the *fiscal* Espinosa reported to the Viceroy
on the proposal. He suggested that the father guardian give his views on
the matter and act accordingly, doing what he deemed best for the good of
the missions.[12] Record of His Excellency's wishes is not found, but ap-

[10] Martín de Alarcón to the Viceroy, January 27, 1707, A.G.N., Provincias Internas, Vol. 28, p. 79.

[11] Alarcón, as other early Spanish explorers, made the naïve assumption that
the Nueces River, the upper portion of which flows toward the Río Grande, joined
that stream. It was not until 1747, during the Escandón *entrada,* that Captain
Joaquín Orobio y Basterra discovered that the Nueces actually flows into the Gulf
of Mexico by way of Corpus Christi Bay.

[12] Dr. Espinosa, "Informe," February 18, 1707, A.G.N., Provincias Internas,
Vol. 28, p. 81.

parently he declined to approve the proposal, for nothing more is heard of it.

Less than a month later Alarcón ordered into Texas from Presidio de San Juan Bautista a force under the command of Captain Diego Ramón, again serving as its leader after an absence of unspecified duration. At least partially responsible for this expedition, and possibly for Alarcón's proposal for moving Mission San Bernardo as well, was an epidemic of smallpox which had visited death upon scores of Indians at the gateway missions, as well as those in the neighboring wilds. Through the years the white man's malady played the major role in subjugating the Coahuiltecans. "By 1800 most of the south Texas Coahuiltecans had disappeared, having been destroyed by disease or absorbed into the Mexican populace."[13] One of the worst epidemics of the *viruela* came in 1706. The Spaniards had brought the disease, but, mercifully, they had also brought the Franciscan priests who worked unceasingly among the afflicted.

The Creator, knowing the little constancy of these miserable Indians in their good intentions, visited them mercifully in the two missions of San Juan and San Bernardo with an epidemic of smallpox. The Christians were favored with the holy sacraments of penitence and extreme unction, while the heathens were baptized. More than a hundred died.[14]

Until the epidemic ran its course, the missionaries scarcely ever stopped to rest for as much as an hour. Aided by two or three Spaniards from the presidio, they carried food to the sick, for hardly any of the Indians remained on their feet. Those who did were employed at digging graves and burying the dead. They were allowed to rest at intervals "because the malignancy of the fever which infested the air was insufferable."[15]

When all members of a family succumbed to the raging disease, their huts and ranch buildings and all that they had owned were put to the torch to prevent spread of the pestilence. The sky above the Valley of the Circumcision was black with the smoke.

As the epidemic subsided at the gateway missions, news came from the wilds of the large number of natives who were dying of the malady with-

[13] W. W. Newcomb, Jr., *The Indians of Texas: From Prehistoric to Modern Times*, p. 37.

[14] Isidro Félix de Espinosa, *Crónica de los colegios de propaganda fide de la Nueva España*, p. 776.

[15] *Ibid.*, p. 776.

out knowledge of Christ. One of the ministers—by his failure to give a name one may assume it was Espinosa himself—accompanied by Captain Ramón and several soldiers, went to *la tierra adentro,* the interior, "to redeem all the souls he could with holy baptism." Thirty leagues distant he found a large number of natives whom the disease already had afflicted. He persuaded them to come with him to the mission, lest he be "grieved that they die as beasts in the countryside."[16] That very day four persons had died of smallpox in the village; for that reason the Indians were preparing to abandon the site in an attempt to run away from the illness, which they believed to be a living creature.

"It is a ridiculous custom which these barbarians observe in the hope of freeing themselves of the smallpox," says Espinosa. When one of their number became covered with the pox, the Indians would place him under a shade and surround him with thorns to keep the demon disease confined. There the victim would be left alone, with only a supply of drinking water for solace. "If he is not helped and God as father does not succor him, he most surely dies." His body would be consumed by the carnivorous animals and birds. These Indians in flight, meanwhile, would strew thorns along the path behind them to impede the pursuit of Demon Smallpox. If the disease attempted to pursue and encountered the sharp thorns, the evil would be broken and lose its strength, according to the native superstition.[17]

When this particular band of Indians was brought to the Río Grande missions, the missionary inquired if others of their nation remained abroad who were ill. They told of one who had been left to his fate amid his encirclement of thorns. The benevolent minister, accompanied by a soldier and a kinsman, went to seek the stricken man. A brother of the ill one rode on the same horse with the padre, so that he might indicate the spot where the victim had been left.

He was found still alive, with the smallpox only beginning. The missionary had him mount his horse, with the brother riding behind him to hold him on. Since the horse was spirited, the priest walked, leading the animal, "in order to save that soul whose own kinsmen already had left him in the countryside as lost."[18] He brought the ailing man safely to the

[16] *Ibid.,* p. 776.
[17] *Ibid.,* pp. 776–777.
[18] *Ibid.,* p. 777.

mission, and when the Indian had recovered, the same missionary baptized him.

The epidemic left the missions of the Río Grande depopulated to such an extent, says Father Espinosa, that the minister of San Juan (himself) was obliged to go with a force of soldiers at the beginning of the Lenten season to seek other rancherias of natives to replace those who had died in the missions.

8. WITH SWORD AND CROSS

THE JOURNEY, not without its dangers, would cover many leagues. Before the start the missionary heard the confessions of all the military men, "that they might perform their duty with the church."[1]

Governor Martín de Alarcón had written orders for the expedition on February 25, 1707, two days short of a month after he had proposed removal of Mission San Bernardo to the Río Frío. To join eleven soldiers and four *vecinos* from Ramón's Presidio de San Juan Bautista the Governor sent eight soldiers from the Presidio of San Francisco de Coahuila and eight citizens of the Villa de Santiago de la Monclova, with powder and ball and provisions.[2]

There seems to have been some difference of opinion as to what the expedition was all about. To Father Espinosa the purpose was finding a new crop of neophytes for his mission. Alarcón's order stated:

They shall go in pursuit of the enemy who is found on the San Marcos River. . . . In order that the punishment of the enemy not fail, the campaign shall be carried out with all secrecy and vigilence, which with the help of God

[1] Isidro Félix de Espinosa, *Crónica de los colegios de propaganda fide de la Nueva España*, p. 777.
[2] Order of Martín de Alarcón, February 25, 1707, A.G.N., Provincias Internas, Vol. 28, p. 52.

cannot go astray. . . . The execution is of much importance to the greater service of His Majesty.[3]

The difference of opinion was typical of the divergent view of the religious and the military. It is to the credit of Captain Ramón that he was able to satisfy both purposes. His diary reveals that he dealt out punishment to recalcitrant savages with one hand and welcomed them to pueblo and mission with the other. Ramón pointed out that the expedition resulted from the ruin threatened by an uprising of the Ladino Indian nations, "accomplices in the murder of Spaniards and in the theft of their horses." The *indios ladinos* were creating disturbances in Nuevo León, particularly in the regions where new settlements were being made, continually stirring up the mission Indians.[4]

With some urgency attached to the expedition, the small force left the Presidio de San Juan Bautista just twelve days after Governor Alarcón had issued the orders. Ramón already had sent out Indian scouts to locate the native villages between the Río Grande and the Nueces and to make alliances with any Indians who were disposed to be friends with the Spaniards. Taking a guide and interpreter from Mission San Juan, with Father Espinosa as chaplain, the thirty-one soldiers and citizens rode out of the *plaza de armas* March 9, 1707, "marching in good form by the route to the northeast to challenge the Río Bravo." Herded along with the expedition was a *caballada* of 150 horses. The necessary provisions and ammunition were carried by 20 pack mules.[5]

---

[3] *Ibid.*

[4] Diego Ramón, "Diario de la jornada que executado el Sargento mayor Diego Ramón," March 9–April 8, 1707, A.G.N. Provincias Internas, Vol. 28, p. 53. The complete diary is contained in *ibid.*, pp. 53–71.

[5] *Ibid.*, p. 55. The "route to the northeast" would have been by way of Pacuache Crossing, also known as Paso de Diego Ramón, instead of Paso de Francia. Diego Ramón's list of the members of his expedition (*ibid.*, pp. 53–54) includes the following: Fray Isidro de Espinosa and *sargento mayor* Diego Ramón (*cabo superior*); Ygnacio Guerra, sergeant of the flying company of San Juan Bautista, and Río Grande soldiers Baptista de Treviño, Sebastián de Villa Franca, Nicolás Flores, Francisco Hernández, Ascención Maldonado, Santiago Ximénez, Matías García, Juan del Toro, Sebastián de Lara, and Carlos de Lara; citizens of the Río Grande, Joseph de Longoria, Antonio de Longoria, Diego de Charles, and Mateo de la Cruz Hernández; soldiers of Presidio de San Francisco de Coahuila, Miguel Minchaca, Antonio Maldonado, Diego Ximénez, Agustín Ponce, Antonio de Luna, Diego Minchaca, Juan Cortinas, and Alonso Olivares; citizens of Monclova, Capitán Don Joseph Antonio de Ecay Múzquiz, the *alférez* Cristóbal Rodríguez, Cris-

Five women mounted on horseback followed along as far as the river crossing. Ramón confessed ignorance as to whether they were "motivated by love of husband or by feminine curiosity."[6] Little water flowed outside the main course of the river, and the crossing was made without danger to the soldiers or their horses. Camp was made by some pools of water on the other side, only two leagues distant from the presidio.

The following day, March 10, the company marched northeastward eight leagues (about twenty miles) without significant event. On the eleventh, after traveling four leagues, Ramón sent Sergeant Ygnacio Guerra with two soldiers and an Indian interpreter on a scouting expedition, to seek Indian signs. Four leagues farther on Guerra and his companion came upon fresh footprints, which led them to the bank of the Nueces River at its juncture with the Arroyo de Caramanchel, northeast of present Carrizo Springs. Finding the Nueces not fordable with their pack animals, they crossed the stream on a foot log, leaving one soldier on the west bank to guard the horses. A short distance beyond the stream the scouting party came upon an Indian who was desperately ill. Through the interpreter Guerra asked him if he wished to be a Christian and receive the water of baptism, and the Indian replied that he did. The Sergeant baptized him "and shortly gave the soul to God."[7]

While Guerra scouted the countryside for signs of enemy Indians, Joseph de Maldonado, *el chico,* a citizen of the Villa de Santiago de la Monclova, went hunting for game to supply the company's larder. While stalking a deer he became lost. When he failed to rejoin the company, Captain Ramón sent four soldiers to look for him, but the four returned without finding any sign.

The company, meanwhile, had reached the ford on the Nueces, some distance upstream from Guerra's foot log crossing. Ramón ordered a halt for the night near present Crystal City, six leagues from the previous camp. Then he sent two other soldiers back to the area where the tracks of Maldonado's horse had last been seen as he pursued the deer. As the two soldiers proceeded across a plain which was hidden from view of the camp and which offered no landmark by which to tell directions, they met

tóbal de Carbajal, the *alférez* Joseph de Maldonado, Antonio de Luna el viejo, Nicolás Quiñones, Sebastián Maldonado, and Joseph de Maldonado el chico.

[6] *Ibid.,* p. 55.

[7] *Ibid.,* p. 56.

the lost man and led him to camp. Ramón, in his diary, manifested elation: "What a happy day, to have gained a soul for Heaven from such as there are in these regions, obscured from the Gospel. A Catholic Christian was found."[8]

Next day, after a late start, the company marched upstream, meandering with the river, trying to stay out of the dense growth of timber that lined the stream's banks. At last the stream was crossed with difficulty, as many of the horses bogged down on the muddy banks. Camp was made on the east bank.

March 13: "I requested the Reverend Father Friar Isidro de Espinosa to say prayer Mass in order that his Divine Majesty might give us light for the good purpose to which the journey is directed. His Fatherhood said Mass on a portable altar."[9] Afterward Father Espinosa went into the dense timber away from the camp for solitary meditation.

Following the Mass an Indian described as a heathen came to Ramón and, through the interpreter, asked how he might be "converted to the Catholic Faith like those of our party." The other Indians offered to guide Ramón to the camp of the Pacque nation, said to include the ones "who stirred the spirits of paganism."[10] Ramón was preparing to march the company upstream when a member of the Pacque tribe, whom he had sent from San Juan Bautista as a spy, reached the Spanish camp. The native had kept track of the movements of the band while trying to win friends among it for the Spaniards.

The spy guided the company downriver to the ford, where he said he had left the others of his tribe three days before. But when the company reached the crossing, the Indians had vanished. The spy picked up the trail, and one league distant found the encampment of twenty-one men, women, and children. They were given tobacco and provisions in an effort to win their friendship. Ramón ordered camp made near the rancheria, at some pools of water, probably near present Big Wells, ten leagues from the morning start.

Next day, March 14, the twenty-one Indians marched with the Spaniards to a campsite four leagues downstream, where they waited for the friendly savages to gather in those who were scattered among the timber

---

8 *Ibid.*, p. 56.
9 *Ibid.*, p. 57.
10 *Ibid.*, p. 57.

along the banks of the Nueces. Ramón sent gifts of tobacco, knives, and biscuit to the scattered Indians, to entice them into pueblo and mission.[11]

The following day camp was moved four leagues farther downstream to better pasture, nearer the Indians being sought. The place was at an estuary which offered good fishing, probably the mouth of San Roque Creek, west of present Cotulla. A portable altar was arranged and a huge cross erected in order that Father Espinosa might conduct the Mass. The camp remained here six days while the company provided itself with fish, and spies went out to seek the savages in the wilds.

On the seventeenth the chaplain celebrated Mass in the early morning. Later, while the friar was having breakfast, a friendly Indian brought news to Captain Ramón that a band of Indians had come into camp, "disposed to be received in the manner which they recognized would make us happy." Each one kissed the habit of the Father Chaplain. Ramón came and placed his hands on their heads "in the manner used to show friendship." All the Indians, thirty-four of the Assares nation, young and old, were seated in a circle. The Captain regaled them with the usual gifts of tobacco, knives, and biscuit. Through the interpreter Castillo he told them of the King's desire for the redemption of their souls. "All responded that they would accordingly give due obedience to His Majesty, gathering themselves in pueblo and mission in order that they might be educated in the mysteries of our Holy Catholic Faith."[12] Then Ramón had Castillo ask them if they were of the enemy Indians who had molested the Spaniards previously.

The Indians admitted that they lived close to those of whom the Spaniards asked, although there was enmity between their tribes. This bad blood resulted from the fact that the Indians now addressing the Spaniards had refused to join the enemy Indians in killing Spaniards and stealing their horses. Such activities, they claimed, were inspired by some Ladino Indians who had come from the other side of the Río Grande, in the direction of the setting sun, from Nuevo Reino de León and Presidio de San Gregorio.

Satisfied with their replies, Ramón arranged for the Indians to place their camp near that of the company. The Captain chose three runners

[11] *Ibid.*, p. 58.
[12] *Ibid.*, p. 59.

from their number to be sent to spy upon the enemy, ordering that they be provisioned with food and tobacco. They covered themselves with mud as a camouflage and departed.

Still in camp on the eighteenth, Father Espinosa again celebrated Mass and heard confessions of some of the soldiers. The following day was the day of St. Joseph, and again Mass was sung, the chaplain administering the sacraments to the natives who confessed. The day was set aside for the Feast of the Precept, with the Indians in camp joining the Spaniards in praying "for our devotion and for obedience to His Majesty." Ramón noted that the natives prayed "in the manner which the enemy Indians and disturbers of the infidel nations from this part of the northeast had learned from spying."[13] The camp where the company had remained the better part of a week was given the name of St. Joseph.

Following Mass three additional Indians volunteered to seek out the rancherías of the enemy Indians. With provisions and tobacco they embarked quite happily on their mission.

For two more days the company remained at St. Joseph. Mass was said each day. More fish were caught and the horseherd was gathered in preparation for a move, whenever the runners should return from the field. Liberal gifts of tobacco and rations were given the Indians in camp, who joined in the prayers.

On the afternoon of the twenty-first, the first two groups of spies returned to camp with great fanfare, indicating they bore good news. Ramón gave each his ration and a cigar and listened to their report, translated by the interpreter Castillo.

The smokes of the enemy camp had been sighted, they told him, indicating the location. He decided that a third party of three Indians would go to spy on the enemy further. This group left at daybreak, March 22. With the pasture in this area depleted, the camp was moved four leagues downstream, stopping on the higher bank of the river overlooking a ford. This camp, probably southeast of present Cotulla, was the place of rendezvous with the Indian scouts on their return. The Indians who had been gathered placed their camp nearby. The following day sixteen Indians of the Pasti nation came in, and Ramón had the usual gifts of tobacco and corn passed among them in a gesture of friendship.

[13] *Ibid.*, p. 60.

They said through the Interpreter Castillo that they had a great desire to know me, and they would help me punish the enemy Pelones and Ladino Indians, who had been urging these same ones to go out and do damage to the Spaniards. I answered them that my first wish and that of the Father Missionary was that they should receive the water of Holy Baptism and give obedience to His Majesty, as his subjects, together with the other members of their families. They embraced this proposal and took residence in the camp.[14]

On March 24 Ramón took a force and went out to meet the spies in preparation for making an attack on the enemy camp. He chose nineteen of the most expert soldiers, and some twenty-five of the friendly Indians went along. Two leagues from camp they met the spies, who pointed out the location of the enemy, in two separate rancherias. Three leagues farther on camp was made for the night.

Next morning the combined Spanish and Indian force resumed the march in the direction pointed out by the spies. After three leagues a halt was made to allow time for chasing a deer. The animal was caught, says the diary, and half the carcass was divided among the soldiers and half among the Indians.

After lunch Ramón sent the spies out ahead with orders to return at midnight to some pools of rainwater three leagues farther on, where he planned to camp near the enemy. At the pools the company spent a miserable night, as a spring storm blew in. Haughty claps of thunder rolled across the sky as tongues of lightning split the darkness. Short, heavy showers fell intermittently until dawn. Several hours overdue, the spies reached camp after daybreak to report on their reconnaissance of five enemy rancherias.

Ramón held war council and found that Indians and Spaniards alike felt the time had come to strike. Because of the turbulent weather, the force was yet undetected by the hostile Indians; such would not be the case if they waited until the weather cleared. Ramón agreed, and the stealthy march was begun, the force moving almost noiselessly behind the spies. Already smoke from the enemy camps could be seen spiraling into the leaden sky.

---

[14] *Ibid.*, p. 62. The word *ladino* means "sly," "cunning," or "crafty." Here it seems to be the name applied to a tribe of Indians. Elsewhere it seems that *los indios ladinos* should be translated as "crafty Indians."

The *sargento mayor* had advised his followers that under no circumstances were Indians to be killed if they made but little resistance; his instructions called for taking them alive.[15] With the cry of "Santiago," invoking the name of the apostle, St. James, the force fell upon the Indian villages, Ramón forgetting temporarily his own instructions. A shower of arrows greeted them, but the missiles fell harmlessly against the soldiers' armor. Five warriors were slain, and three were taken alive, along with twenty-two women, children, and babies at breast.

Through the interpreter, Ramón asked the captives how many had escaped from the attack. The Indians replied through the interpreter and with signs that two had escaped: one Indian man and an old woman who had just left to hunt for rats to eat. On hearing the noises of battle, these two would have gone to the large rancheria where dwelt the Ladino Indians who had stolen horses from the Spaniards. Three of the five killed were Ladinos, said the captives.

Ramón hastily attended to baptizing the wounded, since Father Espinosa had remained in camp when the force left for the battle. Both the soldiers and the Indians who had gathered to go to Espinosa's mission, San Juan Bautista, had expressed concern for his safety, causing him to stay behind.[16]

Ramón sent Sergeant Ygnacio Guerra with twelve men in search of the *ranchería grande,* the large village, renewing his instructions that no Indian was to be killed without urgent necessity. Guerra took as a guide one of the three warriors who had just been made prisoner. Ramón himself remained with the rest of the squadron standing guard over the prisoners, waiting anxiously for the return of his men. As his apprehensiveness was mounting, Guerra's men fired the victory signal from a short distance away, and Ramón ordered that the signal be answered with two musket shots. Guerra arrived quickly to report to the Major.

After traveling hardly more than a league—probably to a point on Salado Creek in northeastern Webb County—the squadron had encountered twenty-six adult Indians in war formation, each with a bow, two quivers of arrows, and a shield. The Indians shouted insults in the Mexican language, loosing many arrows at the Spaniards. Compelled to attack the Indians, the small body of men killed five and wounded several others.

[15] *Ibid.,* p. 64.
[16] *Ibid.,* pp. 64–65.

The remainder took flight through the dense wood. Proceeding to the rancheria, Guerra and his men found only ten boys and girls, all others having fled into the wood. "The rancheria was composed of fifteen huts made of mares' skins from some herd they had robbed."[17] The enemy Indians circled and came back to attack the Spaniards again but were repulsed.

Ramón arranged first to ease the pain of a wounded Indian, "since the friendly Indians did not kill him in coldblood."[18] Then, through the interpreter, he informed an old Indian man that he was releasing him to return to the *ranchería grande;* he should admonish his tribesmen to end the atrocities they had committed against the Spaniards and make peace with them. He was to tell them that should they gather themselves in pueblo and mission they would be assured of many conveniences, both spiritual and temporal, and that the King would favor and protect them.

The soldiers with Ramón, the leader explained, were ordered to the King's ministry, to bring peace with the Indians and resurrection of their souls. His Majesty had provided presents, which he was now sending to them by the old Indian, of tobacco, biscuit, and other pleasing gifts.

The old Indian departed, and the company began the march with the prisoners back toward the camp they had left to make the assault. That night when they made camp, Ramón ordered the guard doubled on the prisoners and the horseherd in the officially prescribed manner. The enemy remained near, and he was taking no chances.[19]

When next day they reached the place where the rest of the force was camped, Ramón was informed by Father Espinosa that Corporal Miguel Minchaca had permitted some Indian families left in his charge to escape. On March 28 the *sargento mayor* freed some other natives, then sent soldiers to follow them. When all were gone, he departed himself, and, following the signs, he was able to recapture some of the Indians, whom he brought back to the camp. He had Castillo examine them to ascertain why they had fled, inquiring if they were in league with the enemy. Ramón pointed out their error and invited them to come with the other heathen Indians in the camp to gather themselves in pueblo and mission, "that they might enjoy particular benefits in their souls and in their per-

[17] *Ibid.,* p. 65.
[18] *Ibid.,* p. 66.
[19] *Ibid.,* p. 66.

sons, and have comfort instead of inconvenience and uneasiness, as they would have in maintaining their roots in the field." He included a stern warning that the Spaniards would punish them severely if they continued to molest the mission Indians and the Spanish settlements.[20]

The company remained one more day at the camp by the ford on the river which had served as base since March 22, seeking without success the other fugitives. Two Indians who had escaped the skirmishes did come to the camp.

Recorded the *sargento mayor:*

I received them with love and gifts, asking them the cause of their coming. They said they were sent by their captain in order that I would pardon them their transgressions, since they acknowledged that they had opposed the Spanish nation and its benefits; henceforth they would molest no one. I told them through the interpreter that the will of His Majesty was that they be converted to the Catholic faith, that they give obedience to His Majesty, and that I in his Royal name pardon them their transgressions and accept them in Pueblo and Mission.[21]

Ramón told the emissaries to inform their chief that he would march slowly on the return trip to give his band time to overtake the Spaniards and accompany them on the way to the missions. One of the Indians had come to him earlier to inform the major that he was from the Mission San Bernardo. He was among the enemy Indians, he said, as the result of having been lured to a *mitote,* or savage dance, by some Ladino Indians of the Pelones nation,[22] who had been the disturbers of the Indian nations of the interior. He had brought horses and Spanish clothing for the mission in order that Ramón might pardon him. On his own volition this Indian remained in the Spanish camp while his companion, laden with gifts of tobacco, returned to bear the message of welcome to his tribesmen.

The next day, March 30, Ramón headed his company homeward, "thus to improve the place for soliciting new heathens in order to gather them into the missions." The missions, he noted at this point in his diary, were exhausted of people as a result of smallpox which they had suffered this present year. Many of the mission Indians had died in the epidemic "in

---

[20] *Ibid.,* p. 67.

[21] *Ibid.,* pp. 67–68.

[22] *Ibid.,* p. 68. Here, perhaps, the translation should be "some crafty Indians of the Pelones nation."

which His Sovereign Majesty increased His glory, winning many souls to enjoy eternal repose, as they died on having just received the water of the Holy Baptism."[23]

On the thirty-first the *sargento mayor* started his company marching toward his presidio, almost due west. He himself took a squadron of soldiers to seek out more natives who would go with them to the missions. "I had such good luck that in a short distance I encountered four rancherias of Indians of the Pacuq [sic] and Puyuas nations, composed of 21 persons." He proposed that they accompany him to the presidio and missions, which they agreed to do willingly. Ramón then bade the Indians send up a smoke signal so that his company would know to come this way. It did so shortly. The savages then joined the others who had been gathered for the missions, and the caravan continued its march. Camp was made again at some pools of rainwater, "with the customary vigilance"— an indication that Ramón was allowing his new Indian friends no opportunity for treachery.[24]

On April 1 the march was begun in earnest for the presidio. The danger of a revolt among the Indians who traveled with him, either as prisoners of war or voluntarily with the promise of entering one of the missions, apparently weighed on the leader's mind. The entourage "traveled all day with extreme urgency" before a halt was made in late afternoon on a watercourse (probably San Lorenzo Creek, Dimmitt County). While some of the company caught fish, others went out into the countryside and returned at nightfall laden with wild turkeys. Thus the larder was replenished, and the caravan was able to resume the march next day. The evening of April 2 halt was made just four leagues short of the Río Bravo.

After an early start April 3, Ramón's company and the host of Indians arrived at the river, where the crossing was made without hazard, as the stream was low. As the soldiers approached the presidio, Ramón placed his company in formation and fired the accustomed volley to announce their triumphant return from twenty-six days in the wilderness. Following behind the vanguard of soldiers as they marched toward the settlement came the new mission Indians, chanting prayers in unison. The Indian prisoners were confined within the main body of soldiers, after which came the horses and pack mules, and then the rear guard. They marched

[23] *Ibid.*, p. 68.
[24] *Ibid.*, p. 69.

first to the Mission of San Juan Bautista, adjacent to the *plaza de armas*.[25]
All the Indians except the prisoners remained in the mission, and Father
Espinosa "received them anew with demonstrations of rejoicing." The
others went on to the *plaza de armas,* where Ramón placed them in some
houses of the fort and posted sentinels to guard them until Governor
Alarcón should determine their disposition.[26]

The same day Ramón dispatched a letter by courier to inform the Governor of the favorable outcome of his expedition. The messenger returned
April 8 bearing the Governor's thanks to Ramón for his accomplishments.
Apparently on the Governor's instruction, Ramón separated the Indian
prisoners as to sex and turned them over to the missionaries. He explained
to them that they were being freed to receive education and teaching in the
Christian faith, which the padres would give them, and to be baptized. If
they remained in the mission they would receive nourishment, clothing,
and good treatment; "otherwise they would be punished with all rigor of
justice." [27]

Thus Diego Ramón wrote the end to the account of his twenty-six–day
journey into the wilderness, during which he and his men had endured
many discomforts and faced many hazards, all in the service of God and
king. He signed it "together with the leaders and other persons of most
consequence," including Sergeant Guerra, Don Joseph Antonio de Ecay
Múzquiz,[28] Cristóbal Rodríguez, and Cristóbal de Carbajal.

[25] Note description of location of the Mission San Juan Bautista. This bears out
other indications that the mission was moved (about 1741), and that the site
known today, a short distance west of the village of Guerrero, Coahuila, is not the
original, which apparently was in the present village of Guerrero, as was the
presidio.

[26] *Ibid.,* p. 70.

[27] *Ibid.,* p. 71.

[28] Captain Ecay Múzquiz, as will be seen, succeeded Don Diego Ramón as commandant of the Presidio of San Juan Bautista on Ramón's death in 1724. Vito
Alessio Robles (*Coahuila y Texas en la época colonial,* p. 311 n.) observes that
almost all document transcripts carry the name as Eca y Múzquiz, but that it
should be Ecay Múzquiz. "The real name of General Don Melchor Múzquiz, who
was President of the Republic, was Melchor Ecay Múzquiz." I therefore follow the
style used by this eminent Mexican historian.

9. A PLAN FOR TEXAS

W HEN Diego Ramón led the *entrada* of 1707, Padre Olivares was absent from the Río Grande missions, having been summoned the year before to take his turn as guardian of the College of Querétaro. The aging friar chafed at the call which took him from his charge, the Mission San Francisco Solano. This mission had remained in the Valle de San Ildefonso (near present Zaragoza, Coahuila), where Olivares had moved it in 1703. Now as he went to Querétaro, he left Friar Francisco Hidalgo as minister of the mission and president of the missions of the Río Grande. With Hidalgo was Friar José González, a religious layman.

On reaching Querétaro, Olivares was to send a priest who would fill his place at San Francisco Solano during his extended absence. He chose Father Jorge de Puga, who had served two years at Mission San Juan Bautista during the early part of its life. On the death of Father Marcos de Guereña, Father Olivares had sent Father Puga to Querétaro to give formal notice to the College. Puga had remained there until Olivares came to serve as guardian.

In sending Puga to Mission San Francisco the new guardian had a two-fold purpose: he wanted someone who would fill his place with zeal and at the same time would make badly needed material improvements. While not eager for the assignment, Father Puga accepted it with resignation and soon after Easter he hastily undertook the long journey. He hardly even stopped to rest at the missions of San Juan Bautista and San Bernardo, before going on to Valle de San Ildefonso. With Father Hidalgo serving as president of the gateway missions, Father Puga was placed in charge of Mission San Francisco. The major need of that mission, he observed, was for a larger church, as the neophytes were overflowing the present one. Borrowing an escort of soldiers from Presidio de San Juan Bautista, he took a work party of Indians and traveled northward some fifteen leagues to the San Rodrigo River. Soon enough timber was felled to build the larger church and some cells.

Needed for use in transporting the logs were leather ropes, but leather to make them was not available at the neighboring missions. With Father Hidalgo's consent Puga set out for the haciendas near Monterrey, a hundred leagues to the south. Going from place to place, he heard confessions and gathered cowhides, until at last, well into the summer, he was ready to return to the Valley of San Ildefonso.

One evening circumstance brought him to a hacienda whose owner lay gravely ill. There appeared no hope for the man's survival. Father Puga, eager to be on his way, heard his confession and prepared him to receive the other sacraments. Moved by the tears of the wife, the priest prayed that the man might be sustained for her consolation until the final hour. For several days the ill one wrestled with death, delirious from the high fever. He endured death's agony, but death did not come. Father Puga, moved by the intense suffering of the man and the sorrow of his wife, raised his eyes to a crucifix which hung above the bed and prayed a desperate prayer: "Lord, if this soul is not required in Thy court, preserve his life and place his sentence upon me. Though miserable and unworthy, I am thy minister to the end."[1]

The rest of the story, in Espinosa's eyes, revealed God's direct intervention in response to a humble servant's prayer. The ill one began his recovery. Father Puga left the *señora* consoled and took leave to return to his mission. On the road he began to feel ill. He attributed the feeling to the July sun, and for that, he knew, there was no remedy. He pressed onward until, on the eve of the day of St. James, he reached the Mission San Juan Bautista, where Father Espinosa was minister. His face was flushed, and he complained of feeling pain over his entire body. Espinosa brought refreshment, which made him feel better, and urged him to remain until he was completely recovered. Father Puga, however, stayed only long enough to attend Mass on the holy day, then set out upon the final sixteen leagues of his journey, his pain much alleviated.

Hardly had he reached San Francisco Solano when his fever returned, and he realized that he was dangerously ill. At the mission was Father Diego Xavier de Cervantes, who was preparing to leave for Querétaro.

[1] Isidro Félix de Espinosa, *Crónica de los colegios de propaganda fide de la Nueva España*, p. 852.

Since Father Hidalgo was absent, Father Puga asked Cervantes to stay and hear his confession. Then he drew from his brief case a sealed envelope which contained the general confession of his life and handed it to his confessor. With profuse tears he repeated the confession orally. The fever mounted, and the priest gave him the sacred viaticum before he lost consciousness.

When Hidalgo returned, Cervantes began his journey to Querétaro. At the Mission San Bernardo he encountered Father Espinosa, who had come from San Juan Bautista to ask Cervantes to stay and care for his mission while he went to visit Father Puga.

Espinosa reached Mission San Francisco to learn that extreme unction had been given the ailing priest the day before. As the end drew near, the three religious—Espinosa, Hidalgo, and Friar José González—took turns going into the church to pray. When the last of the three returned from prayers, as if on signal, the patient began the agony of death, and his fellow religious committed his spirit to the hands of the Creator.

A short time later, Friar José traveled into Nuevo León, giving to those along his way an account of Father Puga's death. Unknowingly, he gave the report to the very couple whom the priest had visited. As he gave the news of Father Puga's death, tears rolled down the cheeks of his host. The Lord, through His mercy, said the man, had commuted his own death sentence in answer to the unselfish prayer of this servant of God; he was not certain of his own salvation, but he would always believe Father Puga to be a saint.

When Father Espinosa in 1709 left the service of the gateway missions for the first time since his coming, he carried Father Puga's remains to the College of Santa Cruz de Querétaro, where a proper funeral was held.[2]

The year 1707 had been most eventful for the gateway missions. First had come Governor Alarcón's plan for the removal of the Mission San Bernardo to the Frío River in Texas; then the successful Ramón expedition across the Río Grande to punish the Pelones and to seek new people for the smallpox-ravaged missions; and finally the strange death of Father Puga.

---

[2] The story of Father Jorge de Puga is told in *ibid.*, Book V, Chapter XXXVII, pp. 849–853 (new edition). The chapter is entitled "Exemplary Life of Padre Fray Jorge de Puga, Apostolic Missionary, and His Happy Death."

Yet the most significant events of the year were not so easily perceived. Steps were taken which eventually would lead to the re-entry into the land of the Tejas. Father Hidalgo had been with Father Damián Massanet at the first East Texas missions, established and shortly abandoned following the discovery of Sieur de La Salle's ruined Fort St. Louis on Espíritu Santo (Lavaca) Bay. Unlike Massanet, Hidalgo had not been defeated by the experience. He quickly returned to the mission outposts of northern Coahuila to assist first in the founding of Santa María de los Dolores, then in 1699 in the planting of San Juan Bautista on the Río de Sabinas. When hardships befell the Mission San Juan, and its Indians fled, he followed them to establish the mission again, still farther from the bases of civilization. As was now the case with Father Olivares, he had been called away from his mission for a time to serve as guardian of the College of Querétaro. But he had never forsaken his primary goal: to go back to the land of the Tejas and to carry on the work which had been so poorly begun; to teach these Indians the Gospel.

"Father Hidalgo promoted vigorously and untiringly during these years the re-establishment of the missions among the Tejas Indians, which he promised without costs to the Royal Hacienda."[3]

Father Pedro de la Concepción Urtiaga, as procurer of the missionary colleges, went to Spain during Father Hidalgo's last year as guardian of the College of Querétaro (1703) and remained until 1705. He was charged to negotiate in the Spanish court for a renewal of the missionary effort in Texas. His urging resulted in formulation of new plans, but they bore no fruit because of Spain's preoccupation with the War of Succession.

Father Hidalgo, meanwhile, had succeeded in arousing the interest of the viceroy, Duke of Alburquerque. Through Father Lucas Alvarez de Toledo, commissary general of the Indies, he made a lengthy report to King Philip V which won some favor but brought no action.

In this same year of 1707 Don Gregorio de Salinas Varona had left his previous post as governor of Nuevo León to become governor of Santa María de Galve. From his headquarters at Pensacola he sent disturbing news to the capital of New Spain. The French governor of Mobile had dispatched twenty-five armed Canadians, accompanied by one hundred

---

[3] Lino G. Canedo, Introduction to Espinosa, *Crónica*, p. xxxvii.

Indians, to explore the approaches to Spanish territory to the west. They carried two boatloads of merchandise, hoping to establish trade with the Spanish provinces of Nueva Vizcaya, Nuevo León, and Coahuila.[4]

On receipt of this news, the Viceroy instructed the governors and military commanders in those provinces to use all means at their disposal to prevent introduction of French merchandise and intrusion of the foreigners. River crossings and mountain passes were to be watched closely, with friendly Indians utilized to bring information on movements of any intruders.

San Juan Bautista, situated near the already famous Paso de Francia, or French Crossing, on the Río Grande, was particularly affected by the order. It appears quite likely that this alert, coupled with other circumstances, may have contributed to the removal of Mission San Francisco Solano from Valle de San Ildefonso back to the Río Grande, five leagues north of San Juan Bautista and San Bernardo, in 1708.

The War Council in the capital urged the Viceroy also to make contact with the Tejas Indians and their neighboring tribes in order to use them in preventing the intrusion of the French traders. This proposal set the stage for the Espinosa-Olivares-Aguirre expedition of 1709.

At this time Father Olivares was in Querétaro as guardian of the college. On quiet winter evenings in the secluded Mission San Francisco Solano, he and Father Hidalgo had discussed means of bringing about a return to Texas. Father Olivares favored such a move, but the official stance of the college, less optimistic than its guardian, opposed it; the college had neither the missionaries nor the means to carry out such an undertaking, and certainly not without financial support from the Crown. But certain prerogatives went with being guardian, and Padre Olivares was not easily thwarted. He called upon Father Espinosa at San Juan Bautista for a report. In accordance with his instructions Espinosa gave information on the status of the missions of the Río Grande and an appraisal of the plan of Father Hidalgo. He ended the report—dated Mission of San Juan Bautista, December 11, 1708—with the recommendation that a new *entrada* to Texas be made.

It seems, however, that the viceroy, Don Francisco Fernández de la

---

[4] Carlos Eduardo Castañeda, *Our Catholic Heritage in Texas,* II, 21.

Cueva, Duke of Alburquerque, already had issued orders calling for an expedition, in response to the report from Salinas Varona. The Viceroy issued a decree in general assembly August 7, 1708, "in which his Excellency determined and commanded, with the approval of the general assembly," that the expedition go as far as the San Marcos River. Pedro de Aguirre, serving temporarily as captain of the Presidio de San Juan Bautista del Río Grande in the absence of Diego Ramón, was to accompany the Querétaran friars with an escort of fourteen soldiers.[5]

Under the Viceroy's instructions Father Olivares left the College of Querétaro and proceeded to the gateway missions, arriving early in the spring of 1709. He was to go personally with the expedition, stated purpose of which was to determine the truth of reports that the Tejas had moved west to the San Marcos (probably meaning the Colorado), in order to be nearer to the Spaniards. Olivares chose as his personal companion on the journey Father Espinosa, the minister of Mission San Juan Bautista, who would keep a diary of the journey.[6]

The two priests and fifteen military men departed from San Juan Bautista on April 5, crossed the Río Grande at Paso de Francia, and spent the night at Real de Cuervo, or Crow Camp, four leagues from their starting point. Details of this expedition are amply covered elsewhere, but it is significant that once again Spanish explorers looked upon the future site of San Antonio and recorded their observations. On April 13, Father Espinosa noted, "we came to an irrigation ditch, bordered by many trees and with water enough to supply a town. It was full of taps or sluices of water, the earth being terraced." They named the water San Pedro Spring. Nearby was a populous rancheria of Indians of the Siupan, Chaulaames, and Sijames tribes—about five hundred in all. "The river, which is formed by this spring," wrote the diarist prophetically, "could supply not only a village but a city." To the river they applied the same name given to it in 1691 by Don Domingo Terán de los Ríos: San Antonio de Padua.[7]

Continuing northeastward the expedition reached the Colorado River

---

[5] Gabriel Tous (trans.), *The Espinosa-Olivares-Aguirre Expedition of 1709,* p. 14; Castañeda, *Our Catholic Heritage,* II, 22.

[6] Espinosa, *Crónica,* p. 684. Espinosa, diarist of the expedition, here says the expedition went to the Trinity River, instead of the San Marcos (or Colorado).

[7] Tous, *Espinosa-Olivares-Aguirre,* p. 5.

on Thursday, April 18. On both sides of the river they saw many herds of buffalo. "This caused us no little surprise, not having found even old tracks of them from the San Marcos to the Río Grande."[8] This statement seems to indicate that the Spaniards who, as Espinosa observed elsewhere,[9] killed buffalo by the hundreds for their tongues and tallow may have penetrated Texas much more than had the organized religious or military expeditions. (Indeed it seems that even the Spaniards of this expedition, consisting of seventeen persons, killed a good many more buffalo than they had use for, taking eleven in three days' time.)

The Spaniards encountered on this trip a Yojuan (Tonkawa) chief called Cantoná, who apparently was known to some of them from an earlier *entrada*. Cantoná informed the expedition that the Tejas had not come west as reported; only a few of that nation were ever known to leave their country to go to the Colorado in search of buffalo. The Indian called Bernardino, whom the Spaniards had known from the day of the earlier missions, was chief of all the Tejas. The Yojuanes informed the expedition that this chief was "adverse to all matters of faith, never having been made to live like a Christian, and that he had escaped from the mission on the Río Grande with some Indian women who had been left there."[10] The Spaniards decided to go no farther. They had already come as far as Captain Aguirre's instructions allowed, and indications were they would not be welcome in the land of the Tejas.

Cantoná was commissioned to take to the governor of the Tejas a paper cross given him by the missionaries and to tell them that the Spaniards had come to search for them. He was to show them the cane he had, in order to convince them, and to tell them to go to the missions on the Río Grande, where they would be welcomed by Spaniards. Cantoná promised to carry out the instructions, and the Spaniards began their march for the Río Grande.

At this point in his diary Espinosa wrote a lengthy description of the flora and fauna, later incorporated into the *Crónica*. He also observed that some fifty Indian nations inhabited the region, not including those men-

[8] *Ibid.*, p. 7.
[9] Espinosa, *Crónica*, p. 764.
[10] Tous, *Espinosa-Olivares-Aguirre*, p. 9.

tioned by the natives as coming from the interior. "The number of souls that are without the light of the Gospel are innumerable and remain to be conquered . . . They are very friendly to the Spaniards and covet greatly their dress. . . . They learn our language with ease and we have not found a nation that objects to the reception of our holy Catholic faith."[11]

It was a promising field indeed; so promising, in fact, that Espinosa asserted, ". . . this is the best of all the lands discovered and the natives are particularly suited for the reception of the truths of our holy faith and for the extension of the domains of the royal crown."[12]

On Sunday, April 28, the little caravan recrossed the Río Grande, now flowing more water than it had twenty-three days earlier. The travelers reached the Mission San Juan Bautista at 3:30 in the afternoon.

The Espinosa-Olivares-Aguirre expedition proved nothing as far as reestablishment of the East Texas missions was concerned. It showed to be erroneous the reports that the Asinai, or Tejas, nation, eager for intercourse with the Spaniards, had moved their habitation westward in order to be near them; this was the negative result. The positive accomplishment of the expedition was increased familiarity with the land and the other Indian tribes. This knowledge would be useful when the time should come for planting permanent settlements.

Perhaps the most solid achievement of the journey was reconnaissance of the upper San Antonio River. The picture of this location would remain vivid in the mind of Father Olivares—as the memory of his early work among the Tejas remained with Father Hidalgo—until at last he was able to return and plant a mission there.

Soon after the seventeen Spaniards returned to San Juan Bautista both Olivares and Espinosa left the gateway missions to return to Querétaro, perhaps traveling together. Espinosa spent the next several years as *maestro de novicios* at the college. Olivares, before his return to San Francisco Solano, made a voyage to Spain to plead the cause of Texas missions before the King.

Father Hidalgo, meanwhile, remained at Mission San Francisco on the Río Grande as the lone advocate of a return to the Tejas with ministers,

[11] *Ibid.,* pp. 11–12.
[12] *Ibid.,* p. 13.

in order to complete the instruction he had given them nearly seventeen years earlier. His efforts, apparently, availed nothing; contradictions and difficulties met him at every turn. He was looked upon with disdain by his associates; even some of the menials mocked his singlemindedness. In the lonely hours when the rest of the mission slept, he lay awake pondering ways to achieve that which he was convinced was his life's purpose. The solution seemed to elude his tortured mind. Yet in the frustrating years during the absence of his companion, Olivares, and the young and precocious Espinosa, a plan began to take shape for Padre Hidalgo.

Perhaps a plan was forming also in the thoughts of Captain Diego Ramón, who had returned to his presidio shortly after the expedition came back from Texas, relieving the interim commander, Pedro de Aguirre. Ramón had sons and daughters who had married and given him grandchildren. He had sacrificed much of what should have been his, as well as theirs, in the service of the Crown. Now nearing sixty, he had been in military service since he was fifteen. He had achieved advantages during his long service on the frontier, but he was far from being wealthy. He had, perhaps, treated his family unjustly in placing his career ahead of their comforts. Now he could see little better for his children than he had attained for himself. Perhaps it was time that he showed them more consideration.

Who is to say whether the thoughts of the priest or the military man, Hidalgo or Ramón, had a greater effect on the future? The two men, in many respects, were not unlike each other. Both were aging now; each one had a crafty mind, though each employed it in a different way. Each was dedicated to his profession, though inclined somewhat toward disillusionment. And each was willing to apply somewhat drastic measures to achieve goals which he considered to be justified. Which, indeed, bore the greater responsibility for steering Spain onto the course she would one day follow in Texas?

A different approach was being taken, meanwhile, by Father Olivares, who had scarcely returned to Querétaro before he was named procurer for the missions and was asked to go to Spain to meet with the King and his prelates. He carried a letter from the Duke of Alburquerque to His Majesty, King Philip V, dated in México on October 11, 1709. His principal purpose seems to have been to urge the establishment of a new missionary college, in order that more priests might be trained for the mission field. Wrote the Viceroy to His Majesty:

> The spiritual progress which the fervor of the regular order of St. Francis has attained in only a few years . . . has been diffused with great advantage in the good example of the Catholics and conversion of the infidels, penetrating to the most remote habitations of paganism. It is attributed to Divine Providence that so few operators as these religious . . . have been able to carry on so effectively the preaching and teaching of the religion. Yet one wishes that those engaged in the extension of these kingdoms might be many more . . . I am not able to leave to plead in the sovereign comprehension of Your Majesty that the foundations of this institution be increased. This mainly is what the commissary of these missions, Friar Francisco Esteves [sic], in the city of Puebla, attempts. On his request Friar Antonio de San Buenaventura y Olivares passes personally to that kingdom.[13]

Olivares, said the Viceroy, was obliged to present to His Majesty those matters which would in time save the Royal Hacienda the great expense of bringing missionaries from Spain. Many were the gains to be made, said the Duke, "by increasing the number of these apostolic missionaries in proportion to the need of these vast provinces, in order that in all parts and at the same time the fruit of the evangelical law may be achieved."[14] The commissary general of Franciscans had offered to provide an unused monastery in the province of Tepeaca for use as an apostolic college, thereby saving building costs, though he was not able to help in other ways.

Father Olivares at first thought himself well received in the court of the Catholic King. But it soon became apparent that all was not as well as it seemed. An undercurrent of opposition was discernible as the rustic priest related his experiences and observations in the wilderness of far-off Coahuila and Texas. Soon Olivares found himself being shuffled aside, his prelates advising him against pressing his cause further. Resignedly, the priest departed before he had made a nuisance of himself and returned to Querétaro.

On the surface his mission was a signal failure, but he had planted in

[13] Espinosa, *Crónica*, p. 836.
[14] *Ibid.*, p. 836.

high places some ideas which years later bore fruit to the benefit of the missionary colleges in México.[15]

[15] *Ibid.,* p. 837.

10. THE FRENCH CAVALIER

WITHDRAWAL from the East Texas missions in 1693 had not been Father Hidalgo's idea in the first place. He loved the simple souls of the heathen Indians, and although some of the Tejas manifested a marked belligerence toward the Spaniards, others returned the padre's devotion. He gave his all to his task as missionary, ranging far afield from the Mission San Francisco, visiting the many rancherias that were scattered all the way to the land of the Cadodachos, fifty leagues or more. Always he saw countless heathens, and always he felt extreme sorrow at the great number who could not be brought into the church. His zeal inspired great love and admiration among some of the Indians, and now, as he whiled away the dark hours at San Juan Bautista, he felt a twinge of guilt. Had he, in his human weakness, failed his people, the Tejas? With remorse he recalled the words of the chief of the pueblo of his mission, when the Indian leaders observed that the missionaries were about to leave.

"Father," asked the chief, "why are you leaving us? What wrong have my people and I done you? Have we not served faithfully in every circumstance? Have we not sowed for you every year? In your ministry to the Indians, have you not found helpers?"

Friar Francisco now considered his reply to have been a lame one. He offered weakly, "This action does not depend on me, but on my companion, who is my superior. He goes for his own reasons, and I cannot remain alone."[1]

[1] Juan Domingo Arricivita, *Crónica seráfica y apostólica del Colegio de la Santa Cruz de Querétaro en la Nueva España, segunda parte,* p. 219.

The chief was not satisfied. He urged the father: "If you will remain, I give you my word to build you a dwelling house, and church where you may say Mass, and those of my house and family will pray without ceasing every day."

Father Hidalgo looked around him at the church and houses in flames, recalling the harsh threats of Chief Bernardino, who had been responsible for bringing matters to such a pass. His answer to the gentle soul before him was made sharp by this bitter memory: "Why you and your family and not all the Indians?" he retorted.[2]

The Indian replied softly: "Can you be ignorant, Father, of the great inequality which there is among this people? Have you not experienced in this matter that they are very willful? But I give you my word I will not be found wanting."[3]

These were the words that stuck in Father Hidalgo's consciousness. They were a fervent appeal of one who earnestly desired salvation; yet he, an apostolic missionary, had turned away. He *must* go back.

Failure confronted Father Hidalgo at every turn. Yet he did not abandon his goal of returning to the land of the Tejas to renew the missionary effort begun in 1690. Some sources, without clear documentation, say that he made frequent trips from San Juan Bautista into Texas, while tenaciously advocating Spanish reoccupation of the province.[4]

He may well have gone personally to investigate the plight of the Tejas, but, in any event, he gathered information regarding these Indians from whatever source possible: from the buffalo hunters who crossed the Río Grande from the settlement of San Juan Bautista; from Indians who came to the gateway after ranging to the borders of the Asinai nation; from the various expeditioners who penetrated beyond the Great River. Most certainly did he ply with questions the members of the Espinosa-Olivares-Aguirre expedition of 1709 when they returned with secondhand news of the Tejas.

Eagerly he awaited the day when he would be permitted to go back and continue his apostolic task. As the years passed, his hope grew dimmer. His petitions, and those of his fellow missionaries, fell on deaf ears. But the prayers of Friar Francisco did not.

[2] *Ibid.*, pp. 219–220.
[3] *Ibid.*, p. 220.
[4] E.g., Vito Alessio Robles, *Coahuila y Texas en la época colonial*, pp. 425–426.

In almost constant meditation upon his personal obsession, he awoke one day with a plan. He viewed the situation as he had never been able to before, and from this new insight he derived a course of action. Various writers have ascribed diverse motives to the persistent priest: he schemed with cleverness to maneuver toward his goal; or guileless, and in all humility, he took a tentative step which had unforeseen repercussions, and yet bore fruit by producing the desired result. Whichever is the case, his action would be responsible for placing the very foundation stones of Texas.

Father Hidalgo might have reasoned that the Spanish occupation of Texas in the first place had resulted from French rivalry. La Salle's settlement on Espíritu Santo Bay had galvanized officials of New Spain to action. The friar may also have reasoned that a similar threat could cause the Viceroy to order a return to Texas. French intrusion had been rumored ever since the East Texas missions had been abandoned in 1693. In response to each threat a new investigation was made, but each time the alarm had seemed unworthy of major concern. Yet the French definitely were pushing against the borders of New Spain, looking hungrily toward a lucrative fur trade with the Indians west of the Mississippi, and perhaps toward the mines of México. As early as 1700 one Louis Juchereau de St. Denis is said to have headed a French expedition up the Red River. Somewhat later this same man was to claim that he had crossed Texas in 1705, making contact with the Spaniards at San Juan Bautista. If such was the case, the Spaniards at this advanced outpost were singularly silent on the matter.

Father Hidalgo certainly was aware of the French interest in Texas. He should have been able to foresee the probable reaction of the Viceroy to any new intrusion by Spain's number one colonial rival. Historians, therefore, have been prone to ascribe a certain amount of calculating design to his act of writing a letter to French authorities. On January 27, 1711,[5] he wrote to the governor of Louisiana, inquiring of the welfare of the Tejas and asking for French cooperation in establishing a mission for those Indians. To make certain that his letter reached its destination he made three copies and sent each by a different route. How the zealous

[5] Gerardo Mora, "Relación hecha por Don Luis de San Dionis y Don Medar Jalot del viaje que ejecutaron desde la Móvila hasta el Presidio de Diego Ramón," A.G.N., Provincias Internas, Vol. 181, p. 11.

friar would have justified such an act cannot be known, but the result is not disputed. Whatever the missionary's thoughts were as he dispatched the letter, he may well have despaired that it would ever bear fruit before he learned, almost four years later, that it had reached the French governor at Mobile.

While fraught with frustration over his inability to bring about a return to the Tejas, Father Hidalgo busied himself with the work of the Mission San Juan Bautista, seeing that it was not neglected as a result of his preoccupation. His case seems to parallel the story of the ninety and nine, for many sheep already had been brought into the fold at San Juan. In 1710 he reported that 318 persons had been baptized, with 104 married in ecclesiastical ceremonies, and 172 given final rites and burial. After making this report he remained at his post two more years, then returned in 1712 to the College of Querétaro. It was there in 1714 that he learned the fate of his historic letter.[6]

Two and a half years after it was written, the letter came to the hand of Antoine de la Mothe, Sieur Cadillac, who had just taken office as governor of Louisiana. In his new position Cadillac was to be the major commercial agent of Antoine Crozat, holder of the government concession for a monopoly of trade in Louisiana for a fifteen-year period. The French colony was to be treated entirely as a commercial enterprise; conquest and colonization were secondary goals. Cadillac set immediately upon his task of establishing trade with México by sending a merchandise ship to Veracruz, offering a trade for livestock and other necessities. But Spanish officials turned the ship back with a stern warning that the ports of New Spain were closed to all foreign commerce.

With such a rebuff the future of Cadillac's enterprises appeared grim indeed. But the letter from Father Hidalgo opened new possibilities: why not an overland trade route which would direct the commerce of the North México provinces to the Mississippi Basin? Cadillac would be glad to help the Spanish missionaries establish missions among the Asinai Indians. What better way to make the contact with the Spaniards which was necessary to establish trade? The undertaking would be delicate, but he had at his disposal the very man with the qualifications to carry it out: Louis Juchereau de St. Denis. Cadillac immediately sent for St. Denis, the

[6] Arricivita, *Crónica seráfica*, p. 221.

commandant at Biloxi, and issued him a passport on September 12, 1713. He was to take twenty-four men and as many Indians as necessary and go in search of the mission of Father Hidalgo. There he would purchase cattle and horses for the French province of Louisiana. The party set out from Mobile in late September.[7]

After pausing briefly at Biloxi, the expedition proceeded up the Red River. At the site of Natchitoches the Frenchmen constructed two log storehouses, where St. Denis left part of his merchandise and a guard of ten men. Twenty-two days' travel brought them to the Asinai (Tejas) nation, where they found an abundance of cattle and horses.

"Because these natives had retained their deepseated respect for the Spanish name," St. Denis was to inform Spanish officials later, "they had not killed their cattle, hoping that they would return. The horses and cattle left by the Spaniards had increased to thousands of head."[8]

The French party began immediately to barter for livestock and buffalo hides; trading was so brisk that St. Denis is said to have returned to Louisiana for a new supply of goods.[9] It appears doubtful that the leader himself returned, but at this point all but three of the twenty-four men who accompanied him took leave to return to Mobile.[10]

Among the Tejas, St. Denis found many individuals who had continued to practice the Christian religion after the Spaniards departed. These asked him to seek the return to their country of Father Hidalgo, "who had lived among them with outstanding knowledge of their language and customs," and of "a secular Vizcayan, Captain Urrutia, who had been among them ten years, including the time of Father Hidalgo."[11]

At last St. Denis decided to push on toward the Spanish settlement on the Río Grande, first reporting to Governor Cadillac that Father Hidalgo had not been found among the Tejas. In the march southwestward St. Denis and his three French companions were accompanied by Chief Bernardino and twenty-five of his Tejas braves. His own men who remained were Penicault, Pierre Largen, and Medar Jalot. The latter served the

[7] Mora, "Relación," p. 11; Charles Wilson Hackett and Charmion Clair Shelby (trans.), *Pichardo's Treatise on the Limits of Louisiana and Texas,* I, 219.

[8] Gerardo Mora to the Viceroy, A.G.N., Provincias Internas, Vol. 181, p. 6.

[9] Ross Phares, *Cavalier in the Wilderness: The Story of the Explorer and Trader, Louis Juchereau de St. Denis,* p. 45.

[10] Mora to Viceroy, A.G.N., Provincias Internas, Vol. 181, p. 6.

[11] *Ibid.,* p. 6.

leader as chef, valet, surgeon, and, when the occasion arose, public relations representative, self-appointed or otherwise.

On the Colorado the party was attacked by a reported two hundred hostile Karankawa warriors. The bloody engagement lasted from eight o'clock in the morning until two o'clock in the afternoon. St. Denis, a cool tactician in every instance, employed his men effectively. The attackers were driven off, with twelve men and a woman killed, "not to mention those who may have fallen dead or wounded in the dense wood."[12] Two of the Tejas were slightly wounded. Chief Bernardino confidently informed the Frenchmen that the battle had ended the trouble they would have from the enemy. Twenty-one of his warriors turned back the next day, while Bernardino and three others continued on to the Río Grande.

The party of eight, arriving at the San Antonio River, encountered a village of Indians who were friends of the Spaniards. They looked upon the future site of the city of San Antonio and proclaimed it "beautiful and fertile; very suitable for a settlement and worthy of a good presidio."[13] The Frenchmen had no way of knowing that Don Domingo Terán de los Ríos and the Reverend Fathers Espinosa and Olivares also had marked the spot as the place where a prosperous settlement would one day rise. St. Denis did not tarry long. He turned his face determinedly toward the Río Grande, and the presidio of Captain Don Diego Ramón.

Life at the gateway missions and presidio moved along at its same leisurely pace. Hardly, even, was notice taken when in 1713 Captain Diego Ramón, like other frontier commanders, received from the Viceroy specific orders against admitting foreign traders or foreign merchandise into Spanish lands. If any foreigner crossed the frontier, the commanders were advised, he was to be arrested and the Viceroy notified.[14] But still life went on as usual, the padres instructing their neophytes, the soldiers regulating Indian affairs, the *vecinos* bending sinuous muscle to wrest a

[12] *Ibid.,* p. 7. Antonio Bonilla (Elizabeth H. West [trans.], "Bonilla's Brief Compendium of the History of Texas, 1772," *SWHQ,* 8, No. 1 [July, 1904], 24) says of the attacking Indians, "Of course they must have been Apaches."

[13] *Ibid.,* p. 8.

[14] Paul Horgan, *Great River: The Río Grande in North American History,* p. 331.

living from the gray dirt of the Río Grande Plain—"as if tomorrow would always be the same as yesterday."[15]

But summer came, and out of the July heat rose a spiral of dust to the eastward, an object of curiosity, an omen of the change. "Events of July 19, 1714, jarred San Juan Bautista from its complacent slumber into a state of panic. From that day on, the tempo of life on the Río Grande was never the same. The Spanish would thereafter be obliged to watch a rival, guard a border, and prevent—or promote—smuggling."[16]

The mission Indians brought first word of the approaching caravan. The news gave rise to wild speculation. Later in the day a lookout spied the invaders from the tower at the edge of the plaza, counting their number as four Frenchmen and four Indians, no more. Captain Ramón alerted his garrison and waited.

The flamboyant St. Denis, impeccably dressed in tailored linen, strode boldly toward the presidio guards, calling out in good Spanish that he wished to see the commandant. Taken to the presence of Diego Ramón, he exhibited poise and self-assurance as he told the Captain his motives for coming. There was the letter from Father Hidalgo expressing concern for the Tejas Indians. He had set out from Louisiana with the hope of purchasing grain and cattle from the missions thought to exist among the Tejas. On finding the missions abandoned, he had continued his march to the Río Grande.

Captain Ramón glared back at the poised, fearless Frenchmen through narrowed, dark eyes. Then he told him of the Viceroy's order forbidding the entry of foreign merchandise or traders into Spanish territory. He had no alternative but to arrest the intruders.

It was a most unusual imprisonment, but then St. Denis was a most unusual man. The "prison" was the Ramón household. More than being a prisoner, St. Denis was a guest, and a most entertaining one. Indeed he and the Ramóns enjoyed each other. The Frenchman and Don Diego, both veterans of the frontier and knowledgeable of political as well as military matters, had much in common. Their interchange filled a mutual need.

St. Denis was not particularly troubled by his "imprisonment," terms of which forbade his leaving the presidio. He was disappointed, however,

[15] Phares, *Cavalier,* p. 49.
[16] *Ibid.,* p. 49.

to find that Father Hidalgo, who was responsible for his coming, was not to be found at San Juan Bautista. On July 20, the day following his arrival, the French cavalier wrote to the Franciscan priest at the College of Querétaro, informing him of his arrival at the gateway and urging him to speed his return.

The same courier who carried St. Denis' letter to Father Hidalgo also carried one from Father Alonso González, dated San Juan Bautista, July 21, and another from Captain Ramón, dated July 22. Father González observed that the way had been opened by the coming of the Frenchman for work among the Tejas Indians.[17] The commandant opined that "If His Majesty (whom God preserve) does not object to [the French] populating the Pueblos of the Naquitoses, the French will be masters of all this land." Don Diego urged Father Hidalgo to continue his efforts in order that the *entrada* he was seeking might be made, "and that I might have the happiness of accompanying it."[18]

But to the Viceroy, Ramón evidently wrote in a different manner, reporting that Father Hidalgo had asked the French for armed support. He also forwarded St. Denis' papers, including Father Hidalgo's letter to the French authorities in Louisiana.[19] The Viceroy, according to Arricivita, was satisfied with the conduct of Ramón in the episode; "but the Venerable Padre was not pardoned of many mortifications of his spirit . . ."[20]

Once officials in the capital were notified, there was little to do at San Juan Bautista but wait. "Days passed into weeks, and no reply came from higher authority. The alarming incident of the Frenchmen's arrival turned into a prolonged *fiesta*."[21]

St. Denis has given rise to a spate of legends. As though his true exploits were not sufficiently daring and dashing, others of a spurious nature have been attributed to him. It has become almost impossible to separate the two. The known facts are sufficiently dramatic to belong in a novel. While "imprisoned" at San Juan Bautista he wooed and won the seventeen-year-old granddaughter of Diego Ramón. She was lovely, dark-haired Manuela, daughter of Diego Ramón II.

[17] *Ibid.*, p. 52.
[18] Lino G. Canedo, Introduction to Isidro Félix de Espinosa, *Crónica de los colegios de propaganda fide de la Nueva España*, p. xl.
[19] Mora, "Relación," p. 11.
[20] Arricivita, *Crónica seráfica*, p. 222.
[21] Phares, *Cavalier*, p. 54.

While Jalot, the valet skilled in the art of the press agent, spread tales of the love affairs and duels of his master, Manuela herself is said to have been promised to the governor of Coahuila, her grandfather's superior.[22] If such were the case—which is extremely doubtful—it was a complicating factor for the Ramóns. They were subjected to the blandishments of St. Denis, whose primary objective was the instigation of a trade agreement which would be profitable to the French; in fact, it appeared that such trade was essential for the French to maintain their hold in the New World.

Skillfully it was suggested to the Ramóns that St. Denis might be a profitable connection, through which they might become rich in intercolonial commerce. Spain might relax her stringent trade laws, and St. Denis might become the commandant on the French side of the frontier, as Captain Ramón was on the Spanish side. The advantages of an alliance between them were worth pondering.[23]

As summer wore into fall and autumn into winter, St. Denis was busy not only with his quest of Manuela's lovely hand but with gathering information pertinent to his plans for trade. He learned, for example, that sixty-one leagues distant was the mining camp of Boca de Leones (present Villadama, Nuevo León), where there were enterprising merchants who would welcome an opportunity to acquire imported goods to dispense to their customers, and who were willing to barter with unmarked silver. On February 15, 1715, he dispatched this information by secret courier to the governor of Louisiana at Mobile. Still the wait for official word from the city of México went on.

But officials in the capital had not forgotten. Their attention to duty became woefully apparent on a day in late March, when an officer and twenty-five men rode in from Monclova. They took St. Denis, along with his man Jalot, away in chains. Bound for the city of México, the dapper Frenchman now must account to the viceroy, Duke of Linares, for his unauthorized entry into Spanish territory.

---

[22] The governor, according to Phares (*ibid.*, p. 61) was Don Gaspardo Anya, though Coahuila never had a governor by such a name. Governor from 1712 to 1714 was Pedro Fermín de Echeverz y Subisa. Interim governor from 1714 to 1716 was Juan Valdez (Herbert Eugene Bolton, *Guide to Materials for the History of the United States in the Principal Archives of México*, p. 478).

[23] Phares, *Cavalier*, p. 61.

Left behind was a grieving Manuela Ramón, who was perhaps grieved the more because it was her uncle, Domingo Ramón, who headed the escort of soldiers. Or did Don Domingo simply go along to plead St. Denis' case? In either event he was handily on the spot when St. Denis reached the capital. Legend has it that Manuela's gallant lover was taken first to prison in the provincial capital, where the Governor offered him his freedom if he would but renounce his claim to her. In truth, however, this account appears to have no merit except that it makes a good story. It was in the city of México that St. Denis' fate would be decided.

11. NIGHT OF TERROR

S T. DENIS' DEPARTURE left the gateway settlement of San Juan Bautista bleak and desolate. Manuela was not alone in her grief. The entire settlement had been shaken by the uprising of March 6, probably three weeks before the soldiers had come for her lover. Almost all the *vecinos* of the presidio faced the labor of rebuilding what the Indians had destroyed in their wild orgy of revenge.

The occurrences of that fateful day caused the Spaniards of Presidio del Río Grande, as well as the missionaries of San Juan Bautista and San Bernardo, temporarily to forget St. Denis and all the problems he posed. This was the time, says Father Espinosa, when the Indians of the two missions gave the greatest proof of their inconstancy. All the Indians of both missions joined in the rebellion.

Espinosa had returned to the gateway from Querétaro and was stationed at Mission San Bernardo, across the arroyo a short distance from the presidio. Friars Alonso González and Pedro Muñoz were at San Juan Bautista. Father Olivares, apparently, remained at San Francisco Solano, which had been moved in 1708 to San José, five leagues north of the other missions. The Indians of the gateway missions now had been fifteen years under the padres' instruction, and their revolt was a severe blow to the ministers; however, the uprising was aimed not at the priests but at the soldiers of Captain Ramón's presidio.

Several days previously the heathen Indians who lived in the vicinity had gathered at the settlement, claiming that the soldiers had killed some of their kinsmen for stealing horses and meat animals. It had been a hard winter, and provisions were scarce. The Indians, Espinosa indicates, felt justified in killing the livestock for food. But the commandant brooked no protest; he rounded up the women and children of the protestants and impounded them at the presidio. The complaining Indians had kinsmen in Mission San Bernardo who were greatly provoked at these doings. The Christian Indians went first to their minister—evidently Father Espinosa himself—and the priest accompanied them to the presidio to petition for the release of the captives. But the plea was to no avail. The soldiers claimed the captives were prisoners of war, taken legally.

The exasperated natives gathered all the friendly nations from the surrounding countryside. The heathens, joined with the mission Indians, surrounded the missions. At the stroke of midnight, Ash Wednesday, they fell upon the presidio in such a manner that "it seemed that all the furies of hell had been released."[1] The attacking horde shot arrows into animals which the soldiers had left tied in the plaza. Then they set fire to all the haylofts and thatched roofs. With the many fires and the screams of the presidio's women it appeared indeed as a hell. The few soldiers took refuge in the *casas de terrado,* the stone or adobe buildings with flat roofs. The presidio was so poorly manned that scarcely eight muskets could be employed. These were effective only in preventing the Indians from hurtling missiles of fire through the doorways.

The holocaust continued until dawn. None of the Spaniards was killed, a fact which Espinosa attributed to "the special providence of Heaven, because the innocents were intermingled with the guilty." It was the corporal of the guard on the horseherd in the pasture some distance away who brought the attack to a conclusion. Having heard the yells and seen the flames from the pasture, he decided to create confusion by stampeding

[1] Isidro Félix de Espinosa, *Crónica de los colegios de propaganda fide de la Nueva España,* p. 780; Book V, Chapter XXVI, contains an account of the uprising.

the horses. As the herd thundered into the plaza, the frightened Indians fled. "The oppressed presidials were able to breathe again."[2]

Although the missions were not the prime target of the attack, the difficulty did not pass so easily at Mission San Juan Bautista, which had not one soldier for its protection. Friar Alonso González and Friar Pedro Muñoz, watching from the mission as the Indians danced amid the flaming ruins of the presidio, were terrified. They observed that all the Indians of their mission, as well as those of San Bernardo, had broken the restraints of their Christian teaching and joined the heathen savages in the attack. Surely, reasoned the padres, they meant to turn on the missions when finished with the presidio.

The two frightened priests took refuge in the stone granary, which was completely fireproof, hoping that help would come. After several hours, however, with no relief in sight, they abandoned their refuge to flee south. Not daring to return to their cells, they went as they were, coatless and hatless, and without food. With the two priests went a lay brother, an Indian who had come with Father Muñoz from Querétaro, and a small boy, the son of a soldier, whom the padres were teaching to read.

They stopped for the remainder of the night in a wood, half a league from the mission. At sunup, seeing that no one came to their rescue, they set out walking for the Mission Santa María de los Dolores de la Punta. Their sustenance for the day consisted of four turtles, which they found in the road. The turtles were roasted over a fire, with the shells serving as plates.

Tired out from hard travel, expecting to be overtaken at any minute by pursuing Indians, each of the four said his confession in preparation for death. Later on, when they had covered some twenty leagues, they saw the expected horde of Indians coming, and they were certain that the time had arrived. They hastily repeated their prayers, offering their souls to God as His sacrifice.

Without harming them, the Indians, of the Payuguan nation, surrounded the four travelers and told them they were to go with them to their rancheria. For eight days they remained with the Indians, listening each night as the savages debated whether to kill them or give them their freedom. Their captors allowed them no food; but again Providence inter-

2 *Ibid.*, p. 780.

vened, and a Christian Indian woman, who had been taught by Father Espinosa at the Mission San Bernardo, found opportunity to bring them field rats, roots, and herbs to sustain them.

At last the padres obtained their freedom by offering to pay the Indians if they would let them proceed to Dolores de la Punta. Two Indians were sent with them to receive the reward. Resuming their journey for Mission Dolores, they arrived at the abandoned site of the Mission San Miguel on the Sabinas River. The mission hut was still standing, and in it they found a pumpkin, "half eaten by mice but the other half still fresh and edible."[3] The six men dined to their satisfaction. Coming at last to the Mission Dolores, they were welcomed with chiming bells and tears of joy and thanksgiving that they had reached safety. The two Indians were given their ransom, a cloak of fine cloth, a pair of white trousers, and two packages of tobacco. Father Muñoz exchanged experiences with his friend, Father Antonio Margil de Jesús, now at Dolores Mission, and made preparations to return to San Juan Bautista.

The night of the attack at the gateway had found Mission San Bernardo somewhat better prepared than San Juan, for Father Espinosa had received secret information from a faithful Indian girl. With two soldiers and a citizen staying at the mission, he began at once to secure the doors of the monastery and to make fortifications. They remained watchful all night, observing the goings on at the presidio, not daring to leave the mission, which was long since surrounded by swarms of Indians.

With assurance that the riot was directed not at the mission but at the presidio, Espinosa was concerned principally for the missionaries of San Juan, who were not forewarned as he had been.

When quietness came with the dawn, the padre signaled several times by ringing the bell, but no Indians came. Nor did a single soldier come from the presidio to see how the missionaries had fared. Terror had taken possession of the presidials. Realizing this the Indians of Mission San Juan returned. Finding the doors open and the missionaries gone, they entered the monastery and helped themselves to all that was edible and to other items that would be useful or amusing to them in their flight for the interior. Yet they left behind an indication that the padres' teaching had

[3] *Ibid.*, p. 381; Eduardo Enrique Ríos, *Life of Fray Antonio Margil, O.F.M.*, p. 110.

not been in vain: they touched nothing in the church. Although they had access to all the buildings, they harmed none of the ornaments or vessels. They at least had learned a respect for the sacred.

In the afternoon Father Espinosa, certain that the trouble was over, left San Bernardo. Joined by some soldiers, he went to reconnoiter the Mission San Juan and found it grievously plundered. Afterward he surmised that the Indians were not alone in availing themselves of the spoils. He theorized that some men had gone from the presidio to see about the padres; finding the doors open and the padres gone, they proceeded to help themselves to what they wanted.

Several days later word came from Dolores de la Punta that Father González and Father Muñoz were safe.

Weeks went by and the Indians remained at liberty in the *montes*. Nor was there word from St. Denis, perhaps languishing in jail. For Manuela the months grew long with waiting, but she was not alone in her desolation—the missions, too, were desolate. At both San Juan Bautista and San Bernardo the padres worked forlornly alone, doing the menial chores left undone when the Indians fled following the night of terror. There were none left either for them to instruct or to labor in the fields.

Following the uprising Father Muñoz had returned to Mission San Juan. Though he was grieved that the Indians remained in the wilds, he set to work on the projects most needed at the mission. He was able to hire some *vecinos* from the presidio to help him lay out a cemetery. He went out and gathered in some heathens of the Pampoa nation, but they were poor subjects for the *doctrina*. In order to keep them satisfied he found it necessary to slaughter many livestock from the mission herds to feed them. The Pampoas told him frankly: "We will be with you until the meat and the corn are gone."[4] From all the multitude that he fed and cared for, he gained only a small child, whom he restored to life from the point of death, and one family who chose voluntarily to remain with him out of gratitude for the care he had given.

The heat of summer took hold of the gray land without word from the fugitive Indians, or from the capital. In July, Father Antonio Margil de Jesús came to the gateway settlement. He came on horseback because walking was slow and painful, but because of his double hernia he suf-

[4] Espinosa, *Crónica,* p. 782.

fered even more pain from the animal's jogging. It was an unfortunate time for the venerable priest to visit the missions. When he preached at Mission San Juan he had only the indifferent presence of the Pampoa Indians. Mission San Bernardo had no one to hear him but the two priests and a pair of visitors. In the parish church of the presidio he preached to the soldiers, the citizens, and their families, but all in all it was an empty experience. He was convinced from this visit not only that founding missions beyond the Río Grande was futile, but also that the gateway missions themselves were bleak failures. He returned in mid-July to St. Mary of Sorrows.[5]

Those at the gateway, meanwhile, had no inkling of what was going on in the faraway city of México, nor of the effect which events transpiring there would have on their lives. Eagerly they awaited news. At last, into autumn, St. Denis came riding back, bringing in vivid, sparkling detail news of all that had occurred: He had been before the Viceroy. There had been questions, which he had answered straightforwardly and consistently. He had made a written declaration, telling how he had come seeking the mission of Father Hidalgo, never dreaming that the Spaniards would not be overjoyed at the prospect of trade with the French. Not finding Father Hidalgo among the Asinais—who spoke with great affection of the Spaniards and expressed a desire to have the Spanish padres return and establish missions among them—he had proceeded on to the Río Grande. He told it so simply.

The *fiscal*, Doctor Espinosa, had warned the Viceroy of some of the implications of St. Denis' coming: The French had learned the route to the Río Grande; they could with impunity introduce their merchandise into the northern provinces in violation of the orders of the King. Orders should be issued to the governors to prevent such incursions by the French, he suggested. Furthermore, the Viceroy should make provision for Fathers Olivares and Hidalgo and one other religious to proceed to the province of the Tejas without delay to establish a mission. They should be accompanied by a guard of twenty or twenty-five soldiers. By such means further French intrusion could be prevented.[6]

---

[5] Ríos, *Margil*, p. 110.

[6] Gerardo Mora, "Relación hecha por Don Luis de San Dionis y Don Medar Jalot del viaje que ejecutaron desde la Móvila hasta el Presidio de Diego Ramón," A.G.N., Provincias Internas, Vol. 181, pp. 12–14.

The general junta which met August 22, 1715, gave its endorsement to these recommendations.[7] Choice of a commander for the soldiers was left to the Viceroy. The *alférez,* Domingo Ramón, who had lived his entire life on the frontier, was conveniently available. And possibly to assuage any embarrassment St. Denis had suffered at having been brought in chains to the capital city, the official named him conductor of supplies at a salary to equal that of Alférez Ramón. Instead of one mission, four would be established.

At this point St. Denis and Jalot departed the capital, leaving Ramón to make arrangements for the expedition. St. Denis hurried back to San Juan Bautista to resume his courtship of Manuela, whom he hoped to marry before going again into the Texas wilderness.

Legend has it that St. Denis was confronted at this point with opposition of Diego Ramón, Manuela's grandfather. Don Diego is said to have challenged his prospective grandson-in-law to go into the wilderness, seek out the Indians who had fled from the missions the previous March 6, and persuade them to return.[8]

With the fate of the Presidio del Río Grande, and of St. Denis' suit for Manuela's hand, in the balance—so the story goes—the Frenchman crossed the Río Grande, treated with the Indians in Spanish, and led them back to the gateway settlement. The facts of the case are disclosed in the transcript of a hearing convened twenty-two years later, in 1737, by Father Miguel Sevillano de Paredes. In an effort to show the vital role that soldiers of the presidio played in the work of the missions, Sevillano elicited testimony to show that Diego Ramón himself, aided by a small band of soldiers and Father Francisco Ruiz, had brought the Indians back.[9] Some of the soldiers who testified actually had taken part in the

[7] Report of Junta, in *ibid.,* pp. 16–24.

[8] See Ross Phares, *Cavalier in the Wilderness: The Story of the Explorer and Trader, Louis Juchereau de St. Denis,* pp. 85–88. This story and many others concerning the legendary exploits of St. Denis were concocted originally by the Abbé Prevost. See Charles Wilson Hackett and Charmion Clair Shelby (trans.), *Pichardo's Treatise on the Limits of Louisiana and Texas,* IV, 313–314. Pichardo (*ibid.,* p. 312) observes that ". . . almost everything that Prevost writes concerning the journey of St. Denis is false . . ." and (p. 314), "thus far Prevost, whose account must not be given credence because it contains almost nothing that actually happened, and among the few facts that it does contain there are many mistakes."

[9] Testimony of Nicolás Maldonado, A.G.N., Provincias Internas, Vol. 32, p. 43, and of Nicolás Minchaca, p. 59. Espinosa (*Crónica,* p. 782) attributes the feat to

expedition, which was made in October. In a rancheria of more than eight hundred, the runaways were found. Agreeing to return to the missions, they asked only that they be allowed three days to complete their pecan harvest. The Indians then returned to the Mission San Bernardo. One Christian Indian woman, having given birth the night before, followed the people of her pueblo with her husband at a more leisurely pace. It was the last such uprising at the gateway missions, "although the missionaries have never lacked opportunity for exercising their patience."[10]

Even though it seems evident that St. Denis was not the prime mover in the return of the Indians to the gateway missions, he had won a place in the hearts of the Ramón family. Plans for his marriage with Manuela moved forward with full ceremony. Clothes and other wedding accessories were brought from Monclova after a shopping trip that lasted a month.

San Juan Bautista was a riot of color and gaiety. The pomp and ritual of old Spain blossomed. The entire population turned out, and Indians and Spaniards together lined the bridal path in phalanxes as the procession wound its way from the commandant's house up the gentle hill to the chapel. No detail of dress which the frontier could afford had been overlooked.[11]

Seven priests are said to have officiated at the altar. The wedding festivities lasted three days, during which there was firing of muskets and revelry the likes of which the northern frontier had never before witnessed and would not soon forget.

It was fitting that this marriage of Louis Juchereau de St. Denis and Manuela Ramón should be celebrated with such ceremony; its consequences would be far-reaching.

"a missionary who had founded the Mission San Juan, and for whom the Indians had a special love," saying that this priest went into the wilderness alone to treat with the natives. He evidently referred to Francisco Hidalgo, the error doubtless having been caused by the identical first names. But Sevillano shows the priest did not act alone.

[10] Espinosa, *Crónica,* p. 782.

[11] Phares, *Cavalier,* p. 90. Phares apparently envisions the wedding in one of the mission churches at their latter-day sites, rather than in the presidio chapel on the plaza, or one of the older mission churches.

12. BACK TO THE TEJAS

WHILE THE GATEWAY settlement was preoccupied with the festive wedding, the bride's uncle, Domingo Ramón, was bringing his Texas-bound expedition northward. Following his appointment as commandant on September 30, 1715, he had left the capital to proceed to Saltillo. There he recruited as soldiers men with families; this time the Spaniards were bent on colonizing as well as on converting the Indians. He also gathered the livestock and other essentials for the venture.

On February 17 the expedition left Saltillo on a northward course which lay between the Monterrey road and the Monclova road. Five missionaries who had departed from Colegio de la Santa Cruz de Querétaro had not yet reached Saltillo. While many missionary priests had volunteered for service in the Texas wilds, there was one obvious first choice: Father Francisco Hidalgo, a former guardian of the college, "the one who most desired the conversion of the Tejas."[1] With him from Querétaro went Friars Gabriel de Vergara, Benito Sánchez, Manuel Castellanos, and Pedro Pérez de Mezquía. With a viaticum given them at Santa María de las Charcas, they proceeded to Saltillo. Here they were detained ten days on charity. Domingo Ramón sent a sergeant and six men to escort them to his camp at the Nacatas Bridge, which they reached March 3.

Father Antonio Margil de Jesús waited at Boca de Leones to head the friars from the College of Guadalupe de Zacatecas, who would round out the contingent of missionaries to the Tejas. The friars of Zacatecas— Matías Sáenz de San Antonio, Pedro de Mendoza, Agustín Patrón and two lay brothers, Friars Javier Cubillos and Francisco de San Diego, and one oblate, Friar Domingo de Urioste—already waited at the Río Grande gateway.

[1] Isidro Félix de Espinosa, *Crónica de los colegios de propaganda fide de la Nueva España*, p. 685.

Don Domingo procured livestock and other supplies as he marched northward. As he approached Boca de Leones he gathered in the horses, oxen, and goats which Father Margil had obtained for him. A mule train brought corn from Mission de la Caldera.

Friars Hidalgo, Sánchez, Vergara, and Castellanos went to the Mission of Santa María de los Dolores at La Punta (Lampazos) on April 2 to spend Holy Week. Two religious remained in camp to hear confessions and to celebrate Mass.[2]

Domingo Ramón's expedition moved slowly toward San Juan Bautista. Hooves of a thousand cattle stirred the gray dust skyward, prodded along slowly by twenty-one soldiers—four less than had left Saltillo, the number reduced by desertions. Eight women and two children rode in ox carts, while the five friars from Querétaro plodded alongside. Two months had elapsed since Don Domingo had left Saltillo.[3] The friars had been on the road from Querétaro almost three. On April 18, after breaking camp at Amole Creek, the expedition marched seven leagues over a wide expanse of grassland. Two leagues from the Presidio del Río Grande the caravan crossed a creek of running water (Arroyo de Castaño). Coming to meet them was the captain of the presidio, Don Diego Ramón, his officers, and men, who lined either side of the road and fired a salute as the expedition approached. Don Domingo's men "returned the courtesy by saluting with our bows and arrows."[4]

Father welcomed son, and soldier welcomed soldier. Father Espinosa, president of the Río Grande missions, and the friars of Zacatecas, already waiting at the gateway, came to welcome their brother missionaries. The entourage marched on toward the presidio. Passing near the *plaza de armas,* it circled and came to a halt in some cornfields close to one of the missions and pitched camp.

Next day the camp remained in the same place while Don Domingo procured provisions from the presidio and made other arrangements for crossing the Río Grande at Paso de Francia and entering the unsettled wilderness of Texas.

[2] Paul J. Foik (trans.), *Captain Don Domingo Ramón's Diary of His Expedition into Texas in 1716,* p. 6.

[3] Eduardo Enrique Ríos, *Life of Fray Antonio Margil, O.F.M.,* p. 115.

[4] Foik, *Ramón's Diary,* p. 7. Ríos (*Margil,* p. 115) says St. Denis also was among the welcoming group.

Father Margil, having remained behind to procure additional supplies for the trip, now was crossing the desert in the tracks of the convoy. As he stumbled along on sore feet, a high fever overtook him. Traveling alone, he was able to reach Los Juanes Creek, a day's journey from the presidio, but could go no farther.

How news of his condition reached the gateway settlement is a mystery, but the word came about eight o'clock the evening of April 19. Father Espinosa, in company with two of the Zacatecan friars and two soldiers from the fort, hastily departed in the darkness to go to his aid and bring him to the missions.

Next day, April 20, Domingo Ramón marched his caravan two leagues through the marsh and mesquite thicket to the banks of the Río Grande del Norte. Finding the water at low ebb, the soldiers turned the point of the drove of livestock into the water. With the Captain personally supervising the operation, more than one thousand goats swam the stream with a loss of only twelve. Domingo Ramón wrote in his diary, "I set up my camp on the other side of the river with extreme happiness."[5]

But breaking the ties was not easy. The religious still remained behind at the missions. Father Espinosa, for one, had business to finish up before departing. The friars just come from Querétaro had brought with them a patent from the prelate of the college designating Espinosa as president of the Queretaran friars chosen to enter Texas. They brought another patent in blank, in order that he might appoint whomever he chose as president of the Río Grande missions.[6] He selected Friar Pedro Muñoz, who must yet be informed as to the president's duties.

A soldier of the Presidio del Río Grande who had joined the *entrada* also had unfinished business. The man, named José Galindo, was taking a bride. The sergeant of Don Domingo's company, now on the other side of the river, asked permission to go back to the fort to serve as best man. With an eye for increasing the population of his colony, Don Domingo approved. The wedding festival lasted two days. Two more days were spent in gathering in the supplies collected by the missionaries.

And while the caravan waited, Louis Juchereau de St. Denis utilized

[5] Foik, *Ramón's Diary*, p. 8.
[6] Espinosa, *Crónica*, p. 685.

every moment to the fullest. Arrival of the caravan had interrupted his honeymoon.

Father Margil remained gravely ill, and the other religious wished to wait for his recovery. Instead of getting better, however, his condition worsened. On Saturday, April 25, Mass was sung in the Mission of San Bernardo, celebrating the Feast of St. Mark the Evangelist. A procession was formed, and rogation prayers proper to the day were offered for the success of the coming journey. At the conclusion of the ceremonies, the sacred viaticum was administered to Father Margil, who remained with dangerously high fever.

That afternoon the departing religious returned to Father Margil's bedside to bid him farewell. Tears flowed freely as he spoke to each as a father, giving religious advice and encouragement for the undertaking. Then he embraced each one, and Fathers Hidalgo, Sánchez, Vergara, and Castellanos left to cross the Río Grande to join the caravan on the other side. They gave thanks to His Divine Majesty for having chosen them for so glorious an enterprise.[7]

Father Espinosa remained to put in order the missions which had been of his charge. He and Father Matías Sáenz stayed with Father Margil that night. In the afternoon of the following day, after Father Margil had risen to bless them as they knelt before him, they, with Friar Pedro de Santa María y Mendoza, set out to cross the river. They left Margil in the care of the lay brother, Friar Francisco de San Diego.[8]

On the other side of the river, the procession of soldiers who waited greeted the arrival of the last group of priests by firing a salute. There was rejoicing throughout the camp, for now the march could be resumed toward the land of the Tejas.[9] A sermon was given, the start of a practice to be repeated every third day. And some who had not yet taken Easter Communion did so. In the evening the *alabado* was sung.

As the march got under way April 27, Captain Domingo Ramón made a list of the persons in the caravan, now numbering seventy-five. At the head of the party marched the dignified and resolute Father Friar Isidro

[7] *Ibid.*; Gabriel Tous (trans.), *Ramón Expedition: Espinosa's Diary of 1716*, p. 4.
[8] Ríos, *Margil*, pp. 116–117.
[9] Tous, *Espinosa's Diary*, p. 5.

Félix de Espinosa, president of the Franciscans from the College of
Querétaro. With him came the now white-haired Father Friar Francisco
Hidalgo, who in his prime had spent almost two years among the Tejas;
he had grown old while making every possible appeal for a return to the
land of this heathen nation, but now, notwithstanding his age, he walked
erect and his countenance glowed with spiritual delight; at last the dream
which had obsessed him for twenty-three years was to be realized. Then
came Fathers Matías Sáenz, Benito Sánchez, Manuel Castellanos, Pedro de
Mendoza, and Gabriel de Vergara, and lay brothers Javier Cubillos and
Domingo de Urioste.

Behind the religious came twenty-five mounted soldiers, besides the
Captain. They included Don Domingo's brother, Alférez Diego Ramón
II. There came also a number of men and women whose purpose was to
settle the new country, and the three Frenchmen, St. Denis (conductor of
provisions), Medar Jalot, and Pierre Largen, and a number of drovers
and muleteers to look after the livestock.[10] There were sixty-four oxen,
four thousand horses and mules, and more than one thousand sheep and
goats.

As might be expected, considering the diversity of peoples who made
up the expedition, its purpose was in the point of view. "To the missionaries it was a great spiritual campaign to save the souls of the Indians; to
the officials at Mexico City it was an emergency campaign to save the vast
territory of Texas for Spain; to St. Denis and the Ramóns it was primarily
a commercial venture."[11] And what was it to the private soldier and the
settler? Adventure? A new opportunity in a new land? Perhaps. But it
would also be hardship and privation and heartbreak.

From the expedition's cast of characters two were missing. Father
Antonio de San Buenaventura y Olivares, who had stood with Father
Hidalgo as the first choice to undertake the missionary effort among the
Tejas, asked to be excused.[12] Also missing was José de Urrutia, one of the
soldiers who had remained among the Tejas in 1693, when the mission-

---

[10] Carlos Eduardo Castañeda, *Our Catholic Heritage in Texas*, II, 46–47.

[11] Ross Phares, *Cavalier in the Wilderness: The Story of the Explorer and
Trader, Louis Juchereau de St. Denis*, p. 83.

[12] Castañeda (*Our Catholic Heritage*, II, 62 n.) says "because of age and in-
firmities." He cites a letter of Fray Joseph Díez to the Viceroy, of February 10,

aries had withdrawn. Having returned to San Juan Bautista about the time of its move to the Río Grande in 1700, he had guided expeditions of missionaries into *la tierra adentro,* the interior land, several times. He had proved his worth as an interpreter. Father Margil had pleaded to have him accompany the 1716 *entrada.* Alférez José Ramón of Boca de Leones, brother of Don Domingo and Diego Ramón II, with his mother and two brothers-in-law as witnesses, told Margil that it was essential that Urrutia accompany the expedition.[13] But Urrutia had just been named protector of the Indians in Nuevo León; the Viceroy determined that he was indispensable in that position.[14]

Out across the level expanse of the Río Grande plain stretched the caravan, motley in appearance, monotonous in movement, cacophonous in sound. Above the lowing of oxen, the clank of horns, the bleating of sheep and goats, the squeak of cart wheels, and the epithets of the mule-skinners, rang the brisk command of the military officers, the shouting of directions. And beneath was the muffled thud of constantly hammering hooves upon the Texas earth, as varas stretched into leagues.

Behind was left a San Juan Bautista that would never be the same again. A feeling of emptiness pervaded the settlement as the last cloud of dust from the departing caravan settled over the Río Grande.

Toward evening of the second day a messenger came back from the caravan across the river, as yet barely ten leagues away. It was none other than St. Denis himself, who told of the tempest which had struck the camp the night before, shortly after a sermon was given, with such violence that the missionaries had been moved to raise their voices "in suppli-

---

1717, found in A.G.N., Provincias Internas, Vol. 181, p. 220. Olivares' advanced years and ailments are mentioned in this letter, however, in an entirely different connection. Robert Carleton Clark ("Louis Juchereau de Saint-Denis and the Re-establishment of the Tejas Missions," *SWHQ,* 6, No. 1 [July, 1902], 4) says "Le Page du Pratz speaks of a jealousy that existed between Olivares and Hidalgo, and says that they then besought Saint-Denis to prevent Olivares from going on the expedition, on account of his jealous and turbulent disposition." If this is so, no Spanish source is found to support it. It seems rather that Olivares declined to go because he had another plan in mind: founding a settlement on the San Antonio River.

[13] Fray Antonio Margil to the Viceroy, February 26, 1716, A.G.N., Provincias Internas, Vol. 181, pp. 46–48.

[14] Viceroy's endorsement of May 25, 1716, *ibid.,* p. 49.

cation to the Mother of Sorrows and to the saints of our devotion."[15] Tent stakes were uprooted and canvas swirled skyward, with priest and soldier hanging on for dear life. The rain came in torrents, but presently it went as suddenly as it had come.

Passing up Real de Cuervo, or Crow Camp, for lack of water, the caravan had reached Diego Ramón Ford (El Paso Pacuache), two leagues off course. Here the storm had struck about eight o'clock in the evening. The wind had scattered the supplies and transported a sentry, horse and all, for several yards. Horses, oxen, and mules had stampeded, but all had been found, the Frenchman related.

History has recorded that St. Denis returned to San Juan to procure another Indian guide for the expedition. Almost any excuse would have sufficed to bring him back for one last night with his bride, whose lot was to remain behind with her grandparents until her husband had made a place for her. The next day St. Denis mounted his horse and again rode northeastward for Paso Pacuache. He was soon swallowed in the vast, empty distance. Henceforth word from the caravan in Texas would be infrequent.

The fevered face of Father Margil turned eastward to follow the Ramón *entrada,* but his bloodshot eyes could not penetrate the distance. He knew his fellow missionaries expected never to see him again, but as he lay on his cot at Mission San Bernardo, his strong will—or his enduring faith—took charge of his weakened body. His condition began to improve. On June 13, after celebrating the feast of St. Anthony of Padua, he began the journey to overtake his companions. He and Father Agustín Patrón and the lay brother, Friar Francisco de San Diego, set out from San Juan Bautista on horseback. In July they overtook the caravan beyond the Trinity River, and learned that the four missions already had been established. By early in the next year there would be a total of six.

Unlike the first East Texas missions, these looked like a serious attempt to colonize the region. There was a big difference also in the attitude of the French. The first time the Spaniards had found the French threat already abated, but now the French were well established and stood in threatening posture on the threshold of Spanish territory. There could be no turning back now for the Spaniards.[16]

---

[15] Tous, *Espinosa's Diary,* p. 5.
[16] Robert S. Weddle, *The San Sabá Mission: Spanish Pivot in Texas,* p. 9.

But there was more to the new venture than the founding of missions, or the extension of the Spanish dominion. Soldiers as well as priests were able to observe signs of an intense commerce which had been developed between the French and the Indians. The natives owned muskets, clothing, and knives of French origin. Diego Ramón II himself soon went with St. Denis to Mobile, where it is said he negotiated the sale of horses brought from Texas. They returned to the Tejas missions laden with merchandise, which Captain Domingo Ramón planned to send to the Río Grande on the backs of the mules belonging to His Majesty, King Philip V of Spain.

Part II
MOTHER OF MISSIONS
1716-1772

13. PADRE OLIVARES' DREAM

WITH THE DEPARTURE of Captain Domingo Ramón and his caravan of seventy-five persons bound for the wilds of Texas, San Juan Bautista's role on the frontier underwent sudden change. Previously the gateway settlement had been the most advanced colony on the northeastern frontier of New Spain. It was the launching point for all the expeditions which went beyond, and the haven, with a veneer of civilization, to which they happily returned. But now it was no longer a fledgling; it had attained maturity, and parenthood.

The expedition which had just departed represented the first bird launched from the nest. While the youngster tried its wings, the parent would suffer many an anxious moment. Indeed the filial relationship between the old settlement and the new ones-to-be was more than figurative. At the head of the *entrada* was a son of San Juan Bautista's own Captain Diego Ramón. Another son and a grandson—not to mention the new grandson-in-law—also rode in the ranks. And among the priests who would minister to the Tejas Indians were two—Hidalgo and Espinosa—who had devoted many years to the Río Grande missions. Indeed the new settlements in *la tierra adentro* were the progeny of San Juan Bautista. They were her flesh-and-blood offspring.

To the fruit of her womb San Juan Bautista would ever have a responsibility. The gateway would be the nearest point of contact with civilization for the new settlements two hundred leagues beyond. When they needed help she must provide it.

Left behind to man the gateway were the very old, and the very young.

Among them were three lonely persons. Don Diego Ramón, now well
past his prime at age sixty-five, looked longingly after his two sons, recalling the day when he had ridden forth at the head of his troop to chastise the Pelones or to look for the Cerro de Plata. Even his wife was not
beside him now. Doña María was with her two daughters and another
son, José, at Boca de Leones.[1] In his household remained Manuela, heavy
with the Frenchman's child, and probably her mother, Don Diego's
daughter-in-law.

Another lonely soul was Father Pedro de Muñoz, whom Espinosa had
chosen to take his place as president of the Río Grande missions. While
awed by the responsibility, Father Muñoz was pleased with the vote of
confidence. How well he measured up depends on the point of view. The
peevish Father Olivares would judge him harshly. Father Espinosa's
judgment would be tempered with heartfelt gratitude.

Besides Father Muñoz and Captain Diego Ramón, there was still
another who wistfully watched the departure of the Domingo Ramón
expedition from the gateway. This person was Father Pedro Pérez de
Mezquía, who had been chosen for the new Tejas missions and had made
the trip northward from Querétaro as far as the Río Grande. For some
unexplained reason, however, he remained at San Juan Bautista when the
entrada departed. One of the first disclosures of difficulties in the new
East Texas missions would come in a letter addressed to him.[2]

Under ordinary circumstances time was of no essence on the Río
Grande. Life moved slowly; there was no need to fret over the comings
and goings, because they took so long to happen. But now it was different;
the community of San Juan Bautista waited almost breathlessly for some
word from the expedition in Texas.

And what of Father Olivares? Was he among the lonely and the
anxious? He remained at his isolated Mission of San Francisco Solano in
the Valley of San José, a dozen miles from the main gateway settlement
of two missions and a presidio. Even though he had been offered first
opportunity, along with Father Hidalgo, to help carry the Gospel back to

[1] Fray Antonio Margil to the Viceroy, February 26, 1716, A.G.N., Provincias
Internas, Vol. 181, p. 47.

[2] Lino G. Canedo, Introduction to Isidro Félix de Espinosa, *Crónica de los
colegios de propaganda fide de la Nueva España*, p. lxii n.; Francisco Hidalgo and
Manuel de Castellanos to Pedro Pérez de Mezquía, October 6, 1716, A.G.N.,
Provincias Internas, Vol. 282, pp. 215–219.

the land of the Tejas, he had chosen to stay behind. He knew the journey was long and the way was hard; the aches in his body and the growing impatience of his temperament told him that it was time to step aside and make way for younger, more durable men.

Yet, in all probability, these factors had nothing to do with the decision he made. And the choice, once made, was not in the least distasteful to him; it was part of his plan—a plan at least as coldly calculated as that of Father Hidalgo for bringing about a return to the Tejas. The trip he soon undertook to the capital of México was a part of the scheme also. His intent was to convince the Viceroy of the feasibility of planting a mission at the headwaters of the San Antonio River.

Father Olivares' mind was far too busy to permit loneliness to creep in. Before news of the nascent Tejas missions reached San Juan Bautista, he left the Río Grande and journeyed southward. At Querétaro he learned from the guardian, Fray Joseph Díez, of the distress in the new foundations, and likely saw in it a circumstance which would lend support to his own plan. Díez had just received letters from Domingo Ramón and the missionaries in Texas which informed him of their urgent needs. As Olivares prepared to proceed to the capital for an audience with the Viceroy, Díez asked him to take the letters.[3]

At the high seat of government Olivares advanced his plan. He described Texas as a most fertile field for missionary activity, basing his description on observations made during his several penetrations beyond the Río Grande. From the tenor of his report it seems obvious that he came before the Viceroy as his own representative, not that of the missionaries in East Texas. He found the new Viceroy, Baltazar de Zúñiga, Guzmán Sotomayor y Mendoza, Marqués de Valero, Duque de Arión, a most interested listener.

As Olivares told of the country between San Juan Bautista and the eastern missions, he drew heavily on the written reports of others who had entered, including Espinosa's 1709 diary. Adding pertinent facts from his own knowledge, he sought to win the Viceroy's support for planting a mission in the very heart of the region he described, which would be the fulfillment of his cherished dream.

The attributes of the beautiful and fertile country of the province of

[3] Fritz Leo Hoffman (trans.) in Fray Francisco Céliz, *Diary of the Alarcón Expedition into Texas, 1718–1719*, Introduction, p. 15.

the Tejas (or Asinais), from the Río Grande missions to the new ones now being attempted, could not be over emphasized, said Olivares. He gave a lyric recitation of its many advantages: the wild hemp, the grape-vines, mulberries for silk culture, the pecans with such tasty meats, the large live oaks with edible acorns, the many wild turkeys.

"So numerous are the deer that they appear as flocks of goats. The buffalo are many; so great is their abundance that they appear as large herds of cattle."[4]

But of greater value are his remarks concerning the Indians. These were the Coahuiltecans, which had been missionized on the Río Grande and with which he would deal principally at the projected mission on the San Antonio River. Indeed this loose-knit tribe has played a greater role in the history of Texas than is generally recognized.

The nations which we have come to know and to deal with are fifty, not counting those of which we have little knowledge. Their languages are differ-ent; only by means of signs are they understood among all the nations. They are governed, and conduct their trade, with signs.

Their customs are generally the same. Some are more spirited than others. They are very warlike among themselves, and they kill one another with ease, for things of little consequence, as they steal horses or women from each other.

Yet their presence is agreeable. They are of smiling countenance and are accommodating to the padres and Spaniards. . . . When they come to their rancherias they freely give them what they have to eat. They are very fond of Spanish dress. Soldiers often give them a hat, cloak, trousers, or other garment in pay for the work they do. . . .

Learning is easy for them, and they acquire use of the Spanish language with facility. All of them desire to be Christians. . . . Everyone asks the water of Baptism.[5]

The Indians willingly guided the Spaniards into their country, said Olivares, showing them the fruits of their land and pointing out the rivers and other landmarks. They had shown them a river sand which contained a trace of gold, said the padre, who emphasized that minerals were present in quantity, including the Cerro de Plata, or Mountain of Silver. Evi-dently the venerable father's enthusiasm was running away with him.

[4] Fray Antonio de San Buenaventura y Olivares to the Viceroy, November 20, 1716, A.G.N., Provincias Internas, Vol. 181, p. 127.
[5] *Ibid.*, pp. 127–129.

"We have not recognized formal idolatry among these Indians," the priest continued; "some abuses, yes, and there are some witchdoctors among them. . . . These serve as healers, and if the cure fails and the patient dies, they pay with their lives."[6]

One fine point about the Indians, Olivares observed, was that they did not intoxicate themselves. But in their *mitotes,* or general dances, they partook of a drink prepared from the peyote cactus and other herbs. This drink produced "disturbances of feelings and causes them to see visions and fantasies."[7]

On the other hand the natives were much inclined to the domestic life and occupied themselves with such tasks as making bows and arrows, in which great pains were taken. The women tanned and dressed the skins of the bison which the men killed, painting the leather robes and garments in a most curious manner with the dyes they made from various plants and minerals. They also made from deerskins a very soft, pliable white leather which they used to barter with the Spaniards.

Most of these Indians, when settled in Pueblo, are nimble and resourceful in the extreme, as is seen and experienced in the missions which we have founded on the Río Grande. They dress themselves in tanned deerskins, and the women the same, although they are covered to the feet with all honesty. This is worthy of admiration among people without light of the Gospel. The men spend little concern on their dress, as some of them go about naked. But the women, even though they are very young, adhere to honest dress in the best manner which those regions permit.

They take part in *mitotes,* or dances, when they wish to go to war or when they have attained some victory over their enemies. They do this dance as if gripped by the hands by which they suffer various abuses, and these dances are causes of the murders which they commit on each other.

. . . At little cost a multitude of Infidels may be converted to the society of our Holy Mother Church, and obedience of our Catholic King (God keep him). There only remains to be given the powerful patronage of the Catholic Majesty and the assistance of his arms . . .[8]

Just when Father Olivares' letter arrived in the capital is not clear; the only date found on his report is that of the endorsement of the *fiscal:*

[6] *Ibid.,* p. 129.
[7] *Ibid.,* p. 129.
[8] *Ibid.,* p. 130.

November 20, 1716. On that same day the *fiscal* endorsed another instrument from the pen of the hearty old friar, also addressed to the Viceroy.

Your Excellency has ordered me to tell the necessities and things needed for the founding of the mission of the Río de San Antonio de Padua, of which Your Excellency indicates that I may be the founder. I certainly wish for the goal of the King our Lord and Your Excellency to be attained, with the desired Catholic zeal. Therefore, I say that my intention is to relocate the Mission of San Francisco Solano, which I founded with the Indians of the Jarame nation. Very few of them remain in said mission and are presently employed in working the lands. Your Excellency's desires will be served if I gather them in said place, along with the Payayas, Sanas, Pampoas, and others. These neighboring tribes should come to make up a pueblo of three or four thousand Indians.[9]

Olivares had seen and instantly loved the area of the headwaters of the San Antonio River in 1709. He had dreamed of returning there, as Father Hidalgo had yearned for his Asinais. At last he had been given an opportunity to offer his plan to a willing viceroy. From that point on there was a chain reaction.

The padre went on to observe that the new mission site would be bordered on the north by the land of the dreaded Apaches. He asked that ten soldiers be assigned "for the protection of my person while I gather these nations."[10] He also asked that some citizens be sent to settle, with land and water rights to be offered as an inducement. Listing the needs of the new mission, he first named the items for the church, then those for the sustenance of himself and his companions, then the kitchen supplies.[11]

Olivares' plan for the new mission on the San Antonio won approval of the viceregal advisers. They recommended that, in order to provide the requested escort of ten men for the missionary, eight be taken from Presidio de San Juan Bautista and two from the Presidio of San Francisco de Coahuila. These soldiers would not be missed, in the opinion of the *fiscal;* most of the Indians who troubled these presidios soon would be congregated by Father Olivares in missions at San Antonio.

Reports of the *fiscal* were presented to the general junta December 2. The junta agreed that immediate occupation of the San Antonio River was desirable; necessary expenses should be paid from the Royal Treas-

9 *Ibid.,* p. 131.   10 *Ibid.,* p. 131.
11 List of supplies contained in *ibid.,* pp. 131–134; also see Carlos Eduardo Castaneda, *Our Catholic Heritage in Texas,* II, 79–80.

ury. Five days later the Viceroy named Don Martín de Alarcón as governor of Texas. Alarcón had been appointed the previous August 5 as governor of Coahuila, a post he had also held earlier from June 6, 1705, to October 13, 1708. During that time he had urged the removal of Mission San Bernardo from the Río Grande to the Frío River in Texas.[12] He had sent Captain Diego Ramón, accompanied by Father Espinosa, into Texas to punish the Pelones and to bring in Indians to repopulate the missions ravaged by smallpox. Now, while serving as governor of Coahuila, he also would serve as "Captain General and Governor of the Province of the Tejas and such other lands as might be conquered."[13]

The Viceroy then issued orders that Father Olivares should be furnished with all he needed for the mission on the San Antonio River. Within two weeks the supplies were gathered and he was ready to start. From the Viceroy he received a patent which would enable him to get help from provincial governors and presidio captains along the way. Among other things, he wanted the soldiers in Nuevo León to escort him to Presidio de San Juan Bautista del Río Grande, to protect him and his companions, and the supplies for his projected mission, against the dangers he knew to exist in that area.[14]

Olivares set out upon his journey to the North without waiting for Alarcón. At the College of Querétaro he selected two religious companions and in their company resumed his journey.

On February 10 Father Joseph Díez, guardian of the College of the Holy Cross at Querétaro, wrote to the Viceroy, reporting that Father Olivares had departed on the road northward the day before. He had with him all that was necessary for relocating the Mission San Francisco Solano on the San Antonio. Father Díez expressed concern, however, that Alarcón was making no move to begin the journey. He feared that the delay, coupled with Father Olivares' advanced years, might spell disaster for the project. Father Olivares, said Díez, had asked to be excused from the task because he was "ill and burdened with years," but the guardian had insisted that he go.[15]

[12] See Chapter 7 of this study.
[13] Canedo note in Espinosa, *Crónica*, p. 733.
[14] Petition of Olivares, December 28, 1716, in A.G.N., Provincias Internas, Vol. 181, p. 214.
[15] Fray Joseph Díez to the Viceroy, February 10, 1717, in *ibid.*, p. 220.

By March 24 Olivares was in Saltillo. All the while he was casting glances over his shoulder, hoping to see Alarcón coming up behind. With news that the Governor was detained, he felt a growing concern lest the project not be carried out as expeditiously as he had desired.

At Monterrey, Olivares obtained the promised escort to accompany him on toward the Río Grande. He reached the gateway missions May 3 and promptly presented to Captain Diego Ramón and retiring Governor Joseph de Ecay Múzquiz the Viceroy's order for ten soldiers to serve as an escort for his train on the journey to the San Antonio River. But instead of action he received excuses. The officials said they would have to consult with the Viceroy before complying with the request—their garrisons were so reduced that they could not hazard weakening them further, even on His Excellency's order, unless the Viceroy was acquainted with the situation first.[16]

Father Olivares now felt impatience and peevishness, his lifelong enemies, taking hold of him. He well knew the foolishness in proceeding beyond the Río Grande with a train of supplies and gifts for the Indians without an adequate military escort. Eager as he was to get on with the expedition, he must await the new governor. Yet he knew that waiting near the Presidio de San Juan Bautista would be very nearly as hazardous for his supplies as would an unprotected journey into the Texas wilds.

"I resolved to retire to the Mission of San José, distant some four leagues from the Presidio del Río Grande, in order to avoid the many thefts which the soldiers were committing in the vicinity of said Presidio, of livestock as well as anything else they could lay hands on."[17] Not even such isolation, however, could quell his rancor. He vented his feelings and voiced his opinions in a letter to Alarcón.

Before Olivares was gone from the capital, Alarcón had requisitioned from the Viceroy the seventeen hundred head of livestock, the implements, weapons, corn, and tobacco, which he said were necessary for the expedition and the establishment of a warehouse in the province of the Tejas from which to provision the missions. He notified the Marqués de Valero of his plans to depart immediately for the interior provinces to recruit fifty soldiers for the expedition. He asked for and got pay in advance for himself and all his men, beginning in January, 1717. Yet

[16] Olivares to Viceroy, June 27, 1718, *ibid.*, pp. 247–248.
[17] *Ibid.*, p. 248.

when Father Olivares reached San Juan Bautista, Alarcón was not yet in Saltillo. When Alarcón did reach Saltillo in June, he was to be diverted from the pursuit of the new endeavor which so consumed Father Olivares. Back into the picture had come the fast-dealing, ambiguous Frenchman, St. Denis, who had arrived April 19 at San Juan Bautista with a mule train of contraband merchandise for trade with the Spaniards.

14. CONTRABAND AND FRUSTRATION

WITH ST. DENIS came his father-in-law, Alférez Diego Ramón. They brought with them the mules which had transported supplies for the new missions and presidio to East Texas. Captain Domingo Ramón was returning the mules, which actually belonged to the government, for the use of the new governor-appointee, Don Martín de Alarcón. It is the height of irony that these very same mules, the property of His Majesty King Philip V, carried on their backs the merchandise which was to precipitate such a tempest.

"Somewhere north of the Río Grande, St. Denis left the main party and hastened on to San Juan Bautista. A messenger had apparently contacted him with exhilarating news. The cumbersome mule caravan moved much too slowly for a man traveling to see his young wife and his firstborn."[1] The infant daughter was named Luisa Margarita.

News of St. Denis' coming and the merchandise he brought had preceded him to México. "So much ado was made about the matter from one quarter or another that before the end of April Grandfather Ramón had to seize the goods to save his own political career."[2] Don Diego Ramón confiscated seven mule loads of the merchandise and so advised the

---

[1] Ross Phares, *Cavalier in the Wilderness: The Story of the Explorer and Trader, Louis Juchereau de St. Denis*, p. 115.

[2] *Ibid.*, p. 117.

Viceroy. But the seizure did not end the matter, nor did it remove Don Diego from suspicion.

St. Denis was indignant—or feigned indignation.[3] In the company of a servant, Miguel de la Garza, *vecino* of San Juan Bautista, he set his course for the capital to protest before the Viceroy the abuse he suffered at the hands of his grandfather-in-law. Having obtained on the way a letter of commendation from Friar Joseph Díez, guardian of the College of Querétaro, St. Denis reached the city of México in June, about the time Governor Alarcón was arriving in Saltillo. While St. Denis was stating his case before the Marqués de Valero, Alarcón was reading the somewhat upsetting letter he had received from Father Olivares. The impatient friar was trying his best to stay out of the way and mind his own business at Mission San Francisco Solano while waiting for Alarcón to reach the gateway. He was not, the letter indicated, succeeding very well.

The crotchety old missionary's letter was filled with complaints against his one-time friend and co-worker, Don Diego Ramón. No longer did the commandant of the Presidio del Río Grande maintain strict discipline among his troops, Olivares charged. The soldiers slaughtered the livestock of the missions at will and abused with impunity the peaceful Indians. Captain Ramón was most indolent about prosecuting and punishing the offenders.[4]

Olivares, according to the letter, had reached San Juan Bautista on May 3 with the intention of proceeding immediately to the San Antonio River in order to plant crops that year. Ramón, however, had refused to grant him the escort ordered by the Viceroy. He could not spare him the eight men, noted Olivares acidly, though he was able to take a larger number and go to Monclova to see the bullfights.

The Presidio San Juan Bautista was a sorry sight indeed:

I have witnessed and experienced [wrote Olivares] all that these holy religious in charge here suffer, as a result of the negligence of Captain Ramón and the haughtiness of the Indians, who, encouraged by the captain, have lost all respect for the soldiers as well as for the *Padres*. The whole country from Coahuila to the Tejas is in revolt and there is no nation we can trust. . . . Your Lordship will see for himself how the Indians steal from the Spaniards and

---

[3] Vito Alessio Robles, *Coahuila y Texas en la época colonial*, p. 437.
[4] Olivares to Alarcón, June 5, 1717, A.G.I., Audiencia de México, 61-6-35, Dunn Transcripts, pp. 19–22.

will notice many articles which they have exchanged with those of Nadadores and Parral.[5]

As for St. Denis, said the doughty old friar, Captain Ramón and all his kinsmen were in league with him. Frenchmen came and went freely at the presidio, he reported; five were quartered there at that very time, and one planned to marry a Spanish woman. Three others were engaged in a mining operation near Presidio de Coahuila. In the opinion of Olivares, Ramón had embargoed a quantity of the French merchandise while permitting the entry of many other French merchants.

Captain Ramón, concluded the priest, had surrounded himself with a dependable cadre of followers; the entire region north of Saltillo was full of "Ramonistas." Alarcón, in order to restore order, would find it necessary to recruit soldiers in other provinces.

Father Olivares may well have written this letter from spite. If he did, it boomeranged. The letter so aroused Alarcón that he launched an investigation of the French mercantile operation, in which the Ramóns were suspected of complicity. This involvement caused delay in his starting the journey toward the San Antonio River. Olivares was the first to resent his procrastination and to ascribe wrong motives.

Alarcón, on the strength of the padre's letter and other reports he had picked up along the way, wrote to the Viceroy from Saltillo on June 27. Enclosing the letter from Olivares to support his opinions, he charged that Captain Diego Ramón, his sons Domingo and Diego, the protector of Indians of Nuevo León,[6] and St. Denis were associated in a mammoth contraband enterprise "of such a nature that all this region is full of contraband merchandise," of which but a small part was embargoed in order to conceal the main operation.[7] St. Denis should be detained in the capital, said Alarcón, and the Ramóns, father and son, should be removed from their posts on the Río Grande. Only with control of the activities of these three directors of the enterprise would it be possible to end the illicit trade, he opined.

While Alarcón marched northward to the Presidio of San Francisco de

[5] *Ibid.*, translated in Carlos Eduardo Castañeda, *Our Catholic Heritage in Texas*, II, 83.

[6] Joseph de Urrutia was protector of Indians in Nuevo León at this time.

[7] Alarcón to the Viceroy, June 27, 1717, A.G.I., Audiencia de México, 61-6-35, pp. 22–23.

Coahuila, where he would gather more information on the case before proceeding to San Juan Bautista, the letters went south to the Viceroy. St. Denis had reached the capital about the middle of June and was busily engaged in advancing his cause. But suddenly the agile Frenchman, who had always appeared to be master of his fate, found himself ensnared in a most difficult web of circumstance. First word of his coming with the mule train of merchandise had reached the Río Grande ahead of him, causing the seizure of his goods. Then Father Olivares, acting pettishly because Diego Ramón had refused to do his bidding, had written his incriminating letter. Although his accusations may have been ill-founded, they very nearly ruined both St. Denis and the Ramóns.[8] The impetuous Alarcón was set in motion by Olivares, and he in turn had an effect on the Viceroy. When St. Denis arrived in the capital, he found that the Duke of Linares, who had trusted him enough to send him along with Domingo Ramón's expedition as conductor of supplies, had been replaced by the more suspicious and less placable Marqués de Valero. Then came letters to the Viceroy from Gregorio de Salinas Varona at Pensacola. This official related that St. Denis had formed a company in Louisiana for introduction of contraband merchandise into New Spain with complicity of his kinsmen, the Ramóns—Don Diego at San Juan Bautista and Don Domingo of the Presidio of the Tejas. Merchandise valued at thirty thousand pesos had been sent to San Juan Bautista, he reported; St. Denis should be placed under arrest.

As a result of all the letters—from Olivares, Alarcón, and Salinas—St. Denis was imprisoned July 12, 1717, his case to be investigated by Judge Juan de Oliván. This magistrate took from the Frenchman his declaration, which constitutes a firsthand description of Texas as St. Denis saw it in the course of his various expeditions.[9] It also constitutes the best explanation available of what St. Denis' intentions were, though history has been reluctant to accept his statements at face value.

He declared that he had sold all he owned—his plantation and his slaves—at the French fort of St. John on the Mississippi. He had taken the proceeds, and three years' pay as captain, and converted them into merchandise worth 5,500 pesos in Mobile. He had brought this merchan-

[8] Phares, *Cavalier*, p. 123.
[9] Charmion Clair Shelby, "St. Denis's Declaration Concerning Texas in 1717," *SWHQ*, 26, No. 3 (January, 1923), 165–183.

dise to México, he declared, for use in establishing his business of buying cattle, by which he hoped to support his family. His wife was a Spanish subject; he considered himself a citizen of the Presidio of San Juan Bautista del Río Grande and planned to make his home there. He had forsaken his own nation, he told the Spanish officials, in order to come and live with the Spaniards and serve the Spanish king, because such were the greater loyalties of himself and his wife. Therefore, he had brought his thirteen bundles of merchandise—mostly Brittany linen but also some serge, flannel, and woolen cloth, a small box of laces, and a case of thread—to the Río del Norte. But his wife's own grandfather, being a conscientious servant of his king, had seen fit to seize the goods, pending instructions from the Viceroy. This act necessitated St. Denis' trip to the capital of México to inform His Excellency and to seek return of his merchandise. He did not know why he had been imprisoned.

The Frenchmen who had come with him to San Juan Bautista, he claimed, were two of his cousins who assisted him in bringing the merchandise; by this time (September 18) they likely had returned to Mobile, since he had been detained so long.[10]

While St. Denis languished in the national prison of México, Governor Alarcón arrived August 3 at Monclova, and took formal possession of the government of Coahuila from Joseph Antonio de Ecay Múzquiz two days later.[11] By the time he reached San Juan Bautista he had worked himself into such a state—with the aid of Olivares' letter and fragments of information he had gleaned in Monclova—that his plans for entering Texas became quite secondary. His primary goal was to get at the bottom of the business of illicit trade with the French and corruption in high places at the Presidio of the Río Grande.

On the arrival of the new governor, it is said, several Frenchmen who had been living at the gateway settlement fled to Mission San Bernardo, where they were given asylum. Alarcón summoned the president of the missions, Father Pedro de Muñoz, and interrogated him. The missionary friar informed the Governor that he knew facts which no one could ignore: many French merchants had entered; the number of soldiers in

---

[10] *Ibid.*, pp. 173–174.
[11] Cabildo of Monclova, Certification, August 6, 1717, in A.G.N., Provincias Internas, Vol. 181, p. 221.

Ramón's presidio was not the full complement, while horses and arms were insufficient; a great indiscipline existed among the soldiers. But more specific testimony the Governor was unable to elicit.

From all he was able to learn Alarcón concluded that twenty loaded mules had arrived at San Juan Bautista instead of seven, carrying twenty-nine bundles and one box, and that most of the cargo had been rapidly conveyed, on the mules sent by Domingo Ramón, to Boca de Leones. Alarcón demanded that Don Diego deliver the embargoed goods, and Ramón gave up only thirteen bundles and the box. The Captain admitted that the merchandise had come on his son's mules, but if they had brought more than he had delivered, he declared he was not aware of it.

Alarcón continued to seek testimony from disinterested persons about the presidio and found there were none. Father Olivares, he soon determined, was accurate on at least one point: the entire area was populated with "Ramonistas." He talked with one Juan Valdés, only to learn that he was a son-in-law of Don Diego. He interviewed Antonio Martínez Ledesma, who turned out to be an intimate friend and confidant of Don Diego. He interrogated Francisco Hernández and learned that he was *alférez* of the company of Domingo Ramón, having come from the Tejas country bearing special messages.

Meeting a wall of evasiveness, Alarcón had no alternative but to end his investigation. He ordered the merchandise deposited with Father Muñoz and reported to the Viceroy his conviction that more merchandise had entered than had been confiscated. Captain Diego Ramón and the missionary fathers, he observed, preferred to appear to obey the letter of the law, rather than actually uphold the spirit of the law.[12]

St. Denis, master diplomat, really had no cause for alarm—only cause for impatience. Since diplomacy is the natural enemy of agitation, the French interloper did not let impatience rule. Despite the reports of Salinas Varona, Olivares, and Alarcón—not to mention the evidence supplied by the embargoed merchandise itself—he maneuvered so dextrously that he won both his release and an apology.

12 Alessio Robles, *Coahuila y Texas*, pp. 439–440. For an account of the investigation by Alarcón, including an inventory of the goods seized, see Charmion Clair Shelby, "St. Denis's Second Expedition to the Río Grande, 1716–1719," *SWHQ*, 27, No. 3 (January, 1924), 204–208.

Judge Oliván, in reporting to the Viceroy on November 4, 1717, asked that St. Denis be given his freedom and that his merchandise be returned to him. The Spanish officials may have been influenced, as they were calculated to be, by the prisoner's subtle reminder regarding the arms the Indians used. The natives west of the Tejas, where the Spaniards might conceivably find help, used bows and arrows, he pointed out. But the Natchitoches and some of the Tejas tribes, known to be under French influence, used firearms.[13] Yet Oliván continued his investigation two months after the date of the declaration, and in the end his findings confirmed what St. Denis himself had told him. The reports of Alarcón and Olivares, he believed, were exaggerated.

On November 22 the prisoner was released on bond with instructions against leaving the city. At last he was permitted to sell his merchandise but still was enjoined against returning to Texas. The proceeds from sale of the goods were absorbed by living costs, apparently, while he spent long months in the capital awaiting final disposition of his case.[14]

A letter from Father Hidalgo urging that St. Denis be released and sent to Texas produced no results.

All the nations between here and the Río Grande [wrote the padre from Mission San Francisco de los Tejas] are clamoring for the French Captain Don Luis de San Dionissio. They have great love for him, and he promised to place them in Mission on the road between the Río Grande and here. . . . He promised to come with his wife to live among them when the Spaniards came, and the Indians offered to gather themselves in pueblos when he should come with his family. Certainly, if this gentleman does not come, sent by his Excellency, with some title, the Indians cannot be gathered without great expense, many Spanish people, and many years' work. And what is more important, many souls will be lost because many will die without Baptism.[15]

At last St. Denis' patience wore thin. He was eager to return to his family on the Río Grande. At this point he is said to have made a threat that he could provoke the Indians of East Texas to a general uprising, and

---

[13] Shelby, "Declaration," pp. 175–176; Phares, *Cavalier*, p. 135.

[14] Shelby ("St. Denis's Second Expedition," p. 214) says St. Denis presumably went to the Río Grande to secure his goods, which were "sold promptly for a very good price in Nuevo León."

[15] Fray Francisco Hidalgo to Fray Joseph Díez, March 11, 1718, A.G.N., Provincias Internas, Vol. 181, p. 224.

the viceregal authorities responded by ordering his arrest. St. Denis was forced to flee, which he did September 5, 1718. Almost six months later, he reached Natchitoches, February 24, 1719.[16] Speculation has it that he had spent most of the intervening time with his family at San Juan Bautista.

The international marriage, having resulted from such romantic circumstances, turned into a frustrating experience of one long separation after another. Manuela still remained in her grandfather's house at San Juan Bautista. Not until 1721 was she able to join St. Denis. During that year he was named commandant of the French fort at Natchitoches and Fathers Isidro Félix de Espinosa and Antonio Margil de Jesús petitioned the Viceroy to permit Manuela to begin the journey across Texas to join her husband.[17]

Hardly anyone who has concerned himself with a study of St. Denis concedes the possibility that the adventurous Frenchman seriously intended to settle in México with his family and become a Spanish subject, as he stated in his declaration. No one, apparently, believes that he acted from any motivation in bringing his goods to México except a desire to build a rich mercantile business for himself and the French colony. Yet there appears to be a strong possibility that the behavior of St. Denis after he was caught up in the whirlwind of Spanish harassment became quite different from what it might have been without such persecution. True St. Denis most assuredly saw the advantages of mercantilism on the Spanish frontier. He was not above stretching a law for personal gain. But if the Spaniards had been less obsessed with the idea of a French conspiracy to violate their borders with illicit trade, had they taken St. Denis in good faith and permitted him to settle on the Río Grande, he probably would have done so.

It appears that what St. Denis really wanted was to live at San Juan Bautista with Manuela and to rear his children there. Given the opportunity, he would have engaged in commerce between the Río Grande and the East Texas settlements in the vicinity of Nacogdoches, and, later on, San Antonio. But Spanish officials suspected—and history's judgment is that they were correct in their suspicions—that sooner or later he would have been unable to resist the temptation to carry his trade into French

[16] Shelby, "St. Denis's Second Expedition," p. 214.
[17] *Ibid.*

territory in violation of Spanish laws. In conceding a fingertip the Spaniards could have lost a hand.

So they made the Frenchman suffer. They kept him in jail, then required him to stay in the city of México. He could not go back to Texas,
or even to his wife and child on the Río Grande. But in dealing such
punishment on St. Denis, they imposed an even greater hardship on some
of their own people: the missionaries and soldiers on the eastern borders
of Texas.

15. MIRACLE IN THE *MONTES*

NEWS OF THE DIFFICULTIES which surrounded the nascent missions
among the Tejas reached San Juan Bautista in a letter from Friars
Francisco Hidalgo and Manuel de Castellanos. Dated October 6, 1716,
the communication was addressed to Father Friar Pedro Pérez de Mezquía, who had come from Querétaro with the missionaries of the 1716
entrada but had remained on the Río Grande.

One of the first drawbacks encountered by the friars had been a strange
illness which afflicted both religious and military. Father Hidalgo—his
mission of San Francisco was hardly more than a quarter of a league from
the presidio where Father Castellanos served as chaplain—was one of the
first victims. From July until the first of October his body alternately
shook with chills and burned with fever. "But now, thanks to God, I am
convalescing and have strength to work in the vineyard of the Lord."
Friar Manuel had been stricken much later, but his condition already was
improved.[1]

[1] Francisco Hidalgo and Manuel de Castellanos to Pedro Pérez de Mezquía,
October 6, 1716, A.G.N., Provincias Internas, Vol. 181, p. 215. The illness would
appear to be malaria. Much the same information as contained in this letter is
found in Mattie Austin Hatcher (trans.), "Description of the Tejas or Asinai
Indians, 1691–1722," Part III, Hidalgo to Fray Isidro Casas and Hidalgo to the
Viceroy, *SWHQ*, 31, No. 1 (July, 1927), 50–62.

Four missions had been placed in the Tejas country, but the Indians had failed to gather. Much work by the missionaries had been in vain, but all the effort would not be lost if more soldiers could be sent: "This place today is severely lacking of the military; some have fled, others are in bed sick."[2]

Furthermore, the Indians were idolators. They had houses of worship, and in the house of the principal idol they kept a perpetual fire. The Christian instruction of the Indians had not begun, because their dwelling places were spread over such great distances, and it was necessary for the priests to go about from place to place to contact the Indians. The only alternative would be to remove or burn their idols and destroy their pagan temples, but in order to make the Indians subject to the King and the Church in this manner, one hundred soldiers would be needed.

Despite the idolatry of the Indians, however, they treated the friars cordially. On the day of St. Francis many men and women had come to take part in the sung Mass.

Most of the Indians were found in the region beyond, and the French, already settling on the Mississippi, planned to move upstream and settle among these more populous nations. They had been among the Nachitoz people for three years and had the Indians well subjected, with a guard of more than one hundred soldiers.

The letter asked that all the pertinent news of the French settlement on Mobile Bay and the Río de la Palisada (Mississippi) be transmitted to the Viceroy. Diego Ramón, brother of Captain Domingo Ramón, had reconnoitered those settlements, the Captain himself being ill at the time. "This report will enable His Excellency to meet the situation and provide the needed military, because this nation [France] is spreading extensively."[3] Most of the Frenchmen were farther inland, in the region of the Missouri River, one hundred leagues beyond the Cadodachos (Red River), according to the Frenchmen themselves. Where the Missouri and the Mississippi run together, Father Hidalgo was told, was a French settlement, including two missions founded by the priests with the French company.

The French padres intend to place a mission in the Caynio [Cheyenne] nation, which the Frenchmen say has five thousand Indians and is up the

[2] Hidalgo and Castellanos to Mezquía, A.G.N., Provincias Internas, Vol. 181, p. 215.
[3] *Ibid.*, p. 217.

Missouri River one hundred leagues, and in the Pani [Pawnee] nation, fifty leagues higher up, where three arms join to make this river so copious. The Frenchmen go there by canoes and trade with these nations, and have provided them with guns and with many other things in which the Frenchmen trade. On the middle arm some Frenchmen have reconnoitered a great city of other people, very well dressed and with organized government. At the time Don Luis [Louis de St. Denis] departed from Mobile, one hundred and fifty Frenchmen went out to reconnoiter this great city; hence news of it is had in Mobile.[4]

Hidalgo—evidently the writer of the letter, though Friar Manuel put his name to it also—did not emphasize the dire need in which the missionaries found themselves as much as he might have.

"We have great needs, although God is not failing to meet them. Even in these conflicting wants, already mentioned, we have God until such time as the grandness of His Excellency shall remedy such calamity."[5]

Father Pérez de Mezquía at San Juan Bautista read the letter with interest. At first opportunity he sent it on to Father Joseph Díez, guardian of the Colegio de la Santa Cruz at Querétaro. Father Díez attached a note and dispatched it to the Viceroy.

Most Excellent Sir:

As Chaplain (although unworthy) of Your Excellency and loyal vassal of our great Monarch, Felipe Quinto [Philip V] (God preserve him) I give news to Your Excellency of the state of the extended Provinces of Texas, Cadodachos, Nachitoos, etc., which you will see by the attached writing from one of my Religious of the Río Grande Missions. I do not doubt that your zeal for defending the Crown of Spain will apply appropriate measures for obstructing the damage threatened by the intervention of the French in those regions. My obligation is to ask God to assist Your Excellency with perfect health and to keep you in all felicity. From this Apostolic College of Your Excellency of the Most Holy Cross of Querétaro, December 29, 1716.

Your least chaplain is at Your Excellency's feet.

Fr. Joseph Díez[6]

---

[4] *Ibid.,* p. 217. It is interesting to observe that news of the Indians on the upper reaches of the Missouri was transmitted to San Juan Bautista and thence to the capital.

[5] *Ibid.,* p. 216.

[6] Fray Joseph Díez to the Viceroy, December 29, 1716, *ibid.,* p. 125.

The viceroy, Marqués de Valero, already had acted to provide for the needs of the Tejas missions before receiving these letters. On December 15 he ordered that four thousand pesos be paid to Don Martín de Alarcón, the new governor of Coahuila and Texas, for purchasing provisions for the East Texas missions. A combination of circumstances, however, prevented the immediate dispatch of needed supplies and aid. Indeed it seems that these new settlements were temporarily forgotten in all the fuss over the new *entrada* to plant a mission settlement on the San Antonio River, and the frenzy over contraband trade with the French. Although Alarcón received funds to provide the aid in December, he lingered in the capital until well into the following spring, making arrangements for his expedition.

When at last he reached Saltillo, in June, 1717, he involved himself in the investigation of the St. Denis affair to such an extent that his coming journey to Texas became secondary. By the time he reached San Juan Bautista and there brought his probe to frustrating conclusion, most of the year 1717 was gone.

St. Denis, who would have supplied the Tejas missions if he had been free to do so, whiled away the months in the national prison. Regardless of official views, the missionaries—excepting Olivares, of course—saw no harm in St. Denis. They were dismayed by his misfortunes, for well they knew the help he had been to them in settling among the Tejas Indians. His aid had extended to helping them build their churches, as well as establishing some degree of rapport with the natives. In their view he was "worthy of eternal remembrance."[7] But thanks to the Viceroy's order, no longer would he be in position to help them.

Hardly had Alarcón realized the futility of his investigation of St. Denis and the Ramóns than he found himself at loggerheads with Father Olivares. The petulant old man had been responsible for launching Alarcón on the investigation, but then had grown venomous with impatience while the Governor carried it out. Furious at the refusal of Ramón and Ecay Múzquiz to turn over to him the ten soldiers who were to form his escort, he appealed to Alarcón. In response to the viceregal order for eight men from San Juan Bautista and two from Presidio de Coahuila, which Olivares sent him, Alarcón took the eight from Ramón's garrison. But

[7] Elizabeth H. West (trans.), "A Brief Compendium of the History of Texas, 1772," *SWHQ*, 8, No. 1 (July, 1904), 28.

instead of assigning the men to Olivares to take care of the supplies he had stored at Mission San Francisco Solano, the new governor placed them under his own orders. During the eight months more which they remained on the Río Grande, the soldiers performed no service at all, according to Olivares.[8]

The aging friar now was at the point of peevish faultfinding. About the middle of September he observed that Alarcón had not obtained the required number of soldiers for the expedition, nor the families who were to form the new settlement. He hastened to write to the Governor, urging Alarcón to give him the ten soldiers so that he himself might proceed to Texas. Alarcón refused. Met with repeated denials, Olivares protested that most of the men Alarcón had enlisted were not married, as the Viceroy had stipulated, that their character was not of the best, and that many were not of Spanish blood. Alarcón replied acidly that he did not have an apostolic college from which to recruit his men, that in Coahuila there were only "mulatos, lobos, coyotes, and mestizos."[9] All hope of cooperation between the two leaders vanished.

Alarcón had procrastinated until winter was at hand, and it was evident that he planned to delay the start of the expedition until the following spring. Still no supplies had been sent to the missionaries at the far-flung Tejas missions. Information which came to the Río Grande revealed that the past growing season had not alleviated the plight of the missionaries; drouth had cut short the crops of corn and beans. The religious looked with dread at the approach of winter, and the urgency of their messages increased. The president of the Río Grande missions, Father Pedro Muñoz, finally succeeded in prodding Alarcón to action.[10] On November 17, 1717, the Governor began making preparations to send the supplies to the missions. Fifteen soldiers were chosen to go with Father Miguel Núñez de Haro, a Zacatecan friar, and the supply train. It was December

---

[8] Olivares to the Viceroy, June 22, 1718, A.G.N., Provincias Internas, Vol. 181, p. 149.

[9] *Ibid.,* pp. 250–251. In this letter Olivares reviews the entire row for the Viceroy, including Alarcón's comment concerning the quality of the men available. Carlos Eduardo Castañeda (*Our Catholic Heritage in Texas,* II, 87) defines the terms: a "mestizo" is a Spanish-Indian cross, a "lobo" of Negro and Indian blood, and a "coyote" the offspring of a mestizo and an Indian.

[10] Isidro Félix de Espinosa, *Crónica de los colegios de propaganda fide de la Nueva España,* p. 725.

before the caravan crossed the Río Grande and started on its long journey
to take the supplies and a bundle of letters to the missionaries with the
Tejas.

Winter had begun in earnest. Cold, wet northers lashed at the little
band, making travel slow and difficult. The group pushed onward until
January 28 when, on reaching the Trinity River, it found itself unable to
go farther. Espinosa says the river was spread out more than two leagues
in width. Regardless of the accuracy of this estimate, the stream could not
be crossed. "This effort which might have been the salvation of that
province turned out like the fleet aground on the beach." The raging
stream and forty leagues still stood between the relief party and the
missions.[11]

Father Núñez was not one to give up easily. He sent eleven of the
soldiers back, while he and the four others remained with the supplies,
hoping that the floodwaters would recede and they could continue to the
missions. But the rains increased. Cold and miserable, the five men remained camped in the wilderness two more months. During that time
they subsisted on some roots and a little corn given them by Indians.[12]

The eleven soldiers who had turned back, meanwhile, reached San Juan
Bautista and reported to Alarcón. The Governor sent out two military
expeditions to aid Father Núñez, but each reached the Colorado only to
find it at flood stage and turned back.

At last Father Núñez also was compelled to turn back. In desperation
he decided to leave the supplies and the packet of letters concealed in an
oak grove, near the shore of a lake. On top of the boxes and chests were
placed the packsaddles. Over them was stretched his tent. Then the padre
wrote a message to his brothers in the Tejas missions and gave it to some
of the Indians who had remained on the Trinity's west bank to hunt.
When the water went down, he told them, they were to take to the fathers
at the missions the news which was upon the paper. He dared not tell the
Indians what the news was. He ventured only to hope that the dispatch
eventually would reach its destination, and that the starving missionaries

---

[11] Ibid.; Fritz Leo Hoffmann (in Francisco Céliz, *Diary of the Alarcón Expedition into Texas, 1718–1719*, p. 38) says the relief expedition stopped fourteen
leagues west of the Trinity and forty-eight leagues from the East Texas settlements.

[12] Hoffmann note in Céliz, *Diary*, p. 38.

would come and find sustenance in the bundles left in the wilderness.[13] On March 30, 1718, the missionary and the four soldiers, with the pack mules, started back for the Río Grande.

The situation among the East Texas missions, meanwhile, had become desperate. In February, Father Espinosa wrote of their plight to the guardian, Father Joseph Díez. Apologizing for repeating himself, he pointed out that he had received no reply to a report on the condition of the missions which he had sent the previous November. He could only say again what he had said before: "Each day we find ourselves in greater need of clothing and sustenance. The necessities for celebrating the mass have been finished."[14] Perhaps, he suggested, it would be possible for the guardian to have sent to them the provisions which should already be at San Juan Bautista. If this aid arrived during that year, the need would be remedied.

All of us, with good health and the glory of God, are very content, working in His vineyard. Even though it is so wild, we have feasted ourselves with around 100 baptized who were in danger of death, and with the epidemic the gospel of our God has been divulged and much of Satan's stronghold has fallen. The illness is not ended, and we hope to gain more souls, which is the only goal of our poor little labors.[15]

A Frenchman who had been with Father Díez the previous August had brought word of his good health, but no written message; all the letters were at San Juan Bautista awaiting the regular courier.

"By the time you receive this, you may already have taken action, for if aid does not come, I fear all will be lost, and with good reason. God grant that you may send a lay religious to bring what may be offered from the Río Grande."[16] Espinosa had no way of knowing of the effort already being made to bring the supplies to the missions.

While Father Núñez and the soldiers were waiting for the East Texas streams to subside, Alarcón and Olivares made final preparations to embark for the San Antonio River. All the supplies, livestock, and equip-

[13] Espinosa, *Crónica*, p. 725.
[14] Fray Isidro Félix de Espinosa to Fray Joseph Díez, February 28, 1718, A.G.N., Provincias Internas, Vol. 181, p. 228.
[15] *Ibid.*, p. 228.
[16] *Ibid.*, p. 229.

ment had been gathered at San Juan Bautista. At last the Governor's *entrada* was launched April 9, when he crossed the Río Grande with seventy-two persons, not including Father Olivares, who still sulked in the Mission San Francisco Solano at San José. Besides the people—a chaplain, soldiers, mule drivers, and families—there were seven droves of pack mules and large herds of cattle and goats. There were 548 horses, of which the Marqués de Aguayo had given 300, in addition to having furnished all the cattle for the expedition.

The chaplain, who also served as diarist, was Friar Francisco Céliz, whom Espinosa refers to as "a religious from Coahuila."[17]

Alarcón reached the future site of San Antonio on April 25, having encountered Father Núñez and the four soldiers returning from the Trinity. The meeting has been placed at six leagues west of the Medina River. The Governor got firsthand an account of the sufferings of the group, which he had already seen written in the harsh lines of the friar's face. The priest was pale and emaciated. While the men with Núñez proceeded on to San Juan Bautista to carry the disappointing news, Núñez went with Alarcón to the San Antonio River to await the coming of Father Olivares.

This missionary, impatient as he had been to begin the new undertaking, had waited until April 18 to depart from San José. Olivares was the only priest in the party. Father Francisco Ruiz, a veteran of four years in the gateway missions, had been assigned to accompany him, but had died before leaving the Río Grande. A lay religious, Friar Pedro Maleta, was with Olivares, as were enough other persons to transport all the property. They brought the supplies which had been stored at the mission all winter, and all the property of the mission which was being transplanted. Olivares himself said later that not one Indian had remained at the mission, although numerous ones from the San Antonio River area had come to visit him during the winter. He had told more than 150 visitors of plans to establish the mission in their country and of the great desires that the King and the Viceroy had for them to be converted and live in civil

---

[17] Espinosa, *Crónica*, p. 736. Actually Céliz was minister of the Mission of Dulce Nombre de Jesús de Peyotes, which belonged to the Franciscan province of Jalisco, but it seems strange that Espinosa, who was to travel with the expedition beyond San Antonio, did not refer to him by name. Castañeda (*Our Catholic Heritage,* II, 91) mentions missionaries as being a component of Alarcón's caravan, but it appears Father Céliz was the only religious in the entourage.

settlements. To prove his sincerity he showed them the many supplies he had stored in the mission and distributed some of the gifts. The Indians promised that they would wait for him at the San Antonio River. With the supplies, gifts for the Indians, and the mission ornaments from the ne'er-do-well mission of San Francisco Solano—which was destined for a role that no one dreamed of—he and his few companions crossed the river.

Since José de Urrutia had guided him into the Frío River country in 1703, Olivares had dreamed of establishing a mission in Texas. From the time he had come with Father Espinosa and Pedro de Aguirre in 1709 he had envisioned a mission on the beautiful San Antonio River. He reached the San Antonio on May 1. That same day Governor Martín de Alarcón gave him possession of the site of the Mission of San Antonio de Valero, in the name of His Majesty, King Philip V, by express order of His Excellency, Marqués de Valero.[18] Four days later Alarcón founded the Villa de Béjar, three-quarters of a league upstream from the mission, and thus became the founder of modern San Antonio.

With the departure of Captain Domingo Ramón's expedition, San Juan Bautista, the gateway to Spanish Texas, had changed its rôle; no longer the most advanced frontier outpost, she had become the mother of Texas missions. With the departure of Alarcón and Olivares, this new rôle was confirmed. The gateway missions, which had been three almost from the beginning, now were only two. San Francisco Solano must keep her date with destiny.

From San Juan Bautista on May 30, Captain Diego Ramón reported the failure of Father Núñez to reach the Tejas missions with the supply train. The cargo, consisting of mail for the missionaries, clothing which had been gathered at San Juan Bautista, and the badly needed provisions, had been left hidden in a wood. Since many people were known to inhabit the region, Ramón wrote, he feared that it was lost. "Presently the said religious is found at San Antonio with the Reverend Father Olivares."[19]

On June 17, Alarcón returned to San Juan Bautista for additional sup-

[18] Castañeda, *Our Catholic Heritage,* II, 94, citing Mission Records, San Fernando Cathedral, San Antonio, Texas.

[19] Diego Ramón to the Viceroy, May 30, 1718, A.G.N., Provincias Internas, Vol. 181, p. 236.

plies before going on to Espíritu Santo Bay and the East Texas missions. In the meantime letters had arrived from the missionaries in East Texas, telling of their desperate circumstances and renewing their appeal for help. Father Pedro Muñoz, president of the Río Grande missions, volunteered to go to the Trinity, try to find the supplies left by Father Núñez, and deliver them to the missionaries in East Texas. Considering the likelihood that the Indians had found the cache and used up its contents, he gathered all the provisions he could from the mother missions. In the new cargo he thoughtfully included wine and candles for celebrating Mass. He set out June 27 with a lay brother, an *alférez,* and nine soldiers, part of whom had been with Father Núñez and would be able to guide the way.[20]

On July 21 they approached the site of the cache. While still a day's journey distant Father Muñoz sent the lay religious and two soldiers, who knew the hiding place, ahead to look for the supplies. If they found them intact, they were to return as quickly as possible, firing their muskets to signal the good news.

They found the cargo just as it had been left beside the lake which they had come to call Laguna de las Cargas, and returned loose-reined to inform Father Muñoz and the other soldiers. When they fired their muskets, says Espinosa, a large number of shots was heard in answer. Knowing that it was none of their own people, the small party searched the area of the camp without finding a footprint. The mysterious volley was taken as an indication of "the invisible custody which had hidden for so long the succor of those ministers of God from the eyes of the Indians."[21]

Indeed the recovery of the merchandise did seem little short of a divine miracle. Not far from Father Núñez' camp had been the wintering ground of some of the Tejas Indians who had come west to hunt buffalo. They had seen the Spaniards come with loaded mules; they had seen them leave with the mules unloaded. The trail of the beasts remained plainly evident eight months later. Surely the Indians had seen it. And the wood was so sparse that any one traveling through could easily spot the cargo, half hidden in a motte. Small wonder it seemed to Father Espinosa that "Heaven favored the cargo."[22]

[20] Espinosa, *Crónica,* p. 729; Hoffmann in Céliz, *Diary,* p. 39.
[21] Espinosa, *Crónica,* p. 729.
[22] *Ibid.,* p. 729.

The provisions were not even damaged by the weather. Only the pack-saddles, which had been placed on top of the boxes and chests, had suffered detriment.

Almost at the same time Father Muñoz' party was arriving at Laguna de las Cargas, an Indian brought to Father Espinosa, at his Mission of Nuestra Señora de la Purísima Concepción, on July 22, 1718, the letter which Father Núñez had given him the previous March. The writing was faded almost beyond legibility, but Espinosa was able to make out the words. They told of the futile effort to reach the Tejas missions with the cargo and described the place at which it had been left. Espinosa read the startling news and took the letter to Captain Domingo Ramón. Although the captain had little hope that Indians had spared the cargo, they gathered their mules and set out for the lake west of the Trinity to make a search. "The day of the glorious Lady Santa Anna, after having said Mass, we went to meet with those who had come from the Río Grande, at the place where the cargo had been hidden. Our joy was doubled, causing all of us to shed many tears."[23]

It had been more than two years since the missionaries had arrived to begin their work among the Tejas. Until the happy meeting on what now would be called Santa Anna Lake, they had received no aid of any kind. Nor had they received news of the happenings back in México. Until they read the letters which Father Núñez had left with the cargo and talked with Father Muñoz and his party, they did not know that Martín de Alarcón had been named governor of Coahuila and Texas. They were unaware that the Governor and Father Olivares already had arrived to establish a new mission and village on the banks of the San Antonio River, cutting in half the distance to the nearest Spanish settlement.

The Tejas missionaries had news of their own to impart, of the privation and hardship they had endured in maintaining themselves among the Indians. First drouth, then flood had ravaged the crops of the Indians, and the daily bread—which was made of corn in that land—was almost wholly lacking. There was not even grain with which to make tortillas. If at any time meat was to be had, a handful of corn was cooked as a substitute for bread. Salt was completely lacking. When there were beans to eat,

[23] *Ibid.*, p. 730.

they were so insipid because of the lack of salt that they might well have taken the place of a purgative. Game was not to be found, and hence there was no meat. Only on rare occasions did the Indians, sympathetic with the missionaries' plight, bring a quarter of venison, but the meat was tasteless without salt. Often the Spaniards went days at a time with nothing to eat which they could savor.[24]

But necessity is industrious, and one of the missionaries observed the abundance of crows fluttering about the trees each morning. With his musket he was able to get food every day. "The darkness and toughness of it [crow meat] was repugnant to the appetite, but need gave it such flavor that for the greater part of the year it made a tasty dish." Fast days posed a difficulty, but herbs were gathered from the fields, and some nuts were found with which to season them. Leaves of the wild mustard plant were served as a palatable salad, especially if salt could be found to season it.

Though the cord had to be drawn tighter about the priestly habit, food was not actually the most urgent necessity: what the ministers really needed was candles with which to observe Mass. They saved the tips of the candles they had brought and melted them down to be used again, until every bit of wax was consumed. Then they resorted to candles of tallow. Wine was so scarce that only a drop was put into the cup. It was Father Margil who came to the rescue. The aged and experienced priest lacked necessities for the *mesa* but not for the *misa*—for the table but not for the Mass. He traveled thirty leagues to bring to Father Espinosa an earthen jar of wine.[25]

Father Muñoz and his party returned to the Mission Concepción with Father Espinosa and Captain Ramón, helping to transport the supplies which had been retrieved from the wilderness, as well as those which he himself had brought. This priest appears to have been a man of action rather than words. At the East Texas missions, he likely found himself in an awkward position, as the missionaries read the letters which had come with the supplies. The packet included a copy of the first set of instructions issued to Don Martín de Alarcón, in the autumn of 1716, from which "it was surmised that the Most Excellent Viceroy had given various providences in favor of the Province of the Tejas."[26] Espinosa exercises

[24] *Ibid.*, p. 725.
[25] *Ibid.*, p. 726.
[26] *Ibid.*, p. 730.

great restraint to keep from indicting Alarcón for his failure to send supplies when they were needed. Yet he makes it quite plain at this point that the missionaries, in reading the instructions, could scarcely avoid comparing the Governor's orders against his performance. Between the two was a considerable gap. The instructions sounded most encouraging. They called for more aid to be supplied the Tejas missions, more soldiers to protect them, and a sister settlement only half as far away as San Juan Bautista. There was only one flaw: the instructions had been issued almost two years previously; Alarcón was to proceed from San Antonio de Padua to the Tejas missions, to bring them grain and cattle and to strengthen them with replacements for the soldiers who had died or deserted. Yet nothing had yet been seen of the Governor, and the word from Father Muñoz was that he had reached the San Antonio River to plant a settlement three months previously.

Father Margil called Father Espinosa to the Mission of Dolores and proposed a meeting of the missionaries to determine what should be done. If the response to the Viceroy's instructions to this point was indicative of what might be expected in the future, the missions would not be able to survive. With Espinosa's concurrence the six missionaries met together and decided that the Viceroy should be informed of "all that had happened."[27] Two missionaries, one from each college, should go to the capital to report and to correct impressions of what was going on in Texas that were quite contrary to fact. At Margil's insistence, Espinosa went with Friar Matías Sáenz de San Antonio. Friar Muñoz accompanied them to San Antonio de Padua, where Espinosa learned that Alarcón planned to go immediately to Espíritu Santo Bay and thence to the East Texas missions. Feeling that it would be wise for him to accompany the Governor, he turned his letters over to Father Sáenz and wrote a lengthy letter to the prelate of his college. Sáenz and Muñoz departed for the Río Grande without Espinosa.

Father Muñoz stopped at his mission on the Río Grande, and Father Sáenz went on alone.

Long before Father Sáenz arrived in the city of México in November, Captain Diego Ramón's letter from San Juan Bautista had reached the Viceroy, informing him that the supplies taken to Santa Anna Lake prob-

---

[27] *Ibid.,* p. 736.

ably were lost. On June 27, 1718, the Viceroy discussed before a *junta de hacienda* the problem of aiding the missionaries. The junta, still unaware that the supplies had been retrieved, appropriated another four thousand pesos for the relief of the East Texas missionaries.

On his arrival Sáenz informed the Viceroy of the hardships which had been suffered during the first two years of the East Texas settlements. Spain, he said, was running a great risk of losing the settlements to the French who had a fort on the Red River and were building many more along the Mississippi.[28]

Governmental action seldom came in a hurry, and Friar Matías became impatient. In February, 1719, he left the capital with only the amount appropriated previously.

In the meantime Alarcón had visited Espíritu Santo Bay and the Tejas missions, but he left no more satisfaction among the missionaries than he had found.

His *entrada* [writes Espinosa] accomplished nothing more than visiting the missions, and giving presents to the Indians, and adding six or seven soldiers to replace the twenty-five who had deserted. All we religious saw on this occasion the dispatch and grand providences which the Señor Marqués de Valero had given on the one hand, and on the other we saw the governor enter without bringing what had been promised us.[29]

They could only pin their hopes on Friar Matías' success in México, not knowing that he had already failed.

Even after the mission and presidio had been founded on the San Antonio River, San Juan Bautista continued to succor the far-out settlements. The mother of the Texas missions was obliged to perform many and varied services in fulfilling her role of parenthood. Frequently the assistance needed was of a material nature. From her storehouses she must furnish what the Texas missions could not produce for themselves. Not always was the material aid provided from San Juan Bautista as dramatic as the expeditions of Father Núñez and Father Muñoz. Often the establishments in Texas needed building material, pottery, or livestock of one kind or another.

There were times, however, when the lack was spiritual rather than

[28] Hoffmann in Céliz, *Diary*, p. 39.
[29] Espinosa, *Crónica*, p. 736.

material. Such a need arose early in the life of the Mission San Antonio de Valero, the transplanted San Francisco Solano. At the new location Father Olivares and the lay brother, Pedro Maleta, ministered to the Xarames and other Indians whom they were able to gather from the immediate vicinity. Olivares was the mission's only priest. Before the venture was a year old, he suffered a painful accident when his horse slipped upon a wooden bridge across the river, not far from his mission. In the fall the padre's leg was broken. Apparently infection set in, for Espinosa records that "he was placed in grave danger, and it was necessary to send to the missions of the Río Grande for a confessor."[30]

Again it was Father Friar Pedro de Muñoz who answered the call. He drove his horses so hard that he covered the eighty leagues in forty hours, Espinosa relates, not stopping on the way. With a priest at his side Father Olivares felt much better. After confessing, he had his leg set by a soldier. Although confined to his bed for a long period, he recovered and regained his vigor.[31]

And then, in mid-summer, 1719, there came to Presidio de San Juan Bautista del Río Grande a new cry for help. This time it came from the missionaries on the eastern Texas frontier, who had learned by means of an unprovoked attack on a Spanish settlement that France and Spain were at war.

Fully aware of what the French could do if reinforced by the Indians to whom they had supplied firearms, the Spaniards already had abandoned the Tejas missions and presidio. If these establishments were to be reclaimed, help was needed from the presidios of Béjar, San Juan Bautista, and San Francisco de Coahuila.

[30] *Ibid.*, p. 735.
[31] When he was well he moved the mission from the west to the east bank of the river, so that it would not be necessary to cross the bridge. "A terrible hurricane in 1724 demolished this mission's *jacales* for the Indians, and the mission was moved again, this time only 'two gun-shots distance' from the earlier site. The move was completed by 1727, to the spot where the present Alamo stands" (Lon Tinkle, "The Alamo," in *Six Missions of Texas*).

16. CHANGING OF THE GUARD

IN THE DEAD HEAT of summer word of the French attack on the Mission San Miguel de los Adaes reached San Juan Bautista. The dispatches, dated July 2, 1719, were contained in a double mailing issued by Fathers Espinosa and Margil. They gave the information to the presidios of San Antonio de Béjar and San Francisco de Coahuila, as well as to the viceroy, Marqués de Valero, and to the missions and the presidio on the Río Grande. Urgent was the plea for help.[1]

The hammer had fallen at San Miguel in mid-June. Somehow news that France and Spain had been at war with each other for more than five months had not yet reached the Spanish frontier in Texas. The French commander at Natchitoches, Philippe Blondel, on receipt of the news had moved quickly to capture the nearest Spanish outpost, ten leagues distant. Manned only by a lay brother and one soldier, the mission was easy prey for Blondel and his band of seven. The Frenchmen gathered up the mission's sacred vessels, ornaments, and meager provisions, then raided the henhouse. This last move was his mistake. The chickens flapped their wings; the captain's horse shied and spilled him in the dirt. The lay brother, with the attention of his captors diverted, dashed into the woods. He reached Mission Nuestra Señora de los Dolores on June 22 to impart to Father Margil all that he had been able to learn from the attacking force: Pensacola had been captured by the French on the outbreak of war between Spain and the Quadruple Alliance.[2] One hundred soldiers were said to be on their way from Mobile. Retreat to the Río Grande appeared to be the only course left for the Spaniards. Margil buried the implements, packed the ornaments, and made for Mission Concepción.

---

[1] Isidro Félix de Espinosa, *Crónica de los colegios de propaganda fide de la Nueva España,* p. 741.

[2] The Quadruple Alliance of England, France, Holland, and Austria was

It was from this latter mission that the startling news which now spread rapidly through the Río Grande settlement of San Juan Bautista had been written. The soldiers at Presidio de los Tejas, said the communication, had lost spirit, because many of them were only boys, poorly clothed and without arms or mounts. Eight of the soldiers were married men, and their wives set up a clamor for withdrawal before the French came marching. "Nothing sufficed to arrest the current of this misfortune."[3]

The great fear of the Spaniards stemmed from a lack of confidence in their own relationship with the Indians. The fact that many Indians carried French muskets led them to fear that the natives would ally themselves with the French cause. It seemed prudent that the Spaniards retire some distance and wait for reinforcements of men and supplies. As Captain Ramón and his soldiers escorted the citizens and livestock toward safety, Espinosa, Margil, and two soldiers returned to Concepción—after giving the Captain a written waiver of responsibility—to spend twenty days consoling the Indians, many of whom were reluctant to let them go. During this time they composed the appeal for help, which was written in Espinosa's hand.[4]

The news which came to San Juan Bautista spread from presidio to mission, and Father Pedro Muñoz, still president of the missions, was greatly upset. Always the man of action, he set about organizing an expedition to go to the aid of his fellow missionaries. Little information is found concerning his efforts, but it seems that his request for a sizeable force of soldiers met rebuff by Captain Diego Ramón, and perhaps also by Alarcón, who now was preparing to relinquish his post as governor of Coahuila. Rare was the military commander in New Spain who was willing to risk his own security to go to another's aid until he was forced to.

In September, however, a small force was raised at the insistence of Father Muñoz and one of his fellow missionaries at San Juan Bautista.

---

formed in 1718 to oppose the plans of the first minister of Philip V, Alberoni, and of the new Queen Isabel de Farnesio, who sought the recovery of the Italian dominions lost by Spain in the Peace of Utrecht. The outbreak of hostilities with France did not take place until January 9, 1719. At the end of this year Alberoni fell, and the war ended (Lino G. Canedo in Espinosa, *Crónica*, p. 739 n.).

[3] Espinosa, *Crónica*, p. 738.

[4] *Ibid.*, p. 738.

The expedition, which may have contained a few soldiers but most likely was made up of civilians, crossed the Río Grande and headed up the Camino Real, the long road to the land of the Tejas. With it went a letter from Father Muñoz saying there was no hope of sending further help.

Espinosa and Margil had remained at Mission Concepción until, on July 14, they received word that Domingo Ramón was retiring farther than had been agreed upon. The two missionary priests now had a disagreement over their course of action: Espinosa wanted to stay, Margil to go after the others. At last Espinosa reconciled the Indians to their going, and five days later, after crossing several streams that were dangerously swollen, they overtook the others in a lonely expanse of wilderness at the edge of the Tejas country.[5] "Making sojourn as the children of Israel, we maintained ourselves on the frontier of the Tejas all the months of August and September, waiting for aid," Espinosa relates.[6]

Living conditions were so poor in this wilderness region—with provisions of unsalted meat and flour full of impurities—that Espinosa resolved at the end of September to go personally to San Antonio and San Juan Bautista to seek help. The padre and a few soldiers had traveled twenty leagues in the direction of San Antonio when they came upon the tracks of a number of horses. They followed the trail and soon overtook the small caravan sent by Father Muñoz. The newcomers were guided by Espinosa back to the camp where the others remained, and there the padre read the letter that had been brought from Muñoz, taking in its disheart-

---

[5] *Ibid.*, p. 742; Eduardo Enrique Ríos, *Life of Fray Antonio Margil, O.F.M.*, p. 122. Eleanor Claire Buckley ("The Aguayo Expedition into Texas and Louisiana, 1719–1722," *SWHQ*, 15, No. 1 [July, 1911], 14) says the fact that the two presidents remained twenty days at Concepción is evidence that the missionaries wished to remain, despite the French threat.

[6] Espinosa, *Crónica*, p. 742. Henri Folmer (*Franco–Spanish Rivalry in North America, 1524–1763*, p. 226) says that after the flight of the missionaries, the French occupied some of the Spanish missions but did not go beyond the Neches River. A plan for driving the Spanish from Texas, presented to the Duke of Orleans, called for a naval expedition to the mouth of the Río Grande and seizure of the Presidio of San Juan Bautista. "Though Orleans did not order the execution of this ambitious plan, he did ask, as has been stated, that the western boundary of Louisiana be fixed at the presidio of San Juan Bautista and the Río Grande. Thus the name of this forlorn little frontier post entered into European diplomacy."

ening news: No force of soldiers could be raised to help restore the religious to their missions.

A few days later, on October 3, the entire camp began the move to San Antonio. Father Margil and the seven other religious went to the Mission of San Antonio de Valero; Espinosa decided to continue with the relief expedition on to San Juan Bautista to make a personal appeal for the necessary action to reclaim the East Texas missions.

In December, 1719, Espinosa returned to San Juan Bautista, where he had served as president of missions until the start of the 1716 *entrada.* There he was met by his successor, Father Muñoz, who informed him of recent political developments. Alarcón, feeling himself caught in a squeeze between what the missionaries needed and demanded and what he was able to get the Viceroy to provide, had tendered his resignation early in the year. Joseph de Azlor y Virto de Vera, Marqués de San Miguel de Aguayo, wealthy *hacendado* of Coahuila, having offered his life, his fortune, and his sword, had been chosen to succeed Alarcón as Governor. He now was preparing to lead a new expedition into Texas.

Father Espinosa was gladdened, though anxious, at the news. His anxiety stemmed from his concern for restoring the missionaries to the Tejas missions. Eager to know that adequate provision was being made to reclaim the land of the Tejas, he importuned Father Muñoz to go to the hacienda of the Marqués de Aguayo to learn what steps were being taken; he wished to know just when such a move might be expected.

Espinosa felt a keen sense of urgency; such delays as those experienced previously would be intolerable now. The other missionaries were quartered temporarily in straw huts at San Antonio. Much needed to be done in Texas, but while they waited for help to arrive, their time was being wasted.

Just why Espinosa asked Muñoz to go to the Marqués instead of going himself is not explained. Perhaps Espinosa felt himself too personally involved to make an effective appeal to the new Governor, though he did make one later to the Viceroy. It seems that Muñoz never got around to fulfilling the request, possibly because word had come that the Marqués de Aguayo was not at his hacienda but in Monclova, where Father Espinosa would be going shortly.

As Espinosa feared, the return to the Tejas missions was delayed a year and a half. Although a company of soldiers crossed the Río Grande during the interim, they went no farther than San Antonio.[7]

Espinosa left San Juan Bautista late in December and went on to Monclova, where he held a preaching mission. Both Martín de Alarcón and the Marqués de Aguayo attended his services, but if he discussed with either of them the needs of the Tejas missions, he fails to mention it.

Early in 1720 he went on to Querétaro and thence to the capital for a conference with the Viceroy himself.[8]

The new governor of Coahuila and Texas, Marqués de Aguayo, meanwhile, gathered five hundred men for the new expedition to Texas from the districts of Celaya, Zacatecas, San Luis Potosí, and Aguascalientes. Severe drouth caused many of his horses to die en route to Monclova, and additional animals had to be brought in from the various haciendas. By the time these reached Monclova it was September. In mid-October six hundred mules that had left the city of México the previous April arrived at Monclova, carrying the clothing, arms, powder, and six cannon which had been secured on orders of the Marqués. At this time came word that a truce had been effected between Spain and France. Aguayo's hope of driving the French from Texas and Louisiana was to be denied. He would be limited to defensive warfare, to founding a settlement on Espíritu Santo Bay, and to restoring the Spanish priests and settlers to their rightful positions.[9]

Don Fernando Pérez de Almazán was chosen as lieutenant governor and captain general and was placed in charge of the troop, which was divided into eight companies. On November 16 the Governor ordered Pérez to set out with the expedition; he himself was detained by matters of government of the province.

The diarist of the expedition, Father Juan Antonio de la Peña, notes that the route as far as the Río Grande was well known; therefore, it could have been no other than the one which led to San Juan Bautista.

While summer drouth had occasioned previous delays, floods now hampered the expedition. Three weeks' wait was necessary to cross the Río de Sabinas, and even then a soldier was drowned and several others

[7] Espinosa, *Crónica*, p. 742.

[8] For details of this meeting see Carlos Eduardo Castañeda, *Our Catholic Heritage in Texas*, II, 123–124.

[9] Peter P. Forrestal (trans.), *Peña's Diary of the Aguayo Expedition*, p. 6.

had narrow escapes. Five days later, on December 20, the troop reached the Río Grande, now more than a musket shot in width and more than a rod and a half deep. Pérez de Almazán ordered rafts to be built, and after Christmas was celebrated—many of the soldiers observing the occasion at the Presidio of San Juan Bautista—the crossing began. Severe weather hampered the operation, with rain, snow, and intense cold. Fifty swimmers worked in the water to pull the rafts, each of which carried six packloads at a time. On orders of the Marqués himself, who had just arrived with Father Espinosa, the swimmers were sustained with brandy, chocolate, and plenty of food.[10] Also joining the expedition at the Río Grande at this time were Captains Alonso de Cárdenas and Juan Cortinas with their companies, and Friar Benito Sánchez, who had been among the missionaries entering Texas in 1716, and who had served as minister of the Mission of San José de los Nazonis. Sánchez probably had come with Espinosa on his journey to seek aid and had served temporarily at Mission San Juan Bautista while Espinosa went on to the capital. While the crossing was effected, the two waited in the nearby missions.

The Aguayo expedition was the biggest yet to cross the Río Grande at the gateway, and would hold the record until Santa Anna's army came this way in 1836. Not only did the crossing set a new record as to size; it also set a new mark in time consumed. With the crossing begun shortly after Christmas, it was March 23 before the last of the expedition had reached the other side. A contingent of one hundred men had gone on ahead, for on February 2 news came to the gateway concerning an old acquaintance of the settlement: none other than Louis Juchereau de St. Denis himself.

The word from Captain Matías García of the Presidio de San Antonio de Béjar, received by him from Indians of the Sanas[11] tribe, was that St. Denis and other Frenchmen were holding a convocation of many tribes thirty leagues beyond that settlement. The Governor held a council of war

---

[10] *Ibid.*, p. 9.

[11] Sana, Chanes, Zana, Canas, Chanas. A Tonkawan tribe, for which the Llano River (Río de las Chanas) first was named. It appears likely the name *Llano* is in this case a corruption of *Chanas,* since *Llano* (plain) is not descriptive of the terrain through which the Llano River flows. The Sanas, or Chanas, Indians entered San Antonio de Valero Mission from 1740–1749, says Fritz Leo Hoffmann in Francisco Céliz, *Diary of the Alarcón Expedition,* p. 35 n.

and decided immediately to send Pérez de Almazán and two companies on to San Antonio.

As the crossing neared completion, Aguayo received word that the Indians were gathered beyond the Brazos, and he concluded that the rumor regarding St. Denis was correct. The Governor sent for Friars Espinosa and Sánchez at Mission San Juan and speeded up the work at the river in order to cross the last of the expedition two days earlier than he had planned.

On the final day Aguayo distributed clothing to sixty Indians from the nearby missions who had helped in taking the rafts and the livestock across the river. The natives had worked faithfully since the crossing had begun almost three months previously, and the governor had kept them supplied with meat and corn.

On Monday, March 24, he and eight companies, minus the detachment already at San Antonio, continued the march beyond the Río Grande. Each company had 350 horses, 600 head of cattle, and 800 sheep, and the Marqués had with him 600 muleloads of clothing, provisions, and baggage—a total of some 14,600 head of livestock. Another 500 muleloads of food, war supplies, and clothing had been sent ahead. A considerable quantity of provisions remained in storage at Presidio de San Juan Bautista through foresight that proved indispensable later on.

Marching by the road to Real de Cuervo, or Crow Camp, the expedition ended the day at Las Rosas de San Juan,[12] five leagues from the Río Grande.

When the Aguayo expedition at last left the Río Grande and headed out on the Camino Real toward San Antonio and the most far-flung mission outposts of the Tejas, it left behind arrangements for provisions to follow. A small coastal vessel would bring supplies from Veracruz to Espíritu Santo Bay, to be transported on to the Tejas by means of mule train, but other supplies were to enter the province by land as well. From the borders of the kingdom of León[13] Aguayo's men were busy gathering livestock which would be driven up the road to the East Texas mission settlements and as far as Los Adaes (present Robeline, Louisiana), 340

---

[12] Forrestal, *Peña's Diary*, pp. 10–11. Las Rosas de San Juan possibly was a ranch or outstation from San Juan Bautista, occupied by a family named Rosas. *San Juan* would refer to its proximity to San Juan Bautista.

[13] *Ibid.*, p. 57.

leagues from the point of origin. This drove of four hundred sheep and three hundred cattle, said to be the forerunner of the cattle drives which were to play such an important role in the later history of Texas, passed by San Juan Bautista in late summer, 1721, and crossed the Río Grande at Paso de Francia.

For fear that the coastal vessel bringing supplies to Espíritu Santo Bay should suffer some disaster, Aguayo had ordered that two hundred loads of flour and one thousand fanegas of corn be gathered at San Juan Bautista. The vessel made its voyage safely, but a disaster of another sort created an urgent need for the supplies. News of the loss came to San Juan Bautista by means of Aguayo's messenger in midwinter. The expedition, said the courier, had encountered severe weather while returning from the East Texas missions. In the blizzards and ice storms horses had died by the hundreds. The men had traveled on foot, even, in an attempt to spare the horses. Running low on supplies, Aguayo met at a place called El Encadenado, four leagues from the San Marcos River, a convoy bringing thirty loads of provisions from the ship.

Welcome as the provisions were, they came with bad news: A raging fire had swept through some of the buildings at Presidio de San Antonio de Béjar; sixteen soldiers' huts had been destroyed. But the worst was the loss of the granary, with the seven hundred bushels of corn and the supply of flour. Not one ear of corn was saved. The Governor's order which the messenger carried was that mules should be brought from Saltillo to transport the supplies stored at San Juan Bautista to San Antonio immediately.

Once again there was a flurry of activity at the gateway as the soldiers and citizens of San Juan Bautista strove to relieve an emergency in Texas. In a few weeks the mules came from Saltillo. They were hastily loaded with corn and flour, and the train embarked on the road to San Antonio. Eight hundred horses gathered from Guadiana and other places were sent as remounts for Aguayo's plodding troops. The train reached San Antonio safely, and the succor provided from San Juan Bautista saved the day for Spaniards in Texas. The supplies proved to be sufficient to meet the requirements of the Governor's troops and of the Presidio of San Antonio.[14]

Another messenger from the Governor stopped briefly at San Juan

[14] *Ibid.*, pp. 59–60; Juan Agustín de Morfi, *History of Texas, 1673–1779*, pp. 222–223.

Bautista early in February, carrying the Governor's report to the Viceroy. The Aguayo expedition had reached San Antonio; although almost all of its five thousand horses and seven hundred mules had been lost, all the men were well.

Such messengers from the Aguayo expedition commanded intense interest at the Río Grande settlement, particularly among the Ramón family. The Governor, it was learned, had met with St. Denis, who had become commander of the French fort at Natchitoches the previous year. Also in the previous year, his bride, Manuela, had at last left San Juan Bautista with their children to join the dapper Frenchman. Received by the Marqués de Aguayo, St. Denis had announced that if the Spanish governor were willing to do likewise, he, as commandant of the forces on the entire frontier, would observe the truce now in effect between France and Spain. The Marqués replied that he would be glad to observe the truce, provided the French commandant would immediately evacuate the province of Texas and withdraw all his soldiers to Natchitoches.

For once St. Denis found himself confronted with a Spaniard he could not evade. He tried in vain to convince Aguayo that the Adaes country was unhealthful, that the soil was too poor for farming. But the Spaniards had been there; they knew about the country around the Mission San Miguel. St. Denis recognized their determination and the futility of any effort to dissuade them. He withdrew to Natchitoches. The Marqués de San Miguel de Aguayo then established the Presidio of Los Adaes, which in years to come would serve as the Spanish capital of Texas. The missions which had been abandoned in 1719 were reactivated.

The messenger went on south from the gateway but returned to San Juan Bautista toward the end of the month, this time carrying the Viceroy's commendation for the Marqués de Aguayo. After brief respite, he turned his mount toward the Paso de Francia, splashed across the Great River, and again disappeared into the lonely expanse of Texas wilderness.

When Aguayo departed from Texas in May, 1722, he left ten missions, where there had been seven prior to the 1719 retreat, four presidios where there had been two, and 268 soldiers instead of the 60 or 70 before.[15] Two of the presidios—Los Adaes and Espíritu Santo (La Bahía)—were located at points where foreign aggression was most feared.

---

15 Castañeda, *Our Catholic Heritage,* II, 148.

Left in command of the garrison at La Bahía was Don Domingo Ramón, leader of the 1716 entrada, son of Don Diego Ramón of Presidio de San Juan Bautista, uncle by marriage of St. Denis, and a true son of the Spanish frontier.[16] The Marqués de Aguayo, if he had a reason for bringing Don Domingo to La Bahía instead of returning him to Presidio de los Tejas, apparently did not choose to reveal it. His reason may have been the family relationship—and perhaps trade relationship—of Domingo Ramón and St. Denis. The troublesome Frenchman, as he might have been described by almost anyone charged with the responsibility of enforcing Spain's laws on the eastern frontier, now was commandant of the French fort at Natchitoches, and, therefore, in position to be more troublesome than previously. The Spanish leader who would deal with him must not have his decisions weighted down by family ties. It was a circumstance which would cost Domingo Ramón his life.

The decade which began with Aguayo's *entrada,* 1721, had brought many changes for those whose names are found in the cast of characters of the story of San Juan Bautista. One of the founders of the Mission San Juan Bautista, aged and failing, retired on September 8, 1720, from the mission which he had moved from the Río Grande, San Antonio de Valero. Father Antonio de San Buenaventura y Olivares was succeeded by his co-worker, Friar Francisco Hidalgo. Olivares returned to the Colegio de la Santa Cruz de Querétaro, where he lived out his days.[17]

An important event also occurred in the life of Father Isidro Félix de Espinosa. This missionary, who had spent many years in the service of God and king at the Río Grande missions, was named on October 25, 1721, as guardian of the College of the Holy Cross at Querétaro. He was to succeed Father Diego de Alcántara, who had resigned four months before the end of his term. On receiving word of his appointment, Espinosa hastily departed from the Mission Concepción in East Texas.

---

[16] Forrestal, *Peña's Diary,* gives the name of La Bahía's commander as José Ramón; it appears that he confused Domingo with his brother José, who lived at Boca de Leones and as far as is known never made an official entry into Texas. Buckley ("The Aguayo Expedition," p. 32) says Aguayo, while still at the Río Grande, sent forward a company of forty soldiers under Domingo Ramón to occupy Espíritu Santo Bay: "They probably came as far as San Antonio with the detachment under Almazán."

[17] Edward W. Heusinger, *Early Explorations and Mission Establishments in Texas,* p. 78.

Reaching San Juan Bautista in the winter of 1722, he paused briefly for a visit with his friend, Father Pedro de Muñoz, and hurried on southward over the long, winding road to the Colegio de la Santa Cruz de Querétaro.[18]

Time was running out, meanwhile, for Señor Capitán Don Diego Ramón, the elder. He had never quite escaped from the cloud he had been placed under by Don Martín de Alarcón's investigation of his part in the St. Denis affair. Pichardo records that the king, in a royal cedula dated January 30, 1719—the same one that ordered St. Denis to be sent with his wife to live in Guatemala—ordered that Don Diego be removed from the Presidio of San Juan Bautista and that he be given another post so distant that he would be unable to communicate with the French.[19] But orders were slow in being carried out, and this one, because of unexplained delays, would be thwarted altogether.

Don Diego, in this year of 1722, was past seventy years of age. He still held onto his command, but it did not take an astute observer to see that the post was not as it had once been. The aged captain had grown lax and inattentive. No longer able to enjoy the long ride to Monclova to see the bullfights as he once had, he kept close to his presidio. Even his rides over his hacienda of Santa Mónica, in which he had taken such great pleasure, had grown less frequent. Naturally the hacienda was the choicest spread to be found in the vicinity of the gateway; it had the greatest abundance of water for irrigation to be found on any of the farms and ranches, even those of the missions.[20] But the hacienda, like the presidio, was suffering from lack of attention.

The old man's spirit appeared to be gone. No longer able to cross the Río Grande himself, he could only sit and gaze wistfully into the distance whence his sons and his grandsons had gone. In his thoughts he must have relived his own life in that of his son Domingo, now in a new presidio on the frontier, at the Bay of Espíritu Santo. But then the stunning blow fell. Out of the Texas wilderness, early in the year 1724, came a messen-

[18] Lino G. Canedo, Introduction, Espinosa, *Crónica,* p. lii.

[19] Charles Wilson Hackett and Charmion Clair Shelby (trans.), *Pichardo's Treatise on the Limits of Louisiana and Texas,* I, 224.

[20] Jorge Cervera Sánchez in Fray Juan Agustín de Morfi, *Descripción del Territorio del Real Presidio de San Juan Bautista del Río Grande del Norte, y su Jurisdicción, Año de 1778,* p. 306 n.

ger bearing ill tidings. It was the messenger's unpleasant lot to tell Don Diego that his son Domingo was dead.

The story was long in unfolding, but when the facts were fully known, it was evident that Domingo had been inept in his administration of the Presidio of Nuestra Señora de Loreto (La Bahía), and in his handling of the unruly Karankawa Indians. His son who succeeded him temporarily, another Diego, was even worse. The name Ramón, which had long stood with pride on the northern frontier of New Spain, was dragged through the dirt.

The trouble had begun December 15, 1723. A mission Indian entered the house of a soldier of the presidio to ask for a piece of beef. While he waited he shook from his blanket a cloud of dust which settled upon a metate where the soldier's wife was grinding corn. Angered, the woman called her husband, who threw the surly savage from the house. In the aftermath of the incident the entire Indian population became aroused. Don Domingo rounded up what Indians he could, including all the women and children and a few men, and imprisoned them in a small hut. From the crowded prison he planned to remove them a few at a time to be hanged. Some of the Indians tried to escape, and Captain Ramón and a few soldiers approached the hut to force them back. The Captain was seized and drawn into the hut. He managed to escape and ordered his soldiers to charge. One of the Indians then rushed at Ramón and stabbed him in the breast with a large pair of scissors. On Ramón's order a cannon was fired at the hut, opening a hole through which all the Indians escaped except one squaw. Don Domingo ordered that this unfortunate one be hanged. Eight days later, December 23, he himself died of the wound he had received.

Young Diego Ramón, Domingo's son, took command on his father's death. But an official investigation of goings on at the presidio resulted in formal charges of negligence being brought against him. Gambling was rampant at the post; the soldiers were in rags, their arms unfit for service; discipline was nonexistent. Young Diego was summarily removed from command.[21]

---

[21] Fernando Pérez de Almazán to the Viceroy, May 1, 1724, A.G.N., Provincias Internas, Vol. 181, pp. 322–327. See Castañeda, *Our Catholic Heritage,* II, 180–184, and Hodding Carter, *Doomed Road of Empire: The Spanish Trail of Conquest,* pp. 109–110.

The name Ramón still would be heard in Texas for years to come. But never again would it command the respect which once had been accorded Don Diego, the elder. Perhaps the old soldier, in his grief, realized the inevitability of this dire circumstance, and was hastened thereby into his own grave. Early in the year 1724 at the Presidio of San Juan Bautista del Río Grande, Captain Don Diego Ramón cheated the royal decree of 1719 which had called for his removal to another command post. The old soldier's death at the age of seventy-three was due to natural causes.[22]

Don Diego's worldly possessions consisted primarily of his hacienda, Santa Mónica, which passed to his son Diego. The command of Presidio de San Juan Bautista del Río Grande, which had belonged to Don Diego ever since its founding, with the exception of short intervals when he was on leave, went to Don Joseph Antonio de Ecay Múzquiz, a Creole Spaniard who had previously served as interim governor of Coahuila in 1717 and 1718, being relieved by Don Martín de Alarcón. Prior to that time he had served many years as an officer in Coahuila.[23]

With the increase of the missions and presidios in Texas, the traffic over the long road through northern México and through the gateway at San Juan Bautista also multiplied. A detail of nine soldiers was assigned permanently to escort missionaries and supply trains on their way to Texas as they traveled north from Saltillo to the Río Grande.

In the spring of 1724 a party made up of Father José González, two other missionaries, and two Indians reached Saltillo to find that the escort was not available; it was at the other end of the line, at San Juan Bautista. Friar José, impatient to continue his journey, chose not to wait; the group continued without escort. At Los Hierros a band of Tobosos attacked, killing one of the Christian Indians and badly wounding the other. One of the missionaries took an arrow in the back, the tip of which lodged in the spinal column. Father González lost all his baggage. His four mules were killed.

González carried orders from the Viceroy for Mateo Pérez, a private in

---

[22] Hackett and Shelby, *Pichardo's Treatise,* I, 224 n.; Cervera Sánchez in Morfi, *Descripción,* p. 308 n. 57.

[23] Ecay Múzquiz' name first appears as a witness on documents signed by Alonso de León in 1688 and 1689. It will be remembered that, as an officer of the Presidio de San Francisco de Coahuila, he accompanied Diego Ramón on his *entrada* of 1707.

the Presidio of San Juan Bautista del Río Grande, to proceed to San Antonio to relieve Captain Nicolás Flores y Valdés as captain of the Presidio of San Antonio de Béjar. In fact, the missionary, from Mission San Antonio de Valero, had traveled the distance to the Mexican capital to arrange for the orders personally. He and Captain Flores had clashed over treatment of the Apaches, and it was at the priest's urging that Pérez, an illiterate man who had served at the gateway presidio twenty years as a private, was suddenly elevated to the responsible position. Pérez, humbled by the unexpected trust placed in him, requested the Viceroy to keep his place in the garrison of San Juan Bautista vacant so that he might return to it, should he not prove worthy of the new charge. When Father González and his companions departed from the gateway to proceed to San Antonio, Pérez was with them.[24]

The soldier whom the late Captain Don Diego Ramón had not seen fit to promote in twenty years would never have had his moment of glory in the first place, had it not been for the unfortunate row between Father González of the Mission San Antonio de Valero and Captain Flores. The disagreement stemmed from the fact that González, overcome by his desires for peace with the Apaches, had severely criticized Flores when the Captain found the Apaches' peace overtures insincere. Father Francisco Hidalgo, associated with González in the Mission San Antonio de Valero, supported González in his claims, and the latter went to the capital city to use his priestly influence on the Viceroy.

Mateo Pérez was captain at San Antonio de Béjar for almost a year before Flores, who had been withdrawn to Coahuila, was vindicated and returned to his post at San Antonio. Father González was recalled to the College at Querétaro, but it appears he never reached the college. Castañeda records that he "perished on the road from Texas to the Río Grande."[25]

It was as a result of these events, in the summer of 1725, that Father Francisco Hidalgo retired from his post at the Mission San Antonio de Valero and returned, dejected, to San Juan Bautista. Father Hidalgo had entertained great hope for the pacification of the Apaches, having expressed the belief that the settlement of this wily tribe might already have

---

[24] See Castañeda, *Our Catholic Heritage,* II, 197–198.
[25] *Ibid.,* p. 253.

been accomplished, had the presidios been managed properly.[26] But even with Flores out of the way and Pérez in charge of the Presidio de Béjar, by Father González' own choosing, progress in that direction was still slow in coming.

The Venerable Padre was finding himself already old and oppressed by painful circumstances. Consulting only the robustness of his spirit, he began glorious feats with marked valor. The loving zeal he had for the Apostolic Institute obliged him to ignore the dangers, and to prefer the hope of pacifying those barbarians, and subjecting them to the sacred Laws of the Gospel, to his own life and religious conveniences.[27]

By petition of March 20, 1725, Father Hidalgo and the lay brother, Friar Francisco de Bustamante, asked the president of the Querétaran Missions in East Texas, Father Gabriel de Vergara, for permission to go into the land of the Apaches. It would not be necessary, they said, to send soldiers to protect them. They would be armed with the sincere desire to take the Gospel to the heathen, and with the hope that peace could be brought to the frontiers. Father Hidalgo had been grieved to see the repeated slaughter which resulted from the war with the Apaches. He would risk his life for a chance to end it.[28]

It was a characteristic gesture of the veteran missionary. This was the same priest who had refused to be defeated, as was Father Massanet, by the bitter setback at the first Tejas mission; the same zealous friar who had founded the mission San Juan Bautista on the Río de Sabinas, and who, when the mission's Indians fled, had gone after them to re-establish the mission deeper in the wilderness, near the banks of the Río Grande; the same who had worked and planned for years to bring about a return to the country of the Tejas. But in this daring new plan he met refusal.

Father Vergara submitted the question to the guardian, and the official ruled. Many times in the history of the church, said the Venerable Padre Pedro Pérez de Mezquía—himself a longtime friend of Hidalgo—had the flock been watered with the blood of its pastors. But the rules set forth

[26] *Ibid.*, p. 195, citing Hidalgo to Viceroy, Archivo San Francisco el Grande, Vol. 10.

[27] Juan Domingo Arricivita, *Crónica seráfica y apostólica del Colegio de la Santa Cruz de Querétaro en la Nueva España, segunda parte*, p. 226.

[28] *Ibid.*, p. 225; Robert S. Weddle, *The San Sabá Mission: Spanish Pivot in Texas*, p. 1.

in the Gospel must be followed in making such a decision. The missionaries who content themselves with the fulfillment of the obligations of their charge, said the father guardian, would find enough to suffer; they could compete, in fact, with the most valiant martyrs, who give their lives for the Redeemer but once, while these constant ones die innumerable times for their sheep, prepared at all times to shed their blood for them.[29]

The next year, 1726, Father Hidalgo, suffering great despair at being unable to carry out what he felt to be the last important task of his life, returned to San Juan Bautista. In the mission church he spent much time in prayer before at last, in the month of September that same year, "his soul was delivered to the Lord."[30]

Having attained the age of sixty-seven, Father Hidalgo had followed the religious life fifty-two years, since taking the holy habit at the age of fifteen. He had served forty-three years as an apostolic missionary, some thirty-five years of which were on the frontiers of northern Coahuila and Texas.

17. THE DOUBLE STANDARD

AT SAN JUAN BAUTISTA, 1727 was the year of inspections. Both presidio and missions were brought into the spotlight and a reassessment made of their role in the service of God and king.

When Juan de Acuña, Marqués de Casafuerte, became viceroy in October, 1722, King Philip V had instructed him to have a survey made of the frontier defenses of New Spain with the view to instigating certain reforms. Official dishonesty and wastefulness had crept into the presidial system. To the Viceroy the garrisons of the northern frontier seemed more

[29] Arricivita, *Crónica seráfica*, p. 226.
[30] *Ibid.*

costly than their usefulness warranted, their administration full of defects and abuses, both military and financial.[1]

To gather the information desired, Casafuerte chose Colonel Pedro de Rivera y Villalón, former governor of Tlaxcala and interim commander of the fortress of San Juan de Ulloa, and made him a brigadier general. Rivera began his travels in November, 1724. In the spring of 1727, on returning from his inspection tour to Santa Fé by way of Presidio del Paso del Norte and Sinaloa, he at last reached Coahuila. From Monclova he proceeded to San Juan Bautista and crossed the Río Grande into Texas two leagues northeast of the presidio.[2] At year's end he would return to the gateway, after having made observations that would shake the very foundations of the Spanish conquest of Texas. In the meantime another inspector came to the Río Grande.

Friar Miguel Sevillano de Paredes reached San Juan Bautista late in October. He carried a mandate from the commissary general of New Spain, Friar Fernando Alonzo González, as *visitador* of the missions of the Río Grande del Norte. He included among the missions of "the presidency of the Río Grande," in addition to San Juan Bautista, the Mission San Antonio de Valero, which he had already visited, and that of Santa María de los Dolores de la Punta, where he would compose his report.

Having entered Texas in 1716, Father Sevillano had just finished a period of service at San Antonio de Valero. He was on his way to Querétaro, where he would serve from late in 1727 till 1734 as guardian of the Colegio de la Santa Cruz. His inspection of the missions most likely was inspired by Rivera's inspection of the presidios and by Rivera's recommendations. Sevillano, who would have learned at San Antonio of the tack Rivera was taking in his recommendations, tuned his own report to meet the forthcoming one of the military man.

For years to come the two men—Sevillano as guardian of the College of Querétaro, Rivera as special adviser to the Viceroy—would be aligned against each other on the questions of how the missions should be managed and what help the presidios should lend to the missions. Each man,

---

[1] Retta Murphy "The Journey of Pedro de Rivera, 1724–1728," *SWHQ*, 41, No. 2 (October, 1937), 126.

[2] If the direction is given correctly, this would be Pacuache Crossing, rather than Paso de Francia.

of eminent stature and influential position, stood on the observations he had made during his inspection tour this year of 1727. The irony is found in the fact that they had not inspected the same establishments. While one surveyed missions, the other examined presidios. Each saw a different side of the coin. The controversy is typical of the divergent points of view always present in the two arms to which the conquest of New Spain was entrusted: the religious and the military.

That Sevillano included San Antonio de Valero among "the missions of the Río Grande del Norte" may in itself be significant. This mission, which would become known as the Alamo, was at this time the only Querétaran mission on the San Antonio River. The Mission of San José y San Miguel de Aguayo had been founded by Father Margil in 1721 for the Colegio de Nuestra Señora de Guadalupe de Zacatecas. The Mission of San Francisco Xavier de Nájera was shortlived, having been abandoned in 1726, before permanent quarters were erected. San Antonio de Valero, although moved from the Río Grande in 1718, remained under the jurisdiction of the "presidency of the Río Grande." The *visitador* himself explains by giving the history: "This Mission was founded first near the Mission of San Juan Bautista and that of San Bernardo on the Río Grande, with the name of San Francisco Solano. The Indians left it because of the scarcity of water, and the Mission was moved to a place fifteen leagues distant from the Río Grande, and given the name of San Ildefonso."[3]

But the Indians who came to the new location were few, and the trouble from the Gavilanes and other hostile Indians was great, Sevillano recalled. Tired of seeing their kinsmen slain, the converts asked that the mission be moved again to a place three leagues from the Mission San Bernardo, where the pueblo with the name of San José was established. This place also had little water, and the people of the Xarame nation were not pleased to have to come so far from their native land, on the Río de San Antonio, in order to enter the mission. Then one day, without warning, they stole away from San José and returned to their homeland. In time the mission was moved to the San Antonio River, where it was established with only five Indians, and given the name of San Antonio de Valero. Following a hurricane in 1724, when the mission buildings were

[3] Fray Miguel Sevillano de Paredes, "Visita de las Misiones del Río Grande," A.G.N., Historia, Vol. 29, p. 37.

destroyed, it was moved to a more commodious site.[4] In the ten years since the mission was moved, the Xarames had been gathered in from the surrounding area along the San Antonio River. They had been joined by the Payayas, Yerbipiames, Muruabes, and Pacuaches: a total of 273 Indians comprising sixty families. Materials had been gathered to build a church of stone, but the present church was of *jacal,* a straw hut, though a spacious one. During the three years since the mission had been moved, the principal concern had been with water development; an aqueduct, which would enable the mission to succeed in a material way, had been built, taking precedence over the building of the church, one missionary pointed out. The other missionary noted that the mission was near to the Apache Indians, who had twice robbed the pastures; hence it was considered necessary to make the church a bastion of defense, strongly built of stone. Time had been required to obtain the stone and to find stone masons, not an easy quest, because few were willing to come to such a dangerous region.[5]

Completing his visit to San Antonio de Valero by October 16, Sevillano de Paredes reached the Mission of San Juan Bautista on October 24. He spent three days in that mission, then proceeded to San Bernardo. In each mission he examined the books of administration and census and the inventories of mission property and made observations on spiritual and temporal matters.[6]

Padre Sevillano found the Mission of San Juan Bautista with seventy-one families of three nations: Mescales, Filijayes, and Pastalocos. These three and remnants of other nations had a total of 240 Indians, of whom 210 were Christians. The 30 non-Christians were being instructed in the catechism in order that they might receive the sacrament of baptism. Since the mission had been established, 364 Indians had died in the mission, including 260 "well-dressed" adults and 157 small children. This infor-

---

[4] *Ibid.,* p. 38. Not mentioned was the earlier move, about 1719, made by Padre Olivares, from the west bank of the San Antonio River to the east bank.

[5] For the complete remarks of Sevillano de Paredes on San Antonio de Valero see *ibid.,* pp. 35–41.

[6] Although the *visitador* drew separate reports on each establishment, the two gateway missions are treated together here for the convenience of the reader in making comparisons. The following account is based on the author's translation of Sevillano de Paredes, "Visita de las Misiones del Río Grande," *ibid.,* pp. 35–68.

mation was found in the Book of Funerals, the Books of Administration, and the Census of Indians.

At Mission San Bernardo were 200 Indians, forty-five families, made up of five nations: Pacuaches, Pastancoyas, Pastalocos, Pachales, and Pamasu. Of the 200 Indians, 165 were faithful Christians and 35 were being instructed in the catechism in order that they might be baptized. Some pages were missing from the Book of Funerals, which was old and worn, but the *visitador* was able to determine that 156 adults, baptized and well-disposed, and 30 baptized children had died.

Both missions had gathered other Indians who had fled back to the *montes*; the reason for their return to the wilds, he wrote, would be given at the conclusion of his visit to the last mission (Dolores de la Punta). Other nations which the padres had not been able to persuade to try mission life still roamed the wilds.

The ungathered included the nation of the Pampopas, consisting of 500 persons, to be found on the southern part of the Río de las Nueces, beyond the Río Grande, twenty-two leagues distant; the Tixilxos, 300 strong, also on the Nueces River, downstream from the Pampopas; the Patacales, with 400 persons, who had withdrawn from San Juan Bautista Mission and now dwelt to the south; and the Cacho Postales, a small nation which inhabited the country near the Pampopas. These nations, with a combined population of 1,200, came and went from San Juan Bautista, and most of them had kinsmen there. Some 200 members of the Filijayes nation were to come to the mission presently to join their tribesmen already there. Some of them had come into the mission for the observance of Lent, then gone back to their native habitat.

Other Indians of the region, more closely related to those missionized at San Bernardo than at San Juan, included the Pajalaques, 200 strong, inhabitants of the lower San Antonio River, forty leagues distant; the Pacos and the Pantascoyas, containing 100 persons, now joined together in flight from San Bernardo and to be found fifteen leagues away, on the lower Río Grande, at a place called Carrizo; the Panagues nation, small in number, found with other less numerous nations with combined strength of about 100 on the Nueces River, eighteen leagues away; the Pausanes, with population of 300, found sixty leagues away on the San Antonio River, a docile people who had retired after having come to San Bernardo for a year and a half asking to be placed in mission; the Pacuaches, many of whom were residents of the mission, which had 350 members in the wilds, having left because of lack of sustenance, since corn was not to be had; and the other members of the Pacuache nation, who most likely could be induced to come into the mission from their present dwelling place fifteen leagues away.

Proceeding to the inventory of farm implements and livestock owned by the missions, the *visitador* noted that the Mission San Juan had twenty-seven yokes of oxen, twenty-four plowshares, eighteen axes, thirty hoes, two iron shovels, a new cart for hauling corn, with the necessary plow straps and yokes.

The Mission San Bernardo had sixteen yokes of oxen, twenty-three plowshares, nineteen axes, eight sickles, four iron bars, eight pairs of shearing scissors, an iron shovel, and the necessary yokes and straps.

San Juan had more than 800 head of branded cattle with 225 calves for a total of 1,025, and two branding irons. San Bernardo's inventory showed 600 head of branded cattle, with 200 calves already on the ground and more coming—800 head in all. San Juan Bautista had 752 sheep and 400 goats; San Bernardo 465 sheep, 225 goats, and 117 lambs and kids.

The Mission San Juan owned considerably more horses and mules than her sister mission, with 25 broke horses, a herd of 32 mares, 12 burros, and 12 mules; while San Bernardo had only 12 horses and 2 mares, it did count 35 burros with nine sets of harness for these small beasts, which were used to haul corn. The latter mission had two branding irons and a forge for use in shoeing horses.

Produce of the missions included corn and beans, the abundance of the yields depending on the vagaries of the weather. Some years there were chilies enough to last the entire year, but other years there were few or none. Pumpkins and other vegetables were produced, the quantity depending upon the season. At San Juan Bautista some cotton was raised, along with an average annual yield of eight hundred fanegas of corn and nine of beans, though the harvest of beans was often less. San Bernardo had never been able to produce an adequate corn crop, because its supply of water for irrigation was not reliable. The scant crop often was consumed in the roasting ear stage, and usually the mission needed to obtain corn from San Juan each year by the month of June, because it had not been possible to make the fields productive. Only this year had the picture changed. The missionaries of San Juan had run an aqueduct from the Nogales (or Santa Rita) River, twelve or thirteen leagues long, to bring water to its fields. The ditch had not been finished; consequently, only the fields within its reach could be irrigated, the water playing out two leagues from the mission itself. A small flat-roofed house had been built in the field where the water was, to give the Indians who worked there safety in case the Apaches or the Tobosos should attack. These were the two tribes which habitually harassed the missions, the visitor noted; they once had raided the pastures and driven off thirty mares and other horses and smaller animals belonging to the missions.

While the *acequia* of San Juan Bautista Mission had not been finished, it evidently provided enough water so that this mission had no use for that which it had previously brought from the Arroyo de Castaño. Hence, San Bernardo, during this year of 1727, had been able to use the water which previously had been spread to both missions. Fields which could not be cultivated before were now planted. As a result its crops were abundant, with provisions enough to last an entire year having been produced.

Discussing the progress of the missions in temporal matters, Friar Miguel reviewed their history as he was given to understand it. We have already seen that the exact date of San Juan Bautista's early founding on the Río Grande was obscured because of the fact that the mission had been moved without authority from the Sabinas River.[7] This fact is borne out by the erroneous dates given by Sevillano de Paredes:

This Mission of San Juan Bautista had its first foundation on the Río de Sabinas, it seems, the year of 1701 [actually 1699]. It remained there only a very short time; since the Indians revolted, it was necessary to move it. This move was made the year of 1704 [actually January 1, 1700] to the place where it now is found on the Río Grande del Norte, which they call the Valle de la Circunsición. All this is contained in the paper of the foundation and transfer of this mission signed by General Don Matías de Aguirre, who was governor of the Presidio of Coahuila. Thus it is seen that it has been twenty-three years [actually twenty-seven years] since the founding of said mission at this place on the Río Grande.[8]

[7] See Chapter 2 of this study.
[8] Sevillano de Paredes, "Visita de las Misiones," pp. 44–45.

Friar Miguel goes on to relate that San Bernardo was founded "at this place on the Río Grande in 1703 [probably 1702], a year before the Mission of San Juan Bautista was moved from the Río de Sabinas" to its present site, two musket shots from San Bernardo, which had never been moved. "All this is contained in the Books of this Mission under the signatures of the Reverend Father Friar Francisco Estévez and Friar Francisco Hidalgo, who rest in peace."[9]

At the beginning twenty head of cattle had been placed in each mission, and they had reproduced under the watchful care of the missionaries, who had "applied their care to the increase of the temporal in order that the spiritual edifice might be established."[10]

The small livestock, from scant beginnings, given as alms for the padres, had increased from year to year, and the herd of mares had been diligently tended.

But not all the efforts of the missionaries had been directed at building the herds of livestock or bringing water to the *labores*. At San Juan Bautista a church had been built with three well-adorned altars, of which the main one had a large and beautiful gilded ciborium so that the elements of the sacraments could be deposited without risk. Since the sacristy was small and dark, a larger one was being made, which would be well lighted. By the time the report reached the commissary general, this improvement would be finished. The church had a belfry with four bells. A monastery, which had a spacious portico, had been made with sufficient cloister, containing seven cells, an office, and a ladder mounting to the choir loft. A handbell was kept by the principal door of the monastery, which also included a refectory and kitchen. A part of the establishment was a large corral with a wide gate with lock which was called *puerto del campo*. Near this "haven from the country" was a large cell, made especially for the convenience of visiting missionaries: "for when the news comes that the missionaries from Texas are entering."[11]

From this corral another gate led to the pen where the hens were kept. A path left by a door from the cloister, leading to the large orchard, which was surrounded by an adobe wall. This was truly an ornamental garden, with fig trees and other kinds, as well as plantings of vegetables. All the

9 *Ibid.*, p. 52.
10 *Ibid.*, p. 52.
11 *Ibid.*, p. 45.

conventitos, the little monasteries, had clean, whitewashed walls; the doors which looked from the cells to the outside had lattice of hardwood.

The village for the Indians was made up of fifteen flat-roofed houses, seventeen thatch-roofed adobes, and rancherias. Little by little work was being done to make the entire village of *terrado,* replacing the thatch with flat roofs. A stone gallery had been constructed which held more than a thousand fanegas of corn. There was a corral of adobe and stone, with stalls for the mares, and two other corrals for the cattle, one of stakes, the other of stone.

The Indians had some little gardens, with fig trees and vegetable plantings. A little ranch had been made on the lands of the Mission San Juan. After the aqueduct to bring water from the Arroyo de Castaño had been built, a gallery for corn and a small stone house for the Indians was erected on the ranch to encourage the Indians to live and work there as much as possible, making a contribution to the upkeep of the mission.

Like San Juan Bautista, the Mission San Bernardo also had a beautiful church, with altar and furniture well adorned. There were two cells, two offices, and a kitchen, "all enclosed under one door with its patio."[12] A large corral had been constructed, with two rooms built into the walls— the rooms, having just been built, as yet had no roof. There was a large gallery of stone, and two other corrals for the cattle; an orchard with different kinds of fruit trees had been started, and vegetables for the mission were also grown there. The pueblo consisted of five flat-roofed houses, sixteen of adobe and *jacal,* plus all the rancherias. This mission had two bells in its belfry.

Although the Mission San Bernardo had shown gains on the one hand, in some respects it had been left behind. The reason for its lack of progress had been a scarcity of corn to feed the Indians, who seized the excuse to flee back to the wilds in search of liberty and leisure. But with the improved supply of water it was hoped that crops would be more abundant in the future, and San Bernardo would at last begin to prosper.

Both of the gateway missions had the necessities for divine worship, including sacred vessels and ornaments for celebrating mass, and "all that is conducive to the correct administration of the Holy Sacraments."[13]

[12] *Ibid.,* p. 52. The church in existence at this time was not the stone church which still stands, as will be seen.
[13] *Ibid.,* p. 46.

The Christian doctrine was taught in the morning, and in the afternoon the missionary explained the text of the doctrine in terms appropriate to the limited understanding of the Indians.

It is evident to all in this Presidio del Río Grande that the Indians know the expounded principal mysteries of Our Holy Faith, since they have been heard to say it in the church and in the plaza. They begin by responding to the articles of faith, the sacraments, and the rest by the sign of the Holy Cross. . . . The Spaniards should confess that they do not know the Doctrine as the Indians know it.[14]

At San Bernardo, Sevillano observed, "The Indians pray the Rosary every Saturday together in the Church, singing some devotionals and the Litany of Our Lady. Many Indian men and women confess, but few take communion, since most are uninitiated. They were born to their ideas, having come from the wilds."[15]

The Indian men and women of Mission San Juan, being more advanced in the faith, went to the presidio every Saturday with the Rosary of the Virgin, singing in procession, to assist the presidials "in the devotional function." Most of the Indians heard Mass every day of their own volition. Many of the baptized confessed and took communion, and were accustomed to the sung rosary as well as other devotional songs which they had been taught. "They have quit their diabolical songs, and it was common for the boys and girls, and even the *indios grandes* [to be heard] singing the *Padre Nuestro* and *Ave María* by the pueblo."[16]

The sacraments were administered to the Indians with great care, the ill were assisted in the spiritual and the temporal, and the dying were carefully attended until the last, then buried "without profit" by the missionary. The religious went personally to console, to give medicine and food to the ill Indians. The Indians often were clothed with apparel purchased with the alms which the King gave for provisionment of the missionary. The priest also assisted in ministering to the presidio, preaching to the soldiers and the citizens, and to those who lived on scattered ranches, administering the sacraments to them.

Father Sevillano was able to visualize continued progress in the two

[14] *Ibid.*, p. 47.
[15] *Ibid.*, p. 53.
[16] *Ibid.*, p. 47.

missions, with more nations of Indians expected to come to be mission-ized. "When these pagans come to this Mission," he said of San Juan Bautista, "they are received and treated kindly." The Filijayes and the Pampopas nations gave indication that they would come to join the mission, "because they are not as peevish of soul as they once were." They made no resistance to the explication of the Christian doctrine. "It is hoped in God our Lord that if there is encouragement by the military, many souls will be won for God in this Mission."[17]

The Pacuaches, especially, would come to the Mission San Bernardo if they but had the encouragement of the military, Father Sevillano theorized. One of the reasons they remained in the *montes* was the lack of sustenance in the mission, but the mission had been blessed just this year with the remedy. However, the Indians must have the encouragement and help of the soldiers.

The commissary visitor finished his report on San Bernardo on October 28, 1727, and proceeded to the Mission of Santa María de los Dolores de la Punta, at present Lampazos, Nuevo León, to begin his inspection there November 4. Only twelve families, fifty-one persons, of two nations (Pitas and Pajalves) were found, all baptized Christians. The rest were fugitives in the *montes*. Among the items lost when the Tobosos Indians struck the mission in 1714 were its record books. Just the previous May 3 the enemy Indians had driven off thirty-three horses.

As for the produce of this fourth and last mission of the presidency of the Río Grande, it was more uncertain than the rest. The other three missions had only the inconstance of the weather to consider; but to the inequality of the seasons here was added the inconstance of the Indians. Some years there was no harvest because the seasons did not allow it; other years there was none because the Indians fled and there were no workers. Many times since its founding in 1698 had the mission been set back by the natives' infidelity.

The Indians in this mission, observed the visitor, were the least advanced of any to be found in the four missions of the group, as a result of their repeated flights; the missionaries could not instruct them in Christianity and government when they were absent.

On finishing his report on Mission de los Dolores, the *visitador* set

---

[17] *Ibid.*, p. 48.

himself to the painful task of giving a "comprehensive general account" of all the missions he had visited. For this purpose he had gathered reports from each of the religious on how the produce and livestock of the missions were expended, the reasons for the flight of the *gentiles,* as well as some Christians, away from the missions; what factors induced them to forsake their barbarous life in the first place, and the methods used in teaching the catechism. On the latter point he noted that by mandate of the commissary general, scripts of the catechisms of the Father Maestro Ripalda had been placed in each mission of the presidency, as well as in each of the Querétaran missions of the presidency of the Tejas, and these were explained to the Indians in terms appropriate to their intelligence.

As for how the livestock and produce were expended, he reported that in the missions of San Juan Bautista, San Bernardo, and San Antonio de Valero, two large beeves were killed for sustenance of the Indians each fifteen days. A beef was killed whenever there was a wedding, for *fiestas* as Christmas and Easter, or at any feast time. This practice was not followed at La Punta, however, because there were so few cattle. A hundred head of sheep and goats were drawn each year for distribution to the Indians as an inducement for them to remain in the missions. Whenever an Indian asked for one to eat, it was given him. An animal would also be killed for any ill person. The religious were maintained from this same livestock, though the Indians took the greater part.

The corn grown in the mission *labores* was divided among the Indians, by nation, at a designated hour each day. If the year was abundant and a surplus was produced, it was bartered to the presidials for cloth to dress the Indians. But in the lean years, no corn was traded in the presidios; all was consumed by the Indians.

The beans grown provided rations for Lent and for fast days, as long as they lasted. Through the paternal diligence of the missionaries, watermelons, cantaloupes, and pumpkins were planted; the fruit was given to each Indian according to his service and stability. Such items as salt, soap, and brown sugar loaves were divided among those who were most deserving, as a means of keeping them "friendly and constant in the missions."[18] This practice was common in all the missions, the visitor stated.

Each year, observed Father Sevillano, the King gave each religious 450

18 *Ibid.,* p. 62.

pesos. In these missions the amount was expended by the legal representative *(síndico)* for cloth, tools, tobacco, glass beads, and rosaries for the Indians, and to keep the tools and implements used by the Indians on the farms in good repair. Even so, it often was necessary to make clothing for the Indians from the used cloaks and tunics of the missionaries, especially to clothe the nakedness of some of the Indian women.

Great changes had been wrought by the missionaries in the lives of the Indians, Sevillano believed. Without the padres' kindly teaching many dying children would have gone unbaptized, and many adults "who we believe are mercifully gained for God, dying, as they died, baptized, sacramented, and disposed."[19] Without the encouragement of the missionaries the Indians would still dwell as irrational souls in the *montes,* as was proved in those areas where the priestly influence was not felt.

Yet the Indians of the missions still were not able to govern themselves; it was therefore necessary to withhold from them their freedom of choice —and their corn and their cattle. If the means of their sustenance were left to them, not a bone would remain within two months. Then, with pretext of having to hunt deer and buffalo for food, they would return to the wilds. Such had been the case in other missions which had allowed the Indians to take their cattle and use them as they saw fit. These Indians were now found in the *montes* without form of missions.

Those natives who fled the missions of the Río Grande to return to their native habitat, said the visitor, did so only in search of their liberty, "that they might indulge themselves in their ancient vices without having anyone to apply the rein to their bestial appetites."[20] It was difficult for them to see themselves as being subject to the captains of the presidios. From the beginning it had been the custom to follow the fugitives and bring them back to the missions from the hills and the woods, but no longer was this done, apparently because of a lack of cooperation on the part of the presidial captains. As a result the march of the Gospel was halted; many were the missions which could be founded and innumerable the pagan souls which could be saved with the application of only a gentle force by the military—in the opinion of Father Sevillano, who may have been right, but who also was a missionary himself. The missionaries, he contended, could not go alone to the *montes* to bring the fugitive

---

[19] *Ibid.,* p. 63.
[20] *Ibid.,* p. 63.

Indians in; aside from the obvious risk of going without armed protection, they had no knowledge of the places where the fugitives had
gone. Nor did it seem prudent to leave the missions exposed to attack, the
Christian Indians to die without sacraments should some emergency arise.
The soldiers could easily bring them in, said the commissary visitor, as
was evidenced in the uprising of Indians at San Juan Bautista and San
Bernardo, when only sixteen men with the religious sufficed to draw more
than five hundred barbarians armed with bows and arrows from the
rancheria grande and to obtain their return to the missions.[21]

It had been imagined, recalled Father Sevillano, that the coming of the
inspector general of the presidios (Pedro de Rivera) would bring a
remedy to this ill which hampered progress of the missions. But the actual
result of Rivera's visit had been quite to the contrary. The Brigadier had
ordered back to their presidios the soldiers assigned to the missions to
protect the missionaries and to instruct the Indians and make them work.
Rivera had given such instructions at San Juan and San Bernardo, and
only at the strenuous protest of the mission president had he agreed to
stay the order until he returned from Texas.

At San Antonio de Valero the military inspector had taken away the
guard even though the missionaries were left exposed to the ravages of
the Apaches. If Texas were left as the Brigadier intended, said the missionary visitor, all would be finished. It was a notorious outrage against
the missionaries, and a matter not to be passed over, he asserted.

"The inspector says the King does not wish the Indians forced, yet he
does not acknowledge that the spiritual baptisms are subject to the laws of
the Church and of the King, and that [the Indians] are obliged to be
compelled to complete the obligation which they have contracted: of
being subject to the Church and the Catholic King."[22]

It was quite possible for the religious themselves to work the fields, care

---

[21] *Ibid.*, p. 65. This statement evidently refers to Diego Ramón's *entrada* of
1707, when he was accompanied by Father Isidro Félix de Espinosa. Although
Ramón had a force of thirty-one soldiers and citizens, sixteen is the number he
took from San Juan Bautista. The others came from Presidio de San Francisco de
Coahuila (see Chapter 8 of this study). The *rancheria grande* mentioned here,
however, was on the Nueces River and is not to be confused with the one on the
Brazos, as is done in Walter Prescott Webb and H. Bailey Carroll (eds.), *The
Handbook of Texas*, II, 435.

[22] Sevillano de Paredes, "Visita de las Misiones," p. 67.

for the livestock, and do the other temporal things, said Sevillano. With help of the soldiers they could perform these tasks and still extend the catechism, administer the sacraments, and meet other spiritual necessities; but without such help, it would be impossible. Without the firm hand of the padre and the soldier, the Indians refused to work and drifted back to paganism. Even so the *visitador general* was withdrawing the aid of the military, forbidding the soldiers to go out and bring in fugitives: "Without doubt it is the end of all."[23]

Immediate action to repair this damage would bring an increase to the missions; but that which was needed for the Gospel to make progress was the encouragement of the military.

Thus Father Miguel Sevillano de Paredes concluded his report at the Mission of Santa María de los Dolores—St. Mary of Sorrows—November 4, 1727, subscribed to by the secretary of the visit, Friar Francisco de Bustamante. Then the commissary visitor turned his steed southward over the long winding road to Querétaro, where he would assume the responsibilities of guardian of the College of the Holy Cross. As successor to Padre Pedro Pérez de Mezquía he would serve until 1730, during which time he was the titular head of the Querétaran missions. At the same time Pedro de Rivera was the principal adviser to the Viceroy. The battle lines were already drawn. Even before the Brigadier had issued his report and made his recommendations to the Marqués de Casafuerte, Father Sevillano had spelled out the basis for his opposition. In the coming years he would frequently resort to the arguments presented in his report on the Río Grande Missions in making appeals to the Viceroy and to the King.

[23] *Ibid.*

18. THE ISLANDERS

MANY OF THE RECOMMENDATIONS to come out of the *visita* of Don
Pedro de Rivera, so objectionable to Father Sevillano and the Col-
lege of Querétaro, stemmed in the first place from the ideas put forth by
a priest. Castañeda blames the evil result on the irresponsible tack taken by
Friar José González, in his effort to have Captain Nicolás Flores of the
Presidio of San Antonio replaced by a private from San Juan Bautista.[1]

The fruits of Rivera's visit may be summarized as follows: The presidios of Texas were reorganized, the personnel sharply reduced. The
oldest presidio, that of Nuestra Señora de los Dolores de los Tejas, was
abolished. Three of the missions in East Texas were removed to the banks
of the San Antonio River.[2] There were many other effects not so easily
discernible. Perhaps the overall result was the lessening of cooperation
between religious and military and, consequently, a deterioration in the
relationship of the missionaries with the Indians. As Sevillano de Paredes
had pointed out in his own visit to the Río Grande missions, no longer
would soldiers be assigned to protect the missions and to help the missionaries instruct the Indians. No longer would the soldiers go out to bring in
fugitives. The natives were quick to sense the weakening of the grasp
upon them. Henceforth the priestly task would be more difficult.

In December, 1727, the visitor general's party, having traversed South
Texas from Presidio de la Bahía at its new location on the Guadalupe
River, forded the big river and beat a dusty trail into the Presidio of San
Juan Bautista del Río Grande. He made skimpy notes on the gateway
fortress, observing that it maintained a company of thirty-three, including
the captain, officers, and chaplain, who drew pay, and that it had the

[1] Carlos Eduardo Castañeda, *Our Catholic Heritage in Texas,* II, 197.
[2] *Ibid.,* p. 267.

quantity of powder which the Brigadier had prescribed.[3] The soldiers were well equipped and well trained. The annual cost of maintaining the post was 10,200 pesos, with the soldiers paid 300 pesos per year, the captain 600.[4]

Then the *visitador general* settled himself to the task of compiling his thoughts and observations on Texas, which, as he saw it, had only three real settlements: Los Adaes, Béjar, and La Bahía. On January 1, 1728, he finished his work at San Juan Bautista and departed by his former road to Monclova, where similar work detained him three weeks.[5] When at last he reached the capital he spent four months compiling his report. Then he became private counselor to the Viceroy in all matters pertaining to the frontier outposts. When the many complaints regarding his reforms began to pour in, he himself ruled on their validity. And it might be said that the complainants in such cases did not have a prayer.

In the wake of Rivera's inspection trip to Texas arose various circumstances which created new demands on San Juan Bautista. The three Querétaran missions in East Texas, left without military protection, were moved first to the Colorado River, then to the San Antonio. Large numbers of Indians were congregated at the new sites, and provisions had to be brought in. From San Juan Bautista 800 fanegas of corn were supplied at a cost of fourteen reales each, plus four and a half pesos for transportation; 250 head of cattle were purchased at the Río Grande missions for six pesos and two reales per head, not counting transportation costs to San Antonio.[6]

Many were the protests, meanwhile, which poured into Rivera's own hands regarding the action he had brought about. The missionaries vehemently protested the removal of the mission guards, but Rivera, as might have been expected, failed to give heed. At San Juan Bautista, Rivera had pointed out to the Viceroy, each of the missions kept two soldiers to act as managers and overseers of the mission farms. This prac-

[3] Pedro de Rivera, "Proyecto y Visita," A.G.N., Provincias Internas, Vol. 29, p. 141.

[4] Vito Alessio Robles, *Coahuila y Texas en la época colonial*, p. 477.

[5] Retta Murphy, "The Journey of Pedro de Rivera, 1724–1728," *SWHQ*, 41, No. 2 (October, 1937), 137.

[6] Fray Pedro Pérez de Mezquía to the Viceroy, May 4, 1731, A.G.N., Provincias Internas, Vol. 236, p. 39.

tice had originated at the time of the establishment of the presidio, but many Indians had since been congregated and had adopted the ways of civilized men; the presence of the soldiers no longer was necessary, he said. If the missionaries felt that a Spaniard could do guard duty better, they could obtain the services of one of the civilian settlers in the vicinity. The conditions which prevailed at San Juan Bautista, said Rivera, were true also of other Franciscan and Jesuit missions all along the frontier. In his opinion the soldiers should be returned to their presidios.

Father Sevillano, the guardian of the College of Querétaro, thwarted by Rivera, addressed himself directly to the King. Pointing out the difference in the nature of the Indians along the Río Grande and in Texas from those in the Mexican interior, he cited instances in which the two soldiers assigned to the missions had saved life and property. In 1722, for example, the Tobosos had attacked some religious who were approaching San Juan Bautista. Their baggage was lost, but two soldiers and a party of mission Indians from San Juan arrived in time to save their lives. In 1728 the Apaches had attacked the Mission of San Juan Bautista and stolen the entire horseherd. The two soldiers who guarded San Juan stood off the savages with their musket fire until help came from the presidio.[7]

In view of this direct appeal to the monarch, Rivera may have realized at last that it was time to retreat; on his advice the Viceroy agreed that one soldier should be provided each mission during the daytime, returning to the presidio at night. For the missionaries half a loaf was better than none.

In the meantime, it was decreed that the guard of twelve men stationed at Saltillo to provide escort for missionaries and mission supplies between that point and San Juan Bautista and thence on to Texas should be abolished. The service would be performed by soldiers of the Presidio of San Francisco de Coahuila, at Monclova, which had received an added increment of ten men back in 1721. Escort would be provided for no more than four trips per year.

But the removal of the East Texas missions to the San Antonio River had increased the number of trips now being made between San Antonio and the Río Grande. The missionaries were not always able to wait for the quarterly trip of the soldier escort, and their urgency frequently led to disaster. On January 9, 1731, for example, two missionaries, Fray Sal-

[7] Fray Miguel Sevillano, Memorial to the King, November 12, 1729, in Archivo del Colegio de la Santa Cruz, 1716–1749, pp. 3–4.

vador de Amaya and Fray Francisco de Bustamante, with a special escort of five men from Presidio de Béjar, on their way to San Juan Bautista, fell victim on the Medina River of an attack by fifty Apaches. A woman was killed, a child captured, and the baggage lost. The Apaches grew bolder, and the following April 17 a party of eighty hostiles surprised a group of soldiers driving a herd of horses to the Río Grande at the same place the missionaries were attacked. All the horses were lost. And on June 25 Father Benito de Santa Ana and Brother Esteban Zaes Monge, traveling from San Antonio de Valero to the Río Grande, were attacked by Apaches who killed two soldiers of the escort, drove off all the horses, and took the personal baggage.[8] And once again Rivera was forced to yield; he recommended that the Viceroy instruct the presidios of San Antonio de Béjar and San Juan Bautista to provide an escort of eight men and a corporal for the missionaries whenever it was necessary for them to travel to and from the Río Grande to get provisions.

Father Sevillano de Paredes also raised his voice to the King regarding the end which had been brought to the practice of sending soldiers out to bring back fugitive Indians. His appeal reiterated the arguments he had presented to the commissary general in the report of his visit to the missions of the Río Grande in 1727. Since that time conditions had grown no better; the fears expressed in the earlier report had been fully justified.

Father Joseph González, apparently a different missionary from the one who had raised the ruckus at San Antonio, now was president of the missions of the Río Grande, headquartered at San Juan Bautista. With him were Fathers Francisco Vergara, Joseph Hurtado, Benito Sánchez de Santa Ana, Salvador de Amaya, Luis de la Cruz, and Antonio de San Juan.[9]

In June, 1729, the King granted the urgent petition of Fathers Sevillano de Paredes and Matías Sáenz de San Antonio to send twelve additional missionaries from Spain to work in the Querétaran missions in Texas and on the Río Grande. They reached New Spain in November, 1730, the year that Sevillano was succeeded as guardian by Father Pedro Pérez de Mezquía. When the retiring official terminated his guardianship,

---

[8] Pérez de Mezquía to the Viceroy, August 8, 1731, A.G.N., Provincias Internas, Vol. 236, pp. 47–48.

[9] Castañeda, *Our Catholic Heritage*, II, 254.

which had come at a most difficult time, the brigadier, Pedro de Rivera, still held firmly to his post as personal adviser to the Viceroy.

In the meantime soldiers of the Presidio de San Juan Bautista were busy escorting a growing number of travelers to Texas.

Despite its wealthy potential, Texas fell far short of acquiring economic independence [says Alessio Robles]. All the settlements were precarious and were required to provision themselves of goods in México, Saltillo, and San Juan Bautista del Río Grande. From Saltillo [via San Juan Bautista] came almost all their provisions.[10]

The hooves of plodding mules stirred a spiral of brownish gray dust across the Río Grande plain from the Great River to San Antonio. The backs of these wiry little animals carried the sustenance of the Texas missions. Some of the trains formed at the gateway settlement, while for others, coming from the south, San Juan Bautista was but a welcome oasis on the long trail. With the trains rode the soldiers of Presidio de San Juan Bautista del Río Grande, mounted on foam-flecked horses, toughened by a difficult environment. The soldiers carried muskets ever at the ready to defend themselves and their charges against surprise attack by the dreaded Apaches.

The padres traveled on muleback or walked alongside, their loose-fitting habits flapping in the Gulf breeze, their bare or sandaled feet stirring the trail dust to mingle with the clouds which rose from the hammering hooves of the beasts of burden.

Yet the settlements in Texas needed more than just the sustenance which could be brought to them from Coahuila on the backs of mules. It needed settlers. Almost since 1716 the missionaries had recognized the need to bring in Spanish families to form a civilian settlement adjacent to the missions. In 1719 the Council of the Indies recommended that the King issue orders for transporting two thousand families from the Canary Islands and Galicia to Texas by way of Veracruz. The plan, which called for founding a number of settlements, beginning at Espíritu Santo Bay, did not meet royal favor. In 1722 the Marqués de Aguayo asked that two hundred families be sent in order to place a colony near each of the Texas presidios and on the bay, so that the Texas settlements could be made

[10] Alessio Robles, *Coahuila y Texas,* p. 514.

permanent. He was joined in his proposal by the viceroy, Marqués de Valero.

Such ideas were discussed for years, during which time Pedro de Rivera characteristically sought to debunk Aguayo's plan and substitute one of his own.[11]

At last, on March 27, 1730, the first ten families of an expected four hundred embarked from Santa Cruz, Tenerife, uncertain as to their actual destination. The Canary Islanders arrived in Veracruz, by way of Havana, the following June 30, and rested there while details of the remainder of their journey were being worked out. Largely through the influence of Rivera it was decided to send the colonists overland to San Antonio de Béjar instead of by sea to Espíritu Santo Bay, as had been contemplated. In August they proceeded to Cuautitlán, where they remained two and a half months before starting the long march to Texas on November 15.[12] By that time there had been several changes in the make-up of the colonists. Two persons had died at Veracruz, one on the road to Cuautitlán, and two infants during the stay at Cuautitlán.[13] There had been five marriages also; hence, the number of families had increased from ten to fifteen. Some of the original group had fled, no longer desirous of finding a home in the wilderness, and two Canary Islanders, already in México, joined the group when they found their sweethearts among it. (Theirs were two of the five marriages.)

The fifty-six persons arrived at Saltillo on January 29, 1731, thoroughly exhausted. Here they rested while Captain Matías de Aguirre, on orders from the Viceroy, supplied them with eighty-six horses, seventy-seven mules, sixteen yokes of oxen—a plow, an axe, and a hoe to go with each one—and sixteen *metates* with corresponding *manos,* none of which, it is said, did the viceregal government ever pay for.[14]

In mid-February the colonists arrived at San Juan Bautista, and once again tragedy struck the group. A little girl, María Rodríguez Granadilla,

[11] See Castañeda, *Our Catholic Heritage,* II, 268–278.

[12] *Ibid.* See also I. J. Cox, "The Early Settlers of San Fernando," *SWHQ,* 5, No. 1 (July, 1901), 142–170.

[13] The statement of Cox ("The Early Settlers of San Fernando," p. 143) that the only death of the journey was Juan Cabrera at Veracruz, and that of Paul Horgan (*Great River: The Río Grande in North America,* p. 338) that the only casualty, a five-year-old girl, died at San Juan Bautista, evidently are in error.

[14] Alessio Robles, *Coahuila y Texas,* p. 471.

five years old, died there. Her father, Juan Rodríguez Granadilla, had been the first person to die on the journey, having succumbed at Veracruz. The death of the child was the only one to occur after the islanders left Cuautitlán.

The captain of the Presidio of San Juan Bautista, José Antonio de Ecay Múzquiz, under instructions from the Viceroy, provided an escort to take the colonists on to San Antonio.

It was his responsibility, according to the detailed instructions, to get them safely across the Río Grande, and on to their destination by way of Las Rosas de San Juan, Caramanchel, Charcos de la Tortuga, the Frío, the Hondo, Charco de la Pita, and Arroyo de los Payayas.[15] On March 9, 1731, the islanders reached their new home, having consumed the better part of a year in their journey.

The *isleños* left their worn-out horses at Presidio de San Juan Bautista, and it appears that the animals became the center of a controversy which lasted some months. Late in 1731, Juan Leal Goraz, a leader among the colonists, arrived in the city of México with a petition from his fellow islanders asking that the horses left at the Presidio of the Río Grande be given to them. Actually the horses belonged to the government, having been provided only to take the settlers to their destination. By decree of November 28, 1730, the colonists had been provided with other livestock, but no mention was made of horses. Furthermore, the Viceroy was provoked at the presumptuousness of one of the islanders in coming to the capital to confront him with such an issue. He rebuked the Texas governor, Juan Antonio Bustillo y Ceballos, for allowing the man to leave the province and ordered that Canary Islanders not be permitted to do so in the future. Nevertheless, he granted the request of Leal, and the horses were distributed among the colonists.[16]

With only fifteen families having been transported from the Canary Islands to settle in Texas, the project was ended. The fact that no more settlers were sent is directly traceable to Pedro de Rivera, who "was sincere in his recommendations, but he failed to see the far-reaching implications of his short-sighted policy, dictated by his mania for economy and to some extent by his personal aversions to the view of the Marquis of Aguayo."[17]

[15] Castañeda, *Our Catholic Heritage*, II, 294.
[16] Cox, "The Early Settlers of San Fernando," pp. 150–154.
[17] Castañeda, *Our Catholic Heritage*, II, 283–284.

Once again Spain had turned away from a course which might have helped her hold on to her far-flung New World empire.

The coming of the islanders added to the strings of pack mules that beat the dusty trail from Coahuila to San Antonio, sometimes starting from San Juan Bautista, sometimes originating elsewhere and only pausing there for a rest.

A large portion of the finished materials for their houses, and of living necessities (for the time at least) had to be transported on pack animals from the interior of México. This was the case with supplies for the presidial garrison [at Béjar], and must necessarily continue for some time for the new colonists.[18]

During much of the tenure of Juan de Acuña, Marqués de Casafuerte, as viceroy, the hand of Pedro de Rivera was felt in the manipulation of affairs pertaining to management of the missions. When Casafuerte died in 1734, however, to be succeeded by Juan Antonio de Vizarrón y Guiarreta, archbishop of México, Rivera had already departed México (1732) to become president of the Audiencia of Guatemala. Nevertheless, the deleterious effects of his influence would be felt among the northern settlements for years to come. Even though the efforts of Father Sevillano and Father Mezquía had helped to counteract some of these results, the Rivera influence was much in evidence at San Juan Bautista in 1734. It could be seen in the relationship between presidio and missions, a fact which troubled a thirty-five–year–old missionary named Alonso Giraldo de Terreros.

A native of Cortegana, in the Spanish province of Huelva, Terreros had come to New Spain with his parents when he was yet a small child. He had prepared himself for missionary work at the College of the Holy Cross in Querétaro, to enter the priesthood July 14, 1721, when he was twenty-two years old.[19]

Before coming to San Juan Bautista he had served in one of the East Texas missions. In 1729, on July 20, he joined with the other priests of those conversions, in placing his name to a "Representation of the Religious" which protested the suppression of Presidio de los Tejas under order of Rivera. If the garrison could not be kept, the missionaries pleaded,

18 Cox, "The Early Settlers of San Fernando," p. 150.
19 Robert S. Weddle, *The San Sabá Mission: Spanish Pivot in Texas*, p. 39.

then His Excellency should order the religious returned to their college.[20] Father Terreros was rapidly becoming known for his living faith and missionary zeal, his concern for his fellowman, and his desire to spread the Christian Gospel among the Indians. Seldom if ever did he shrink from debate when he knew he was right. Often did he grieve when his firm stance embroiled him in controversy and his zeal provoked animosity. In his thirty-seven years as a missionary on the frontiers of New Spain, he would render valuable service to God and king, until at last he achieved the crown of martyrdom.

Father Terreros, arriving at San Juan Bautista in the early 1730's found the gateway missions caught in the backwash of Rivera's reforms. The work of the missionaries was being seriously hampered by the restrictions placed upon the services they could obtain from the soldiers. Whether he acted on his own initiative or on instructions from Father Sevillano—who may have felt that his own effectiveness had been impaired by his repeated pleas—is not known. Nevertheless, he went to the heart of the matter. From among the papers dealing with the founding of the gateway settlement, he produced the documents which showed the reasons for the placing of the presidio. Convinced that he held an effective weapon, he took the papers and made the long journey to the capital to present himself before the Viceroy-Archbishop June 17, 1734. He made his appeal as follows:

The Count of Moctezuma, when he was viceroy, had ordered by dispatch of March 28, 1701, the establishment of a flying company of thirty men and one officer; the purpose of the company was to travel over the lands of the Río Grande missions, helping the missionaries to govern and to provide other assistance conducive to the stated purpose of the missions; the dispatch had been thoroughly abused through the years, but the missionaries considered its directive to be unalterable. He asked assurance of such from the Viceroy-Archbishop.

The superior dispatch, in full context, was reviewed by the high official, including a summary of the appeal for protection made by Father Antonio de San Buenaventura y Olivares, whose death had been plotted by some of the barbarous Indians.[21]

[20] *Documentos para la historia de Texas o Nuevas Philipinas, 1720–1779,* Vol. 12, pp. 92–95.
[21] San Juan Bautista, "Testimonio del Decreto de Fundación del Presidio de

Plainly evident from the *testimonio* was one fact: The missionaries who had founded the gateway missions had gone out alone, without guarantee of permanent military protection, to extend the dominion of both Majesties. The military came later, and then only because soldiers were needed to help carry on the work of the missions. The religious purpose behind establishment of the presidio stood out from every angle.

The missionaries and the officer in charge together designated the place where the flying company was stationed. The company was to consist of thirty men and an officer "for assisting the mission of San Juan Bautista . . . for use in going over the lands in order to free the Missionaries and inhabitants from the invasions of the barbarians."[22] The company should be divided into three squads of ten men each, two of the squads to travel continually over all the country "for protection of the religious, the increase and conversion of Christianity, discovering of the settlements and designs of the French. . . . The other squad shall be maintained always in company and assistance of the missionaries, without losing sight of them, in order that it may defend them against the barbarous nations."[23]

There is little indication that the relationship between the religious and the military improved appreciably as a result of Father Terreros' appeal based on history. In years to come this very priest would be at the center of a storm which revolved around the divergent points of view of "these two parallel and inevitably conflicting agencies."[24]

San Juan Bautista," A.G.N., Historia, Vol. 29, pp. 69–75. See also Chapter 4 of this study.

[22] *Ibid.*, pp. 72–75.

[23] *Ibid.*

[24] Weddle, *San Sabá Mission,* p. 142; Paul D. Nathan (trans.) and Lesley Byrd Simpson (ed.), *The San Sabá Papers: A Documentary Account of the Founding and Destruction of San Sabá Mission,* p. 115.

19. UP THE RIO GRANDE

UNFORTUNATE as Rivera's advice on mission matters was, his tour bore fruit of another kind. At the start of his official journey viceregal counselors had suggested that his trip include exploration of the Río Grande from San Juan Bautista to La Junta de los Ríos, where the Río Grande was joined by the Río de los Conchos. Rivera, finding himself unable to pursue this suggestion without slighting his main business of inspecting presidios, kept the idea in mind until he returned to the capital. Then he proposed a special expedition to explore the region upstream from San Juan Bautista. The viceroy, Marqués de Casafuerte, ordered the governor of Nueva Vizcaya, Ignacio Francisco de Barrutia, to organize the expedition.

Chosen to head it was Captain José de Berroterán, commandant of the Presidio of San Francisco de los Conchos. Berroterán would organize a force made up of troops from the presidios of Conchos, Mapimí, San Francisco de Coahuila, and San Juan Bautista. Starting point for the exploration was to be San Juan Bautista. For Berroterán and his troops from Conchos, the task of reaching the point of beginning was a major one. From San Juan Bautista he was to proceed up the Río Grande over country which few men had traveled since the unauthorized *entrada* of Gaspar Castaño de Sosa in 1590. This was country occupied by hostile Indians who preyed relentlessly upon the frontier settlements of Nueva Vizcaya and Coahuila. It included some of the most rugged and inhospitable terrain the Spaniards had yet attempted to conquer.[1]

The Río Grande, from El Paso to La Junta de los Ríos, near present

---

[1] This is the area which James Manly Daniel ("The Advance of the Spanish Frontier and the Despoblado") has termed the Despoblado, "a great arid, unpopulated region that comprises three fourths of western Coahuila, a third of Chihuahua and Trans-Pecos Texas region" (pp. 1–2). The northward advance of settlement in colonial México, says Daniel (p. iii), split and by-passed the Despoblado,

Presidio, Texas, had been traversed in 1683 by Juan Domínguez de Mendoza, who with Friar Nicolás López established six missions in the vicinity of La Junta. But the region between that point and San Juan Bautista remained virtually unknown, the river's dark chasms an unexplored mystery.

Berroterán's purpose was threefold: to explore the country, to look for a site for a new presidio, and to find and punish the natives who had laid waste to north Mexican settlements. The fact that he was more conscious of the Indian threat than his instructions intended probably was due to the influence of the officers of Presidio de San Juan Bautista. However, it brought criticism upon the head of Berroterán from Don Pedro de Rivera himself.

From his remote presidio in Nueva Vizcaya, Berroterán set out January 13, 1729, traveling southeastward to Mapimí. By a circuitous route he arrived at his starting point, San Juan Bautista, March 15, to remain there several days waiting for detachments from Monclova and Mapimí to catch up. He spent the time gathering supplies for the expedition.[2]

On March 20 the *alférez*, Diego Jiménez, arrived from the Presidio of San Francisco de Coahuila with fourteen men and supplies, and twenty Indians from the pueblos of Caldera and Santiago. Berroterán, on March 26, presented an *escrito* to Don Joseph Antonio de Ecay Múzquiz, requesting his assistance in charting the course of the expedition, and his advice as to the best method of apprehending the enemy Indians. Ecay Múzquiz was asked also to "convene the most experienced and intelligent persons to be found in the jurisdiction, who have done military service . . . to express their feeling on matters appropriate to the service of both Majesties," and the best manner of carrying out the expedition.[3]

---

which was avoided because it was generally unfit for settlement by Europeans of the time. Failure of the Spaniards to settle the area left a broad and deep gulf in the northern frontier between El Paso and San Juan Bautista. This area was used by nomadic and warlike Indians of the Big Bend and the Edwards Plateau as an avenue to strike settlements far south of the Río Grande.

[2] José de Berroterán, "Relación Diaria de los acaecimientos que ocurrieron en la expedición de José de Berroterán," A.G.N., Historia, Vol. 52, p. 14. For published accounts of the expedition see Vito Alessio Robles, *Coahuila y Texas en la época colonial*, pp. 480–487, and Carlos Eduardo Castañeda, *Our Catholic Heritage in Texas*, II, 336–347.

[3] José de Berroterán to Joseph Antonio de Ecay Múzquiz, March 26, 1729, A.G.N., Historia, Vol. 52, p. 1.

Ecay Múzquiz' reply appears to have been partly responsible for the expedition's outcome. The commandant of San Juan Bautista noted that he had a detachment of fifteen men, and the lieutenant of his presidio, Joseph Hernández, ready to join Berroterán's force of seventy-three brought from the other presidios. "With the commandant is formed a company of eighty officers and soldiers who are prepared and equipped in every way possible, pursuant to the primary goal of the Most Excellent Lord Viceroy of surprising and punishing the enemy Indians of the Javilanes [Gavilanes] and allied nations who are molesting with murder and theft the dominions of His Majesty."[4] Besides the eighty-nine soldiers from the presidios, Ecay Múzquiz pointed out, there would be forty-six Indian allies, including contingents from the missions of San Juan Bautista, San Bernardo, and Dulce Nombre de Jesús de Peyotes, as well as those from Caldera and Santiago, and the six which Berroterán had brought from his own presidio.

Noting a suggestion that the force be divided—one part to survey the Sierra de Santa Rosa, the other to follow the Río Grande—Ecay Múzquiz strongly advised against it. Should the enemy Indians be overtaken in the Santa Rosa range, he pointed out, experience had demonstrated that they would take refuge on the peaks and eminences. Provisioned with jars of water, the Indians would be invulnerable in these positions, even though their numbers might be small. The limited number of soldiers which could be sent into this region would be unable to dislodge them. Should the soldiers make an attack, the Indians could defeat them without loosing an arrow, simply by casting rocks from the heights. Thus the Spaniards would waste ill-spared energy and effort, and the Indians, having successfully defended themselves, would be more arrogant than before.

Furthermore, the detachment from the Santa Rosa Mountains would find difficulty traversing the rugged country, to make a rendezvous at La Junta de los Ríos with the force proceeding up the Río Grande. The distance was great, the land sterile and without water, totally impracticable for marching cavalry. In years past, the now aging commandant recalled wistfully, during the governorships of Cuerbo y Valdés, Gregorio de Salinas, and Don Linán de Padilla,[5] expeditions had been made into that

[4] Joseph Antonio de Ecay Múzquiz, "Informe," March 27, 1729, *ibid.*, p. 3.
[5] *Ibid.*, p. 4. Ecay Múzquiz evidently refers to Simón Padilla y Córdova, Coahuila governor from 1708 to 1712.

territory. Some of these he had commanded himself; others were led by the late Captain Don Diego Ramón, the first commandant of Presidio de San Juan Bautista. Always pursuit of the natives had to be abandoned, the troop to return to the presidio. "We were not able to maintain ourselves or to overtake the Indians for the reasons mentioned."[6]

Since the expedition also was to seek a site for the Presidio of Sacramento, Ecay Múzquiz noted, it would be unlikely that two forces traveling over separate routes would be able to get together on their recommendation. Division of the force would render impossible the attainment of the principal goal: that the enemy Indians should be surprised and punished.

Since there were experienced officers in his presidio besides himself, the commandant Ecay Múzquiz called them into council, to give their feeling and opinions. These were Lieutenant Joseph Hernández, who would lead the San Juan Bautista troops on the expedition with Berroterán; Alférez Santiago Jiménez, who would accompany him; Captain Diego Ramón, son of the late commandant of the presidio, who had inherited his father's Hacienda de Santa Mónica nearby; Captain Andrés Ramón, either a son or a grandson of the late captain; and Captain Manuel Rodríguez. "They have served, as I have, many years in the Presidio de Coahuila and in this one."[7]

The council outlined in detail the route Berroterán should follow during the early part of the journey, suggesting camping places and the procedure of sending out Indians to reconnoiter the country ahead of the main force. The document submitted by Ecay Múzquiz reveals the extent of the knowledge which the San Juan Bautista company had of the territory up the Río Grande prior to the expedition. It emphasizes the intractable nature of the Indians which dwelt along the stream.

With the company to depart from the presidio March 28, the council suggested that the first stop should be at Santo Domingo, six leagues distant. Spies and runners should be sent out the following day at daybreak to reconnoiter San Rodrigo Spring, in order that the camp might be moved there without being detected by the enemy. At this location, abundant of water and pastures, five leagues beyond Santo Domingo, sojourn should be made while the spies went out to seek the enemy Indians. These scouts,

[6] *Ibid.*, p. 4.
[7] *Ibid.*, p. 4.

it was suggested, should be most vigorous and skillful in order to seek out the enemy on the borders of the Sierra de Santa Rosa and along the borders of Arroyo de la Bavia.

Spies also should be sent ahead to reconnoiter the headwaters of the San Diego River and the places of refuge in its ravines where the enemy Indians were known to cross going to and from their camps in the canyons and deep woods along the Río Grande.

These being their dwelling places, our spies should be able to discover them without being detected. Then the body of the company, leaving its camp and equipage with security, can attack and achieve the goal of surprising them and punishing them, which is the principal one which the sovereign mandate of His Excellency calls for.[8]

Ecay Múzquiz observed that the official instructions forbade "doing damage to the Indians of the Cíbolos nation, because they are friends of the Spaniards, if treated kindly and courted." But, said the Captain, "In all the years I have served in these regions, I do not know, nor have I heard of such a nation of Indians."[9] In the fifty leagues along the Río Grande above San Juan Bautista would be found only enemy Indians, rebels against the Royal Crown: Apaches, Jumanes (sic), and Pelones nations, the ones which molested the presidios of San Antonio de Valero (Béjar) and San Juan Bautista. "We do not know what the distance will be by land to the juncture of the Río Grande with the Conchos, because we have never traveled over these parts; for this reason it seems appropriate that the company should go all in one body."[10]

In the *plaza de armas* of the Presidio de San Juan Bautista del Río Grande on March 28, 1729, there passed in review before Captain José de Berroterán the eighty-nine soldiers and officers—fifty-eight from Nueva Vizcaya, fifteen each from Monclova and San Juan Bautista—and the forty-six Indian auxiliaries about to march out into the unknown. Each man was found to be armed and equipped in the proper manner of his kind, Indian or soldier, and moderately well prepared. The march was begun immediately, and, as Ecay Múzquiz and his council of officers had suggested, the company traveled seven leagues the first day to Santo Do-

[8] *Ibid.*, p. 6.
[9] *Ibid.*, p. 7.
[10] *Ibid.*, p. 8.

mingo, some distance beyond the former site of the Mission of San Francisco Solano. Berroterán dispatched eight scouts to reconnoiter the San Rodrigo and San Antonio rivers. Next day the company arrived at the San Antonio and paused to await news of the reconnaissance. Finally on the afternoon of the thirty-first two of the Indians came in to report that they had found no trace of the enemy.

On April 1 march was resumed toward the northwest, to the San Rodrigo without having had word of the enemy. Before dawn next day Berroterán dispatched ten spies with orders to reconnoiter the San Diego River, Real de las Vacas, and other watering places in the vicinity, "where I had been assured the enemies had their regular habitation."[11]

About noon the next day a messenger came from San Juan Bautista bearing a letter from Ecay Múzquiz which he had received from the Coahuila governor, Manuel de Sandoval. Saltillo and Parras had been attacked by hostile Indians. Large herds of horses had been driven off and several dead were left in the wake of the raid.

The Governor appealed to Berroterán to send one detachment of his troops back to the Presidio of Coahuila, another to proceed to Santa Rosa, and another to block the passes and occupy the strong points around Cuatrociénegas. The Captain immediately called a council of his officers, who agreed that the proposed measures would be too late to be effective; the result would be only the loss of the expedition's objectives.

The march was proceeding slowly enough as it was. The Indian scouts reported having seen tracks of Indians hunting buffalo eight or ten leagues from the camp. The commandant, assured that the trail was made by a large number of Apaches, went in pursuit. Four days later the trail led to a band of Pacuache Indians—known to be friends of the Spaniards—on a buffalo hunt. The Pacuaches were asked if other Indian nations were known to be in the vicinity, and they gave assurance that there were none. So much time gone for naught.

Berroterán sent six more scouts to reconnoiter the banks of the San Diego River and another six to the Real de las Vacas, a noted crossing on the Río Grande a short distance below present Ciudad Acuña. But then the commandant realized that the Indian auxiliaries from Coahuila were playing a game with him. Having learned his plan of keeping the troop

[11] Berroterán, "Relación Diaria," p. 16.

idle while the spies sought out the enemy, they were prolonging their excursions. Meanwhile, provisions needed for the rest of the journey were being consumed, hastening the time when the return must be made. The Captain wrung his hands and waited for the Indians to come back to camp. At last he summoned the two officers from San Juan Bautista, Lieutenant Joseph Hernández and Alférez Santiago Jiménez, and the one from Presidio de Coahuila, Diego Jiménez, to ask how they might proceed without the Indians. The officers strongly advised against such a plan. The Captain then proposed that they examine the soldiers of their presidios to learn if perhaps there were some soldier who knew the country well enough to guide them onward. This was done, but no one was found.

That night, however, the Indians returned, and with news of having found signs of the enemy, in the region which Berroterán had been ordered to explore.

Reaching Real de las Vacas on the eleventh, Berroterán sent his Indians out to survey the Paso de las Síboras (Cíbolas), stopped to wait a day while the scouts returned, and then marched seven leagues on the thirteenth to the ford.[12] More time was lost on the fourteenth, the leader finding himself without anyone who could direct the course of the march. Then it was learned that the river ahead ran through deep canyons and was inaccessible for watering the horses. At last, on the fifteenth, word came of a watering place six or seven leagues beyond. Getting a late start, the camp moved to the new location, which was reached just in time for evening prayers.

On the eighteenth the force crossed the Río Grande, and the following day continued upstream, traveling near Shumla, Langtry, and Osman.[13] Berroterán continued to send out his scouts, but now the chief concern was for finding available water instead of enemy Indians. Nevertheless, he still guarded against surprise attack as he marched up the left bank, covering thirty leagues on this side of the river.[14] The explorers informed him that up ahead the canyon of the Río Grande cut deep inside craggy rock walls. He continued along the river until he came to a suitable cross-

---

[12] Castañeda (*Our Catholic Heritage,* II, 341) and Alessio Robles (*Coahuila y Texas,* p. 484) say the expedition was at a point near present Comstock, Texas.

[13] Says Castañeda (*Our Catholic Heritage,* II, 342).

[14] Reaching the vicinity of Dryden, says Alessio Robles (*Coahuila y Texas,* p. 485).

ing on April 23. Fearful that he would not be able to regain the right bank should the river rise, he crossed over to wait until April 28 for the scouts to come in. When they arrived they informed the leader that the region they had explored was extremely mountainous with no water to be found whatsoever.

Once again the hesitant Berroterán called a conference, and it was determined, in view of the diminished supply of provisions, that it would be impossible to continue on to La Junta de los Ríos. The Captain ordered that the troops from the two presidios in Coahuila, Monclova and San Juan Bautista, return by way of Nadadores, effecting an exploration of the country along the way, on which they would make a detailed report. His own men from Conchos would proceed directly to their presidio.

The morning of April 29 the two groups split, the soldiers from Coahuila taking a southeasterly course toward Nadadores. Berroterán and his men marched south across dry and desolate country. As they pushed hard to reach the next water hole, horses and mules became crazed from thirst. Dead and weakened animals were left along the trail. Reaching one watering place, the force rested several days before advancing toward the next. At last, on May 16, it reached the Presidio of San Francisco de los Conchos, and Berroterán turned his thoughts to the report he would make to the Viceroy. He forwarded his *informe* on May 28.

The report was subjected to careful scrutiny by Brigadier Rivera, whose reaction was a snort of dissatisfaction. It was examined by the *auditor de guerra*, Oliván y Rebolledo, who agreed that the expedition had been very nearly a complete fiasco. Berroterán, these two officials perceived, had lacked zest for the campaign. Instead of making his own reconnaissance, he had entrusted this vitally important phase of the expedition to his Indian scouts. He had exercised poor judgment and manifested a lack of energy. He had failed utterly in his number one objective: to explore the country from San Juan Bautista to La Junta de los Ríos.

The hardships Berroterán thought he had suffered meant nothing to Rivera. If the leader had really prosecuted his assignment under difficult circumstances, the Brigadier believed, he would have lost many more horses; the twenty-eight animals he had left scattered along the trail were nothing compared to the hundreds lost by Domingo Terán de los Ríos and the Marqués de Aguayo.

As for the difficulties Berroterán encountered in crossing the dry country, said Rivera, he could have avoided them simply by following the river, as his instructions called for. But Rivera himself was not in possession of all the facts, and some of his opinions were as precipitous as the Río Grande canyons, which, it should be remembered, he had never seen. Berroterán's real error was in the extreme caution he had exercised in the early stages of his journey. This excessive care caused him to consume too much time and too great a portion of his provisions before he ever reached the arduous part of his task.

The one redeeming feature of his expedition, in Rivera's eyes, was that he had opened new routes from his presidio in Nueva Vizcaya to San Juan Bautista. The march from Mapimí to San Juan Bautista, said the two viceregal advisers, was the first of its kind; the route followed from San Juan Bautista up the Río Grande and across country to the Presidio de Conchos, had covered a large area previously unexplored, opening a new communication route.

Still the main objective had not been attained. His Excellency, said Rivera, should issue orders for a new expedition as soon as possible. But several years would pass before any move at all would be made to carry out this proposal of Rivera and the area in question was thoroughly explored.

Meanwhile, the Indian attacks on Nueva Vizcaya, Nuevo León, Coahuila, and Texas intensified. San Juan Bautista, like other settlements in these provinces, suffered. Conditions at the Río Grande presidio in 1734 are described eloquently in the report of Coahuila Governor Blas de la Garza Falcón, on his official visit to the outposts of his province.

Most Excellent Sir:

Having proceeded . . . with my visit in this Province, as will be evident to Your Excellency by the attached reports and lists of inhabitants of the Pueblos, I give news of the state in which they are found. Arriving at the Presidio del Río Grande del Norte, I found its company complete, well equipped and supplied with munitions, although subjected to the continued warfare which the Apaches are making on it. While I was in the Presidio on my visit they drove off the *caballada* of one citizen, and it had been but a few days since they had stolen other horses. At this time I received a dispatch . . . in which Your Excellency ordered that ten soldiers be sent from this Presidio to that of San Antonio. I sent the ten soldiers in prompt compliance, even though you have placed me in this Province to build it up, in order that any invasion by the enemies, which attack the said Presidio del Río Grande as well as that of San Antonio, might be repelled. Taking away ten soldiers will make it impossible for them [the people of San Juan Bautista] to defend themselves from the continued attacks which are being made daily, especially with the Presidio composed of only thirty-two soldiers, thirteen of whom are in custody of the horse-herd, four are in the missions, and the ten have gone to the Presidio de San Antonio, making twenty-seven [that are absent]. This leaves only five in the Presidio, including the officers, who remain unable to furnish escort for the mails which cross from the interior, or to make war and defend themselves. This I place before Your Excellency, in order that you may handle it as you see fit.

Although this Presidio has forty auxiliary citizens living on the lands of the pueblos of the Indians of San Juan Bautista and San Bernardo, the father missionaries will not consent for them to build houses for their abode, lest they be encouraged to lay claim to the land. The Indians have more than enough land and water, and the *vecinos* should be able to avail themselves of it. Many of them asked me for permission to leave this place, they are so vexed at finding themselves denied. I communicate this to Your Excellency, since you may find that a villa should be placed here.[15]

Thus the problems of the gateway settlement were brought into focus. The difficulties described by Govenor Garza Falcón were the very ones which cast a long shadow into the future, shaping the community's destiny. The *vecinos*—those persons who had come to settle near the presidio and the missions—were being crowded out; in essence, the missions were choking the life from the community as a whole, a fact which would become increasingly evident with the passing years. So few settlers could obtain land in the vicinity that the settlement did not even have enough people to defend it. Such was the situation, while San Juan Bautista still occupied a place of strategic importance on the Río Grande frontier.

Possibly the report of Garza Falcón, coupled with appeals from the citizens of Nueva Vizcaya, caused the Viceroy once again to turn official attention on the unoccupied and largely unexplored stretch of river between San Juan Bautista and La Junta de los Ríos. The missions in the vicinity of the meeting of the rivers still remained without protection. The Indians at La Junta had revolted ten years previously, in 1724, and Nueva

---

[15] Blas de la Garza Falcón, "Visita del Río Grande," April 27, 1734, in A.G.I., Audiencia de México, 61-2-18, pp. 34–35.

Vizcaya citizens petitioned for a new presidio. The idea languished and died. In the face of repeated incursions by hostile Indians, new appeals were made. It was partly as the result of these that the reconnaissance of Captain José de Berroterán had been ordered, but his expedition did little or nothing to alleviate the situation. The attacks continued and the governors of Coahuila and Nuevo León renewed their pleas to the Viceroy.

The new Viceroy, by decree of August 29, 1735, ordered the governor of Coahuila, Garza Falcón, and the captain of Presidio de San Juan Bautista, Joseph de Ecay Múzquiz, to explore the route which Berroterán had followed. They were to reconnoiter both banks of the river in search of an appropriate site for the proposed Presidio de Sacramento. Of prime consideration in choosing the site should be its strategic position with relation to the trails of the Apaches.

When the orders reached him October 23, the Governor was engaged in a campaign against the Tobosos. He sent instructions immediately to Captain Ecay Múzquiz at San Juan Bautista to make ready to join the expedition with twenty men.

The Governor left Monclova on December 12, 1735, with twenty soldiers, ten Indian guides, several herders, and servants. As he proceeded northward toward San Juan Bautista, he found the country depopulated, the haciendas untended as a result of the repeated Indian raids.

Between the Álamo Seco and the Río de Sabinas the Governor's force observed many wild mustangs, descendants of the mounts left lame and starving along the Spanish trail to Texas, or of those which had escaped to the wilderness during stampedes. Three mules loaded with provisions were lost in crossing the Río de Sabinas, but the cargoes were saved. Still more wild mustangs, the *caballada mesteña*, were seen north of the Sabinas.

On the seventeenth, after traveling off the road for eight leagues, the force came to the cattle ranch of Captain Ecay Múzquiz, eight leagues short of San Juan Bautista, and stopped here to spend the night. From the manager of the hacienda it was learned that on the day before, three Indians from the nearby Mission of Dulce Nombre de Jesús de Peyotes were attacked while working in their fields by ten mounted and well-armed Apaches. One of the mission Indians was killed, another wounded. The third escaped to inform the padre at San Juan Bautista. A squad of soldiers from the presidio was sent out promptly to pursue the attackers.

Picking up the Apaches' trail the following day, the soldiers estimated the marauding force to contain seventy Indians. Any intention of giving pursuit was promptly rationalized: The Indians had not inflicted much damage; their number was large, their arms superior to those of the Spaniards. If the soldiers should pursue, they would leave the mission without protection, easy prey to the Apaches.[16]

Next day, after the chaplain of the expedition, Friar Joseph Antonio Rodríguez, had said Mass, the Governor's force marched the final eight leagues to the Presidio of San Juan Bautista, and Garza Falcón halted his troop in the *plaza de armas*. The following morning the soldiers and *vecinos* of the presidio were ordered to provision themselves with biscuit and beef for the reconnaissance, which was to begin the following Thursday, the twenty-second. Then a parade was formed around the *plaza*.

But on the twenty-first, word came that the trail of the mounted enemy Indians had been seen at Nogales Spring, near the mission of Dulce Nombre de Jesús. A squad of soldiers was sent to defend the mission and pursue the enemy. On Friday, the twenty-third, the force returned at four in the afternoon, saying the hostiles had fled up the Río Grande, in the direction the reconnaissance was to be made. The Captain and the Governor, in hasty council, decided to dispatch ten Indian auxiliaries on Sunday, which was Christmas Day, to reconnoiter the country upriver. The start of the march was delayed on the twenty-seventh, because a fierce norther was blowing. At last, after Father Rodríguez said Mass, the expedition got moving. It consisted of 51 soldiers, 38 Indians, 6 muleteers, 40 pack mules, and 380 horses. Following the route of Berroterán, as had been ordered, Governor Garza Falcón and Captain Ecay Múzquiz led their force up the right bank of the Río Grande.

Don Blas waxed eloquent as he described the country they traveled over: ". . . a fertile plain of pastures and low hills, abundant of water, very commodious and agreeable."[17] It would be a site for future settlements, he said of the area of Santo Domingo, with ranches and fields, and irrigation waters to run over the breast of the earth to make it productive. Reaching the Río de San Antonio, not yet forty miles from San Juan Bau-

[16] Blas de la Garza Falcón, "Diario y Derrotero de Don Blas de la Garza Falcón and Don Joseph Antonio de Ecay y Múzquiz," A.G.I., Audiencia de México, 6-2-8, 1733–1738, pp. 119–120.

[17] Garza Falcón, "Diario y Derrotero," p. 123.

tista, the soldiers found the country full of wild horses, and the camp was provisioned with wild turkeys.

After passing a night on the San Rodrigo River, they struck the San Diego River fifteen miles south of present Del Rio. It was this region which most impressed the Governor. The river was running a good stream and had deep pools, edible fish, and good stands of timber along its banks. That night the spies sent out before the company left the presidio came in to report that they had been unable to pick up the trail of the hostiles.

On the morning of January 1, 1736—"the day of the circumcision of the Lord"[18]—the chaplain said Mass. Garza Falcón then chose twenty-five men and three friendly Indians to make a reconnaissance of the river to its source. Traveling three leagues upstream, they found two points suitable for drawing out water, one on either bank. Arable land was abundant on one bank but not on the other. The supply of hardwood, stone, and soil suitable for adobe, and terrain which offered a good defensive position, suggested a likely site for a presidio. Garza Falcón and Ecay Múzquiz were so taken with the place that they decided to remain here several days, going over the region thoroughly, and even felling timber for use in the stockade of a future presidio. Meanwhile, they sent the Governor's son, Miguel de la Garza Falcón, with thirty soldiers and ten Indians, to reconnoiter the country fifty leagues beyond. The Viceroy's order asked specifically that this reconnaissance be made to see if the banks of the Río Grande were as impossible as Berroterán had reported them to be.

Setting out January 4, 1736, Don Miguel traveled nine leagues northward to reach a spring at the head of a creek, not far from present Ciudad Acuña, Coahuila. He encountered an Apache trail on the way, and remains of Indian fires at the spring warned him that the enemy was near. Continuing the march northwestward up the Río Grande on January 5, the party covered eight leagues. Snow began to fall the next day, but the explorers pushed on, crossing from one bank of the stream to the other, finding many springs, though the terrain was rough and the soil poor. Many of Garza Falcón's horses went lame, and several were left beside the rugged, snow-banked trail.

The snow continued to fall January 6 and 7, but the Spaniards

18 *Ibid.*, p. 125.

pressed on up the Río Grande, following the stream as closely as possible. The night of the seventh they camped in a deep ravine surrounded by hills. At the crest of one of the hills they found silhouetted against the snowy sky a large wooden cross, standing upright, as it evidently had been placed by some unknown Spanish explorer who had been here previously, perhaps by Berroterán. They called the place La Santa Cruz de Mayo. Next morning, at the "Holy Cross of May," the decision was made to turn back.[19]

Retracing their steps, Don Miguel's men were able to return to the camp on the San Diego in three days of stiff marching to rejoin Don Blas and Captain Ecay Múzquiz. Next day all the campaigners began the retreat to Presidio de San Juan Bautista, which they reached January 15. The Governor, although severely ill, began immediately to compile his report, which he sent to the Viceroy on January 17.[20]

The Governor's advanced age and poor health prevented him from doing more. His death came shortly after the expedition ended, but not until he had recommended to the Viceroy that the new presidio be erected on the Río de San Diego. While a fort at this location would be of no more benefit to the missions at La Junta de los Ríos than would San Juan Bautista itself, it would serve to deter Indian attacks on the Coahuila and Nueva Vizcaya settlements. The Viceroy gave approval December 22, 1736. The new fort, only twenty-four leagues from San Juan Bautista, would be called Presidio de Sacramento, the name having been chosen before the Berroterán expedition was made.[21]

In recognition of the services of Miguel de la Garza Falcón as *alférez* and lieutenant in his father's command for twenty years, he was named commandant of the new presidio. He had journeyed to the capital personally to solicit the appointment before the Viceroy. Another son of Don

---

[19] *Ibid.*, p. 131. Castañeda (*Our Catholic Heritage*, III, 206) fixes the farthest point of their march as "either Indian Creek or Canyon, south of Dryden," in Terrell County, Texas. Daniel ("Advance of the Spanish Frontier," p. 176) notes that no mention was made in the diary of crossing the Pecos and concludes that the expeditioners mistook the Pecos for the Río Grande and followed it northward to the vicinity of present Pandale.

[20] Garza Falcón, "Diario y Derrotero," pp. 117–132.

[21] Joseph Antonio de Ecay Múzquiz, "Informe," March 28, 1729, A.G.N., Historia, Vol. 52, p. 4.

Blas—Clemente de la Garza Falcón—was named to succeed him as governor of Coahuila. It seems, observes Alessio Robles, that this family had established its own feudal system in northern Coahuila.[22]

As a result of an attack by Apaches upon a party from the settlement of Dolores de la Punta, Governor Clemente de la Garza Falcón made an inspection of presidios early in 1738. He went first to Sacramento, which still was in the building stage. He found the new presidio without a chaplain; the commissary of missions had given permission for the aged Friar Francisco de Céliz, diarist of the Alarcón expedition of 1718, to administer the sacraments, but the unsteadiness of his advanced years caused him to suffer several mishaps, and it was necessary to restore him to his monastery. Friar Alonso Giraldo de Terreros, missionary at San Bernardo, visited the presidio about this time, perhaps in connection with filling the chaplaincy, and issued a report on the progress of construction. In 1739, however, the fort was moved fifty leagues to the Valley of Santa Rosa (present Melchor Múzquiz, Coahuila), at the headwaters of the Río de Sabinas.

Unlike the Berroterán expedition, the Garza Falcón–Ecay Múzquiz excursion was not intended to reach La Junta de los Ríos. It was aimed primarily at finding a site for a new Coahuila presidio—and at determining the accuracy of Berroterán's reports on the incredible terrain he found along the Río Grande. If Berroterán, Garza Falcón, and Ecay Múzquiz, in their travels upriver, had proved anything at all, it was that the river was the wrong approach to La Junta de los Ríos from San Juan Bautista. This fact would be borne out some years later by another Coahuila governor, Don Pedro de Rábago y Terán.

But before San Juan Bautista would play an additional rôle in exploration of the Río Grande, it must deal with another pompous official whose mishandling of colonial affairs would be very nearly as disastrous as that of Pedro de Rivera.

22 Alessio Robles, *Coahuila y Texas,* p. 548.

20. A CROSS TO BEAR

"T HE TROUBLES experienced by the missionaries as a result of the continued attacks of the Apaches," says Castañeda, "were not half as detrimental to the progress of the missions as the misunderstandings with Governor Carlos Benites Franquis de Lugo."[1] The fact that Franquis governed Texas and not Coahuila did not exempt the missions of the latter province from the deleterious effects of his unreasoning behavior.

Franquis had just come from Spain with a royal appointment as governor of Tlaxcala when in 1736 Viceroy-Archbishop Vizarrón made him interim governor of Texas to succeed Manuel de Sandoval. Franquis, of violent nature, set immediately upon a stormy course which assured his name of a place in history but won him also the enmity of almost every missionary and presidial official from Saltillo to Los Adaes.

Arriving at Monclova in August, the new appointee vented his wrath upon the Coahuila governor, Clemente de la Garza Falcón, accusing him of laxity in protecting settlements of the province against Indian attacks. Proceeding on to San Juan Bautista, he flew into Captain Ecay Múzquiz because there was no escort waiting to conduct him to San Antonio, although the Captain had not been apprised of his coming. Leaving in a huff, he went on to San Antonio without the escort, arriving unannounced September 26, 1736. But Captain Ecay Múzquiz and San Juan Bautista had not heard the last of Governor Franquis, who made himself obnoxious to all by claiming that the presidios of Coahuila, as well as those of Texas, owed him the same obedience due the Viceroy or the King.

San Antonio soon was in turmoil. Only a short time was required for San Juan Bautista to be included in the upheaval. Franquis, on November 19, wrote a high-handed letter to Captain Ecay Múzquiz, demanding

[1] Carlos Eduardo Castañeda, *Our Catholic Heritage in Texas,* III, 49.

to know what authority the Captain had for continuing to station guards in each of the missions over which the Río Grande presidio had jurisdiction. Ecay Múzquiz, apparently not prone to letter writing, showed the missive to Father Miguel Sevillano de Paredes who, having served his term as guardian of the College of Querétaro, had returned to the gateway as president of the Río Grande missions. The Captain asked the padre's advice, and Father Sevillano offered helpfully to answer the letter himself.[2] While the priest's intentions undoubtedly were good, the letter would have been better left unanswered; his sincere reply only fanned the fire.

The mission guards were being continued, Sevillano advised Franquis, by special authority of the Viceroy. And was not the Governor perhaps exceeding his authority by giving orders to the captain of San Juan Bautista, who really was subject to the governor of Coahuila? If what he heard was correct, he continued—that the mission guards had been removed at San Antonio—he would have to journey to the capital to take the matter up with the Viceroy. This he would do "in order that the Blood of Christ may not have been shed in vain for the salvation of those unfortunate Indians, whom Divine Providence has brought into the fold of the Church through the hardships of the missionaries and the blood they have shed."[3]

As for reports that the mail of the missionaries had been tampered with, wrote the priest, he refused to believe them; the Laws of the Indies imposed severe penalties for such an act.

The Governor saw nothing but insult in the letter. He angrily replied that it was not the place of the missionary to meddle in affairs of his office, that the captain of San Juan Bautista was as much subject to his own orders as to those of the governor of Coahuila, that he would not tolerate such liberties on the part of the priest without seeking satisfaction.[4]

Father Sevillano did not make reply; instead he waited for the Governor's wrath to cool. But the storm in San Antonio raged on. The president of the San Juan Bautista missions was kept informed by frequent letters from the missionaries in Texas, when the letters were allowed to pass.

---

[2] Benito Franquis de Lugo to Joseph Antonio de Ecay Múzquiz, November 19, 1736, A.G.N., Misiones, Vol. 21, Part 1, pp. 97–98.

[3] Fray Miguel Sevillano de Paredes to Franquis de Lugo, November 22, 1736, in *ibid.*, p. 101, quoted in Castañeda, *Our Catholic Heritage*, III, 52–53.

[4] Franquis to Sevillano, November 30, 1736, in *ibid.*, pp. 103–104.

There were repeated instances of messengers bound for San Juan Bautista being stopped and searched after having left San Antonio.

A courier named Chirino arrived at the Río Grande presidio to testify before Captain Ecay Múzquiz, Lieutenant Joseph Hernández, Don Gaspar Lombraña, and Padre Alonso Giraldo de Terreros, minister of Mission San Bernardo. Chirino had been intercepted by Alférez Juan Galván, and all mail not bearing the official seal was taken from him. Two soldiers from San Juan Bautista, Nicolás Rodríguez and Nicolás Ramón, were searched as they returned with mail from San Antonio. The man who searched them was Mateo Pérez, now a lieutenant at San Antonio de Béjar —the same soldier who, some years before, had been taken from his private's billet at San Juan Bautista to serve briefly as captain of the Presidio de Béjar. Pérez, who was acting on orders of Governor Franquis, made it obvious that he was interested only in mail of the religious. Finding none, he let the rest of the dispatches pass. But he failed to look under the soldiers' saddles. If he had, he would have found what he sought.

With such definite instances of mail tampering, Father Sevillano wrote a full report to the Viceroy, sending along copies of all the correspondence which had passed between himself and Ecay Múzquiz and Governor Franquis.[5]

His "Consulta Apologética," dated February 15, 1737, detailed all the abuses suffered by the missionaries in Texas and on the Río Grande since the arrival of Governor Franquis. The guardian of the College of Querétaro, Friar Pedro Muñoz, delivered the memorial to the Viceroy. The result was a new enjoinder to Franquis that he should improve his relationship with the missionaries and restore the soldiers to guard the missions, under penalty of suspension. The Governor refused, however, and his removal from office was ordered under date of July 11, 1737. He was instructed to retire to San Juan Bautista while the resident judge, Fernández de Jáuregui, investigated his official conduct.

Franquis was brought to San Juan Bautista in the company of Fray Francisco Vergara, Lieutenant Joseph Hernández of the Río Grande presidio, and a squad of soldiers under Corporal Bartolomé Torralba. The deposed Governor turned the trip into a ludicrous affair by his repeated scoffing at the missionaries in general and Father Sevillano in

---

[5] Miguel Sevillano de Paredes, "Consulta Apologética," *ibid.*, pp. 93–96.

particular. He constantly referred to Sevillano, whom he blamed for all his troubles, as "jawbone of a rabbit" and "the death mask." All the religious, he asserted, were but missionaries of Satan. In camp in the evenings, he encouraged a soldier named Pedro Salinas, a noted mimic, to do an imitation of the old priest preaching a sermon. The words he put into Father Sevillano's mouth were hardly complimentary: "Hey, why is it the ladies are going to San Bernardo to Mass? Is it because Father Alonso [Giraldo de Terreros] is good looking and I am old?"[6]

Franquis relished the performance, and even worse, commented Sevillano later, so did Father Vergara, who had forgotten his holy profession to join in the Colonel's mirth. The incident evidently hit Sevillano in a tender spot. At his insistence an investigation of the matter was held at San Juan Bautista, with Captain Ecay Múzquiz taking testimony from Hernández, Torralba, and the soldier Pedro Maldonado. Each one corroborated the story Father Sevillano had heard, and the transcript of their testimony ran to three thousand words.

It was, however, an empty show. On his arrival at San Juan Bautista, Franquis stole away without permission to go to the capital and present his case before the Viceroy. The act apparently availed him nothing. His trial lasted several years. Freed at last, he was appointed an officer in the garrison at Veracruz, where once again he came under a cloud for trying to asssume more authority than he had.

Franquis, in little more than a year as governor of Texas, had very nearly ruined the province. Fortunately San Juan Bautista was not directly affected by the unreasonable measures he had imposed, but it was caught continually in the swirling backwash of the controversy. An example is found in a letter from the Texas Governor to Ecay Múzquiz of July 15, 1737—a very short time before Franquis received word of his suspension.

A new missionary had come to San Antonio to serve at the Zacatecan Mission of San José. He informed Franquis that a train of supplies for the Zacatecan missions had arrived at San Juan Bautista but was held at the gateway for want of escort. The Captain, he said, had refused to furnish the soldiers needed. Thus Franquis was inspired. He did not inquire

[6] San Juan Bautista, Proceedings of Investigation at San Juan Bautista, October 5, 1737, A.G.I., Audiencia de Guadalajara, 67-2-27, p. 179. Entire proceedings are contained in *ibid.*, 177–188.

of the Captain's difficulties, or suggest that the supplies be sent on as soon as possible. Instead he issued a curt order for Ecay Múzquiz to send the train without delay, and a threat to the effect that if an escort were not provided, he would take drastic measures.[7]

During this period there arose other irritating incidents which were unrelated to the Franquis affair. One Alejandro de Uro y Campa went before the Ecclesiastical Cabildo of Guadalajara and the judges of the treasury and made certain claims regarding the missions of San Juan Bautista: they had large herds of cattle and sheep, he said, and many cattle had been sold. They raised abundant crops and had numerous horses and mules; the missions had been in operation almost forty years; they had previously paid tithes and had discontinued the practice without reason; the neophytes were in fact capable of governing themselves.

Such were the statements used by Uro y Campa, the agent for tithes for Coahuila, in an effort to obtain the order he needed to collect tithes from the gateway missions. Sevillano's protest was instantaneous: the agent's assertions were unfounded. He called for an investigation. In conducting the hearing Captain Ecay Múzquiz cooperated admirably; apparently here was a military man who was seldom found at cross purposes with the religious.

Testimony was given by Sergeant Nicolás Maldonado, age fifty-five; Francisco de Salinas, age sixty; Alférez Diego Ramón, *vecino* and *hacendado* of the Valley of Santa Mónica, son of the late commandant, now sixty years of age; and Joseph Minchaca, forty-eight—all of whom had lived at San Juan Bautista almost from its beginning. Two of the witnesses, Sergeant Maldonado and Salinas, had served as *mayordomo* in the missions, supervising the Indians and assisting the padres. Minchaca had been on at least one expedition to return fugitive Indians to the missions.

Statements from Friar Mariano de los Dolores, at the Mission of San Antonio de Valero, and Friar Francisco de Céliz, diarist of the Alarcón expedition of 1718 and missionary at Dulce Nombre de Jesús de Peyotes, also were entered in the record, which consists of 8,500 words. The testimony given in response to Father Sevillano's ten questions offers a

[7] Franquis to Ecay Múzquiz, July 15, 1737, A.G.N., Historia, Vol. 524, Part 3, pp. 748–749.

clear picture of the life of the missions from their founding, the purpose they served, and their accomplishments.[8]

The hearing was convened by Captain Ecay Múzquiz in the Presidio of San Juan Bautista on October 17, 1737. Ecay Múzquiz sat as judge, assisted by two Spaniards, Domingo de Monzón and Gaspar de Lombraña. The testimony of each of the deponents closely paralleled that of the others. Each was duly sworn "by God our Lord and the sign of the Holy Cross."[9]

In response to the questions drawn by Father Sevillano they testified that the herds of sheep and cattle were the common property of the Indians of the missions. The livestock did not belong to the missionaries of San Juan, San Bernardo, and Nuestra Señora de los Dolores de la Punta, who had no property of their own.

The missionaries had a small number of saddle horses for use in going from one mission to another, and to other places where their ministry took them. These were the property of the Apostolic Chair, having been purchased for the use of the missionaries from Lieutenant Mateo Pérez. But the main herd of horses and mules, like the cattle and the sheep, were the common property of the mission Indians. Even these were few, because of repeated raids by the Apaches.

The crops raised on the mission lands also belonged to the Indians. From one year to the next hardly enough was raised to feed the neophytes. It was well known that for several years beans had been brought from Monclova because the local yields were so short. As for the sale of cattle, only in 1731 had small droves been sold, and these to help the new missions which had just been moved from East Texas to San Antonio. On rare occasions since that time a few cattle had been sent to feed the Indians at San Antonio. Some cattle had been sent to Monclova in exchange for flour and wine to celebrate the Mass. Cattle from the missions had occasionally been furnished to the Presidio of San Juan Bautista, in exchange for clothing or tools for the Indians of the missions. All the witnesses agreed the missions had never paid tithes previously, though they could not say what had been done in the missions at La Punta and Peyotes.

They acknowledged that the first mission had been initially established at this site in 1703 (actually 1700), but the Indians did not yet have the

[8] Fray Miguel Sevillano de Paredes, "Representación," contained in A.G.N., Provincias Internas, Vol. 32, pp. 36–64.

[9] *Ibid.*, p. 40, *et seq.*

ability to manage their own affairs. The Indian population of the missions was ever changing. Many of them ran away, and new ones had to be brought to take their place. On two occasions the missions had been moved after being partly destroyed in Indian raids, and forced to make new beginnings.

In the uprising of 1715 virtually everything had been lost; all the Indians had fled back to the wilds. The Indians assaulted the presidio, robbed the Mission San Juan, and destroyed the herds of mares belonging to the citizens of the presidial town. The same Indians who took part in the rebellion, however, were returned to the missions for a new beginning, brought back by Captain Diego Ramón—father of one of the witnesses—accompanied by the Reverend Father Friar Francisco Ruiz. This missionary later died in the Mission San Bernardo, shortly before he was to depart with Father Olivares to transfer the Mission San Francisco Solano to the San Antonio River in Texas.[10] One of the witnesses, Joseph Minchaca, testified that he was among the soldiers who went with Don Diego and Father Ruiz to bring the Indians back.[11]

The Indians living in the missions were not ready for self government, the witnesses agreed; if they were left to themselves, they would consume everything in a few days, then return to their nomadic life in the *montes.*

Apparently the tithes were never paid, but the controversy dragged on interminably. It was not until three years later, in 1740, that the representation of Friar Mariano Francisco de los Dolores y Viana to the Viceroy succeeded in getting the order rescinded.[12]

While the Franquis unheaval was at its zenith and the storm over payment of tithes was brewing, Captain Ecay Múzquiz was involved also in the founding of a new mission. On September 5, 1737, he served in lieu of Governor Clemente de la Garza Falcón to give possession of lands for the new Mission of San Francisco Vizarrón, a short distance from the Mission of Dulce Nombre de Jesús de Peyotes. Since 1734 Fray Joseph Rodríguez had sought official sanction for the mission. On September 29, 1735, the Viceroy Vizarrón issued an order that "in the marked bounda-

---

[10] *Ibid.,* p. 43; Lino G. Canedo (Isidro Félix de Espinosa, *Crónica de los colegios de propaganda fide de la Nueva España,* p. 739 n.) says Father Ruiz served four years in the missions of the Río Grande.

[11] Sevillano, "Representación," p. 59.

[12] *Ibid.,* pp. 62–64.

ries of the village of Dulce Nombre de Peyotes, Fray Joseph Rodríguez may found the Mission of San Francisco Vizarrón." The mission of Peyotes should not be moved, said the Viceroy, because the Indians had already built its church and houses.[13] Cervera Sánchez gives this version of the founding of San Francisco Vizarrón:

> Under date of September 25, 1736, Don Clemente de la Garza Falcón sent the order to the Captain of the Río Grande that he should give possession to Father Rodríguez. On October 17, 1736, Captain Ecay y Múzquiz [sic] replied to the governor that he was ready to give possession to Father Rodríguez when the *padre* advised him that he had gathered the Indians. On March 26, 1737, Father Rodríguez went to the Río Grande to tell the Captain that he already had the Pausanes Indians near the Mission, in the Mission of Peyotes. Finally, on April 4 that year, Captain Múzquiz was in the Mission of Peyotes to give Father Rodríguez possession. This took place solemnly on April 5, 1737, as he took possession of the lands and waters of Mission San Francisco Vizarrón.[14]

Ecay Múzquiz gave possession of the lands to the Indians and named the necessary officials—*alcalde, regidor, alguacil, mayor,* and *fiscal*—from among them. He marked as the boundary of the new mission's lands the road which linked Dulce Nombre de Jesús with the Presidio of San Juan Bautista del Río Grande.[15]

Thus San Juan Bautista continued to carry water on both shoulders; while providing succor to the missions of Texas, escorting supply trains, and serving as way station, it still must function in Coahuila. It must provide men for exploration and settlement, and protection for the new settlements which were founded.

The founding of San Francisco Vizarrón probably was the last in which Don Joseph Antonio de Ecay Múzquiz took part. The following year, 1738, he died at Presidio de San Juan Bautista.[16] His death apparently followed the pattern of his life: it came quietly, with little fanfare. This was not a flamboyant man, such as Don Diego Ramón, the elder; but he

[13] Jorge Cervera Sánchez in Fray Juan Agustín Morfi, *Descripción del Territorio del Real Presidio de San Juan Bautista del Río Grande del Norte, y su Jurisdicción, Año de 1778*, pp. 296–297 n.

[14] *Ibid.* See also Don Juan Gutiérrez de la Cueva, "Informe de las Misiones de la Provincia de Coahuila," A.G.N., Californias, Vol. 29, p. 219.

[15] Morfi, *Descripción,* 308 n.

[16] *Ibid.;* Alessio Robles, *Coahuila y Texas,* p. 492.

had served almost half a century on the northern frontier of New Spain, during the period when the most stirring history was being made; and like Don Diego, he left descendants who would carry his name deep into the story of Texas.

He was succeeded by Don Joseph Hernández, formerly lieutenant of the garrison, who like his predecessor had served many years in the presidios of Coahuila and San Juan Bautista. In 1729 Hernández had served with José de Berroterán on his expedition up the Río Grande, leading the troops from San Juan Bautista. One of the oldest citizens of the Río Grande outpost, he was described as being especially knowledgeable regarding the surrounding country, standing alongside Diego (the younger) and Andrés Ramón.[17]

Don José served on a temporary basis until his appointment by royal decree the following year, 1739. He filled the post until his own death in 1744, when he was replaced by Captain Manuel Rodríguez, a native of Monclova, Coahuila, where he was born in 1697. Although Rodríguez was forty-seven years old at the time of his appointment as commandant of the Presidio de San Juan Bautista, he was to serve at that post for twenty-eight years, surpassing even the tenure of Diego Ramón himself.[18]

Manuel Rodríguez had first come to the Presidio del Río Grande on January 3, 1717, to serve two years as a soldier. In 1720 he was found in the company of the Marqués de San Miguel de Aguayo, then governor of Coahuila, as a volunteer on a campaign against the rebel Toboso Indians. He gave good account of himself.

While serving as a captain of militia he took part in 1721–1722 in three campaigns conducted by Don Blas de la Garza Falcón against the Tobosos, the latter one punishing the Indians severely for their raids in the Saltillo area and bringing an end to the incursions.

In 1732 both he and his younger brother, Vicente Rodríguez, accompanied Governor Manuel de Sandoval on an expedition against the Tobosos, overtaking them in the vicinity of La Bavia. The Indians were defeated, and thirty-four prisoners taken by the Spaniards. Rodríguez was back in time to join Don Juan Antonio de Bustillo y Ceballos, governor of Texas, on an expedition against the Apaches. These Indians were defeated

[17] Morfi, *Descripción,* 308 n.
[18] *Ibid.*

in a bloody battle on the San Sabá River in present Menard County, Texas, December 9, 1732.

After serving twelve years as a captain of militia in Coahuila, Rodríguez became *alférez* in the Presidio of Sacramento on June 1, 1737, then lieutenant in the Presidio del Río Grande (San Juan Bautista) October 22, 1738. In 1739, when Captain José de Urrutia of Presidio de Béjar waged a campaign against the Apaches, Don Manuel took along a picket from the San Juan Bautista company. Like Bustillo's of 1732 this expedition also reached the San Sabá River, surprised an Indian camp, and took a large number of captives.[19]

It is evident that when Rodríguez was elevated to the captaincy of the Presidio del Río Grande on December 1, 1743, he was a seasoned veteran of the frontier and its Indian wars. His experience would stand him in good stead during the twenty-eight years he was to serve as commandant.

[19] Manuel Rodríguez, Service Record, A.G.N., Provincias Internas, Vol. 25, pp. 301–303.

21. NEW ROADS TO TEXAS

IN THE YEAR 1745 Padre Fray Alonso Giraldo de Terreros joined the long list of missionaries to be elevated to the guardianship of the College of the Holy Cross of Querétaro after serving at San Juan Bautista.[1] That year the missionaries at San Antonio were reaching out to carry the Gospel to corners not yet touched by Christianity.

The period from 1731 to 1745 had not been noted for geographical expansion, but rather for development in areas already settled. But the next seventeen years would be marked by considerable efforts at exploration and settlement of new territory.[2]

[1] Lino G. Canedo in Isidro Félix de Espinosa, *Crónica de los colegios de propaganda fide de la Nueva España*, p. 215 n.
[2] Herbert Eugene Bolton, *Texas in the Middle Eighteenth Century*, p. 42.

In 1745 plans were being made to establish missions on the San Xavier River (today's San Gabriel); a settlement was about to be born which would affect the lives of many persons now living at San Juan Bautista. These projected new conversions would live and die in tragedy.

The missionaries of San Juan Bautista and San Bernardo had intentions of reaching out themselves to the uncivilized areas. They were planning, this year of 1745, an expedition to the natives who inhabited the lower Río Grande. This excursion was prevented, however, by an uprising at Mission Santa María de los Dolores de la Punta (Lampazos Naranjo, Nuevo León). Some of the coastal tribes joined in this revolt, and it seemed inadvisable for the missionaries to go among them at such a time.[3]

During this year, also, Father Francisco Xavier Ortiz, under orders of the commissary general of missions, Friar Juan Fogueras, made an official visit to the missions. He noted the progress of the conversions and made recommendations for improvement.

By this time San Juan Bautista and San Bernardo had baptized more than 1,000 Indians each, many of them having come from north of the Río Grande. Living in the two missions were 940 Indians, including 389 that had not been baptized.

The unbaptized neophytes [says Bolton] were mainly newcomers, and their number is an indication of the current activity among the outlying tribes. The discrepancies between the total numbers baptized and the numbers remaining at the missions is explained partly by runaways, but chiefly by deaths, for the majority of the adult baptisms were made at the deathbed, while disease at all times made sad havoc among the children.[4]

The missions of the Río Grande, like those on the San Antonio and the Guadalupe,[5] had made good progress in the temporal. In all respects the missions on the Río Grande, being older, were far in advance of those at San Antonio. Agriculture prospered, manufactures had been well established, and both missions had completed fine stone churches.[6]

[3] *Ibid.*, p. 16.
[4] *Ibid.*, p. 19.
[5] The Mission Nuestra Señora del Espíritu Santo de Zúñiga was at this time located on the Guadalupe. It was moved to the San Antonio River at present Goliad, along with the Presidio of Nuestra Señora de Loreto (La Bahía) in 1749.
[6] Says Bolton (*Texas in the Middle Eighteenth Century*, p. 21). Just how fine the churches were may be questionable. A few years later Friar Diego Jiménez

But in this year of 1745 the settlement of San Juan Bautista del Río Grande stood at the brink of change. A detachment of soldiers from the presidio, ranging downriver on reconnaissance, discovered a crossing on the Río Grande. The name of the patrol's leader, Jacinto de León, was given to the ford, hereafter known as Paso de Jacinto.[7] The soldiers had no inkling of the significance of their find; they had no way of knowing that here would spring the town of Laredo, and that future expeditions would by-pass San Juan Bautista and Paso de Francia in favor of a safer trail and a crossing at Paso de Jacinto.

The middle years of the century were busy and significant ones for San Juan Bautista. The period was marked by intensified interest in the regions not previously explored to satisfaction; primarily these regions were those along the Río Grande, both above and below the gateway.

Permanent settlements had been established in Nuevo Reino de León, Coahuila, Nueva Vizcaya, New Mexico, and Texas. Yet along the Gulf Coast from the Pánuco River to the Guadalupe River in Texas lay a vast territory still unsettled and largely unexplored. Included in the area were the Sierra Gorda and the present state of Tamaulipas, as well as the fertile valley of the lower Río Grande, between San Juan Bautista and the coast. Exploration of the region had been urged for years. In 1746 José de Escandón, *corregidor* of Querétaro, was chosen to head the conquest of Seno Mexicano, and plans moved forward under the impetus of the capable new viceroy, the Count of Revilla Gigedo.

Escandón approached the problem of exploration and colonization as he would a military campaign. His plan was to penetrate the area from seven different points at the same time, all the expeditions converging at the mouth of the Río Grande. He set January, 1747, as the starting time. From Pánuco 150 men were ordered to begin the march January 20, the same time as 200 men from Villa de Valles. Escandón would march at the head of 150 soldiers from El Jaumave on January 24. Nuevo León

---

launched the building of a new San Bernardo Church. San Juan Bautista had just made a short move, the distance of two rifle shots, four years before, in 1741, according to Fray Francisco Xavier Ortiz ("Visita de las Misiones de San Juan Bautista y de San Bernardo del Río Grande del Norte en la Provincia de Coahuila hecha por el Reverendo Padre Visitador Fr. Francisco Xavier Ortiz," A.G.N., Historia, Vol. 29, p. 95).

[7] Carlos Eduardo Castañeda, *Our Catholic Heritage in Texas*, III, 173.

troops would come in three detachments, from Cadereyta, Villa de Linares, and Cerralvo. The Coahuila troops, to be gathered by Governor Pedro de Rábago y Terán, would cross the Río Grande at San Juan Bautista and follow the left bank of the stream, while the Cerralvo force marched down the right bank so that the two groups could give each other aid in case of surprise attack.

Fifty men from La Bahía, joined by fifty from Los Adaes, were to march south as close to the coast as possible to reach the mouth of the Río Grande. In such a manner the entire area would be explored and mapped from all directions at once.

Until the exploration was begun, little more was known of the area than had been understood in 1705, when Governor Martín de Alarcón of Coahuila wrote of plans to reach the Frío River from San Juan Bautista by canoe. His plan was to paddle down the Río Grande to its juncture with the Nueces and thence up the Nueces to the Frío. Captain Orobio y Basterra from La Bahía, in his trek of 1747, was the first to discover the fallacy of Alarcón's plan. On reaching Corpus Christi Bay, he wrote, "This river of Las Nueces, which until now was thought to join the Río Grande del Norte, enters the sea at this place."[8]

Possibly because Coahuila Governor Rábago y Terán was in ill health, the downriver trip fell to Miguel de la Garza Falcón, commandant of Presidio of Santa Rosa María del Sacramento. Garza Falcón rode at the head of twenty-five soldiers from his own presidio, and fifteen from Monclova, ten militiamen—four from Monclova and two each from Santa Rosa, Valle de San Matías, and San Juan Bautista—and twenty-five Indians from the missions of San Juan Bautista and San Bernardo.

Fully equiped and provisioned, the force splashed across the Río Grande on January 21, 1747, having been delayed several days on the Sabinas River by a furious snowstorm. It followed the left bank downstream, in a southeasterly direction, staying close to the river. It was not feasible to carry out Governor Rábago's orders to explore the country back from the river, because of the lack of water.

The Coahuila troops reached the mouth of the Río Grande on March 3. Garza Falcón reported that he had found the country barren, short of

---

[8] *Ibid*, p. 144; José de Escandón to the Viceroy, October 27, 1747, A.G.N., Provincias Internas, Vol. 179, Part 1, pp. 241–247. For Alarcón's plan see Chapter 7 of this study.

grass as well as water, and covered with mesquite and similar brush. The land was low and of poor fertility, and because of the lack of an adequate water supply, he deemed it unfit for settlement.

The company passed thirty-eight rancherias of the coastal tribes, whose chiefs were friendly. The Indians told them of many other nations who dwelt on the other side of the river.

The leader of the Coahuila troops gave his name to a ford a few miles below present Laredo, known as Don Miguel, or Garza, Crossing.

Arriving at the coast, Garza Falcón failed to establish rendezvous with the troops from La Bahía and Los Adaes, as his instructions had provided. The La Bahía contingent had been delayed by snows, that of Los Adaes by a water shortage. For this failure he was excused by Rábago y Teran, who noted that Don Miguel had proceeded with persistence in the face of difficulty and had at all times conducted himself in a soldierly manner.

After passing a few days among the Indians of the coast, Garza Falcón began the homeward trek. Having traveled 186 leagues each way, the Coahuila company unsaddled at Monclova on March 28.[9]

The greater part of San Juan Bautista's role in the Escandón movement was quickly done with; but not so the effects to be felt by the gateway settlement. In this new area, to be called Nuevo Santander, after Escandón's native province in Spain, fourteen towns and fourteen missions were planned. The settlement, like the exploration, would be under the capable management of Escandón, new count of Sierra Gorda and knight of the Order of St. James. In response to a call from the colonizer for volunteer settlers, there resulted in 1749 on the lower Río Grande "the first great land rush within the present limits of the United States."[10]

In March, 1749, the first settlement, Nuestra Señora de Santa Ana de Camargo, was established across the river from present Rio Grande City, Texas, by Captain Blas María de la Garza Falcón and forty families from Nuevo León. The founding of Reynosa quickly followed. Missions were planted near each settlement. The settlers of each received fifty sitios (five leagues) of land on the north side of the Río Grande. With such encour-

9 Report of Governor Pedro de Rábago y Terán on the expedition of Miguel de la Garza Falcón, contained in Escandón's report to the Viceroy, October 26, 1747, A.G.N., Provincias Internas, Vol. 179, pp. 240–241.

10 Castañeda, *Our Catholic Heritage*, III, 156. Many documents pertaining to the settlement of Seno Mexicano are found in A.G.N., Historia, Vol. 29, Part 2.

PLATE 1. This unexcavated mound is the last site (after 1741) of Mission San Juan Bautista, established at present-day Guerrero, Coahuila, in 1700.

PLATE 2. Near the village of San José, from which Mission San Francisco Solano was moved in 1718 to San Antonio to become known in later years as the Alamo. Ruins like these could be of old mission buildings.

PLATE 3. The stone walls of Presidio de Monclova Viejo still stand on a hill over-looking the San Rodrigo River in northern Coahuila.

PLATE 4. The outline of buildings which once stood inside the walls of Presidio de Monclova Viejo.

PLATE 5. Paso de Francia as seen from the Mexican side of the Río Grande. The river flows through a maze of islands both above and below the crossing.

PLATE 6. View of the Pecos River Canyon where it joins the Río Grande, soon to be under the waters of Amistad Lake. In this vicinity Captain Vicente Rodríguez of Presidio de San Juan Bautista led his troops in Indian battle June 6, 1773.

PLATES 7–8. Church of the Mission San Bernardo, begun in the 1760's by Father Diego Jiménez and never finished. The ruins still stand a short distance north of Guerrero, Coahuila.

PLATES 9–10. Mission San Bernardo.

PLATES 11–12. Mission San Bernardo.

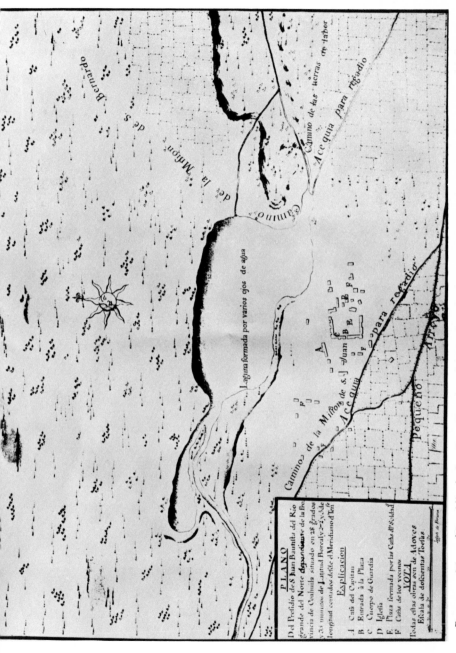

PLATE 13. Map of Presidio de San Juan Bautista del Río Grande drawn by Joseph de Urrutia, lieutenant of infantry, who assisted the engineer, Nicolás de Lafora, on the Rubí expedition (1767).

PLATE 15. Ruins of the customs house at old Pacuache Crossing, six miles northeast of Guerrero, Coahuila.

PLATE 14. Where the Camino Real emerged from Paso de Francia on the Texas side of the Río Grande, it started erosion which has formed this large gully on the Tovar Ranch, Maverick County.

PLATES 16–17. Ancient crypts are seen in the Guerrero cemetery, said to have been the burial ground in mission times. Many gravesites are marked with only a flat stone on top of the ground.

PLATE 19. View of a flat-roofed stone building—*casa de terrado*—of the presidio. The *presidencia municipal* is in the background.

PLATE 18. Arched doorway of an ancient building of presidio days, now approaching ruin.

PLATE 20. Thatch-roofed building of presidio times.

PLATE 21. Typical ruins which mark the site of Presidio de San Juan Bautista inside the village of Guerrero, Coahuila.

PLATE 22. This building, now the home and store of Señorita Profesora Aurora Botello G., was originally the home of the pay-master of Presidio de San Juan Bautista. Enscribed beams give the date of 1810, when the house, which is one block west of the plaza, was given a new roof.

PLATE 23. The *casa de capitán* of Presidio de San Juan Bautista del Río Grande at the time of the Rubí expedition is located at the northwest corner of the plaza.

PLATE 24. A street in Guerrero, Coahuila.

PLATES 25–28. Different views of an original presidio building at the south-east corner of the plaza. Note remains of a double archway.

PLATES 29–32. The Guerrero church, built in the early 1800's, now is kept locked and is opened only on request. Seen from the church belfry is the plaza, originally the *plaza de armas* of Presidio de San Juan Bautista. The modern school across the plaza stands on the site of *cuerpo de guardia* of the presidio.

PLATE 33. This camp of Company E, Texas Rangers, was located at Pacuache Crossing on the Río Grande near the mouth of Cuervo, or San Antonio, Creek.

PLATE 34. Two United States soldiers of Company L, Third Battalion, Third Infantry, at the ruins of the customs house in Texas near the Pacuache Crossing on the Río Grande, 1918 or 1919.

agement the settlers flocked to Escandón's province of Nuevo Santander. Some of the more venturesome souls actually went beyond the colonizer's plans for settlement, establishing themselves on land of their choice, then asking Escandón's approval. In such a manner the third settlement of the new province—Nuestra Señora de los Dolores—came into being, and with it a new set of circumstances for San Juan Bautista, which to this point had been the only real gateway to Spanish Texas. Now a new gateway was about to open.

While Indian hostility many times had held back settlement, Dolores is an example of how colonization was pushed forward by the bellicose natives. The Eastern Apaches, pressed upon from the north and east by the mounted Comanches and Wichitas, were ranging farther southward.

All the neighbors of the Apaches had become their enemies . . . Their backs were against the wall in the struggle to hold their own land against many aggressors. Provoked by the Spaniards' founding of missions for their enemies, the Apaches moved southward to sweep through Bandera Pass and raid San Antonio, or across the Río Grande to attack Spanish settlements in northern México, always stealing as many horses as they could.[11]

The ranches of Coahuila were being made to suffer, and the long-established trail between San Juan Bautista was known and being watched by the sanguinary Apaches. Travelers on the trail had long courted disaster in the form of Indian attack, and it was not too surprising, though none the less tragic, when it came in the summer of 1749.

The victims were Father Francisco Silva, a Zacatecan friar who had been assigned to a projected settlement on the Nueces River to be called Villa de Vedoya, and his escort of soldiers. Father Silva had left Seno Mexicano to go first to San Antonio, then to San Juan Bautista, in search of supplies for the settlement about to be founded. He reached San Antonio and departed for San Juan, escorted by eight soldiers. Five leagues from the Río Grande the band of hostiles attacked. Not long after the massacre some mission Indians from San Juan Bautista, carrying the mail to San Antonio, came upon the scene of death.

It was said that the nine murders were the work of the Apaches, "but this is not known for certain, because no one remained alive to tell."[12]

[11] Robert S. Weddle, *The San Sabá Mission: Spanish Pivot in Texas,* pp. 11–12.
[12] Fray Gaspar Gómes to the Commissary General, February 11, 1751, in A.G.N., Historia, Vol. 29, Part 2, pp. 375–376.

The death of Father Silva on July 5, 1749, evidently deterred the settlers of Vedoya, for the settlement was never established. Captain Diego González had crossed the Río Grande at San Juan Bautista with a band of colonists and soldiers from Nuevo León and a quantity of supplies before the year was out, bound for the site which had been selected. But the next spring Escandón received word that the Nuevo León families had withdrawn to Arroyo Salado in Nuevo León, where Captain González had died. They had found the Nueces site unsuitable and the Indians hostile.[13]

If the attack upon Father Silva's party had dissuaded these would-be settlers, it would have quite a different result for another new colony.

One of the Coahuila livestock raisers who suffered from Apache depredations was José Vásquez Borrego. His large hacienda, San Juan del Álamo, lay halfway between Monclova and San Juan Bautista, twenty-five leagues from each. The Indians repeatedly raided his herds until at last he sent scouts to seek a more suitable area in which to carry on his operations.

Independently of Escandón, Vásquez Borrego at last established his ranch beyond the Río Grande, within the bounds of Nuevo Santander. He then proposed in July, 1750, that his new hacienda be incorporated into the new colony as one of its settlements. His request was granted, and he received a grant of fifty sitios of land and exemption from taxes for a period of ten years. Thus the community of Nuestra Señora de los Dolores, twenty-one miles southeast of present Laredo, was born.

Vásquez Borrego began operating a ferry on the Río Grande, and when in 1753 the opportunity presented itself he asked Escandón to grant him an additional fifty sitios of land for this service. Escandón permitted him to charge a reasonable fee instead.[14]

As a result of the ferry the main road began to turn away from San Juan Bautista. The massacre of Father Silva's party was too fresh in the memory; the trail had been subjected too long to the ravages of the Apaches. The more southerly route could be traveled with less danger. By 1755 almost all the traffic bound from the interior of México to La Bahía, San Antonio, and Los Adaes crossed on Don José's boats at Dolores. The

13 Bolton, *Texas in the Middle Eighteenth Century*, p. 296.
14 Castañeda, *Our Catholic Heritage*, III, 165–166.

old road south of San Juan Bautista, which for so long a time had been the only road, now appeared almost abandoned. But still San Juan Bautista was the anchor post, the hub of the large wheel whose spokes were trails into the pagan land, which remained to be conquered.

A second settlement north of the Río Grande came into being May 15, 1755, when Tomás Sánchez, with a land grant from Escandón, founded Villa de Laredo, with only four families. The new village was at Paso de Jacinto, discovered ten years earlier by Jacinto de León and his party of soldiers from San Juan Bautista. Like Vásquez Borrego, Sánchez operated a ferry on the Río Grande, affording an alternate crossing for travelers to and from Texas. Just three years later it was reported that roads connected Laredo with San Antonio de Béjar, Monclova, Dolores, La Bahía, and Revilla.

The towns on the lower river drew more and more of the traffic to Texas away from the crossings at San Juan Bautista. Two-wheeled *carretas,* cattle herds, and pack trains chose the more peaceful routes downriver in preference to the Apache menace of the older trails. The new settlement forged rapidly to the front.

22. TO THE MEETING OF THE RIVERS

REASONS FOR THE POPULARITY of the new roads to Texas, which crossed the Río Grande farther downstream, were becoming increasingly apparent at San Juan Bautista. During the 1740's Apache raids on northern Coahuila intensified. In the earlier part of the decade the menace worsened also for the Spanish settlement at San Antonio. Captain Manuel Rodríguez at San Juan Bautista faced the necessity of taking action to bring relief to both the parent settlement on the Río Grande and its offspring in Texas.

In the autumn of 1744, less than a year after he had become commandant of Presidio del Río Grande, Don Manuel was joined by his brother, Vicente. The junior by two years, Vicente also had a long record of service in Coahuila and had been on many campaigns against the Tobosos[1] and the Apaches. Having served as *alférez* for three years previously in the Presidio of Sacramento, he now became lieutenant of his brother's Presidio of San Juan Bautista. Hardly had he taken the new post, October 11, 1744, than he was called upon to make preparations for assisting Captain Toribio de Urrutia of San Antonio de Béjar with a campaign against the Apaches. They pursued the aggressors to their village, probably on the San Sabá River, and punished them severely.

In 1747 Don Vicente took a force from San Juan Bautista to join Governor Pedro de Rábago y Terán in "another campaign against said Apache Indians for the hostilities which their cruelty had committed on this Presidio del Río Grande, whose punishment was happily attained."[2]

The following year, 1748, Don Manuel himself accompanied Governor Rábago on a campaign against the Apaches, joining "in putting a stop to their continued thefts, in punishing them, and in taking 95 of them prisoners."[3] He led a campaign himself from San Juan Bautista in 1750, about which it is recorded only that one Indian was captured.

For years the various Apache nations had harassed the mission settlements at La Junta de los Ríos. The missionaries had withdrawn in 1724 to San Felipe de Chihuahua, there being no presidio at La Junta to protect them, and carried on their work from there. Shortly after Don José de Escandón began his exploration of Seno Mexicano, the vigorous new viceroy, Count of Revilla Gigedo, turned his attention on the Río Grande

[1] By 1735, says James Manly Daniel ("The Advance of the Spanish Frontier and the Despoblado," p. 29), the Tobosos had largely disappeared, those who had not been killed by the Spaniards having joined the Apaches. At the same time the Comanches were pushing against the Apaches from the North. The Apaches thus moved into "the Despoblado" and succeeded the Tobosos as the bane of the Spaniards.

[2] Vicente Rodríguez, Service Record, A.G.N., Provincias Internas, Vol. 25, p. 300. This statement, written by Manuel Rodríguez, leaves one to wonder if it refers to the expedition of Rábago y Terán to La Junta de los Ríos. It evidently does, for, as will be seen, a contingent of troops from Presidio of San Juan Bautista, led by the lieutenant of the company (Vicente Rodríguez) accompanied the Governor to La Junta late in 1747.

[3] Manuel Rodríguez, Service Record, *Ibid.*, p. 302.

above San Juan Bautista. He called for a report on this sector, and the *auditor,* Marqués de Altamira, informed him of the need to reinforce the nearly defunct missionary effort at the meeting of the rivers.

The Viceroy promptly issued orders to the governors of Coahuila and Nueva Vizcaya. A simultaneous movement was planned, similar to Escandón's approach to Seno Mexicano, with all the units converging on La Junta to re-establish the six missions which had been abandoned because of Apache hostilities. Captain José Berroterán, still commandant of the Presidio of San Francisco de los Conchos, would be responsible for selecting a suitable site for a presidio.

Instructions to Governor Rábago y Terán called for gathering information from the most experienced and knowledgeable persons concerning the practicability of relocating Presidio de Sacramento. This post, if placed on either bank of the Río Grande, suggested the Viceroy, might render better service. It would serve to complement a new presidio at the confluence of the Conchos and the Río Grande, as well as that of San Juan Bautista. With such a series of forts the entire province of Coahuila would be protected against invasions from the bellicose Apaches who came from beyond the Río Grande.[4]

In this suggestion the Count of Revilla Gigedo showed advanced thinking. Some years later, under the Royal Regulation of 1772, a line of forts would be established in an effort to block the trails of access to marauding savages from the north.

Governor Pedro de Rábago y Terán, when he had recovered from an illness, relayed the Viceroy's orders to his presidio commanders. At San Juan Bautista fifteen men were chosen to accompany the lieutenant, Vicente Rodríguez, on the march with the Governor. Rábago y Terán, with twenty soldiers and ten mission Indians from the Presidio of San Francisco de Coahuila, marched out of Monclova on November 10, 1747. He rendezvoused at Presidio de Santa Rosa María del Sacramento with the force from San Juan Bautista on November 15. Augmented by thirty soldiers from Sacramento—headed by Captain Míguel de la Garza Falcón— the combined force included sixty-five soldiers, with 540 horses, 99 pack

[4] Instructions of the Viceroy, Don Juan Francisco Güemes y Horcasitas, Count of Revilla Gigedo, to Pedro de Rábago y Terán, June 22, 1747, A.G.N., Historia Vol. 52, pp. 126–127.

mules, and the *gente de servicio,* the service personnel required for tending the mules and their packs.[5]

Early on the morning of the sixteenth the chaplain of the expedition, Padre Fray Manuel María Neri, said Mass in the Presidio of Sacramento, "and we left from said presidio with the accustomed order, the three squads in one body, and taking the western course with some inclination to the north."[6]

Actually the force followed Arroya de la Bavia northwestward across Coahuila and did not strike the Río Grande until it reached the vicinity of present Big Bend National Park.[7] For this route there was good reason. The previous expeditions of Berroterán and Miguel de la Garza Falcón, who started upriver from San Juan Bautista, had proved the utter impossibility of following the Río Grande all the way to La Junta. Rábago cut across country to strike the river near to his destination, thus avoiding some, but not all, of the rough country which lay along its course.

Two days' travel out of Sacramento, on Arroyo de Álamos, a messenger came from the lieutenant of the presidio, apprising the Governor of the theft from a ranch in his district of two herds of mares, two nights previously. The Governor, without hope of success, sent a squad of ten soldiers to pursue the marauders in the direction of the headwaters of the San Rodrigo River, a hard day's ride to the north.

On the eighteenth the force remained in camp while Rábago, with Vi-

---

[5] Pedro de Rábago y Terán, "Diario de la Campaña executado por el Governador de Coahuila, Don Pedro de Rábago y Terán," A.G.N., Historia, Vol. 52, pp. 143–145. The complete diary is found on pages 143–191.

[6] *Ibid.,* p. 145. This departure was from present Melchor Múzquiz, Coahuila. Carlos Eduardo Castañeda (*Our Catholic Heritage in Texas,* III, 214) has mistakenly placed the expedition on the Río Grande, "a few miles above Del Río," by November 19, some two hundred miles off course. The key to this error lies in the fact that the presidio of Sacramento had been moved from its original site on the San Diego River to Melchor Múzquiz, far to the south. Ignoring that portion of the diary covering travel from Monclova to Sacramento, Castañeda states that the expedition traveled northwest fifty leagues from Sacramento on the San Diego River to reach the Río Grande.

[7] Vito Alessio Robles (*Coahuila y Texas en la época colonial,* p. 564) says the expedition first crossed the river above San Vicente Ford, near the Coahuila-Chihuahua boundary, at Chisos Crossing, to which Rábago applied the name Santa Rita. Daniel ("Advance of the Spanish Frontier," p. 19) says the crossing was at San Vicente, near the later site of the presidio by that name. Rábago y Terán ("Diario de la Campaña," p. 157) substantiates Alessio Robles.

cente Rodríguez and Captain Garza Falcón went to reconnoiter a stream five leagues beyond, which they called Río Escondido.[8] Resuming travel the nineteenth, the Spaniards turned northwest, following an old Indian trail up the Arroyo de Álamos to reach Las Rosas de San Juan, six leagues from the previous stop.

It is noteworthy [Don Pedro observed in his diary] that this route was followed because the margins of said upper Río Grande had already been reconnoitered as far as the San Felipe River, on both banks, even to the ford called San Vicente, and it offers no facility whatsoever for settlement, except on the rivers of San Rodrigo, San Diego, San Antonio, Santo Domingo, and San Ildefonso.[9]

On November 21 the expedition came to La Bavia, future site of a presidio by that name in the new line of defense established along the Río Grande after 1772. Finding water at this location, Don Pedro called a day's halt while his scouts went out to reconnoiter the country.

By November 25 rugged terrain slowed the pace of the march, with only two leagues logged for the day. Still in "Arroyo de Álamos,"[10] the force made camp beneath a hill called "Cuesta de San Xavier." A difficult climb faced Rábago's men the following day. Leaving the horseherd in an arroyo on the slope of the mountain, they began the grueling labor of raising the packs up a high cliff. They followed a trail which had been made by the enemy Indians. Since they had not been able to reconnoiter the high ground beforehand, springlike tension gripped the men as they ascended the steep path; the enemy could be lurking in any one of the many ravines that cut the rim of the mesa.

[8] Not to be confused with the river by that name which flows into the Río Grande at present Piedras Negras, this one joined Arroyo de la Bavia five leagues above the Camino Real from Sacramento to San Juan Bautista (Rábago y Terán, "Diario de la Campaña," pp. 146–147).

[9] Rábago y Terán, "Diario de la Campaña," p. 147. Rábago's difficult wordage evidently contributed to the aforementioned erroneous conclusion as to the route the expedition followed. The San Vicente Ford mentioned here is near present Del Rio and not to be confused with the one at the southernmost point of the Big Bend. The San Felipe River referred to is San Felipe Creek, which rises in southeastern Val Verde County, Texas, and flows southwest eleven miles to join the Río Grande at Del Rio.

[10] Arroyo de Álamos actually is the head of Arroyo de la Bavia, which becomes the Río de Sabinas. It appears here (*ibid.*) that the name Arroyo de Álamos is used interchangeably with La Bavia.

At last, after an arduous three leagues, they reached the pass in the mountains. The Governor gave the precipitous trail the name of Cuesta de los Suspiros. From the summit of the Hill of Sighs they could survey the country on the other side. Sighs of exhaustion gave way to sighs of relief, for their view into the distance revealed no signs of the dreaded enemy Indians. At nine o'clock that night the squad of soldiers which Rábago had sent out to scout the road ahead came into camp. Although they had covered much territory, they had failed to find water. The governor ordered another squad of ten men to make ready to ride forth at dawn.[11]

In the morning the horseherd had to be brought up from the arroyo on the side of the mountain, where it had remained through the night. With the train assembled, the march was begun in a southwesterly direction, still following the trail of the enemy Indians, the danger of surprise attack still eminent. The trail remained difficult, and just as dangerous as the one of the previous day, but it was downgrade, except for one high hill which had to be skirted.

Safely past the hill, the troop turned down an arroyo, following it northwestward. But the arroyo's potholes were dry, and only a little water, too fetid for the men to drink, was found. They camped that night after eight leagues' travel at a place which the Governor called San Pedro. The site was near the arroyo which joins the Río Grande just above Boquillas del Carmen. In the middle of the night the squad of soldiers who had left at dawn to scout ahead for water returned with welcome news. They had found an arroyo farther on with an abundant water supply.[12]

At eight o'clock on the morning of the twenty-eighth, Rábago went to make a personal reconnaissance of the trail indicated by his scouts. It was time well spent. Near the spring he observed the ashes of thirty Indian fires. The marks of the Indians' travois still were seen upon the ground, and on the decomposed carcass of a horse was the brand of one of the *vecinos* of Santiago de la Monclova. "Thus we came to full knowledge that these were the Indians who, on last October 5, had stolen some horses

---

[11] Rábago y Terán, "Diario de la Campaña," p. 152. The pass crossed by Rábago's men November 26, 1747, is in the Sierra del Carmen, twenty-seven air miles southeast of Boquillas.

[12] *Ibid.*, p. 153.

from the Valley of Las Ajuntas and killed a servant of the Señor Conde de San Pedro del Álamo at his hacienda."[13]

The surrounding area was surveyed, and many trails were found, all of which seemed to join at this one point. Rábago had come upon the first watering place used by the marauders following their raids on the settlements of Coahuila. If this one refuge could be eliminated, he reasoned, the raids from this quarter would be stopped. He suggested a presidio here would cut off the retreat of the Indians who were ravaging the settlements.

From the spring, which he named Santa María del Socorro, he sent out two squads to explore the country to the north and west, one led by the lieutenant of San Francisco de Coahuila, the other by Vicente Rodríguez of San Juan Bautista.[14] The first squad returned the following afternoon, having been unable to find a pass through the mountains. Some of the soldiers and Indian auxiliaries had climbed a high peak to look down upon the Río Grande where it cut through the rugged country in deep chasms, but there was no access to the stream itself, because of its precipitous walls.

At midnight Lieutenant Rodríguez and the soldiers of San Juan Bautista rode in from the north with a different story to tell. They had encountered many trails of the enemy, well marked by the tracks of their horses and mules. The Governor theorized that these could only be those of the herds of mares stolen from the vicinity of the Presidio of Sacramento on the fifteenth, joined, perhaps, by other small herds. Arriving at the Río Grande, Rodríguez and his Indian spies had surveyed its banks, locating a ford where many trails, both old and new, converged to cross. Travois and horse tracks testified that this was the principal crossing of many Indians.

On December 1 Don Pedro ordered the camp moved four leagues in the direction of the Rio Grande, to some pools which were given the name San Andrés, the feast of St. Andrew having been observed the day before. Reveille came early the day following, and the march was resumed on a northerly course, between towering canyon walls, overshadowed by craggy

---

[13] *Ibid.*, p. 154.
[14] *Ibid.*, p. 155. Names of these officers are *not* given in the diary. The name of Vicente Rodríguez is supplied because it is definitely known that he *was* the lieutenant of San Juan Bautista, as Rábago describes him, at that time.

peaks. Still seeing the tracks of the enemy, the company reached the Río Grande "farther up than the ford called San Vicente."[15] The Governor ordered a crossing at the new ford, which he named Santa Rita, located just above Mariscal Canyon. In what is known today as Big Bend National Park, Rábago's men made camp.

The following two days the Governor made an extensive personal reconnaissance, finding the country to be extremely mountainous, the river boxed in by high walls on either side—"between mountain and mountain, which is uncrossable."[16] He observed that the mountains, like those on the other side, contained many lustrous minerals. While a squad of soldiers looked upriver for future campsites, a band of auxiliary Indians explored the mountains to the north.

On the fourth the march was resumed, with four leagues traveled to a point almost due south of Emory Peak. The following day many abandoned Indian camps were found, and three horses which the enemy had left behind. In the river canyon at one point were found some springs which gushed warm water. Making camp in a glen, where he found Castillian poplars (Álamos de Castilla) and willows in profusion, Rábago noted that no other white man had ever traversed the north bank of the Río Grande in this vicinity.[17] The place, to which he gave the name Santa Bárbara, probably was near present Castalon.

From this point on it is difficult to determine exact locations, because the rough country caused many meanders. Distance traveled in the upstream direction probably was much less than actually logged. The route was circuitous. On the sixth the explorers traveled south, then west, then north, to arrive at a field where pumpkins had been planted; the place apparently had been abandoned by the Indians just before they arrived. They named it Real de las Calabazas, likely somewhere near the mouth of Santa Elena Canyon and Terlingua Creek.

Because of the broken country the Spaniards had to abandon the course of the river on the seventh. Again meandering in three directions, across deep arroyos, over stony hills, and through thorny brush, they reached a place near the river where a giant cottonwood grew and there was ample pasture. The place was named Álamo Grande. On the eighth they found

[15] *Ibid.*, p. 157.
[16] *Ibid.*, p. 158.
[17] *Ibid.*, p. 160.

many old Indian camps and two dead horses with brands of Coahuila ranches. That night it began snowing, and they marched in a blizzard the following day to the Arroyo de Mezquital. Heavy snow again fell during the night, keeping the voyageurs in camp on Sunday, December 10. The chaplain said Mass in a tent.

On December 13 Rábago y Terán and his men came to an Indian camp which had been abandoned ten or twelve days previously. The camp bore signs of a *mitote* or scalp dance having been celebrated there: A horse had been roasted on the spot, and a totem pole with blood stains from the fresh scalps that had been hung upon it was found. On the river nearby they discovered a ford which was named Paso de Rábago, where they made camp preparatory to crossing the next day.[18]

After reaching the south bank of the river on the fourteenth, Rábago led his company over frozen ground and rugged terrain for four days, following Indian trails and carefully observing signs of the enemy's presence. The soldiers felt themselves constantly watched by hostile eyes. Surprise attack might come at any moment. On the afternoon of December 18 a portion of the vanguard, mounting a hill, saw spirals of smoke in the distance. "Not knowing from what settlement it might come," wrote the Governor, "I kept myself on said hill and sent to make reconnaissance a squad of soldiers in the charge of the lieutenant of the Presidio del Río Grande, by the same trail which we had followed to this place."[19]

Lieutenant Vicente Rodríguez returned with news that the smoke came from the Pueblo of Nuestra Señora de Guadalupe, where he found no *justicia mayor,* but an Indian governor and one minister of the order of St. Francis, Padre Fray Francisco Sánchez. The priest had placed his mission at the disposal of the company, which at last had arrived at the meeting of the rivers.

With this news, so greatly longed for after the imponderable labors of cold, lack of water, snow and ice, and considerable loss of horses and mules, I took up the march for the mission. The missionary received us with chiming bells, because of the great jubilation which he felt on seeing conquered such impossible tasks as those of this passage. After giving thanks to His Divine Majesty

[18] Apparently near present Mulato, as Alessio Robles (*Coahuila y Texas,* p. 565 n.) says.
[19] Rábago y Terán, "Diario de la Campaña," p. 169.

and my Lady of Guadalupe we left the church and camped in the plaza of said pueblo, having traveled this day . . . some twelve or thirteen leagues.[20]

Father Sánchez was the only missionary in the Mission of Guadalupe. It was situated below the confluence of the Conchos and the Río Grande, while the Mission of San Francisco, of which Father Lorenzo Saavedra was minister, was above the meeting of the rivers. These two missions were on the right bank of the Río Grande. On the left bank were the missions of San Cristóbal and San Antonio de los Puliques, the former directly in front of the confluence, the latter farther downstream.

That night the Governor had a long conference with Father Sánchez, who was totally discouraged by the lack of success he was having with the Indians. The natives did as they pleased in the absence of a military force to keep them subjected.

Captain Joseph Idoiaga, with his force from Nueva Vizcaya, had been at the Mission Guadalupe but had departed for El Cajón, ten leagues up the Río Grande. While awaiting news from him, Rábago crossed the river and reconnoitered the ruins of the missions of San Antonio de los Puliques and San Cristóbal. Back on the right bank two days later, he visited the scattered villages of Christian Indians, then returned to the Mission of Guadalupe.

In the Indian villages he saw many herds of horses and mules bearing brands of the citizens of Saltillo, Nuevo Reino de León, Santa Rosa, San Juan Bautista del Río Grande, Monclova, and the ranches of those districts. The soldiers, having observed on their journey across Coahuila and Nueva Vizcaya the trails which the Indians used for making their raids, were eager to accost the savages and claim the stolen livestock. Rábago issued orders forbidding it; the horses should be regained only by trading for them.

The Governor also learned that a Pampopa Indian woman from the Mission San Bernardo and another from San Juan Bautista were held captive among the mission Indians of La Junta, who claimed they had purchased them from the Apaches. Rábago gave the captors to understand that the Indian women were not to be sold as slaves, since both had been baptized in the Río Grande missions and one of them had a living hus-

[20] *Ibid.*, p. 170.

band waiting for her return. Joined by the two priests, he prevailed upon the Indians of La Junta to deliver their captives to him.

The Governor made a reconnaissance of the area between the Río Grande and the Conchos, then went up the Conchos to the Mission of San Juan. Going and coming, he traveled twelve leagues. Captain Idoiaga, meanwhile, wrote that his return would be delayed several days. Rábago waited until the twenty-eighth, then moved across the river to begin his return to Coahuila next day.

After crossing the Río Grande again at Paso de Rábago, the Governor's force reconnoitered the right bank on the return trip. It followed an old Indian trail through what would seem to be almost impenetrable country, passing the future site of Presidio de San Carlos and proceeding along the south rim of Santa Elena Canyon. After having passed near Santa Rita Ford to a campsite four leagues downstream, Rábago divided his force on January 7. He placed all the soldiers except those from Monclova in charge of Captain Garza Falcón of Presidio de Sacramento and sent them back the way they had come. With the rest of the company he returned by a more direct route, reaching Monclova on January 13. The main body of the company reached Sacramento with worn-out horses three days later. Lieutenant Rodríguez and the soldiers from the Río Grande presidio proceeded on to San Juan Bautista,[21] presumably with the two Indian women released by their captors at La Junta de los Ríos.

The Coahuila governor sent his report to the Viceroy on January 23, relating details of his expedition over 348 leagues of unexplored country, stalked constantly by hostile Indians, especially at the mountain passes and the water holes. This route diary has value even today, since the area which Rábago traveled has yet to be completely explored. With the information contained in his report, says Alessio Robles, it was possible to establish several presidios to close the route by which the Indians of the North came to attack Coahuila and Nueva Vizcaya.[22]

Although Rábago strongly advocated establishment of the long-awaited Presidio del Norte at the meeting of the rivers, eleven years would pass before it finally was founded on the Texas side of the Río Grande, near

---

[21] *Ibid.*, p. 190.

[22] Alessio Robles, *Coahuila y Texas,* p. 568. The presidios, however, failed in the purpose for which they were founded, as will be noted later in this study.

the present town of Presidio. In the meantime Don Pedro de Rábago would be called to serve another cause, and the soldiers of Presidio de San Juan Bautista del Río Grande would be divided to assist new settlements to the north.

23. BRINK OF SACRIFICE

H ARDLY was a settlement launched or a move made on the northern frontier of New Spain during the first half of the eighteenth century without the direct involvement of San Juan Bautista. Even after Escandón's downriver settlements turned the tide away from the first and foremost gateway to Spanish Texas, it continued to furnish supplies, services, and manpower for extension of the kingdom. Such names as Ramón and Ecay Múzquiz would still be heard on the far limits of the Texas frontier, as the descendants of these first two commandants of Presidio de San Juan Bautista del Río Grande went forth to serve.

Troops and auxiliaries of San Juan Bautista had aided both Escandón in settlement of Nuevo Santander and Don Pedro de Rábago y Terán in his reconnaissance from Coahuila to La Junta de los Ríos. The Franciscan priests at San Antonio, meanwhile, pressed out upon new missionary frontiers. Their latest endeavor was a settlement of three missions on the San Xavier River (now known as the San Gabriel, near present Rockdale) for Indians of the Tonkawan, Attacapan, and Karankawan nations.

"The missions met trouble from the start. Raiding Apaches drove away the mission Indians. Disputes arose between the missionaries and the antagonistic governor, Pedro del Barrio y Espriella."[1]

Before a permanent presidio was authorized, thirty soldiers were assigned to protect the missions, arriving in March, 1748. The first contingents of soldiers came from the presidios of La Bahía and Los Adaes.

---

[1] Robert S. Weddle, *The San Sabá Mission: Spanish Pivot in Texas,* p. 32.

Families of converted Indians came from San Antonio and the Río Grande missions to aid in the new missionary endeavor. Cattle and other supplies also were obtained from these places, with payment to be made when possible.[2]

On July 7, 1749, the Viceroy approved a plan proposed by the *auditor*, Altamira, for increasing the San Xavier garrison to forty-eight men. To provide the additional eighteen he suggested that four soldiers from Monclova and ten from Sacramento be sent to San Juan Bautista to serve; from San Juan sixteen men should be sent to Béjar; from Béjar eighteen should be sent to San Xavier. It was a roundabout way of getting it done, but on August 28 the sixteen men from San Juan Bautista arrived at Béjar, on the way to San Xavier.[3]

In accordance with the Viceroy's instructions, the commandant at Béjar, Toribio de Urrutia[4] appointed Diego Ramón III as lieutenant of the garrison. Ascensio Rasso was named *alférez*. Governor Barrio, angry at not being consulted, countermanded Urrutia's orders, appointing Lieutenant Juan Galván to serve as lieutenant. Ramón, said the Governor, was a mulatto who had been degraded for offenses he had committed while he was an officer at La Bahía.[5] Neither Rasso nor Ramón could read, and Ramón could write "only under the direction and counsel of the Rev. Father Fray Mariano de los Dolores."[6] Controversy flared anew, and Barrio sent Galván back to San Xavier over the protests of Father Dolores.

On July 9, 1749, Father Benito Fernández de Santa Ana reached San Juan Bautista on his way from the Texas missions to the city of México. He was going to the capital to counteract the hostile reports of Barrio and to present his plans for an Apache mission. When he arrived at the Río Grande he learned that approval already had been granted for the in-

---

[2] Herbert Eugene Bolton, *Texas in the Middle Eighteenth Century*, p. 192.

[3] *Ibid.*, pp. 206, 211. See also Elizabeth H. West (trans.), "Bonilla's Brief Compendium of the History of Texas," *SWHQ*, 8, No. 1 (July, 1904), 47.

[4] Toribio de Urrutia, the son of José Urrutia, had succeeded his father as commandant at Béjar.

[5] This was the son of Domingo Ramón, leader of the 1716 *entrada* into Texas. Young Diego Ramón, when his father was killed in an Indian uprising at La Bahía in 1723, succeeded him as commandant, serving until an investigation revealed the deplorable conditions that had arisen. Juan Antonio Bustillo y Ceballos was named to replace him. What had happened to Diego Ramón during the years which separated this incident from the San Xavier affair is obscure.

[6] Bolton, *Texas in the Middle Eighteenth Century*, p. 212.

creased garrison at San Xavier, but he decided to continue his journey anyway. As a result of this decision Barrio was discredited in México, and a new investigation ordered before the presidio could be established at San Xavier. Chosen to make the inquiry was José Joaquín de Ecay Múzquiz of the Presidio of Sacramento—probably a son of the late commander of San Juan Bautista, José Antonio de Ecay Múzquiz. He arrived in Texas to begin the survey in June, 1750.

Ecay Múzquiz, in the report of his investigation, favored establishment of a presidio and maintenance of the missions at the San Xavier site, instead of moving them to the San Marcos River, as Barrio had insisted. Eight months passed before consent was given, and Felipe de Rábago y Terán, nephew of Don Pedro, the governor of Coahuila, was named captain. It was a stroke of tragedy for the San Xavier missions. Felipe de Rábago was to attain new heights of infamy in the annals of the Spanish mission movement in Texas.

On his way north from the capital, Felipe de Rábago stopped for a lengthy stay at Monclova, possibly for a visit with his uncle, though one must wonder what the two could have had in common. Late in November he passed San Juan Baustista, where there could have been no indication of the future relationship he would have with that settlement, and thence on to San Xavier to relieve Ecay Múzquiz on December 11, 1751.

The San Xavier missions, whose story has been adequately told elsewhere, were ill-starred from the beginning. The misfortunes of the venture set the Texas mission movement back perhaps for decades, and at this point it almost caused the death of the Río Grande missions of San Juan Bautista and San Bernardo.

The new missions in Texas had demanded increasing expenditures, taxing the royal treasury beyond reason. The requests came at a time when Escandón was launching his unparalleled colonization plan; a new presidio was being considered at La Junta de los Ríos; proposals had been made for a new mission at La Bahía; and every presidio in Texas, Coahuila, and New Mexico was clamoring for an increased garrison. Father Santa Ana burned with zeal for the conversion of the Apaches and had even proposed abandonment of the San Antonio missions and removal of the Presidio de Béjar to the Pedernales River to this end.[7]

[7] Carlos Eduardo Castañeda, *Our Catholic Heritage in Texas*, III, 302.

Early in 1750 this zealous friar, in the capital to advance his Apache mission plan, was rebuffed by the authorities, his request flatly refused. The news was sent to the missions at San Juan Bautista and those at San Antonio by the guardian of the College of the Holy Cross, Father Francisco Xavier Castellanos.

The relationship between these circumstances and the proposal to end the missionary effort on the Río Grande is left to conjecture. It appears likely that the idea stemmed both from the financial difficulty resulting from the San Xavier fiasco and from the hope that the resources of the Río Grande missions could be directed to converting the Apaches. The suggestion appears to have originated with Father Alonso Giraldo de Terreros, who had returned to San Juan Bautista after ending his term as guardian in 1748 and was now serving as president of the Río Grande Missions. The college of La Santa Cruz planned to turn the wealth of these missions—long reputed to be excessive—to the better support of San Xavier. The gateway missions, it was suggested, should be turned over to the secular clergy.

Under date of November 28, 1751, the college ordered Terreros as president to send a thousand goats to San Xavier missions, "in order that, with this subsidy, those new sons of the church may have the means with which to continue Christian and civilized life."[8] With the letter was one to Father Mariano de los Dolores, instructing him to send at once a religious to take the goats away. Father Terreros was to use his own judgment as to other items from the old missions which could be used in the new. In February, Fray Miguel Pinilla, passing by on his way to San Xavier, took charge of the goats at San Juan Bautista. Further instructions were issued at this time that each mission should send to San Xavier as many horses as might be spared.[9]

But suddenly there was a change of plan. It was to be many years before San Juan Bautista missions were secularized or suppressed. Events transpiring at San Xavier turned the tide. When Felipe de Rábago arrived in December to take charge of the presidio, he came with the wife of one of his soldiers as his mistress. When the husband complained threaten-

[8] Bolton, *Texas in the Middle Eighteenth Century*, p. 239, citing Discretorio to Terreros, November 28, 1751.

[9] *Ibid.*, p. 240, citing Discretorio to Terreros, February 21, 1752.

ingly, he was placed in irons, though he managed to escape and take refuge with the missionaries. The presidio chaplain, Father Miguel Pinilla of the Mission Candelaria, succeeded in sending the woman back to San Antonio, but in so doing he won the enmity of the Captain. These events led Father Mariano de los Dolores to propose, such a short time after winning establishment of the presidio, that it be abolished. Dolores was not the most benign of the missionaries, and it was with some justification that officials at the college decided he should be removed in the interest of harmony. He would be "promoted," in the words of the guardian, to the presidency of the Río Grande missions. Father Terreros would be put in his place as president of the missions of San Antonio and San Xavier.[10]

The instructions came to Father Terreros: He was to go at once, leaving Father Miguel Placido de Alaña in charge at San Juan Bautista until Friar Mariano could come from Texas. On his arrival at San Antonio, Friar Alonso was to deliver to Dolores the order to go to the Río Grande to take charge. Actually, it was no promotion for Dolores. The guardian confessed as much in his letter to Terreros, saying never before had the college been in such need of the wisdom and prudence which had brought peace to the missions under Father Terreros' direction.

And Friar Mariano, when he got news of the planned switch, was not to view it as an advancement. It created in him an enmity toward Terreros which endured for years and, as was so often the case with bickering among officials on the frontier, this ill feeling may well have affected the course of history adversely. But the plans, as it developed, were only academic.

Before Terreros, as the instrument of peace, could begin the journey to Texas, the situation at San Xavier became irreparable.

Another adulterous affair between the wife of a soldier and one of Rábago's favored subordinates came to light when the woman told of the relationship in her confessional. The matter shortly was public knowledge, and the woman's lover accused Father Pinilla, the presidio chaplain, of violating the seal of the confessional. Rábago forbade Pinilla from ministering as chaplain to the garrison and banished him from the presidio. The priest excommunicated the garrison, February 19, 1752.

In the aftermath Friar Juan José de Ganzábal and the soldier, Juan José

---

10 *Ibid.*, p. 255.

Ceballos, whose wife had been Rábago's mistress, were slain in a plot apparently perpetrated by Rábago. The Captain was removed to command the Presidio of Sacramento in Coahuila, where he was to face a prolonged investigation.

Rábago, conducted on his forced journey under guard, found occasion to resent the treatment he received at the behest of Captain Manuel Rodríguez of Presidio del Río Grande. He protested in a letter written from Presidio de Sacramento to the viceroy, now the Marqués de las Amarillas, that Rodríguez had crudely emphasized his status as a prisoner by keeping him under heavy guard.

> Even a chief of such well-known merit and experience might have accorded honorable treatment in delivering me under arrest, with the manner appropriate to an innocent and destitute officer who is humbled at the feet of your Excellency with great submission, imploring your powerful protection and mercy . . .[11]

Captain Miguel de la Garza Falcón was sent from Sacramento to replace Rábago at San Xavier.

The death knell had sounded for the ill-fated missions on the San Xavier. As if the hand of God had marked the spot in retribution of the sins committed there, the river ceased to flow, standing in stagnant pools. Most of the Indians had fled, and pestilence decimated the ranks of those who remained.[12]

Among the fatalities was Miguel de la Garza Falcón. His successor was Don Pedro de Rábago y Terán, governor of Coahuila the previous ten years. Rábago, at the insistence of the missionaries, at last took matters into his own hands. He moved the missions and the presidio to the San Marcos River, where many had urged that they be placed years before.

Prior to Don Pedro's departure from Coahuila, however, his name appears in connection with two other incidents in which the San Juan Bautista settlement played a part. In response to a petition by twenty-two

---

[11] Felipe de Rábago y Terán to the Viceroy, Marqués de las Amarillas, March 26, 1756, A.G.N., Provincias Internas, Vol. 22, p. 104. Rábago had been at Sacramento several months when he wrote this letter, since he wrote from the same place December 13, 1755 (*ibid.*, p. 102). Manuel Rodríguez, in his statement of his service record, strangely, tells of having assisted "the captain of Santa Rosa, Don Felipe de Rábago," in a campaign against the Julimeños in 1755 (A.G.N., Provincias Internas, Vol. 25, 302). This document is dated November 1, 1764.
[12] Weddle, *San Sabá Mission*, p. 34.

vecinos of the Presidio de San Juan Bautista del Río Grande, the viceroy, Count of Revilla Gigedo, issued a decree December 29, 1749, for the founding of San Fernando de Austria. Alessio Robles calls this settlement the most important one in Coahuila in the second half of the eighteenth century.[13] It was founded February 1, 1753, not far from the earlier mission site of San Ildefonso (San Francisco Solano) from 1703 to 1708.

The request for this new village appears to have been one of the first ominous signs of the future in store for the civilian settlement around the Presidio of San Juan. The community was literally being choked to death. The missions of San Juan and San Bernardo held title to the lands and waters surrounding the presidio and village; there was no opportunity for a *vecino* to obtain land nearby on which he might raise crops and live-stock. Even the haciendas of the Ramón and Ecay Múzquiz families lay some distance away to the south. Those who had tried settling on the other side of the Río Grande had found themselves cut off from the pro-tection of the presidio and exposed to the ravages of the Apaches. Their lands soon were abandoned.

Thus it appeared, as the eighteenth century passed the halfway mark, that citizens of the Río Grande settlement must look elsewhere for oppor-tunity. The names on the petition included some of San Juan Bautista's oldest families: Juan José Vázquez Borrego, Jerónimo Flores, Pedro José Zepeda, Juan Antonio Ramos, Juan José Rodríguez, José Navarro, Juan Flores, Nicolás Sánchez, Juan Olvera, Joaquín Flores, Andrés de la Garza, Francisco de la Garza, Diego Jiménez, Mateo Rodríguez, Pedro D. Charles, José Guardiana, Petra Longoria, Javier Jiménez, José Pérez, Juan Guajardo, Francisco Reducindo, and Manuel Flores.[14]

Governor Pedro de Rábago, on his general visit to the settlements, was at San Juan Bautista at the time. Accorded the honor of officiating in the founding of the settlement, he was accompanied by Friar Juan Rubio de Monroy, from the Mission of Santa Rosa de Nadadores. The Governor, assisted by the *vecino* Jerónimo Flores, made with his own hands the cross which was placed at the cemetery.

Thirty-six *pobladores* were listed at the time of the founding, but some

13 Vito Alessio Robles, *Coahuila y Texas en la época colonial*, pp. 571–572.

14 *Ibid.*, p. 572. It is pointed out (pp. 571–572) that the name of San Fernando de Austria was changed to San Fernando de Rosas in 1827 and again to Zaragoza, the name presently used, in 1868.

of the settlers apparently became dissatisfied with the new location and withdrew, for when Friar Antonio de Aguilar came in 1756 to take charge of the local church, he found but twenty. The infant settlement, however, was destined to surpass its parent, and in 1762 the number had grown to forty-seven. The Governor, on arriving at the spring known as Las Ánimas, proceeded first to divide the lands and waters among the colonists, and to measure off a square, marking the site for the church and government buildings. He bestowed the name of "San Fernando de Austria, Valle de las Ánimas," and named Jerónimo Flores as general procurator of lands and waters. Leaving eighteen men and the Franciscan priest to cut timber for construction of the first houses, the Governor returned next day to the Presidio of San Juan Bautista del Río Grande to complete his inspection.

A presidial force of twenty-one men under command of Vicente Rodríguez also was established at the settlement, nine of them in the new village and twelve at the neighboring ranch of San Ildefonso.[15]

During the first quarter of a century, the transplanted *vecinos* of San Juan Bautista who formed the new village on the Río Escondido apparently failed to prosper. In 1778 Teodoro de Croix and Friar Juan Agustín de Morfi visited the settlement, and Morfi wrote in his diary:

Although the territory is suitable for a metropolis, the village is nothing more than a miserable hamlet. The houses are little cabins of sticks, with grass roofs. If there are some which have walls of stone and mud, the roofs always are the same, unless the continued attacks in which the Indians set fire to them force the people to make flat roofs. Of this they already have some examples.[16]

The other venture in which both Governor Rábago y Terán and San Juan Bautista figured was the establishment of the first Spanish mission for the Apaches. It followed the year after San Fernando de Austria was founded, and in the same general locality.

The Franciscan friars at the San Antonio missions, notably Benito Fernández de Santa Ana and Mariano de los Dolores, had sought for years

---

[15] According to his service record (A.G.N., Provincias Internas, Vol. 25, pp. 299–300), Vicente Rodríguez still was considered lieutenant of Presidio de San Juan Bautista del Río Grande.

[16] Juan Agustín Morfi, *Viaje de Indios*, pp. 246, quoted in Alessio Robles, *Coahuila y Texas*, p. 574.

to win establishment of an Apache mission. Their effort, however, became mired in the tedium of official red tape.

The Apaches themselves were willing. For a time they had come to San Antonio in large bands, proposing to camp there until a mission was founded for them. But the missions of San Antonio were not prepared to take them in, and establishing new missions elsewhere would be time-consuming. The Apaches were not disposed to wait.

Bands of this generally hostile nation frequently visited the vicinity of San Juan Bautista, sometimes in broad daylight to slake their curiosity concerning the Spaniards by conversing with them in the villages, sometimes in the dark of night to plunder and kill. The president of the Río Grande missions, Father Terreros, had on various occasions talked with members of the Natagés, a branch of the eastern Apaches, who visited Presidio del Río Grande and frequently committed depredations in the area. With patience and zeal the padre had sought to induce these Indians to accept Christianity and settle themselves in a mission.

Now turned away by the priests at San Antonio, they came to see Father Terreros, who yearned for the conversion of the Apaches, much as Francisco Hidalgo had longed to return to finish his work among the Tejas. Father Terreros turned to Governor Pedro de Rábago y Terán.

Rábago now was under orders transferring him to the Presidio of San Xavier, to fill the command post left vacant by the death of Miguel de la Garza Falcón. He nevertheless wrote to the Viceroy on June 3, 1754: Peace treaties had been made with the Apaches, said the Governor, and as a result more than nine hundred of them—chiefly Natagés, Cíbolos, and Tucubantes—were camped along both banks of the Río Grande, near the new settlement of San Fernando de Austria.

Although the Indians appeared to desire settlement in missions, Rábago said, he himself had doubts. Suggesting that Captain Manuel Rodríguez of Presidio San Juan Bautista be instructed to make an investigation in cooperation with the missionaries, he proposed to treat the Indians as guests until the Viceroy's pleasure was known.[17]

The viceregal advisers were skeptical, but they approved the investiga-

<hr/>

[17] Castañeda, *Our Catholic Heritage,* III, 356; Bolton, *Texas in the Middle Eighteenth Century,* p. 80; See also William Edward Dunn, "Missionary Activity among the Eastern Apaches Previous to the Founding of the San Sabá Mission," *SWHQ,* 15, No. 3 (January, 1912), 196–200.

tion. Rábago, meanwhile, proceeded to his new assignment, in which he was called upon almost immediately to explore the possible site of another proposed Apache mission, on the San Sabá River in Texas. Left to serve in his stead was the lieutenant governor, Juan Antonio Bustillo y Ceballos, who received his instructions at Monclova on November 22. He departed December 2 for San Juan Bautista, arriving on the ninth. Four days later he proceeded, in the company of Lieutenant Vicente Rodríguez and Father Terreros.

They traveled upstream to meet the Indians on the river not far from present Eagle Pass-Piedras Negras. Though the Indians expressed a preference for a mission site on the San Rodrigo, a more suitable site was found at San Ildefonso, eighteen leagues west of San Juan Bautista and two leagues from San Fernando de Austria. A council was held with the chiefs of a large band of Apaches camped nearby and mission life was explained to them. The Indians agreed to the terms. Bustillo y Ceballos then gave possession on December 21, 1754, bestowing the name San Lorenzo. The new mission was to be under the protection of the twelve soldiers placed the year before at the *estancia* of San Ildefonso.[18]

Friar Alonso de Terreros, who deserves to be called the apostle and martyr of the Apaches, remained in charge of the mission, another offshoot from San Juan Bautista. By the beginning of March, 1755, fifty-two Apaches were living at San Lorenzo. The number increased to eighty-three by the end of the month. The neophytes all came from the other side of the Río Grande, where they were being pressed upon by the mounted Comanches and Wichitas.

The buildings erected and the *acequia* constructed, Father Terreros found it necessary to go to Querétaro, and possibly to the capital, to seek support for his venture. He left Friar Diego Martín García, who had previously served at San Antonio, in charge. The following June, Friar Martín was replaced by Friar Félix Gutiérrez Varona, who had seen service at the disaster-prone San Xavier missions. This priest worked hard and earnestly to win the nomadic Apaches to Christianity, but his zeal was not enough. When the geese flew south in the autumn the Indians grew

---

[18] The site of San Ildefonso, says Jorge Cervera Sánchez (in Fray Juan Agustín Morfi, *Descripción del Territorio del Real Presidio de San Juan Bautista del Río Grande del Norte, y su Jurisdicción, Año de* 1778, p. 307) was on the hacienda of Vicente Rodríguez).

restless. On October 4 they rose up, sacked the mission, and set fire to the buildings while the awe-stricken padre watched helplessly.

Leveled at a stroke, the mission would never rise again. The Spanish Franciscan missionaries had had their first bitter taste of Apache faithlessness. "The Apaches' quest for missions, in every case, was to endure only as long as it suited their convenience. And in every case this was just long enough to get the Spaniards into trouble."[19]

Yet the experience at San Lorenzo had strengthened, rather than weakened, the argument for placing missions in the Apaches' own country farther north.

[19] Weddle, *San Sabá Mission*, p. 22.

24. PROVIDENCES OF 1756

ALL ALONG THE NORTHERN FRONTIER of New Spain the Apaches had become a dreaded menace. They were being driven from their homeland on the southern plains by the Comanches and the Wichitas, only to find themselves hemmed in on the south by the Spaniards. Indeed the whole situation stemmed from the coming of the Europeans: by introducing the Indians to the horse, they had upset the cultural balance maintained so long among the tribes.

As a result the mounted Plains Indian possessed new capabilities as a hunter and as a warrior. He could range great distances in pursuit of the buffalo, his principal source of food. As the horse came into wide use among the various tribes, it gave rise to new conflicts. Ferocious wars over hunting grounds resulted, and the out-numbered Apaches had to give ground, retreating southward. When they found a new enemy in the way, they made war upon him.

At first the Spaniards won victories over these irate mounted warriors, because they held the advantage of firearms over bows and arrows.

"For twenty years, more or less open warfare with the Apaches, with short intervals of illusory peace, was the pattern of border life."[1] The Apaches from time to time showed signs of softening, and the Spaniards, particularly the Franciscans, entertained notions of settling them in missions. It was an idea which the Apaches came to encourage, though they doubtless did so without realizing the full implications of the bargain to be made. "With the Comanches and the Wichitas pressing on them from the north and east, and the Spaniards from the south, the Apaches realized the time had come to choose sides. They chose the Spaniards. That they did so with reservations seems hardly surprising, for the Spaniards were the intruders in the Apaches' land."[2] One attempt at an Apache mission had failed, but in this year of 1756, events in the evolution of a second venture moved rapidly forward.

In fact 1756 was full of significant events of many kinds. Word came to San Juan Bautista early in the year that Don Pedro de Rábago y Terán had died on the San Marcos River, where he had moved the San Xavier settlement the previous summer. Left in command of the San Xavier garrison on the San Marcos was Diego Ramón III. But Don Diego's grandson still was not considered worthy of command, and a search was being made in the other provinces for a permanent commander.

Hardly a year before Don Pedro de Rábago's death he had led an expedition to the San Sabá River, a follow-up to one conducted in 1753 by Juan Galván. The purpose of both explorations was to seek a suitable site for an Apache mission. Rábago's findings were being pondered, this spring of 1756, by the Viceroy's advisers in the capital city.

News of another important change now came to San Juan Bautista from the south. Agustín de Ahumada y Villalón, Marqués de las Amarillas, had come to New Spain as viceroy, succeeding Juan Francisco de Güemes y Horcasitas, Conde de Revilla Gigedo. The new official had taken the helm without departure from the course; he continued to steer toward an Apache mission on the San Sabá River.

And in Querétaro, awaiting an opportunity to help the San Sabá project along was the former San Juan Bautista missionary and champion of

---

[1] Lesley Byrd Simpson (ed.), Introduction, *The San Sabá Papers: A Documentary Account of the Founding and Destruction of San Sabá Mission*, pp. xiii–xiv.

[2] Robert S. Weddle, *The San Sabá Mission: Spanish Pivot in Texas*, p. 24.

the Apaches, Friar Alonso Giraldo de Terreros. His occasion was not long in coming.

While much was afoot which pointed toward expansion of the kingdom of both Majesties, 1756 also found the mission settlements torn by dissension. Missionaries disagreed as to procedure. The continuing conflict between religious and military thrived, partly as the outgrowth of the disastrous San Xavier affair, in part over the coming San Sabá venture. It was the year of another official visit ordered by the commissary general of Querétaro, Friar José Antonio de Oliva. The task of inspecting the missions and reporting to Oliva fell, as it had in 1745, to the *padre visitador,* Friar Francisco Xavier Ortiz, apostolic procurator of the college. In the view of Ortiz, part of his task was to console the missionaries and put an end to abuses they had suffered.

The *visitador* arrived at San Juan Bautista on Holy Monday, April 13, 1756, happy to reach the oasis because he was suffering from an upset stomach. He was weary from travel, he said, even though the country was in good shape, with plenty of grass for the horses, and members of his party had been required to walk but little on the way. Observance of Holy Week, he wrote at last, had prevented his settling immediately to the task of replying to Commissary General Oliva, whose letter he had received at Monclova. He had been prevented from replying there by long conferences with the Governor, and the road had offered no facilities for writing. He wrote the following Saturday, "repeating the great desire which drives me, to give satisfaction with all preciseness possible to the confidence of Your Most Reverence and the Apostolic College." From what he was able to see thus far, he wrote, satisfaction would be given for the calumnies which had been spread, and the result would be "for the greater glory of God, the welfare of souls, and the luster of our Holy Habit." The visit was necessary, he believed, "for conciliating spirits and extirpating abuses which have caused the missionary fathers to suffer unprecedented labors. I repeat, Your Most Reverence, that time is necessary for clearing up these things justly; without noisy clamor they may be established peacefully and firmly."[3]

On the preceding day, a feast day, reported the visitor, the patent which

[3] Fray Francisco Xavier Ortiz to Fray José Antonio de Oliva, April 18, 1756, A.G.N., Historia, Vol. 29, pp. 29–30.

he carried from the commissary general was read to all the religious of the presidency. The president of the Texas missions (Father Mariano de los Dolores) assisted, while all the religious of the Río Grande missions gave due obedience and attention. This done, Ortiz had determined to start immediately for the San Antonio Missions and would cross the Río Grande the following Monday, April 20. This decision was influenced by the fact that Texas Governor Jacinto de Barrios y Jáuregui was then at San Antonio. "His presence can assist greatly the task, as well as the foundation of the new conversions of the Apaches." Ortiz had been informed by both the visiting priest from San Antonio and the religious at San Juan Bautista that this undertaking would come soon. "I will manage to give full account to Your Most Reverence, according to what experience has taught me."[4]

Father Ortiz would not actually make his official inspection of the San Juan Bautista missions until near the end of the year, but at this point he had already formed an opinion on what their future should be.

What I consider indispensable [he wrote] is that the College ask the Señor Viceroy to free these two missions of San Juan and San Fernando [San Bernardo]. With these Indians it seems to have complied with the institution, heedful that they are catechized and instructed politically, and have sufficient means for their livelihood. If such is not the case there is no hope that it ever will be.[5]

According to the *padre visitador* the Río Grande missions should be turned over to the secular clergy; their suppression as missions would enable the expense of maintaining them to be directed at founding new ones. "In little time the others would be able to attain the state in which these are found today. . . . Especially is this needed if we are to proceed with the conversion of the Apaches, Comanches, and others."[6]

Once again the zeal of a missionary priest was giving rise to the suggestion that the Río Grande missions be suppressed in order to provide the means for new conversions. Fortunately for San Juan and San Bernardo, however, such a course was delayed until a thrust was made into the San Sabá River country. The outcome of that venture was to remove from all consideration the plan to suppress the older missions in favor of extending religion to the Apaches and the Comanches.

---

[4] *Ibid.*, p. 30. [5] *Ibid.*, p. 30. [6] *Ibid.*, pp. 30–31.

Father Ortiz departed from San Juan Bautista as planned on April 20 and arrived seven days later, on the twenty-seventh, at San Antonio de Valero. He read his patent to the assembled missionaries and proceeded two days later to the San Marcos River. On returning to San Antonio in June, he wrote to Oliva that the Apaches were showing every indication of peace and friendship "and most appreciable disposition for being congregated and converted to our Holy Faith," regarding the missionaries "with love, respect, and reverence."[7]

Ortiz had completed his visit at San Marcos but delayed sending his report until he had finished with the inspection of the Río Grande missions. In the meantime, he wrote, the commissary general might rest assured that he had found nothing against any of the missionaries: only admiration for their constance in suffering, their zeal for the salvation of souls.

Ortiz seems to have had his preconceived notions of what the findings of his visit to the missions would be. He now reported accordingly.

By the time Ortiz returned to San Juan Bautista to complete his visit in December, much progress had been made in planning the mission for the Apaches. On April 29, 1756, Friar Alonso Giraldo de Terreros was summoned for a conference with the viceroy, Marqués de las Amarillas. He was informed that his cousin, Don Pedro Romero de Terreros, was considering sponsorship of missions for the Apaches on condition that Friar Alonso would be placed in charge of the new conversions. To this the padre readily agreed. Then he and his cousin worked out the details whereby Don Pedro would give four thousand pesos during the first year to each mission founded, up to twenty, for the Apaches and other tribes north of San Juan Bautista.[8]

On May 18, Colonel Diego Ortiz Parrilla, governor of Sonora, was named to succeed Don Pedro de Rábago y Terán as commandant of the San Xavier Presidio. After relieving the temporary commander, Diego Ramón III, he would take the San Xavier garrison of fifty, remove twenty-two men from San Antonio de Béjar, and recruit an additional twenty-seven to form a one-hundred-man garrison for the Presidio of San Luis de las Amarillas on the San Sabá River at present-day Menard.

---

[7] Ortiz to Oliva, June 14, 1756, *ibid.*, p. 23.
[8] Weddle, *San Sabá Mission*, p. 40.

The eventful year of 1756 was drawing to a close when, early in December, two expeditions traveling in opposite directions met at San Juan Bautista. Ortiz had come back from Texas to complete his visit and to compose his report before going on to Querétaro. Traveling in the opposite direction were Father Terreros and his band of missionary priests of the colleges of Querétaro and San Fernando de Méjico. They had with them nine Tlaxcalteco Indian families from Saltillo, who would assist in the new mission for the Apaches. Close behind Terreros came Colonel Diego Ortiz Parrilla, who brought with him the twenty-seven soldiers he had recruited on the way north. He had finished gathering his men at Monclova. To come later was Father Francisco de la Santísima Trinidad, who presently was scouring the settlements of northern México, seeking supplies for the new Apache mission. The travelers spent a few days at the gateway before taking up the march anew for San Antonio, where they spent a winter of discord. This dissension set the new mission to be founded in the spring off on the wrong foot.[9]

The state in which this plethora of visitors late in 1756 found the settlement of San Juan Bautista makes for interesting speculation. Don Manuel Rodríguez had been removed as captain of the presidio the previous October 27 by order of the interim governor, Don Miguel de Sesma y Escudero.[10] Serving in his stead and holding Rodríguez under arrest pend-

[9] Said to have been with Father Terreros when he arrived at San Juan Bautista were Friars Joaquín de Baños and Diego Jiménez from the College of Querétaro and José de Santiesteban and Juan Andrés from the College of San Fernando de Méjico. Baños, however, appears to have been traveling instead with Father Ortiz, and to have remained with him at San Juan Bautista when the others left for San Antonio. It was Baños as secretary of the visit, who signed, on December 11, Ortiz' report of his inspection. Since the Terreros party arrived at San Antonio on December 14, Baños surely came later. Customary travel time between the two settlements was about one week. Father Trinidad, however, was able to overtake the group before it reached San Antonio, and therefore to arrive at the same time. (See Weddle, *San Sabá Mission,* pp. 43–44; Father Terreros to Don Pedro de Terreros, February 26, 1757, A.M.S.F.; Fray Francisco Xavier Ortiz, "Visita de las Misiones de San Juan Bautista and San Bernardo del Río Grande del Norte en la Provincia de Coahuila hecha por el Reverendo Padre Visitador Fr. Francisco Xavier Ortiz, 1756," A.G.N., Historia, Vol. 29, Part 1, p. 108.)

[10] Sesma or Lesma. Vito Alessio Robles (*Coahuila y Texas en la época colonial*) and Herbert Eugene Bolton (*Guide to Materials for the History of the United States in the Principal Archives of México*) give it as Lesma, while the document transcripts give the name as Sesma.

ing investigation of the unspecified charges against him was Manuel de Cós, lieutenant at the Presidio de Santa Rosa del Sacramento.

The new governor had come to the province the previous spring. The Viceroy, on December 13, 1755, had issued an order for Rodríguez to provide a force of twenty-five or thirty soldiers, with the customary citizens or auxiliary Indians, when they should be asked, to meet the incoming official and escort him to the capital at Monclova. Rodríguez replied more than three months later, March 28. He stated that he was sending the soldiers to San José de Anelo, eighty leagues from San Juan Bautista, to meet the Governor, who, it developed, would be responsible for keeping Rodríguez under arrest more than a year. Lieutenant Cós filled his post as commandant of Presidio del Río Grande until November 30, 1757. At last, word came from the Viceroy that Rodríguez, freed of all charges, was to be restored to his command. Both he and Father Diego Martín García, president of the San Juan Bautista missions, wrote statements praising the manner in which Cós handled the assignment.[11]

In the meantime, the visitors to San Juan Bautista may have been puzzled, but they were not detained by the strained circumstances they found in the presidio.

Father Ortiz watched the missionaries, then Parrilla and his soldiers, as they set out for the river crossing, and then went on about the business of his *visita*. He began the inspection of San Bernardo on December 6, taking careful inventory and examining the record books in order to give full report to the commissary general, Oliva.

Since his previous visit in 1745, the visitor noted, 392 Indians had been baptized in San Bernardo, bringing the total to 1,490 since the mission was established in 1703. While the books failed to list marriages, the mission had 100 families, consisting of 297 persons, not including the 150 who had fled to the *montes*. The missionaries presently were exerting every effort for their return. Since the mission's founding, 963 Indians had died there after receiving the sacraments.[12]

----

11 Viceroy to Manuel Rodríguez, December 13, 1755, A.G.N., Provincias Internas, Vol. 22, p. 4; Rodríguez to Viceroy, March 28, 1756, *ibid.*, p. 5; Manuel de Cós to Viceroy, January 30, 1758, *ibid.*, pp. 105–106; Manuel Rodríguez and Fray Diego Martín García, Certifications, *ibid.*, pp. 110–111.

12 Ortiz, "Visita de las Misiones," pp. 102–103. Data on San Bernardo are found in pp. 102–108.

San Bernardo's church at this time consisted of a single stone building, 27 varas long and 4¾ varas wide, and was quite old, in the view of Ortiz. Its chancel was on two levels, with a communion rail of turned mesquite wood. The main altar, which was upon a table of cypress, included a sculptured image of the patron, St. Bernard; a painting 2 varas high, in gilded frame, of the Lady of Sorrows; gilded sculpture images of the Lady of the Assumption and St. Joseph, with silver crowns, and of the Lady with Palm; and paintings of the princes St. Michael and St. Gabriel.

An image of the Crucified Savior adorned the Altar of the Holy Christ, with the Lady of Sorrows and San Juan of Armazón at the sides. A sculpture signified the Immaculate Conception at the Altar of the Most Pure.

On through the church went the *visitador* and his secretary, from the main church to baptistry and sacristy, inventorying in minutest detail. The pulpit was of hardwood, on a turned base, adorned by moldings. There were two large benches of cedar for the *cabildo* and two of cypress, one confessionary, and a copper trough for holy water, situated on a stone pillar made with lime mortar. In the baptistry a small table stood between the door and the window. Upon it rested a copper baptismal font with cover. There were a hardwood cross, a painting of the baptism of Christ, and three containers for holy oils. The sacristy had a painting two varas high of St. Bernard, an image of St. Thomas, and paintings signifying the soul in grace and in purgatory. Functional items included a copper basin for washing the hands, a large locker for the ornaments, five chests with inlay, fitted with locks, and a large clothes closet with three divisions.

And so on through the ornaments and holy vessels, the household linens, and furniture of church and sacristy. There were two bronze incense burners and spoons, eleven large bronze candlesticks, four medium ones, and two small ones, three hand bells for the altars, two irons for making communion wafers, robes for the acolytes, and clothing bags of white damask and black satin.

The church had a large patio and a two-bodied tower, in poor condition, but with three good bells. The monastery and pueblo were huts of *jacal,* the monastery with only five cells. Ruin was setting in, and a league distant, on a more commodious and healthy site, a new mission was being built. The new mission had a church of adobe, roofed with tule, quite a decent affair, in the opinion of Ortiz. Stone cells, supported by mesquite,

were being readied, as was a shop twenty-nine varas long with roof of
beams and tablet. Adjacent to the new mission were good fields with
abundant water.[13]

Necessary license for the move to the new mission, said the visiting
priest, was conceded on petition of the pueblo.

San Bernardo had nine hundred head of cattle, which reproduced abun-
dantly in the *montes,* and six thousand sheep and goats. There were three
hundred broke horses and colts, a like number of mares, and one hundred
burros. Wool from the sheep and cotton harvested on the farms supplied three looms in the mission's textile mill, which had fifteen spinning
wheels.

Finished with San Bernardo, the visitor went on to San Juan Bautista
on December 9.

After examining the books of the Mission San Juan, Father Ortiz concluded rightly that the mission was founded in 1699 on the Río de Sabinas and wrongly that the year of its move to the Río Grande was 1704.
In 1741, he noted, it had undergone a short move—the distance of two
rifle shots—to the present site, which offered greater conveniences than
the previous one.[14]

Baptisms had been somewhat fewer in recent years than those of San
Bernardo. Since the last visit in 1745, 238 Indians had received the holy
waters, making a total of 1,400, both adults and children, to be baptized
from the start of mission records in 1700. Deaths from the beginning
numbered 1,140, including 250 since the last visit, all having been given
proper burials. All the adults had received the holy sacraments, excepting
only some who were killed by the Apaches.

The census showed that San Juan now had only 224 Indians; however,

[13] *Ibid.,* pp. 106–107. Jorge Cervera Sánchez (in Juan Agustín Morfi, *Descripción del Territorio del Real Presidio de San Juan Bautista del Río Grande del
Norte, y su Jurisdicción, Año de 1778,* p. 315.) says that two leagues to the north
of the San Bernardo Church which was not finished (the one still standing in ruin
just north of Villa de Guerrero) was the site of Misión Nueva, which was not
finished either. This source says the location was "one league from Río Bravo, in
front of Pacuache Ford."

[14] Ortiz, "Visita de Misiones," p. 95. This latter statement gives confirmation to
previous indications that the Mission San Juan first was located on the plaza, in
the present Villa de Guerrero. Data on the inspection of San Juan are found on
pp. 94–101.

in the Texas missions there were more than 100 fugitives from San Juan Bautista, and continued efforts were being made for their return.

The missionaries had the additional duty of ministering to the presidio, as well as to some neighboring ranches, at least until new arrangements could be made by the authorities. For the administration of the presidials there were three books, in which were recorded baptisms, deaths, and marriages, as Father Ortiz had stipulated on his previous visit. "Also ordered on that occasion was that the College should place an additional minister in this mission and in that of San Bernardo, since the King paid for only one, and this was done."[15]

San Juan's church was of stone blocks, plastered on the outside. It was thirty-four varas long and seven wide, with double tower, and choir loft. The main altar was adorned with an oval-shaped picture of the Lady of Light, an effigy of Talla, one of St. John the Baptist, another of St. Francis, and one of St. Anthony. There was a ciborium of gilded sculpture, and mirrors with gilded frames.

A second altar contained an image of the Crucified Christ on a cross two varas wide, an image of the Holy Lady, and one of St. John, mounted on pedestals, with appropriate vestments. A third altar consisted of an image of Jesus the Nazarene, the cross set upon a hill, two varas high, and smaller sculptured images of the Christ child, St. Francis, and Santa Rosalia. Curtains were of Toledo satin.

The church proper contained two confessionaries, with an effigy of the Crucified Savior, three benches of cypress, an enscribed stone fountain for holy water, and a satin curtain.

A cotton curtain covered the door of the baptistry, with one of Toledo satin over the ciborium. The baptismal font was of copper, with shells of silver and bronze. Sculptured heads were of pecan wood.

The choir's place was behind turned pecan wood railing, on cypress benches. It was equipped with a music stand, "turned and painted."

In the tower were six bells, one of 10½ arrobas,[16] another of 8½, still another of 8, and the others of 4 each.

The usual articles, mostly of silver, furnished the sacristy. Household

[15] *Ibid.,* p. 96.
[16] One arroba equals 25.36 pounds.

linen and ornamental draperies and cloth included fine imported fabrics of satin, silk, taffeta, and brittany, in rich colors of purple and crimson, often embroidered in gold and silver. The sacristy was adorned in the same manner as that of San Bernardo, with an effigy of Christ; paintings of Santa Catarina, of the Lady of Sorrows, and of St. Joseph; and a sculpture of the "Holy Exceomo." On the functional line were a bronze hand basin, a copper washing trough, the iron for making communion wafers, three writing desks, well painted, and ten bookcases with locks.

Construction of the monastery was of block and stone, roofed with beams and tablet, with whitewashed walls. It was on a square with eight cells—two for the ministers, the others for guests and for use as offices. The porter's office had three arches of stone masonry, roofed with beams and tablet. A block and stone building thirty varas long housed the textile mill, where the Indians worked the wool and cotton produced on the mission lands. The gallery for corn was of corresponding quality, with stone pillars in the middle. It had ten windows and was roofed with cypress.

The mission's pueblo was pleasing to the visitor, since it was on a suitable site. It had two areas of houses, one with twenty houses of block and stone, containing as many families. They were roofed with thatch, and all had doors. Each house was twenty varas long and of corresponding width. The other group of houses was not finished, the families living meanwhile in grass huts.

Like San Bernardo, the Mission San Juan had ample lands for pastures, fields, and orchards, irrigated from a good *acequia,* with regular planting of corn, cotton, beans, and chile to feed the Indians. At the roundup there were 1,000 head of cattle, 12,000 sheep and goats; 400 broke horses and colts belonged to the mission, with 380 mares.

There were four looms in the mill, where the Indians spun the cotton and wool and wove it into fabric for their own clothing. It had "all the necessary equipment as evidenced by the inventories."[17]

Still at San Juan Bautista a month later, Father Ortiz sent his report to the commissary general, along with letters from the Coahuila governor and the lieutenant of San Xavier (Diego Ramón III). In his letter of

---

[17] *Ibid.,* p. 101. It will be noted that the report of the Ortiz visit informs on the missions in reverse chronological order, San Bernardo having been visited first.

transmittal he reviewed all the controversies being suffered in the San Antonio missions. The attached letters, he said, would leave "a good understanding of the injustices with which many have sought to obscure the condition of the Apaches, their number, their peacefulness, and their conduct from the Father President of those [San Antonio] missions."[18]

After reaching Querétaro, Ortiz wrote again to Oliva on April 16, recommending a plan for management of the missions and for extending the missionary effort northward. The plan serves only to show the naïveté with which the Spaniards sought to move out upon the northern frontier. Ortiz suggested appointment of a commissary visitor for the Texas missions, who would be independent of all of them in order that he might make impartial judgment and keep the authorities informed of the progress and the needs of each mission. The six old missions of the college could be delivered to the *ordinario* (ecclesiastical judge) and a custody formed, freeing the missionary colleges "to move ahead to the Apaches, Comanches, and other nations."[19]

At this point the Spaniards were ignorant of the true nature of the Apaches and, more especially, the Comanches. They soon would be enlightened by means of the daring venture on the San Sabá River.

At the conclusion of the visit at San Juan Bautista, Friar Joaquín Baños departed for San Antonio to join the other missionaries bound for this new endeavor. Within the year he would be back again, bringing disillusionment and dire predictions for the fate of the Apache mission. But even one of his experience could not discern the tragedy that lay ahead.

---

[18] Ortiz to Oliva, January 11, 1757, A.G.N., Historia, Vol. 29, Part 1, p. 26.
[19] Ortiz to Oliva, April 16, 1757, *ibid.*, p. 32.

25. ILL WIND FROM THE PLAINS

Fᴵʀꜱᴛ ɴᴇᴡꜱ of the disappointment that was being experienced at the
new Mission Santa Cruz de San Sabá came to San Juan Bautista in
midsummer, 1757. Hardly three months had passed since the mission was
founded amid bickering of the missionaries with one another, rancor between religious and military leaders, and disillusionment of all at the total
absence of the Apaches. The traveler who bore the news to the Río Grande was Friar Benito Varela, the first of the missionaries to lose patience
with the new enterprise. Varela was bound for Querétaro, where he
would be given another assignment by the missionary college.

The priest may have traveled with Lieutenant José Joaquín de Ecay
Múzquiz, who served as official courier for Colonel Parrilla. In his new
garrison of one hundred men—the largest in Texas—Parrilla had drawn
Ecay Múzquiz and Alférez Diego Ramón, one the son and the other the
grandson of a former commandant of Presidio de San Juan Bautista.
While Múzquiz did courier service, however, Ramón was sent to México
to prison by order of the Viceroy on unspecified charges.[1]

On this trip the courier may well have carried letters from two other
priests at San Sabá—Diego Jiménez and Joaquín Baños—asking permission of the college to retire from the new mission. In due course leave was
granted, and these two also appeared at San Juan Bautista, in early
autumn, brimming over with disappointment and disillusionment. The
money which Don Pedro Romero de Terreros had provided for establishment of missions among the Apaches was being squandered without
result; who would answer to him for it?[2] After a brief rest from their

---

[1] Paul D. Nathan (trans.) and Lesley Byrd Simpson (ed.), *The San Sabá
Papers: A Documentary Account of the Founding and Destruction of San Sabá
Mission*, p. 52.

[2] Robert S. Weddle, *The San Sabá Mission: Spanish Pivot in Texas*, p. 60.

journey Jiménez and Baños took leave from San Juan Bautista and headed south to Querétaro. The time would not be long, however, until their return to the Río Grande to fill a new assignment, in the course of which they would be concerned again with saving Apache souls.

It was winter when another traveler reached the gateway, headed in the other direction. He was Father Miguel de Molina from the College of San Fernando,[3] who might be compared with the Gonzales men of a later time; just as they stole purposefully into the Alamo to die for Texas, Padre Molina, equally as full of purpose, marched willingly into the baited trap that was the San Sabá Mission.

Early in March, Lieutenant Ecay Múzquiz came again to San Juan Bautista, with three soldiers. They were en route to the Presidio of Santa Rosa del Sacramento to meet a new parish priest and escort him to San Sabá. Ecay Múzquiz brought news of a threatened Indian attack on the northernmost settlement, where Father Molina had recently arrived. The Apaches still had not settled in the mission.

At this point the San Sabá River seemed far away and irrelevant to those who talked with Ecay Múzquiz on the Río Grande. But suddenly, on a chill March afternoon, a rider came hurrying in from the river crossing, bringing news to the gateway that left it in a state of shock: the Comanches and their allies, more than two thousand strong, had demolished the Mission Santa Cruz de San Sabá and murdered its inhabitants. Captain Manuel Rodríguez received the news in letters from Toribio de Urrutia, commandant of Presidio de San Antonio de Béjar, addressed to Governor Angel de Martos y Navarrete at Monclova.

. . . this Province is under enemy attack. Indeed, it is my opinion that at this moment the Presidio de las Amarillas is totally destroyed, for the Colonel [Parrilla] has written to the commander of a convoy bringing supplies to the Presidio, to abandon the supplies and approach the Presidio by a roundabout route, since the road has been occupied by the enemy. In the same letter he . . . states that he will keep me informed of developments if he is still alive.

Up to the present time, however, I have had no further word from him and must therefore presume the complete ruin of the Presidio.[4]

---

[3] The missionary College of San Fernado de Méjico was established in 1731, in Mexico City. It was to share with the College of Querétaro the administration of missions on the San Sabá River, where one of its priests would be martyred.

[4] Nathan and Simpson, *San Sabá Papers*, p. 11.

Captain Manuel Rodríguez digested the letters hurriedly. Urrutia, in his message to the Governor, pointed out that he had only five soldiers in his presidio, the others being dispersed among the missions. If the raiding Indians should sweep down upon San Antonio, he would be unable to cope with them. ". . . I beg and pray that I be given all available aid in this extreme emergency from each of the presidios under the authority of your Worship."[5]

Urrutia appended a second letter to the Governor, advising him of the testimony of a soldier who had just arrived: the Father President, Alonso Giraldo de Terreros, and Father José de Santiesteban, had been killed; most of the soldiers also had been killed, the rest badly wounded—fortunately a statement later to be proved much in error—and the soldier had escaped at night, on foot, carrying Father Molina on his back. Doubt would be cast later upon the soldier's story.

Near panic spread across the northern frontier of New Spain. Manuel Rodríguez hastily provided a relay rider to take the message on to Santiago de la Monclova. That no time was lost along the way is borne out by the fact that Urrutia's letters of March 20 reached the Governor the afternoon of March 23. The Governor worked late into the night, issuing dispatches to the presidial commanders and to the governors of neighboring provinces. On learning of the savage attack of the Comanches and their allies at San Sabá each of the presidios was paralyzed by fear. They felt that they themselves were in danger of surprise attack from the daring savages, goaded by their victory.[6]

Reaction to the news at San Juan Bautista is not recorded, for Don Manuel Rodríguez' letter to the Governor, which accompanied that of Toribio de Urrutia, apparently has not been preserved. In reply, however, Don Manuel received his instructions from Martos y Navarrete under date of March 23:

Your letter was received today at about five o'clock in the afternoon.

In view of this calamity, and for the greatest benefit to the royal service, it is imperative that we take all precautions and adopt the strictest diligence to safeguard most zealously the frontiers of this Province. . . . I direct that you proceed to concentrate all your troops in that fort, with the exception of those required at the Villa de San Fernando [under Lieutenant Vicente Rodríguez],

---

[5] *Ibid.*, p. 11.   [6] Weddle, *San Sabá Mission*, p. 92.

and that you issue powder and ball and provide the same for the inhabitants and *rancheros*. You will put all your forces on the alert and see to it that they hold themselves in readiness for any expedition that may be required, and above all for vigorous defense if need be. This is our most important duty, together with the preservation of the Missions, where I direct you to hold inspections of the Indians armed with bows and arrows, to make sure that they, as well as our own troops, are ready to fulfill their obligations.

I have been informed that the horses at the Presidio are weak and diminished in numbers. I accordingly order your worship to request, command, and require the Reverend Missionary Fathers to turn over to you the horses of their Missions.[7]

But whatever orders he issued to San Juan Bautista and the other garrisons, Governor Martos had no intention of sending reinforcements either to Toribio de Urrutia at Béjar or to Parrilla at San Sabá. He revealed as much when, two days later, he informed the Viceroy of the difficulties at San Sabá:

The post is so remote . . . and so isolated that no matter what I might wish to undertake in this urgent necessity, it would be of no avail because of the great distance and the extreme aridity of the whole region. . . . I have concluded that I ought to strengthen and supply the frontiers of my command against whatever may occur.[8]

No help was sent to San Sabá. News came out of the north of the new set of circumstances which existed on that frontier:

[The mission massacre] represented the initial contact of the Spaniards with large numbers of hostile Indians equipped with firearms and skilled in using them. . . .These new enemies, incited by the alliance of the Apaches with the Spaniards, had formed a strong alliance themselves. . . . The San Sabá massacre marked the beginning of Comanche warfare with the white settlers in Texas.[9]

To the gateway settlement of San Juan Bautista southbound couriers of Parrilla came, bearing proposals to the viceroy, Marqués de las Amarillas, for coping with the new situation. In midsummer a messenger returned from the south with new instructions for Parrilla. The San Sabá com-

---

[7] Nathan and Simpson, *San Sabá Papers,* p. 20.
[8] *Ibid.,* pp. 24–25, cited in Weddle, *San Sabá Mission,* pp. 92–93.
[9] Weddle, *San Sabá Mission,* pp. 101–102.

mander was to convene at San Antonio de Béjar a junta to plan a campaign for punishing the northern tribes. Captain Don Manuel Rodríguez of Presidio del Río Grande received orders to be present for the junta October 4. He, like the other officials summoned to attend, found excuses for not doing so. When the junta finally met January 3, 1759, Rodríguez was present, along with Jacinto de Barrios y Jáuregui, governor of the province of Texas; Angel de Martos y Navarrete, governor of Coahuila; Manuel Ramírez de la Piscina, captain of the Presidio of La Bahía; José de Castilla y Terán, of the Presidio of Monclova; Parrilla and Lieutenant José Joaquín de Ecay Múzquiz, of the Presidio of San Luis de las Amarillas.[10]

"Not since the days of the Aguayo expedition to drive the French out of Texas had plans been made on such a scale."[11] San Juan Bautista would furnish twelve soldiers, six militiamen, and twenty Indians. Other contingents would come from San Sabá, San Antonio, La Bahía, Monclova, Santa Rosa del Sacramento, the Missions of Dulce Nombre de Jesús de Peyotes and San Francisco Vizarrón (five Indians each), San Bernardino de la Candela, San Fernando de Austria, San Pedro de Gigedo; the haciendas of Álamo, Cantatores, Ciénegas, and Sardinas; Nuevo Reino de León, Nuevo Santander, Saltillo, San Luis Potosí, and Charcas.

The expedition, bent on punishing the Indians of the northern tribes for their attacks on San Sabá, got underway from San Antonio the middle of August. It went first to San Sabá, then set its meandering course northward.

The story of that expedition has been told elsewhere[12] and the purpose here is merely to relate the part which San Juan Bautista played in it. After surprising a Tonkawa camp somewhere beyond the Brazos Clear Fork, killing 55 Indians and taking 149 prisoners, Parrilla employed one of the captives as a guide. The Indian led him to the vicinity of present Spanish Fort, on the banks of the Red River north of Nocona, where the Wichitas, Comanches, and other enemy tribes waited in fortified position.

---

[10] Mariano de los Dolores to Fray Joseph García, February 11, 1759, A.M.S.F.

[11] Carlos Eduardo Castañeda, *Our Catholic Heritage in Texas,* IV, 117.

[12] Weddle, *San Sabá Mission,* pp. 118–128; Robert S. Weddle, "What Happened at Spanish Fort?" *Fort Belknap Society Yearbook,* 4 (1965–1966), 9–19; Robert S. Weddle, "The San Sabá Mission: Approach to the Great Plains," *Great Plains Journal,* 4, No. 2 (Spring, 1965), 29–38.

In attempting to take the village, Parrilla found himself opposed by Indians both mounted and on foot who appeared to have had the benefit of European military training. In one of his reports he told of seeing a French flag flying from the stockade. In his assault (on October 7, 1759) he lost nineteen killed and fourteen wounded. When his captains called a muster that night, it was determined that nineteen were missing, in addition to the Apaches, who had scattered to fight as Indians rather than soldiers.[13]

The company of the Río Grande, made up of the men of the Presidio of San Juan Bautista and those of Presidio of Santa Rosa, commanded by Manuel Rodríguez, counted four casualties: one dead and three wounded. Two Indians from Mission San Bernardo were missing, including one who had retreated to the wood when his horse was killed.

Many of the officers had experienced close calls, including Don Manuel—a bullet had creased the front skirt of his cuirass, but he was unharmed. Shots struck the cuirass, the saddle, and the shield of the lieutenant of the Río Grande company, Don Santiago Monéo, but he was not hurt. The *alférez* of the company, Don Nicolás Rodríguez, had his shield pierced three times by bullets, and one crashed into his saddle tree, but he was not hurt.[14]

One of the most decisive battles in the history of Texas had been fought; though the Spaniards fought with valor, they failed to take the fort and to demonstrate the superiority they had claimed. Thenceforth the forces of New Spain must tread lightly in dealing with the Comanches and their allies.

Parrilla's withdrawal was orderly, despite published accounts to the contrary. The troop passed the night near the battlefield, then withdrew a short distance the following day to an arroyo which offered pasture and water, here to wait three days. From this place, which he called Bear Camp, Parrilla dispatched the first news of the battle.

On October 18 two Indian runners arrived at Mission San Antonio de Valero, carrying Parrilla's message to Father Mariano de los Dolores. Friar Mariano copied the letter October 20 and sent it on to Father Diego

---

[13] Diego Ortiz Parrilla, "Testimonio de Parrilla," A.G.I., Audiencia de México, 92-6-22, Dunn Transcripts, 1759–1761, pp. 222–223.

[14] *Ibid.*, p. 226.

Jiménez, now serving as president of the Río Grande missions at San Juan Bautista. Thus the news came back to the gateway settlement, which, as many times before, had sent its men to faraway places in the service of God and king.

Father Mariano interrogated the two Indian runners to obtain a clearer picture of the battle than Parrilla offered. He was able to get this news regarding casualties:

The two Indians affirm only that they saw five of ours dead in the canyons, one Indian from Concepción, another from San Joseph [San Antonio], and three from San Juan Bautista, including one from Peyotes.[15]

[Father Dolores concluded by saying:] I request your reverence at the first opportunity to send this letter to our Father Guardian, so he may have this news . . . to relieve his anxiety and that he may help us pray to God to bring well being to the Colonel. The evident danger is of losing this province.[16]

Father Jiménez read the message with a sad recollection of his own experiences with the San Sabá Mission enterprise, and with a feeling of vindication for his misgivings. He refolded the letter and sent it at first opportunity to Father José García, guardian of the College of Querétaro.

Parrilla's force, making an orderly withdrawal, reached San Sabá on October 25. The commander immediately called his officers into council to determine whether a new campaign should be undertaken against the northern tribes. Overruled, he determined to take his force as soon as possible to San Antonio and disband it, despite the fact that his officers had advised a month's rest at San Sabá before continuing on to Béjar.[17]

His lieutenant, Don José Joaquín de Ecay Múzquiz, in whom Parrilla placed the greatest reliance, was ill and unable to remain in charge of the San Sabá garrison. The commander quickly arranged for Captain Manuel Rodríguez of San Juan Bautista to take over his post temporarily. Rodríguez may have left San Sabá before spring, but if he did, he shortly returned. Parrilla, in making his reports of the campaign, suggested to the Viceroy that he come to the capital to explain personally the new forces at work on the northern frontier. He returned to Presidio of San Luis to

---

[15] Fray Mariano de los Dolores to Fray Diego Jiménez, October 20, 1759, A.M.S.F.

[16] *Ibid.*

[17] Weddle, *San Sabá Mission*, p. 127.

await a reply to the proposal. The permission came in April and Parrilla departed, again leaving Manuel Rodríguez in charge. Parrilla was never to return.

Charles III was now king of Spain, and Joaquín de Monserrat, Marqués de Cruillas, was viceroy. New policies regarding the northern frontier were to be placed into effect, and the experience which Parrilla had gained would not be used. He was to be replaced by Felipe de Rábago y Terán, who had been exonerated of crimes at the San Xavier Missions and was being restored to the command of his garrison, which now formed a part of the Presidio of San Luis de las Amarillas. Parrilla would command the Presidio of Santa Rosa and, in time, would be governor of Coahuila.

When Rábago arrived at San Sabá to take over the garrison, September 30, 1760, he found Manuel Rodríguez still in temporary command. Though the record is not clear, it seems likely that Vicente Rodríguez, Don Manuel's brother and lieutenant in charge of the small garrison at Villa de San Fernando, was in command of Presidio de San Juan Bautista del Río Grande during the Captain's prolonged absence.

The new viceroy may have forgiven Rábago for his part in the murders and adulteries of San Xavier, but the missionaries in San Antonio had not. Father Mariano de los Dolores, for example, viewed his return to Texas as jeopardizing the peace of the entire province.[18] Knowing the enmity with which he would be met in San Antonio, Rábago wisely avoided going there. Since there was no other established trail to San Sabá except the San Antonio road he made a new one.

The trail which Rábago opened went north from Villa de San Fernando de Austria and crossed the Río Grande near present Del Rio. Although it took him through rough country, it was a trail he would have need of in the future. *Persona non grata* in San Antonio, he must obtain supplies from the northern Coahuila settlements, principally from San Juan Bautista and Villa de San Fernando.

At the Río Grande missions, it seems, was Rábago's only friend among the missionaries. He was Friar Diego Jiménez, one of the six missionaries who had founded the ill-fated Mission Santa Cruz de San Sabá, now president of the Río Grande missions. When Rábago—who apparently made

---

[18] *Ibid.*, p. 149.

a genuine effort for a time to reform himself—found the Apaches favorably inclined toward missions, he wrote to Friar Diego for help and advice. Thus San Juan Bautista became deeply involved in the new effort to win these nomadic Indians to the way of the Cross.

Late in October two messengers from Rábago came to the Río Grande bearing an urgent message for Friar Diego. The zealous padre hastily read the news that one of the principal Lipan chiefs, El Cabezón, had declared his people ready to be settled and live in peace with the Spaniards. Rábago urged the priest to come at once, before the Indians had time to change their mind. Jiménez departed immediately for San Sabá.

After talking personally with some of the chiefs and hearing their mission desires, the missionary still was not convinced. He wrote November 4:

> . . . I can place little faith in their words which they have so often failed to keep, and I shall not believe their sincerity until I see them already congregated in missions with the necessary means for their maintenance. Nevertheless, the zeal of Felipe de Rábago y Terán, his experience, and his insistence persuade me to believe that after the will of God, it will be through his efforts more than through anything else that any hope for reducing these nations can be entertained.[19]

By November 23 Father Jiménez was back at the Mission San Bernardo, which he had chosen as his residence while serving as president of the missions of the Río Grande. He reported again to the commissary general: The Apaches, suffering from hunger, had gone on a buffalo hunt not far from the San Sabá River to provision themselves for the winter. On their return they had agreed to be congregated on the upper Nueces River, thirty or forty leagues from the Río Grande. A second mission was planned twelve or fourteen leagues beyond, on the Chanas (Llano) River, and a third on the San Sabá. The priest himself had examined the three rivers and found them to offer the necessary facilities. Captain Don Felipe, he said, had spared no effort to make the necessary arrangements for settling the Apaches, and many souls would be saved as a result.

---

[19] Fray Diego Jiménez to Fray Manuel de Nájera, Commissary General, November 4, 1761, A.G.N., Historia, Vol. 28, p. 194. (Translated by C. E. Castañeda, in Juan Agustín Morfi, *History of Texas, 1673–1779*, p. 396.)

. . . I must confess to your reverences that never before have I seen the Indians less opposed to being congregated than at present, though I have observed their attitude ever since we settled San Sabá. I say *less opposed*, because all these Indians, if I am not mistaken, agree to be congregated half willingly and half unwillingly, as if constrained. This is their attitude until their barbarous nature, softened by instruction in the catechism, becomes more amenable to divine grace.[20]

Jiménez suggested that the two missions on the Río Grande could furnish corn and tobacco for the Apaches until the necessary supplies were sent by the commissary general. But the allowance formerly given San Juan and San Bernardo had been canceled; their income was small, their expenses large, and they were being maintained only with difficulty. If the small surplus of the Río Grande missions were turned to the support of the Apaches without recompense, it would be impossible to maintain the older missions in the future.

Missionaries had been appointed for the Apache missions, noted Jiménez, and he expressed the hope that they would not be long in coming.

Once again the two old missions on the Río Grande were being deprived for the sake of new undertakings in Texas. No provision was made by the missionary college or by the government for this drain upon the mother missions, a fact which is evidenced by cancellation of the allowance which they had enjoyed in the past. And still once more did the threat of ending the older missionary effort hover above the Valley of the Circumcision; these missions stood in danger of being bled to death by their offspring.

But Father Jiménez believed in pressing forward. The inaction at San Sabá, when the Apaches failed to congregate, had been more than he could endure. In company with Friar Joaquín Baños he had hurried back to Querétaro for a new assignment. Returning again to San Juan Bautista, he had expressed confidence in Felipe de Rábago, for whom all others had only suspicion and mistrust. Because of the priest's faith in this man of questionable character, new missions were being founded for the Apaches; but they were being founded contrary to the Viceroy's plans, and they would never receive his recognition. This was a contingency,

---

[20] Jiménez to Nájera, November 23, 1761, A.G.N., Historia, Vol. 28, p. 196. (Translated in Morfi, *History of Texas,* p. 399.)

however, on which Diego Jiménez had no time to wait. He must take the Apaches in while they were willing. By early February, 1762, two missions had been established (at present Camp Wood and Montell), and Jiménez' old companion, Joaquín Baños, was on hand to help him run them.

While the missionaries labored to take the Gospel to the Apaches, the soldiers of San Juan Bautista Presidio amused themselves in the nearby pueblos. They attended the fiestas and added to the noise by firing their guns, putting on a show for the ladies. Such actions drew a warning from the Viceroy. Captain Manuel Rodríguez was instructed that the soldiers should conserve their powder, and not allow themselves to become the ridiculous object of the villagers' diversion.[21]

26. MISSIONS IN THE CANYON

FRIARS Jiménez and Baños, together with Friar Diego Martín García, prepared under date of February 7, 1762, a report on the condition of the missions of the Presidency of the Río Grande. On that date Jiménez and Baños were at the new Apache mission on the Nueces; yet they began the document with a description of the missions of San Bernardo and San Juan Bautista and the province of Coahuila, in greater detail than should have been necessary for any official of New Spain, even the viceroy, Marqués de Cruillas:

The Presidency of the Missions of the Río Grande del Norte contains four missions, two of them three quarters of a league apart, two short leagues from the Río Grande, fifty leagues from the capital of the Province, 280 from México. The capital is the Villa de Santiago de la Monclova, and the Province is called San Francisco de Coahuila, Nueva Extremadura. It has a Governor

21 Viceroy to Manuel Rodríguez, June 24, 1762, A.G.N., Provincias Internas, Vol. 22, p. 5.

who resides in said Villa, and contains some settlements of Indians and Spaniards, though shapeless, and some Missions of Infidels belonging to the Holy Province of Xalisco, and those of the College of the Holy Cross of Querétaro.

For its defense it has three Presidios with 160 soldiers, more or less. To the east of said Province is the Nuevo Reyno de León, and part of the new Colony of Escandón. To the west are pastures and other haciendas of its *Marqueses,* bordered by Nueva Vizcaya: to the south is the Villa de Saltillo, and to the north is the Río Grande del Norte.

The climate is more dry and cold than otherwise, and said Province includes many deserts which offer no utility because of the scarcity of water. This Province produces corn, wheat, cotton, chile, and some wine, with an abundance of mules. Minerals are not lacking, although they are of poor quality.

The two missions referred to are San Juan Bautista and San Bernardo.[1]

San Juan Bautista, it was noted, had to its credit 1,434 baptisms of all ages and both sexes since its beginning. Though the report does not take notice, it may be observed that only 34 baptisms had been accomplished since Father Ortiz' visit in 1756, a considerable slump from previous times. Marriages in the church numbered 343 (a statistic which Ortiz failed to mention), and 1,066 had died with the sacraments.[2]

The mission now had 216 Indians—a decline from 224 since Ortiz' report—and these comprised 54 families. Of the total, 150 took communion and confessed. Many of the mission's Indians were of the Pampopas, Tilojayas, and Pacholocos nations, and some from the Tuzan nation, which were gathered here to save the expense of founding new missions for them elsewhere. Even so, the mission populace did not increase "because the epidemics and other illnesses consume them, and they die, as is the case in all our Missions."[3]

During the last year the missionaries of San Juan had begun to seek the conversion of the Tuzan Nation, "with enough work, great cost, and little

[1] Diego Jiménez, "Relación del Estado de las Misiones de la Presidencia del Río Grande del Norte, pertenecientes al Colegio de la Santa Cruz de Querétaro," A.G.N., Historia, Vol. 29, Part 1, pp. 108–109.

[2] *Ibid.,* p. 110. Fray Francisco Xavier Ortiz ("Visita de las Misiones de San Juan Bautista y de San Bernardo del Río Grande del Norte," *ibid.,* p. 108) listed 1,140 deaths in 1756. All of these had received the holy sacraments, he stated, except some who had been killed by the Apaches. Assuming death figures contained in both his report and that of Jiménez and Baños are correct, the Apaches had taken a heavy toll of San Juan Bautista Mission Indians prior to 1756.

[3] *Ibid.,* p. 110.

or no encouragement from the Presidio."[4] The Indians were brought from the *monte* by the eastern route—from the sea coast. Five heathens from the Tuzan or Carrizo nation were presently being catechized for baptism. The progress of the Indians in Christianity, generally speaking, was almost unbelievable; the evidence was more than superficial: they confessed, took communion, fasted, heard Mass, and assisted in the divine offices and daily explication of the doctrine, which was made by interpreter. Even so, Jiménez observed, as Father Morfi was to observe some years later:

> But all this is done on command in a grade of piety so familiar that they are hardly recognized as Christians; that is, speaking of the common and excepting those few of both sexes in whom is distinguished some degree of devotion. The majority have affection more for the *monte* and their barbarous liberty than for the mission and for the rational, political, and Christian life. . . . and it is necessary on their return from the wilds to begin the catechism almost as if they had never been Christians. . . . Although the mission itself is old, its founders already dead, almost all the Indians are new. It is no wonder, therefore, that there is found in the missions barbarity which they should not have, being as old as they are.[5]

The Indians, continued the report, were maintained in community. They sowed and raised livestock in common and consumed them under direction of the minister. By such a method some of the mission produce was conserved; everyone received equal benefit from the work, to which the Indians were naturally adverse. Some of the produce was exchanged for goods which they needed more. This trading was done under direction of the minister because the Indians did not yet have the capacity for provisioning themselves. Under no circumstance did the padre appropriate anything to his own use; even his stipend was converted into items useful to the Indians, and the priest was maintained poorly from the common store of the Indians.

San Bernardo, since its founding in 1703, had served the Ocanes, Canuas, Catuxan, Pazchal, Pamulum, Pacuaz, Pastaloco, Papanac, and Tuamca nations, and others of small number. This mission seems to have been considerably more active since Father Ortiz' visit than had its sister

[4] *Ibid.*, p. 110.
[5] *Ibid.*, pp. 111–112.

mission. Baptisms, had increased 128 to a total of 1,618, and 377 persons comprising 91 families and some orphans lived in the mission, compared with 297 persons in 1756. From the founding there had been 383 marriages, according to the Jiménez-Baños-García report, although Ortiz had said the mission had no matrimonial records. During the previous five years there had been 116 deaths, making a total of 1,079. The discussion of San Bernardo was hastily ended with the observation that "the condition, government, and other matters of these Indians are in all ways like those of the Mission of San Juan."[6]

Then the writer proceeded to the main reason for writing in the first place: the new Apache missions on the Nueces.

The ministers of San Bernardo presently are seeing after the conversion of the Apache Indians, which it appears will be attained through the efficiency and perseverence of Captain Don Felipe de Rábago y Terán. . . . The other two missions of this presidency are those of Santa Cruz and Nuestra Señora de la Candelaria, which are just being founded. They remain in embryo until the approval of the Superior Government is obtained.[7]

Embryonic they were indeed. The Mission Candelaria (at present Montell) was still in the process of being founded. San Lorenzo de la Santa Cruz, founded just two weeks previously (at Camp Wood), had baptized only five Apaches. But the entire nation of Lipan Apaches, according to those who had gathered, numbered close to five thousand—a figure which undoubtedly was somewhat exaggerated.

Situated in the Valle de San José (called El Cañon), the two new missions were fifty leagues from those of the Río Grande. They were situated on a fluent river which rose ten leagues to the north and was fed by numerous springs. The many hills which surrounded the valley were said to have mines, and there was an abundance of cedar, live oak, cottonwoods, elms, pecans, and other hardwoods to suit any purpose. Those who had traveled beyond said there were other suitable sites for villages, especially between Valle de San José and the San Sabá River. In this area were found the Río de las Chanas (South Llano) and Cañon de las Lechugas y Trancas (North Llano and Bear Creek, Kimble County). The writer had seen the San Sabá and knew it to have many good sites for

[6] *Ibid.*, p. 113.
[7] *Ibid.*, p. 113.

villages. In the land that had been occupied until now by the Apaches could be founded a populous province, even a kingdom, with settlements extending from San Juan Bautista to New Mexico.[8]

But the whole thing was only a Jiménez dream. It was much like Father Hidalgo's vision of converting the Tejas, like that of Father Terreros of founding effective missions on the San Sabá. Even had the Viceroy granted the needed support for the new missions of El Cañon, the Jiménez vision could not have come true. The Apaches were still nomads. They had not changed—and would not change—their leopard spots. They would not permanently exchange their ancient freedom for the white man's religion and civilization's shackles.

Nevertheless, the principal effort of the missions of San Juan Bautista and San Bernardo for the next several years was to be directed at converting the Apaches. With tools and several yokes of oxen brought from San Juan Bautista, Fathers Jiménez and Baños set about putting the new establishments in order. The Apaches enjoyed the novelty of the clothing and trinkets which the padres had brought from the Río Grande and feasted on the brown sugar loaves, corn, and beans which the older missions had provided. A number of Christian Indians from San Bernardo assisted the padres in instructing neophytes in the doctrine and in the work of the missions. By no means safe from Comanche attack, they were guarded by twenty soldiers provided by Captain Felipe de Rábago y Terán. But appeals for a garrison for El Cañon went unanswered, as did requests for other government support. Rábago's problems were compounded by having to split his garrison at a time when the enemy northern tribes were growing bolder.

During the first year of the missions Father Jiménez appears to have spent most of his time at El Cañon, in neglect of the missions on the Río Grande. After a time Father Baños withdrew and Father Miguel Antonio de las Cuevas came to take his place. Near the end of the year a formal request from the Viceroy, dated October 1, 1762, came to the priests on the upper Nueces. It called for a report on the progress of the missions and for the missionaries' recommendations. From Mission San Lorenzo, on January 24, 1763, they stated their case without equivocation: given a competent garrison of soldiers to defend the Apaches against their ene-

[8] *Ibid.*, pp. 114–115.

mies and to inspire fear and respect among the Indians, and with financial assistance for maintaining them until a crop could be harvested, the missions would succeed—without these benefits there was scarcely a hope for the Apaches' settlement.[9]

The Indians had changed their outlook since his experience with them at the time of the founding of the Mission Santa Cruz de San Sabá, Father Jiménez believed. At that time they had expressed fear of settling in villages, lest the immobility cause them illness; they had disdained the idea of baptism. But now they heard the divine word with pleasure.

They have helped with some of the work, and are persuaded that they have to maintain themselves by their labor and permanence in the Missions, as others who are settled. With this goes the pleasure of their offering us their children to be baptized; and if the adults are ill, they call us for the same thing. They have not left the mission without our permission, and then they have left as surety some horses, their wives, and children. These and other things convince us of the good condition of these Indians for being settled.[10]

Presently gathered in the missions, said Jiménez, were some four hundred Lipan Apaches, whose total number was said to be something less than three thousand. The Lipans gave assurance of the settlement of the Natagés, Pelones, Mescales, and Apaches proper—the Indians who had recently been raiding in Coahuila—because they were their relatives or close friends and spoke the same language. But Jiménez readily admitted that such a possibility appeared remote. Besides, it would not be wise to attempt such a feat unless His Excellency saw fit to provide an adequate number of soldiers and some financial assistance for the undertaking.

Furthermore, the Indians of the North, who had destroyed the Mission Santa Cruz de San Sabá, pressed hard upon the Apaches. After the founding of the Nueces missions the Plains Indians had penetrated the Hill Country to destroy numerous rancherias. This persecution forced the Apaches to keep on the move, without fixed habitation.

Already the enemy knows of these Missions because they have spied upon us; soon they will come to destroy these Pueblos. They will find no resistance

[9] Diego Jiménez, "Informe que hacen los Rdos. Padres Fr. Diego Ximénez y Fr. Miguel Antonio de las Cuebas al Exmo. Señor Virrey," January 24, 1763, A.G.N., Historia, Vol. 29, p. 169.

[10] *Ibid.,* pp. 169–170.

because our Lipans only seek to hide themselves in these critical times. The soldiers who accompany us are, in proportion to the enemies, very few and inept. Only God will defend us, if indeed we do not perish.[11]

An armed force was required, also, said the priest, because it was necessary to instill fear in the mission Indians in order to contain them during their frequent unrest. The simple souls were subject to a thousand diabolical schemes suggested to them by "the common enemy." To one chief, while he was at San Sabá butchering meat, for example, the Devil had appeared in a dream, telling him that the Spaniards had departed from the Nueces missions, taking the horses, the women, and the children of the Indians. The anxious chief hurried southward, only to find his family safe and peaceful, the young people applying themselves to the Christian doctrine.

Then the Demon suggested to the chief that his wife and the other Indian women had been cohabiting with the priests and soldiers and with the Indians from the Río Grande missions who assisted the missionaries. What measures the aroused chief would take the padre did not know, for the Indian had left the mission in a sulk and had not returned.

Another chief had conceived the notion that the Spaniards had gathered the Apaches in the missions to kill them. He suggested that before other soldiers came to join those already here, the Indians should kill them instead. This chief went about to all the Indian leaders, attempting to organize them in an uprising. "But God, by means of them, defended us; they answered him that, had they doubted our sincerity they would have fled."[12]

The one aroused chief had gone into the wilds alone and had not returned.

The Indians, with horses and firearms, observed Jiménez, were haughty; when they went unpunished for their misdeeds, they were more so. With the present lack of military force, they could not be chastised; they were introduced to Christianity only as it suited them, and as a result all would be lost if a garrison were not provided.

Emphasizing the need for financial assistance, Jiménez pointed out

[11] *Ibid.,* p. 171.
[12] *Ibid.,* p. 172.

that the Indians were arrogant and restless, without fixed abode. There being no food, it was necessary at times to feed them corn from seed stock, or to allow them to leave the missions to hunt for game. "And as the wolf always leads the sheep astray, thus the common enemy, seeing the Indians away from their pastor, assails them with a thousand temptations. These influences determine whether they return to the Mission or go back to evil-doing with the others."[13]

Quite likely this report stirred the Viceroy's curiosity concerning the missionary effort and the Presidio of San Sabá, which was supposed to protect it. Desiring an impartial appraisal, he wrote to Captain Manuel Rodríguez on the Río Grande, July 15, 1763. The high official asked Rodríguez to inform him on the material condition of Presidio de San Sabá; the condition of its garrison, its armament, and its clothing; movements of enemy Indians against the fort; and the need for moving the presidio to another location.[14]

While the San Juan Bautista missionaries concerned themselves with making Christians of the Lipans, the other Apache nations continued to harass the settlements of northern México. Official eyebrows raised at the effort Father Jiménez was making; to many, an Apache was an Apache, whether he be Lipan or Mescalero. Early in September, 1763, the interim governor of Coahuila, Lorenzo Cancio Sierra y Cienfuegas (1762–1764), called upon the religious of the Presidency of the Río Grande to clarify their position and to explain political aspects of dealing with the Apaches: Had the Mescaleros been inclined peacefully toward the Spaniards? Were they considered to be Apaches, like the Lipans? If they had committed atrocities, what measures should be employed in curbing their raids? What governors had made campaigns against them in the past? Jiménez, as "president and minister of these missions of the Río Grande del Norte," replied from San Juan Bautista.[15]

According to a paper found in the mission archives, wrote the padre, the war with the Indians of the North had begun in 1722. These Indians

---

[13] *Ibid.*, p. 173.

[14] Joaquín de Monserrat (Marqués de Cruillas), Viceroy, to Manuel Rodríguez, July 15, 1763, A.G.N., Provincias Internas, Vol. 25, Part 2, p. 227.

[15] Diego Jiménez, "Repuesta de los PP. al Sr. Cancio a varios puntos de un Informe," September 19, 1763, A.G.N., Historia, Vol. 29, Part 1, p. 173.

were commonly called Apaches, without distinction as to nation until later communication with them had established that several nations were included under the one name.

The bloodthirsty hostility with which they had harassed the settlers of Coahuila and Texas was well known, observed Friar Diego; they had killed and captured Spaniards and mission Indians and stolen many horses and cattle. Campaigns had been made against them by Governor Manuel Antonio Bustillo y Ceballos, Captain Urrutia, and Governors Juan García de Pruneda and Pedro de Rábago y Terán, besides the continual patrols made from Presidio de San Juan Bautista and other frontier posts. Peace had been made with the Lipans in San Antonio, the friar noted, but the armistice was not general, because Indians of another Apache nation had been responsible for killing Friar Francisco Silva and his escort of soldiers in the vicinty of the Río Grande missions.

The Lipans and the Mescaleros, Jiménez was convinced, were quite distinct. While intertribal marriages may have been made in earlier times, such was not the practice now. Though the two groups did maintain a kind of commerce with each other, it had become minor, and the Lipans had allied themselves more with the Spaniards. From the time the Lipans came into the missions, the Mescaleros had begun to steal horses from them. The Mescaleros had sought in vain to enlist the help of the Lipans in resisting Spanish arms, but instead the Lipans offered to help the Spaniards in their campaigns against the Mescaleros.

Regarding the most effective means of dealing with the hostiles, Jiménez pointed out that reconnoitering enemy territory had proved of value in discouraging them from their atrocities. Reconnaissance made it easier to pursue the Indians in order to punish them for their offenses, since it familiarized the Spaniards with enemy territory.

The purely defensive war, as is practiced, is not sufficient to remedy the losses which are being experienced and it truly is risky, because many times a sizeable number of enemies is kept in ambush. The soldiers come following the few wrong-doers and are surrounded; they may perish without effecting punishment or recovering the theft.[16]

Cancio, in asking for the report of Jiménez, apparently was seeking testimony supporting his own effectiveness in dealing with the Apaches.

[16] *Ibid.*, p. 177.

Jiménez reassured him. Some of the thefts and murders, he noted, had occurred during the regime of Don Jacinto de Barrios y Jáuregui as governor. Barrios had found reason to send Lieutenant Vicente Rodríguez, with an adequate force, to pursue the offenders. But since no result was discernible from the campaign, it was natural to assume that it had never been made. None of Cancio's predecessors, emphasized the padre, had been able to stop the incursions. "It is known here that Your Lordship has kept the Troop [of Presidio de San Juan Bautista] in continuous movement, making patrols, lending support, pursuing the enemies with him on whom they have visited theft and kidnaping and killing, containing the haughtiness of the barbarians."[17]

Some members of the Apache nations had been coming to Villa de San Fernando de Austria to trade, Father Jiménez noted, and no good could come of it. The Indians were acquiring a knowledge of Spanish settlements and defenses which could prove ruinous, for the Indians lacked Christian instruction, having spurned offers to come into the missions.

Governor Cancio's concern was more than academic. Early in 1764, enemy Indians from the Plains swept down upon the Presidio de San Sabá and an outpost near San Antonio. Captain Felipe de Rábago at San Sabá appealed for more arms and ammunition, which he apparently never got, following a severe attack by Comanches.[18] Shortly after learning of that raid, Cancio wrote to Viceroy Cruillas, he was advised that some of the missionaries of San Antonio, along with some soldiers and servants, had been caught by a raiding party at a place called Puerto Viejo, six leagues from Béjar, the night of January 26. One Spaniard had been killed and two wounded. Cancio quite naturally feared that the missions of El Cañon would be the next target.

Having advised the Missionaries of the Río Grande of the risk which the ministers at El Cañon faced, I ordered the Captain of the Río Grande, with the rest of the troop which remained with him, including those of the Missions, to proceed to El Cañon. He was to leave his Presidio garrisoned by the citizens.[19]

[17] *Ibid.,* p. 178.
[18] Lorenzo Cancio to Cruillas, March 3, 1764, A.G.N., Provincias Internas, Vol. 25, p. 263; Robert S. Weddle, *The San Sabá Mission: Spanish Pivot in Texas,* p. 163.
[19] Cancio to Cruillas, March 3, 1764, A.G.N., Provincias Internas, Vol. 25, p. 263.

A letter had just reached Cancio from the father president of the missions at El Cañon, along with one from Captain Manuel Rodríguez, who already had arrived there. The Captain's investigation had led him to believe that the attack on Puerto Viejo was attributable to Apaches, rather than Comanches. With this news the fears of Governor Cancio grew; he saw in the belligerence of these two ferocious tribes the threat of ruin for the provinces of Texas and Coahuila.

The immediate threat subsided, and the soldiers returned to their presidios; but Cancio's fears were well grounded.

The missions on the Nueces were almost three years old when on December 26, 1764, Friar Diego Jiménez reported again to the commissary general on the accomplishments of the missions of the Presidency of the Río Grande since October, 1758. While the mission president had been occupied with the new conversions on the Nueces, the Río Grande missions of San Juan and San Bernardo had declined.

The Indian population of San Juan Bautista had been reduced by almost half, from 216 to 109, since the report of February 7, 1762. At San Bernardo the census had declined from 377 to 325. The Indians were subject to being drawn by instruction in political and Christian life. Yet because of their natural proclivity to their ancient liberty and their aversion to work and to maintaining themselves peacefully in villages, the missionaries had wasted many years of continuous labors.[20]

Some years were lost in their entirety, others for the most part, all to some extent. During the five years of his tenure as president, Friar Diego reported, 70 children and 16 adults had been baptized in Mission San Juan, 38 had married; 56 adults and 50 children had died. During the same period 128 children and six adults had been baptized in Mission San Bernardo; 44 had married; 103 children and 84 adults had died.

On four occasions the padres had gone out in company with some soldiers and some settled Indians in search of new subjects for conversion. Twice, when the missionaries were unable to leave the missions because each had only one priest, they sent soldiers and well-taught Indians for the purpose. The effort was frustrated: because the soldiers had been occupied in chastising the hostile Indians of the provinces, the Indians did

[20] Diego Jiménez, "Relación de las Misiones de la Presidencia del Río Grande del Norte desde Octubre de 58 Hasta Diciembre de este Año de 1764," A.G.N., Historia, Vol. 29, Part 1, p. 180.

not welcome them. In all the excursions thirty-three heathen Indians were gained, and sixty-four who had strayed from the missions were brought back. At the date of writing seventeen others remained in flight, and they were being sought.

The reason for the decline of the Río Grande missions, however, appears to have lain not so much in the lack of Indians as in that of priests. All of the reports of Jiménez' time show little real concern over the conversions on the Río Grande. He deals with them in cursory manner in order to get to the main business: that of the Apache missions in the Valle de San José. This report was no exception.

The two new missions, San Lorenzo and Candelaria, fifty leagues to the north, each had more than four hundred Lipan Indians. Many of them were warlike and treacherous, and none were well taught, because of the long delay of the Viceroy in providing soldiers. Only in certain seasons were provisions available; the Indians often went out in search of food, and at the same time, struck a blow at their enemies, the northern tribes. But Friar Diego still had hopes that the Viceroy would provide soldiers, who would do the Lipans' fighting for them, and food to obviate the necessity of their going on hunts. This done, he believed, "these villages will be put in final form and three additional ones can be founded with the other people of this group."[21]

Though Jiménez was dissatisfied with progress, the Lipans still brought their children for baptism. When an adult became ill, he often would send great distances for a priest. When a smallpox epidemic struck the missions, the missionaries baptized *en articulo mortis* forty children and twenty-seven adults at San Lorenzo, two adults and five children at Candelaria. "The chiefs of this partiality assure us of the settlement of the rest of the Apaches, which they say are 4,000. Although they have already made peace with our people, we judge their conversion will require much time, especially if the providences of the Lord Viceroy are not forthcoming."[22]

There was no doubt, wrote Jiménez, that these barbarians, who were without light, without king, and without God, practiced formal idolatry and worshiped idols under the tutelage of a witch doctor, though they had no temple or other designated place for sacrifices. Only those were

21 *Ibid.*, p. 181.   22 *Ibid.*, p. 182.

allowed to worship who burned incense to the idol, blowing out smoke through the mouth. The idol was half a body of human form, made of leather, painted to make it appear lifelike.

Although we are ignorant of the sacrifices which they make to them, it seems that the enemies they kill in their *mitotes* or festivals are sacrificed to the idol, following processions and many ceremonies, which is done with lances. From the Idol, the Demon speaks to them through the witch doctor, telling them whether their enemies are near or far, whether the buffalo, by which they are sustained, is at great distance or close at hand; whether the ill ones, which they heal by diabolical methods, are living or dead. In the blessing of houses or new tents, the witch doctor prophesies the bad or good outcome of the new abode. When there is drouth or storm the witch doctor is the one to whom the others turn for petition and conjuration.

After the missionaries have undeceived them, they have more faith in them than in their *hechiceros*, because of what they have experienced in the conjurations. Many ask the Holy Cross for defense, and carry it with demonstrations of reverence.[23]

The Apaches recognized a head chief who made judgments over his tribesmen. They believed in immortality, and when a tribesman died, they left him all his belongings in the belief that he was only going to live with others of their nation in lands not far away. Most of the Indians had more than one wife, and wives were easily put aside; men with only one felt inferior.

The light of the Holy Faith, wrote Jiménez, should be extended to these people, who had ample cause for being as they were; certainly, he knew, the King repeatedly informed his viceroys that settlement of the heathens was his primary concern, but much opportunity was being lost by the long delay. Only with an adequate garrison of soldiers could the Indians be kept from their barbarous licentiousness.

Whether the soldiers and the financial support which Friar Diego so earnestly sought could have saved the missionary effort on the Nueces is unknown, for they were never provided. Soon the Comanches began to follow the Apaches back from their hunting and raiding expeditions in the north and to harass the missions. When in 1767 the King's inspector general, the Marqués de Rubí, passed El Cañon on his tour of frontier forts, he found the Candelaria Mission abandoned because of Indian dep-

23 *Ibid.*, pp. 182–183.

redations. Mission San Lorenzo was in the care of two missionaries, Fathers Rivera and Santiesteban, who at this time had no Indians to teach. Thirty soldiers and an officer from Presidio de San Sabá guarded the establishment.[24]

In June, 1768, Felipe de Rábago y Terán, harassed by the northern Indians and by disease, moved his garrison without authority from San Sabá to El Cañon. The following spring he was relieved by Manuel Antonio de Oca, who made a feeble attempt to reoccupy Presidio de San Sabá but shortly brought the garrison back to El Cañon. Here it remained until June, 1771, when the Spanish settlement on the upper Nueces River finally was abandoned.[25]

27. ISLE OF THE MALAGUITAS

DURING THE LATE 1760's expeditions from San Juan Bautista reached from Padre Island to El Paso. In 1766 Colonel Diego Ortiz Parrilla led the march to explore the coastal isle for signs of settlement by other European nations. Captain Manuel Rodríguez was at the head of a troop which traveled to El Paso in 1769. The force directed itself against the hostile Indians who continued to raid Coahuila from their strongholds in the rough country along the Río Grande above San Juan Bautista. Other campaigns of smaller proportions were made almost continually against the marauding savages who frequently raided Coahuila horseherds and murdered citizens.

Prior to the two major expeditions, however, these same two officers,

[24] Weddle, *San Sabá Mission*, pp. 167–168; Nicolás de Lafora, *Relación del Viaje que hizo a los Presidios Internos situados en la Frontera de la América septentrional perteneciente al Rey de España*, pp. 186–187.

[25] See Hons Coleman Richards, "The Establishment of the Candelaria and San Lorenzo Missions on the Upper Nueces," for a concise narrative of the missions of El Cañon.

who had fought side by side against the Comanches and the Wichitas on the Red River in 1759, joined to act in another matter: that of granting a tract of Texas land to a former soldier and long-time citizen of San Juan Bautista.

Parrilla, having been deposed as commander of the Presidio de San Sabá in 1760, served as interim governor of Coahuila from June 18, 1764, until December 9, 1765. During this period, as well as for a time before and after, the colonel of dragoons also was commandant of the Presidio of Santa Rosa María del Sacramento. Since his term as governor was a short one, there appears to have been little to distinguish it.

On February 23, 1765, Parrilla was pleased to be visited by an old friend, Don Antonio de Rivas, *vecino* of San Juan Bautista. A man of action, as well as of vanity, Parrilla likely took great delight in swapping remembrances with Don Antonio, who at one time had served with him in Texas.[1] And the Governor would have been pleased to find himself in position to help Don Antonio achieve an ambition. For Rivas came bearing a petition.

Antonio Rivas had been born in the town of Santander in Castile, the son of Don José de Rivas Cacho and Doña María Sierra. A resident of Presidio de San Juan Bautista twenty-five years, he had married Francisca Hernández, also a resident of the presidio, and she had borne him ten children.[2] His petition set forth:

> That having a large family and some stock, without owning any property in which to maintain said stock, and there being as there are vacant lands on the other side of the Río Grande, and notwithstanding the frequent dangers resulting from the frontier Indians still continuing and there being no vacant lands on this side of the river in this jurisdiction, I pronounce and register twenty *citios* of land for pasturage of cattle, etc., and five for sheep, etc.[3]

[1] Herbert Eugene Bolton (*Texas in the Middle Eighteenth Century*, p. 276) says Rivas was one of those who accompanied Parrilla when he left San Antonio in January, 1757, to examine the mission site on the Guadalupe River at the request of Father Mariano de los Dolores; therefore, Rivas probably was with Parrilla at the founding of Presidio de San Luis de las Amarillas on the San Sabá River in April of that year.

[2] The will of Antonio Rivas, in *Abstract of Title to Antonio Rivas Grant in Maverick County, Texas (Except Three Leagues and 6130 Acres)*, p. 5.

[3] *Ibid.*, p. 3. He set out the description of the land, the bounds running from opposite the mouth of Penitas de Abajo Creek, which enters the Río Grande from the Mexican side, to the ford on Arroyo de San Ambrocio, thence along the high

Since it was the desire of His Majesty that his dominions be populated, responded Parrilla:

> . . . in his royal name I hereby grant and adjudicate to petitioner, Don Antonio de Rivas, for himself, his children, heirs and successors . . . the 20 *citios* for cattle, horses, etc., and five for sheep, goats, etc., under the terms and boundaries expressed, with the watering places on the Río Grande del Norte. I command Don Manuel Rodríguez, Chief Justice of the Garrison of San Juan Bautista de Río Grande del Norte, that as soon as the interested party presents him this grant, to proceed to receive official information . . . in regard to these *citios* . . . and after having done all that he is required, he will put him in possession of the aforesaid *citios*.[4]

Don Antonio presented his petition to Captain Manuel Rodríguez at Presidio de San Juan Bautista on March 10. Rodríguez examined one Sergeant Miguel San Miguel and four other witnesses, all of whom told him that a traveling merchant, Don Joseph Días de Oropeza, had possessed the land for about one year and eight months but had removed his livestock, and that the lands had remained vacant and abandoned seven or eight years.

In view of the testimony Don Manuel Rodríguez saw no reason for delay in giving Don Antonio possession of his land grant. He decreed on March 11 that it be done the following day. Afterwards he wrote this account:

> At the place and point called El Paso de Francia on the other side of the Río Grande del Norte, about two leagues more or less from this garrison of San Juan Bautista . . . I, Captain and Chief Justice, went to the place, and there being no neighbors on the four sides of the lands, only what was said about the settlement of Joseph Días de Oropeza, the citation was omitted, and . . . I took said Don Antonio Rivas by the hand and walked him over a portion of the lands . . .; and said Antonio walking over said land, pulled weeds, threw stones, sprinkled water out of the river, and made other motions of true possession, which possession he took quietly and peacefully, without any contradictions from any person.[5]

---

hills of that creek to Rositas de San Juan (Las Rosas de San Juan being a frequently mentioned point on the road to San Antonio), then to the head of Arroyo de la Cueba and along that creek to its juncture with the Río Grande, and down the Río Grande to the starting point. This area took in both key crossings on the Río Grande: Paso de Francia and Paso Pacuache.

[4] *Ibid.*, p. 3.   [5] *Ibid.*, p. 4.

Antonio Rivas apparently lived in the happy possession of his land beyond the Río Grande some fourteen years. But on October 1, 1779, in the Royal Presidio of San Juan Bautista del Río Grande del Norte, he lay severely ill. Feeling that death was nigh, he summoned the captain, now Don Manuel de Cerecedo y Velasco, and in his presence made a will. He provided for disposal of his personal property, including one rock house and some livestock, and for settlement of some debts. Listing the names of his children by his wife, Francisca Hernández, he named Manuel de Luna as testamentary executor in the first place, his son Andrés de Rivas in the second. After having satisfied all debts, if it was recognized that there was something left of his estate, "it is my wish that something be distributed among my above named children, with mine and God's benediction."[6]

In order to trace the history of this land grant made in 1765 a bit farther, it is necessary to get ahead of our story.

The immediate disposition of the land grant is not recorded. The Rivas family—children, grandchildren, and great-grandchildren—continued to live on the right bank of the Río Grande, in the vicinity of the Presidio of San Juan Bautista del Río Grande. Political upheaval in the years which followed cut them off from their inherited land, largely in present Maverick County, Texas.

First came the Mexican War for Independence; then the Texas Revolution, after which the new Republic laid claim to all the land to the left bank of the Río Grande. At last came the war between México and the United States, which unequivocally confirmed the Río Grande as an international boundary. With the end of that conflict, it was quite apparent that if the heirs of Antonio Rivas ever were to establish claim to this land, they must do so immediately. On April 4, 1848, the great-grand-children of the original grantee gave power of attorney to a Mexican lawyer named Vicente Garza, authorizing him to seek out the lost documents which would establish their ownership of the land grant. The documents, according to the instrument, had been lost by Don Antonio's executor; "none of us have received what belongs to us in justice."[7]

[6] *Ibid.*, p. 5.
[7] *Ibid.*, p. 5. This instrument was signed in the "city of Guerrero" April 4, 1848.

But the heirs of Don Antonio apparently had no money with which to finance the search. When Vicente Garza began to pressure for some sort of recompense, they made him, on May 9, 1848, at Guerrero, a full partner; in exchange for making the search at his own expense he was to receive half the land he recovered.[8]

On January 8, 1872, the state of Texas granted to the heirs of Antonio Rivas "28 leagues, 10 labors, 448,867 square varas of land . . . in Maverick Co. on the east bank of the Río Grande about 25 miles below Eagle Pass, being the quantity of land they are entitled to by virtue of the grant of land made to Antonio Rivas by the Government of Spain for 25 sitios of land, dated Feb. 23, 1765 [sic]."[9] Vicente Garza got his share, though it had taken years of effort.

Much more interesting history goes with the Antonio Rivas land grant, but it does not form a part of this story.

Don Diego Ortiz Parrilla, when he authorized a land grant to an old soldier, had no idea of the involvements the piece of land would have.

When Parrilla was relieved as governor of Coahuila by Don Jacinto de Barrios y Jáuregui, he remained for a time as commandant of the Presidio of Santa Rosa. In this capacity he was to undertake the exploration of the Gulf Coast.

In 1765 rumors were brought to San Juan Bautista by the Malaguita Indians, natives of the coastal region who had been gathered recently into the missions, that the English had formed a settlement along the coast, not far from the mouth of the Nueces River.

First to investigate these reports was Colonel José de Escandón, who communicated in May and June of 1766 that he had found no English settlements. He further asserted that there was no place along the entire coast which might be settled.[10] But the rumors had sounded convincing, and to make absolutely certain of Escandón's findings, Parrilla was ordered to the coastal region. At San Juan Bautista he gathered a number of the coastal Indians to serve as scouts and guides and formed his body of troops for the march to the coast.

[8] *Ibid.*, p. 7.
[9] *Ibid.*, p. 4.
[10] Bolton, *Texas in the Middle Eighteenth Century*, p. 105.

The expedition was launched from San Juan Bautista early in September, 1766, proceeding first to Santa Petronilla, a ranch near the mouth of the Nueces, where Parrilla established his camp. From here he sent twenty-six soldiers and nine Indians of the missions of San Juan and San Bernardo to explore the long island which lay along the coast, called Isla de San Carlos de los Malaguitas (Padre Island). The party, headed by officers Eugenio Fernández, Joseph Antonio de la Garza Falcón, and Mateo Martínez, crossed a shallow body of water and found itself on a narrow, flat, stretch of sand, with no reliable source of drinking water. It was noted that the island extended from its northern end, opposite the southern shore of Corpus Christi Bay, in a southerly direction, inclining to the west, for fifty-five leagues parallel to the main coast line, about two leagues distant. It was also about two leagues from the island's southern tip to the mouth of the Río Grande.

On the southern end they found ruined rancherias, evidently used for a short time each year by coastal tribes gathering food from the sea. The party had to dig shallow wells in the sands, as the Indians did, to obtain drinking water. They found no wood except on the outward side, where the debris from shipwrecks had washed up with the tide. Several canoes and small boats lay along the shore, and the explorers came to the broken hulk of a twenty-gun vessel, which they burned. No stone or other building material was found, and the little grass which grew from the sand was coarse and unfit for livestock. Two old Indian chiefs told the Spaniards they visited the island often and frequently saw ships passing at a distance.[11]

Heavy rains and swollen streams prevented Parrilla from exploring Corpus Christi Bay—which he is credited with naming—and from proceeding along the coast to Presidio de San Agustín de Ahumada del Orcoquisac (near present Wallisville). He turned up the Nueces to seek a crossing in order to reach Presidio de la Bahía (present Goliad) and traveled forty-two leagues before he was able to cross. Finally reaching La Bahía, he decided against attempting to go farther and contented himself with interrogating soldiers from Presidio de San Agustín whom he found there. He learned that the soldiers at La Bahía, as well as those

[11] Diego Ortiz Parrilla, "Testimonio de las Diligencias practicadas por el Coronel Don Diego Ortiz Parrilla," A.G.I., Audiencia de Guadalajara, 104-6-13 (Dunn Transcripts), pp. 12–15; Parrilla to Viceroy, *ibid.*, pp. 3–4.

from Presidio de San Agustín, were familiar with the coast from Matagorda Bay to the Nueces and had made frequent expeditions there to reconnoiter wrecked vessels and to pursue mission Indians in flight.[12]

Parrilla's thoroughness in collecting information from everyone who had something to contribute—including Cujan and Karankawa Indians of the Mission of Nuestra Señora del Rosario—is reminiscent of his procedure following the San Sabá Mission massacre.[13] His reports, consequently, were the first to give detailed descriptions of Mustang, St. Joseph, and Matagorda islands and of Cópano (Santo Domingo) Bay. These reports were in addition to those made by his own officers of their reconnaissance of the Isle of the Malaguitas and Culebra Island.

Returning to Coahuila the following April (1767), Parrilla forwarded his reports to the Viceroy. With maps to substantiate his views, he expressed the opinion that there was no danger of the English occupying any of the islands.

Soon after his return from the Texas coast, Parrilla disappears from the Coahuila-Texas scene. Commanding the Presidio of Santa Rosa later that year was Captain Don Vicente Alderete.

While Parrilla wound up his affairs in Coahuila, and Captain Manuel Rodríguez chased Indians, measures were being taken by order of the King of Spain which would change the face of New Spain's northern frontier. The King's inspector general, the Marqués de Rubí, was touring the frontier forts. His recommendations would be revolutionary, but those who had been responsible for dealing with the savage menace on the frontier, as had Parrilla and Rodríguez, would be quick to see the advantages.

[12] Depositions taken by Parrilla from various persons at Presidio de la Bahía during October, 1766, are found in *ibid.*, pp. 20–24.

[13] See translated documents in Paul D. Nathan (trans.) and Lesley Byrd Simpson (ed.), *The San Sabá Papers: A Documentary Account of the Founding and Destruction of San Sabá Mission.* Parrilla, unable to make complete exploration of the coast, apparently spent the winter at La Bahía, preparing maps and documents, which eventually were forwarded to the King.

28. THE SAVAGE FRONTIER

A NEED FOR FRONTIER REFORM was quite apparent, this spring of 1767, as the incoming governor surveyed the military forces of Coahuila. The new official, Jacinto de Barrios y Jáuregui, late of Texas, observed that Coahuila had only three presidios—Monclova, San Juan Bautista del Río Grande, and Santa Rosa María del Sacramento—with a combined force of just 117 men. Of that number 95 were assigned to duties outside the presidios, leaving the forts themselves manned by 11 men, not allowing for extra escort duty, for pursuing the enemy, or for illness.

San Juan Bautista, for example, had a complement of thirty-two men, including the subalterns: Four men were assigned to the Villa de San Fernando (which also had 10 from Santa Rosa and 6 from Monclova); four were on duty at the missions of San Juan and San Bernardo; four were billeted with the principal guard; seven guarded the horseherd; and eight were assigned to escort the supply trains of Presidio de San Sabá. This latter figure alone seems to indicate the magnitude of Indian trouble in northern New Spain. San Sabá, the most advanced outpost on the northwestern Texas frontier, was gradually being squeezed to death by the hostile tribes of the north. Supply lines were cut off, and the people were starving. The three Coahuila presidios had a total of thirty men assigned to convoy duty on the San Sabá lifeline.[1] Even that number, however, was not enough. San Sabá was not alone in suffering the bloody harassment of the mounted warriors. A state of continued warfare gripped Santa Rosa as well, a circumstance which soon involved the officers and men of Presidio de San Juan Bautista.

Colonel Don Jacinto de Barrios did not remain long as governor of

---

[1] Jacinto de Barrios y Jáuregui, "Estado que manifiesta la fuerza de los Tres Presidios de esta Provincia de San Francisco de Coahuila, y las distribuciones de ellas," May 3, 1767, A.G.N., Provincias Internas, Vol. 25, pp. 427–428.

Coahuila. His departure left Captain Manuel Rodríguez in charge as interim governor. He reported to the Viceroy:

> . . . on February 7 [1768], with license of Your Excellency, the Colonel Don Jacinto de Barrios departed from this Capital [Monclova], leaving me charged with the command of this Province, and he told me that on returning to my Presidio I should leave Don Francisco Flores in political authority.[2]

As interim governor and commandant of the province, Rodríguez had availed himself many times of Don Francisco's assistance, he related, leaving him in political charge when he went on military expeditions.[3] He asked for and received the Viceroy's approval for granting his assistant the title of political lieutenant general.[4]

By this time the Marqués de Rubí had come and gone on his inspection tour of the presidios of New Spain, from the Gulf of California to Los Adaes. In some instances he had issued instructions on the spot, in others he had let the presidial commanders wait for word to sift down through official channels. At Presidio de Santa Rosa, for example, the inspector general had ordered that a diary of operations be kept. The new commandant, Vicente Alderete, who had recently replaced Parrilla, began keeping the diary January 20, 1768. From that document several interesting facts, as well as a general picture of conditions on the frontier, may be drawn:

> February 21—Two soldiers left from this presidio in company of the Captain Commandant of this Province, who was proceeding to his Presidio del Río Grande . . .
>
> March 7—Two soldiers left from this Presidio with letter to His Excellency which came from Presidio del Río Grande, charged by the Commandant of the Province, Don Manuel Rodríguez, that they should carry it to Coahuila.
>
> March 11—Two soldiers left from this Presidio with letter of the Royal Service, sent by Lieutenant Commandant Don Joseph de Castilla for the Com-

---

[2] Manuel Rodríguez to the Viceroy, Marqués de Croix, November 26, 1768, A.G.N., Provincias Internas, Vol. 22, p. 11.

[3] Ibid. Vito Alessio Robles, (*Coahuila y Texas en la época colonial*, p. 570) says Francisco Flores substituted many times for Governor Parrilla and Governor Barrios but fails to mention Manuel Rodríguez in any manner or form. Barrios, says Alessio Robles, delivered the government on February 6, 1768, to José Castilla y Terán, a statement obviously in error.

[4] Viceroy to Rodríguez, December 17, 1768, A.G.N., Provincias Internas, Vol. 22, p. 12.

mandant of the Province, Don Manuel Rodríguez, which they carried to the Presidio del Río Grande, returning the 15th.

March 16—Seventeen leagues distant from this Presidio the Apache Indians killed a herdsman from the hacienda of the Marqués de Baldivieso on the lower Sabinas River. He was brought to this Presidio for burial three days after his death. I advised the Commandant of the Province, Don Manuel Rodríguez, of this news by means of two soldiers, who left immediately for the Presidio del Río Grande to look for a minister, since the Chaplain and Priest of this Presidio was ill.

March 23—The Commandant of the Province arrived at this Presidio, bringing with him the two soldiers who went to look for a Minister, whom they did not bring because of not having providence in those missions. Although with difficulty because of his illness, the said chaplain managed [the funeral service].

March 24—During the night the Apaches stole herds of mares from two *vecinos,* pastured two leagues from this Presidio. A squad of eight soldiers has just returned, having searched the avenues of the enemy Indians without finding any tracks. The said Indians on this same day entered behind said squad. Said commandant of the Providence being found here, he determined to make a campaign with soldiers from the Presidios and some *vecinos* who voluntarily enlisted, it being planned for April 20.

April 9—The Apaches stole a herd of white mares and eight broke horses from the ranch of a *vecino* five leagues northeast of this Presidio, on the other side of the Río de Sabinas, of which news I advised the Commandant of the Province, who was found in this Presidio, and on the same day had gone six leagues away to give possession of some land to a citizen. With the news he returned to make arrangements for the planned campaign.

April 16—At 8 o'clock in the morning I received news that on the 15th, during the night, the Apaches killed a citizen five leagues from this Presidio, tending his sheep with two boy herdsmen, who were carried away by said Indians. I advised the Commandant of the Province by means of two soldiers who left to overtake said Commandant, who on the 15th day had marched for his Presidio del Río Grande to make preparations for the campaign referred to. Then the supernumerary sergeant left with 12 soldiers to pursue the said Indians, who were three, according to the tracks . . .

April 18—The Mescalero Apaches killed two herdsmen of the cattle of the Marqués de Baldiviezo, 15 leagues from the Presidio. Their bodies, thrown into the depths of the Río de Sabinas, were recovered by other shepherds and brought to this Presidio for burial.

April 21—The Commandant of the Province arrived at this Presidio with soldiers from his Presidio and some citizens of his district. On this day he began to gather soldiers, citizens, and Indian auxiliaries from the Missions to make the said campaign.

April 26—A soldier left from this Presidio, to join with another from Coahuila, to carry a letter sent by the Commandant of the Province to His Excellency.

April 27—Fourteen soldiers, including the Alférez Don Eugenio Fernández and the supernumerary sergeant, departed from this Presidio in the company of the Commandant of the Province and the other troops of soldiers and citizens to go against the Mescalero Apaches who are harassing this Province.

May 9—At nine o'clock in the morning a Moso servant brought news that he had found in the country a league and a half distant a dead man, while he was out searching for his horses. I proceeded with a soldier and other persons who followed me to give faith of the case, and I found that the man had been slain by the Apaches, because the fatal wound was made with an arrow. As we followed the tracks another arrow was found in the trail, which was barely discernible because it had rained the night they killed him. The same night they had stolen from that area a herd of mares whose trail could not be followed because of the heavy rain.

June 9—The Commandant of the Province and the fourteen soldiers, including the *alférez* and the rest of the troop from the Presidios, and the citizens who accompanied them, arrived at this Presidio.[5]

Fruits of the campaign are not given in the diary, probably signifying that there were none. The force was dispersed June 17, and the Commandant returned to Presidio del Río Grande. On the twenty-fifth eight Mescalero Apaches raided to the very outskirts of Monclova, killing two shepherds and driving off a number of horses. Two soldiers left from Santa Rosa on the twenty-seventh to carry the word to Captain Rodríguez at San Juan Bautista.

On July 5 another raid at Monte de las Minas, a league from Santa Rosa, resulted in the death of a Moso Indian. Eight soldiers rode in pursuit but could not overtake the fleeing Apaches. With tired horses the soldiers returned after giving chase for five leagues. Two soldiers went to inform Rodríguez. Three days later it was necessary to send two more soldiers to San Juan Bautista, carrying an envelope to Rodríguez from the

[5] Vicente Alderete, "Diario de las operaciones del Real Presidio del Santísimo Sacramento y Valle de Santa Rosa," January 20–July 18, 1768, *ibid.*, pp. 323–329.

Viceroy. On the sixteenth the *comandante de la provincia* returned with the four soldiers to Santa Rosa. At this point the diary is terminated.

In September, Rodríguez was ordered to gather what troops he could from the province and join with Captain Don Lope de Cuéllar, military commandant of Chihuahua, in waging a campaign against the enemy Indians. Rodríguez reported that no more than thirty-nine soldiers could be spared from the three presidios of the province.[6] On December 2 he reported from Monclova: "In order to chastise the pride of the frontier enemy Indians I have placed under arms not only those of this province, presidials as well as citizens, but also the surrounding territory, as Your Excellency ordered me to do in your letter of September 3 last."[7]

With still no more than 117 men on full-time military duty and all but 22 of these on assignment outside the three presidios, Rodríguez had to reach out wherever possible to gather in additional men. If the situation had changed by the spring of 1769, it was only for the worse. The sanguinary Apaches continued their relentless raids.

> In compliance with the precise obligation of my charge [wrote Captain Rodríguez], I can do no less than make evident to Your Excellency the grievous ravages which the enemy Indians are committing daily. I have been obliged to bring in the *vecinos* of the Presidio de Santa Rosa from their country estates. . . . In all the province there is no road that is passable without calculated risk of meeting the barbarous Indians' advance. Although I have applied the best possible means of containing them and punishing their insolence, it has not been possible to attain this objective because of the sad plight of the horses of the three Presidios of this jurisdiction. Nothing more than a defensive maneuver can be made.[8]

He was still awaiting word from Captain Don Lope de Cuéllar to collect the available soldiers and militia and begin the projected campaign. Don Manuel feared he was being blamed for the delay, when actually his rôle was only to support Cuéllar.

> For when the time comes, I have asked help from the Governor of Nuevo Reyno de León, who has offered me thirty men. And in that regard the garrison of San Sabá has been transferred to the place of El Cañon, where it serves

[6] Manuel Rodríguez to Marqués de Croix, September 8, 1768, *ibid.*, pp. 314–315.
[7] Rodríguez to Croix, December 2, 1768, *ibid.*, p. 13.
[8] Rodríguez to Croix, March 19, 1769, *ibid.*, p. 19.

no purpose, if indeed it ever has; . . . the captain who commands it should be ordered to give whatever aid called for in order to protect this Province and to pursue its enemies.[9]

Word came post haste from the Marqués de Croix that the Captain of Presidio de San Sabá was to supply "the assistance which might be asked and needed."[10]

April came, and Don Manuel still waited for the start of the campaign. He attended, meanwhile, to the lack of equipment and clothing which hampered the effectiveness of his troop, fortunately finding "an angel" to provide their needs. The benefactor for the public good was Don Gregorio Sánchez Navarro, a Monclova merchant, who generously supplied clothing, horses, and provisions for Don Manuel's troop.[11]

By letter dated April 24, Lope de Cuéllar informed Rodríguez that he planned to begin on the first of June the campaign which had been ordered the previous August 8. The expedition was to be directed "against the Barbarous Indians which have terrorized Nueva Vizcaya and this Province [Coahuila]."[12] An earlier start had not been possible because arms and other assistance promised by the Viceroy had not arrived, said Cuéllar, who advised Rodríguez that he planned to march for La Junta de los Ríos, designating the trail the latter should follow to meet him there.

In consideration of this information [wrote Rodríguez], I have decided to begin my own march on the sixteenth of the following month [July] . . . traveling in solicitude of the juncture of the Río de Conchos with the Río Grande, west from this Presidio [San Juan Bautista], to reconnoiter one and the other side of the rugged mountains in which the enemies hide themselves. From the meeting of the rivers I will communicate the results to Cuéllar in order that the effort may succeed in a general chastisement.[13]

The interim governor Rodríguez planned to take with him 87 officers from the three Coahuila presidios, together with 30 from Nuevo León and 91 militiamen, and a number of mission Indians, making a total force of 285. But these were only plans. When the force assembled it was shy

[9] Rodríguez to Croix, March 19, 1769, *ibid.*, p. 20.
[10] Croix to Rodríguez, May 27, 1769, *ibid.*, p. 21.
[11] Rodríguez to Croix, April 11, 1769, *ibid.*, p. 25; Croix to Rodríguez, May 27, 1769, *ibid.*, p. 26.
[12] Rodríguez to Croix, May 29, 1769, *ibid.*, p. 27.
[13] Rodríguez to Croix, May 29, 1769, *ibid.*, p. 27.

by 100. Only 9 soldiers would be left in the Presidio of Santa Rosa, 7 at San Juan Bautista, 8 at San Francisco de Coahuila, and only a few armed Christian Indians to guard the missions.

This manpower shortage had caused Rodríguez to call upon Captain Manuel Antonio de Oca, who had replaced Felipe de Rábago y Terán in command of the San Sabá garrison, now at El Cañon, in accord with the Viceroy's authority. Oca maintained the horseherd of his troop at Villa de San Fernando (present Zaragoza), and frequently hauled grain from there to El Cañon, forty-five leagues distant. On Rodriguez' request he agreed to station 30 soldiers at San Fernando, enabling the commandant to take the 13 soldiers regularly assigned there from the three Coahuila presidios to assist the campaign. Thus Oca would be responsible for the protection and defense of San Fernando during Rodriguez' absence.[14]

In the Presidio of Santa Rosa María del Sacramento on July 18, 1769, the interim governor and commandant concluded his general review of the 145 soldiers and 40 auxiliaries who would launch the campaign the following day. From the Royal Presidio of San Juan Bautista del Río Grande were 4 officers: the commandant's brother, Lieutenant Vicente Rodríguez, and Sergeant Don Miguel de San Miguel, Corporal Xavier Cadena, and Corporal Xavier Minchaca. Other officers included the captain of Santa Rosa, Vicente de Alderete, and Juan Miguel de Martiaren, Joseph Castilla y Terán, Manuel de Soda, and Eugenio Fernández.

Soldiers from the Río Grande presidio numbered 20, with 2 citizens. There were 8 Indian auxiliaries from the Mission San Bernardo and 7 from Mission San Juan, each equipped with bows and arrows, shields, and three horses, with three loads of provisions for each mission. The Mission of Dulce Nombre de Jesús de Peyotes furnished 2 Indians on foot and 8 who were mounted, each with bow, arrows, and shield, 2 with firearms, and four muleloads of provisions for all of them.

Each of the soldiers carried a gun (*escopeta*), a shield, a bullet pouch, with one hundred balls and two *libres* of powder for each regular, fifty balls and one *libre* of powder for each citizen. The *caballada* included twelve horses for Lieutenant Vicente Rodríguez, while the rest of the troop had from six to eight horses per man. The lieutenant had three pack loads of supplies, while each of the soldiers had half a load.[15]

[14] Rodríguez to Croix, May 29, 1769, *ibid.*, p. 28.
[15] Manuel Rodríguez, "Lista y revista que en dicho día se hizo de la tropa,

The following morning Don Manuel Rodríguez, now at seventy-one, well past the age when he might have left such arduous tasks to men half his age, was up before his troop. He dashed off a hurried note to the Viceroy, explaining that he was sending the list of the soldiers and citizens because he felt His Excellency should know the names.

Today I undertake the march on the route to the northwest to face what the campaign has to offer: the advances, ambushes, countermarches, which will be adjusted to suit the primary objective for which the superiority of Your Excellency has ordered me. . . . At the feet of Your Excellency, Your most Reverent Subject, Manuel Rodríguez.[16]

It would be the old soldier's last campaign. But he undoubtedly was happy as he rode out of the Presidio of Santa Rosa María del Sacramento at the head of his troop, into the July dawn. Ahead lay countless leagues of dusty, unmarked trail, with water holes far apart, every mountain pass and stream crossing a possible ambush.

Turning westward Don Manuel led his troop through the Bolsón de Mapimí, "an elevated desert shaped like a huge pouch and rimmed with mountains."[17] Following the pocket northwestward, he reached the Río Grande near the Chisos Crossing, used more than twenty years earlier by Don Pedro de Rábago y Terán. After more than a month in the saddle, the troop reached Presidio del Norte at La Junta de los Ríos on August 25, but failed to find Don Lope de Cuéllar as expected. Don Manuel sent out Indian scouts to see if they could cut the trail of the other arm of the expedition, but they returned without success. Governor Rodríguez then dispatched the *alférez,* Don Eugenio Fernández, with a squad of soldiers to the Villa de Chihuahua to learn which way Don Lope had gone from there. Meanwhile, the troop would rest its horses, which were completely worn out from hard travel over rugged country, and the Commandant would take advantage of the break to advise the Viceroy of developments.[18]

vecinos del Real Presidio de San Juan Bautista de Río Grande, assie de Armas, Caballas, y municiones de boca y guerra," *ibid.,* p. 41 bis.

[16] Rodríguez to Croix, July 19, 1769, *ibid.,* p. 31.

[17] Paul Horgan, *Great River: The Río Grande in North American History,* pp. 740–741.

[18] Rodríguez to the Viceroy, August 26, 1769, A.G.N., Provincias Internas, Vol. 22, p. 42.

After a time Rodríguez took his force on up the Río Grande, finally reaching the "Presidio del Paso del Río del Norte." On the way he encountered a band of Indians with a herd of stolen Spanish mares. He took the animals on to El Paso and left them in the custody of the lieutenant of Socorro, Don Diego Tiburcio.

By a squad of soldiers of the Presidio of El Paso he sent word to Cuéllar that he was waiting for him to arrive before proceeding against the enemy Indians. Cuéllar replied under date of October 22, saying that he was not free to join in the campaign just then. He suggested that Rodríguez return to Coahuila. On the return march the Coahuila troop engaged a band of thirty-two savages and killed three of them. Seven mares and four colts wearing His Majesty's brand were retaken and would be kept in Rodríguez' care until instructions were received from the Viceroy for their disposition.

Rodríguez returned to Presidio de Santa Rosa on December 12. He immediately dispersed his force, sending the various components back to their respective presidios. Completing his diary, he sent it on to Viceroy Croix.[19]

Evidently the expedition from Santa Rosa to El Paso, by way of La Junta de los Ríos—the first of its kind ever undertaken—fell short of complete success because Lope de Cuéllar failed to come up to his part of the bargain. But Don Manuel made an observation on the trip which he felt made the excursion entirely worthwhile. He did not wait till he returned to Presidio del Río Grande to communicate his idea to the Viceroy:

> On the discovery which I have made on this Campaign to the Presidio del Paso del Río del Norte, I have affirmed that it would be an easy matter to open trade from here with that settlement, with no more than a convoy which may be given the *vecinos* by the presidios of this Province.[20]

Such trade would be beneficial to both areas, he believed, as well as facilitating the movement of arms from one presidio to the other.

It was a plan which Don Manuel thought worthy of pursuing. Not long after his return from the arduous journey to the west, he was happy to find himself relieved of the duties of interim governor and comman-

---

[19] Rodríguez to the Viceroy, December 21, 1769, *ibid.*, pp. 43–44. This diary, which Rodríguez transmitted with this letter, has not yet come to light.
[20] Rodríguez to Croix, December 23, 1769, *ibid.*, p. 48.

dant of the province, which burdens he had borne almost two years. Don Manuel lost no time in taking his plan up with the new governor, Don Jacobo de Ugarte y Loyola. Back at his own presidio of San Juan Bautista the following March (1770), he wrote to the Viceroy of his conference with Ugarte, who had offered all possible help in establishing communication with El Paso del Norte.[21]

Don Manuel felt that his plan, if carried out, would be instrumental in breaking up certain alliances among the Indians and in putting an end to their depredations upon Coahuila and the other northern provinces. Coahuila, he noted, was infested with hostiles. The Lipan Apaches had formed a pact with the Bidais and other nations in the direction of Texas, which were providing them with firearms. The Lipans were gathering midway between San Juan Bautista and the Presidio de Béjar, and they were implicated in recent murders and thefts. Several citizens of the Laredo area, forty leagues from San Juan, had become frightened, and some had moved near the Río Grande presidio to seek its protection.[22]

Indians of the Mission del Carrizo, which was under Rodríguez' jurisdiction, were joining with the Mescalero Apaches and other hostiles who lived in the region between San Juan Bautista and El Paso, in alliances similar to those which had in times past come close to bringing ruin upon Coahuila. The Indians of Carrizo Mission, Rodríguez explained, were those who previously had given trouble in the missions of Julimes at La Junta de los Ríos, joining with the Apaches to make raids into Coahuila, inflicting deadly ravages. Finally a presidio had been placed at La Junta to contain them; fearing punishment, they had moved to Coahuila some fourteen or fifteen years previously and gathered at the Mission of Vizarrón, only ten leagues from San Juan Bautista. At last they deserted the mission, stealing all its horses. "I went out with the troop to return them," related Don Manuel. "They repulsed us, and we considered ourselves fortunate to escape with our lives; since they had joined with many enemies, we could not contain them."[23]

Later the Indians, who were of the Julimeños nation, established themselves in a mission founded one league from Vizarrón, called El Carrizo, where they had remained nine or ten years. The pueblo lay at the edge of

[21] Rodríguez to Croix, March 16, 1770, *ibid.*, p. 56.

[22] *Ibid.*, p. 56.

[23] *Ibid.*, p. 57.

a range of hills whence came the enemies of the Spaniards, untamed savages who were friends and kinsmen of those in the mission, to raid the settlements, including San Juan Bautista. Just recently they had struck the encomienda of the Presidio of Santa Rosa. Joined by the hostile Apaches, they had killed three persons. Three Julimeños were captured. Although the Governor had suggested that the three Indians be imprisoned, Rodríguez hesitated to punish them in that manner, lest it cause the others to flee from the missions and return to the *montes*.

There is no doubt, Most Excellent Sir, that unless these Indians are punished for their excesses, they will persist in them, with grave damage to these provinces. I believe also that if only the three accused are punished, all the others will retire to join themselves with our enemies.[24]

To avoid losing these souls while preventing further ravages by the recalcitrants, Rodríguez suggested that the entire pueblo might be transported to Havana, or some other place which the Viceroy should decide upon—far from the province of Coahuila.

I am obliged to suggest to your superior understanding [continued Rodríguez] that efficient communication of arms would be facilitated with those of El Paso del Norte if four Presidios were placed on the borders of the Río Grande del Norte, in the places reconnoitered on my campaign, some 40 leagues apart: one presidio in the place of El Cajón, halfway between Presidio of El Paso and that of La Junta, which has been depopulated, at Julimes; another at the place of San Vicente, or Santa María, and the fourth at the place of Las Vacas, or of San Felipe [Ciudad Acuña or Del Río]. In this manner the presidios would form a cordon [extending] from here. The passage of the Indians to the Provinces, to harass them, would be avoided, and their conversion to our Holy Faith could be hoped for. Since the enemies have to retire from our lands by a route to the north, they would have no place to retire to if the Río Grande were occupied. Thus good lands could be settled, and in some parts many mines discovered. If settlement is not done in this manner, it will be necessary for His Majesty to spend much, and these Provinces to suffer much, for want of prompt punishment of said enemies because they live so far away.[25]

In a general way it was the plan which was adopted and incorporated into the Royal Regulation of 1772, after the recommendations of the Marqués de Rubí.

24 *Ibid.*, p. 58.   25 *Ibid.*, pp. 58–59.

29. NEW LINE OF DEFENSE

CHARLES III was new on the throne of Spain, but he was not altogether unaware of what was going on at the far-flung outposts on New Spain's frontiers. Rumors not wholly to his liking reached his royal ears —rumors of profiteering by presidial commanders, of mismanagement, and waste. He rightly suspected that some of the presidios had outlived their usefulness. Other questions concerning the management of Spain's New World empire called for investigation also: the acquisition of Louisiana, for example. What should be done with this new territory, which posed an enigma in so many ways? The new king needed answers. To find them His Majesty called upon the Marqués de Rubí, field marshal in the Royal Army. Rubí arrived in México early in February, 1766, to begin a thorough inspection of the frontier. He was to report the status of each presidio, from the Gulf of California to Los Adaes.

Rubí and Nicolás de Lafora, captain of engineers, who traveled with him, went first into New Mexico, as far north as Santa Fé, then on to the Gulf of California. They returned to Monclova, Coahuila, June 15, 1767, and from there launched the leg of their journey which took them into Texas. The route went north to Presidio de Santa Rosa María del Sacramento, where they noted that a garrison of fifty-two men was maintained. Crossing the Río de Sabinas three leagues beyond, the expedition came on the second day to Villa de San Fernando de Austria. On July 14 it reached the Río Grande, having crossed the San Antonio and the San Rodrigo rivers, and forded the Great River between El Moral and Jiménez, just above present Quemado, Texas. A Pausán Indian was drowned in the crossing.

The first Texas settlement to be reached was the San Juan Bautista off-shoot in the Valle de San José, where Fathers Rivera and Santiesteban remained in the Mission San Lorenzo with no Indians to teach, but with thirty-one men from the Presidio de San Sabá for their protection.[1]

The Texas tour took them to the Presidio de San Sabá, thence to San Antonio, Nacogdoches, Los Ais, Los Adaes, San Agustín de Ahumada, and La Bahía. With his final presidial inspection completed, Rubí set out on November 12, 1767, for San Juan Bautista.

The only settlement along the route was Laredo, a village of sixty huts which straddled the Río Grande. . . . Rubí's party crossed the river at that spot and made the journey into San Juan Bautista in four days.[2]

.   .   .   .

On the 22nd [says Lafora] . . . we arrived at the presidio of San [Juan] Bautista del Río Grande, situated at 28°35′ north latitude and 272°5′ longitude, computed from the Tenerife meridian. Its cavalry company is composed of 33 men, including the captain, lieutenant, and one sergeant. Its annual allotment amounts to 10,245 pesos. Moreover, each soldier, including the lieutenant, is given six pounds of gunpowder, as is the practice in all the presidios which his Majesty has on the frontier. There are also forty settlers with their families. Many have left to settle at La Bahía and the new town of San Fernando [de Austria] because of lack of farm land which has been taken over by the nearby missions of San Bernardo and San Juan Bautista. The first has 101 families, and the second 33 families from the various tribes mentioned in the description of this province. Among them are many Borrados, who are still savages. From both missions 170 men could be armed, some using bows and arrows, some pikes, half-moons [*medias lunas*], and a few, shotguns. The spiritual care of these people and the administration of the presidio is entrusted to three priests from the College of Our Lady of Guadalupe of Zacatecas. They receive an annual stipend of 450 pesos each.[3]

[1] Robert S. Weddle, *The San Sabá Mission: Spanish Pivot in Texas*, p. 168; Nicolás de Lafora, *Relación del Viaje que hizo a los Presidios Internos situados en la Frontera de la América septentrional perteneciente al Rey de España*, p. 187; Lawrence Kinnaird (trans.), *Frontiers of New Spain* (translation of Lafora, *Presidios Internos*), p. 147.

[2] Kinnaird, *Frontiers of New Spain*, p. 34. At each of the presidios visited, both Lafora and his assistant, Joseph de Urrutia, lieutenant of infantry, prepared a map. Urrutia's map of San Juan Bautista appears in David Hotchkiss, *Spanish Missions of Texas from 1776 Including the Battle of the Alamo—1835 (sic)*, as Map No. 11, and is reproduced in this volume by special permission of Hotchkiss and the British Museum, which owns the original map.

[3] *Ibid.*, p. 187. The statement that the Río Grande missions were under the College of Zacatecas is in error. When removed from the care of the College of

The Rubí party departed eight days later, on November 30, for Monterrey. Two leagues from the gateway settlement it crossed the Arroyo de Castaño and continued southward, over rolling hills covered by a low growth of mesquite, huisache, and cat's-claw.

Rubí's report of his inspection was sharp with criticism. He had found the frontier presidios lax in discipline, poorly manned and equipped, and weakened by the profiteering of their commanders. The major exception to the rule was San Juan Bautista and its aged captain, Don Manuel Rodríguez. While some of the commandants had been found guilty of profiteering at the expense of their troops—Don Angel de Martos y Naverrete at Los Adaes, for example—Rubí found that San Juan Bautista's captain had paid his troops out of his own pocket for three years. Rodríguez, observed the inspector at the conclusion of his visit, was found to be a most unselfish servant of the King, his reputation for zealously serving His Majesty entirely unimpeachable. Not only had he served well during the twenty-four years he had been at the helm of the Presidio of the Río Grande; his service went back many years, to the time when the rebel Tobosos were committing atrocities. The Marqués also found occasion to praise Don Manuel's ability in the management of his soldiers, who regarded their commandant with love, confidence, and respect: "All these factors make your merit commendable and yourself worthy of receiving the benefits of the Royal Gratitude, to which purpose I shall gladly devote my report, committing myself to relate your most zealous and punctual performance of duty."[4]

Don Manuel, said the inspector, had never used his position for personal gain. He had been attentive to such matters as the equipment of his troop; unlike those of some other presidios, San Juan Bautista's weapons were all of one caliber. Thus the possibility of finding the troop without firepower because its ammunition was the wrong size was avoided.

There were minor details at San Juan Bautista which needed to be corrected: a more strict uniformity of clothing should be adhered to; to avoid misunderstandings in the keeping of accounts, each soldier should be given a memorandum book, in which entries would duplicate those in the

---

Santa Cruz de Querétaro in 1772 they were transferred to the province of Guadalajara, as will be seen.

[4] Marqués de Rubí to Manuel Rodríguez, November 29, 1767, A.G.N., Provincias Internas, Vol. 22, p. 71.

books of the commandant; prices of the various commodities should be posted prominently in the *cuerpo de guardia,* the guard station; duties at the mission should be rotated among all the soldiers; the captain should reach a definite agreement with the ministers concerning the time the soldiers were to spend in the missions.

Concerning depredations by the Lipan and Mescalero Apaches, Rubí observed, the presidio captain had full authority under the ordinances governing the frontier forts to deal with them as he saw fit. He observed that the last three expeditions made from Presidio del Río Grande, led by the lieutenant commandant, Vicente Rodríguez, had been successful and apparently had gone a long way toward intimidating and containing the barbarians. These vigorous campaigns stood in sharp contrast to the lethargy found in some other posts, which seemed to lack the initiative, even, for pursuing their attackers. "Upon this particular I am persuaded that Your Grace needs no other stimulus than that of his interest in the good of the service."[5]

Not even Lafora, whose diary became most critical of the administration of the presidios and the presidial commanders in general, dealt harshly with the gateway fort.

When the Royal Regulations of 1772 were issued by Charles III, calling for establishment of the defensive line across the northern frontier, as Rubí had recommended, Presidio de San Juan Bautista was to remain where it was. The best barrier to be had for the provinces of Nueva Vizcaya and Coahuila, from La Junta de los Ríos to San Juan Bautista, the Regulations observed, was the Río Grande del Norte itself. The river's course, from one point to the other, was 240 leagues. The river was impassable at many places along the way. The defense line should take advantage of the natural barrier, the presidios of Cerro Gordo, San Sabá, Santa Rosa, and Santiago de la Monclova to be relocated close to the banks of the Río Grande at open places between San Juan and La Junta. In short the relocated forts would block the war trails of the hostile Indians from the north. The four were useless where they were; San Sabá, in fact, was worse than useless; it was an actual detriment at its old location, it was observed.[6]

---

[5] *Ibid.,* p. 74.
[6] Sidney B. Brinckerhoff and Odie B. Faulk, *Lancers for the King: A Study of*

Between the presidios of La Junta and San Juan Bautista the terrain should be reconnoitered scrupulously by the commandant of the frontier of Nueva Vizcaya and the governor of Coahuila.

The commandant of Nueva Vizcaya was to restore the troops from Julimes to their old presidio at La Junta. With those from Cerro Gordo and San Sabá he was to make a reconnaissance of the Río Grande, establishing soldiers of the former in a new presidio on the banks of the river. The Coahuila governor, Jacobo de Ugarte y Loyola, should unite the two companies of Santa Rosa and Monclova, and explore the country between San Juan Bautista and the confluence of the San Diego River and the Río del Norte. With these two companies he would erect two new presidios, one to guard the Villa of San Fernando de Austria to its back and the other to be located near the mouth of the San Diego River.

Ultimately, Presidio de San Sabá, whose garrison had been withdrawn from the Mission San Lorenzo to San Fernando de Austria, was placed almost on the boundary of Coahuila and Nueva Vizcaya (present Chihuahua). It overlooked San Vicente Ford on the Río Grande across from the present Big Bend National Park, blocking one fork of the Comanche war trail. Cerro Gordo became San Carlos, between San Vicente and La Junta, not far from Pedro de Rábago's Río Grande crossing in 1747. Presidio de Santa Rosa María del Sacramento was placed on the banks of the San Diego River, where it became known as Aguaverde, and Santiago de la Monclova became Monclova Viejo, situated on the San Rodrigo River.[7]

While the reconnaissance was underway the Commandant was to send adequate forces under capable officers to drive all enemy Indians to the other side of the Río Grande, "and his is not to consent under any pretext

---

the Frontier Military System of Northern New Spain, with a Translation of the Royal Regulations of 1772, p. 57.

[7] Vito Alessio Robles, *Coahuila y Texas en la época colonial*, pp. 573–574. The author visited the sites of Monclova Viejo and Aguaverde in the summer of 1965. Monclova Viejo was built of stone, and its outer walls still stand, serving as a pen for livestock. Aguaverde, made of adobe, has melted away. The site, though hidden by a dense growth of mesquite, has been discovered and badly victimized by treasure seekers or other irresponsible diggers. It should be noted that Brinckerhoff and Faulk (*Lancers for the King*) have confused Aguaverde and San Vicente (or San Sabá) and have failed to discern that Aguaverde was the transplanted Santa Rosa (see map, *ibid.*, p. 80).

that the Lipan Apaches be allowed to remain in the district of Coahuila nor congregate in the shelter of the presidio of San Juan Bautista."[8]

As for San Juan Bautista, one league from the Río Grande, it was found to be at the latitude which corresponded to that designated for the line of defense, and should remain at the place it had always occupied; its company should be increased to the full complement prescribed for all the frontier presidios

. . . in order that its detachments can defend the many avenues and fording places near the front and sides of the presidio. And in conjunction with the troops from Monclova and those from San Antonio de Béjar, which will be contiguous with this presidio, they can halt the invasions of the enemies; it is to be kept in mind that the ten Indians assigned as scouts for the company in this presidio, and the others in the line from it to San Buenaventura, are to be selected from the Julimeños because of their warlike spirit and tested bravery.[9]

The new defense line was not completely established for several years. It became apparent, as segments of the line began to fall into place, that one Indian trail into Coahuila from the north was being left open. To close this route Presidio de San Antonio Bucareli de la Bavia was founded by Captain Rafael Martínez Pacheco. Construction on the additional fort, situated in La Bavia Cañon, was begun in 1774. Four years were required for completion.[10]

From La Junta the defense line was extended westward to the Gulf of California with the presidios of San Eleazario, El Carrizal, San Buenaventura, Janos, Fronteras, Tucson, and Altar. East from San Juan Bautista was Presidio de la Bahía del Espíritu Santo. Between La Bahía and San Antonio a detachment of twenty men was stationed at Arroyo del Cíbolo.

San Antonio, to succeed Los Adaes as capital of Texas, and Santa Fé were Spanish settlements permitted by the Royal Regulations to remain above the defense line.

Rubí, in laying the foundation for the New Regulations, had main-

[8] Brinckerhoff and Faulk, *Lancers for the King,* p. 59.

[9] *Ibid.* The Julimeños were a tribe which had inhabited northeastern México before the coming of the Spaniards. In 1737 they were gathered into the Mission San Francisco Vizarrón, not far from San Juan Bautista.

[10] Alessio Robles, *Coahuila y Texas,* p. 577; Hugo Oconor to Teodoro de Croix, "Report on the Condition of the Interior Provinces," July 20, 1777, A.G.I., Audiencia de Guadalajara, 104-6-18.

tained that the foreign threat had vanished with the cession of Louisiana to Spain. He failed to consider the possibility that within a few short years the English colonies would separate from the mother country to form a new nation whose people would incubate ideas of "Manifest Destiny."

For a number of years the northern frontier in Texas had been static, unable to advance. The Rubí inspection and the resultant Royal Regulations signaled a retreat. The real reason for such a withdrawal was that the Plains Indians made it necessary.[11] The San Sabá Mission episode, although it had accomplished little toward pacifying the Apaches, had aroused the Comanches and initiated warfare between that wily tribe and white settlers in Texas. It was obvious that Spaniards could not hold out against them at far-flung outposts like San Sabá. Rubí, however, felt that the solution to peace with the Comanches lay in severing relations with the Apaches, perhaps joining with the northern tribes in war against them, and even turning one Apache tribe against another in the hope that they would exterminate each other.

As the New Regulations were implemented, the war with the Apaches was prosecuted with limited success, as was the attempt to make peace with the Comanches. Nonetheless,

... the Royal Regulations of 1772 showed that the emphasis on the northern frontier had shifted from a religious effort to a military one. As church and state were wedded under the Spanish government, the Spaniards on the frontier still came with the sword in one hand and the cross in the other, but the Royal Regulations clearly indicated that it was the sword that was in the right hand.[12]

While such far-reaching alterations were being made in the military system on the frontier, the religious arm also came to grips with change. In 1767 the King had expelled the Jesuits from all the Spanish dominions, and in New Spain this meant a general redistribution of the missionary forces of the northern frontier. For more than a century the missionary work of the Pacific Slope and among the Tarahumara Indians had been in the hands of the Jesuits. Their place in Lower California was now taken by the Franciscans of the three missionary colleges. "To offset this new burden the College of Santa Cruz in 1772 asked and secured permis-

[11] Weddle, *San Sabá Mission,* p. 174.
[12] Brinckerhoff and Faulk, *Lancers for the King,* p. 7.

sion to renounce its missions in Coahuila and Texas. Those in Texas were taken over by the College of Zacatecas and those in Coahuila by the Province of Santiago de Jalisco."[13]

Few recruits had entered the College of Querétaro in recent years, and it was becoming increasingly difficult to replace the aged and disabled missionaries. It therefore sought to be relieved of the four missions at San Antonio and two at San Juan Bautista, which were in a prosperous condition, in the midst of well-established communities. Well provided with permanent churches, supplied with all the necessary ornaments and sacred vessels, they possessed adequate quarters for the ministers and sufficient cultivated and irrigated lands. Their administration would entail no hardships on whoever should take them over. These missions, however, were not ready to be placed under the care of seculars, because there were many neophytes who were still under instruction; new groups had been brought in regularly to replace those who had died in the frequent epidemics and those who had returned to the *montes*.

The province of Jalisco (Guadalajara) and the College of Zacatecas readily accepted the missions. The viceroy, Antonio María de Bucareli y Ursúa, issued a formal decree for the transfer on July 28, 1772. From Guadalajara would come the proper number of missionaries as soon as possible to take charge of San Juan Bautista and San Bernardo. Those worthy of the greatest trust were to be chosen to receive the missions from the ministers presently in charge. The transfer was to be effected with all the proper formality under accurate inventory of the spiritual and temporal belongings of each of them.[14]

The commandant of San Juan Bautista Presidio, however, viewed the move apprehensively. He feared the neophytes would completely abandon the missions after the Queretaran missionaries had withdrawn. The garrison and the *vecinos* of the pueblo, who felt likewise, presented their case in writing and forwarded it to the Viceroy. Citing numerous examples in which the change of missionaries had caused the abandonment of missions, they suggested that the same was likely to happen to those on the Río Grande. The discontented neophytes, they feared, might ally

---

[13] Herbert Eugene Bolton, *Texas in the Middle Eighteenth Century*, p. 109.
[14] Carlos Eduardo Castañeda, *Our Catholic Heritage in Texas*, IV, 263.

themselves with hostile tribes and lead them to the settlement to take vengeance for pretended wrongs.

The Viceroy's advisers and officials of the College of Querétaro took the matter under consideration and eventually the Discretorio assured Bucareli that, despite the fears of the well-meaning citizens of San Juan Bautista, the Indians themselves would be entirely indifferent to the change; in their simple way, they probably would view with enthusiasm the coming of new missionaries to minister to them. Even should they choose to run away, the garrison at Presidio de San Juan Bautista was sufficient to arrest their flight. Satisfied, the Viceroy then repeated his previous orders and instructed the commander of the Presidio del Río Grande and the governor of Texas to witness the transfer in person, or to delegate persons to represent them.[15] But during this year of 1772 many other problems had arisen at San Juan Bautista which had to be settled before this matter could be finally consumated.

30. END OF AN ERA

D ON Manuel Rodríguez, as interim governor and commandant of the province of Coahuila, probably was as much responsible as any other man, excepting the Marqués de Rubí himself, for the line of presidios established along the Río Grande under the Royal Regulation of 1772. Having surveyed the region from San Juan Bautista to El Paso in 1769, he had suggested the location of presidios to block the war trails of the Indians of the North in order to cut off their raids on the north Mexican provinces. But the old campaigner was never to see the line of defense es-

[15] Ibid., p. 264, citing Juan Domingo Arricivita, *Crónica seráfica y apostólica del Colegio de la Santa Cruz de Querétaro en la Nueva España, segunda parte,* pp. 440–441.

tablished. After more than half a century in the service of his king, his time ran out.

Don Manuel's death evidently was not unexpected. When the end came, the various members of his family seemed to know exactly what course to take, and lost no time in taking it. It seems strangely incongruous that the family of such a selfless man should be so completely dominated by selfish thoughts almost before the body was cold in its crypt. His eldest son wrote immediately a petition in his own behalf to the viceroy, Antonio María Bucareli y Ursúa, who had taken office the previous August.

Most Excellent Lord Viceroy:

I, Señor Don Francisco Rodríguez, legitimate son of Don Manuel Rodríguez, who was captain of this Presidio of San Juan Bautista del Río Grande del Norte, and who died on this date [February 11], submit to Your Excellency that he, my father, served the King Our Lord (God keep him) more than fifty years, as soldier, officer, and Captain, with the gracefulness of manner, valor, and fortitude, which is well known in these interior provinces, as Your Excellency can discern from the attached from the Senor Marqués de Rubí. After so many years of service, he has left us, our deceased Father, in total poverty, and with many debts, not because His Grace spent anything on pomp or vanity; nor had he any vice whatsoever, except for maintaining his Troop (as everyone knows), and that the principal attention of His Grace was not to accumulate wealth but for the greater and more exact fulfillment of both Majesties.

During his illness, which was extended, my deceased Father wrote to Your Excellency, asking of your Piety that his position should be conferred upon me, for the support of his large family, and for the satisfaction of his debts. This letter has not reached the hands of Your Excellency, I know not why. That which places me at the feet of Your Excellency is humbly to request of your Piety and compassionate zeal to grant me the position of said Captaincy, whose honor I shall discharge as a son of my Father, whose great attention and glory was to shed his Blood in service of both Majesties. I await the great mercy of Your Excellency's favor.

May the Divine Majesty preserve the important Life of Your Excellency for the protection of the poor many years. Presidio de San Juan Bautista del Río Grande del Norte, February 11, 1772.

Francisco Rodríguez[1]

[1] Francisco Rodríguez to Viceroy Bucareli, February 11, 1772, A.G.N., Provincias Internas, Vol. 22, p. 69.

Taken without the plea for a concession for himself, the son's letter forms a beautiful tribute to Don Manuel. Unfortunately, it appears that advancing his own station was uppermost in the mind of Francisco, rather than memorializing his father. Little is known of this eldest son of Don Manuel, who apparently had not even served as a soldier in his father's presidio. Evidently he acted on impulse, and his methods defeated his purposes.

He had to wait three days for his uncle, Vicente Rodríguez, acting commandant of the presidio, to provide him with a copy of the remarks which the king's inspector, Marqués de Rubí, had addressed to Don Manuel.[2] In the meantime he induced his mother, the captain's widow, to write to the Viceroy also.

Doña Antonia Rodríguez Morales recounted that her late husband's service career had extended over more than sixty years.[3] Before receiving the King's patent as captain of Presidio del Río Grande in 1743, he had served as *alcalde ordinario* of the Villa de la Monclova, and as soldier, corporal, sergeant, *alférez,* and lieutenant. The letter of Rubí would attest to the efficacy of his service. Since Rubí's visit Don Manuel had made two campaigns against the Apaches; the latter one, made on orders of the superior government, constituted a vigorous war to punish the Apaches for the many and repeated raids they had made on Coahuila and Nueva Vizcaya. He had pursued them all the way to the Paso del Norte, in the jurisdiction of New Mexico, over a route which no other leader had yet traveled.

So unselfish was the conduct of the late captain during the twenty-nine years he had commanded Presidio de San Juan Bautista—said his widow —that on the day of his death he had left her nothing except a large family, including three sons. The oldest, now thirty-one, was in her opinion qualified to fill his father's former post. His appointment would bring

[2] Marqués de Rubí to Manuel Rodríguez, November 29, 1767, *ibid.,* pp. 71–75, quoted in preceding chapter. Vicente Rodríguez' certification was witnessed by Antonio de Rivas.

[3] Antonia Rodríguez Morales to Viceroy Bucareli, February 14, 1772, *ibid.,* pp. 67–68. Note that Francisco Rodríguez said his father had served God and king more than fifty years, rather than sixty. The widow exaggerates. Don Manuel was about seventy-five at the time of his death, having been born in 1697 at Monclova. His service record (A.G.N., Provincias Internas, Vol. 25, p. 301) shows he had served forty-two years in 1764.

comfort to her in her widowhood, her poverty, and her advanced years, as well as to her large family.[4]

Don Manuel's widow and his son were not the only ones to see opportunity in his death. The Coahuila governor, Jacobo de Ugarte y Loyola, recommended two of his favorites from Villa de San Fernando for appointment as *alférez* and lieutenant of the Río Grande presidio. He also wrote in behalf of the widow's plea, and the Viceroy responded that, sympathetic as he was for the plight of the widow of Don Manuel, he could not grant her petition to alleviate her poverty, because the late captain was responsible for his own investments; the appointment of a new commandant could not be influenced by the fact that the family was left destitute.[5] Some months later Bucareli got around to appointing Eugenio Fernández as lieutenant of Presidio del Río Grande, in accord with Ugarte's wishes.[6] Vicente Rodríguez had ascended to the captaincy, though the appointment had not yet been made official. He was only two years younger than his brother, and would not have long to serve, but he nevertheless was preferred to his thirty-one–year–old nephew.

In view of the interim appointment, made by the Viceroy subject to the approval of the King, Don Vicente reported on the employment of the company of the Presidio del Río Grande. Of the thirty-two soldiers on duty, not including two subalterns, four were on guard duty in the presidio, seven guarded the horseherd, eight were assigned to the four missions of the presidio's jurisdiction, with thirteen kept in reserve in order to be able to repel any attack by the hostile Indians, for the citizenry had few arms with which to protect themselves.

The eight soldiers who spent each day at the missions, with the title of *mayordomo*, were employed in the care of cattle, brood mares, and other property of the Indians. Don Vicente doubted that it should be the duty of soldiers actually to defend the missionaries, in view of the royal ordinances in effect since shortly after the visit of Pedro de Rivera in 1727. Times had changed, he noted; if at that time the Indians were considered

4 *Ibid.*, pp. 67–68.

5 Viceroy to Ugarte, March 3, 1772, A.G.N., Provincias Internas, Vol. 24, Part 1, p. 105.

6 Viceroy to Eugenio Fernández, August 20, 1772, A.G.N., Provincias Internas, Vol. 22, p. 77.

to be idle, such was no longer the case. The natives were sociable, adept in agriculture and other arts. Besides the two missions no more than a gunshot distant from the *plaza de armas,* San Juan and San Bernardo, the presidio's jurisdiction also included the missions of Dulce Nombre de Jesús and San Francisco Vizarrón. These latter two were the distance of a rifle shot apart, and two rifle shots from the settlement of San Pedro de Gigedo, nine leagues from the Presidio de San Juan Bautista del Río Grande.

The Captain closed by asking the Viceroy to inform him whether the soldiers should continue in the missions or return to the presidio.[7]

In another letter bearing the same date Don Vicente described the condition of the Mission of San Francisco Vizarrón. Ten years previously some families of *indios norteños* from Chihuahua had gathered there. These northern Indians were living as apostates in the fields, committing murders and thefts. The minister of the mission at that time had brought half the Indians in and sent the others to the place called Carrizo, a league distant. The Indians at Carrizo had got out of hand and, in Don Vicente's opinion, should be compelled to abandon their licentious life and join their kinsmen at Vizarrón.[8]

Meanwhile, the soldiers of San Juan Bautista had protested the appointment of Don Eugenio Fernández as lieutenant of the presidio. Don Vicente, who had recommended the appointment in the first place, evidently gave permission for his soldiers to send two representatives, Francisco Longoria and Francisco Flores, to the capital to protest to the Viceroy. His Excellency was not pleased. He curtly advised Rodríguez that he had no business sending soldiers from the province at a time when the citizenry as well as the governor of Coahuila were crying for an increase in military protection. The soldiers were sent back to their duties, and Rodríguez was advised that license for soldiers to come to the capital for the purpose of asking superior resolutions should be granted only in cases of extreme urgency.[9]

A month later Bucareli informed Rodríguez that, in all propriety, the

---

[7] Vicente Rodríguez to the Viceroy Bucareli, September 12, 1772, A.G.N., Provincias Internas, Vol. 22, pp. 78–79.

[8] Vicente Rodríguez to Viceroy, September 12, 1772, *ibid.,* p. 80.

[9] Viceroy to Vicente Rodríguez, September 29, 1772, *ibid.,* p. 61.

King had seen fit to confer upon him the captaincy of the Río Grande Presidio, which he had been serving under the Viceroy's interim appointment.[10]

Still later, the Captain was advised that he should continue the soldiers of his garrison in the employment in which they were occupied; His Excellency's resolution on whether the service his soldiers were giving him in the missions should be discontinued would come later. Don Vicente also was to take whatever action he considered necessary to curb the licentiousness of the *indios norteños* who inhabited the place of Carrizo.[11]

But these were only the minor matters with which Don Vicente had to concern himself in the first few months of his captaincy. The year 1772 had been a busy one, full of import for San Juan Bautista: settlement, presidio, and missions. On September 10 King Charles III had issued his Royal Regulations redesigning the frontier defense establishment. Then, on November 22, the Coahuila governor, Jacobo de Ugarte y Loyola, had at last sent final orders to Captain Vicente Rodríguez for the transfer of the two missions, San Juan and San Bernardo, from the College of the Holy Cross to the province of Jalisco. Rodríguez sent word to Friar Diego Jiménez, still serving as president of the Río Grande missions, that Friar Luis de Lizarrana of the province of Jalisco was ready to receive the missions. The transfer of Mission San Juan Bautista was begun November 27.

With inventories to be taken of all the accouterments of church, Indian quarters, shops, farming and stock handling equipment, and livestock, it was a time-consuming task. First a list of every item in church, baptistry, and sacristy was prepared, containing approximately the same items as those listed in 1756 by Father Ortiz. From the church Jiménez, Lizarrana, and Rodríguez proceeded to the Indian quarters to inventory houses, equipment, furnishings, and utensils; thence to the implement shed and stable of the farm, a league distant from the mission. Then on to the ranches, six or seven leagues southeast of the missions, to round up the stock and make a count. San Juan Bautista was found to possess 672 branded cattle, 698 horses, mules, and donkeys, more than 5,300 sheep, and 657 goats. Also inventoried was all the equipment of the carpenter shop, the blacksmith shop, the textile mill, the diningroom, the kitchen,

10 Viceroy to Vicente Rodríguez, October 28, 1772, *ibid.*, p. 62.
11 Viceroy to Vicente Rodríguez, December 8, December 9, 1777, *ibid.*, pp. 63, 64.

and the stores in the warehouse. The administration books were examined, revealing that ninety-six Indian males and seventy-three females were living in the mission at the time. It was December 15 before the inventory was completed and the team went on to make a similar count at San Bernardo.

Declared Captain Rodríguez for the record:

Aware of the care, vigilance, and constancy with which the said Reverend Father President and his missionaries have labored in the fulfillment of their duty, the education of the natives, and the teaching of the catechism, as well as in the efficient administration of the temporal interests of the missions, I hereby declare the College of Querétaro exonerated from all further responsibility and thank its missionaries for their faithful services.[12]

So ended a charge which the College of the Holy Cross of Querétaro had begun at this location January 1, 1700—almost seventy-three years previously—when Father Francisco Hidalgo followed a bunch of runaway Indians from the Río de Sabinas into the Valley of the Circumcision.

A similar inventory was made of the possessions of the Mission San Bernardo and given to Father Lizarrana. San Bernardo was found to have 1,204 head of cattle, 6,900 sheep, more than 900 goats, 835 mares, 212 horses, and 101 mules.

Though at this stage San Bernardo had only a few more Indians than did San Juan Bautista, it may be noted that the former mission had larger numbers of livestock and apparently possessed considerably more wealth than did the latter. This condition may be due in part to the fact that Father Jiménez, with his attention divided between the Río Grande missions and those on the Nueces, had given attention to the mission of his residence (San Bernardo) while neglecting the other.

Jiménez, in fact, has been given credit—or blame—for construction of the San Bernardo Church which stands in ruin just north of Villa de Guerrero today. Says Cervera Sánchez: "The ruins of this Mission which are preserved at Villa Guerrero are those of the temple built by Friar Diego Jiménez at the middle of the Eighteenth Century. The construc-

---

[12] Carlos Eduardo Castañeda, *Our Catholic Heritage in Texas,* IV, 265, citing "Testimonio de los Vienes de la Misión de San Juan Bautista del Río Grande del Norte, Año 1772," Saltillo Archives, Vol. 3, pp. 76–134.

tion of this edifice was not finished, since the work remained in the cornicement."[13]

A few years after the transfer Father Juan Agustín Morfi was to write of San Bernardo and the former president of the Río Grande missions:

> Being minister of this mission, the former guardian of the College of Santa Cruz, Fray Diego Jiménez, began the construction of a beautiful temple that would shine in any community.
>
> It is all of rock . . . and was up to cornicing and near to being finished, but being so ill-suited to the place, with such expense required to finish it, there is no hope of doing so.[14]

Thus it appears that the Franciscans of the province of Jalisco took the unfinished stone church of San Bernardo along with its wealth of live-stock and farm land. It is difficult to determine whether any part of the church ever was used. Though the main church and the *cruceros* appar-ently never were given a roof, the baptistry dome, which is still intact today, was completed, as was the arched stone roof of the sacristy.[15]

While San Juan Bautista at the time of the transfer had 169 Indians of both sexes, San Bernardo had 185, including men, women, and children, all well instructed in the tenets of the Catholic faith. All those over seven years of age went to confession and received communion at least once a year. They were provided with proper clothing, including shoes and stock-ings, which they wore when attending church. All had been taught a trade; they were skilled as farmers or as tradesmen. As this mission was transferred to the custody of the province of Jalisco, Captain Rodríguez

---

[13] Jorge Cervera Sánchez in Juan Agustín Morfi, *Descripción del Territorio del Real Presidio de San Juan Bautista del Río Grande del Norte, y su Jurisdicción, Año de 1778*, p. 315, n. 87.

[14] Juan Agustín Morfi, *Viaje de Indios y Diario del Nuevo México*, p. 203.

[15] Paul Horgan (*Great River: The Río Grande in North American History*, p. 325) assumes this church had served from the mission's beginning in 1703: "Saint Bernard's lifted in 1703 a grace new to the river, for with its creation the curve arrived in the Spanish architecture of the Río Grande. The circle was frag-mented and used in the stone arches of the great doorways, the barrel vaultings of the nave and the refectory, and the stone door of the baptistry. . . . The Franciscan style was now formed . . . Across the wastes of México Saint Bernard's high walls and baptistry dome were a signal of haven for wayfarers coming to the wide valley from the south."

reiterated the tribute he had paid to missionaries in transferring San Juan.[16]

The missions of the Río Grande, like the presidio, had come to the end of an era. They were placed in new hands.

[16] Castañeda, *Our Catholic Heritage,* IV, 266, citing "Testimonio de la Entrega de la Misión de San Bernardo del Río Grande del Norte a los Rds. Pds. de la Santa Prova. de Xalisco. Año de 1772," Saltillo Archives, Vol. 3, pp. 34–74.

Part III
PRESIDIO OF THE LINE
AFTER 1772

31. SWORD ABOVE THE CROSS

WHILE THE Marqués de Rubí had submitted his recommendations to a council of war in México's capital city early in 1769, his plan was subjected to a thorough study before the King handed down the Royal Regulation, September 10, 1772. In the meantime the Indian situation in the northern provinces only worsened. Spanish military forces were totally inadequate to cope with the ferocious raids of the Apaches, and often the garrisons were content to sit quietly in the presidios following an attack, rather than go out in pursuit. Thanks to the Rodríguez brothers, fearless and energetic, the garrison of Presidio de San Juan Bautista probably was more active in the pursuit of marauding Indians than was that of any other fort on the northern frontier. Soon Don Vicente, though seventy-three years old, would undertake another vigorous campaign against the Apaches.

Hugo Oconor,[1] as commandant inspector of the Interior Provinces, was

[1] Hugo Oconor, born in Dublin in 1734, expatriated himself after the failure of Irish rebellions against England. Like many another Irishman who had lost his birthright or prejudiced his freedom in conflict with Protestant England, he sought a haven with Spain. An officer in the Regiment of Volunteers of Aragón when it was ordered to Cuba in 1763, he quickly rose to the rank of major and was elected to membership in the Order of the Knights of Calatrava. In 1765 he was sent to Veracruz and thence to the capital of México, where he caught the eye of the Viceroy Marqués de Cruillas, and was sent to Texas to perform certain urgent duties. On August 28, 1767, he became governor ad interim of the province and was therefore the principal officer in Texas when the Rubí inspection was made (David M. Vigness, "Don Hugo Oconor and New Spain's Northeastern Frontier, 1767–1776," *Journal of the West,* VI, No. 1 [January, 1967], 28–30).

given the job of effecting the new Royal Regulation. His first task was to dislodge a band of Mescalero Apaches who were raiding out of the Bolsón de Mapimí. Next he was to select the new sites for the presidios of Julimes, San Sabá, Cerro Gordo, Santa Rosa, and Monclova. He would review and revitalize these garrisons, then move on to follow the same procedure with the presidios farther west.

Oconor's campaign dislodged the Mescaleros and drove them northward from the Bolsón de Mapimí early in 1773, but still raiding bands visited their wrath on Coahuila. Oconor's presence was required at San Antonio in the spring and summer of 1773, since the East Texas missions were being suppressed and the settlers moved to San Antonio. He appointed Captain Raphael Martínez Pacheco[2] at Villa de San Fernando to act in his stead. Martínez Pacheco had no troops but those of the undermanned presidios with which to rid the beleaguered province of the menace.

On the night of May 24 word came to the Villa de San Fernando of the latest in a series of bloody attacks. At a place called San José, ten leagues southwest of San Fernando, the Mescalero Apaches had killed seven cart drivers and taken a number of captives, including an aged woman, three small boys, and one youth of twelve. Captain Martínez Pacheco fortunately had at his command a portion of the garrison which had been withdrawn from Presidio de San Sabá. He immediately gave orders for the lieutenant of San Sabá, Don Alejo de la Garza Falcón, and the *alférez,* José Antonio Pérez, to take fifty-two men into the field the following day.[3]

Martínez sent a hurried messenger to Presidio del Río Grande, where Captain Vicente Rodríguez, at three o'clock the following morning, awoke to receive the news. Hastily gathering eleven soldiers and ten Indian auxiliaries from the Mission San Bernardo, with the necessary supplies, Don Vicente and his lieutenant, Félix Pacheco, were underway for San Fernando by midmorning. The small force reached the village, fourteen leagues distant, at seven o'clock that evening.[4] A third contingent of

---

[2] See Walter Prescott Webb and H. Bailey Carroll (eds.), *The Handbook of Texas,* II, 322, for a sketch on this controversial figure.

[3] Martínez Pacheco to the Viceroy, June 11, 1773, A.G.N., Provincias Internas, Vol. 22, p. 405.

[4] Vicente Rodríguez, "Diario de las Operaciones de Don Vicente Rodríguez,

twenty-six men came from the presidios of Monclova and Santa Rosa, to make a total force besides the captain of three officers and ninety-nine soldiers. On May 26, at seven o'clock in the morning, the second part of the force rode out of Villa de San Fernando de Austria "with orders to pursue the infamous murderers to their lands and rancherias, which was done by the most difficult routes . . ."[5]

Following the Camino Real southwestward, the troop came to San José, where the men viewed the seven new graves which had resulted from the recent Apache raid. Setting out again on the Camino Real toward the Presidio of Santa Rosa, they soon left the road to head northward, following the trail of Lieutenant Garza Falcón. Their march impeded by heavy showers, the men covered twenty leagues that day, by Captain Rodríguez' reckoning.[6]

After marching two leagues on the twenty-seventh, Rodríguez' company came to the place where Garza's men had spent the night. Here they saw another grave, of the woman whom the Indians had captured, then killed. Hastening on to overtake Garza, Rodríguez came up to him at five o'clock that evening. The entire force camped together for the night, and Don Vicente logged twenty-two leagues for the day.

On the twenty-eighth, still meandering northward, the united force cut the trail of the fleeing Indians and followed the well-worn path. After six leagues, however, they found the trail barred by an immense hill, which they called Cuesta del Toro because they found the bones and horns of a bull thereon. Descending the hill on the other side, they came into a beautiful valley, filled with trees and green grass, though it was late afternoon before they found water. By the spring they saw an abandoned Indian village. Ironically, the Indians had left a large cross standing at their former camp site. Rodríguez' Indian scouts, exploring ahead, returned with a horse, abandoned by the fleeing savages because it was too weak to travel. The night was passed at the place, which was named Agua de San José de la Peña. The day's travel, by Rodriguez' count, covered twenty-two leagues.

Capitán del Presidio de San Juan Bautista del Río Grande," May 26–June 10, 1773, *ibid.,* p. 412.

[5] Martínez Pacheco to Viceroy, *ibid.,* p. 405.

[6] Rodríguez, "Diario de Vicente Rodríguez," *ibid.,* p. 412.

The march evidently inclined to the west of north, getting into the rough country in the edge of the Serranías del Burro, where the tributaries of the Río Grande sliced the rim of the plateau, forming sharp precipices. Still following the tracks of the enemy on the twenty-ninth, the Spaniards undertook more dangerous climbing, so steep and difficult that they had to dismount and lead their horses. Even so, the ascent was made with great risk, since the horse of Lieutenant Félix Pacheco slipped and plunged down a steep hill, a near miss to sudden death. Conquering this Cuesta del Diablo, or Devil's Peak, the troop looked down upon a plain cut by many canyons. Marching till dusk, having traveled twenty leagues by the log, they found no water and made a dry camp, their tongues thick from thirst. Captain Rodríguez sent four soldiers, together with the San Bernardo Mission Indians, to reconnoiter the country for a water supply, since many trails of wild horses crossed the plain, a sure sign that water was not far distant. The scouts returned to report that they had found an Indian campsite, apparently abandoned some four days previously, in a narrow canyon, where there was a small spring.

Next morning the entire troop moved one league to the spring, there to pause and water and rest the horses. The Indian scouts went out to reconnoiter the trails and water holes. Furious rainstorms lashed the camp that night.

On May 31 the troop traveled west over a steep and stony trail, then turned back to the north. During the day twenty leagues were covered. The scouts raised a fresh trail of an Indian on foot and tried to intercept him before he could warn his people of the Spaniards' approach. The troop continued to march down a canyon until sundown. The scouts did not return that night.

On June 1 the troop proceeded north over a rocky range of hills, the progress much impeded by runoff from the heavy rains. After six leagues they came to an arroyo in which the enemy had camped, but now the arroyo was carrying a flooding stream of water. By Don Vicente's count the day's travel covered eighteen leagues. That night at eight o'clock the scouts returned with the disappointing news that they had been unable to overtake the Indian on foot, who had taken a westerly course.

The march began at dawn on June 2, the troop laboring up a hill, then descending into a rocky arroyo, the horses fatigued from traveling the rugged path. At last they arrived at the Río Grande, only to find it on a rampage. The enemy, unfortunately, had reached the other side ahead of the flood. Captain Rodríguez directed the march downstream, hoping to find a crossing at a place where the river widened, called San Marcelino. He counted the distance as fifteen leagues. Making camp at the ford, where the Indians had crossed ahead of him, Don Vicente sent out his scouts. The troop remained in camp on the third, waiting for the river to go down—a difficult decision, since the scouts came back to report that the enemy Indians were encamped not far distant on the opposite side of the stream.

The crossing was undertaken at daybreak on the fourth. It was not an easy task, and some soldiers came close to being drowned. Two men did lose their horses and most of their equipment. From the left bank of the river the troop marched northward, over hill and arroyos which were almost impassable. The Spaniards now were in the vicinity of the mouth of the Pecos River.[7] Rodríguez entered eighteen leagues in his diary.

They picked up the trail of the enemy on the fifth. Soon after beginning the day's march they found in an arroyo the enemy's recently abandoned rancherias, where they had eaten a horse and left behind one of the captives (presumably dead). With such fresh signs Rodríguez called a halt and dispatched his spies. The scouts came back at three in the afternoon, reporting that they had found where the Indians had slept close at hand the night before. The Captain sent them out again. There would be no more travel by daylight. While waiting for nightfall and further report from his spies, he ordered a review of the troop.

The soldiers mounted up at nightfall, and shortly afterward the spies came in with word that the horseherd of the Indians had been seen not far distant. Rodríguez sent them back to scout the approaches to the enemy camp. He ordered a halt at midnight, four leagues from the enemy, having marched that day and night, by his count, twenty-two leagues.

At three in the morning he ordered Lieutenant Alejo de la Garza to form a squad of five men for the center of the line of attack, with two squads of thirty men for the flanks. At four o'clock the force mounted up. After marching a short distance, with the aged captain right in stride, they were able to make out seven rancherias formed at the top of a hill overlooking a running creek. "We invoked our Patron St. James, and

---

[7] Martínez Pacheco to Viceroy, *ibid.*, p. 405.

our three segments arrived in such good time that the enemy barely had time to take up their arms and put themselves on defense."[8]

The Indians fought bravely for three hours, all of them defending themselves to the death. Some Indian women fought along with the men, but since the Spaniards did not know they were women, they received no special treatment. They died along with the men, also. Eight women, including a very old one who was blind, and eight children were taken prisoners. None of these had entered into the battle.

As for the Spaniards, their losses consisted of several wounded horses and three wounded men, none dangerously. Three Spanish captives taken by the Indians at San José—two eighteen-year-old girls and a twelve-year-old boy—were freed. Recovered also were two hundred horses and mules, which the Indians had driven off from the settlements of Coahuila in five separate raids, and a large number of horses and mules which belonged to the enemy Indians. These included the horseherd of the Mission of Dulce Nombre de Jesús de Peyotes, and the horses of two soldiers of the San Sabá garrison whom the Indians had killed.[9] Two hundred pesos worth of gold and silver vessels taken from one of the Coahuila missions were regained as well.

All the stolen horses and mules and other property would be returned to their rightful owners. The property of the Indians would be distributed among the soldiers and the Indian auxiliaries.

At two in the afternoon Don Vicente broke camp to begin the homeward march, having placed the lieutenant of San Juan Bautista, Félix Pacheco, in charge of the prisoners. By night they had traveled twelve leagues, by Don Vicente's reckoning, and had reached the bank of the Río Grande, evidently some distance above San Marcelino.

Next day the crossing was made between *el agua edionda* and Las Vacas, slightly below present Ciudad Acuña, and the Captain marked eighteen leagues in his diary.

Finding plenty of water and grass and easier terrain on the right bank of the Río Grande, the troop made good time on the eighth. Approaching the Río de San Diego, it made camp in a ravine. Don Vicente counted

---

[8] Rodríguez, "Diario de Vicente Rodríguez," *ibid.,* p. 419.

[9] Rodríguez, "Diario de Vicente Rodríguez," *ibid.,* p. 419; Martínez Pacheco to the Viceroy, *ibid.,* p. 406. Neither of these sources reveals the number of Indians killed in the attack, but it must have been considerable.

the day's travel as twenty-four leagues, the longest day's march of the expedition.

The following day, counted as eighteen leagues, brought the expeditioners to the Río de San Rodrigo, and on June 10, entered in the diary as eight leagues, they reached San Fernando. Lieutenant Pacheco turned the prisoners over to Captain Rafael Martínez Pacheco, and Don Vicente added up the leagues of his expedition to 272, though it appears that all the distances given in his diary are greatly exaggerated.

Captain Martínez Pacheco gathered all the information he could from the officers of the expedition and from the Spanish captives being returned. The following day he composed his report to the Viceroy, which he forwarded along with Captain Rodríguez' diary.

The two Spanish girls who had been captives of the Mescalero Apaches told Martínez Pacheco that the Mescaleros had planned to join with the Lipan Apaches to destroy the two new presidios of Coahuila, along with Santa Rosa and San Fernando.[10] Such plans, wrote the Captain, stemmed from the fact that the Apaches had been able to make so many thefts and robberies without ever having been punished until now, the enemy realizing that the *comandante inspector,* Hugo Oconor, had departed with his entire camp and would not soon return. But with the success of this campaign led by Captain Rodríguez, the other hostiles could be contained until the *comandante* returned with his force to make a general campaign. Just to be on the safe side, however, Martínez Pacheco was sending the lieutenant of Presidio del Río Grande, Félix Pacheco, and a squad of soldiers to Saltillo with the captives. He also sent Sergeant Manuel Carbajal with a squad to alert the frontier haciendas between Monclova and Saltillo of the possibility of a retaliatory Indian raid, and to give assistance to any who needed it. One of the prisoners, the aged blind woman, was being kept at San Fernando, for fear she would not be able to stand the trip; furthermore, it was suggested, she might be willing to receive the Holy Waters of Baptism.[11]

While Martínez Pacheco felt the Indians could be contained temporarily as a result of the expedition led by Rodríguez, he believed that only

---

[10] Martínez Pacheco to the Viceroy, *ibid.,* p. 406. The presidios referred to probably were Monclova Viejo on the San Rodrigo and Aguaverde on the San Diego, which were being built at this time.

[11] *Ibid.,* p. 408.

through completion of all the presidios of the line, at short distances from each other, could the natives be permanently subdued.[12] Knowingly or otherwise, Martínez reflected the thinking of Viceroy Bucareli, regarding frontier defense. While awaiting the Royal Regulation the previous autumn, the high official had written his own views: until the five presidios —Monclova, Santa Rosa, San Sabá, Cerro Gordo, and Julimes—were transferred to the Río Grande, until Oconor could start a general campaign, and until presidio garrisons began to fight outside their walls, the savage menace would continue.[13]

The presidios were being moved, the garrisons were fighting outside the walls, and Bucareli liked the signs; yet he was not to be deceived by high-sounding claims.

You have convinced me [he wrote to Martínez Pacheco] that this happy strike will contain the ideas which the Lipan and Mescalero Apaches had of uniting their forces to attack the Presidios which are being moved. But aside from this reflection, I am not obliged to neglect the movements of the presidial troops. Before making any effort to discount the intentions of the barbarians, I must consider that even though the diary [of Vicente Rodríguez] clearly explained all the operations, it failed to give the number of the enemy which the detachment fought, apparently in order to attribute this victory to gallantry or good leadership. These are things which I take for granted, since a party of 99 men entered into the affair, invoking with living faith the name of our glorious Patron Santiago, and were engaged in the fray three hours. For these reasons it is necessary that Your Grace remedy this obvious defect and see that it does not occur in future diaries. It is not enough to give the number of rancherias. The number of people, more or less, of which they are comprised, and the dead and wounded of both sides, are needed also.[14]

The Viceroy approved of the action Martínez Pacheco had taken to send to Saltillo the Indian women and children who were prisoners. He would issue authority for Lieutenant Félix Pacheco to be reimbursed for daily rations on the trip, the costs to be charged to the commandant in-

[12] *Ibid.,* p. 407.

[13] Bernard E. Bobb, *The Viceregency of Antonio María Bucareli in New Spain, 1771–1779,* p. 137.

[14] Viceroy to Martínez Pacheco, July 13, 1773, A.G.N., Provincias Internas, Vol. 22, p. 409. Martínez replied to these points August 15, 1773, in *ibid.,* pp. 380–383. It had been impossible to fix the number of dead, he reported, because many had fallen unseen in the canyons. He had learned from the Lipan Apaches that only three combatants had escaped, a woman and two men.

spector, as provided in Article 1, Title 8 of the Royal Regulation.[15] The prisoners would be delivered to the Justice, who would divide them among the distinguished families of the *villa*; they would be cared for and their Christian education seen after.

The disposition made of the horses and the mission furnishings taken from the Indians seemed appropriate to Bucareli, "but not the method with which Your Grace is handling the interim commission which was conferred upon you by the Commandant Inspector Hugo Oconor."[16]

Captain Martínez Pacheco, it seems, had assumed more authority than was given him. In the orders he had issued to Sergeant Carbajal—a copy of which he had sent to the Viceroy—he referred to himself as adjutant, or subinspector, of Oconor, the inference being that he was removing himself from the jurisdiction of the Governor of the province. The governor, said Bucareli, viewed this action as being insubordinate. In conceding the military command to the commandant inspector, the Governor had not relinquished his authority over the officers and troop of the presidios, whose duty it was to defend the frontiers of his province. As the Governor's first subaltern, Martínez Pacheco was still obliged to obey his orders, which the commandant inspector had no authority to change. In this matter the Captain was to set an example for the other military leaders of the province.

Closing on a more mellow note, the Viceroy said:

Your Grace shall extend my thanks to Captain Don Vicente Rodríguez, to the subaltern officers, and to the troop which participated in the recent action against the enemy, for the honor with which they have conducted themselves, assuring them that such meritorious effort will be brought to the attention of His Majesty.[17]

The presidial troops continued their movements, even before these instructions from the Viceroy were received, but not all campaigns were to have such a happy result. Hugo Oconor remained at San Antonio, and

[15] Viceroy to Martínez Pacheco, July 13, 1773, *ibid.*, p. 410. The citation of this portion of the Royal Regulation appears to be in error. See Sidney B. Brinckerhoff and Odie B. Faulk, *Lancers for the King: A Study of the Frontier Military System of Northern New Spain, with a Translation of the Royal Regulations of 1772*, p. 29.

[16] Viceroy to Martínez Pacheco, July 13, 1773, A.G.N., Provincias Internas, Vol. 22, p. 410.

[17] *Ibid.*, p. 411.

Captain Martínez Pacheco had to go there in June to turn over his former garrison—apparently that of San Agustín de Ahumada—to Governor Barón de Ripperdá. He left San Fernando on June 13 and returned to San Juan Bautista on August 9. He wrote on July 5 to the captain of Presidio de San Juan Bautista, enclosing a letter from Governor Jacobo Ugarte y Loyola, asking for Rodríguez to go to the aid of Sergeant Carbajal. The Sergeant and his squad had gone in pursuit of enemy Indians who had committed atrocities near Cuatrociénegas.

In council with Lieutenant Alejo de la Garza Falcón of the garrison of San Sabá (still quartered at San Fernando), Rodríguez decided to place José Antonio Pérez, *alférez* of San Sabá, in charge of the expedition. Pérez was put at the head of a troop consisting of thirty-eight soldiers, including sergeants and corporals, from the garrisons of San Sabá, Santa Rosa, and San Juan Bautista, along with eight Indian auxiliaries, to go to the aid of Sergeant Carbajal. Even though Carbajal returned before Pérez got underway, the small expedition was allowed to proceed. It was a tragic blunder. In compliance with the specifics of the new Royal Regulation, the Indian scouts were the Julimeños from the Mission of San Francisco Vizarrón. These were the Indians of whom both the Rodríguez brothers, Vicente and Manuel, had given warning, for they were known troublemakers. Hence it appears surprising that Don Vicente ever put such faith in them. Yet, apparently even he had no indication that they were capable of the treachery of which they were to be suspected.

The subaltern, José Pérez, mounted his troop and departed from the Villa de San Fernando at nine o'clock on the morning of July 25. In accordance with his instructions he rode south to reconnoiter the headwaters of the San Ildefonso, or Santa Rita Creek,[18] above present Morelos. Tramping out all the known haunts of the enemy Apaches, the small force made a westward loop, cut the headwaters of the Río de Sabinas, and headed back to the north. Camp was made the night of July 29 at La Rosita de San Juan, a campsite mentioned by Pedro de Rábago y Terán in his 1747 diary,[19] on the Arroyo de la Bavia. From this point on Pérez followed La Bavia Creek, adhering closely to the Rábago y Terán route.

The course which had been charted for the expedition by Vicente Ro-

---

[18] Also known as the Nogales River, the one from which irrigation water was taken for the missions of San Juan Bautista.

[19] See Chapter 22 of this study.

dríguez and Alejo de la Garza would have taken Pérez to Rábago's old campsites of San Pedro and Santa María del Socorro, as far as San Vicente Ford, just across the Río Grande from the southernmost point of present Big Bend National Park. There appears to be no connection between the choice of the route and the fact that the San Sabá garrison soon was to be established at this location, as the new Presidio de San Vicente. In any event Pérez failed to reach his destination.

Reaching the place of La Bavia on the thirtieth, he kept the troop there an extra day to rest the horses. On August 1 the Indians went on ahead to explore the mountainous country, seeking out signs of the enemy. In order to allow the scouts time to locate and report any danger signs Pérez kept the troop in camp till noon. With the troop, the horseherd, and the pack train arranged in good order, he marched five leagues to reach at three o'clock in the afternoon a high hill, the Cerrito de las Cabras, which seemed to have been planted right in the middle of the trail. Instead of attempting to mount the crest of the hill, as Pedro de Rábago might have done, the troop chose a path around its brow. As the vanguard turned a corner of the hill it came face to face with a band of Apaches lying in wait. A shower of arrows rained upon the Spaniards, and five men tumbled from their saddles. Caught by complete surprise, the soldiers did not even have time to put on their *cueras,* the thick leather jackets which served as armor. With a sudden outcry the attacking savages dashed over the Spanish troop so quickly that many were unable to fire their guns before they were gone. Even so the soldiers' first volley killed three Indians, so close upon them that their clothing was powder burned.[20] But with the shout and the outburst of gunfire from the troop, the horseherd and the pack mules stampeded.

Considering the large number of the enemy—later estimated at 250, both on foot and mounted[21]—Pérez rallied his troop and let the horses and mules go. The animals were quickly seized by the enemy, but the capture of the horses and mules bought the soldiers a chance. They seized the advantage of terrain and made ready to withstand an attack. Within an hour the Indians had the horses and mules corraled, and returned in force to make the assault.

[20] Martínez Pacheco to the Viceroy, August 25, 1773, A.G.N. Provincias Internas, Vol. 22, p. 394.
[21] Martínez Pacheco to the Viceroy, *ibid.,* p. 389.

The troop defended with valor, though several of the soldiers fell wounded, and many of the horses were wounded or killed. Seeing that the number of the enemy was overwhelming, Pérez decided on a fighting withdrawal. Those soldiers who had lost their horses mounted behind the saddles of others, while the wounded were borne on litters between two horses. But the Indians swooped down upon the Spaniards and surrounded them, and many more horses were killed. Pérez was forced to dismount his men and make another stand. Again the soldiers fought bravely, killing and wounding many Indians, as night moved in and visibility faded. In the dusky haze it appeared that the enemy Indians and the Indian auxiliaries of the Spanish troop were joining together. One could be told from the other only by the helmets which the Julimeños wore. It seemed the entire troop would perish.

For a time Pérez, with four men at his side, and Sergeant José de la Garza, with six, formed a defensive line. Pérez held the right, Garza the left, but then the Indians drove a wedge between them. It was every man for himself.

Near dawn Pérez, ignorant of Garza's fate, decided to avail himself of the darkness and the undergrowth upon the hill. The five men, leading their tired horses, stole through the brush, leaving the Indians in mastery of the field.

One soldier who had become separated from the others when the Indians first rushed upon them still cringed alone in the brush during the last stages of the fighting. He could hear the firing of Sergeant Garza's men close at hand, but the shots were fewer and fewer. At last the shooting stopped. For a time there was dead silence in the arroyo below, and the soldier lay breathlessly still, lest he divulge his hiding place to the enemy. Then there arose from the direction whence he had heard the firing a more awesome sound: the wails of the Indians, bemoaning the loss of their dead. Pérez' small force had been cut to pieces, but thirty-eight brave men had made the Indians pay a dear price.[22] The battle had lasted twelve hours—till four-o'clock in the morning of August 2—and the fighting had covered nine leagues, from Cerrito de las Cabras to the Arroyo de los Cabezones.

By August 6 Pérez and the four soldiers who had escaped with him

---

[22] Martínez Pacheco to the Viceroy, *ibid.*, p. 394.

reached the Valley of Santa Rosa (probably the site of the presidio, now being moved to the San Diego River). After getting help started on the way for any of his men who might still be able to use it, Pérez wrote his report of the encounter.[23] As yet he had no idea of the extent of the casualties his troop had suffered. The full story of the battle would be slow to unfold, and would be talked about and conjectured upon for many months to come.

On August 10 Captain Martínez Pacheco, just returning from San Antonio, reached Villa de San Fernando de Austria to hear for the first time the news of the disaster. The village was without troops, because all had joined a new expedition up the Arroyo de la Bavia, hoping to rescue any of Pérez' men who remained alive, perhaps wounded and on foot, among the rugged hills and canyons.

Four days later, on the fourteenth, Governor Jacobo de Ugarte y Loyola reached San Fernando, bringing Pérez and the four soldiers who had made their way to the Valley of Santa Rosa. Ugarte also brought news that Sergeant Carbajal had reached Arroyo de los Cabezones, Creek of the Big Heads, to learn the full extent of the Spanish loss. He found the dry stream bed strewn with the decaying corpses of fourteen soldiers, including Sergeant Garza. Carbajal, himself with only a small squad, dared not continue on to the Cerrito de las Cabras, for he saw fresh Indian signs; there was no sense in inviting repetition of the disaster. Not until sometime later was Captain Martínez Pacheco able to piece together a complete casualty list for his official report: twenty-one dead and nine wounded. The dead included nineteen soldiers, a muleteer, and an Indian who was with the troop during the battle. Of the soldiers twelve were of the garrison of San Sabá, which also had six wounded. San Juan Bautista counted five dead, with one corporal wounded. Two of the dead and one of the wounded were from Santa Rosa.[24]

None of the Indians of the missions of Peyotes, San Bernardo, and San Juan Bautista, excepting the one killed, took part in the battle. Pérez firmly believed that he had seen some of them at dusk, fighting on the side of the enemy, and was convinced that they had turned traitors. The

[23] José Pérez, "Derrotero que con el favor de Dios, empieza hacer el Alférez de la Compania de San Sabá, Don Joseph Pérez," *ibid.*, pp. 396–400.

[24] Martínez Pacheco to the Viceroy, August 25, 1773, *ibid.*, pp. 391–392.

soldiers of Presidio del Río Grande, he wrote in his report, had told him of the treacherous nature of the Julimeños, whom it now appeared had delivered the troop for massacre by the enemy Apaches.[25]

Martínez Pacheco, however, did not subscribe to Pérez' suspicions. He had interrogated the Indians of Carrizo and was satisfied that it had not happened as Pérez suspected. Only by circumstance, the Captain believed, did the hostile Indians, just returning from a raid to the south, happen along at the precise moment the Spanish troop was moving up the Arroyo de la Bavia. It was easy for them to see, theorized Martínez, that the Spaniards' number was small; hence they lay in wait at the Cerrito de las Cabras to visit their destruction upon the soldiers. But it was no easy victory for the Indian force, believed to have been made up of Mescaleros, Jileños, Natagés, and Julimeños, armed with bows and arrows. Sergeant Carbajal had seen in the Arroyo de los Cabezones many signs that the natives' toll had been heavy. Their principal gain consisted of 250 horses, 10 pack mules and their cargo, and 6 saddle mules, badly needed by the Indians, for at the time of the attack they did not have enough mounts for all their warriors.

On the night of August 15 Captain Vicente Rodríguez reached Villa San Fernando, having come from San Juan Bautista on orders from Martínez Pacheco and Governor Ugarte. The following day the Governor convened a junta to determine the methods to be employed in defending the frontier. One of the points of major concern was the state in which the late disaster had left the garrison of San Sabá, which was one of the principal forces for defense of the province. The garrison had lost twelve men. Even those who had survived the massacre had lost horses, arms, and equipment. It was decided that Martínez should inspect the San Sabá company and determine the men who could be placed under arms to join troops from the other presidios to seek out and punish the enemy Indians.[26]

On the seventeenth the Governor departed for the Valley of Santa Rosa, and thence for Monclova, to gather citizens to augment the military force.

On August 21 Martínez Pacheco sent fifteen men and a corporal from

25 Pérez, "Derrotero," *ibid.*, p. 400.
26 Martínez Pacheco to Viceroy, *ibid.*, pp. 390–391.

San Juan Bautista, with fourteen friendly Indians, to the Presidio of Santa Rosa. Two days later José Pérez departed for the same post with forty men of the San Sabá garrison. The forces gathered at Santa Rosa—which evidently means the new location of Santa Rosa, known as Presidio de Aguaverde, on the San Diego River. There they were to wait for Martínez Pacheco, who would bring ten men from the Monclova garrison, which also had moved by this time to the San Rodrigo River, where it would be known as Monclova Viejo.[27]

In the meantime, Martínez was completing his report on Pérez' battle with the Indians, and he attempted to fix the blame—squarely at the feet of the San Juan Bautista Captain, Vicente Rodríguez.

In the first place, he noted, there was no reason for the expedition on which Pérez had been sent. Plans had called for his going to aid Sergeant Carbajal; when Carbajal returned, Pérez' trip should have been canceled. Never, he emphasized, should so small a company have been sent over such a long and dangerous route. Captain Rodríguez, he noted acidly, had taken a force of sixty-seven when he was only going to the new site of Presidio de la Monclova to remove from the vicinity some Lipan Indians who had never offered any indication of enmity. In pursuing the loose Indians who had raided in the center of the province, Rodríguez had taken ninety-nine men and three officers, giving himself such an advantage that he had no trouble in obliterating the enemy camp. Yet this same captain had sent thirty-eight men through the heart of enemy country, over rugged terrain, on an expedition which was supposed to extend all the way to San Vicente Ford. It had been an easy matter for the enemy 250 strong, to observe the small numbers and to launch their deadly attack. That the entire force was not wiped out was due only to the strength and valor of the soldiers and the fortitude of the *alférez*.

Most Excellent Sir, this loss of soldiers who were so well known for their strength and valor, and their horses and arms, has been very painful to me, and it is very damaging to the service. And what a pity to see the poor widows and their children left in such an unhappy state![28]

Even though Martínez Pacheco would place all the blame at the feet of Vicente Rodríguez, however, there is no certainty that Pérez himself was

[27] *Ibid.*, pp. 394–395.
[28] *Ibid.*, p. 393.

not at fault, particularly in the light of subsequent happenings. Some military leaders are disaster prone.

Pérez, like George Armstrong Custer a century later, may have been such a leader. Like Custer in his battle with Black Kettle's Cheyennes on the Washita, Pérez had committed a tactical error which could well have ended his career, and certainly should have taught him a lesson. Like Custer he lived to fight another day, to meet a worse disaster, only by quirk of circumstance. Custer's nemesis was at the hands of the Sioux on the Little Big Horn. Pérez, five years after the affair up La Bavia Arroyo, led twenty-two men from Presidio de San Vicente into an Apache death trap at a place which took its name from the crosses which marked the soldiers' graves: Las Cruces.[29]

Apparently, however, the affair in Arroyo de la Bavia bore fruit in one sense. It revealed an oversight which had been made in planning the new line of defense. This was an invasion route of the hostile Apaches which had been overlooked. It must be closed. The means of closing it was Presidio de San Antonio Bucareli de la Bavia, which Martínez Pacheco began building in 1774.[30]

By September, 1774, the new line of defense was complete "from sea to sea," except for some interior works at Monclova (Viejo), Santa Rosa (Aguaverde), and three presidios of the province of Sonora.[31] Hugo Oconor, therefore, could begin preparing for the most ambitious and most comprehensive campaign against the Indians ever attempted on the northern frontier. His plan, formulated early in 1775, called for putting nine large forces, totaling 2,228 men, in the field. Each was to start from a different point on the frontier, to punish the Apaches and drive them back from the left bank of the Río Grande.

In practice, however, the grandiose plan fell far short. The projected nine forces dwindled to three. These were led by Captain Manuel Muñoz of Presidio del Norte at La Junta, Captain Martínez Pacheco of Presidio

---

[29] Robert S. Weddle, *The San Sabá Mission: Spanish Pivot in Texas,* p. 182; Vito Alessio Robles, *Coahuila y Texas en la época colonial,* p. 578.

[30] Alessio Robles, *Coahuila y Texas,* p. 577; correspondence of Eugenio Fernández, A.G.N., Provincias Internas, Vol. 22, pp. 82–88.

[31] Hugo Oconor, "Papel Instructivo," July 20, 1777, Audiencia de Guadalajara, 104-6-18, pp. 49–50.

de San Antonio Bucareli de la Bavia, and Coahuila Governor Jacobo de Ugarte y Loyola. In its outcome the campaign fell far short of success.

Governor Ugarte y Loyola reviewed his force in the *plaza de armas* of Presidio de San Juan Bautista del Río Grande, preparatory to departure September 22, 1775, a month behind schedule. From the presidios of Monclova Viejo, Aguaverde, San Vicente, and San Carlos, as well as Río Grande, he had 184 men. Captain Vicente Rodríguez, though now seventy-six years old, was one of the principal leaders. It would be his last major campaign.

From San Juan Bautista the troop marched upriver to Monclova Viejo, crossed the Río Grande, and traveled northward for the abandoned Presidio de San Sabá. While Ugarte kept his main force in camp at Aguaje de las Vacas (probably Bear Creek, present Kimble County), Captain Rodríguez took forty-five soldiers over the divide to the San Sabá, seeking out the hostiles in the vicinity of the old fort abandoned six years previously. Rodríguez found only buffalo-hunting Lipans encamped along the river. He promptly returned to the main camp, and the force headed back to the Río Grande, crossed to Aguaverde, and prepared for the second phase of the campaign.

After exchanging 233 worn-out horses and resting one day, the troop recrossed the Río Grande, marched up the Río de San Pedro (Devil's River)[32] to its headlands, then turned west to the Pecos. After joining his force with that of Martínez Pacheco, Ugarte sent eighty-eight men under Vicente Rodríguez "on a swift march to the Sierra de Guadalupe" to reconnoiter Indian trails and watering places.[33] Rodríguez marched upstream until November 19, cutting the cold trail of Captain Muñoz from Presidio del Norte but never finding him. Having followed the Pecos into the present limits of New Mexico, Don Vicente reconnoitered the Guada-

[32] Jacobo de Ugarte y Loyola, "Diario de lo executado por el Destacamento mandado del Governador de la Provincia de Coahuila," September 22–December 30, 1775, A.G.N., Provincias Internas, Vol. 24, p. 261. It is said that Texas Ranger Captain John Coffee (Jack) Hays, after riding far across barren, rugged, and dry country, came to the forbidding gorge of this stream and asked his Mexican guide the river's name. He was told that it was the Río de San Pedro. "Saint Peter's, hell," exclaimed Hays, "it looks like the devil's river to me" (Webb and Carroll, *Handbook,* I, 495).

[33] Ugarte y Loyola, "Diario," pp. 263–264.

lupe Mountains and returned to the main force at Paso de Gálvez on December 2.[34]

While Ugarte waited for Rodríguez' return, he sent five Indian auxiliaries and two citizens who had served as soldiers in the old Presidio de San Sabá to reconnoiter the headwaters of the Río Florido (Concho) for sign of the Apaches. Ugarte intended that the scouting party should follow the route laid out in 1761 by a force from San Sabá.[35] The two ex-soldiers, having been members of that expedition from San Sabá, believed that they could find the way. Six days later, however, they returned, unable to find the trail to take them over the wide expanse of dry country to the Concho's headsprings. Having wandered about lost over the extensive plains until their horses grew weary and their provisions ran low, they had to follow their own trail back to camp.

The expedition, returning to the Río Grande along the same route by which it had come, was attacked by a band of hostiles on the Devil's River and lost three men before reinforcements put the savages to flight. Making camp at the juncture of the Devil's River and the Río Grande, Ugarte sent one hundred *hombres de cuera* and thirteen auxiliaries under Lieutenant Alejo de la Garza Falcón of Presidio de San Vicente (San Sabá) and the *alfereces* of Presidio del Río Grande and San Carlos to pursue and punish the Indians on the headwaters of the Río de San Pedro.[36] The Indians fled for the Nueces and San Sabá rivers, however, and Garza's force returned to Aguaverde January 9, 1776. Its only accomplishment consisted of forcing the Indians to move their camp farther away from the Spanish line of defense along the Río Grande.

[34] See "Derrotero" of Vicente Rodríguez, November 1–December 2, 1775, A.G.N., Provincias Internas, Vol. 24, pp. 275–282.

[35] See Weddle, *The San Sabá Mission,* p. 151, and Robert S. Weddle, "The San Sabá Mission and the Permian Basin," *The Texas Permian Historical Annual,* 4 (December, 1964), 33–39. The latter contains a translation of the report of the expedition from San Sabá to the Pecos by Felipe de Rábago y Terán.

[36] The *alférez* of Presidio de San Juan Bautista was Balthasar de los Reyes, that of San Carlos, Ramón Marrufo. See Alejo de la Garza Falcón, "Derrotero," A.G.N., Provincias Internas, Vol. 24, pp. 283–288, for a complete account of the expedition.

32. PADRE MORFI'S VISIT

THE YEAR 1776, so full of import for the English colonies, was not completely devoid of significance for the northern provinces of New Spain. Spanish military forces were on the move all along the northern frontier. The war went worse for the Apaches. Where the troops of San Juan Bautista del Río Grande and the other presidios of the line had failed to establish contact with the enemy Indians the previous year—in the Sierra de Guadalupe—the Comanches struck them a hard blow. Several hundred Apaches were killed.[1] The presidial troops kept pressing the harassed remnants.

"By 1776, then, the line of presidios recommended by Rubí had been established and the Indians had been forced to retreat. . . . Thus was marked the end of an era and the beginning of a new concept with respect to the Interior Provinces."[2]

On August 22, 1776, Charles III appointed Teodoro de Croix governor and commandant general of the Interior Provinces of New Spain. Placed under Croix' jurisdiction were Texas, Coahuila, Nueva Vizcaya, Sonora, and Sinaloa, New Mexico, and the Californias, which for most practical purposes became a separate governmental unit independent of the Viceroyalty of Spain.

Croix arrived in México on December 22, 1776, to begin preparations for a tour of inspection. Father Juan Agustín Morfi was ordered by the father provincial of Franciscans to accompany the tour as chaplain.[3] The trip started from the capital August 4, 1777. It was to extend to all the

---

[1] Bernard E. Bobb, *The Viceregency of Antonio María Bucareli in New Spain, 1771–1779*, p. 143.

[2] *Ibid.*, pp. 143–144.

[3] Carlos E. Castañeda, Introduction, Juan Agustín Morfi, *History of Texas 1673–1779*, p. 18.

provinces of the new commandant general's jurisdiction. From the city of México the expedition traveled northward to reach the Río Grande in December.

Father Morfi, who wrote extensively of his observations on the journey, gives a view of San Juan Bautista through the eyes of an outsider. At the time of his arrival at the gateway to Spanish Texas, in December, 1777, he was a stranger to the frontier. The people and their customs were foreign to him. He could not reconcile them with his own experience, or with his ideas of what they ought to be. But he did not permit this inability to deter him from candid comment.

It would not be the last time for San Juan Bautista to come under the critical eye of an outsider.

The expedition stopped for the night of December 20 at the Mission San Francisco Vizarrón, not far from that of Dulce Nombre de Jesús de Peyotes and the Villa de San Pedro de Gigedo. Morfi rose early to say Mass, and the party departed from Vizarrón by eight o'clock to travel over an immense plain which in itself was strange to the father chaplain's eyes. They rode past a long string of desolate ranches, abandoned because of the ravages of the Apaches.

Just three leagues west of San Juan Bautista was the Rancho del Salitrillo, owned by one N. Quintero, *vecino* of the presidio, whose lands extended along the road from Peyotes, beyond the place called Palo Alto.[4] The ranch had two good houses, a *cocina,* or kitchen, an oven, and corrals, but it now stood vacant because of the Apaches' depredations.

On the south side of the Camino Real lay the lands of the Mission of Peyotes, extending to Palo Alto, which marked the halfway point of the day's journey. The plain gave way to a forest of mesquite.

After a brisk ride of twelve leagues, the Valley of the Circumcision lay before them. Riding past the rambling stone and adobe buildings and walls of the Mission San Juan Bautista, they came, in another quarter of a league, to the *plaza de armas,* the military plaza of Presidio del Río

---

[4] Jorge Cervera Sánchez (Juan Agustín Morfi, *Descripción del Territorio del Real Presidio de San Juan Bautista del Río Grande del Norte, y su Jurisdicción, Año de 1778,* p. 310) says Palo Alto was the name given a motte of live oaks in front of the Hacienda de Santa Mónica. At this place at the beginning of the nineteenth century, savage Indians destroyed a caravan en route from San Juan Bautista to Peyotes. The Rancho del Salitrillo, known by the same name today, is found between Guerrero and Villa Union.

Grande. The post commandant had his troop formed in the plaza to receive the visitors. Going through the formality of a muster, the *comandante* had his secretary announce that anyone having complaint against his officers should come forward and be heard. Evidently no one did. "This done we went to the church to dismount and from there to our lodgings."[5]

As Father Morfi walked about the settlement drinking in the sights and sounds which issued from the two missions, the presidio, and the village, his ears caught the strains of a moving melody sung by some Indian girls. "There is no doubt that if they believe as well as they sing, few religious communities have any advantage over them."[6]

A bustle of activity centered around the *plaza de armas*. Ten soldiers rode in from San Antonio de Béjar, bringing documents from Governor Barón de Ripperdá and escorting some citizens who had come to trade.

Croix, meanwhile, busied himself with arrangements for crossing "the desert" between the Río Grande and San Antonio, and dispatching letters and reports. But in keeping with the time and place, life at the Presidio del Río Grande ceased to flow at midafternoon.

On getting up from siesta we found the fort full of Lipan Apaches. It was the band of Josecillo el Manso, who under the guise of peace had come to find out what was going on. This José is Christian, a son of the Mission of Peyotes, who was captured by the Lipans when six or seven years old and was raised among them. Through industry and shamelessness he came to be a chief. He is very bold and has done great damage in the province, and makes much to-do over his having received the waters of baptism.[7]

Now Josecillo was loudly ordering food and supplies from the Spaniards. He wanted corn, tobacco, bridles, and, above all, powder and lead, "but seeing his petitions unattended to, he shortly settled down and lowered his voice."[8] The other Apaches of his band, including the women, meanwhile, distributed themselves among the people gathered in the streets and in the plaza. The Indians had made friendships among the *vecinos* of the presidio, but Morfi observes that such relationships were of

---

[5] Juan Agustín Morfi, *Viaje de Indios y Diario del Nuevo México*, p. 315; *Ibid.*, pp. 315–330, deals with the visit to San Juan Bautista.

[6] *Ibid.*, p. 315.

[7] *Ibid.*, p. 316.

[8] *Ibid.*, p. 316.

little advantage to the Spaniards and endured only as long as they enabled the Indians to do mischief; these "friends" of the Apaches usually were the first victims of their fury.

The following day broke with a dense fog hovering close over the low, flat land of the Río Grande plain, curbing the activities of the visitors. The Lipan chief, Josecillo, determined to make trouble, came to the presidio with the accusation that some of the Indians of the Mission San Bernardo had stolen his bridle. The officers to whom he complained recognized that he was lying. They told him to go and find the thief and bring him in; then would the stolen article be returned to him and the culprit punished. His scheme frustrated, the troublemaker departed quietly.

Morfi packed a lot of observations into his commentaries, as well as a considerable number of outspoken judgments.[9] In general he believed that the settlement came nowhere near to living up to its potentialities, either in the spiritual or the temporal. His eyes saw a dirty little village where people lived in needless squalor, a rich land which was going to waste because the inhabitants were too indolent to work it, scores of savages who paid lip service to the religious dogma but had hardly any understanding of the sacred words they spoke in the ritual.

Since the flying company of Captain Diego Ramón was established here in 1701, Morfi noted, settlers gravitated to the protection of the troops. Gradually a considerable settlement for farming and business grew up around the presidio, and the village now was the third largest of the province of Coahuila. It had some eight hundred souls, including the soldiers and their families. The settlement, however, had neither the regularity of a town nor the form of a fort. The houses were of adobe, built without comfort or beauty and, being outside the plaza, exposed to Indian attack

[9] According to Morfi's diary, the Croix party remained at San Juan Bautista only three days, December 21–24. His *Descripción del Territorio del Real Presidio de San Juan Bautista del Río Grande del Norte, y su Jurisdicción, Año de 1778* (contained in A.G.N., Historia, Vol. 29, pp. 185–204, and published, in Spanish, with introduction and notes by Jorge Cervera Sánchez, in 1950 as a "Sobretiro del Tomo LXX, Nos. 1–3 del Boletín de la Sociedad Mexicana de Geografía y Estadística") is dated at San Juan Bautista, January 23, 1778. On returning from Texas the Croix expedition spent from January 22 to January 28 at San Juan Bautista before going on to Monclova Viejo, Aguaverde, and Santa Rosa, and thence westward by way of La Bavia, San Vicente, and San Carlos to the Gulf of California. It returned to the capital in June, 1781.

or whatever. The plaza was large and well formed (square) and almost closed on all sides by buildings. The only entrance was through narrow little alleys.[10]

To the northwest of the presidio was a beautiful lake of clear water, fifty yards wide, a quarter of a league long and more than two varas deep. Source of the water was some springs at Paso Hondo (Deep Ford) on the Arroyo de Castaño, a league and a half northwest of the presidio. It was impounded by a wall of stone which the people of the presidio had built. A network of ditches carried the water to the individual lots of the town, but the ditches formed a marsh and rendered the place unsanitary, in Morfi's opinion. The lake abounded in fish and waterfowl.

Fronting the plaza from the west was the *cuerpo de guardia,* poorly formed and old. Adjacent to the guard station stood the house of the Captain, the only building inside or outside the plaza that was white-washed. Across the plaza on the east side was the site where the church should have been built:

It is remarkable that in seventy-eight years so little effort has been given to the material improvement and adornment of the House of God. The church, only a few years old, was planned on a small scale, not being proportioned to the size of the population. It is found still near to its beginnings, and the father chaplain is required to say Mass in a little room which was meant for a sacristy, without doors, without whitewash, and without other adornment except for the altar table and one loose Cross of wood leaned against the wall.[11]

In fairly recent times lumber needed for the roof had been obtained from the missions; the foundation for the church was laid, and the walls were raised two varas. "At this stage they happened to notice that distance between the walls exceeded the length of the beams that were to reach from one to the other. They discontinued work, leaving the timber exposed to the weather. . . . It is no exaggeration to say that now it is not fit for horse stables."[12] The chaplain of the presidio supplied the spiritual

[10] Morfi, *Descripción,* p. 305; *Viaje de Indios,* p. 327.
[11] Morfi, *Descripción,* p. 305. The present church in Villa de Guerrero, says Cervera Sánchez, was not finished until the nineteenth century, possibly not until the missions had disappeared. The present bells of the church were made in 1851 in commemoration of the 150th anniversary of the presidio. All the bells of the missions were moved to other places (*ibid.,* p. 306 n.).
[12] Morfi, *Viaje de Indios,* p. 327.

needs of the community, holding the title of *cura* and ecclesiastical judge of all the citizens, by authority of the archbishop of Guadalajara.

The part of the church used was a little room without doors, barely big enough for the priest and his assistant. It had no sacred vessels of its own, but borrowed ornaments, books, bell, and other essentials from the missions. The soldiers looked to the citizens to provide the church's needs; the citizens responded by looking to the soldiers—an obvious stalemate which was reflected in the miserable condition of the church.

The captain of the presidial company, Morfi noted, also served as principal civil and criminal justice of the presidio and its jurisdiction. This authority extended to the population of San Pedro de Gigedo, the missions of Dulce Nombre de Jesús de Peyotes and San Francisco Vizarrón, in addition to those of San Juan and San Bernardo, now administered by the province of Jalisco. Also included in the jurisdiction were the various ranches. Among them were Santa Mónica, the ranch belonging to the Ramón family, San Blas, Carmen, and San Nicolás.[13]

By the census which the Señor Comandante General Caballero de Croix ordered this past year of 1777, we know that without counting the good families and houses of the soldiers which make up the garrison there are in this jurisdiction 420 men, 344 women, 242 male children, 203 female children, 5 male slaves and 12 female slaves, 6 churches, 4 monasteries, 86 houses of stone, 60 of adobe, 55 cultivated plots (*solares*), 40½ *caballerías* of divided land, 349 sitios of large and small livestock, 76 teams of mares . . ., 192 yokes of oxen, 2,030 head of cattle, 12,215 of sheep, 2,945 of goats, 561 of broke horses, 124 broke mules, 55 burros, and 35 swine.

By the same census it is evidenced that, excluding always the soldiers, the armament which there is in all the jurisdiction, for its defense, is reduced to 68 smoothbores, 23 rifles, 29 pistols, 17 blunderbusses, 29 swords, 33 lances, 20 *cueras* [leather jackets], 59 shields, 113 saddles, 107 bridles, 97 saddle blankets, 91 spurs, 129 bowmen [*hombres de arco y flecha*].[14]

[Father Morfi noted the arid nature of the region, the extreme cold in winter and heat in summer.] But it is very healthful and suited for the com-

---

13 Cervera Sánchez (Morfi, *Descripción*, p. 297) makes notes to the effect that while the Hacienda de Santa Mónica is one of the oldest in the Municipio de Guerrero, having been the property of Captain Diego Ramón and afterward of his son by the same name, the other ranches named by Morfi are not known by such names today.

14 Morfi, *Descripción*, pp. 297–298.

fortable permanence of those who are born here, and even for those of other countries who are gathered and settle here.

The lands are generally fertile, delightful, abundant in pastures. . . . It has all that is possible to wish for, for raising all kinds of crops, horses, and cattle. The springs of water are sweet, many, and abundant; the air pure, the sky happy, the land productive, the rains regular of season. Everything offers a thousand conveniences, and it is doubtful that another site in all the province is better suited for a numerous population.[15]

Crops harvested, Morfi noted, were pepper, beans, and corn, which were produced in such abundance that, after the jurisdiction was supplied, enough was left to provision the neighboring presidios of the line, even as far as San Vicente, part of the colony of Nuevo Santander, Nuevo Reino de León, and various settlements of the province of Coahuila.

Even so, in Morfi's forthright opinion, the lands were not cultivated as they should be:

The little active nature of these people—not to say complete laziness—permits them only to do the work that is absolutely necessary. . . . The abundance of corn and beans of which I have just spoken is due only to the work of the Indians and to the diligence and activity of the missionaries of the four Missions. The others (except in rare instances) sow little, care for it badly, and make the small produce from their labor serve for gambling and other vices which dominate them, living all year long in total poverty and misery in this land of fertility and abundance.[16]

In such a state Morfi found "the land most apt for all kinds of crops, vegetables, groves of trees, fruit orchards, raising of livestock." Only a little wheat and barley had been sown, but the suitability of the land for the production of these crops had been demonstrated. With an abundance of irrigation water going to waste, he said, "It seems incredible that these people do not dedicate themselves to the sowing." The only explanation

[15] *Ibid.,* p. 298.

[16] *Ibid.,* pp. 299–300. Cervera Sánchez observes (in note, p. 300) that from the first years of founding of the missions, the religious complained constantly that the soldiers of the presidio were inclined to gambling and other vices, Captain Diego Ramón having been accused of abandoning the service to go to Monclova with his soldiers to see the bullfights. It may also be recalled that Friar Marcos de Guereña, in the early years of San Juan Bautista, prosecuted the gambling vice among the soldiers.

for such a reprehensible omission, in his view, was "their little application and imponderable indolence."[17]

The absence of a mill in the entire jurisdiction doubled the cost of
grinding wheat into flour, since the grain had to be taken to Monclova,
Candela, or Santa Rosa. Yet the people lacked the vision which enabled
them to see the advantage a mill would offer the entire jurisdiction, as
well as to the three presidios of Río Grande, Monclova, and Aguaverde.[18]

The people were just as negligent in planting cotton, and because of
this lack of application, people went about completely naked, "the women
not finding one piece of blanket with which to cover their flesh." If cotton were grown, not only could the people dress themselves, but it also
would give them something to do. "By this means some licentiousness
could be avoided."[19]

Morfi saw garlic, onions, lettuce, tomatoes, turnips, radishes, carrots,
broccoli, cauliflower, and other vegetables harvested in abundance where
industry was applied in planting and cultivating. Peas and lentils did well
in this locality; only someone to plant them was lacking.

Fruit trees which did well in the region were peach, walnut, fig, pome-
granate, and grapes, with many wild grapevines growing along the
creeks, indicating the land's suitability for vineyards. Morfi, like Espinosa,
Olivares, and other chroniclers, noted that mulberry trees were present:
"trees useful for raising silk worms, whose name is yet ignored in this
country."[20] Citrus fruits were not suitable because of the cold winters, but
there were cantaloupes, watermelons, and many tasty wild fruits.

---

[17] *Ibid.*, p. 300. On a recent visit to Guerrero the writer observed small patches
of wheat growing at the edge of the village. Morfi's appraisal of the capabilities
of the land appears to have been quite accurate.

[18] At the end of the eighteenth century, says Cervera Sánchez (*ibid.*, p. 300 n.
32), the Mission San Bernardo had a mill: "There is presently a place which
carries this name [?] where a mill existed in the Nineteenth Century. This land
belonged to Don Marcos Hernández, who was the *Jefe Político* of the District in
the year 1847. As the springs which provided the water for turning the mill were
exhausted in the year 1886, no mill was to be found in the Villa de Guerrero."

[19] *Ibid.*, pp. 301–302.

[20] *Ibid.*, p. 302. See Isidro Félix de Espinosa, *Crónica de los Colegios de Propaganda Fide de la Nueva España*, pp. 761–764, and Fray Antonio de San Buenaventura y Olivares to the Viceroy, November 20, 1716, A.G.I., Provincias Internas,
Vol. 181, p. 127 (cited in Chapter 13 of this study).

Everyone of this jurisdiction complains of the lack of hardwood for building material for their houses, but in reality they should complain only of themselves. . . . No one of them is ignorant that these trees have always done well when they are transplanted; but everyone wishes that nothing be required for their care and culture, but that they produce their natural bounty for himself alone.[21]

Like many a frontier settlement of a later day, north of the Río Grande, San Juan Bautista had its "mustangers." Commerce of the area, the visiting padre observed, was restricted to trading in corn and livestock. With wild horses abounding in the countryside, some men of the settlement were accustomed to going out to catch them, for their own use and for trade.[22] With the end of Indian hostilities, Morfi predicted, the country would be populated with cattle, and the same wild horseherds could be domesticated to make an abundance of horses and mules. But the savages must be pacified before agriculture and commerce could thrive: "The poor merchant who wishes to expend his labor and to expose his life and his goods to the notorious risks of the road is rare; only one or two merchants have settled in the presidio, and not another is found in all the territory."[23] In the meantime the inhabitants must pay the exorbitant prices asked, because they had no other recourse.

No easy lot was that of the citizens of the presidio. "It is not possible now for the *vecinos* to work with any hope of advantage, because land is most scarce, with hardly enough space available for a building lot."[24] From this situation arose repeated complaints, with some justification, against the missions of San Juan Bautista and San Bernardo, which had laid claim to extensive lands for the use of the Indians, thus denying opportunity to the citizens.[25]

[21] Morfi, *Descripción*, p. 303.

[22] The wild horseherds of which Padre Morfi speaks, says Cervera Sánchez (*ibid.*, p. 303 n.), were formed in the seventeenth century, when the horses escaped from the Spaniards in Texas. Even at the middle of the nineteenth century, parties of horsemen from the Río Grande went to catch mustangs in Texas. It should be remembered that Don Blas de la Garza Falcón found many wild horses between San Juan Bautista and the Sabinas and San Diego rivers in 1734.

[23] *Ibid.*, p. 304. As Cervera Sánchez points out (*ibid.*, p. 304 n.), this time was long in coming. The Indians were raiding some ranches along the Río Grande as late as 1881.

[24] *Ibid.*, p. 306.   [25] See Cervera Sánchez, *ibid.*, p. 306 n. 52.

The lands that were available were poorly divided, said Morfi. The heirs of the three old captains, Diego Ramón, José de Ecay Múzquiz, and José Hernández, were the masters of large tracts, possibly as much as fourteen or fifteen leagues. Little of this land was made to produce as it should; many ranches had been depopulated by the Indian raids. Land titles were confusing, with some grants overlapping others, and already violent quarrels were resulting.

Situated on a smooth hillock a quarter of a league west from the presidio was the Mission San Juan Bautista. From its founding in 1699 to 1761 it had baptized 1,434 souls, administering the sacraments of marriage and of death to 1,066 persons. The mission church, noted Morfi, was large and in the shape of a cross. "The little care this part has had for the past few years is noted in the walls, since the portal, the tower, and one of the chapels are noticeably out of plumb and in danger of falling."[26]

Morfi observed that the main altar was quite suitable, the sacristy rich in good ornament and sacred vessels, the monastery large and well built with comfortable living quarters for six religious. The huts for the Indians, as was usually the case, were cramped, miserable little rooms which joined with the monastery to form a plaza. The workshop where the blankets were made, the granary, and all the offices were adequate and in good condition. The mission possessed immense lands for cultivation and for pasture, where innumerable livestock could be maintained.

The missionaries, not content with the water from the springs, had abandoned them for the *vecinos* and soldiers and had gone to the head of Santa Rita Creek to bring an irrigation ditch a distance of twenty leagues. It yielded even more water than was needed. From the ditch had been taken small, brownish pearls with which a necklace had been made for the image of the Virgin in the church.

The produce of the missions had, in former times, been quite plentiful, but incursions of the Apaches and the frequent changes in administration had taken their toll. "However, they eat as well today as they did when

---

[26] Morfi, *Viaje de Indios,* p. 319. Nothing remains of the Mission San Juan Bautista except mounds of earth. Cervera Sánchez (Morfi, *Descripción,* p. 314 n.) says all the stone was sold during the last century for use in reconstructing houses in the village of Guerrero.

the land was covered with beeves." Living at the mission at the time of Morfi's visit were 135 persons of all ages and sexes, "as miserable as those of Peyotes and as Christian as the Apaches."[27]

In one corner of the plaza a little pond had been made for the Indian women to wash their clothing. In Father Morfi's presence four catfish nearly half a vara long had been caught from the pool.

But the Spanish of these parts do not eat fish, and they consider it the worst of misfortunes if necessity compels them to. As proof of this statement I refer to what I myself heard. A son-in-law of Lieutenant Colonel Vicente Rodríguez, speaking in the presence of many about hardships which the said officer had suffered on his campaigns, told me there had been an occasion when he had to eat poisonous snakes, grasshoppers, rats, and even fresh fish. The voices that use such an example to express the worst of miseries are the same that are to lead the native people to a proper civilized life.[28]

A short half a league from San Juan Bautista was the Mission San Bernardo, in which had been performed 1,618 baptisms, 383 marriages, and 1,073 burials since its founding. Its church was a small, dark "canyon" of adobe, the altars without adornment, though the sacristy was better fitted out than that of San Juan Bautista. Many of the ornaments and sacred vessels had been taken out for use at the church of the presidio. Friar Diego Jiménez, when he was minister of this mission, had begun construction of "a beautiful temple that would shine in any community." Built of limestone, it was up to the cornicing and near to being finished, with thousands of pesos having been spent on it. "But being so out of proportion to the place, and so much expense required to finish it, there is no hope of its succeeding."[29]

The convent was small and miserable, the living quarters uncomfortable. The Indian huts, behind the monastery, were wretched affairs, but the granary and workshop were well built and spacious.

This mission is the richest in the province because it has the greatest number of Indians, the most fertile land, the most pastures. [Morfi found the greatest

[27] Morfi, *Viaje de Indios*, p. 320.
[28] *Ibid.*, p. 320.
[29] *Ibid.*, pp. 321–322. See also Cervera Sánchez, in Morfi, *Descripción*, pp. 315–316 nn. 87, 88.

disorder to prevail, even though 3,000 loads of corn had been gathered.] The produce of the field is plentiful, and the presidios of these provinces get a great part of their meats and grain here; even so, the Indians do not, on this account, eat or dress better, nor do they have any rest. An irrigation canal equal in every respect to that of San Juan Bautista has been dug by the Indians. Each year the ditch of each mission has to be cleaned out; the natives do this work without neglecting their chores in fields and workshop. And they say the Indians are lazy![30]

While the two missions had been managed by the College of Santa Cruz de Querétaro, the King maintained two ministers at a salary of 450 pesos annually in each one. But when they were given over to the province of Jalisco in 1772, only one missionary was kept in each mission.

As for the progress of civilization and religion among the natives over the period of more than half a century, Morfi agreed with the judgment of the missionaries of the College of the Holy Cross, who had founded and operated the missions so many years:

> Progress of these Indians in Christianity is almost imperceptible. . . . They confess, they take the sacraments, they fast, they hear Mass, and attend prayer and explanations of the doctrine; but all this is as commanded and with a grade of piety so low as hardly to be recognizable as Christianity. It is not difficult to discover the causes of their failure. . . . These Indians will never be made Christians until they are first made men.[31]

Father Morfi having reached such conclusions, the party of the *comandante general* of the Interior Provinces mounted and rode northeastward from the Presidio del Río Grande on December 24, 1777, at twelve o'clock noon. The expeditionary chaplain, until he reached the Rio Grande two leagues distant, continued to observe what he considered to be great opportunity going to waste. The beautiful plain, he noted, was watered most of the way to the river by the overflowing waters from the mission and the village; but still the land was not cultivated. "We passed through a small forest of mesquite to arrive at the famous Río Grande del Norte, which we forded at the crossing called La Francia."[32] As his

[30] Morfi, *Viaje de Indios*, pp. 322–323.

[31] *Ibid.*, p. 323.

[32] Morfi (*Ibid.*, p. 328) either was confused or took poetic license with the name "Paso de Francia." Since it traveled northeast to reach the ford, the expedition obviously crossed at Paso Pacuache, not Paso de Francia as Morfi says.

mount splashed belly deep into the muddy but gently flowing river, Padre Morfi counted the horse's steps to the other side: 180. Like many another Spanish caravan before it, the expedition made camp on the opposite bank.[33]

[33] Morfi, *Viaje de Indios,* p. 329. "From what I could learn from people who know the country," says Morfi, "it continues to the mouth without waterfalls or rapids." He suggests the possibility of navigation from Presidio de Río Grande to the Gulf. Actually, rapids exist a short distance downstream. Navigation possibilities were studied some years later, as will be seen, and found to be nil.

33. FADING OF THE MISSIONS

WHEN TEODORO DE CROIX, as the new commandant general, began his inspection tour of the Interior Provinces, he had in his possession an eighty-four–page report by Hugo Oconor.[1] His health broken from intensive efforts to drive the hostile Indians back and establish the new line of presidios, Oconor was destined for a less strenuous assignment as governor of Guatemala.

The retiring *comandante inspector* had given heart and soul to establishment of the defense line, with the firm conviction that it was the answer to the Indian problem. Croix, however, chose to wait and form his own evaluation. He was singularly unimpressed by Oconor's description of how the garrisons of the various presidios covered the entire frontier by means of constant patrols from one fort to the next.

Each patrol lasted fifteen days. A portion of the troop of Presidio de la Monclova, for example, would march to the juncture of the Río Escondido with the Río Grande and thence to San Juan Bautista, returning by the same route. A squad from San Juan Bautista would cross the Río

[1] Hugo Oconor, "Papel Instructivo," July 20, 1777, Audiencia de Guadalajara, 104-6-18, pp. 7–91.

Grande and proceed to the banks of the Nueces, where it would meet the squad from Presidio de San Antonio de Béjar, then would return to its own presidio by the same road.[2]

Similar patrols were maintained between each of the presidios of the line, from La Bahía (Goliad) to the Gulf of California. But Croix knew the number of the presidials was not sufficient for the task. The cost of maintaining the presidios at their advanced location, in his opinion, far out-weighed the results they achieved.

While Croix believed the newer presidios poorly placed, he felt, however, that San Juan Bautista was excellently situated. It served its purpose of defending the frontier at this point, and was an important link in the communication with Texas.[3]

Eventually Croix recommended abandonment of the other Coahuila presidios of the line, but thought San Juan Bautista was indispensable. Removal of the various garrisons to San Fernando, Santa Rosa, and Monclova, in A. B. Thomas' words, "shortened the line of Coahuila, tightened up the defense at critical points, and tied the well-placed presidio of San Juan Bautista into a coordinated plan."[4]

At the time of the Croix inspection visit to San Juan Bautista late in 1777, Captain Vicente Rodríguez had served that post for thirty-six years. Having retired several months earlier, he remained active. That same year he had petitioned for sanction to establish a settlement at San Ildefonso, near Villa de San Fernando and lying within the bounds of his own hacienda. Most of the inhabitants of the new village would have been his sons and grandsons. But his request was denied.[5] In February, 1777— some ten months prior to Croix and Morfi's visit in December—his com-

---

[2] *Ibid.*, pp. 67–68.

[3] Alfred Barnaby Thomas (ed.), *Teodoro de Croix and the Northern Frontier of New Spain, 1776–1783*, p. 50.

[4] *Ibid.*, p. 54. See also Bernardo Gálvez, *Instructions for Governing the Interior Provinces of New Spain,* translated and edited, with Introduction, by Donald E. Worcester, p. 11. The record is obscure, but some of these presidios evidently were regarrisoned after a time; later mention of their activities is found in various studies.

[5] Jorge Cervera Sánchez in Juan Agustín Morfi, *Descripción del Territorio del Real Presidio de San Juan Bautista del Río Grande del Norte, y su Jurisdicción, Año de 1778,* p. 307 n. 53.

mand post was given to Manuel de Cerecedo y Velasco.[6] Despite his advanced years, Don Vicente continued to go on short expeditions, even after his retirement with the rank of lieutenant colonel.

Cerecedo was a young man, by comparison to Rodríguez, seeking experience to help him broaden his military career and win promotions. He arrived at San Juan Bautista only a few months before the appointment of Colonel Juan de Ugalde as governor of Coahuila, November 23, 1777.[7] Ugalde, on whose recommendation Croix was to act in removing the garrisons of the presidios of the line in 1781, was an energetic military leader whose job was to combat the Apache menace and drive the hostile Indians back beyond the Río Grande. Cerecedo would be called upon to help him.

Between May, 1779, and March, 1783, Ugalde made four campaigns and inflicted defeats of varying degree on the Mescalero Apaches in northern Coahuila and along the Pecos River in Texas. The first got underway May 3, 1779, and lasted until June 12. It accomplished little.[8]

The second lasted seventy-four days, from November 22, 1781, to January 23, 1782. On this excursion the Governor's force hit the Mescaleros three times in their rancherias. Both the first and second campaigns were made to the rough country along the Río de San Pedro (Devil's River) and the Pecos, in Texas.

Manuel de Cerecedo y Velasco, as *comandante* of Presidio del Río Grande, was one of the captains on the third expedition, which began June 4, 1782. Its objective was to punish the Mescaleros for recent ravages on the settlements of Parras and Álamo and the haciendas of Anaelo and Mesillas, as well as others of Nuevo León and Coahuila. Ugalde led his force upon the savages in their own strongholds in the Bolsón de Mapimí. He attacked and defeated them in four thrusts, killing six, wounding two, taking thirty-eight prisoners, and releasing six Spanish captives. The Spaniards also destroyed 120 Indian tents.[9]

The fourth campaign was the longest, consuming all of autumn and

[6] Manuel de Cerecedo y Velasco to the King, July 21, 1788, A.G.N. Provincias Internas, Vol. 22, p. 97.

[7] Walter Prescott Webb and H. Bailey Carroll (eds.), *Handbook of Texas,* II, 816.

[8] Juan de Ugalde, "Campaña del Coronel Dn Juan de Ugalde," A.G.N., Historia, Vol. 29, pp. 206–207.

[9] *Ibid.,* p. 210; Cerecedo to the King, pp. 97–98.

winter of 1782–1783, from September 18 to March 9. The chaplain of Presidio del Río Grande, Father Onofre Castellón, was both chaplain and surgeon of the expedition, which carried 213 men, plus 48 muleteers to manage the two hundred *cargas* of provisions. The Spaniards first tramped out the headlands of the Río de San Antonio, west from Villa de San Fernando, and the foothills of the Serranías del Burro. Farther west they attacked a rancheria at the Sierra del Pino, then returned briefly to San Fernando early in October to deposit prisoners and replenish supplies. November found the force in the Bolsón de Mapimí, northwest of Monclova. From November to March it tramped out the Bolsón, the Trans-Pecos, and the Big Bend areas without making contact with the elusive enemy.

At last, on March 3, Ugalde's scouts found a sizeable Indian camp in the rugged heights of the Sierra del Carmen. Despite the fact that the enemy held the advantage of terrain, and all possessed firearms as well as bows and arrows, Ugalde's officers led an attack which put the hated Mescaleros to flight. Seven Spaniards fell wounded in the battle, six by arrows, one by a rifle ball. Father Castellón's best efforts as a surgeon could not save the latter; he then ministered to him as a priest.

The Governor's force despoiled forty-three tents of the enemy and loaded eighty-one captured horses and mules with plunder from the Indian camp in the high sierra. The homeward march began the next day.

Thus ended a campaign which had lasted just seven days short of six months. The results were not impressive. Only six Indians had been killed, with twelve taken captive and one Spanish captive released. In ten engagements of the four campaigns nineteen Indians were killed, two chiefs wounded, sixty-seven prisoners taken, eight Spanish captives redeemed, and 744 horses and mules taken. Twelve rancherias were despoiled, the enemies' equipment, weapons, and provisions taken from them. The Spaniards lost three killed.[10]

Soon after the campaign ended, Ugalde became involved in a row with Teodoro de Croix, and the Governor was the loser. He was removed from office the very next month, April, 1783. For three and one-half years he served at the Mexican capital. When he returned to the north it was the year 1786, and he was second in command to a new commandant, Jacobo

[10] "Ugalde, Campaña," pp. 239–240.

de Ugarte y Loyola, but soon to become commandant general himself. Once again he took the field against the Apaches.

In 1788 Don Manuel de Cerecedo y Velasco, having been relieved as commandant of San Juan Bautista, recited his part in the third Ugalde campaign as he sought from the King a promotion to lieutenant colonel and permission to return to Spain.[11] By September 13 the commandant general, Ugarte y Loyola, had given Cerecedo permission to proceed on his journey to the south, and he had already reached the city of México. By January 16, 1789, the former San Juan Bautista commandant had received permission to go to Spain at first opportunity.[12]

As Ugalde's Indian campaigns continued, a Coahuila force met disaster on August 22, 1789, at the hands of the Lipan Apaches. Twenty men, including a sergeant from San Juan Bautista, were slain by the Indians.[13]

In 1790 Ugalde, with the aid of some Comanche allies, dealt the Lipans and Mescaleros a severe defeat at Arroyo de la Soledad, in the Texas Hill Country. The Lipans retaliated by hitting the settlements whenever they could. In July, 1790, they stole two herds of mares from Mission San Bernardo, after killing all the stallions. The same day thirty broke horses were driven off from Mission San Juan Bautista. A few weeks later the Lipans stole eight mules and horses from twelve different *vecinos* of San Juan Bautista.

It would be many a day before Indian troubles ended on the Río Grande.

Soon the trouble was with the Comanches, as well as with various Apache nations. Early in 1795 half a dozen Comanches stole into the vicinity of San Juan Bautista and drove off a herd of cattle belonging to the missions. A band of Lipans stalked the marauders to the San Sabá Canyon, took them by surprise, and recovered the stolen cattle, which were returned to the missions.[14] The Lipans, it seems, still hovered close

---

[11] Cerecedo to the King, pp. 97–98.

[12] Cerecedo to the Viceroy, September 13, 1787, and January 16, 1789, A.G.I., Provincias Internas, Vol. 22, pp. 89–90, 99.

[13] Report of Juan de Ugalde for year 1789, A.G.N., Provincias Internas, Vol. 160, p. 393. Details are obscured by the badly smudged original manuscript and illegible handwriting.

[14] Robert S. Weddle, *San Sabá Mission: Spanish Pivot in Texas*, p. 190; Carlos Eduardo Castañeda, *Our Catholic Heritage in Texas*, V, 116–117.

to the missions, afraid to divest themselves of the Spaniards entirely, lest they be gobbled up by the voracious Comanches.

In February, 1797, Comanches stole some three hundred cattle from Mission San Bernardo. A detachment of soldiers and mission Indians overtook the raiders near the old Presidio de San Sabá, recovering most of the cattle.

Since the implementation of the new Royal Regulation of 1772, many changes had been brought to bear on San Juan Bautista. While the missions of San Juan and San Bernardo continued to function after a fashion, they no longer held the rôle of importance which once was theirs. Dominant feature of the once-proud gateway to Spanish Texas now was the fort, which was coming more and more to be known not as Presidio de San Juan Bautista but as Presidio del Río Grande. In 1772 new Spanish policy had dictated that, while sword and cross should march together, the sword should play the dominant part. Such a position was evident in many ways. Some military expeditions were made and diaries written without so much as a mention of the expeditionary chaplain, least of all the holding of a religious service during the campaign. While the religious once had occupied a prominent place on such excursions—writing the diaries, holding Mass at regular intervals, and confessing the soldiers and granting absolution before battle—they now were thrust into the background.

Not only is the part of the priest on the military expedition drawn into obscurity, but life at the missions as well. Few descriptions of the activities of the Río Grande missions are found after 1772. In a report signed at Monclova on February 15, 1790, however, Don Juan Gutiérrez de la Cueva[15] brings us up to date on San Juan and San Bernardo.

In 1781 the *comandante general,* Teodoro de Croix, had arranged a transfer of the Coahuila missions from the Franciscans of the province of Jalisco to the religious of the Colegio de Propaganda Fide de Pachuca. Father Manuel Gorgón had taken charge of San Juan Bautista, Father Antonio Ruiz of San Bernardo. They had done well with the administration of the missions. Each missionary received an annual stipend of 450

---

[15] Juan Gutiérrez de la Cueva took possession of the government of Coahuila in November, 1788, as interim governor, and served until March 4, 1790. As *ayudante inspector* of missions he visited the missions of Coahuila late in 1789 or early 1790.

pesos, payable in the *casas reales* of San Luis Potosí, on certification of the governor of Coahuila.

The mission churches were well maintained. Although one wall of San Juan's was out of plumb, Father Gorgón planned to repair it. Improvement plans also were in the offing at San Bernardo, where the church presently in use was the first one built for that mission. Standing nearby was the huge stone church begun a quarter century ago by Father Diego Jiménez but never finished. The baptistry dome and the vaulted roof of the sacristy were complete, but the rest of the structure still was uncovered, although the walls were of sufficient height. The present missionary, said the *ayudante inspector,* planned to finish it.[16]

In the two missions under the jurisdiction of Presidio del Río Grande, the looms stayed busy, weaving cloth for blankets and clothing from the wool and cotton produced on mission lands. None of the goods was sold outside, however, as all was needed by the Indians of the missions.

At this time San Juan Bautista Mission had only 63 Indians, San Bernardo 103. They were rapidly fading to insignificance.

In 1797 the *vecinos* of Presidio del Río Grande, having long hungered for the expansive and fertile mission fields, petitioned for division of those lands.[17] Nevertheless, almost three decades must pass before their petition would be granted.

If the missions had begun to fade, they still were taking part in the founding of new villages in northern Coahuila in the early part of the nineteenth century. San Juan Bautista, though no longer giving birth to new missions, still filled a rôle as mother of settlements.

On February 20, 1801, the village of Nava was founded twenty-five miles to the west on the road to San Fernando and given the name of the current commandant general of the Interior Provinces, Pedro de Nava. Taking part in the act of founding, which was done under supervision of Governor Antonio Cordero y Bustamante, were Friar Manuel Gorgón, president of the missions of the Río Grande and minister of the Mission San Juan Bautista; Friar Antonio López, minister of the Mission San

---

[16] Juan Gutiérrez de la Cueva, "Informe de las Misiones de la Provincia de Coahuila," February 15, 1790, A.G.N., Californias, Vol. 29, p. 227. Plans to finish San Bernardo Church were never carried out.

[17] José Placido y Monzón, "Petition of *Vecinos,*" A.G.N., Misiones, Vol. 20, pp. 18–19.

Bernardo; Friar Blas de Serrano of Sweet Name of Jesus Mission at Peyotes; Pedro Nolasco Carrasco, captain of Presidio del Río Grande; Francisco Iglesias, superior justice of the district; Tomás Flores, political lieutenant of the Villa de San Fernando, also representing the authorities of
the Villa de Gigedo.[18]

With all the form and ceremony attendant to the founding of the
ancient missions and villages, Governor Cordero proceeded with the new
settlers and all his attendants to the place designated for the main plaza
and the church. A cross was erected and an arbor built, and the padres
blessed the place where the church was to rise. After celebration of the
Mass the boundary markers were placed on its lands, and the town lots
were marked off. One of the corner markers was placed on the bank of
"the old San Bernardo irrigation ditch."

> This work done [recorded the Governor], I proceeded, accompanied by the
> same crowd, to the place designated for the main plaza of the settlement and
> proclaimed in a loud voice, "This is the Village of Nava!" upon which the
> settlers, through intercession, committed this land of the glorious apostle San
> Andrés to the Omnipotent for time immemorial.[19]

While the irrigation ditches of the missions of San Bernardo and San
Juan Bautista were contiguous to the lands allocated to the new settlement,
the *pobladores* were not to use the water from them. They were permitted
to take water from a spring, called Ojo de Afuera, four leagues west of
the village, which also supplied water for the missions.

> It is well understood that neither above nor below the source of water of said
> spring will they be able to attempt any work, as it would deplete the supply
> of water which the missions of San Juan and San Bernardo get from the same
> source. . . . To avoid damage to the *acequias* of this village and to the adjacent
> ones of the two missions referred to, they are not to pasture livestock . . . on
> the lands above said village, nor on those contiguous to the *acequias* of the
> missions, but only on the lands downstream. They should keep in mind that in

---

[18] Vito Alessio Robles, *Coahuila y Texas en la época colonial,* p. 583. This
source also contains a list of the first settlers, both of Spanish origin and those of
Tlaxcaltecan extraction. Judging from the names, many of them must have been
descendants of early soldiers and citizens of San Juan Bautista.

[19] *Ibid.,* p. 585. This source goes into considerable detail on the founding, which
is omitted here.

consequence of the establishment [of this village] the mission of San Juan Bautista has been obliged to take water from the spring called Paso Hondo.[20]

The *vecinos,* noted the Governor, should not contest the right of the Mission San Juan to take all the water it needed. In view of the effort the mission was making for the benefit of the new settlement, the villagers should join with the other three missions—San Bernardo, Peyotes, and Vizarrón—to help San Juan Bautista with the work connected with taking the water from Paso Hondo. Until its own irrigation system was complete, Villa de Nava could use the excess from the *labor* of Las Masas, which belonged to the Mission San Bernardo and was watered by the old San Bernardo irrigation ditch.

Much, meanwhile, was happening all across the northern frontier of New Spain. Settlers on the northeast extremity, having been uprooted by the Royal Regulation of 1772, had gravitated back to their old homes to establish permanently the town of Nacogdoches. The English colonies had thrown off the shackles of the mother country and formed a new nation. Spain, in possession of Louisiana since France awarded her the prize in 1762, stood face to face with this strapping youngster, already flexing its muscles and looking westward with hungry eyes.

Soon adventurers from the new United States dared trespass upon the Spanish dominion of Louisiana and Texas, and it was more than a rumor that some of them had the blessing, if not the support, of highly placed officials in the American government. One was the filibuster Philip Nolan, who rode at the head of a band of youthful recruits on his fourth expedition into Texas as the year 1800 drew to a close. Disaster stalked the adventure-hungry band until, on the morning of March 21, 1801, the American "mustangers" awakened in their crude fort on the Brazos to find themselves surrounded by a Spanish troop from Nacogdoches. Nolan, refusing surrender, was killed, his men borne off in chains to San Antonio and thence to México.[21]

Ellis P. Bean and the other survivors of the Nolan expedition may have been the first Anglo-Americans to visit the Spanish Presidio del Río Grande, but Bean fails to specify the route by which they were conducted

[20] *Ibid.,* p. 586. Paso Hondo was on the Arroyo de Castaño some distance southwest of San Juan Bautista.

[21] See Bennett Lay, *The Lives of Ellis P. Bean,* pp. 13–27.

to the interior. Regardless of the route, Nolan's men were the first of a long line of gringos to spill over into Spanish territory. Many others would come to the Río Grande settlement by force or favor to look with eyes oriented to foreign surroundings, to speak from prejudices formed by an alien civilization.

In 1803 Spain, persuaded that Louisiana in the hands of France would be a lasting buffer against the aggressive Americans, re-ceded that territory to the French, only to learn later that France had contracted its sale to the United States months before the transfer took place. The new American nation now cast a long shadow over Spanish territory. Ill-defined boundaries, the continued intrusions of filibusters into Texas, and numerous plots and schemes by American citizens or officials contributed to the hostile attitude of the Spaniards.[22]

These factors also influenced Spanish exploration, particularly in quest of a new route to connect San Antonio and Santa Fé. Until the latter part of the eighteenth century the Santa Fé–San Antonio journey could be made only by way of El Paso, Chihuahua, Monclova, and San Juan Bautista. But while the Spaniards in Texas sought a connecting trail with Santa Fé, so did the Americans from the north and east. One such American expedition was headed by Lieutenant Zebulon Montgomery Pike of the United States Army.

Under orders of the Army's chief, General James Wilkinson, Pike and his seventy-four–man crew ascended the Arkansas River, then crossed to the valley of the Río Grande. When captured by a Spanish force, Pike claimed to be unaware that he was in Spanish territory. He and his men were conducted to Chihuahua for interrogation before they were allowed to return to Louisiana, by way of San Juan Bautista.

En route to Presidio del Río Grande from Chihuahua, Pike, his friend Dr. John Hamilton Robinson, and six American soldiers traveled in the company of Captain Mariano Varela (whom Pike referred to as "my friend Barelo").[23] Varela was traveling under orders to proceed to the Río Grande and to take command of the presidio. He had never seen

22 Weddle, *San Sabá Mission*, p. 193.
23 Castañeda, *Our Catholic Heritage*, V, 347; Elliott Coues (ed.), *The Expeditions of Zebulon Montgomery Pike to Headwaters of the Mississippi River, through Louisiana Territory, and in New Spain, during the years 1805–6–7*, II, 690.

the place, but he was happy about his new assignment, because it had been described to him in glowing terms. Upon his arrival, however, his enthusiasm evaporated. According to Pike ". . . he found himself miserably mistaken, for it was with the greatest difficulty that we obtained anything to eat, which mortified him extremely."[24]

Pike had advance notice of an American who had arrived at Presidio del Río Grande the previous year and was practicing medicine there. On his arrival, at eight o'clock the evening of June 1, 1807, Pike sent for the man to examine him, as he had been requested to do by General Nemesio Salcedo,[25] commandant of Interior Provinces. The moment the man entered the room Pike could tell that he was not what he pretended to be. ". . . I discovered he never had received a liberal education or been accustomed to polished society."[26]

The man, who gave his name as Martin Henderson, professed a love for frontier life which had led him on a solitary trek across the Texas wilderness. The story he told might have paralleled that of Felipe Mendoza in 1705, but for one thing: it was pure falsehood.

The imposter would not attempt to pass himself off on his fellow Americans as a physician; he hoped, however, that they would not betray him, for he only prescribed samples and was careful to do no harm. Pike quickly concluded that the fellow was an agent of Aaron Burr's and, debating in his own mind whether to denounce him as such to the commandant (Captain Varela), he decided against such a course, lest the man be innocent. But at that crucial point one of Pike's men entered the room and informed him of the man's true identity. His name was not Henderson but Trainer; he had come across Texas not because of a thirst for adventure but to avoid prosecution for murder. As a hired killer he had slain one Major Bashier in the wilderness between Natchez and Tennessee. Taking the Major's own pistols from him while he took a noon nap, Trainer had used these weapons to shoot the officer through the head as he slept. The governor of the state, a friend of the Major's, had posted a large reward, thereby forcing Trainer to flee.

Pike reported the circumstances to Captain Varela, who immediately placed Trainer in jail to await instructions from Governor Cordero y

---

[24] Coues, *Expeditions*, II, 690.
[25] See Eugene Hollon, *The Lost Pathfinder: Zebulon Montgomery Pike*, p. 152.
[26] Coues, *Expeditions*, II, 690–691.

Bustamante. Pike learned later, on reaching San Antonio, that the murderer was to be sent to "some place of perpetual confinement in the interior," and he appended, "thus vengeance has overtaken the ingrate and murderer when he least expected it."[27]

The business done, it was time for entertainment. "In the evening we went to see some performers on the slack-rope, who were no wise extraordinary in their performances, except in language which would bring a blush on the cheek of the most abandoned of the female sex in the United States."[28]

Despite his friendship for Captain Varela, Pike liked Presidio del Río Grande less and less the following day as he whiled the hours until their departure at five o'clock in the afternoon. "In the day time [we] were endeavoring to regulate our watches by my compass, and in an instant that my back was turned some person stole it. I could by no means recover it, and I had strong suspicions that the theft was approved."[29]

One of the more pleasant experiences of the day was a tour of the town and "all the missions," escorted by a priest—"a very communicative, liberal, and intelligent man."[30] During the tour Pike estimated the town had 2,500 inhabitants.

Enjoyable as was the tour with the priest, Pike and his companions were excluded when mealtime came.

> The captain went out to dine with some monks who would have thought it profanation to have had us as their guests. We saw no recourse for a dinner but in the inventive genius of a little Frenchman who had accompanied us from Chihuahua. . . . He went off and in a very short time returned with a table-cloth, plates, a dinner of three or four courses, a bottle of wine, and a pretty girl to attend on the table. We inquired by what magic he had brought this about, and found that he had been to one of the officers and notified him that it was the wish of the commandant that he should supply the two Americans [Pike and Robinson] with a decent dinner. . . . We took care to compensate them for their trouble. This we explained to Barelo in the evening, and he laughed heartily.

27 *Ibid.*, p. 694.
28 *Ibid.*; Hollon, *Lost Pathfinder*, p. 156.
29 Coues, *Expeditions*, II, 694.
30 *Ibid.*, pp. 694–695.

We parted from the captain with regrets and assurances of remembrance. Departed at five o'clock . . .[31]

Pike, his companions, and their escort crossed the Río Grande and encamped at a ranch on the other side, seven miles from San Juan Bautista. The next morning they set out across Spanish Texas, Pike's description of which did nothing to turn back the tide of North American invaders: "It has one of the most delightful temperatures in the world. . . . Take it generally, it is one of the richest, most prolific, and best watered countries in North America."[32] Nevertheless, when Pike saw the Stars and Stripes at Natchitoches, just one month after his arrival at San Juan Bautista, his reaction was one of unbridled joy.

While the hungry expansionists of the United States breathed offensively upon the Spanish colonies, internal trouble was brewing within the limits of New Spain. It was the same kind of trouble which England already had experienced in her colonial possessions, the same which had brought into existence this brash young nation that now pressed upon the borders of Spanish possessions.

[31] Coues, *Expeditions,* p. 695.   [32] Hollon, *Lost Pathfinder,* p. 157.

34. DEATH TO THE *GACHUPINES*

IN THE YEAR 1810 a part of the *cuerpo de guardia* of Presidio del Río Grande was repaired. The paymaster's quarters and office were given a new flat roof, with beams of cypress wood hauled all the way from the Río de Sabinas by oxcart. Carved into the beams, together with the year of the rebuilding, was a religious message: "Hail purest Mary, conceived without original sin. . . . Praised be the sweet names of Jesus, Mary, and Joseph."[1]

[1] *Ave María Purísima sin pecado original concevida Se fecha el año 1810. Alabado sean los dulces nombres de Jesús, María y José.* The building, still stand-

Juan José Díaz was at that time commandant of the Presidio del Río Grande. On April 27, 1810, he was ordered by Don Antonio Cordero y Bustamante, governor of Coahuila, to officiate in the founding of a new settlement. Díaz was to distribute lands to settlers who wished to establish homes in the new Villa de Palafox on the left bank of the Río Grande some distance below San Juan Bautista.[2]

Named for a Spanish patriot who had won distinction opposing the forces of Napoleon in Spain, Palafox was inhabited by families from the older settlements of Coahuila. "A regular map was drawn for the lay-out of the town, and Captain José Díaz was put in charge of its development."[3] Official approval of the project finally came from the Commandant General in September, along with an expression of regret that the King's treasury could not bear the expense of erecting the public buildings for the new village, as was the custom.

While most of the offspring of San Juan Bautista outdid the parent, this settlement was the exception. Abandoned from 1818 to 1826 because of Indian depredations, it finally was destroyed in 1829.[4] Details of its tragic story, apparently, have been lost to posterity.

While paeans of praise were being inscribed in the roof beams of the paymaster's house, and while the Commandant went out to form a new settlement, storm clouds gathered over México. On that fateful day, September 16, 1810, the holocaust erupted with the *Grito de Dolores,* the mighty outcry, and the Creole priest, Miguel Hidalgo y Costilla, led his proletarian hordes into a bath of blood. The lines were quickly drawn between the "haves" and the "have-nots"—the wealthy and powerful *gachupines,* or native Spaniards, joined by the more opulent Creoles

---

ing, presently serves as the store and dwelling of Srta. Profa. Aurora Botella G. (Personal interview, April 8, 1967).

[2] Carlos Eduardo Castañeda, *Our Catholic Heritage in Texas,* V, 433. This source gives location of Palafox as "about halfway between Presidio de Río Grande and Laredo," but S. B. Wilcox ("Laredo during the Texas Republic," *SWHQ,* 42, No. 2 [October, 1938], 83) gives the location of San José de Palafox exactly as thirty-seven miles northwest of Laredo. Wilcox observed that some ruins were still visible in 1938, though the village was never fully rebuilt after the Indian attack of 1818.

[3] Castañeda, *Our Catholic Heritage,* V, 433.

[4] Walter Prescott Webb and H. Bailey Carroll (eds.), *Handbook of Texas,* II, 325.

(Spaniards born in New Spain) on the one side; the Indians, *mestizos,* and run-of-the-mill Creoles on the other.

By September 20 Hidalgo had fifty thousand followers, mostly armed with farm tools and shouting "Death to the *gachupines!*" Royalist General Félix María Calleja moved to intercept the seething mass at San Luis Potosí. An appeal went out to the provincial governors to send him troops.

Governor Antonio Cordero y Bustamante responded quickly from Coahuila. He "gathered the commandants of the presidial companies stationed at Monclova, La Bavia, Aguaverde, San Vicente, and San Juan Bautista del Río Grande and ordered them to prepare their troops to march to San Luis Potosí" to be placed under orders of Calleja.[5]

In addition, two companies of volunteers were raised October 8 from Monclova Viejo and Presidio del Río Grande. Another three companies of lancers were placed under arms at Monclova, San Buenaventura, and San Juan Bautista—or Río Grande—November 14, the latter under José de Jesús Rodríguez. All the settlements of Coahuila were ordered to mobilize their militia units to defend the province against invasion by the rebels. But rebel sentiment, long dormant, soon would stir to life in Coahuila also.

Hidalgo, successful in the early stages, hesitated, then turned away from the city of México to head back to Guanajuato. His force and that of General Calleja met at Aculco. Merely the sight of Calleja's five columns in excellent military formation, executing commands in precision, was enough to unnerve the untrained rebels. Calleja, pressing Hidalgo's rear, held mass hangings for the citizens who had sided with the rebellion; corpses by the scores dangled from jury-rigged gallows at the principal crossroads.

Hidalgo proceeded with his slaughter of the *gachupines.*

In January, Calleja, with six thousand well-armed regulars and militia, marched upon Hidalgo's mob of eighty thousand at Guadalajara. Despite the disparity of numbers, the tide turned for the Royalists in the South.

In the North the spirit of insurgence blazed in white heat. The rebels soon held Coahuila from one end to the other, and the road to Texas pos-

---

[5] Vito Alessio Robles, *Coahuila y Texas en la época colonial,* p. 630; an indication that the presidios ordered abandoned by Teodoro de Croix were regarrisoned later, or else kept the same names at new locations.

sessed a sudden appeal. Forces of both opposing factions, each laden with huge sums of money, soon would be heading for San Juan Bautista, still an important gateway. One side would never reach that gateway. The other would, but with regret that it had.

As the rebel forces pressed upon him from all sides, Coahuila Governor Cordero capitulated, and was captured as he attempted to flee. With the collapse his treasurer, Manuel Royuela, sought to escape with the state funds. Royuela decided to go to San Antonio de Béjar, where he believed the tide of revolution had not yet spread. With his wife, Doña María Josefa Sánchez Navarro, and their six sons, he proceeded northward in January, 1811, escorted by a sergeant and sixty men.[6]

Knowing the location of the forces of the insurgent governor, Pedro de Aranda, Royuela's caravan skirted Monclova and proceeded to Presidio del Río Grande. They arrived on January 15, not knowing of the trap that waited there. The judge of the village of Río Grande, Salvador Carrasco, and the commandant of the presidio—now Antonio Griego, who had succeeded Juan José Díaz—lay in wait to attack the Treasurer's force and seize the government funds, said to exceed 300,000 pesos. When the time came, they decided to employ a ruse instead.

While the Treasurer and his family and the officers of the militia were treated as welcome guests, agents of the insurgents were at work on the soldiers of Royuela's escort. Most of them were won over to the rebel cause by persuasion. As the caravan prepared to depart for Béjar next morning, January 16, 1811, the population of the village suddenly gathered in a mob and fell upon the Royalists. The *alférez*, Ignacio Elguézabal, the sergeant, a merchant, and an official of the treasury were killed. Royuela and his family were imprisoned.[7]

Less than a week later the garrison at San Antonio went over to the insurgent side; Captain Juan Bautista Casas took over the company of Álamo de Parras, stationed in the old Mission San Antonio de Valero, the transplanted San Francisco Solano. Casas placed Governor Manuel María de Salcedo and Colonel Simón de Herrera y Leyva, commandant of the auxiliary forces of Texas, under arrest. On orders from Miranda he sent them and a number of other officers, in the charge of Captain Vicente Flores and thirty mounted men, to San Juan Bautista. Most of the prison-

---

[6] *Ibid.*, pp. 634–635.
[7] *Ibid.*, p. 635.

ers merely wore handcuffs, but special treatment was accorded the Governor: he was transported in chains.[8]

A week later the party from Texas reached Presidio del Río Grande, where the presidial officers apparently cooperated to the fullest in putting the prisoners up for the night and providing a new escort to take them on to Monclova and eventually to the Sánchez Navarro hacienda near Santa Rosa.

In the meantime dissension had set to work on the insurgent army in the South. Ignacio Allende had taken the command from Hidalgo, making the instigator of the revolution virtually a prisoner in his own camp. Allende directed the march northward and arrived February 24 at Saltillo, where accord was reached and Hidalgo was given a figurehead title of generalisimo. Great fiestas were held in celebration, including a solemn Mass of thanksgiving, with Fray Bernardo Conde officiating.[9]

The revolutionary leaders, aware that General Calleja blocked the southward route to San Luis Potosí, determined to march for the United States. Their purpose was to use the sizeable war chest they had accumulated to purchase the arms they were unable to get in México. Encouragement for such a move came with word of Captain Casas' coup at San Antonio de Béjar; all the road ahead, it seemed, was in the hands of revolutionists. But far too much was taken for granted as the insurgents marched northward, bound for the gateway at Presidio del Río Grande.

The loyalist treasurer, Royuela, had not been nearly as lax in his providences. His dastardly capture at Presidio del Río Grande would be avenged in full measure. Among other accomplishments, he had convinced one of his guards, the retired Creole Captain Ignacio Elizondo, that he had everything to lose and nothing to gain by fostering the rebel cause. Elizondo, more than a trusted ally of the insurgents, was a keystone. Though his loyalties changed under Royuela's influence, he continued to masquerade as an ardent revolutionist. Soon he was "guarding" Governor Salcedo and company at the Sánchez hacienda.

Royuela's work also had included the placing of two important spies— the Baron de Bastrop and a former officer of Presidio del Río Grande, Sebastián Rodríguez—in the northbound caravan of Hidalgo and Allende.

[8] Hodding Carter, *Doomed Road of Empire: The Spanish Trail of Conquest*, p. 206.

[9] Alessio Robles, *Coahuila y Texas*, p. 636.

The spies even served as guides. Unsuspecting, the revolutionists marched ahead, into the baited trap.

Elizondo was not the only one who had changed sides inopportunely for the insurgents. Counter-revolution swept across the northern provinces. Captain Casas was unseated at San Antonio by a Royalist junta. The Texas Royalists sent Captains José María Muñoz and Luis Galán as deputies to inform the commandant general of Interior Provinces, Nemesio de Salcedo, in Chihuahua, of developments in Texas, and to pledge support of the Texas forces in putting down the insurrection.

Instructions to the two deputies were carefully drawn. They carried a false set of papers for the benefit of revolutionaries whom they might encounter; the true message, not trusted to writing, was to be given to Nemesio Salcedo orally. Pledging faithful observance of the instructions, the two officers set out at noon on March 8, 1811, for Presidio del Río Grande.

In the afternoon of the fourth day they came to the crossing on the Río Grande. Fording the wide but shallow passage, they found before them the weathered buildings of the ancient gateway to Spanish Texas. Before them, too, they recognized, was a crucial test. They approached with caution; whatever the sentiments of the town, it was of the utmost importance that the deputies appear to be on the right side.

In the village they were welcomed first at the home of the postmaster, Juan Antonio Urtiaga. Soon visitors began to arrive, and the deputies found themselves the center of attention, continually plied with questions about the state of affairs in Texas. First came the curate of the town. With inner misgivings Muñoz and Galán informed him of the recent overthrow of the Casas regime, and of their true mission. The curate's reaction was reassuring: the counter-revolution must not fail; there were many here at San Juan Bautista who were ready to strike a blow for the King.[10]

Then came the commandant of the presidio, who had received a formal request from the two deputies for permission to state their purpose. The captain was intensely interested in what they had to tell him of the happenings in Béjar. He offered to help them along the next leg of their journey to Chihuahua.

Their courage much bolstered, Muñoz and Galán decided to pay a

[10] Castañeda, *Our Catholic Heritage,* VI, 25.

courtesy call on the priest at Mission San Juan Bautista. To their delight they found him to be an ardent Royalist. The minister promised to sing a solemn high Mass and to offer a novena for the success of the mission and the early restoration of royal authority over New Spain.

By the time the two officers from Béjar returned to the postmaster's home, the news they had brought of the Royalist victory in San Antonio had spread throughout the town. While the word generally was received joyously, the two men could not help but notice the hostile stares from dark doorways on either side of the narrow street. After nightfall the Captain came to warn them: the town was divided in its feelings. There were those who sharply resented the news so favorable to the Royalists. For the safety of the visitors he placed a fifteen-man guard on the postmaster's house.

The night passed without incident, and early next morning Muñoz and Galán continued on their way to San Fernando de Austria. As they looked back on the square-roofed buildings of the presidio, the Royalist envoys doubtless entertained questioning thoughts. They had safely cleared the fort where Governor Salcedo and his party, prisoners of the insurgents, had been kept overnight, then sent on to Monclova in the custody of an escort of revolutionists from Río Grande. And it was here, just two months previously, that Manuel Royuela was captured, his protectors massacred. Had the officers of the presidio detected the shifting sands and decided it was time to alter their stance? Or had they actually been powerless to rescue Salcedo from his captors, and to prevent the assault on Royuela's party by the townspeople? The tide of revolution was capricious indeed.

San Juan Bautista was a nerve center of the revolution. It throbbed with the pulse of every move made by loyalist and insurgent, as the fortunes of each ebbed and flowed between interior México and Spanish Texas.

The arrival of Muñoz and Galán at San Fernando gave new impetus to the counter-revolution. The two loyalist officers met Elizondo, who took them to the hacienda where Governor Salcedo was being held "prisoner" until the proper moment arrived to spring the Royalist plot. They joined with Lieutenant José de Rábago, another Royalist who was acting as second in command to the rebel governor, Aranda, and the infiltrating band arranged a party for the pleasure-loving official. The *aguardiente* flowed freely. When the revolutionary leader and his cohorts reached the proper state of senselessness, Royalist forces closed in and captured them all. Among Aranda's papers was a letter which revealed that the insurgent generals and a convoy, leaving Saltillo on March 17, had asked for a military escort to meet them at Acatita de Baján, a short distance below Monclova. It was the kind of opportunity the Royalists had been looking for. They intercepted the revolutionist caravan at Baján on March 21, and their capture of the rebel leaders was virtually complete.

It is significant that others taking part in the Royalist coup besides Elizondo previously had given allegiance to the insurgents. Among these were two former officers of the King at Presidio de San Juan Bautista del Río Grande, Lieutenant Joaquín Rodríguez and Alférez Jesús Rodríguez. Having joined the uprising at Aguanueva, they came back into the Royalist fold in time to take part in the capture of the revolutionary leaders.

One of Elizondo's lieutenants in the operation was Antonio Griego, commandant at Presidio del Río Grande at the time of the assault on the Royalist treasurer, Manuel Royuela. But in this case it was the revolutionists' treasury which was being robbed, and the loot, consisting of well over a million pesos, was deposited with Royuela.[11]

On March 25 Governor Salcedo, who would yet lose his life in the revolution, conducted Father Hidalgo and the principal generals out of Monclova on the march to Chihuahua, and to death before a firing squad.

At San Juan Bautista early in July an armed guard arrived from Béjar, conducting a prisoner to Monclova for sentencing by a court martial. The prisoner was the ex-Captain Juan Bautista Casas, deposed leader of the revolutionists in Texas. A month later the guard returned to Presidio del Río Grande from the South. This time it carried Captain Casas' head in a box. It was being returned to San Antonio to be placed on a pike and displayed in Military Plaza as a warning to others with traitorous sentiments.[12]

The tide of revolution was stemmed temporarily. But during the year following, José Bernardo Gutiérrez de Lara, a *mestizo* blacksmith from Nuevo Santander, went to the United States to confer with Secretary of State James Monroe. Though he and Monroe were unable to come to terms on aid from the United States government, Gutiérrez returned to Texas with an army raised in Louisiana. After withstanding a siege at

11 Alessio Robles, *Coahuila y Texas,* pp. 648, 650.
12 Castañeda, *Our Catholic Heritage,* VI, 21.

Presidio de la Bahía, the "Republican Army of the North" marched on San Antonio and obtained the surrender of Governor Manuel Salcedo, back at his post after his sojourn as a prisoner of the insurgents in México. The governor and sixteen of his officers then were led out of town by a band of revolutionaries, allegedly acting on orders of Gutiérrez, and beheaded, April 3, 1813.

Meanwhile, the friend of Zebulon Pike, Doctor John Hamilton Robinson, had returned to Presidio del Río Grande in the autumn of 1812 as an agent of the United States government. He carried a message for Nemesio Salcedo, the commandant general of Interior Provinces, in the interest of better relations between the authorities of New Spain and the United States. The Spanish official was suspicious, however, and the mission was a signal failure. Robinson returned to Presidio del Río Grande four months later, in February, 1813, to spend several days at the gateway settlement. At San Juan Bautista he proposed himself as a mediator between the revolutionaries and the Royalists. His offer was declined. The forthright and personable Doctor Robinson found a need for his medical skills at the presidio, however. His patient was Colonel Ignacio Elizondo, who had played the major rôle in capturing the revolutionary leaders at Baján. Elizondo, it seems, was suffering more from sickness of the spirit than of the body. He confessed to Robinson his reasons for affiliating himself with the Royalists: While his sympathies lay with independence, he could not abide the lawlessness with which the insurgents sought to attain their goals. If the President of the United States would but extend a helping hand. . . .

Doctor Robinson returned to the United States to give such a report on his conversation with the Spanish officer in April, 1813.[13]

Elizondo remained at Presidio del Río Grande with seven hundred men, well armed and fully provisioned, waiting to be ordered to his next move. The Royalists in México eyed the flaming revolution in Texas with misgivings. Measures must be taken to stop it. Joaquín de Arredondo, governor of Nuevo Santander, just named commandant of the eastern Interior Provinces, prepared for the effort. Early in June, Arredondo, himself advancing toward Laredo, ordered Elizondo to move up to an observation post on the Frío River and to wait for him there.[14] Elizondo, how-

[13] *Ibid.*, p. 93.
[14] Carter, *Doomed Road*, p. 233.

ever, marched on to San Antonio, and on June 20 his force was put to rout in a surprise attack by the Republican Army of the North. Elizondo retreated to San Juan Bautista, but his force returned to Texas to form the advance guard in the Battle of the Medina, August 18, 1813.[15] The Republican Army of the North, now commanded by José Alvarez Toledo y Dubois, was cut to pieces by the forces of Elizondo and Arredondo. No mercy was shown the Mexicans who dared challenge the supremacy of the crown, nor their wives and daughters. Elizondo led a relentless pursuit of fugitives eastward almost to Nacogdoches. Before his return to San Antonio he lost his life in an attack on his person by a demented officer serving under him.

Arredondo, meanwhile, submitted a report to his superiors praising the conduct of his officers in the Battle of the Medina. Among them was one Antonio López de Santa Anna.

Another phase of the revolution had been defeated. Indeed it seemed for a time that the Royalists had been successful in putting down the rebellion. But in the end independence was won, not by bloodshed—of which there had been plenty—but by a plot so clever in design that neither arms nor ideology could successfully combat it.

Author of the plot was Colonel Agustín de Iturbide, who had been ousted from his Royalist command post because of irregularities of many sorts, then reinstated. At the close of 1820 he was found in command of three thousand men in a southern mountainous district near the Pacific coast. Then in February, 1821, having communicated with the patriot leader, Vicente Guerrero, he published his decree called the "Plan de Iguala."

The "plan" declared for independence of México under a constitutional limited monarchy, governed by a member of the Spanish royal family, under the Catholic religion. Through his cleverness "Iturbide had the sympathy of the clergy, the secret well wishes of the aristocracy, and the noisy, enthusiastic support of the proletariat."[16] It was a "something-for-everybody" type of plan, a sort of half-way separation from Spain. Its popularity spread rapidly, and on July 24, 1821, Viceroy Don Juan

---

[15] Henry P. Walker (ed.), "William McLane's Narrative of the Magee-Gutiérrez Expedition, 1812–1813," *SWHQ,* 66, No. 3 (January, 1963), 468.

[16] Clarence R. Wharton, *El Presidente: A Sketch of the Life of General Santa Anna,* p. 7.

O'Donojú signed away Spain's dominion over México and her outlands. After O'Donojú's death hardly more than two months later, the Spanish government repudiated his capitulation; the idea of rule by a Bourbon prince was abandoned, and Iturbide became Emperor of México, May 19, 1822.[17]

San Juan Bautista—Presidio del Río Grande—had been a Spanish outpost, the gateway to Spanish Texas, for almost a century and a quarter. Now, in a political sense, neither the gateway nor Texas was Spanish, but the road between them was not yet closed. San Juan Bautista, which had changed rôles many times, must do so again.

[17] *Ibid.,* p. 12.

35. BUGLE AT DAWN

ONCE AGAIN the settlement of San Juan Bautista underwent transition. No longer a part of Spain, it belonged to an independent México. The sentiment of the people had favored independence from the beginning, although the presidio had remained Royalist since the revolution's early stages.

On July 14, 1815, Rafael González[1] came from Monclova to serve as a first lieutenant in the Royalist company of Presidio del Río Grande. He ascended to the captaincy on May 18, 1818. It was not until July 3, 1821, that González joined the independence movement and pronounced for the Plan de Iguala, and his presidial garrison and the people of the town followed his lead.

González served as a lieutenant colonel in the army of México and, on

[1] See Vito Alessio Robles, *Coahuila y Texas desde la consumación de la Independencia hasta el Tratado de Paz de Guadalupe Hidalgo,* II, 194. Also Walter Prescott Webb and H. Bailey Carroll (eds.), *Handbook of Texas,* I, 706.

August 15, 1824, became governor of Coahuila and Texas.[2] During his term as governor a town was established east of San Antonio de Béjar and named in his honor. The town of Gonzales would be known in later years as "the Lexington of Texas."

After the revolution Mexican soldiers garrisoned Presidio del Río Grande, which afforded protection against Indian raids, served as a way station for travelers to and from Texas, and, in theory at least, guarded against contraband trade.

Electoral procedure for the provinces of the independent nation was established in 1823, with José María Jiménez serving as elector for the Río Grande district.[3] That year also marked the final end, for all practical purposes, of the Missions of San Juan Bautista and San Bernardo, and the other two missions within the jurisdiction of Presidio del Río Grande: San Francisco Vizarrón and Dulce Nombre de Jesús de Peyotes.

Coahuila's first deputy to the Mexican Congress, Antonio Elosúa,[4] viewed the difficult plight of the settlers on the northern frontier and sought alleviation of their problems. Involved in the solution was distribution of the lands of the four missions, which long since had ceased to function as institutions for civilizing the Indians.

Coahuila, observed the former Governor (1820–1822), had been depredated from its beginnings by the barbarous Indians who still were raiding across its borders from the north. It had been settled at the cost of repeated sacrifices by its colonists, who had found it necessary to keep arms ready at all times. Many had lost their property, and even their lives. Often they had seen their toil and sacrifice of years put to naught in minutes, as the savage raiders swooped down upon them, killing *vaqueros* and shepherds and scattering their livestock.

2 He served in that capacity until March 15, 1826. In 1834 González was secretary of the Comandancia of Coahuila and Texas. He died in 1857.

3 Alessio Robles, *Coahuila y Texas desde la consumación,* I, 153.

4 Elosúa, a native of Havana, had come to México in 1802 to serve as an infantry officer. Like Antonio López de Santa Anna he was one of the captains who drew the praise of General Arredondo for his part in defeating the Republican Army of the North in the Battle of the Medina, August 18, 1813. As governor of Coahuila he pronounced for the Plan de Iguala on July 6, 1821, at Monclova. After serving in the Mexican Congress he became *ayudante inspector* of Coahuila and Texas, serving from 1826 to 1833, when he died in San Antonio de Béjar and his body was interred in the chapel of Mission San Antonio de Valero (the Alamo) (Alessio Robles, *Coahuila y Texas desde la consumación,* I, 65).

During the last eleven years, reported the deputy, the people of Coahuila had sustained the most disastrous war of the Comanches and the Lipans. The frontier was depopulated of livestock, and even of people, for many persons had been killed and many others had fled inland in hope of saving the only thing they had left: their lives. Only widows, orphans, and those reduced to poverty by the Indians were to be found on the frontier.[5]

The first step toward remedying the deplorable condition, Elosúa believed, should be that of bolstering the presidios of Monterrey, Santa Rosa, San Fernando, and Río Grande. The soldiers of these garrisons were naked, without arms, on foot, and lacking sustenance; they should be brought into a state of discipline such as that provided for by the Reglamento of 1772, in order that they might defend the territories and that the colonists might dedicate themselves anew to the tasks of the field.

Secondly, the deputy noted, the people who so often were called upon to defend the lands of the North against the Indians had been fighting for property in which they had no ownership. To correct this injustice he asked the President to order that the lands of the four missions under the jurisdiction of Presidio del Río Grande be distributed immediately among "the most worthy inhabitants of the frontier," in accord with the decree of the Spanish Cortes of September 30, 1813.[6]

The missions, said Elosúa, were a living anachronism. They had no neophytes, and for all practical purposes they had ceased to function in 1810. In his opinion they should have been subjected to secularization, "with all its implications," but this had not been done because of the disrupting effects upon the missions of the first wave of insurgence.[7]

In accordance with the Coahuila deputy's petition, the distribution of the mission lands was ordered on July 13, 1823. Yet for some reason the order was not carried out until several years later.

On March 16, 1826, Victor Blanco, the day after he succeeded Rafael González as governor, decreed the division of the lands and waters of the

---

[5] Antonio Elosúa, Petition, June 25, 1823, A.G.N., Californias, Vol. 44, folios 66–67.

[6] *Ibid.*, folio 68. The decree ordered that all missions which had been in existence as long as ten years be delivered immediately to ecclesiastical judges, the missionary religious giving up their government and the lands to be distributed. A copy of the decree is found in *ibid.*, folio 69.

[7] Elosúa, Petition, *ibid.*, folio 69.

missions. He commissioned for the task C. Nicolás Elizondo, who arrived at the Río Grande community July 21 to carry out the assignment.[8] Elizondo gathered in representatives from the neighboring villages to see the job well done. "The oath was administered, Mass celebrated, and the work begun."[9] On January 22, 1829, Miguel de la Peña certified that distribution of the lands was complete.

By legislative decree of August 7, 1827, the vestiges of mission and presidio were erased when the name of the "puesto de Río Grande" was changed to Villa de Guerrero.[10] The new name honored Vicente Ramón Guerrero, a soldier of the revolution, recently an unsuccessful candidate for vice president of México. Guerrero was to be elected President of the Republic in 1829, to die before a firing squad February 14, 1830.[11]

With the advent of the revolution in 1810 the Río Grande missions had faded into oblivion. In the intervening years the number of Indians at the missions had constantly dwindled. Many of the natives retreated to the wilds, a great many others succumbed to the frequent epidemics which visited the population, and still others were absorbed into the Mexican population, which, in actuality, was the ultimate end of the Coahuiltecan race.

The mission buildings fell into disuse and began to crumble away.[12] The stone was sold from the patio walls, then from the churches and monasteries, and was used by the citizens of the nearby villa to build their homes. Religious inscriptions were carved or painted on the roof beams of some of these houses. Today, one block north of the church, just off

---

8 Alessio Robles, *Coahuila y Texas desde la consumación,* I, 253–254.

9 *Ibid.,* p. 254.

10 *Ibid.,* p. 252. Many years passed, however, before the name Guerrero came into popular use. At the same time the name of San Fernando de Austria was changed to San Fernando de Rosas. It became Zaragoza in 1868.

11 Webb and Carroll, *Handbook,* I, 744.

12 Paul Horgan (*Great River: The Río Grande in North American History,* p. 394) says a few mission Indians still lived at San Bernardo: "Now asked to maintain the great stone temple . . . as a local parish church . . . the few families . . . could not do so. The friars were withdrawn." These sweeping generalizations present an erroneous picture. It is extremely doubtful that any effort ever was made to maintain either of the gateway missions as a parish church. "The great stone temple" mentioned by Horgan was the unfinished San Bernardo church, never placed in use. He gives an elaborate description of the ruin of San Bernardo by the weather after the roof of the nave fell in. Again, he refers to a roof that was never put on in the first place.

the historic plaza of Guerrero, stands a roofless building, its walls held together by a single cypress beam. On its underside the beam bears this inscription: "No one passes from this threshold without being healed by the life which, hail Mary, was conceived without original sin."[13]

Today, in this community whose origin had such deep religious roots, no regular church service is held. The church, on the east side of the plaza, is locked except on the rare occasions when a priest comes from Piedras Negras.

Though at the birth of the Mexican nation the community of Río Grande had passed its zenith, it still would be host to many historic personages and events. Its conflict was far from over. The new nation of México was eager—perhaps *too* eager—to attract settlers to the vast territory of Texas. To this end it permitted persons of an alien culture and foreign beliefs to take up land and form colonies. For México this was a grave mistake. Conflicts inevitably arose. Villa de Guerrero, still a gateway to Texas, was drawn into the conflict periodically, until the conflict was finally resolved. But with its missions gone, Guerrero seemed to sink deeper and deeper into oblivion.

By administrative order of February 21, 1828, the seat of government (*cabecera*) of the district of Río Grande was moved from Guerrero to Gigedo, one of the many offspring of the parent settlement. The same decree established the route over which the mails would be carried: from Gigedo, by way of Allende, Morelos, San Fernando de Rosas, and Nava, thence to Guerrero. The *cabecera* was moved from Gigedo to Nava in 1831 before being moved back to Guerrero in 1834.[14]

The decline of Guerrero is shown graphically by the census reports of Coahuila and Texas, 1828–1831. The 1828 census gave the villa 943 persons, while the number had declined to 756 in 1829, to 539 in 1831. By the time of the latter census it was evident that the population of Coahuila was decreasing, that of Texas increasing. While the 1831 census enumerated scholastics in the towns and villages which had schools, no such information was given for Guerrero. Guerrero did, however, show one

---

[13] *Nadie pase del umbral sin hace curar con la vida que, Ave María, fué concevida sin culpa original.* A similar inscription is found in the Marcos Hernández House (1845) just east of the plaza.

[14] Alessio Robles, *Coahuila y Texas desde la consumación,* I, 261, 378.

schoolmaster on its occupational list, as well as one minister, one church sexton, two public employees, two merchants, eighteen stock raisers, forty-six farmers, seventy day laborers, and ninety-two craftsmen. Significantly, no soldiers were listed.[15]

The conflict between the Mexicans and the Anglo-Americans, now taking up land in Texas, came early—assuming various forms and producing sundry results. In many instances differences arose as a result of imprudent laws which had originated in the Spanish regime and were retained by México. A case in point is the regulation of commerce, by which the government would not allow the colonies to trade among themselves, or with other nations except under burdensome restrictions. Dissatisfaction sprang up among the colonists, who sought to evade laws which they considered unjust. They resorted to smuggling and other illegal practices.[16]

Noah Smithwick's story of tobacco smuggling serves as an illustration. The incident he relates also involves Presidio del Río Grande, about the year 1827. Texas colonists, said Smithwick, were permitted under the colonization act to import duty free everything they desired for their own use. In order to take merchandise for trading purposes into México, however, they had to pay a heavy duty. Reserved to the government was the sole right to deal in such luxury items as tobacco and coffee. "Traders had to pay a heavy duty to get their goods into market, and a still heavier duty to get their money out [of México]; so smuggling was largely resorted to, notwithstanding the strict patrol maintained along the border. . . . The principal risk lay in the greed of the Mexican soldiery."[17]

Smithwick sold his unprofitable blacksmith shop at Bell's Landing (Columbia) and invested the proceeds in one thousand pounds of leaf tobacco. With three other colonists—Joe McCoy, Jack Cryor, and John Webber—he set out for México, intent on disposing of the contraband on the black market. The tobacco, in one-hundred–pound bales, was carried on pack mules. The smugglers struck Laredo, only to find some other trader had been there ahead of them; the market was stocked. They proceeded upriver toward Presidio del Río Grande, but rains set in and the

15 *Ibid.*, pp. 328–333.

16 Herbert Eugene Bolton and Eugene C. Barker (eds.), *With the Makers of Texas: A Source Reader in Texas History*, p. 134.

17 *Ibid.*, p. 135; Noah Smithwick, *The Evolution of a State or Recollections of Old Texas Days*, p. 42.

river rose beyond safe fording. "We hid our tobacco out in the chapparral and lay around watching for some chance to cross the river."[18]

Eyeing a goat ranch across the river, Smithwick and Cryor decided to swim their horses over and have a look around. Some Mexican soldiers saw them and set out to cross the river themselves to reconnoiter the invaders' camp. But the soldiers were mounted on frail ponies, and as they entered the current they were carried downstream to a point where the bank was too steep to land. Before they could find a landing place one soldier was drowned.

The soldiers who reached the left bank safely found the tobacco cache and helped themselves to as much as they could carry, "making no attempt to arrest us, as their duty required. To have done so would have necessitated the surrender of the goods to the Mexican government, which they had no intention of doing."[19]

To save the rest of their tobacco the Texans knew they had to move quickly; the soldiers would return. After dark they again swam the river to the goat ranch and, for a price, obtained the loan of a rawhide boat. Back on the Texas side, they loaded the crude craft with tobacco, and, swimming and pulling the boat after them, they ferried their goods to the opposite shore.

Since they had more tobacco than could be disposed of in one small village, they divided the cargo. Cryor and McCoy took theirs to Guerrero, where they procured the aid of the local alcalde. But customs officers learned of the business and arrested the official. Cryor and McCoy managed to escape but had to leave their tobacco buried in the sand.

Webber and Smithwick, meanwhile, proceeded on to Villa de San Fernando, where they established liaison with another Anglo, named John Villars. Villars found them a safe hiding place for their wares in the home of an aged Mexican woman, Doña Petra, the widow of an American.

The tobacco had to be sold in small quantities, but the price was good: up to two dollars per pound. Yet with the loss they had suffered at the hands of the soldiers, and the expenses they incurred in San Fernando, they had no more money than the law allowed. On the return to Texas they cleared customs with ease.

During the postrevolutionary period others came to Guerrero because

[18] Smithwick, *Evolution of a State,* p. 43.
[19] *Ibid.,* p. 44.

the road went that way. In 1833 the steamship *Amos Wright* brought fifty-nine men, women, and children, the vanguard of a proposed colony between the Río Grande and the Nueces, to the Texas coast. The colony to be established was that of the Río Grande and Texas Land Company, organized by Dr. John Charles Beales, a naturalized Mexican citizen.[20] The settlers—English, German, and American—traveled by ox wagon from Cópano to San Antonio. The direct route to their colony, located on Las Moras Creek in present Kinney County, would have taken them across rugged, uncharted country; hence it was decided to follow established trails as far as possible. The Upper Presidio Road brought them to the banks of the Río Grande at Paso Pacuache in early afternoon of March 4, 1834. D. E. Egerton, an English surveyor, had gone on ahead that morning to purchase small stores at Presidio del Río Grande.

The caravan made camp on the left bank of the river and sent a party across the stream to ascertain its depth. It was found to be three feet deep, running three hundred yards wide. After spending the afternoon in preparing the loads for the passage and in repairing the road where it ascended the banks of the river, the travelers crossed next day and made camp on the right bank.[21]

Five miles' travel on March 6 brought them to Mission San Bernardo, just north of Presidio del Río Grande. Dr. Beales saw before him "a small village with about seven hundred inhabitants. There are some large houses in it, and several gardens. The people were very civil to us; altogether, I liked it much better than either Bexar or La Bahía. In the afternoon we, as usual, were visited by nearly all the inhabitants of the place."[22]

The colonists had intended leaving on the seventh, but that morning they found their cattle had strayed some distance and were forced to remain another day. A yoke of oxen was still missing the following day, but it was decided to proceed without the animals. The travelers did considerable trading in Guerrero; Beales purchased two cows and calves and two fat heifers.

From Presidio del Río Grande they traveled northwestward along a trail roughly following the route of José Berroterán in 1729 and Don Blas

[20] See Webb and Carroll, *Handbook*, I, 127–128.
[21] William Kennedy, *Texas: The Rise, Progress, and Prospects of the Republic of Texas*, II, 49.
[22] *Ibid.*

de la Garza Falcón and José de Ecay Múzquiz six years later. First night out they camped at Santo Domingo Spring, twenty miles upriver. The second they made the Río Escondido. Like Garza Falcón and Ecay Múzquiz a century before, they saw a great number of wild horses here.

On March 10 Egerton split off from the caravan to seek supplies at San Fernando, while a crossing was being sought on the Escondido. After fording the stream the colonists encountered five Shawnee Indians trapping beaver (they had caught about forty). "About a mile farther on, we entered on a very fine low plain, with very rich land, forming a kind of extensive bottom to the Río Grande."[23] This was the site of the present city of Piedras Negras, Coahuila.

On March 12 the caravan crossed the Río Grande near present Quemado, a few miles below the mouth of Las Moras Creek, and the following day proceeded northward to the site of their colony. The settlement they established, called Dolores—honoring Beales' wife, María Dolores de Soto—was shortlived. It was abandoned at the outbreak of the Texas Revolution when Santa Anna's army advanced with the avowed purpose of driving all Americans from Texas. A wagon train of retreating colonists was attacked by Comanches on the Nueces River below Espantosa Lake, probably near present Carrizo Springs. All were massacred except Mrs. Sarah Ann Horn and another woman and their small children, who were subjected to living hell as Comanche captives.[24]

Colonization and land matters concerning Texas claimed much official attention in the early 1830's. The citizens of Presidio del Río Grande, during the mission period, had been hemmed in, unable to obtain lands near the settlement. Even in the early years of the Republic, the church had held on to the lands of the adjacent missions. Not until many citizens had departed from the community to settle elsewhere was the situation eased, and then it was too late; the community had lost its opportunity to prosper.

It seems ironic, therefore, that in 1835, some years after the mission lands were divided, the Coahuila-Texas Legislature granted ten sitios of pasture land on the opposite side of the Río Grande to the citizens of

[23] *Ibid.*
[24] See Carl Coke Rister, *Comanche Bondage: Beales' Settlement and Sarah Ann Horn's Narrative.*

Guerrero. The lands lay in front of Pacuache Crossing, on either side of "the road which leads to Béjar."[25]

Before this same session of the legislature came a leading Anglo-Texan in quest of land titles for settlers along the Red River. Benjamin Rush Milam was unfortunate, however, in his choice of companions on the return trip. He traveled with Agustín Viesca, new governor of Coahuila and Texas. Viesca, in defiance of an order of General Martín Perfecto de Cós, to move the state capital from Monclova back to Saltillo, was fleeing to San Antonio with plans temporarily to establish the capital there.

We left Monclova on the 29th of May, and were taken prisoners on the 5th of June, at night [Milam wrote one month later]. The troops had been watching our march all the last day, and knew the only chance we had to get water. They placed themselves in a position to take possession of our horses as soon as it was dusk.

In this situation we were obliged to surrender to twenty-five men—or savages as we may more properly call them. Captain Galán and Lieutenant Rodríguez commanded the party. They will be long remembered. . . .

We were taken to San Fernando, and kept in close confinement for one week. We were not permitted to write or speak to any person except in the presence of an officer, and then only in the Spanish language. From there we were taken to Río Grande, where we were treated somewhat better. From Río Grande we were brought to this place [Lampazos de la Punta, Nuevo León]. From here we expect to go to Monterrey to stand our trial. I hope to be set at liberty. But all is uncertainty.[26]

In the last ten days, Milam continued, two hundred troops had left Lampazos for San Antonio; two thousand more would be on the march within a few weeks, to make an alliance with the Indian tribes and incite the slaves to revolt. Texans, he asserted, must unite, adding prophetically, "The people of Texas will never submit to a dictator."[27]

While being moved toward Monterrey Milam escaped his captors and fled to Goliad. A few months later, he led a force to capture San Antonio

---

25 Alessio Robles, *Coahuila y Texas desde la consumación*, II, 15.

26 Milam to "Dear Jounson," quoted in Bolton and Barker, *Makers of Texas,* pp. 156–158. The capture was near Villa de Gigedo, hardly twenty-five miles from Guerrero.

27 *Ibid.,* p. 158.

from General Martín Perfecto de Cós, who had been sent to Béjar to arrest key rebels and subdue the population.[28] To the Texans' surprise Cós surrendered on the fourth day, but not until Ben Milam had fallen, the victim of a sniper's bullet, to become a martyr to the Texas Revolution.

Other valiant men soon would die on this famous battleground; the general-in-chief Santa Anna already was gathering his force at San Luis Potosí. He would see that his brother-in-law, Cós, the commander of the eastern Interior Provinces, did not keep his commitment to stay out of Texas. Already, at the Texas town of Gonzales—named for the former commander of Presidio del Río Grande—the first defiant shot had been fired from a brass cannon filled with scrap iron. The breach between the Texas colonists and the Mexican government no longer was conveniently reparable; it was easier to kill, and be killed, than to concede error.

The rôle of Villa de Guerrero in the coming conflict would be the same as it had always been: the gateway to Texas. For almost a century and a half the Río Grande settlement had received the caravans marching out for the region beyond the Great River, and those returning. Often its fields had been trampled by the droves of livestock going to serve new colonies in Texas. Many times had its buildings been over-run with visitors, its storerooms stripped to provision the passing hordes. But Villa de Guerrero—still more often called "Presidio" or "Río Grande"—had not yet seen such armies as would pass this way in the infancy of the fatal year 1836.

That it should be so is one of the truly dramatic circumstances of history.

General Antonio López de Santa Anna, now determined to drive all Americans from Texas, had as his first objective the capture of San Antonio de Béjar. He went to considerable pains to shuffle his troops in order to launch his campaign from the historic gateway. Could he have been striving for dramatic effect by sending out from the parent settlement the punishment for the errant child? Could he have had such knowledge or concern for history? Implausible as such questions may seem, he went to great lengths to follow the same trail used by Padre Olivares, when in 1718 he moved the Mission San Francisco Solano to the San Antonio

---

[28] Lon Tinkle, "The Alamo," in *Six Missions of Texas*, p. 20.

River. When the bugles blew that fateful March 6 his troops would storm the walls of Mission San Antonio de Valero. Or call it San Francisco Solano. Or the Alamo.

Historians have perpetuated much confusion concerning the movements of Santa Anna's forces as they marched to Béjar.[29] But there no longer remains a fragment of doubt that all the troops which took part in the assault on the Alamo marched from Guerrero.

Santa Anna began in October to marshal his troops for extinguishing revolutionary sparks in Texas. His second in command, Vicente Filisola, gathered various units at San Luis Potosí. General Joaquín Ramírez y Sesma, heading the First Infantry Division, marched for Laredo with detailed instructions from the *presidente* on December 7. General Filisola took up the march a day later, with orders to join the forces of Ramírez y Sesma and Cós on reaching Béjar. Filisola, reaching Lampazos on December 18, received the first news of the capitulation of General Cós at Béjar. He hurried on to overtake General Ramírez y Sesma the following day at the Río Salado. The river was up and had to be crossed in homemade boats. In the meantime Filisola communicated to General Santa Anna the news of Cós' capitulation. But the chief already had heard. Before Filisola could reach Laredo, he received a complete change of orders:

> The city of Béjar having fallen to the rebels, it becomes necessary to alter the march of this division. I therefore am preparing the order for you to proceed to the Villa de Guerrero, previously known as Presidio de Río Grande. It is necessary to keep the movements of this division secret until you receive further orders."[30]

In a reply from Laredo, Filisola sought to dissuade Santa Anna from his decision to make Villa de Guerrero the base of his operations. He of-

[29] E.g., Horgan (*Great River*, p. 527), Clarence R. Wharton (*El Presidente: A Sketch of the Life of General Santa Anna*, p. 50), and Carlos Eduardo Castañeda (*Our Catholic Heritage in Texas*, VI, 287) all state that Santa Anna's army crossed at Laredo on its way to assault the Alamo. Yet Castañeda (*The Mexican Side of the Texas Revolution, by the Chief Mexican Participants*, pp. 64–70, Santa Anna to the Ministry of War and Marine) stands in clear refutation of that error. The facts reviewed herein are extracted from Castañeda's translated documents in the last mentioned work and two other sources: Alessio Robles, *Coahuila y Texas desde la consumación*, II, and General M. A. Sánchez Lamego, "Storming the Alamo: A Mexican Version," *Dallas Morning News*, March 6, 1966, p. 26-A.

[30] Alessio Robles, *Coahuila y Texas desde la consumación*, II, 95. Alessio Robles terms this change of plan "absurd, unnecessary, and unwarranted."

fered Villa de Mier, in Tamaulipas, as being more advantageous from the standpoint of distances. But the chief's decision held. His detailed instructions crossed Filisola's note on the way: Cós was to return to Monclova; the troops of Filisola and Ramírez y Sesma were to proceed by way of Monclova, "to Villa de Guerrero, previously known as Presidio de Río Grande, with care that both movements be carried out without fail."[31] It was useless to argue.

A sectional force under General José Urrea, previously stationed at Guerrero, had been withdrawn to Saltillo, then directed to Matamoros to protect the port. Urrea was to enter the Texas fight by way of San Patricio, Refugio, and Goliad.

The First Infantry Division—to be known as the Advance Guard Brigade—arrived at Guerrero on January 10, 1836. The Second Infantry Division stood at Leona Vicario, ready to march for Monclova, on the way to the staging area at the old Presidio del Río Grande. Cós, camped at Lampazos, was getting ready to move on to Monclova, where he would join the main force. Many Mexican families had followed his retreat from Texas, and thirty-two men, women, and children died on the road between Laredo and the Río Salado.[32]

By February 15 the Army of Operations against Texas counted on an effective strength of more than 6,000 men and 21 cannons. The forces were made up of 4,473 foot soldiers, 1,024 horses, 182 gunners, 185 sappers, 60 presidial foot, and 95 presidial cavalry.

Santa Anna waxed impatient at the passage of time without visible sign of progress. Eager to get his force moving, he ordered the march before all his supplies were gathered in. Some contingents of troops were left behind, including engineer and hospital corps. The various segments of the old Second Infantry Division, now dispersed into separate brigades, marched hard for Monclova under force of the general-in-chief's gnawing impatience.

The forced marches took their toll; rest and reorganization were required at Monclova. On February 8 the First Infantry Brigade left that point for Guerrero. Other units followed at two-day intervals.

As the march progressed northward it turned into a nightmare. A se-

[31] *Ibid.*, p. 98.
[32] Sánchez Lamego, "Storming the Alamo"; Alessio Robles, *Coahuila y Texas desde la consumación,* II, 99.

vere blizzard struck on the thirteenth as the troop moved toward Hacienda de la Soledad. Snow fell heavily throughout the day, piling up on the road until the column could hardly move. Half-frozen soldiers trudged knee-deep through the drifts. Broken and abandoned vehicles, exhausted horses, and dying men marked the trail from Monclova to Presidio del Río Grande. But through the snow and the mud Santa Anna's troops slogged on, to San Juan de Sabinas, Charcos, San Juan de Allende, and Nava. Finally, on February 17, the first unit reached the old Presidio of the Río Grande.

Santa Anna himself had departed for the Río Grande ahead of his troops. Leaving Saltillo on February 1, he planned to overtake Ramírez y Sesma at Guerrero before the latter began his march to Béjar. He reached Guerrero on February 12, a day ahead of the snowstorm. Thus he missed the spectacle of his men, traveling on half rations of hardtack, falling fatigued beside the snowbanked trail and left to die, with no hospital or ambulance corps—or priest—to attend them.

The chief left Guerrero on the sixteenth, thereby depriving himself of seeing the miserable condition in which his troops arrived at Río Grande. He had shown utter disregard for the welfare of his men all the way. His secretary, Ramón Martínez Caro, later criticized him severely, accusing him of appropriating to his own use funds and provisions contributed for his army.

> The munitions wagons and gun carriages had to be used to carry the numerous patients. On more than one occasion, General Ampudia and I were obliged to put in the wagons . . . some of the dying wretches we found on the road. I remember particularly . . . a poor wretch whom we found, at the point of death, unable to move, loaded down with his gun and pack. We placed him in one of the wagons, but he expired before the day's journey was over. Of course, he, like many others, received no spiritual consolation.[33]

No supplies could be secured from Monclova to Río Grande, said Caro, nor from Río Grande to San Antonio.

> It should be kept in mind that before leaving Monclova His Excellency said that supplies would be found at Río Grande. No supplies were found there. The reader can imagine the horrible distress of the troops, confronted with the

---

[33] Castañeda, *The Mexican Side*, p. 100.

necessity of continuing the march over a distance of more than 100 leagues of desert to Béxar.[34]

General Ramírez y Sesma's Advance Guard Brigade, having rested at Guerrero more than a month, marched on the morning of February 15 down the village's Calle Real and out on the road to Paso de Francia and San Antonio de Béjar. Santa Anna remained behind one more day, writing to the Ministry of War and Marine. The supreme government, he suggested, should send him instructions on the policy he was to observe in dealing with the colonies "after order has been restored."[35] And he proceeded to dictate the instructions to be sent. Obviously, he anticipated a short and successful campaign. His prognosis was only half right.

On the sixteenth the General-in-Chief, his staff and the fifty mounted men of his escort, mostly from the Dolores Cavalry Regiment, rode to overtake Ramírez y Sesma.[36]

For days the citizens of Guerrero watched the bedraggled, miserable, and hungry soldiers trudging in from the south. The people of the small village did what they could to relieve this suffering, but their resources were nowhere near equal to feeding Santa Anna's thousands. The best Guerrero could do was to offer shelter from the weather in some of its vacant buildings, remnants of a more prosperous era.

Santa Anna came up with the Advance Guard Brigade on February 17 to the Nueces. The Texans had destroyed the bridge, and the Mexican soldiers were having to build another. The General-in-Chief ordered a forced march to Béjar, bent on taking the town by surprise the morning of February 22. A violent rainstorm broke over the column the twenty-first, completely inundating the roadless terrain, foiling the General's plans. Not until afternoon of February 23 did the Mexican force stand outside Béjar. The element of surprise had been lost; the Texans were fortified inside the Alamo walls.[37] From the convent tower the Texans flew their flag. It was the Mexican tricolor, with the date 1824 embroidered on the right side in place of the usual eagle and serpent emblem, signifying the colonists' loyalty to the Mexican constitution which had been overthrown by Santa Anna. Also embroidered on the white field were two stars, symbolizing the sister states of Coahuila and Texas.

---

[34] *Ibid.*, p. 100.   [35] *Ibid.*, p. 64.   [36] *Ibid.*, p. 101.
[37] Sánchez Lamego, "Storming the Alamo."

After personally reconnoitering the Alamo defenses, Santa Anna was convinced the Advance Guard was not sufficient for taking the position. He sent an urgent message to General Antonio Gaona to send forward by forced marches at least three battalions of his First Infantry Brigade. Gaona had left Presidio del Río Grande after a five-day rest and was marching toward Béjar fifty kilometers from Guerrero when he encountered Santa Anna's messenger. The following morning he dispatched the three battalions, which reached San Antonio on March 4.

Too much has been written of the events that followed for further review to be needed here. Santa Anna's bugles blew at the north battery at 5 A.M., March 6. The assault began, with General Cós commanding the first column. The silence of the still morning was shattered by the sound of death. By eight o'clock the bloody work was done. The Alamo defenders had perished to the man. Around their broken bodies lay hundreds of other brave men, clad in a different uniform—men who had held to a different creed, and spoken a different tongue; but brave men nonetheless.

The General Santa Anna, whom Texans forever after would call "butcher," proudly wrote: "Victory accompanies the Mexican Army, and at this moment, being 8 o'clock in the morning, it achieved the most complete and glorious one that will perpetuate its memory."[38]

Victory? Yes, but a dear one.

"I could well say," commented one of the Generalisimo's officers later, "with another victory like this, the devil takes us."[39]

Santa Anna wrote of the occasion as one which would perpetuate a memory. In such a prophecy Texans would gladly oblige, as they took up the cry, "Remember the Alamo."

For after the Alamo came San Jacinto.

[38] *Ibid.*
[39] *Ibid.*

36. DECADE OF THE REPUBLIC

W ITH TEXAS INDEPENDENCE, won April 21, 1836, by the rout of
Santa Anna's forces at San Jacinto, the role of Guerrero changed
again. It suddenly became an outpost on an international border. Texas
had two frontiers to guard: the Indian frontier, stretching from the Red
River southward 500 miles to the Río Grande, and the Mexican frontier, reaching from the vicinity of Presidio del Río Grande to the mouth
of the Great River, a distance of 325 miles. Texas claimed the Río
Grande as its boundary with México. Despite this claim, ". . . the area between the Nueces and the Río Grande . . . was after 1835 virtually a no
man's land over which for nearly a decade a predatory and guerrillalike
warfare was waged between Mexicans and Texans."[1] As an outpost on
the border, Guerrero, which of necessity kept a garrison of soldiers, was
constantly embroiled in international incidents.

The people of Presidio del Río Grande, long accustomed to finding a
market for their produce at San Antonio de Béjar, quickly sought to re-
open those trade lines. A number of different parties of traders from the
old gateway settlement appeared at San Antonio in June, 1838. They
brought horses and mules, flour, beans, and other produce. Among the
trading groups were some former residents of Béjar, who evidently had
retreated to the other side of the Río Grande during the Texan uprising.
Some of these remained when the rest of the traders returned to their
homes in northern México.[2] Other traders soon came, and several from
Béjar made profitable trips to Laredo and Villa de Guerrero.

This friendly commerce soon was interrupted, however, by the antics of
troublemakers, of which both Texas and México at this stage seemed to

---

[1] Joseph Milton Nance, *After San Jacinto: The Texas-Mexican Frontier, 1836–
1841*, pp. 3–4.
[2] *Ibid.*, p. 82.

have more than they needed. One of the first to create difficulty was Vicente Córdova. He incited the Cherokee, Kickapoo, and Caddo Indians in East Texas to defiance of authority. Colonel Edward Burleson led a company of seventy-nine volunteers in pursuit of Córdova's combined Indian-Mexican force and overtook it on the Guadalupe. Córdova lost thirty men killed, about half his force. The remainder fled westward from San Antonio, toward Presidio del Río Grande. A company of rangers under Colonel Matthew Caldwell of Gonzales, augmented by volunteers, took up the pursuit and followed as far as the Frío River.[3]

Not long after the separation of Texas, some Mexican military leaders rose in rebellion against the Centralist Mexican government of Santa Anna. The first was General José Urrea, who, like the Texans he had fought in 1836, stood in favor of the Federalist constitution of 1824. And like the Texans, when they failed to make headway toward restoration of the Federalist constitution, the new insurgents sought to form a separate republic. General Antonio Canales took the lead in creating the Republic of the Río Grande, made up of the north Mexican states. In his Republic, Canales sought to include that part of Texas between the Nueces and the Río Grande.

The fortunes of the Federalists see-sawed back and forth until, in the closing months of 1839, the Centralists emerged the temporary victor. "In August, Guerrero, Nava, Morelos, San Fernando de Rosas, and Presidio del Río Grande were retaken or renounced Federalism. . . . After an eleven months' campaign . . . only a few petty rebel leaders—Canales, Anaya, and Zapata—had not surrendered, but had fled to the other side of the Río Bravo."[4]

Canales fled from San Fernando de Rosas with a companion named Carlos Lazo. They likely skirted Presidio del Río Grande to avoid apprehension by the Centralists and headed up the Camino Real to San Antonio. In Frío River country they found six hundred Comanche warriors encamped a short distance from the road, reportedly with orders from the

---

[3] *Ibid.,* pp. 123–130.

[4] *Ibid.,* p. 170. Nance consistently refers to Guerrero, Coahuila, as "Presidio del Río Grande." The Guerrero he mentions usually refers to that in Tamaulipas, but one might surmise in this instance that it refers to Guerrero, Coahuila, near the other villages listed, though no distinction is made.

Centralist commander at Matamoros to intercept all trade between Guerrero and Béjar.

Canales found the Texas government cool to the idea of a Republic of the Río Grande which would include territory on Texas' side of the river. He returned to México, with a number of volunteer Texans, and took up the fight with the Centralists in Nuevo León. Another Federalist leader, Francisco Vidaurri, meanwhile, fought the Centralists on the doorstep of Presidio del Río Grande, at Peyotes, before being soundly defeated at Villa de Gigedo on January 7, 1840.

Downriver, Canales crossed to the east bank of the Río Grande. Proceeding upstream from Mier, he called a convention of delegates to organize the Republic of the Río Grande, comprising the states of Tamaulipas, Nuevo León, and Coahuila, and that portion of Texas lying below the Nueces. The delegates met January 18 near present Zapata and organized a provisional government based on the constitution of 1824.

At Guerrero, Tamaulipas, on February 18, Canales received word that General Mariano Arista was advancing on him with a Centralist force. He immediately took up the march for Presidio del Río Grande, arriving there March 3. He entered the town without opposition. At "Presidio"—Guerrero, Coahuila—the seventy-four Texans in the Federalist army proposed that Canales establish his headquarters on the Nueces, where there would be a better opportunity to recruit Texans. Canales spurned the suggestion, and sixty of the Texans, commanded by Colonel Samuel W. Jordan, left to return to their homes. Canales departed from Presidio del Río Grande on March 15 and took a position at San Fernando de Rosas (present Zaragoza).

Canales had sent Colonel Antonio Zapata and thirty men, including twelve Anglo-Texans, to nearby Morelos to obtain corn and other supplies. This detachment fell into a Centralist trap and was captured March 24 in a surprise attack by Captain Juan Galán, with six men killed. Assisting Galán in the attack were "eighty-eight of his best horsemen from the presidials of Río Grande and Lampazos."[5]

General Arista, meanwhile, had advanced his main force to Peyotes, seven leagues from Morelos. Canales moved from San Fernando on word

[5] *Ibid.,* p. 260.

of Zapata's capture, hoping to free him, and met Arista's vanguard under General Isidro Reyes. Arista brought up the rest of his men, and the two forces squared off in front of Morelos, where the Federalists were protected by a grove of chaparral and two irrigation ditches. The Centralists had the advantage of numbers, thirteen hundred to four hundred, and though Canales' grape and canister took a bloody toll, the Federalists at last were put to rout. Canales himself barely escaped capture.

The real losers were Zapata and the twenty-two men captured with him. They had been caught with arms in hand, resisting troops of the supreme government, and had enlisted Texans, enemies of México, to fight on their side. Texans and Mexicans alike were tried by court martial and convicted of treason against the Republic of México. At 10 A.M. on March 29 they were executed at Morelos. Zapata's head was taken to Guerrero (Tamaulipas), where it was placed on a pike in the plaza to serve as a warning to all those who would follow after him.

Canales and the remnants of his force again fled into Texas. He finally capitulated in a meeting with Arista at Camargo, November 6, 1840, and was taken into the Centralist army as an officer—somewhat more liberal treatment than that accorded the Texan rebels.

Juan N. Seguín returned to San Antonio from his recent participation in the Federalist campaign and reported on rumored Mexican plans for an invasion of Texas. He said he had learned from a conversation with General Arista that the Mexicans could muster immediately between five and six thousand armed men, and that troops already were arranged along the Río Grande. Included were three hundred infantry and two hundred cavalry at Presidio del Río Grande.[6]

Border skirmishes were the order of the times. In the spring of 1841 a force under one Calixto Bravo is said to have left Presidio del Río Grande in pursuit of a party under Antonio Parez from San Antonio. Early in May, Bravo's force of one hundred to two hundred men intercepted a convoy of traders from San Antonio and robbed their caravan.

Trade, nevertheless, continued between Béjar and Guerrero, and other Mexican communities along the Río Grande. The comings and goings at the time-honored gateway during the decade of the Republic of Texas

[6] *Ibid.,* pp. 388–389. This incident gave rise to the beginning of Texan mistrust of Seguín, who is discussed further in Chapter 37 of this study.

were as pegs on which the entire fabric of Texas-Mexican history for that period could be hung.

In 1841 animosity between Texas and its mother country suffered anew from the Texan Santa Fé Expedition. The Mexicans saw in the Texan effort to exert its claim on Santa Fé a new territorial grab by the land-hungry gringos; they arrested the interlopers and bore them southward to prison in México and at Perote Castle. Texans generally viewed the imprisonment as another infamous example of Mexican tyranny. They talked brashly of invading México, and rumors came up from the Río Grande that Mexican forces were preparing for an invasion of Texas. San Antonians elected John C. Hays, a renowned Indian fighter, to lead them in defense against the Mexican invaders.

The Bexar County Committee of Safety, on February 21, 1842, sent two San Antonio Mexicans on the road to Presidio del Río Grande and San Fernando de Rosas to seek information on the coming invasion. The spies failed to reach Río Grande, however, as they were intercepted just beyond the Nueces by Agatón Quiñones, celebrated bandit of Río Grande. Quiñones said he had orders to prevent all communication between Río Grande and San Antonio. He held the two men one day and turned them back to San Antonio on February 26. Two more men were sent, and they, too, were captured. All Anglo-Texans not absolutely needed for defense of the town, meanwhile, fled eastward. A Texan scouting party was fired upon the night of March 4, four miles west of San Antonio, and next morning the Mexican General Rafael Vásquez was before San Antonio, having come up from Lampazos by way of Laredo. The small Texan force, being no match for the five to seven hundred Mexicans, withdrew and left the invaders to the looting of the town. Two days later, on March 7, the Mexicans departed, taking with them all the valuables of San Antonio. The retreating forces, accompanied by some of the San Antonio Mexicans, carried off 132 muleloads of plunder and appropriated all the available carts and wagons they could find in which to carry their loot.[7] Vásquez, with his long caravan of plundered goods, crossed the old ford and led his procession up the Calle Real of Guerrero on March 15. Captain Hays led a small force in pursuit but lacked sufficient strength to make an attack.

[7] Joseph Milton Nance, *Attack and Counterattack: The Texas-Mexican Frontier, 1842*, pp. 47–49.

All in all, the invasion was but a preliminary to the main event sched-
uled some months later.

On June 5, 1842, General Isidro Reyes was instructed by President
Santa Anna to prepare for another attack on San Antonio. To carry out
the maneuver was the brigade of General Adrian Woll, the French soldier
of fortune who had staked his career on Santa Anna's. Woll assembled his
army at Presidio del Río Grande, which furnished fifty-two soldiers under
Captain D. Manuel Flores and ninety-two horses for the campaign. On
August 24 the force marched out of the presidio for the river. Next day
the first of his dragoons began crossing at "Paso de Nogal" in two small
canoes.

It required from the 25th through the 30th—six days—for General Woll
to cross his army, which, according to the report of his quartermaster, Colonel
José María Carrasco, consisted of 957 men, 12 wagons loaded with corn, 150
loads of provisions, 50 or more head of cattle, 2 pieces of artillery and an
artillery train, 919 horses, and 213 mules.[8]

On the thirtieth Woll and his division chiefs crossed and inspected the
troops. In addressing the soldiers, Woll said, ". . . victory will crown your
heroic efforts and a generous country will reward your worthiness."[9] He
neglected to mention that the death penalty awaited those who might
desert.

Next morning General Reyes himself, now commander-in-chief of the
Army of the North, moved with Woll to the head of the line and read a
proclamation, charging the troops to use the name *Santa Anna* as their
battle cry: "This name, magic to Mexicans, will augment your military
valor."[10] Then Reyes returned to the right bank of the Río Grande.
Woll's army marched for San Antonio by a route which lay twenty miles
to the north of the Upper Presidio Road.

This maneuver was designed to take the town by surprise, though it

---

[8] *Ibid.*, p. 311. Paso de Nogal evidently is the same as Pacuache Crossing, six
miles upstream from Paso de Francia. Josiah Gregg (*Diary & Letters of Josiah
Gregg: Southwestern Enterprises, 1840–1847*, I, 256) says, "He started north, that
it might be believed he was going against the Comanches, and then descended
upon San Antonio." While Paso de Francia probably was under surveillance of
Texan scouts, Paso de Nogal, or Paso Pacuache, evidently was not.

[9] Nance, *Attack and Counterattack*, p. 312.

[10] *Ibid.*, p. 312.

fell short of complete success. Nevertheless, Woll formed a tight ring about San Antonio the night of September 10, closing all roads. Vicente Córdova and his Cherokees guarded the streets leading to the Alamo. Completing the arrangement by midnight, the troops rested upon their arms, awaiting the firing of a cannon, which would be the signal to enter the town and seize the Main Plaza.

At 4:30 A.M. the Texans sounded reveille. Woll mistook the signal, ordered the cannon fired, and brought the fog-shrouded city to life. Texans poured forth from their homes and headed for Maverick's corner, Commerce and Soledad streets, where Johnson's Company was fortifying itself inside the home of Samuel Maverick.[11]

Woll's infantry, supported by two pieces of artillery, concentrated fire upon Maverick's corner in an effort to take the plaza, but the Texans' fire, from the flat roof of the Maverick home, was withering. As the Mexicans were thrown into disorder and withdrew, they left two dead and twenty-six wounded in the plaza, according to one source, which says six of the wounded later died.[12]

The triumph of the Texans was short-lived; soon they surrendered under Woll's threat that an army of two thousand (actually about 1,300) of which his force was but the vanguard, would destroy the defenders completely. Woll took sixty-two prisoners; ten later were released, because of youth or promise of future loyalty to México. Among the captives were the district judge, Anderson Hutchinson; James W. Robinson, former lieutenant governor of the Republic of Texas; C. W. Peterson, district attorney; French S. Gray, assistant district attorney; William E. Jones, lawyer and member of Congress; Samuel A. Maverick, lawyer, land speculator, and member of Congress; Andrew Neill, lawyer; James L. Trueheart, district clerk; and David Morgan, interpreter for the district court. "The capture of these men put an end to civil government in San Antonio for eighteen months."[13]

[11] Ibid., p. 318. Rena Maverick Green, *Samuel Maverick, Texan, 1803–1870,* p. 164.

[12] Green, *Samuel Maverick,* p. 164. Nance (*Attack and Counterattack,* pp. 324–325) points out wide variation in Texan reports of Mexican casualties. Woll claimed only one soldier and one musician dead, twenty wounded (Joseph Milton Nance [trans. and ed.], "Brigadier General Adrian Woll's Report on His Expedition into Texas in 1842," *SWHQ,* 58, No. 4 [April, 1955], 526).

[13] Nance, *Attack and Counterattack,* p. 323.

The prisoners were kept under guard in the Maverick house until September 15, then departed from San Antonio under guard of 125 men commanded by Captain Emeterio Posas. The wounded from the fight on Main Plaza were carried on carts. Some of the Texans were permitted to ride their own horses, while others were forced to trade for inferior mounts. One of the fifty-two, J. R. Cunningham, died of a fever en route after Captain Posas had denied the two physicians among the prisoners permission to treat him. He was left in a shallow grave on the west bank of the Leona River, near the Woll road.

Dr. Shields Booker, a few days later, was permitted to treat a Mexican soldier bitten by a rattlesnake, which he was attempting to capture alive (by walking up on its tail) on a bet with one of the officers. The physician lanced the wound and undoubtedly saved the man's life. At least he "got better in a few days."[14]

Eight days after leaving San Antonio on September 23, the prisoners and their escort crossed the Río Grande at the place where Woll had crossed. Maverick's diary entry for the day was as follows:

Crossed the Río Grande in two canoes. Horses made to swim; three or four drowned. Men astonishing swimmers. River here at the upper crossing at Lone Pecan (on east side) [Paso de Nogal or Pacuache Crossing] is about 350 yards wide. Kinto's ranch in sight above. Camped in sheep fold. 10 miles.[15]

At the sheep pen, the prisoners learned for the first time of the death of Cunningham. Next day they were permitted to bathe in the river, then marched six miles to Presidio del Río Grande. The prisoners rested until the twenty-seventh, quartered in an old house fronting the *plaza de armas.* A date on the structure indicated 1776 as the year of its building. The guard which brought the prisoners was ordered back across the Río Grande to meet Woll, but on arriving at the river the soldiers learned that the main force stood a short distance away. They returned to Presidio del Río Grande.

Viewing the old presidial town through unaccustomed eyes, several of the Texans recorded their impressions. To Trueheart it appeared as "a poor miserable place in fast decay."[16] In his succinct description Maverick

---

[14] *Ibid.,* p. 332, citing Maverick diary.
[15] Green, *Samuel Maverick,* p. 176.
[16] Nance, *Attack and Counterattack,* p. 332.

observed that the water was salty and unfit for drinking, the town old, the population "villainous." Sheep and cattle surrounded "the old mission east of town"—Friar Diego Jiménez' unfinished San Bernardo Church, actually more north than east of the village. Maverick estimated the population at one thousand. Good farm lands lay around the village, almost all the way to San Fernando de Rosas.

"Sept. 27th. Passed through rich irrigable prairie all the way to Nava, before reaching which we saw thousands of acres of corn without fence. Soldiers say the land is public." Maverick was more favorably impressed with the populace of Nava, twenty-six miles from Guerrero, referring to "the kind, hospitable people."[17]

At San Fernando de Rosas, some thirty-five miles northwest from Presidio del Río Grande, the march of the prisoners was halted September 28 for several days. On October 4 the San Antonio prisoners were joined there by ten of the Dawson captives. Both groups started toward the capital on October 7.

The story of Nicholas Mosby Dawson's men forms a sequel to that of the fifty-two men taken by Woll at the Maverick home in San Antonio. When news of Woll's invasion reached him at La Grange, Dawson assembled a group of men to reinforce Matthew Caldwell's men from Gonzales and left La Grange on September 16. Two days later scouts returned with news that a battle already was in progress (Battle of Salado). Dawson, marching his fifty-three men toward the Salado River, was discovered by Mexican cavalry a mile and a half short of the battle. As the Texans took cover in a mesquite grove, the Mexicans withdrew from rifle range and brought up two pieces of artillery with which they fired upon the Texas position, killing thirty-five men, including Dawson. Fifteen were captured, among them five wounded. They were marched after the San Antonio prisoners.[18]

In the main engagement the Texans fared somewhat better, losing only one killed and nine wounded. Late in the afternoon Woll retreated from

---

[17] Green, *Samuel Maverick*, p. 176. Nance (*Attack and Counterattack*, p. 332) refers to Nava as being "near the old Spanish mission of San Juan Bautista," an example of the mislocation by many Texas historians of this site which played such an important part in Texas history.

[18] Walter Prescott Webb and H. Bailey Carroll (eds.), *Handbook of Texas*, I, 474. See Nance, *Attack and Counterattack*, pp. 364–381.

the Salado back to San Antonio, having lost sixty killed and a number of wounded. He retired from San Antonio on September 21, marching back toward Presidio del Río Grande. Some two hundred Mexican families who had espoused the Mexican cause left under Woll's protection. It was they who had plundered San Antonio, loading 150 carts with their loot, driving five hundred head of cattle before them.

A Texan force pursued the Mexicans and captured a cannon at the Hondo River. Then an argument between Colonels Matthew Caldwell and John H. Moore over who should lead the troops into battle gave time for the Mexicans to recover; the Texans lost their advantage.

Ten days after leaving San Antonio, Woll's force came on September 29 to the banks of the Río Grande. At ten o'clock the morning of October 1 the army entered Presidio del Río Grande, with its large numbers of stolen Texan livestock and the two hundred families from Béjar, their carts creaking under the heavy loads of stolen goods.

As Woll drew near to Presidio del Río Grande, it is said, General Reyes induced the citizens to form a procession, going out to meet him and accord him the honors of victory. Reyes himself went forth in a garlanded carriage. "Great was the disappointment of the populace when they found the troops all worn down with fatigue and completely dispirited."[19]

The returning general quickly silenced the feeble exclamations which followed, informing Reyes bluntly that there was no cause for rejoicing; his army had won no plaudits by its performance in Texas. Yet to his soldiers he expressed himself differently: "You are returning covered with glory. . . . You have shown yourselves worthy sons of México."[20]

While the able-bodied Dawson prisoners proceeded on to San Fernando de Rosas, where they joined the San Antonio captives, the wounded men remained under guard at Presidio del Río Grande. After two months they grew restive and began to plot their escape, encouraged by a Frenchman, who told them that the Río Grande was low and could be easily crossed. The four men, Milvern Harrell and his uncle Norman Woods, W. D. Patterson, and John MacCredae, decided to act. They had noticed that their soldier guards spent a great deal of time at cards, and it ap-

---

[19] Nance, *Attack and Counterattack*, p. 404.
[20] *Ibid.*, p. 404.

peared their guns were not loaded. On a bright moonlight night the Dawson men made their move.

After the guard had passed the door of the house which served as their jail, the prisoners darted from the building and ran toward the river, stumbling and falling on the rocky ground. Woods, not fully recovered from his wounds, was quickly recaptured. To elude their pursuers the other three avoided the closest ford and traveled upstream ten or twelve miles. At daylight they came at last to the bank of the Río Grande. At a place where the river narrowed they plunged in and started to swim across, Patterson leading the way.

The water was icy cold, and the men were weak from having been confined so long. Only a short distance from shore MacCredae called out that he could go no farther and sank in the deep river. On nearing the Texas bank the other two men got into swift water and were carried rapidly downstream. Then Patterson uttered a cry and sank beneath the raging current. Harrell was left alone, fighting his way for the Texas shore.

By this time I was completely exhausted and was helpless in the current. Thinking every second would be my last, I was suddenly washed upon a rock in the river, and carried high upon it, the water being only about six inches over its surface. . . . It was sleeting now, and I was almost frozen. I decided that I could not reach the Texas side, and knowing that I would freeze where I was, I went back to the Mexican side of the river.[21]

Back on the Mexican side, Harrell ran up and down the smooth beach to restore warmth to his body. Then, mounting a hill to get his bearings, he saw a house in the distance and went toward it. A Mexican man whom Harrell had known in San Antonio came out to meet him, covered his still-shivering form with his coat, and took the Texan inside to a bright fire and a pot of hot coffee brought by the Mexican's wife.

Warmed by the fire and the coffee, Harrell was overcome by drowsiness and asked for a bed. He slept from seven o'clock in the morning till early afternoon—and awoke to find four Mexican soldiers standing over him. They carried him back to Presidio del Río Grande, and then on south to

---

[21] *Ibid.*, p. 405, citing Milvern Harrell's account in the *Dallas Morning News,* June 16, 1907.

join the other Dawson prisoners, and those from San Antonio and Mier, on the way south to Perote's dungeons.[22]

Aroused Texans, meanwhile, plotted retaliation for the predatory raids made by the Mexicans during the year 1842. President Sam Houston appointed Alexander Somervell to organize militia and volunteers and to invade Mexico if the strength of the army was sufficient to indicate a reasonable hope of success. In November, Somervell's spies in Coahuila informed him that there were no troops at Presidio del Río Grande, though eight hundred men under Reyes stood at San Fernando de Rosas, and another two hundred under Vásquez at Santa Rita de Morelos. No other troops were nearer than Monterrey, it was reported. The spies also told of an abundance of provisions in the vicinity of the presidio at Guerrero—a rather strange report, considering the many marches that had passed through. San Fernando was indicated as a likely target for the Texan attack. As word of the impending movement reached the Río Grande, it was Guerrero's turn to suffer invasion jitters. Some of Woll's prisoners were sought out by Mexican officers and soldiers when they received news that Somervell was advancing toward Presidio del Río Grande. The Mexicans wanted "to know how they should surrender and what to say to the Texians to save their lives."[23]

But the smallness of the Texan army saved the Coahuila points from attack. When the time came Somervell marched his 750 men out of San Antonio on the old Presidio Road. This move, however, was only for the benefit of the Mexican spies harbored in San Antonio. The Texan force soon turned south to strike the road to Laredo. After taking that border town, Somervell led his troops on to capture Guerrero, Tamaulipas. But the Texans were in a precarious position, and their leader recognized the

[22] Perote Castle, in the Mexican state of Veracruz, was built between 1770 and 1775 to guard one of the main Spanish trade routes and to serve as a depository for treasure awaiting shipment to Spain. On a twenty-six–acre plot surrounded by a moat the castle was used by the Mexican government as a prison. Most of the Texas prisoners captured by México during the decade of the Republic of Texas were imprisoned there. The captives of the Texan Santa Fé Expedition had spent the winter of 1841–1842 in Perote's dungeons before their release in the spring of 1842. "Accurate records on the number who escaped, who were released through influence of friends, who died from disease, starvation or exposure, and who were killed by Mexican guards are not available" (Webb and Carroll (eds.), *Handbook*, II, 362–363).

[23] Nance, *Attack and Counterattack*, p. 474 n.

fact. When Somervell ordered his force to disband, some 308 men refused to comply. They continued on down the Río Grande on what became known as the Mier Expedition. It was the most disastrous of all the campaigns the Texans made into the area below the Nueces. These headstrong patriots swelled the ranks of the martyrs to the Texan cause in the famous Black Bean Episode and increased the Anglo population of Perote's dungeons.

The attacks on San Antonio in 1842—one of which was launched from, the other returning to, the old mission settlement of San Juan Bautista del Río Grande—did not constitute a renewal of the Mexican effort to subjugate Texas. Nor did the retaliatory strokes on other Texas towns during the decade of the Republic.

The seizure of Goliad, Refugio, and San Antonio must be regarded as a warning to persons outside Texas that México still considered Texas a part of the Mexican nation over which she expected to restore her authority. It was a warning to Texans that they could expect retaliation for any aggression beyond the ancient boundaries of the province of Texas, and that México would condone neither smuggling from Texas nor the extension of Anglo-American settlements beyond the Nueces.[24]

And they served as a warning to the United States that any attempt to annex Texas would constitute "an unfriendly act." Such an admonition, however, could only delay, not prevent, Texas from entering the Union. On British advice the government of México agreed to recognize Texas independence on condition that she not annex herself to another country. In the face of this offer both the Texas Congress and a convention called into session by President Anson Jones voted in favor of annexation. A state constitution was adopted in October, 1845, and approved by the United States Congress on December 29, 1845, date of Texas' legal entry into the Union. Transfer of authority from the Republic to the state was completed February 16, 1846.

[24] *Ibid.*, p. 579.

37. ARMY OF CHIHUAHUA

N O LONGER could the area between the Nueces and the Río Grande remain a "no man's land." The boundary question must be settled. The die was cast as General Zachary Taylor, moving United States troops into the disputed territory, clashed with the forces of Mexican General Mariano Arista, April 25, 1846, in a skirmish near Matamoros. Then, as Taylor advanced into México, Antonio López de Santa Anna accepted appointment as commander-in-chief of "the Liberating Army" to drive the North Americans from Mexican territory.

The North American strategy called for sending one column to take over New Mexico, another to secure control of California, Taylor to march on Monterrey, and still another force to seize Chihuahua.

This latter assignment fell the lot of Brigadier General John E. Wool, sixty-two–year–old martinet and a stickler for detail, who won such nicknames from his troops as "Old Granny Wool." In June, 1846, Wool was ordered to San Antonio to assemble his Army of Chihuahua, preparatory to a march on Presidio del Río Grande to make his entry into enemy-held territory. Before Wool reached San Antonio, however, another regular Army officer proceeded to the historic gateway. Lieutenant Colonel William Selby Harney, in command of six companies of the Second Dragoons, had been assigned to San Antonio to protect the town from Indians. Spurred by rumors of troop concentrations at Presidio del Río Grande, Harney called for volunteers. With some seven hundred who signed up and three of his six dragoon companies, he marched out for the Río Grande.

Reaching San Antonio with the Arkansas Volunteers a short time after Harney's departure was Dr. Josiah Gregg, who had signed on as a civilian government agent—a guide and interpreter. Gregg, who marveled that

Harney's behavior did not win him a court martial, brings us the story of this unauthorized expedition.[1]

As Harney's force approached the river, the two hundred soldiers stationed at Presidio del Río Grande evacuated and fled southward. Harney, with no way of knowing what kind of reception he would receive on the other side, plunged his troops into the swollen stream, running some four hundred yards wide. One man gave out before he reached the other side and drowned. By Gregg's account others were on the verge of being swept under by the swift waters when Mexican citizens from Guerrero came to their rescue, plunging into the water to help retrieve the near-drowning men. Had even a few armed men fallen upon the hapless Americans at this stage, Gregg theorized, the American force would have been cut to pieces.

When the waters of the river receded, a messenger reached Guerrero from General Wool ordering Harney to return to San Antonio. Harney withdrew, leaving three companies behind to guard the provisions he had collected at Guerrero. On receiving word of the withdrawal of the main force, the Mexican troops returned. The small American force panicked, fired the storehouses, and fled back to Texas. The American camp was established on the left bank, and eight men were engaged in crossing supplies for the return trip when the Mexican soldiers came up on the Mexican side of the river. The eight men plunged into the stream and swam for the Texas bank, but three never made it, "either killed or drowned, as was believed." The Mexicans continued to fire across the river at the American camp. A stray bullet killed a mule, "and others wounded."[2]

The Mexicans made the most of the incident. Americans had been repulsed from Mexican soil! Great and heroic, their accounts soon were saying, was the victory. Word went out to Texas that preparations were being made for a formidable resistance to any further attempts to invade México at that point.

It was an interesting array of personages indeed who gathered in San Antonio that summer of 1846, forming themselves into the Army of

[1] Josiah Gregg, *Diary & Letters of Josiah Gregg: Southwestern Enterprises, 1840–1847,* edited by Maurice Garland Fulton, I, 222.

[2] *Ibid.,* p. 223. Gregg learned differently later, however.

Chihuahua and preparing for the march to Presidio del Río Grande. In almost any American military unit in the Mexican War might be found men who would rise to prominence on one side or the other in the nation's coming civil conflict—men whose future relationship with each other, fortunately, could not be foreseen. Wool's Army of Chihuahua was no exception.

In the Arkansas Volunteers, for example, both Lieutenant Colonel John S. Roane and Captain Albert Pike, a company officer serving under him, would serve the Confederacy as brigadier generals in the Trans-Mississippi. Enmities carried over from the Mexican War would cause them to engage in a farce of a duel in which neither was hurt. Pike, who made treaties for the Confederacy with the five civilized tribes and for a time commanded the Department of the Indian Territory, later was falsely accused of disloyalty. It fell the lot of Roane, not unhappily, to issue orders for Pike's arrest.[3]

But future fame considered, Roane and Pike were the lesser lights. There was an engineering officer, twenty-one years in the service and now nearing his fortieth year, who had yet to march into battle. The soft-spoken Virginian rode into the "quaint border town" of San Antonio and reported to General John E. Wool. Wool had met the officer previously on an inspection trip to Fort Monroe. He recognized him as Captain Robert E. Lee.[4]

Among the line officers at San Antonio, Lee found a number of West Pointers, some of whom served in his own corps or in the affiliated topographical engineers. To this latter branch belonged a young second lieutenant named William B. Franklin, who was busily making arrangements to go ahead to the Río Grande with Captain George W. Hughes to lay out a road for the main army. "Sixteen years later, almost to the very day, that same Franklin was to be in command of some very troublesome troops at a place called Crampton's Gap, in South Mountain, Maryland."[5]

Another young officer of whom Captain Lee heard much in San Antonio was an aide-de-camp of General Wool, named Irvin McDowell, first lieutenant of artillery. McDowell was absent from the command at

---

[3] Regarding the duel see Fred W. Allsopp, *Albert Pike: A Biography,* pp. 130–135.
[4] Douglas Southall Freeman, *R. E. Lee: A Biography,* I, 204.
[5] *Ibid.,* p. 205.

the time, but Lee had ample reason in later years to recall his earlier reputation. It was McDowell's threatened march on Richmond from the north
which had to be taken into account when Lee assumed command in front
of the Confederate capital, June 1, 1862.

Lee was assigned to work with Captain William D. Fraser of the Corps
of Engineers, his first duty being to assist in collection of tools for road
and bridge building. Two days after Lee's arrival, while he was still
searching for the needed tools, the topographical engineers set out to find
the best road for Wool's advance. Captain Hughes and three other officers, including young Franklin, rode out of Béjar on September 26 to
overtake their wagons that had gone on ahead.[6]

On Saturday, September 28, about half the Army of Chihuahua
marched for Presidio del Río Grande. Included were six companies of the
Arkansas Volunteers under Colonel Archibald Yell (four companies remaining in San Antonio under Major Solon Borland), four companies of
Illinois Infantry, and two of regular infantry, two companies of Second
Dragoons, and one company of flying artillery—about fifteen hundred
men in all, under command of Colonel Harney.[7]

General Wool, with aides, part of his staff, and a guard of two companies of the First Dragoons, departed September 29. For Lee it was the
first time he had ever ridden with troops against the enemy. The march
followed the route General Adrian Woll had taken in 1842 in making his
surprise attack on San Antonio. Woll had taken the northern route to
avoid detection by Texan spies. Wool took it for a different reason: to
cross the rivers nearer their sources, where they were smaller, thereby
avoiding old crossings which had become silted up.

On orders from General Wool, Gregg rode ahead September 30 with
an order for Colonel Harney to delay his march until the General's party
overtook him. Gregg reached Harney on the Sabinal River, where he remained in camp October 1. Wool's party arrived about noon. The united
force marched on together to the Río Grande.

Eleven days of marching, excluding the day Harney's force was halted
on the Sabinal, brought the Army of Chihuahua to the bank of the international stream, a mile or more below Pacuache Crossing, northeast of
Presidio del Río Grande. One observer attributed the rapidity of the

[6] *Ibid.*, pp. 205–206.
[7] Gregg, *Diary,* I, 233–234; Freeman, *Lee,* I, 206.

march to "the indefatigable exertions of those distinguished officers,"
Captains Lee and Fraser, who built a road and bridged the streams.[8] Camp
was made on the left bank, the main force to remain here until a suitable
campsite was located near the presidio.

At least two men with the expedition recorded their observations of
Presidio del Río Grande, the historic gateway of San Juan Bautista. One
of these was Gregg; the other was Captain George W. Hughes of the
topographical engineers. The two diarists probably crossed the river at the
same time, a day after the arrival at the river, though there is a one-day
discrepancy in dates given. They went with two companies of the Second
Dragoons under Colonel Harney about ten o'clock in the morning to
enter the presidio five miles from the river. The crossing was not the
daring venture which it may at first appear. The evening before, the pre-
fect and the alcalde had come out to meet Wool's column under a flag of
truce. They brought the General the first news he had received of General
Taylor's victory in Monterrey. In view of the circumstances they made offers of submission and gave expressions of friendship. The small force
which entered the Presidio del Río Grande on the morning of Friday,
October 9, therefore, did so with little feeling of apprehension.

Until four days before the arrival of the United States Army of Chihuahua, Colonel Francisco Castañeda had occupied Guerrero with something more than two hundred men.

> The people of the town appeared well pleased at our entrance [wrote
> Gregg], and continued to treat us with great friendship and hospitality; not
> only on account of their natural temperaments, perhaps, but for fear of our
> army: yet it is pleasing to state that no important outrages were committed
> upon them or their property by our troops.[9]

Gregg found the town of Guerrero—still better known to the Americans as Presidio del Río Grande—a place of more importance than he had
imagined. He estimated the permanent population at two thousand persons, though the town now appeared desolate and evacuated, half the
population having fled at the approach of the American force.

> There are many large stone houses, pretty well finished originally, yet now
> rather dilapidated. It is said to be as old or older than San Antonio. There is

8 Freeman, *Lee,* I, 207.   9 Gregg, *Diary,* I, 257.

an old mission building [San Bernardo Church] in the suburbs, but now gone nearly to ruins—coarse architecture. The town and farms are watered from a small stream of sulphurous and brackish water leading to Río Grande. The productions are Indian corn and sugar, chiefly,—though they only make coarse cake sugar here. But few fruits, except figs—some quinces and peaches.[10]

Pecans grew all about the town, but wild fruits appeared to be scarce.

The crossing with Colonel Harney apparently was between Woll's Crossing (Pacuache) and Paso de Francia, camp having been made a mile and a half downstream from the former. Both Gregg and Hughes described the ford as having a smooth, hard bottom, the water 3½ feet deep, the current swift. Hughes noted its width exactly as 816 feet. Several wagons made the crossing but with difficulty. "The Río Grande del Norte at this place," wrote Hughes, "is truly a noble river, with high banks, never overflown, well deserving of its name, 'the Great River of the North'." Colonel Harney and his squadron of Second Dragoons camped at "a very pretty position, near a hacienda about two miles beyond Presidio."[11]

General course of the road from the crossing to the town, Hughes noted, was south fifty-two degrees west, the distance five miles.

It is a town of about twelve hundred inhabitants, pleasantly situated on a small creek, furnishing abundant water for irrigation, flowing into the river a few miles below the ford. There is a good deal of corn, cotton, sweet potatoes, beans, and sugar cane grown in the vicinity, and fruits are plentiful. The town, built of adobes, or unburnt bricks, is in a dilapidated condition.[12] [Hughes, like Gregg, observed the ruins of the Mission San Bernardo's unfinished church a short distance from town.] Its walls are thick, and built of stone, and are still in tolerable state of preservation and might at little expense be rendered a strong defensible position. Within the town is a stone tower, built

10 *Ibid.*

11 George W. Hughes, *Operations of the Army in Texas and on the Río Grande,* p. 17.

12 *Ibid.,* p. 17. It will be observed that Hughes saw adobe buildings, while Gregg saw houses of stone. Samuel Maverick also wrote that the town was built of adobe. The explanation, apparently, is that while the presidio itself was built of stone—of which much evidence remains today—the dwellings of the townspeople were largely of adobe. Many of the dwellings today are old stone buildings —some having been part of the presidio originally, others having been built of stone taken from buildings of the two missions.

for and formerly occupied as a guard-house. The inhabitants are said to be extremely hostile to us, but did not manifest it by any offensive acts, but, on the contrary, were kind and civil in their deportment.[13]

That night Hughes and his companions returned to camp on the Texas side of the Río Grande.

The following morning two lieutenants, Sitgraves and Bryan, went to examine Woll's ford, or ferry, as Hughes preferred to call it, a mile and a half upstream from the camp. They found the river at that point "some six hundred feet wide, very rapid and not fordable." Fronting the ford on the right bank were large plantations of sugar cane, corn, and cotton. In the afternoon Hughes' men made examinations below the camp but found no suitable crossing. Three miles downstream they found the river "broken into several cascades, over which boats can safely pass only in floods."[14]

Such difficulty had been foreseen, however, and an alternate plan was employed.

Today a flying bridge was put in operation by Captain Fraser, of the Engineers, who had built pontoons in San Antonio for the purpose, which was transported to place in wagons. For the purpose of protecting it, and to keep open the communication with San Antonio, where Colonel Churchill still was with the rear-guard and a portion of the supplies, the engineers were directed to construct defensive works on both banks, and two companies of volunteers were left behind as a guard. Lieutenant [William B.] Franklin was occupied with the astronomical calculations.[15]

Lee doubtless had a hand in this [says Freeman]. He probably assisted, also, in choosing and running the lines of the field defenses that General Wool ordered the engineers to construct at the bridgeheads. It was the first earthwork he ever constructed of the general type that he, more than any one man, was to develop in utility.[16]

The captain from Virginia was experiencing much that was new to him. He looked about and observed the restlessness of the men, and their eagerness for battle. In camp in the evening he wrote a letter to his wife. "We have met with no resistance yet. The Mexicans who were guarding the passage, retired on our approach. There has been a great whetting of

[13] *Ibid.*, p. 17.   [14] *Ibid.*, pp. 17–18.   [15] *Ibid.*
[16] Freeman, *Lee*, I, 208.

knives, grinding of swords, and sharpening of bayonets, ever since we reached the river."[17]

On October 12 the entire army, including wagons and artillery, crossed the river on the flying bridge, marched down the five-mile road to Guerrero, and up the Calle Real, the main street, through the old presidial town. The march through was as much as the rank-and-file soldiers of the invading army got to see of the historic village. Camp was made four miles from town, where the grazing was good but the water was bad, "in consequence of which we were compelled to dispense with the soldiers' favorite dish, bean soup."[18]

To the camp came a Mexican officer and two soldiers, under a flag of truce, bringing a copy of the articles of capitulation of Monterrey, one provision of which was an eight-week armistice. The messengers came from Colonel Castañeda, who had withdrawn from Presidio del Río Grande and now was near Santa Rosa on his way to Saltillo. General Wool found nothing in the articles to deter his advance.

The following morning the General ordered Captain Hughes into Guerrero in quest of information concerning the routes to Santa Rosa. In Hughes' opinion the information which he was able to get from the townspeople was not very satisfactory. Lieutenant Bryan, meanwhile, was busy surveying the roads leading out of Guerrero.

Wool's quartermaster was gathering provisions from the merchants and farmers of Guerrero who asked for, and got, a fancy price for their wares.

While the army waited on Hughes' topographical engineers to determine the route by which it would continue the march, a near-starving man found his way into the American camp. He was a survivor of Colonel Harney's raid on the presidio, having been among those ferrying supplies back across the river when Colonel Castañeda's men returned to harass their retreat. The man, a beef contractor named Riddles, had a strange story to tell.

When the Mexicans had begun firing on the party of eight, Riddles recounted, he had jumped into the river, though he could not swim. The current carried him downstream and up against the bank on the Mexican side, where he was able to conceal himself from the enemy. After nightfall he pushed a log into the river and endeavored to steer it to the oppo-

---

[17] *Ibid.*
[18] Hughes, *Operations of the Army,* p. 18.

site bank, but the log was unmanageable in the swift water. He floated down the river twenty or thirty miles. Coming ashore at last, he was once more on the right bank. He walked back to Guerrero and was captured again by two Mexicans who took him to the presidio. There he was imprisoned with two of his companions who had been captured earlier. The night before the three of them were to be taken south to prison in the interior, Riddles again escaped and made his way to the river. He tried the same method of escape, and again his log was carried downriver, to the vicinity of Laredo. Riddles hid out until he felt reasonably certain that Wool's army would have reached the Río Grande, then made his way back upstream.

The other two men who had been presumed dead had been taken south to San Luis Potosí. One of them, named Reed, was sent back to Saltillo, where sometime later he succeeded in finding Lieutenant Franklin of the topographical engineers and thus joined Wool's army.[19]

Also arriving at Wool's camp near Presidio del Río Grande was Brigadier General James Shields, who had come up from Camargo to confirm the news of the capitulation of Monterrey and to take command of one wing of Wool's army.

On the fifteenth the topographical engineers marched out from the camp to reconnoiter the country. Pike's and Preston's companies of Arkansas Volunteers, under Colonel Roane, formed an escort. As Captain Hughes' unit marched out toward Nava, it encountered a shortage of water in the once well-irrigated and highly cultivated land. Dry ditches, empty fields, and houses in ruin stood out on every hand: devastation amid evidences of former prosperity. "It is nothing but a desert waste, abandoned to the dreaded Comanches, or the not less terrible Mescaleros and Apaches who have driven the timid inhabitants from their rural dwellings, and cooped them up within the presidio of the villages, converting this once smiling garden into a howling wilderness."[20]

Two hours after Hughes' departure, at nine o'clock, an alarm was sounded in the American camp, then a call to arms. In a matter of minutes the force of more than two thousand was ready to meet the enemy. Shots were heard in the distance, and the Dragoons rode out to investigate. Soon they returned to report there was no cause for alarm. The

[19] Gregg, *Diary*, I, 290–291.
[20] Hughes, *Operations of the Army*, p. 19.

Mexicans at Presidio were celebrating a feast day, and this called for firing volleys.[21]

The army was to leave for the interior the next day, and General Wool ordered a big review in the afternoon. Afterward the soldiers retired to their tents, many to write one last letter to loved ones far away.

When the army set forth, one company of Arkansas Volunteers under Captain Hunter remained behind at Presidio del Río Grande.

While Wool's Army of Chihuahua marched southward to Saltillo and adventures which do not form a part of our story, the old San Juan Bautista site was being approached from a different direction. In October, 1846, Major General Patterson, commanding the second division, Army of Occupation of México, ordered the United States steamer, *Major Brown,* to investigate navigation possibilities on the Río Grande above the mouth of the San Juan River. Navigation of the Río Grande above this confluence had long been held impracticable, but Patterson felt that a thorough exploration might result in the opening of military communication between Camargo and Presidio del Río Grande. Captain Mark Sterling of Pittsburgh was given the assignment, with a detachment of nineteen privates and one officer, in addition to the regular crew—a total of twenty-seven men.[22]

Each man was provided with musket and ammunition, while provisions for one month were placed on board. The voyage began October 1. Orders called for proceeding almost three hundred miles up the river to Presidio del Río Grande, and as far beyond as possible.

The party reached Laredo without difficulty. Considerable improvement would be needed—$100,000 worth—to make it navigable, but with proper improvement above Mier, boats drawing four feet could readily ply between the mouth of the Río Grande and Laredo. While the *Major Brown* rested at Laredo, however, the river fell suddenly. It was deemed advisable to send a land party on to Presidio del Río Grande to make explorations of the river's course before the steamer attempted to negotiate it. Two of the boat's pilots and one of the engineers, together with Dr. Rackliffe as guide and interpreter, mounted horses and proceeded up-

[21] Paul Horgan, *Great River: The Río Grande in North American History,* p. 740.
[22] Bryant P. Tilden, Jr., *Notes on the Upper Río Grande,* p. 8.

stream. Leaving Laredo on October 29, they traveled by the direct land route to reach Presidio on Sunday, November 1. The plan was to obtain a boat at the historic gateway and follow the river downstream to Laredo. They found the presidial town to contain about two thousand inhabitants.

The town is, without exception, the prettiest one of our southwestern frontier [it was observed]. Nearly every dwelling has its garden or yard; and the whole town is plentifully and conveniently irrigated. Its style of building . . . is tasteful, and even striking in effect, but most wretchedly meagre and insignificant in detail. All the Mexican towns have an appearance of antiquity owing in a very great measure to the materials used for construction, and to a heavy and clumsy solidity of structure, often mis-styled massive.[23]

At Presidio a Captain Moore provided the party from Laredo with a dugout, which had been cut up and sunk on the Texas side of the river. Two and a half days' work, aided by some of Moore's men, made the craft more or less seaworthy. Dr. Rackliffe returned to Laredo the way he had come, in custody of the horses. The other three men from the steamer embarked in their crude boat November 4, to examine the river down to Laredo. A Dr. White and a Mr. Misner from the American force accompanied them to the first falls below, a distance of three or four miles from the camp of the Illinois and Arkansas troops which occupied General Wool's bridgehead.

The voyage was not uninteresting in the least, though it destroyed any idea that the river could be made navigable. With the exploration a spark of hope for Guerrero's future faded and died. The river could not be counted upon to bring back to Guerrero the traffic which no longer traveled the old Camino Real.

From this point [wrote Tilden] a succession of reefs and falls, of from two to three feet, occur at short intervals, for a distance of twenty miles. These reefs in many instances form solid walls from one island to another, the river widening to a breadth of more than a mile, containing in one group more than twenty islands. Several of these reefs were examined from one end to the other, and sounded near their coasts, in the hope of finding some opening, but to no purpose. The only method of passing in safety was, for everyone to get out of the boat, and after heading her over a reef, to force her into the rapids beneath, hanging on to her sides, stem and stern, and then climbing in as she

23 *Ibid.,* p. 26.

floated on below. . . . At a distance of more than fifty miles below Presidio, and on the Mexican side, a high rock rises vertically from the very water's edge to a height of fifty feet. . . . Close by are two rock islands, in midstream, which at high water cannot be covered. Rapids rushing with a tremendous velocity through the passage thus formed render it doubtful, should any steamboat attain this point, whether it will be safe for it to attempt to pass down it in any stage of the river.[24]

The summing up of the voyage contained two predictions, one bright and one grim.

Presidio de Río Grande, which is on the direct route between San Antonio de Béxar and the interior Mexican trading and agricultural towns, must, in time, be compelled to add to the growth and importance of Laredo, while it will derive a reciprocal benefit therefrom. Laredo is destined ultimately to become, and to continue for years, the head of navigation on the Río Grande.[25]

For many a decade travelers across the Río Grande had observed the wide, deep river and speculated upon the possibility of navigation from the sea. But appearances were deceiving. The river's geography was not such that Guerrero, so long a gateway on the overland trail, could become a river port as well.

But the question, as it developed, was only academic anyway. The treaty of Guadalupe Hidalgo, signed February 2, 1848, was ratified by the United States Senate the following March 10. Among other provisions, it confirmed the Río Grande as an international stream, the boundary between the United States and México. This pact would in time contribute to the sealing of the gateway which had served more than a century and a half.

While the treaty was awaiting ratification, American forces remained along the Río Grande as a precaution against renewed hostilities. Stationed temporarily at Presidio del Río Grande was Captain John A. Veatch of the Texas Mounted Volunteers. During this time there came to the old gateway post to talk with Veatch a tragic figure, one who had suffered much from the vicissitudes of Texas' conflict with México.

In the years of turmoil there doubtless were many persons living in

[24] *Ibid.,* pp. 26–27. Tilden is mistaken on the distance, according to Ben E. Pingenot of Eagle Pass; thirty miles would be more nearly correct.
[25] *Ibid.,* p. 29.

Texas who found it difficult to choose sides, who were unsure which side was more closely allied with their interests. Doubtless many who had pledged their loyalties to Texas were driven to the Mexican side by unreasoning persecution on the part of Anglo-Texans. Such a man was Juan N. Seguín, who had become truly a "man without a country."

Seguín, oldest son of Erasmo Seguín, was born in San Fernando de Béjar on October 27, 1806. In 1835 he actively recruited volunteers to take up arms against the Mexican dictator Santa Anna. He was with Bowie in the Battle of Concepción. In 1836 he was commissioned a captain in the regular cavalry and was assigned to William B. Travis' force in San Antonio. He escaped the fate of Travis and his men at the Alamo only because he had been sent through the Mexican lines with a plea for reinforcements. He then took part in the Battle of San Jacinto.

Promoted to lieutenant colonel in May, 1836, Seguín was placed in charge of the military government of San Antonio. It was he who gave military burial to the ashes of the defenders of the Alamo. When in 1837 General Felix Huston ordered that San Antonio should be destroyed, and its inhabitants moved to the Brazos, Seguín defied the order and appealed to President Sam Houston, who upheld him. San Antonio was saved, but Seguín had made an enemy. His persecution began.

Going to the Texas Senate in 1838, Seguín worked to bring about friendly relations between Mexican-Texans and Anglo-Texans. He resigned his Senate post in 1840 to lead Texas volunteers into México to aid Antonio Canales but found the Federalist leaders in México as determined to reconquer Texas as was Santa Anna. He returned to give warning to Texas.

As mayor of San Antonio in 1841, Seguín incurred the enmity of some of the new Anglo-Texans. On the failure of the Texan Santa Fé Expedition, a rumor was widely circulated that he had been responsible for informing Mexican officials of its coming. Business correspondence with Mexican General Rafael Vásquez convinced Seguín that a Mexican invasion of Texas was imminent, and he urged evacuation of San Antonio. When the invasion shortly came, Vásquez spread the word that Seguín was his friend and ally. Many stood ready to believe him.

Such harassment continued until, in April, 1842, Seguín resigned as mayor of San Antonio and went to México. He later claimed that Santa Anna gave him a choice of serving in the Mexican Army or going to prison. When he returned to Texas the following September, Seguín was a member of Adrian Woll's invading force. Those who previously had refused to believe malicious rumors concerning him now regarded him as a traitor.[26]

When Woll withdrew to Presidio del Río Grande, followed by two hundred Mexican families, old Erasmo Seguín—"one of the truest friends Texas ever had"[27]—went along hoping to persuade his eldest son to leave the Mexican service and remain in Texas. He followed as far as the Medina but finally turned back, rebuffed and dejected. Less than six months later many of the San Antonio Mexicans returned to San Antonio saying they had gone to México under the influence of Juan Seguín. Seguín himself at last came to the day when he wished to return also. He appeared at Presidio del Río Grande and sought out Captain Veatch.

Veatch reported to General Mirabeau B. Lamar on February 23, 1848:

Our *Texian-Mexican* Seguín, presented himself a few days since, desiring permission to bring his family—which he thinks is in Saltillo—to this place. He says he will return to Texas and risk consiquences [sic]. He looks care worn & *thread-bare*. He is just from Querétaro and came by way of San Luis Potosí.[28]

Seguín received permission to return to Texas. One must wonder if he ever found happiness in the state for which he had heroically fought, from which he had angrily exiled himself, and to which he now penitently returned. He died outside the borders of Texas, in Nuevo Laredo, in 1889.

[26] Walter Prescott Webb and H. Bailey Carroll (eds.), *Handbook of Texas,* II, 590.

[27] Nance, *Attack and Counterattack,* p. 384.

[28] Veatch to Mirabeau B. Lamar, February 23, 1848, in Charles Adams Gulick, Jr., and Winnie Allen (eds.), *The Papers of Mirabeau Buonaparte Lamar,* IV, Part 1, 193–194.

38. CLOSING THE GATEWAY

FOR ALMOST A CENTURY the Villa San Agustín de Laredo—founded May 15, 1755—had exerted a divisive influence on the traffic crossing the Río Grande to and from Texas. Laredo, from its very beginning, had shared with the older settlement of San Juan Bautista the role of gateway to Spanish Texas. Still the ancient passage by way of Guerrero and Paso de Francia (or Paso Pacuache farther upstream) had remained open and active until the war between México and the United States.

With the founding of other towns in northern Coahuila, however, travelers to and from Texas began to follow yet another trail which by-passed the historic gateway. In 1760 Felipe de Rábago y Terán, on his way to take command of the Presidio de San Sabá, blazed a new trail north from San Fernando de Austria.[1] With Rábago out of favor at San Antonio de Béjar, he had found it necessary to obtain his supplies from the Coahuila settlements. Consequently, the road which linked San Fernando with San Sabá and the missions of El Cañon, on the upper Nueces River, became well traveled. But then the trail north from San Fernando began angling eastward, threading its way along the Río Escondido to a crossing on the Río Grande just below the confluence of the two streams. This new ford, because of the flights of eagles from their nesting places along the lower Escondido, became known as Paso del Águila. The route to San Antonio—quite likely following an old Indian trail—came to be frequented by traders traveling between that settlement and San Fernando, Nava, Santa Rita de Morelos, and the other more western *poblaciones* of northern Coahuila.[2]

---

[1] Robert S. Weddle, *The San Sabá Mission: Spanish Pivot in Texas,* p. 150.
[2] These steps leading to the "closing of the gateway" were evolved by Ben E. Pingenot of Eagle Pass, and I am indebted to him for permission to use them here (Pingenot to author, letter, February 16, 1967).

Following the Texas Revolution such trade was frowned upon by Mexican officials but nevertheless persisted; the hitherto legal trade route became a contraband trail. While hostile Indians might previously have caused caravans to shift their route and travel the more protected road by Presidio del Río Grande, this no longer was the case. The operations now must be carried on in secret. Paso del Águila's business picked up.

In 1841 General Mariano Arista issued an order forbidding Mexican citizens to trade with the Texans. Patrols went out to watch the Río Grande crossings, including Paso del Águila. When General Adrian Woll, in August, 1842, led his invading force from Presidio del Río Grande upon San Antonio, he marched north from Paso Pacuache (Paso de Nogal) to reach the old smuggling trail, hoping to take San Antonio by surprise. The route lay some twenty miles north of the Upper Presidio Road, which had been laid out shortly after 1800 as a more direct route between Presidio del Río Grande and San Antonio de Béjar.[3]

Later the same year (1841), when the Texans began to talk of a retaliatory stroke against the Mexican border towns, General Isidro Reyes moved his main force from Presidio del Río Grande to Paso del Águila. From this new location he felt that he could operate effectively toward either Guerrero or San Fernando de Rosas.[4] No longer just an obscure smugglers' crossing, Paso del Águila had risen to strategic importance.

Texas and United States Army forces were in firm control along the Río Grande following General John E. Wool's invasion at Presidio del Río Grande in the autumn of 1846. Early in 1848 Captain John A. Veatch moved upriver from Laredo to spend some time at the historic gateway presidio, then proceeded on to Paso del Águila. There he collected mineral and botanical specimens and wrote a report to M. B. Lamar at Laredo.[5] It appears likely that Veatch bore an influence in later devel-

---

[3] Joseph Milton Nance, *Attack and Counterattack: The Texas-Mexican Frontier, 1842*, p. 313. There were three roads between Presidio del Río Grande and San Antonio de Béjar: the Camino Real, laid out by Domingo Terán de los Ríos in 1691, later known as Lower Presidio Road; the Upper Presidio Road mentioned here; and the Woll Road, which, with modifications, later became the Eagle Pass Road.

[4] *Ibid.*, p. 449.

[5] Veatch to Lamar, May 26, 1848, in Charles Adams Gulick, Jr., and Winnie Allen (eds.), *The Papers of Mirabeau Buonaparte Lamar*, IV, Part 1, 198–199. See also Mrs. William L. Cazneau (Cora Montgomery), *Eagle Pass, or Life on the Border*, p. 96.

opments which spelled unequivocal doom for the ancient gateway to Spanish Texas.

Hardly a year after the signing of the Treaty of Guadalupe Hidalgo, Captain Sidney Burbank marched with three companies of the First Infantry Regiment from Fort Inge[6] under orders to establish a new fort on the Río Grande. Burbank camped for several days at Pacuache Crossing, the more frequented of the two fords near old San Juan Bautista in recent years. On the opposite side of the river stood Presidio del Río Grande's *colonia militar,* likewise guarding the international gateway.

Burbank, however, was not satisfied with the suitability of this location for a military post. Wood, drinking water, and building stone—three prime requisites—were scarce. Acting, perhaps, on the basis of reports made by Captain Veatch one year earlier, he moved his force thirty miles upriver to Paso del Águila—Eagle Pass—March 27, 1849, to establish a military post later known as Fort Duncan.[7]

The new post filled an important purpose. Traders plying between the northern Coahuila settlements and those of Texas crossed at this point and used the new military road which ran to Fort Inge, Fort McIntosh (Laredo), and San Antonio. The fate of Presidio del Río Grande was sealed.

The historic road to the ancient gateway had split in two, each prong missing Guerrero on a different side. As Laredo drew attention away from Guerrero in the downstream direction, Eagle Pass would do so in the upstream quarter.

During the California gold rush some emigrant trains bound for the gold fields the fastest way possible chose a route across northern México. Some of the trains traveled a modified version of the Woll Road[8] from

---

[6] Fort Inge was founded by Captain Burbank with two companies of First Infantry on the east bank of the Leona River, Uvalde County, March 13, 1849. It was named for Zebulon M. P. Inge, who was killed in the Mexican War Battle of Resaca de la Palma. (Walter Prescott Webb and H. Bailey Carroll (eds.), *Handbook of Texas,* I, 627.

[7] Webb and Bailey, *Handbook,* I, 624; Ben. E. Pingenot to the author, letter, November 8, 1966.

[8] W. H. C. Whiting in *Reports of the Secretary of War With Reconnaissances of Routes from San Antonio to El Paso,* p. 246. Whiting notes that the road followed an old smuggling trail and was somewhat circuitous. He was able to shorten it twenty miles by cutting out some of the meanders. "There is," he re-

San Antonio to the Río Grande, striking the now international stream at Eagle Pass rather than Guerrero. They then angled across Coahuila to Parras, southwest of Saltillo, and thence northwestward to a juncture with other emigrant roads west of Tucson. "Most who followed this route reached the gold fields before those using trails in the United States."[9] But Guerrero got none of this traffic.

Mexican military units along the Río Grande apparently shifted according to the movements of troops of the United States. The military colony of Presidio del Río Grande, which had been situated in front of Pacuache Crossing, opposite the first camp of Captain Burbank's men,[10] moved upriver also, to a point just across from Fort Duncan. From the two military camps eventually rose the cities of Eagle Pass and Piedras Negras.

As early as 1851 Eagle Pass was connected by stage with San Antonio. More and more the traffic was directed away from Guerrero. Where the stage line went, the railroad, in 1882, would follow.

This most historic place on the lower Río Grande [wrote Coues in 1905], has in the course of time fallen between two stools, so to speak. For now one railroad runs from San Antonio nearly S. to Laredo by way of Pearsall, Derby, Cotulla, Encinal, Webb, and Sanchez, and another comes W. to Laredo from Corpus Christi on the Gulf; while a third railroad comes to San Antonio with Eagle Pass by way of Castroville, Sabinal, and Brackettville (Fort Clark).[11]

At Eagle Pass the Texas and New Orleans Railroad joined the Mexican Railway to take the international route away from Guerrero once and for all. Paved highways followed the same pattern.

---

ported, "a great deal of passing both of California emigration and of inland and of Mexican commerce by this place [Fort Duncan]." The date was 1849.

[9] Ray Allen Billington, *The Far Western Frontier, 1830–1860*, p. 232.

[10] Jorge Cervera Sánchez in Juan Agustín Morfi, *Descripción del Territorio del Real Presidio de San Juan Bautista del Río Grande del Norte y su Jurisdición, Año de 1778*, p. 316.

[11] Elliott Coues, *The Expeditions of Zebulon Montgomery Pike to the Headwaters of the Mississippi River, through Louisiana Territory, and in New Spain, during the years 1805–6–7*, II, 690 n. In *ibid.*, p. 692, Coues notes that the name of Presidio de Río Grande used by Pike in 1806 was not yet entirely obsolete (in 1895), "but the place is now better known as Presidio Salto—that is 'Fort Falls,' or the Mexican military post which was established near the falls of the Río Grande. Las Islas, or the isles, is the name of the place on the river where the usually impassable falls or rapids occur, and just above these is the crossing."

While Guerrero's importance as an oft-used gateway had faded not long after the Mexican War, the ancient fords continued to be of strategic importance in border troubles between the United States and México for years to come. In 1857 an American force was stationed at "Camp Pendencia" near Pacuache Crossing. From about 1890 through World War I both the United States Army and the Texas Rangers from time to time had detachments guarding one or both of the two fords of the historic gateway. Some trade was carried on over the fords, though probably only local in nature, and customs houses were maintained on both sides of the river at Pacuache until late in the nineteenth century. From April, 1918, to November, 1919, Company L, Third Battalian, Third U.S. Infantry, was encamped at the mouth of Cuervo Creek, a short distance below Paso Pacuache. The customs house on the Texas side was roofless then, though its walls were still standing, as evidenced by a photograph supplied by Thomas B. Hughes of Shiner, Texas, a member of the company. Hughes and his companions pried the stone lid from what they believed to be the vault of the customs house and killed a rattlesnake inside.[12]

The commerce which flowed back and forth across the Río Grande at the two historic crossings took two forms: legal and illegal. Smugglers forded the stream where once the religious and military forces of Spain, bent on taming a pagan land, had crossed into Texas.

As the years stretched into decades, Guerrero forgot her past glory. The old presidio buildings began to fall to ruin. The name Presidio del Río Grande no longer was heard, that of San Juan Bautista almost completely forgotten. Still Father Jiménez' dream, the grand new San Bernardo Mission church—so grand that it was never finished—remained as a reminder of the settlement's origin. The Mission San Juan Bautista had largely disappeared, the victim of scroungers for building material. Only a mound of earth, an old well, bits of shattered crockery, a piece of clay tile here and there remain to identify the site.

Water still runs through ancient ditches to irrigate the gardens of Guerrero. The fig trees, so abundant in mission times, still grow from the Spanish stock. Old stone buildings abound, some of them crumbling, some in remarkably good state of repair. A few of these ancient structures

---

[12] John F. Woodhill to the author, letter, April 24, 1967.

can be identified as presidial buildings. But the others? *¿Quién sabe? Casas antiguas.* Very old houses.

The parish church stands on the east side of the plaza, as it did in colonial times. Its masonry walls are old and weathered. The stone steps leading to the belfry are hollowed deep by the bellringers of many generations. But the door to the church is locked, except on the rare occasions when a priest comes from Piedras Negras. One wishing to pray at the altar must obtain a key from the *presidente municipal.*

Across the plaza, about where the *cuerpo de guardia* stood, is a new school building. Down by the marsh, where Padre Marcos de Guereña bared his frail body in penitence to allow the vicious mosquitoes to suck his blood, the limestone banks of the creek are notched in giant steps. Here the rock was quarried to build the missions and the presidio.

At the lower end of town is the cemetery, so aptly called "holy ground." Before the gate of this same *campo santo* the errant Coahuiltecans of the missions were made to kneel and face the cross while they received cutting lashes on bare backs to convince them of their error. Beneath the well-kept turf in anonymous graves lie the remains of the natives over whom the padres rejoiced—the ones who received the waters of holy baptism before dying.

Close by the cemetery Guerrero's Calle Real, Royal Street, turns into the Camino Real: the road to Texas that was trod in colonial times by the bare feet of Fathers Hidalgo, Olivares, Margil, and Espinosa; by the Frenchman St. Denis; by Don Diego Ramón and his progeny; by the Canary Islanders; by the Rodríguez brothers, Manuel and Vicente; by Nicolás de Lafora and the Marqués de Rubí; by Padre Morfi and Teodoro de Croix; by Zebulon Montgomery Pike; by Ben Milam, and then by Santa Anna's legions, by Adrian Woll and his Perote-bound prisoners, by John E. Wool, and Robert E. Lee.

The street, deep rutted by the marching processions of history, no longer carries the name of Calle Real. Now it bears the name of a native son who became governor of the state: Lic. Raúl López Sánchez. But a change in name does not alter history.

The past is attested by the thick-walled houses of adobe and quarried stone, some frescoed in pastel shades, some of bare mud bricks or aged and weathered rock. Either makes a cool refuge from the sweltering heat of summer. Guerrero's yesterdays also are bespoken by heavy doors, the flat roofs of its *casas de terrado,* supported by hand-carved cypress beams.

Guerrero is a quiet town. Its pace is atuned more to the wagons and two-wheeled carts, the saddle horses and burros seen on its streets than to the jet age. Almost lifeless in midday, it awakens in the cool of evening. The plaza fills with people, strolling, laughing, talking in the Castillian tongue, somewhat altered by time and place, and by the blending of cultures.

Out away from the town are the proud haciendas with irrigated fields and fat cattle, and the humble goat ranches, tended by the poor but free and independent families who live in adobe huts with roofs of thatch. From the slopes the springs still flow, and near each farmhouse is a small ditch to channel the water to field or garden. One may be inspired thereby to recall Father Morfi's description of the area: "It has all that it is possible to wish for . . .: the springs of water are sweet, many, and abundant; the air pure; the sky happy; the land abundant."[13] Or Father Espinosa's observation: "In flower the lands . . . seem a pleasant garden, an uncultivated paradise; in this . . . is a most beautiful agreeableness."[14]

A dozen miles upstream from Guerrero, among the mesquite, the huisache, and the prickly pear, lies the ancient village of San José. Here stood the Mission San Francisco Solano, which Padre Olivares moved in 1718 to San Antonio, there to become known first as San Antonio de Valero, then as the Alamo. It is at San José that the last tragic episode of the gateway story occurred in three deadly hours on a late December morning, 1917.

Livestock shortages in northern México had given rise to wholesale stealing of cattle from the Texas side of the Río Grande. One method was for a man hidden in the brush on the Mexican side with a high-powered rifle to shoot cattle when they came to the river to drink in late afternoon. Then, after dark, a small band of men would ford the river, dress out the carcasses, and recross the stream to sell the hides and the meat in Guerrero or Piedas Negras.[15]

A raiding party from Guerrero and San José struck June 27 at El Indio

13 Morfi, *Descripción del Territorio,* p. 298.

14 Isidro Félix de Espinosa, *Crónica de los colegios de propaganda fide de la Nueva España,* p. 763.

15 Walter Prescott Webb, *The Texas Rangers,* pp. 495–496.

Ranch on the Texas side and drove off twelve head of cattle. The feat was twice repeated in August, on the tenth and the fifteenth. The ranch manager reported the thefts to Mexican officials and provided names of the offenders, but no arrests resulted.

Matters were brought to a head by the murder of two Americans on an authorized hunting trip on a hacienda in México, ostensibly for having interfered with the thieves' operations. Before the excitement over the killings had died, Mexican thieves crossed the river and made off with 160 goats from the Indio Ranch. The ranch manager sounded the alarm in Texas Ranger headquarters in Eagle Pass at 6:30 P.M. December 29, 1917. "In a short time the few Texas Rangers at Eagle Pass, and three troops of cavalry with a machine gun were en route to the Indio Ranch."[16]

Early the following day a combined force of 150 Rangers, citizens, and soldiers from Fort Duncan crossed into México and followed the goat trail to the village of San José. As the Americans approached the house of a Mexican river guard—whose duty was to prevent smuggling—they saw several freshly slaughtered goats hanging in the trees. A cow wearing the Indio brand was tethered to a tree in front of the house.

A Mexican man and a woman were passing near by, and when the Ranger captain called to them to halt, the woman screamed and ran. Then, as any one of the Rangers might have said it, "all hell broke loose." Mexicans hidden in the brush began firing from a semicircular line eight hundred yards long. The men from Texas hastily dismounted and began firing by platoons, in V-formation. The Mexicans fell back, some of them taking refuge in a house nearer the heart of the village, continuing to fire upon the Americans. By this time the cavalry troop had its machine gun set up. As it riddled doors and windows in the house, the fire from the house was silenced. The Mexicans who were able fled the town.

Recrossing the river from the three-hour invasion of México, both Ranger and Army officers reported six known dead among the Mexicans. Later the number was raised to twelve. But Major E. C. Wells of Fort Duncan learned that seventeen burials occurred in Piedras Negras and three at San José immediately after the fight.

The expected repercussions were heard from Mexican officials, but the effect of the invasion was salutary. The governor of Coahuila himself or-

[16] *Ibid.,* p. 496.

ganized a force to help clean up the border. Some of the bandits were executed, others imprisoned; the gateway was closed against the international thieves.

San José today is a primitive village of perhaps less than one hundred persons. Overlooking the beautiful spring which waters the village stand the ruins of an old stone church. Out among the mesquite and cacti lie the remains of many other stone buildings of ancient vintage. The exact site of the Mission San Francisco Solano has not been found, but when it is, it likely will be on a low hill looking down upon the village and the river a mile distant.[17]

The gateway, now closed, had long been a center of conflict: between Spaniard and Indian, Spaniard and Frenchman, Creole and *gachupín,* Mexican and gringo; most of all it was the center of a conflict of civilizations. The real story is of one culture trying to thrust itself upon another. In such an effort conflict and struggle are inevitable; but it is of these ingredients that history is made.

The fulcrum of the strife in this case was the gateway to Spanish Texas.

[17] Ben E. Pingenot, "San José," typescript of sketch prepared for use in supplement to *The Handbook of Texas.*

BIBLIOGRAPHY

UNPUBLISHED MATERIAL

Alarcón, Martín de. Letters. Archivo General de la Nación, México, Provincias Internas, Vol. 28; Archivo General de Indias, Audiencia de México, 61-6-35, Dunn Transcripts. The University of Texas Library, Austin.

Alderete, Vicente. "Diario de las operaciones del Real Presidio del Santísimo Sacramento y Valle de Santa Rosa." Archivo General de la Nación, México, Provincias Internas, Vol. 22. The University of Texas Library, Austin.

Almazán, Fernando Pérez de. Letter. Archivo General de la Nación, México, Provincias Internas, Vol. 181. The University of Texas Library, Austin.

Barrios y Jáuregui, Jacinto de. Report ("Estado que manifiesta la fuerza de los Tres Presidios de esta Provincia de San Francisco de Coahuila, y las distribuciones de ellas"). Archivo General de la Nación, México, Provincias Internas, Vol. 25. The University of Texas Library, Austin.

Berroterán, José de. Letters. Archivo General de la Nación, México, Historia, Vol. 52. The University of Texas Library, Austin.

——. Report ("Relación Diaria de los acaecimientos que ocurrieron en la expedición de José de Berroterán"). Archivo General de la Nación, México, Historia, Vol. 52. The University of Texas Library, Austin.

Bucareli y Ursúa, Frey Antonio María de, Viceroy. Letters. Archivo General de la Nación, México, Provincias Internas, Vols. 22, 24, Part 1. The University of Texas Library, Austin.

Cabildo of Monclova. Certification. Archivo General de la Nación, México, Provincias Internas, Vol. 181. The University of Texas Library, Austin.

Cancio, Lorenzo. Letter. Archivo General de la Nación, México, Provincias Internas, Vol. 25. The University of Texas Library, Austin.

Castellaños, Manuel de. Letter. Archivo General de la Nación, México, Provincias Internas, Vol. 282. The University of Texas Library, Austin.

Cerecedo y Velasco, Manuel de. Letters. Archivo General de la Nación, México, Provincias Internas, Vol. 22. The University of Texas Library, Austin.

Cós, Manuel de. Letter. Archivo General de la Nación, México, Provincias Internas, Vol. 22. The University of Texas Library, Austin.

Croix, Carlos Francisco de (Marqués de Croix), Viceroy. Letters. Archivo General de la Nación, México, Provincias Internas, Vol. 22. The University of Texas Library, Austin.

Cuebas, Fray Miguel Antonio de las. Report ("Ynforme que hacen los Rdos. Padres Fr. Diego Ximénez y Fr. Miguel Antonio de las Cuebas al Exmo. Señor Virrey"). Archivo General de la Nación, México, Historia, Vol. 29, Part 1. The University of Texas Library, Austin.

Cuerbo y Valdés, Francisco. Letters and reports. Archivo General de la Nación, México, Provincias Internas, Vol. 28. The University of Texas Library, Austin.

Daniel, James Manly. "The Advance of the Spanish Frontier and the Despoblado." Doctoral dissertation, University of Texas, June, 1955.

"Declaraciones de los Indios de los Tejas." Archivo General de la Nación, México, Provincias Internas, Vol. 28. The University of Texas Library, Austin.

Díez, Joseph. Letters. Archivo General de la Nación, México, Provincias Internas, Vol. 181. The University of Texas Library, Austin.

Dolores y Viana, Fray Mariano Francisco de los. Letters. Archivo del Marqués de San Francisco. The University of Texas Library, Austin.

Ecay Múzquiz, Joseph Antonio de. "Informe." Archivo General de la Nación, México, Historia, Vol. 52. The University of Texas Library, Austin.

Elosúa, Antonio. Petition. Archivo General de la Nación, México, Californias, Vol. 44. University of California Library, Berkeley.

Escandón, José de. Report. Archivo General de la Nación, México, Provincias Internas, Vol. 179, Part 1. The University of Texas Library, Austin.

Espinosa, Isidro Félix de. Letter. Archivo General de la Nación, México, Provincias Internas, Vol. 181. The University of Texas Library, Austin.

Espinosa, Joseph Antonio de. Letters and reports. Archivo General de la Nación, México, Provincias Internas, Vol. 28; Archivo General de la Nación, México, Historia, Vol. 29, Part 1. The University of Texas Library, Austin.

Fernández, Eugenio. Letters. Archivo General de la Nación, México, Provincias Internas, Vol. 22. The University of Texas Library, Austin.

Franquis de Lugo, Benito. Letters. Archivo General de la Nación, México, Misiones, Vol. 21, Part 1; Archivo General de la Nación, México, Historia, Vol. 524, Part 3. The University of Texas Library, Austin.

García, Fray Diego Martín. Certification. Archivo General de la Nación, México, Provincias Internas, Vol. 22. The University of Texas Library, Austin.

Garza Falcón, Alejo de la. "Derrotero." Archivo General de la Nación, México, Provincias Internas, Vol. 24. The University of Texas Library, Austin.

Garza Falcón, Blas de la. Reports ("Visita del Río Grande" and "Diario y Derrotero de Don Blas de la Garza Falcón y Don Joseph Antonio de Ecay y Múzquiz"). Archivo General de Indias, Audiencia de México, 61-2-18. The University of Texas Library, Austin.

Gómes, Fray Gaspar. Letter. Archivo General de la Nación, México, Historia, Vol. 29, Part 2. The University of Texas Library, Austin.

Güemes y Horcasitas, Juan Francisco (Conde de Revilla Gigedo), Viceroy. Instructions. Archivo General de la Nación, México, Historia, Vol. 52. The University of Texas Library, Austin.

Gutiérrez de la Cueva, Juan. "Informe de las Misiones de la Provincia de Coahuila." Archivo General de la Nación, México, Californias, Vol. 29. University of California Library, Berkeley.

Hidalgo, Fray Francisco. Letters. Archivo General de la Nación, México, Provincias Internas, Vols. 181, 282. The University of Texas Library, Austin.

Jiménez, Fray Diego. Letters. Archivo General de la Nación, México, Historia, Vol. 28. The University of Texas Library, Austin.

————. Reports ("Relación del Estado de las Misiones de la Presidencia del Río Grande del Norte, pertenecientes al Colegio de la Santa Cruz de Querétaro," "Ynforme que hacen los Rdos. Padres Fr. Diego Ximénez y Fr. Miguel Antonio de las Cuebas al Exmo. Señor Virrey," "Repuesta de los PP. al Sr. Cancio a varios puntos de un Informe," "Relación de las Misiones de la Presidencia del Río Grande del Norte desde Octubre de 58 Hasta Diciembre de este Año de 1764"). Archivo General de la Nación, México, Historia, Vol. 29, Part 1. The University of Texas Library, Austin.

Maldonado, Nicolás. Testimony. Archivo General de la Nación, México, Provincios Internas, Vol. 32. The University of Texas Library, Austin.

Margil de Jesús, Fray Antonio. Letter. Archivo General de la Nación, México, Provincias Internas, Vol. 181. The University of Texas Library, Austin.

Martínez Pacheco, Rafael. Letters. Archivo General de la Nación, México, Provincias Internas, Vol. 22. The University of Texas Library, Austin.

Mendoza, Felipe. Declaration. Archivo General de la Nación, México, Provincias Internas, Vol. 28. The University of Texas Library, Austin.

Mezquía, Pedro Pérez de. Letters. Archivo General de la Nación, México, Provincias Internas, Vol. 236. The University of Texas Library, Austin.

Minchaca, Nicolás. Testimony. Archivo General de la Nación, México, Provincias Internas, Vol. 32. The University of Texas Library, Austin.

Monserrat, Joaquín de (Marqués de Cruillas), Viceroy. Letter. Archivo General de la Nación, México, Provincias Internas, Vol. 25, Part. 2. The University of Texas Library, Austin.

Mora, Gerardo. Report. Archivo General de la Nación, México, Provincias Internas, Vol. 181. The University of Texas Library, Austin.

Oconor, Hugo. "Report on the Condition of the Interior Provinces," including "Papel Instructivo." Archivo General de Indias, Audiencia de Guadalajara, 104-6-18. The University of Texas Library, Austin.

Olivares, Fray Antonio de San Buenaventura y. Letters. Archivo General de la Nación, México, Provincias Internas, Vols. 28, 181; Archivo General de Indias, Audiencia de México, 61-6-35, Dunn Transcripts. The University of Texas Library, Austin.

Ortiz, Fray Francisco Xavier. Letters. Archivo General de la Nación, México, Historia, Vol. 29, Part 1. The University of Texas Library, Austin.

———. Report ("Visita de las Misiones de San Juan Bautista y de San Bernardo del Río Grande del Norte en la Provincia de Coahuila hecha por el Reverendo Padre Visitador Fr. Francisco Xavier Ortiz"). Archivo General de la Nación, México, Historia, Vol. 29, Part 1. The University of Texas Library, Austin.

Parrilla, Diego Ortiz. Letter. Archivo General de Indias, Audiencia de Guadalajara, 104-6-13, Dunn Transcripts. The University of Texas Library, Austin.

———. Reports ("Testimonio de Parrilla," "Testimonio de las Diligencias practicadas por el Coronel Don Diego Ortiz Parrilla"). Archivo General de Indias, Audiencia de México, 92-6-22, Dunn Transcripts, 1759–1761; Archivo General de Indias, Audiencia de Guadalajara, 104-6-13, Dunn Transcripts. The University of Texas Library, Austin.

Pérez, José. "Derrotero que con el favor de Dios, empieza hacer el Alférez de la Compania de San Sabá, Don Joseph Pérez." Archivo General de la Nación, México, Provincias Internas, Vol. 22. The University of Texas Library, Austin.

Pingenot, Ben. E. Letters. In possession of author.

———. "San Antonio Crossing." Typescript of sketch prepared for publication in forthcoming supplement of *The Handbook of Texas*.

———. "San José." Typescript of sketch prepared for publication in forthcoming supplement to *The Handbook of Texas*.

———. "San Juan Bautista." Typescript of sketch prepared for publication in forthcoming supplement to *The Handbook of Texas*.

Placido y Monzón, José. "Petition of *Vecinos*," Archivo General de la Nación, México, Misiones, Vol. 20, University of California Library, Berkeley.

Rábago y Terán, Felipe de. Letter. Archivo General de la Nación, México, Provincias Internas, Vol. 22. The University of Texas Library, Austin.

Rábago y Terán, Pedro de. "Diario de la Campaña executado por el Governador de Coahuila." Archivo General de la Nación, México, Historia, Vol. 52. The University of Texas Library, Austin.

————. Reports (on expedition of Miguel de la Garza Falcón, contained in José de Escandón's report to the Viceroy), Archivo General de la Nación, México, Provincias Internas, Vol. 179. The University of Texas Library, Austin.

Ramón, Diego. "Diario de la jornada que executado el Sargento Mayor Diego Ramón," March 9–April 8, 1707. Archivo General de la Nación, México, Provincias Internas, Vol. 28. The University of Texas Library, Austin.

————. Letters. Archivo General de la Nación, México, Provincias Internas, Vols. 28, 181. The University of Texas Library, Austin.

Richards, Hons Coleman. "The Establishment of the Candelaria and San Lorenzo Missions on the Upper Nueces." Master's thesis, The University of Texas, August, 1936.

Rivera, Pedro de. "Proyecto y Visita." Archivo General de la Nación, México, Provincias Internas, Vol. 29. The University of Texas Library, Austin.

Rodríguez, Francisco. Letter of Petition. Archivo General de la Nación, México, Provincias Internas, Vol. 22. The University of Texas Library, Austin.

Rodríguez, Manuel. Letters, Archivo General de la Nación, México, Provincias Internas, Vol. 22. The University of Texas Library, Austin.

————. Reports ("Lista y revista que en dicho día se hizo de la tropa, vecinos del Real Presidio de San Juan Bautista de Río Grande, assie de Armas, Caballas, y municiones de boca y guerra"). Archivo General de la Nación, México, Provincias Internas, Vol. 22. The University of Texas Library, Austin.

————. Service Record. Archivo General de la Nación, México, Provincias Internas, Vol. 25. The University of Texas Library, Austin.

Rodríguez, Vicente. Letters. Archivo General de la Nación, México, Provincias Internas, Vol. 22. The University of Texas Library, Austin.

————. Reports ("Diario de las Operaciones de Don Vicente Rodríguez, Capitán del Presidio de San Juan Bautista del Río Grande," "Derrotero," November 1–December 2, 1775). Archivo General de la Nación, México, Provincias Internas, Vols. 22, 24. The University of Texas Library, Austin.

————. Service record. Archivo General de la Nación, México, Provincias Internas, Vol. 25. The University of Texas Library, Austin.

Rodríguez Morales, Antonia. Letter of Petition. Archivo General de la Nación, México, Provincias Internas, Vol. 22. The University of Texas Library, Austin.

Rubí, Marqués de. Letter. Archivo General de la Nación, México, Provincias Internas, Vol. 22. The University of Texas Library, Austin.

St. Denis, Louis Juchereau de. "Relación hecha por Don Luis de San Dionis y Don Medar Jalot del viaje que ejecutaron desde la Móvila hasta de Presidio de Diego Ramón." Archivo General de la Nación, México, Provincias Internas, Vol. 181. The University of Texas Library, Austin.

————. Report of Junta concerning. Archivo General de la Nación, México, Provincias Internas, Vol. 181. The University of Texas Library, Austin.

Salazar, Fray Diego de San Buenaventura y. Representation to the Viceroy. Archivo General de la Nación, México, Provincias Internas, Vol. 28. The University of Texas Library, Austin.

Salinas Varona, Gregorio. Report. Archivo General de la Nación, México, Provincias Internas, Vol. 28. The University of Texas Library, Austin.

San Francisco Solano. "Autos of Founding of Mission San Francisco Solano." Archivo General de la Nación, México, Provincias Internas, Vol. 28. The University of Texas Library, Austin.

San Juan Bautista. Proceedings of Investigation at San Juan Bautista, October 5, 1737. Archivo General de Indias, Audiencia de Guadalajara, 67-2-27. The University of Texas Library, Austin.

————. "Testimonio de la Fundación de la Misión de San Juan Bautista, 1699–1701." Archivo General de la Nación, México, Historia, Vol. 29, Part 1. The University of Texas Library, Austin.

————. "Testimonio del Decreto de Fundación del Presidio de San Juan Bautista." Archivo General de la Nación, México, Historia, Vol. 29. The University of Texas Library, Austin.

Sevillano de Paredes, Fray Miguel de. Reports ("Visita de las Misiones del Río Grande," "Consulta Apologetica," "Representación"). Archivo General de la Nación, México, Historio, Vol. 29; Archivo General de la Nación, México, Misiones, Vol. 21; Archivo General de la Nación, México, Provincias Internas, Vol. 32. The University of Texas Library, Austin.

Terreros, Fray Alonso Giraldo de. Letter. Archivo del Marqués de San Francisco. The University of Texas Library, Austin.

Ugalde, Juan de. "Campaña del Coronel Dⁿ Juan de Ugalde." Archivo General de la Nación, México, Historia, Vol. 29, Part 1. The University of Texas Library, Austin.

Ugarte y Loyola, Jacobo de. "Diario de lo executado por el Destacamento mandado del Governador de la Provincia de Coahuila," Archivo General de la Nación, México, Provincias Internas, Vol. 24. The University of Texas Library, Austin.

Valero, Marqués de, Viceroy. Endorsement of letter. Archivo General de la Nación, México, Provincias Internas, Vol. 181. The University of Texas Library, Austin.

Valladares, José Sarmiento (Conde de Moctezuma y Tula), Viceroy. Letters. Archivo General de la Nación, México, Provincias Internas, Vol. 28. The University of Texas Library, Austin.

PUBLISHED WORKS

Alessio Robles, Vito. *Coahuila y Texas desde la consumación de la Independencia hasta el Tratado de Paz de Guadalupe Hidalgo.* Two volumes. Mexico City: n.p., 1945, 1946.

————. *Coahuila y Texas en la época colonial.* Mexico City: Editorial Cultura, 1938.

————. (ed.) *Viaje de Indios y Diario del Nuevo México,* by Juan Agustín, Morfí. Mexico City: Antigua Librería de Robredo, 1935.

Allen, Winnie, and Charles Adams Gulick, Jr. (eds.). *The Papers of Mirabeau Buonaparte Lamar.* Six volumes. Austin: Von Boeckmann-Jones Co., 1924.

Allsopp, Fred W. *Albert Pike: A Biography.* Little Rock, Arkansas: Parke-Harper Company, 1928.

Arricivita, Juan Domingo. *Crónica seráfica y apostólica del Colegio de propoganda fide de la Santa Cruz de Querétaro en la Nueva España, segunda parte.* Mexico City: F. de Zúñiga y Ontiveros, 1792.

Bancroft, Hubert Howe. *History of the North Mexican States and Texas.* Two volumes. San Francisco: A. L. Bancroft & Company, 1889.

Bannon, John Francis (ed.). *Bolton and the Spanish Borderlands.* Norman: University of Oklahoma Press, 1964.

Barker, Eugene C., and Herbert, Eugene Bolton (eds.). *With the Makers of Texas: A Source Reader in Texas History.* New York: American Book Company, 1904.

Billington, Ray Allen. *The Far Western Frontier, 1839–1860.* New York: Harper & Row, 1956.

Bobb, Bernard E. *The Viceregency of Antonio María Bucareli in New Spain, 1771–1779.* Austin: University of Texas Press, 1962.

Bolton, Herbert Eugene. *Bolton and the Spanish Borderlands.* Edited with an Introduction by John Francis Bannon. Norman: University of Oklahoma Press, 1964.

————. *Guide to Materials for the History of the United States in the Principal Archives of México.* Washington: Carnegie Institution, 1913.

———— (ed.). *Spanish Exploration in the Southwest: 1542–1706.* New York: Charles Scribner's Sons, 1908.

————. "Spanish Mission Records at San Antonio," *Southwestern Historical Quarterly,* 10, No. 4 (April, 1907), 297–307.

————. *Texas in the Middle Eighteenth Century.* New York: Russell & Russell, Inc., 1962 (First published in 1915 as Vol. 3 in the University of California Publications in History).

————, and Eugene C. Barker (eds.). *With the Makers of Texas: A Source Reader in Texas History.* New York: American Book Company, 1904.

Bonilla, Antonio. "A Brief Compendium of the History of Texas, 1772" (an annotated translation by Elizabeth H. West), *Southwestern Historical Quarterly,* 8, No. 1 (July, 1904), 3–78.

Botello G., Aurora. *Datos Históricos sobre la fundación de la Misión de San Bernardo y la Villa de Guerrero Coah. Antes Real Presidio de Río Grande del Norte.* Piedras Negras: Privately printed, 1956.

Brinckerhoff, Sidney B., and Odie B. Faulk. *Lancers for the King: A Study of the Frontier Military System of Northern New Spain, with a Translation of the Royal Regulations of 1772.* Phoenix: Arizona Historical Foundation, 1965.

Buckley, Eleanor Claire. "The Aguayo Expedition into Texas and Louisiana, 1719–1722," *Southwestern Historical Quarterly,* 15, No. 1 (July, 1911), 1–65.

Canedo, Lino G. (ed.). *Crónica de los colegios de propaganda fide de la Nueva España,* by Fray Isidro Félix de Espinosa. New edition with notes and Introduction by Lino K. Canedo, O. F. M. Madrid: Academy of American Franciscan History, 1964.

Carroll, H. Bailey, and Walter Prescott Webb (eds.). *The Handbook of Texas.* Two volumes. Austin: The Texas State Historical Association, 1952.

Carter, Hodding. *Doomed Road of Empire: The Spanish Trail of Conquest.* New York: McGraw-Hill Book Company, Inc., 1963.

Castañeda, Carlos Eduardo (trans.). *History of Texas, 1673–1779* by Juan Agustín Morfi. Albuquerque: The Quivira Society, 1935.

———— (trans.). *The Mexican Side of the Texas Revolution, by the Chief Mexican Participants.* Dallas: P. L. Turner Company, 1928.

————. *Our Catholic Heritage in Texas.* Seven volumes. Austin: Von Boeck-mann-Jones Company, 1936–1950.

Cazneau, Mrs. William L. (Cora Montgomery). *Eagle Pass, or Life on the Border.* Edited with an Introduction by Robert Crawford Cotner. Austin: The Pemberton Press, 1966.

Céliz. Francisco. *Diary of the Alarcón Expedition into Texas, 1718–1719.* Translated with Introduction by Fritz Leo Hoffman. Los Angeles: The Quivira Society, 1935.

Cervera Sánchez, Jorge (ed.). *Descripción del Territorio del Real Presidio de San Juan Bautista del Río Grande del Norte, y su Jurisdicción, Año de 1778,* by Fray Juan Agustín Morfi. Mexico City: Sociedad Mexicana de Geografía y Estadística (Editorial Cultura), 1950.

Clark, Robert Carleton. "Louis Juchereau de Saint-Denis and the Re-establish-ment of the Texas Missions," *Southwestern Historical Quarterly,* 6, No. 1 (July, 1902), 1–26.

Cotner, Robert Crawford (ed.). *Eagle Pass or Life on the Border,* by Mrs. William L. Cazneau (Cora Montgomery). Austin: The Pemberton Press, 1966.

Coues, Elliott (ed.). *The Expeditions of Zebulon Montgomery Pike, to Head-waters of the Mississippi River, through Louisiana Territory, and in New Spain, during the Years 1805–6–7.* Three volumes. New York: Francis P. Harper, 1895.

Cox, I. J. "The Early Settlers of San Fernando," *Southwestern Historical Quar-terly,* 5, No. 1 (July, 1901), 142–170.

Croix, Teodoro de. *Teodoro de Croix and the Northern Frontier of New Spain, 1776–1783.* Translated and edited by Alfred Barnaby Thomas. Norman: University of Oklahoma Press, 1941.

Documentos para la historia de Texas o Nuevas Philipinas, 1720–1779. Colec-ción Chimalistac de libros y documentos acerca de la Nueva España, Vol. 12. Madrid: Ediciones José Porrua Turanzas, 1961.

Dunn, William Edward. "Missionary Activity among the Eastern Apaches Previous to the Founding of the San Sabá Mission," *Southwestern Historical Quarterly,* 15, No. 3 (January, 1912), 186–200.

Espinosa, Fray Isidro Félix de. *Crónica de los colegios de propaganda fide de la Nueva España.* New edition with notes and Introduction by Lino G. Canedo, O.F.M. Madrid: Academy of American Franciscan History, 1964.

Faulk, Odie B., and Sidney B. Brinckerhoff. *Lancers for the King: A Study of the Frontier Military System of Northern New Spain, with a Translation of the Royal Regulations of 1772.* Phoenix: Arizona Historical Foundation, 1965.

Foik, Paul J. (trans.). *Captain Don Domingo Ramón's Diary of His Expedition into Texas in 1716. Preliminary Studies,* Vol. 2, No. 5. Austin: Texas Catholic Historical Society, 1933.

Folmer, Henri. *Franco Spanish Rivalry in North America, 1524–1763.* Glendale: The Arthur H. Clark Company, 1953.

Forrestal, Peter P. (trans.) *Peña's Diary of the Aguayo Expedition. Preliminary Studies,* Vol. 2, No. 7. Austin: Texas Catholic Historical Society, 1935.

Freeman, Douglas Southall. *R. E. Lee: A Biography.* Two volumes. New York: Charles Scribner's Sons, 1934.

Fulton, Maurice Garland (ed.). *Diary & Letters of Josiah Gregg: Southwestern Enterprises, 1840–1847.* Two volumes. Norman: University of Oklahoma Press, 1941.

Gálvez, Bernardo. *Instructions for Governing the Interior Provinces of New Spain.* Translated and edited with Introduction by Donald E. Worcester. Berkeley: The Quivira Society, 1951.

Green, Rena Maverick. *Samuel Maverick, Texan, 1803–1870.* (A collection of letters, journals, and memoirs, edited by Rena Maverick Green). San Antonio: Privately printed, 1952.

Gregg, Josiah. *Diary & Letters of Josiah Gregg: Southwestern Enterprises, 1840–1847.* Edited by Maurice Garland Fulton. Two volumes. Norman: University of Texas Press, 1941.

Gulick, Charles Adams, Jr., and Winnie Allen (eds.). *The Papers of Mirabeau Buonaparte Lamar.* Six volumes. Austin, Von Boeckmann-Jones Company, 1924.

Hackett, Charles Wilson, and Charmion Clair Shelby (trans.). *Pichardo's Treatise on the Limits of Louisiana and Texas.* Four volumes. Austin: University of Texas Press, 1934.

Hanke, Lewis. *The Spanish Struggle for Justice in the Conquest of America.* Philadelphia: University of Pennsylvania Press, 1949.

Hatcher, Mattie Austin (trans.). "Description of the Tejas or Asinai Indians, 1691–1722" (Part 3), *Southwestern Historical Quarterly,* 31, No. 1 (July, 1927), 50–62.

———— (trans). *The Expedition of Don Domingo Terán de los Ríos into Texas.* Preliminary Studies, Vol. 2, No. 1. Austin: Texas Catholic Historical Society, 1932.

Heusinger, Edward W. *Early Explorations and Mission Establishments in Texas.* San Antonio: The Naylor Company, 1935.

Hoffman, Fritz Leo (trans.). *Diary of the Alarcón Expedition into Texas, 1718–1719,* by Fray Francisco Céliz. Los Angeles: The Quivira Society, 1935.

Hollon, W. Eugene. *The Lost Pathfinder: Zebulon Montgomery Pike.* Norman: University of Oklahoma Press, 1949.

Horgan, Paul. *Great River: The Río Grande in North American History.* New York: Holt, Rinehart, and Winston, 1954.

Hughes, Major George W. *Operations of the Army in Texas and on the Río Grande (Memoir Descriptive of the March of a Division of the United States Army, under the Command of Brigadier General John E. Wool from San Antonio de Béxar, in Texas, to Saltillo, in México).* Washington: Government Printing Office, 1850.

Inglis, Jack M. *A History of Vegetation on the Rio Grande Plain.* Austin: Texas Parks and Wildlife Department (Bulletin No. 45), 1964.

Kennedy, William. *Texas: The Rise, Progress, and Prospects of the Republic of Texas.* Two volumes. London: R. Hastings, 1841.

Kinnaird, Lawrence (trans.). *Frontiers of New Spain* (Nicolás de Lafora, *Presidios Internos*). Berkeley: The Quivira Society, 1957.

Lafora, Nicolás de. *Relación del Viaje que hizo a los Presidios Internos situados en la Frontera de la América septentrional perteneciente al Rey de España.* Mexico City: Editorial Pedro Robredo, 1939.

Lamar, Mirabeau Buonaparte. *The Papers of Mirabeau Buonaparte Lamar.* Six volumes. Edited from the original papers in the Texas State Library by Charles Adams Gulick, Jr., and Winnie Allen. Austin: Von Boeckmann-Jones Company, 1924.

Lay, Bennett. *The Lives of Ellis P. Bean.* Austin: University of Texas Press, 1960.

Leutenegger, Benedict (trans.). *Life of Fray Antonio Margil, O.F.M.,* by Eduardo Enrique Ríos. Washington: Academy of American Franciscan History, 1959.

Morfi, Fray Juan Agustín. *Descripción del Territorio del Real Presidio de San Juan Bautista del Río Grande del Norte, y su Jurisdicción, Año de 1778.* Introduction and notes by Jorge Cervera Sánchez. Mexico City: Sociedad de Geographía y Estadística (Editorial Cultura), 1950.

――――. *History of Texas, 1673–1779* (translated and annotated by Carlos E. Castañeda). Albuquerque: The Quivira Society, 1935.

――――. *Viaje de Indios y Diario del Nuevo México.* Mexico City: Bibliófilos Mexicanos, 1935.

Murphy, Retta. "The Journey of Pedro de Rivera, 1724–1728," *Southwestern Historical Quarterly,* 41, No. 2 (October, 1937), 125–141.

Nance, Joseph Milton. *After San Jacinto: The Texas-Mexican Frontier, 1836–1841.* Austin: University of Texas Press, 1963.

——. *Attack and Counterattack: The Texas-Mexican Frontier, 1842.* Austin: University of Texas Press, 1964.

——. (trans. and ed.). "Brigadier General Adrian Woll's Report on His Expedition into Texas in 1842." *Southwestern Historical Quarterly,* 58, No. 4 (April, 1955), 523–552.

Nathan, Paul D. (trans.), and Lesley Byrd Simpson (ed.). *The San Sabá Papers: A Documentary Account of the Founding and Destruction of the San Sabá Mission.* San Francisco: John Howell Books, 1959.

Newcomb, W. W., Jr. *The Indians of Texas: From Prehistoric to Modern Times.* Austin: University of Texas Press, 1961.

Phares, Ross. *Cavalier in the Wilderness: The Story of the Explorer and Trader, Louis Juchereau de St. Denis.* Baton Rouge: Louisiana State University Press, 1952.

Pike, Zebulon Montgomery. *The Expeditions of Zebulon Montgomery Pike, to Headwaters of the Mississippi River, through Louisiana Territory, and in New Spain, during the years 1805–6–7.* Edited by Elliott Coues. New York: Francis P. Harper, 1895.

Rister, Carl Coke. *Comanche Bondage: Beale's Settlement and Sarah Ann Horn's Narrative.* Glendale: The Arthur H. Clarke Company, 1955.

Ríos, Eduardo Enrique. *Life of Fray Antonio Margil, O.F.M.* Translated and revised by Benedict Leutenegger, O.F.M. Washington, D.C.: Academy of American Franciscan History, 1959.

Rivas, Antonio. *Abstract of Title to Antonio Rivas Grant in Maverick County, Texas (Except Three Leagues and 6130 Acres).* San Antonio: Texas Title Guaranty Company, 1938.

Sánchez Lamego, General M. A. "Storming the Alamo: A Mexican Version." *Dallas Morning News,* March 6, 1966, p. 26-A.

Schmitt, Edmond J. P. "The Name Alamo," *Southwestern Historical Quarterly,* 3, No. 1 (July, 1899), 67–69.

Shelby, Charmion Clair, and Charles Wilson Hackett (trans.). *Pichardo's Treatise on the Limits of Louisiana and Texas.* Four volumes. Austin: Universty of Texas Press, 1934.

——. "St. Denis's Declaration concerning Texas in 1717," *Southwestern Historical Quarterly,* 26, No. 3 (January, 1923), 165–183.

——. "St. Denis's Second Expedition to the Río Grande, 1716–1719," *Southwestern Historical Quarterly,* 27, No. 3 (January, 1924), 190–216.

Simpson, Lesley Byrd (ed.), and Paul D. Nathan (trans.). *The San Sabá Papers: A Documentary Account of the Founding and Destruction of San Sabá Mission.* San Francisco: John Howell Books, 1959.

Smithwick, Noah. *The Evolution of a State or Recollections of Old Texas Days.* Austin: The Steck Company, 1935.

Steck, Francis Borgia (trans.). *Forerunners of Captain De León's Expedition to Texas, 1670–1675.* Preliminary Studies, Vol. 2, No. 3. Austin: Texas Catholic Historical Society, 1932.

Texas Title Guaranty Co. *Abstract of Title to Antonio Rivas Grant in Maverick County, Texas (Except Three Leagues and 6130 Acres).* San Antonio: Texas Title Guaranty Company, 1938.

Thomas, Alfred Barnaby (ed.). *Teodoro de Croix and the Northern Frontier of New Spain, 1776–1783.* Norman: University of Oklahoma Press, 1941.

Tilden, Bryant P., Jr. *Notes on the Upper Río Grande: (Explored the Months of October and November, 1846, on board the U.S. Steamer* Major Brown, *Commanded by Captain Mark Sterling of Pittsburgh. By order of Major General Patterson, U.S.A., Commanding the Second Division, Army of Occupation, Mexico).* Philadelphia: Lindsay & Blakiston, 1847.

Tinkle, Lon. "The Alamo," in *Six Missions of Texas.* Waco: The Texian Press, 1965.

Tous, Gabriel (trans.). *The Espinosa-Olivares-Aguirre Expedition of 1709.* Preliminary Studies, Vol. 1, No. 3. Austin: Texas Catholic Historical Society, 1930.

————. (trans.). *Ramón Expedition: Espinosa's Diary of 1716.* Preliminary Studies, Vol. 1, No. 4. Austin: Texas Catholic Historical Society, 1930.

Vigness, David M. "Don Hugo Oconor and New Spain's Northeastern Frontier, 1767–1776." *Journal of the West,* VI, No. 1 (January, 1967), 18–30.

————, and Ernest Wallace (eds.). *Documents of Texas History.* Austin: The Steck Company, 1960.

Walker, Henry P. (ed.). "William McLane's Narrative of the Magee-Gutiérrez Expedition, 1812–1813," *Southwestern Historical Quarterly,* 66, Nos. 2, 3, and 4 (October, 1962, January, 1963, and April, 1963), 234–251, 457–459, 569–588.

Wallace, Ernest. *Ranald S. Mackenzie on the Texas Frontier.* Lubbock: West Texas Museum Association, 1964.

————, and David M. Vigness (eds.). *Documents of Texas History.* Austin: The Steck Company, 1960.

Webb, Walter Prescott. *The Texas Rangers.* Second Edition. Austin: University of Texas Press, 1965.

————, and H. Bailey Carroll (eds.). *The Handbook of Texas.* Two volumes. Austin: The Texas State Historical Association, 1952.

Weddle, Robert S. "The San Sabá Mission: Approach to the Great Plains." *Great Plains Journal,* 4, No. 2 (Spring, 1965), 29–38.

————. "The San Sabá Mission and the Permian Basin." *The Texas Permian Historical Annual*, 4 (December, 1964), 33–39.

————. *The San Sabá Mission: Spanish Pivot in Texas*. Austin: University of Texas Press, 1964.

————. "What Happened at Spanish Fort?" *Fort Belknap Society Yearbook*, 4 (1965–1966), 9–19.

West, Elizabeth H. (trans.). "A Brief Compendium of the History of Texas, 1772" (translation of Bonilla), *Southwestern Historical Quarterly*, 8, No. 1 (July, 1904), 3–78.

Wharton, Clarence R. *El Presidente: A Sketch of the Life of General Santa Anna*. Houston: C. C. Young Printing Company, 1924.

Whiting, W. H. C. *Reports of the Secretary of War with Reconnaissances of Routes from San Antonio to El Paso*. Thirty-first Congress, first session (Senate); Executive Document No. 64. Washington: The Union Office, 1850.

Wilcox, S. B. "Laredo during the Texas Republic." *Southwestern Historical Quarterly*, 42, No. 2 (October, 1938), 83–107.

Worcester, Donald E. (ed. and trans.). *Instructions for Governing the Interior Provinces of New Spain, 1786*, by Bernardo Gálvez. Berkeley: The Quivira Society, 1951.

Ximenes, Ben Cuellar. *Gallant Outcasts: Texas Turmoil, 1519–1734*. San Antonio: The Naylor Company, 1963.

INDEX

Acatita de Baján: 370
Aculco: 365
Advance Guard Brigade: 385, 387, 388
Ágreda, María de Jesús de (Mother): 14 and n.
Agua de San José de la Peña: 323
Aguaje de las Vacas: 337
Aguanueva: 370
Aguascalientes: 160
Aguaverde, Presidio: founded, 305; Apache plan to destroy, 327 n.; force gathers at, 335; completed, 336; troops from, in Apache campaign, 337, 365; Garza returns to, 338; need for mill at, 346
Aguayo, Marqués de San Miguel de (Joseph de Azlor y Virto de Vera): expedition of, 159, 160–161, 162, 163–164, 203, 264; sends Domingo Ramón to La Bahía, 165; plan of, 190–191, 192–193; campaign by, 219
Aguilar, Antonio de (Friar): 245
Aguirre, Buenaventura de: at San Juan Bautista, 53; investigates French settlements, 66–67
Aguirre, Matías de: as governor of Coahuila, 53; investigates French settlements, 66; signs paper, 177; supplies Canary Islanders, 191
Aguirre, Pedro de: expedition of, 91, 92, 93, 94, 98, 149; relieved of interim command, 95
Álamo (hacienda): 264
Álamo (settlement): 353
Álamo, Río del: 58
Álamo, the. SEE San Antonio de Valero, Mission; San Francisco Solano, Mission
Álamo de Parras: 366
Álamo Grande: 234
Álamos, Arroyo de. SEE Bavia, Arroyo de la
Álamos, Río de: 21 n.
Álamos de Castilla: 234
Álamo Seco: 206
Alaña, Miguel Placido de (Father): 242

Alarcón, Martín de: on missions, 71–72, 73, 89; and expedition to San Marcos River, 75–76, 86; as governor, 131, 151, 159, 168; trip of, to San Antonio River, 131, 132–133, 147–148; relations of, with Father Olivares, 134–135, 144–145, 149; investigates contraband trade, 135–136, 137–138, 139, 144, 166; sends aid to Núñez, 146; and Tejas missions, 152–153, 154; rebuffs request for soldiers, 157; attends Espinosa's services, 160; diarist of expedition of, 210, 215; plan of, to reach Frío River, 223
Alasapa Indians: 13
Alburquerque, Duke of (Francisco Fernández de la Cueva): interest of, in Texas missions, 90; actions of, against French, 91, 103; calls for expedition into Texas, 91–92; letter from, to King, 95–96
Alcántara, Diego de (Father): 165
Alderete, Vicente: commands Presidio del Sacramento, 289, 291, 296
Alessio Robles, Vito: on Paso de Francia, 5; on relocation of San Juan Bautista, 25; on economic dependency of Texas, 190; on Garza Falcón family, 210; on Rábago y Terán's 1747 expedition, 237; on San Fernando de Austria, 244
Allende. SEE San Juan de Allende
Allende, Ignacio: 367
Altamira, Marqués de: on aid to missions, 229; plans of, 239
Altar, Presidio: 306
Alvarez de Toledo, Lucas (Father): 90
Amarillas, Marqués de las (Agustín de Ahumada y Villalón): Felipe de Rábago protests to, 243; becomes Viceroy, 249; asked to secularize Río Grande missions, 251; confers with Terreros, 252; restores Rodríguez to command, 254; orders arrest of Diego Ramón III, 260; informed of San Sabá massacre, 263
Amaya, Salvador de (Fray): 188–189

dian relations of, 106–107, 227, 228, 237, 264–265, 278, 279, 292–293, 295, 321, 326, 337, 339, 353, 354; soldiers sent from, 130, 144, 155, 168, 223, 239, 243, 334–335, 365; Olivares and, 131, 134–135; thefts at, 132; St. Denis citizen of, 137; Christmas at, 161; provisions stored at, 162; Ramón and command of, 166; Ecay Múzquiz commander, 168; private from, becomes San Antonio commander, 169; inspection of, 186–187, 204–205, 245, 302, 303–304; troops from, in exploration of Río Grande, 196, 197, 198, 199, 200, 202, 203, 206, 207, 210; Berroterán and, 197, 203; Ecay Múzquiz dies at, 218; Rodríguez commander of, 219–220, 253–254, 298, 299; as protection for La Junta de los Ríos, 209; hearing held at, 216–217; assistance from, to northern settlements, 238; San Fernando de Austria founded from, 244–245; investigation from, for Apache mission site, 246–247; misbehavior of soldiers at, 270; Barrios on, 290; traffic from Presidio del Sacramento to, 291; manpower shortage at, 296, 400; forts upriver from, 305; to remain in place, 306; fear of change of missionaries at, 308–309; Francisco Rodríguez seeks captaincy of, 310–312; Vicente Rodríguez captain of, 312, 313–314; Martínez Pacheco sends message to, 322; aid from, for Carbajal, 330, 333; *alférez* of, 338 and n.; Croix at, 340–341, 350; gambling at, 345 n.; navigation from, 351 n.; Cerecedo and command of, 355; dominant over missions, 356; and founding of Nava, 358; Nolan's men taken to, 359; Pike at, 360–363; Palafox founded from, 364; in Mexican Revolution, 366–367, 370, 371, 372; after revolution, 374, 375; soldiers from, confiscate tobacco, 378–379; Viesca brought to, 382; Santa Anna's army at, 385, 386–387, 388; and Republic of Texas, 390, 392, 393, 394, 399, 415; in Mexican War, 402, 405, 409, 410, 411, 417; loses importance, 418; military colony moves from, 419; name of, falls into disuse, 420; mentioned, 165

San Juan de Allende: 377, 386
San Juan del Álamo (hacienda): 226

San Juan del Río: 11
San Juan de Sabinas: 386
San Juan de Ulloa, 172
San Lorenzo, Mission: 248
San Lorenzo Creek: 85
San Lorenzo de la Santa Cruz, Mission: 273, 274, 281–282, 283, 301–302
San Luis de las Amarillas, Presidio de. SEE San Sabá, Presidio de
San Luis Potosí: 160, 264, 357, 365, 367, 384, 410, 415
San Marcelino: 325, 326
San Marcos River: Tejas Indians and, 40, 59, 92; troops sent to, 75; 1709 expedition to, 92; buffalo on, 93; El Encadenado near, 163; moving of missions to, 240, 243; Rábago y Terán dies on, 249; Ortiz visits, 252
San Matías, Valle de: 223
San Miguel, Miguel: 285, 296
San Miguel, Mission: 109
San Miguel de los Adaes, Mission: 156, 164. SEE ALSO Los Adaes
San Miguel el Grande, Villa de: 11
San Nicolás (hacienda): 344
San Patricio: 385
San Pedro (place): 232, 331
San Pedro, Río de: Ugarte marches up, 337; Hays renames, 337 n.; Indian attack on, 338; against Apaches along, 353
San Pedro de Gigedo, Villa de: 340, 344
San Pedro del Álamo, Conde de: 233
San Pedro Spring: 92
San Rodrigo, Río: timber at, 88; reconnaisance of, 201; Garza Falcón-Ecay Múzquiz at, 208; horsethieves near, 230; settlement on, 231; Apaches seek mission site on, 247; Rubí crosses, 301; presidio on, 305, 327 n., 335; Vicente Rodríguez against Apaches at, 327
San Rodrigo Spring: 199
San Roque Creek: 79
San Sabá, Presidio de: Parrilla recruits men for, 252; destruction of, feared, 261; in campaign against northern tribes, 264; Felipe de Rábago commander of, 267, 416; Rodríguez on, 277; Indian attack on, 279; garrison moved from, 283, 296; Parrilla commander of, 284; founded, 284 n.; escorts to, 290; aid from, in Rodríguez' campaign, 294–295; Rubí at, 302; relocated, 304, 305,

port to, 164; appoints Pérez as San Antonio commander, 168–169
Val Verde County: 7
Varela, Benito (Friar): 260
Varela, Mariano: 360–361, 362
Vásquez, Rafael: 393, 400, 414
Vásquez Borrego, José: 226
Vásquez Borrego, Juan José: 244
Veatch, John A.: 413, 415, 417, 418
Veracruz: 10, 162, 190, 191, 192, 214, 321 n.
Veracruz (state): 400 n.
Vergara, Francisco (Father): 189, 213, 214
Vergara, Gabriel de (Friar): sent to Tejas missions, 114, 117, 118; at Dolores de la Punta, 115; and permission for Apache missions, 170
Vidaurri, Francisco: 391
Viesca, Agustín: Milam travels with, 382
Villadama, Nuevo León. SEE Boca de Leones
Villa de Linares: 223
Villa de Valles: 222
Villa de Vedoya: 225, 226
Villa Franca, Sebastián de: 76 n.
Villars, John: 379
Villa Union: 340
Viscarra, Pedro: 22
Vizarrón y Guiarreta, Juan Antonio de: viceroy, 193; Terreros' appeal to, 194; seeks to punish Indians, 198; Berroterán's report to, 203; notices unexplored section of Río Grande, 205; Garza Falcón's report to, 209; and Franquis, 211, 214; authorizes mission guards, 212; orders founding of San Francisco Vizarrón, 217–218

Wallisville, Texas: 288
Washita River: 336
Webb, Texas: 419
Webb County: 82
Webber, John: 378, 379
Wells, E. C. (Major): 423
West Point (U. S. Military Academy): 404
White, Dr. ———: 412

Wichita Indians: press Apaches, 225, 247, 248, 249; Parrilla battles, 264, 284
Woll, Adrian: attacks San Antonio, 394–395 and n., 417; guard meets, 396; in Battle of Salado, 397–398; Wool follows, 405; Seguín serves under, 415; mentioned 421
Woll Road: 417 n., 418
Woll's Crossing. SEE Paso Pacuache
Woods, Norman: 398–399
Wool, John E.: leads Army of Chihuahua, 402–417 *passim*; mentioned, 421
World War I: 420

Xarame Indians: Urrutia lives with, 17 n.; ask for mission, 22; at San Francisco Solano, 31, 49, 130; at San Ildefonso, 54; at San Antonio de Valero, 155; return to San Antonio River, 173–174
Xijame Indians: 42
Ximénez, Diego: 76 n.
Ximénez, Santiago: 76 n.

Yacasol: Ramón crosses, 71
Yell, Archibald: 405
Yerbipiame Indians: 42, 43, 174
Yojuan Indians. SEE Tonkawa Indians
Yruegas, Blas de: 27, 35
Ysiaguan Indians: 31
Yucatán: 19, 50

Zacatecas (district): 11–12, 26, 46, 160
Zacatecas, College of: founding of, 11 and n.; missionaries from, to Tejas, 114, 115, 116; supplies from, to Tejas missionaries, 145–146, 214; founds mission in San Antonio, 173; Río Grande missions said under, 302 and n.; takes over Queretaran missions, 308
Zaes Monge, Esteban (Friar): 189
Zapata, Antonio: 390, 391–392
Zapata: 391
Zaragosa: 54, 87. SEE ALSO San Fernando de Austria
Zepeda, Pedro José: 244
Zúñiga, Baltazar de. SEE Valero, Marqués de